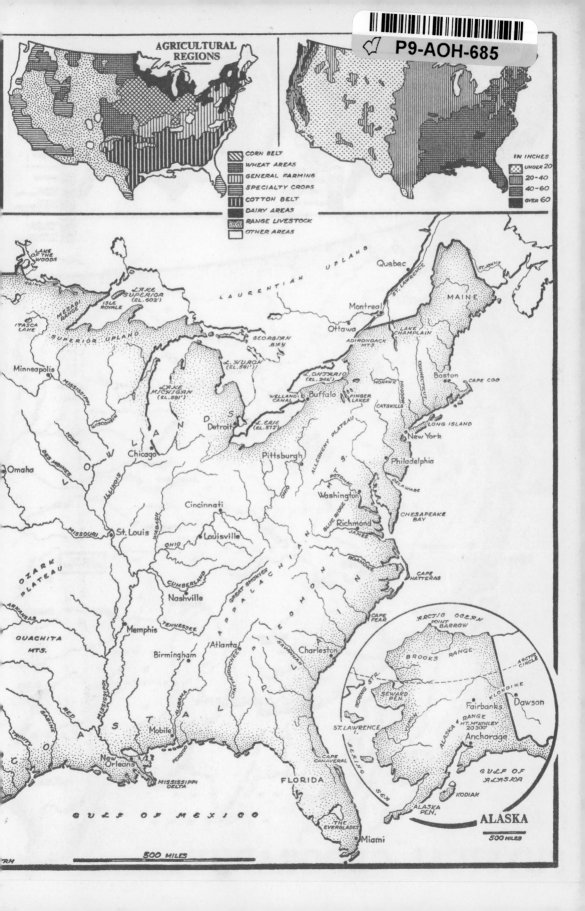

A HISTORY

OF THE

UNITED STATES

[TO 1876]

T. HARRY WILLIAMS
Louisiana State University

RICHARD N. CURRENT
The Woman's College of the University of North Carolina

FRANK FREIDEL
Harvard University

New York   Alfred A. Knopf   1959

L. C. Catalog card number: 59-5580

© *T. Harry Williams, Richard N. Current, and Frank Freidel, 1959*

THIS IS A BORZOI BOOK,

PUBLISHED BY ALFRED A. KNOPF, INC.

FIRST EDITION

To

William Best Hesseltine

Preface

THERE SHOULD BE no need to justify the study of history. The past is worth studying because it is not dead but very much alive. It lives about us in forms that are taken for granted—in laws, customs, institutions, and beliefs which, though intangible, provide an environment as real as the physical world. The past lives also in conscious memory, in a memory that is guided, or misguided, by books, articles, movies, television programs, monuments, restorations, and historical records of various kinds.

The complexity of history (whether history be considered as past conditions and events or as the means of finding out and reporting about them) makes the task of the student and the instructor much more interesting than it otherwise would be, but also much more difficult. If the past were really dead and also simple, a post mortem would be comparatively easy, or (to change the figure) the "bar of history" so often ap-

pealed to could render a final verdict on almost every disputed point. Actually, historians agree upon most of the "facts" of American history. But there are countless facts, and with regard to some of them historians disagree as to which are the more important and which should be picked out and emphasized. Hence historians differ about the meaning or significance of particular phases of the past.

One purpose of a history textbook is to provide, for the beginning student, a guide to an infinitely complex and often controverted story. Of necessity, any text is based upon the researches not of its authors alone but of thousands of historical scholars. In its choice of subject matter and in its handling of controversial issues the book should represent, so far as possible, the consensus of contemporary historical scholarship. At points where there is no clear consensus, the authors have no choice but to rely on their own tentative judgment, unless they are to risk leaving the student in confusion. The student should always bear in mind, however, that the sum of American history is not contained in this or in any other book. Indeed, this book is intended to open the subject, not to close it. The book will have succeeded if, with the indispensable aid of the instructor, it arouses a desire to learn more about American history than is contained between these covers.

This volume includes a number of devices, some of them quite new, designed to make it a more useful and more interesting guide. Chapter bibliographies and a general bibliography provide selected lists of books for further reading. Maps have been conceived and drawn with a view to clarity. Graphs and charts reduce some of the statistical data to a form easily grasped. Other illustrations, which are numerous, have been chosen not as ornaments but as aids to understanding; these are placed near the text material they illustrate, and they are accompanied by rather full explanatory captions. A novel feature is the use of "boxes" which often contain excerpts from contemporary documents; these selections make the volume to some extent a book of readings as well as a textbook. Appendices contain additional documentary and statistical information. The student is urged to make himself familiar, at the outset, with the book as a whole and with all its special features.

One of the chief innovations included in this text is the repetition of the chapter on "The Postwar Nation." This chapter appears as number 31 in the first volume and again as number 1 in the second to accommodate the needs of individual courses, which at the present time exhibit some variation in division between the two terms. Repetition of this chapter affords either a quick review for continuing students or, for newcomers, a detailed treatment of the period of Reconstruction.

Though this book has been put together with considerable care, we are under no illusion that we have managed to escape all errors of fact or interpretation. We will be grateful for suggestions of corrections or other improvements to be incorporated in future editions. Our errors—whatever they may prove to be—are our own. No one else is responsible for them. Certainly they are fewer than they would have been without the assistance of our editors and a number of generous scholars. We are deeply indebted to Roger Shugg, John T. Hawes, Jr., and especially Ray Ginger, who, as an editor at Alfred A. Knopf, Inc., had a truly creative part in the shaping of this book. We are also deeply indebted to the following scholars, who have read and criticized parts of the manuscript: Carl Bridenbaugh, Thomas D. Clark, Charles C. Griffin, Jane L. De Grummond, John Duffy, Holman Hamilton, William B. Hesseltine, Homer Hitt, Arthur S. Link, John Loos, Ernest R. May, J. Preston Moore, Roy F. Nichols, Charles G. Sellers, Jr., Wendell H. Stephenson, George B. Tindall, Joseph Tregle, and Frank Vandiver.

T. H. W.

R. N. C.

F. F.

Contents

List of Illustrations

List of Maps

DESIGNED BY THEODORE R. MILLER

List of Charts

DESIGNED BY VISUAL SERVICES, INC.

A HISTORY
OF THE
UNITED STATES

[TO 1876]

CHAPTER 1

Europe and the New World

Today, an era in human history seems to be coming to an end. Signs of change can be seen in such recent events as the development of atomic energy, the rise of the United States and the Soviet Union as rival superpowers, and the self-conscious stirrings within the so-called "backward areas" of Asia and Africa. Throughout the passing era, which has lasted for about 500 years, the center of world power lay in Western Europe, not in America or Russia, and Europeans reached out to exert their influence upon Asia, Africa, and the Americas. American history began as a result of this expansion of Europe. It began at the start of the era now ending—the "modern" period of European history.

Though the story of the American people is fairly short—it can be spanned by the overlapping lives of a mere half-dozen men—the roots of American culture go deep into the human past. The New World re-ceived its civilization from the Old. Both in Europe and in America this civilization progressed, at least in technological development, more rapidly during the 500 years after the discovery of America than during the 5,000 years before. In time a distinctively American way of life appeared in the United States. Yet, in most essentials, American civilization derived from inherited traditions rather than from uniquely American circumstances. On the prairies of nineteenth-century Illinois, for example, the young Abraham Lincoln had unusual opportunities as a surveyor because of conditions peculiar to the time and place, but his surveying knowledge could be traced back as far as the Egypt of the Pharaohs. The corn planted on the lands he surveyed had been domesticated by the American Indians, but he and his fellow citizens owed far more to the Europeans and their predecessors than to the aborigines of the New World—the first Americans.

The First Americans

There have been many fanciful attempts to explain the origin of the American Indians. According to the myths of the Indians themselves, each tribe sprang from some miraculous act of creation, such as the marriage of the earth mother to the sun father. According to other stories, the first Americans were the Lost Tribes of Israel whom God punished by sending far from home, or they were inhabitants of the "lost continent" of Atlantis who escaped when it sank into the Atlantic Ocean, or they were Asians who crossed the South Pacific on a bridge of islands which afterward disappeared. According to some supposedly scientific theories, the Indians somehow originated in the New World. But no bones or fossils of the ape-like ancestors of men, such as those unearthed on all the other continents, have ever been found in either North or South America. The earliest remains of humanity so far discovered here are little if any older than twenty thousand years.

Most likely the ancestors of the Indians were Mongoloid peoples who began to arrive in America about 20,000 or 25,000 years ago. Seeking better hunting grounds or fleeing from hostile tribes, some of these primitive Asians eventually reached the northwestern corner of Siberia. From there they looked across Bering Strait to the headlands of Alaska, only about thirty-five miles away. In their search for refuge and a richer life they made their way to the new land, either floating from island to tiny island in crude rafts or trekking over on the winter ice. Probably no more than a few families made the first crossing; others followed, and a trickle of migration went on for centuries, then finally ceased. From the northwestern tip of North America the newcomers and their descendants gradually fanned out to populate both the continents. By 1492 there were perhaps a million people north of Mexico, three million in Mexico and Central America, and four or five million in South America.

The Stone Age forefathers of the first Americans brought little with them from Asia, and so the Indians had to develop for themselves such ways of life as they possessed at the time the Europeans arrived. Though neighboring Indians borrowed inventions from one another, the different groups as a whole were so widely scattered that a great variety of native cultures developed.

On or near the Isthmus of Panama, the crossroads of the two continents, where there was the greatest opportunity for the exchange of ideas, the highest civilizations grew up—among the Mayas of Central America, the Aztecs of Mexico, and the Incas of Peru. The Mayas built elaborately carved stone temples and pyramids, bred corn from a kind of wild grass, devised an accurate calendar from astronomical observations, and invented a number system similar to the Arabic and superior to the Roman. At about A.D. 1000 the Mayan civilization was one of the most brilliant then existing anywhere in the world. Living, much as the ancient Greeks did, in loosely grouped city-states, the Mayas were to the Aztecs somewhat as the Greeks were to the Romans. The Aztecs adapted to their own use many Mayan ideas and organized a sizeable empire, a kind of federation with its capital on the site of the present Mexico City. From Cuzco in the mountains of Peru the Incas ruled a more highly centralized and even larger empire, one of the largest of all history, and they constructed thousands of miles of paved roads (or rather pathways, for they had no wheeled vehicles) to hold their empire together.

North of Mexico, within the present area of the United States, no similar talent for political organization was shown. The nearest thing to it was found in the Iroquois league of five nations, covering most of what is now New York. Otherwise, North American Indians seldom advanced beyond a simple tribal government, and they never

Indians had the general features of their Mongoloid ancestors—yellow or brown skin, straight and coarse black hair, and high cheek bones—but there were minor varia-

Tenochtitlán—The Aztec Capital. *This is a model reconstructing the central square. Tenochtitlán, located on the site of the present Mexico City, had a population of about 100,000 in 1502 when the last of the emperors, Montezuma II, began his reign. His empire, covering much of central and southern Mexico, was a rather loose association of city-states from which he collected heavy tribute. The Aztecs developed a complex and magnificent civilization, made up largely of elements adapted from the Mayas and other neighboring peoples. In Tenochtitlán there were surgeons and physicians who are believed to have been as skillful as the best in contemporary Europe, and there were hospitals and nurses. There were also human sacrifices. To appease the Aztec gods, young men and women captives were slaughtered on top of the pyramids. These structures, like those of the Mayas, were comparable in size to the pyramids of ancient Egypt but were used as temples rather than burial monuments. When Hernando Cortez, the Spanish conqueror of Mexico, entered Tenochtitlán in 1519, he found in the central square a rack which held the skulls of about 100,000 sacrificial victims.* (COURTESY OF THE AMERICAN MUSEUM OF NATURAL HISTORY)

attained to science or technology at all comparable with that of the Incas, the Aztecs, or the Mayas.

The numerous and diverse tribes north of Mexico can be classified according to their language, mode of living, and physical appearance, though these classifications overlap in a confusing way. Physically, all the

tions between tribes. The Hopis and Comanches, for example, were short and dark, the Sioux and Navajos tall and relatively light; the Shoshones had broad faces, the Algonkins long and narrow heads. Though customs varied from tribe to tribe, peoples living in the same region usually but not invariably had much in common both because of similar geographical influences and because of imitation or borrowing. Thus on the Great Plains almost all the tribes were nomads who based their life on the buffalo more settled neighbors. There were hundreds of languages, but most of these belonged to one or another of about a dozen linguistic stocks. Men of different tribes

Die figur anzaigt uns das volck und insel die gefunden ist durch den christonlichen künig zu Portigal oder von seinen unterthonen. Die leüt sind also nacket hübsch, braun wolgestalt von leib, ir heübter, halß, arm, scham, füß, frawen und mann ain wenig mit federn bedeckt. Auch haben die mann in iren angesichten und brust vil edel gestain. Es hat auch nyemant nichts sunder sind alle ding gemain. Unnd die mann habendt weyber welche in gesallen, es sey mütter, schwester oder freünde, darinn haben sy kain underschayd. Sy streyten auch mit einander. Sy essen auch ainander selbs die erschlagen werden, und hencken das selbig flaisch in den rauch. Sy werden alt hundert und fünstzig iar. Und haben kain regiment.

Natives of the New World. *This woodcut, made by a German artist about 1505, is the earliest known illustration giving Europeans a pictorial conception of the American Indians. The picture is rather fanciful, and so is its original caption, which (translating the German) says: "The people are handsome in their nakedness, brown and well formed from the kind of life they lead. The heads, necks, arms, groins, and feet of both men and women are partially covered with feathers. The men have precious stones set in their faces and breasts. No one owns property by himself; all things are held in common. The men have wives chosen by their mothers, sisters, or friends; there is no divorce. The people fight among themselves. They also eat one another; when one of them is slain, they hang the meat in the smoke over a fire. They live to be a hundred and fifty years old. They have no government."*

chase, as did the Sioux. On the deserts of the Southwest some were farmers and village dwellers, like the Zuñis and Hopis, while others near them were roving hunters, like the Navajos and Apaches, whose cultures differed completely from those of their with related languages could not understand each other, any more than an Italian could understand a Spaniard, nor were such tribes necessarily alike in their physical features or their cultural patterns. Not only members of the Iroquois league but several other groups, some near, some far away, spoke languages of the same Iroquoian stock.

Without the Indians, American history would have lacked much of its special color and drama, and the modern world would have lacked a number of its characteristic items of food and drink. From the aboriginal cultivators came not only corn but also potatoes, sweet potatoes, chili peppers, tomatoes, tobacco, cocoa, and other novel plants. Speech in the United States was enriched by words of native origin (*moccasin, succotash, Ohio, Winnipesaukee,* to mention only a few), and American thought was colored by numerous elements of Indian lore. Yet one of the Indians' greatest influences on American civilization was negative rather than positive. Despite their kindly aid to the first European arrivals, the Indians became an obstacle to the advance of white settlement, and life on the frontier derived many of its peculiarly "American" qualities from the Indian danger and the Indian wars.

The white man, when he arrived in America, had much to learn from the Indian, but the Indian had far more to learn from the white man. Even the most brilliant of the native cultures, such as the Mayan, were stunted in comparison with the growing civilization of Europe. None of the Indians had an alphabet and—strange to say—none had any conception of the wheel. Whether they would ever have invented such things they of course had little chance to show after the coming of the white man with his magic far more powerful than theirs.

The Quickening of Europe

During the Middle Ages (roughly from A.D. 500 to A.D. 1500) the civilization of Western Europe was in many ways inferior to that of ancient Greece or Rome. After Germanic barbarians had overrun the Roman Empire, the dream of Roman peace and unity lingered on. The countries of medieval Europe were thought to form a single whole, under

the spiritual authority of the Roman Catholic Church and the political authority of what was called the Holy Roman Empire. But kings often asserted power independently of the emperor, and nobles asserted power independently of the kings. Ordinary people, the serfs, tied by custom to the soil, worked the fields while their lords engaged in desultory warfare and chivalric games. Merchants and craftsmen were handicapped by the disorders that prevailed much of the time. Except within the Church, art and learning had few practitioners, and it was left to the monasteries to keep alive the memory of past greatness.

Medieval Europe was backward even by comparison with certain other areas of the contemporary world. Though India and China, like the Roman Empire, had suffered from invasion and conquest, they had fallen upon no "dark age" comparable to that of Europe. The land of the Moslems, extending around the southern rim of the Mediterranean and on to the east of it, supported science, industry, and commerce such as no country of Christian Europe could match. Moslem scholars were familiar with classical learning and far surpassed it in such fields as mathematics, with their Arabic numerals and their decimal system (based on a concept of early India). The wonders of the Far East dazzled the few Europeans who, like the Venetian merchant Marco Polo, got a chance to visit them, and the wonders of the Near East amazed the crusading knights who set out to recover the Holy Land from the infidel.

Forces leading to the awakening of Europe and the discovery of America were set in motion around A.D. 1000 by an outpouring of the Norsemen from Denmark, Norway, and Sweden. These Vikings made conquests as far east as Russia, as far south as France and the British Isles, and as far west as Iceland and Greenland. Two of them, Biarni Heriulfson and Leif Ericson, on separate

Renaissance

voyages, even touched upon the coast of North America, but later attempts at colonization failed, and neither of these men is generally considered the effective discoverer of the New World. Indirectly, however, the Norse did contribute to the subsequent discovery or rediscovery by Columbus. They pioneered in the construction of ocean-going ships, stimulated trade over the area of their widespread conquests, and infused into the life of Europe much of their own energy and daring. Their descendants in France, the Normans (who set up kingdoms in England, Italy and Sicily, and northern Africa), provided outstanding leadership in the Crusades.

The Crusades further encouraged shipbuilding and commerce. In Syria and Egypt the Crusaders got acquainted with a number of exotic goods—spices, perfumes, drugs, silks, china, glassware, gems—which were brought by land and by sea all the way from the Orient. In the Near East some Europeans, especially the Italians, set up trading posts where they exchanged for Oriental commodities mainly the gold, silver, copper, lead, and tin from the mines of Western Europe. These traders sent their imports on to such wholesaling centers as Pisa, Genoa, and Venice, which distributed the goods among merchants from other towns and ultimately among the consumers, remote from the original sources of supply in China, India, or the "Spice Islands" of the East Indies.

This commerce fostered the growth of towns and gave a new importance to town life in Europe. The townsmen or bourgeoisie came to form a substantial "middle" class between the nobles and the clergy above them and the serfs below. They accumulated capital in larger and larger amounts, making possible trading ventures of increasing size and profit. Desiring peace and security, such as would be good for business, the merchants breathed a spirit quite out of harmony with feudalism and its

disorders. In the contests between kings and turbulent nobles, the bourgeoisie came to the support of the kings and thus aided in the rise of centralized national governments.

Increased wealth, leisure, and security, by making possible a greater cultivation of the things of the mind, prepared the way for the Renaissance in Europe. The Renaissance was marked by a changing outlook on life. Formerly, preoccupied with their own sinfulness and weakness, men had viewed their earthly lives as contemptible and had tried to concentrate their thoughts upon eternity. Now, with increasing human self-confidence, they began to show more and more interest in the world about them. Formerly they had relied for their ideas mostly on the authority of the Bible and the works of Aristotle as expounded by the churchmen. Now many became willing to observe, experiment, and test truths for themselves. This changing attitude was involved both in the renewed study of Greek and Roman classics and in the creation of vernacular literatures. It was related also to the multiplication of efforts to control the natural environment by applied science and technology rather than by prayer or magic.

Among the inventions coming into use after the twelfth century were guns and gunpowder, bellows and blast-furnaces, various machines powered by water or wind, movable type and the printing press, the mechanical clock, improvements in ship design and construction, and several devices intended to aid the art of navigation. The compass, at first only a needle magnetized with lodestone and floated in water, told the navigator his direction. He could obtain his latitude by sighting a fixed star with the quadrant, the cross staff, or the astrolabe, and the clock together with certain astronomical data theoretically enabled him to calculate his longitude; but in actual practice he found it next to impossible to make accurate observations from the deck of a rolling ship. So he continued to follow the coasts when feasible, and when he ventured out of sight of land he proceeded (as Columbus did) mainly by dead reckoning, set-

On the European edge of this sea of darkness stood the rising nation-states of England, France, Holland, Portugal, and Spain, each with a strong government and a con-

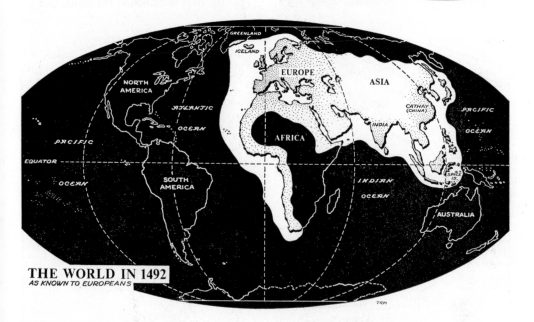

THE WORLD IN 1492
AS KNOWN TO EUROPEANS

ting his course by the compass and finding his position by elapsed time and estimated speed.

Geographical knowledge was still, as in ancient times, a mixture of fable and fact, even though map-making improved remarkably. Mariners, foremost among them the Italians, carefully charted the shore lines along which they sailed, until the coastal areas of almost all the known world had been accurately mapped. On the high seas away from the familiar routes, however, everything remained a matter of speculation. Practical sailors and educated men believed that the earth was a sphere, but many of them underestimated its size. The first globe ever made, the work of a Nuremberg cartographer in 1492, showed an unbroken ocean stretching westward from Europe around to Asia and occupying only about a third of the earth's surface.

sciousness of national unity. These countries, while the most powerful in Europe, were also the most distant from the rich sources of the Oriental trade. In the process of this trade, Italian and Arab merchants added their profits and commissions, and various rulers added their tolls and taxes, so that by the time Oriental wares reached the Atlantic nations the price was outrageously high, and excessive amounts of money were drained away to the eastward. If the middlemen somehow could be by-passed, the Western merchants could gain larger profits for themselves and the Western nations could end the troublesome loss of specie. Here was an adequate motive for finding new routes, entirely by sea, which could be controlled from home. The search for new approaches to the East led to the discovery of new lands in the West, in that presumably empty ocean which lay at the back of Europe.

Westward to the East

Without the wealth of the merchants and the organizing power of the nation-states, the glorious age of exploration would have

ther south. At last, in 1486, Bartholomeu Diaz went clear around the southern tip of the continent, and in 1497–1498 Vasco da Gama proceeded all the way to India. In 1500 the next fleet bound for India, that of

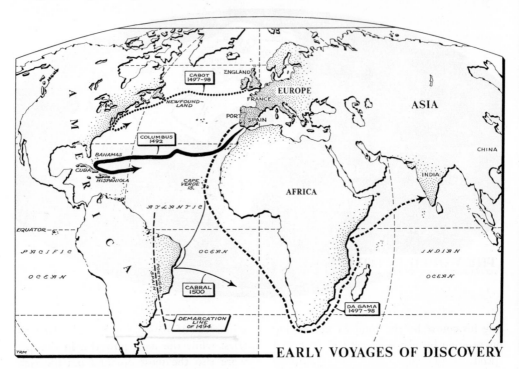

EARLY VOYAGES OF DISCOVERY

been unthinkable. But it would also have been inconceivable without patriotic and religious zeal, skillful seamanship, bold imagination, and courageous leadership.

Portugal early took the lead as an exploring nation. Its maritime supremacy owed a great deal to one man, Prince Henry the Navigator, who devoted his life to nautical studies and to the promotion of exploration. Concentrating upon the western coast of Africa, with the visionary aim of establishing a Christian empire to aid in war against the Moors, and with the more practical object of finding gold, Prince Henry sent out expedition after expedition, some of his mariners going as far south as Cape Verde. After his death in 1460 his work was carried on by intrepid explorers advancing still far-

Pedro Cabral, was blown off its southward course and happened upon the coast of Brazil. So America would have been discovered within a decade even if Columbus had never made his famous voyage of 1492.

Christopher Columbus, who was born and reared in Genoa, got most of his seafaring knowledge and experience in the service of the Portuguese. He was not the first man to think of reaching the East by sailing west, but he was the first to do anything about it. Though an industrious student of geography, he was convinced of the feasibility of his plan as a result of errors rather than special insight. From his reading of Marco Polo's wondrous travel book, from his correspondence with the Florentine geographer Toscanelli, and from other studies and his own calculations, he gathered that the world was smaller than it actually is and that the Asian continent extended farther eastward than it actually does. So he concluded that the western ocean was narrow enough to be crossed on a relatively brief voyage. But he failed to convince the King of Portugal, and as the Portuguese progressed with their own route to the East around Africa, they completely lost interest in the idea of a westward crossing.

Columbus then turned from Portugal to Spain. Though not a maritime people like gon and Isabella of Castile. To Queen Isabella the importunate Columbus appealed for money, men, and ships with which to carry out his project and thereby extend the sway of Christianity and the power and glory of Spain. For several years the Queen withheld her aid, partly because her advisers doubted Columbus' theories and partly because she was busy with Christianizing and conquering Spain itself. In 1492, with the fall of the Moorish stronghold of Granada, the Mohammedans were practically eliminated from Spanish soil, and during that same year

---

The Contract with Columbus

1492

Before undertaking the first of his famous voyages, Columbus drove a rather hard bargain with King Ferdinand and Queen Isabella of Spain. Columbus himself paid about an eighth of the cost of the expedition, obtaining the money from wealthy friends. Ferdinand and Isabella paid the rest. They also agreed to terms that promised to make Columbus rich and powerful, though afterwards they broke their contract with him. His terms were the following:

"First, that your Highnesses as Lords that are of the said oceans, make from this time the said Don Christopher Columbus your Admiral in all those islands and mainlands which by his hand and industry shall be discovered or acquired in the said oceans, during his life, and after his death, his heirs and successors, from one to another perpetually. . . .

"Likewise, that your Highnesses make the said Don Christopher your Viceroy and Governor General in all the said islands and mainlands. . . .

"Item, that all and whatever merchandise, whether it be pearls, precious stones, gold, silver, spices, and other things whatsoever, and merchandise of whatever kind, name, and manner it may be, which may be bought, bartered, discovered, acquired, or obtained within the limits of the said Admiralty, your Highnesses grant henceforth to the said Don Christopher, and will that he may have and take for himself, the tenth part of all of them, deducting all the expenses which may be incurred therein. . . ."

---

the Portuguese, the Spaniards were proud, energetic, and zealous. They were being unified under the strongest monarchy in Europe after the marriage of Ferdinand of Aragon and the Jews who rejected conversion were forced to leave the country. At last Isabella granted Columbus his request. He was to be admiral of the ocean sea, governor of all the lands he might discover, and owner of a tenth of the wealth to be produced therein.

On his first voyage, with the *Pinta*, the *Niña*, and the *Santa Maria* and with ninety

from Asia. On his last voyage, in 1502, he tried to sail around the northwestern end of the continent so as to find the rich and civilized part of the Indies, but he was

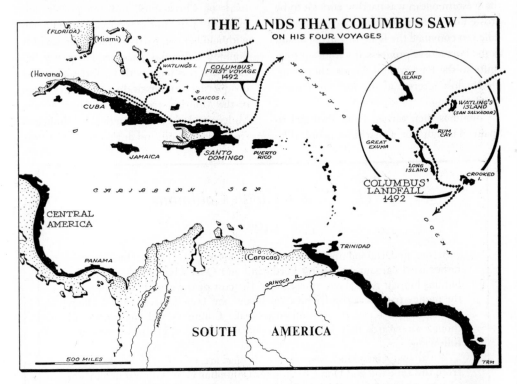

THE LANDS THAT COLUMBUS SAW
ON HIS FOUR VOYAGES

men, Columbus steered as straight as he could for Japan. He thought he had arrived there when, ten weeks after embarking, he landed on Watlings Island in the Bahamas, and he thought he had reached the China coast when he pushed on to Cuba. He returned to Spain with a few natives—he called them "Indians"—but he brought no news of the great Khan's court in China and no samples of the famous wealth of the Indies. The next year, with a much larger expedition, he discovered other islands and left a colony on one of them, Hispaniola. On a third voyage, in 1498, cruising along the northern coast of South America, he passed the mouth of the Orinoco River and surmised that such a large fresh-water stream must emerge from a continent, one separate

blocked by the Isthmus of Panama and succeeded only in exploring the Caribbean coast of Central America. He died still thinking he had been in at least the fringes of the Far East.

At first a hero, then a man in disgrace, Columbus was not even honored in the naming of the land he had discovered. Disregarding his promised monopoly, Spain itself licensed numerous explorers after him, and rival governments sent out expeditions of their own. The Portuguese, who claimed the whole region of his discoveries, promptly dispatched a fleet to the scene (1501). A Florentine merchant, Americus Vespucius, who was aboard, afterward wrote partly fictitious letters describing several visits to the new continent, and a German geographer, Martin Waldseemüller, published one of the letters with the suggestion that the land be named for Americus. The name stuck.

Yet Columbus, for all his misconceptions, deserved the fame that ultimately came to him. He dispelled the terrors of the unknown ocean and led the way to the New World. The explorers of many nations who followed him were but carrying on the work he had begun. Just as he had done on his final voyage, they concentrated their efforts mainly on the search for a water passage which would lead through or around

opened) but they revealed the outlines of both continents and made known the vastness of the territory available for European use.

Spain, turning to the sea as a result of Columbus' initiative, replaced Portugal as the foremost exploring nation. Vasco de Balboa fought his way across the Isthmus of Panama (1513) and gazed upon the great ocean that separated America from China and the Indies. Seeking access to that ocean, Ferdinand Magellan, a Portuguese in Spanish employ, found the strait which now bears his name at the southern end of South

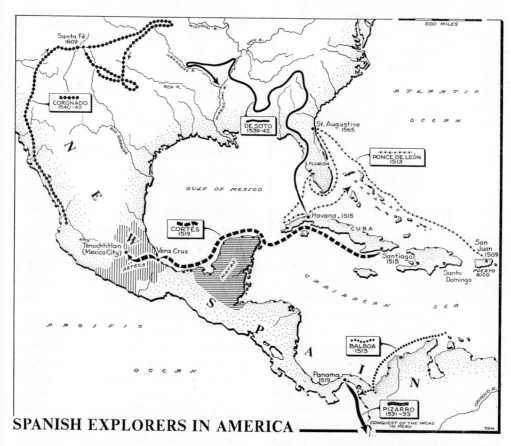

SPANISH EXPLORERS IN AMERICA

the new lands and on to the riches of the Far East. They never found the kind of passage they sought (because it did not exist —until 1914, when the Panama Canal was

America, struggled through the stormy narrows and into the ocean, so calm by contrast that he christened it the Pacific, then proceeded to the Philippines. There Magellan himself fell at the hands of natives, but his expedition went on to complete the first circumnavigation of the globe (1519–1522). By 1550 the Spaniards had explored the

SOME ENGLISH VOYAGES IN THE 16TH CENTURY

coasts of North America as far up as Oregon and Labrador.

England followed Spain as a sponsor of voyages westward in search of the East. John Cabot, Genoa-born like Columbus and inspired by the latter's unsuccessful efforts to reach the Orient, sailed twice to the northwestern coast of North America under the auspices of King Henry VII, the first time in 1497. Much later, after failing to find a northeast passage around Europe, Englishmen began to look for a northwest passage around North America. Martin Frobisher made three trips, the last one in 1578, and discovered Frobisher's Bay, Baffin's Land, and the Eskimos, but not the strait he was

after. Year after year, other Englishmen kept up the search.

Meanwhile, under Francis I, the government of France promoted a series of expeditions to the New World. In 1523–1524 Giovanni Verrazano, a Florentine navigator, followed the shore northward from North Carolina in quest of an opening to Asia for France. Between 1534 and 1541 Jacques Cartier and Jean François Roberval, on separate voyages, tried to find the much-sought passage by pushing up the St. Lawrence River. The Dutch government, a late-comer, commissioned the Englishman Henry Hudson to find an all-Dutch route to Asia, and he was looking for it when, in 1609, he entered the river that afterwards was named for him. Though much valuable information came from all this activity by men of several nationalities sailing under diverse flags, often not their own, the precise relationship of the Asian and North American continents remained something of a mystery until 1728, when Vitus Bering, a Dane in Russian employ, voyaged through the strait that separates the two.

The Spanish Colonies

While remaining an obstacle to those preoccupied with routes to the East, the New World became for others a goal in itself, a source of wealth rivaling and even surpassing the original Indies. The Spaniards, busy making known the configuration of the American continents, were also getting acquainted with their interior and building an American empire. On the basis of Columbus' discoveries and a papal decree, they at first claimed the whole of the New World, but in the Treaty of Tordesillas (1494) they agreed to a demarcation line which left a great chunk of it (Brazil) to the Portuguese. Even so, the area open to Spanish exploitation was so vast and varied that it challenged the human and physical resources of Spain.

The early colonists, beginning with those Columbus brought on his second voyage, settled in the islands of the Caribbean, where they tried without much luck to enslave the Indians and uncover gold. Then (during the same years, 1519–1522, that Magellan's tion of the Spaniards to the mainland. From the island colonies and from the mother country fortune hunters descended upon Mexico in a movement comparable in some ways to the nineteenth-century gold rushes elsewhere in the world. When Francisco

Indians Greet the White Man

1524

In most cases the American natives were very hospitable to the European upon his first approach. Thus Verrazano, exploring for the King of France, reported of his visit to the North Carolina coast:

"While at anchor on this coast, there being no harbor to enter, we sent the boat on shore with twenty-five men, to obtain water; but it was not possible to land without endangering the boat, on account of the immense high surf thrown up by the sea, as it was an open roadstead. Many of the natives came to the beach, indicating by various friendly signs that we might trust ourselves on shore. One of their noble deeds of friendship deserves to be made known to your Majesty. A young sailor was attempting to swim ashore through the surf, to carry them some knickknacks, as little bells, looking glasses, and other like trifles; when he came near three or four of them he tossed the things to them, and turned about to get back to the boat; but he was thrown over by the waves, and so dashed by them that he lay, as it were, dead upon the beach. When these people saw him in this situation, they ran and took him by the head, legs, and arms, and carried him to a distance from the surf. The young man, finding himself borne off in this way, uttered very loud shrieks in fear and dismay, while they answered as they could in their own language, showing him that he had no cause for fear. Afterwards they laid him down at the foot of a little hill, when they took off his shirt and trousers and examined him, expressing the greatest astonishment at the whiteness of his skin. Our sailors in the boat, seeing a great fire made up and their companion placed near it—full of fear, as in all cases of novelty—imagined that the natives were about to roast him for food. But as soon as he had recovered his strength, after a short stay with them, showing by signs that he wished to return aboard, they hugged him with great affection, and accompanied him to the shore, then leaving him that he might feel more secure, they withdrew to a little hill, from which they watched him until he was safe in the boat."

fleet was on its way around the world) Hernando Cortés destroyed the Aztec empire and looted its treasure. The news of silver to be found in Mexico turned the atten-

Pizarro conquered Peru and revealed the wealth of the Incas (1532–1538), the way was opened for a similar advance into South America.

Cortés

Exploration and colonization in Spanish America was primarily a work of private enterprise, carried on by individual leaders, with little direct support from the government at home. Before a man could undertake the job he had to get a royal license. By its terms the king was to have a tenth of the wealth to be produced in the new colony, and the colonizer was to have a tenth in addition to a generous estate, other lands to divide among his followers, and the right for himself and for them to the use of native labor. But he had to equip and finance his own expedition and take the risk of loss or ruin. He might succeed and make a fortune, or through shipwreck or other accident he might lose everything including his life, as many an adventurer did.

The colonial population came only in small part from Spain itself and scarcely at all from other countries in Europe, for few Spaniards were able or willing to emigrate, and foreigners with a few exceptions were excluded from the colonies. Colonial officials were supposed to bring their wives with them, but among the ordinary settlers men outnumbered women by at least ten to one. Naturally, then, most of the Spanish men married Indian women, and a sizeable mixed population grew up. There was nevertheless a manpower shortage, which the Spaniards tried to overcome by forcing the Indians to work for wages. The first experiments with forced labor, as on the island of Hispaniola, resulted in the near extermination of the natives, but Indians continued to work in the mines or on the ranches of the mainland for centuries. As workers on the plantations of the islands and coastal areas, Negro slaves began to be imported as early as 1502, the African slave trade having been established by the Portuguese more than fifty years before that.

The whites exploited the colored peoples, yet the Spanish conquerors were not peculiarly cruel and predatory. Lacking the color prejudice of later English colonists and American whites, the Spaniards treated both the Indians and the Negroes on the whole more humanely than did the English or the Americans. The Spanish reputation for harsh treatment of the natives arose originally from the writings of a sensitive friend of the Indians in the colonies who was himself a Spaniard—Bartolomeo de las Casas. Though overworked and underpaid, the Indians on the *encomiendas* or feudal estates of their Spanish overlords in America were probably no worse off than most of the serfs of continental Europe or even some of the peasants of the British Isles. And if the Spaniards seemed at times to have a monomania for gold and silver, they were in this respect little different from Englishmen such as those at Jamestown who spent their first precious weeks prospecting feverishly for gold. The difference was that the Spaniards, or many of them at least, were fabulously successful. Over a period of three centuries the mines in Spanish America yielded more than ten times as much gold and silver as all the rest of the mines in the world.

The Spanish settlers farmed as well as mined, and they brought in elements of European civilization which, over the centuries, proved far more valuable to the New World than all the gold and silver they took out. They transferred their language and learning, their tools and mechanical arts from the homeland to the colonies. They transplanted grains and fruits and vegetables, including wheat, oranges, lemons, grapes, bananas, olives, and sugar cane. They introduced domestic animals such as cows, pigs, mules, and especially horses, which soon multiplied and ran wild even beyond the colonial frontiers, becoming accessible to the Indians far north on the Great Plains and revolutionizing their way of life. And though the Spaniards brought the sword, they also brought the cross. Priests or friars accompanied every colonizing venture, making each settlement a Christian community and carrying the gospel bravely to the heathen.

The government of the colonies was reasonably efficient and highly centralized. But the Spanish empire did have weaknesses. For one thing, its commercial policy was unusually inflexible and strict. To enforce the collection of duties and provide protection against pirates, the government required all trade with the colonies to be carried on through a single Spanish port and only a few colonial ports, in fleets making but two voyages a year. This system checked the prosperity of many of the colonists, such as those in Argentina, who had to import their Eu-

ropean manufactures and export their own agricultural products through distant Porto Bello on the Isthmus of Panama.

The most serious weakness of the empire resulted partly from the facts of geography. Above Mexico the colonial domain widened out into the whole continent of North America, with no natural barrier such as would limit the aspirations of the Spaniards or provide them with an easily defensible boundary. They could not people the area within this wide border arc thickly enough to make it secure, yet they kept expending energy and resources in trying to hold and even to advance beyond it. The motives for this northward push varied. Such early ex-

Mission San Xavier del Bac. *During the eighteenth century the Spaniards established numerous missions on the northern frontiers of New Spain. One of the finest and best preserved of the churches is San Xavier del Bac, which is located near the present city of Tucson, Arizona. Spaniards visited this area as early as 1539. They were looking for the fabled Seven Cities of Cibola which, according to Indian reports, were full of gold. Eventually missionaries arrived, to Christianize the Indians. Father Eusebio Kino, the most famous of the missionary priests in Spanish America, founded a mission here in 1700. The present church building was constructed in 1797. It was named for St. Francis Xavier, a Spaniard who helped Ignatius Loyola organize the Society of Jesus (the Jesuits) and who served for many years as a devoted missionary in the Far East.* (LIBRARY OF CONGRESS)

plorers as Coronado, De Soto, and Ponce de Leon looked for fabled treasures in the wilderness. Men of religious orders, Jesuit or Franciscan, went out to save souls, the Franciscans establishing a chain of missions which by 1776 extended through California as far north as San Francisco Bay. Frontiersmen moved into New Mexico and Texas to prospect for silver or engage in the Indian trade. Viceroyal expeditions set up remote military outposts, as at St. Augustine in Florida (1565). Indeed, the requirements of defense were always a consideration—defense against the raids of wild tribes and against the colonial thrusts of rival European nations—and *presidios* or fortresses dotted the frontier. But it was a wasting struggle, and in the end a losing one.

These outer reaches of the empire, eventually incorporated into the United States, brought elements of Spanish culture directly into the amalgam of American civilization. Many of these elements are indicated by Spanish words which have become Americanized, words like *ranch, rodeo, corral, lariat, patio,* and *calaboose.* But the influence of Spain's colonial venture upon American history was by no means confined to such direct contributions as these. Contacts, both friendly and hostile, between Spanish-speaking and English-speaking peoples in America affected the development of the United States in ways far too numerous to specify.

Catholic and Protestant

While Spain was building her American empire, the religious unity of Western Europe disappeared, with profound consequences for the colonization of America. As of 1500, the Christian world already was divided between East and West, between the Church of Constantinople and the Church of Rome. But virtually all of western Europe was Roman Catholic and, in spiritual matters, recognized the supremacy of the Pope. Soon

Western Europe itself was divided, between Catholics and those who protested, or Protestants, of whom there came to be many sects. The Protestant leaders intended to reform the Church, and so their movement is known as the Reformation.

The Reformation began in 1517 when Martin Luther, a German professor of theology, challenged the right of the Pope to sell "indulgences" for the remission of sins. Before long, Luther broke completely with the Roman Church. He concluded that man could not find salvation through the Church, its priests, or its sacraments, that man could be saved only by faith, by a thoroughgoing belief in redemption through Christ. Advancing beyond strictly religious matters, Luther advised German rulers to seize Church lands. Rapidly he won converts among both rulers and people.

War ensued between Lutherans and Catholics in Germany. In 1555 the warring factions made a compromise peace, by which each of the German princes was to decide the religion of his subjects. The countries of Southern Germany remained Catholic; those of northern Germany and Scandinavia became Lutheran. Afterwards there was no problem of religious liberty for the Lutheran who happened to find himself in a Lutheran country, or the Catholic in a Catholic country. But there was a problem for the person of either faith who did not share the religious beliefs of his prince.

And there was a problem for those Germans who accepted neither the Lutheran nor the Catholic faith. Starting with Luther's view that salvation was a personal matter, some of the German Protestants went far beyond him in simplifying their creeds and forms of worship. New sects appeared, such as the Dunkers, who practiced rebaptism, and the Mennonites, who believed in direct communion between man and God. Besides, an old sect still existed, made up of the Moravians, followers of John Hus, a Czech who had preached church reform a century before Luther. Sectarians of this kind were not free to worship as they pleased in either the Catholic or the Lutheran countries of Germany.

While Luther was getting his revolt under way, a second great Protestant leader arose, one who was to have a far more direct and important influence upon American civilization. This man was John Calvin. A Frenchman by birth, Calvin studied law and theology in Paris. About 1533 he left the Catholic Church, and then the country. Fleeing to Switzerland, he settled in Geneva, and there he set up a kind of church-state, which he controlled for the rest of his life. He permitted no dissent from his own beliefs.

In his *Institutes of the Christian Religion* (1536), one of the great theological works of all time, Calvin expounded his religious views. The main points, much simplified, were these: God is all-knowing, all-powerful. Man is weak, helpless, born in sin. He cannot save himself by his own efforts: he must rely upon God. Since God knows everything, God knows the future of every soul from the beginning of things, long before the soul is born. God knows whether it is to be saved, or damned. No man can do anything to save his soul, for at birth he already is one of God's chosen, God's elect, or else he is not, and that is that.

On the surface, this doctrine of predestination would seem to imply that human beings might as well enjoy the pleasures of the world, since life here would not determine life hereafter. But such was by no means the conclusion to which Calvin's logic led him. According to his theology, God's elect would give evidence of their future glory by the upright, moral life they lived in this world. Others had a duty to honor God and, regardless, had no choice but to conform. Calvin insisted upon hard work and strict morality. He forbade immodest clothing, swearing, and dancing,

condemned the theater, and provided the death penalty for sex offenses such as adultery.

The Calvinist doctrines, stern and even terrifying as they appear, appealed to many people because of their very forthrightness and puritanical austerity. Calvin gained many followers not only in Switzerland but also in other countries. In France his followers were known as Huguenots, and in the Netherlands as members of the Dutch Reformed Church. In Scotland, whither John Knox carried the message from Geneva, the Calvinists came to be called Presbyterians. In England they were the Puritans.

Neither Calvinism nor Lutheranism, however, caused England to leave the Church of Rome. England broke away because of the political ambitions and marital difficulties of one of her kings, Henry VIII. He coveted the monastery wealth, disliked the loss of money in English contributions to the pope, desired a male heir (which his wife Catherine, daughter of Ferdinand and Isabella of Spain, failed to give him), and fell in love with Anne Boleyn. When the Pope refused to grant a dispensation permitting him to marry Anne, Henry VIII with the cooperation of Parliament made himself (1534) the "supreme head of the Church of England." He was no theological reformer: he kept the main tenets of Roman Catholic doctrine.

After the death of Henry VIII (1547) the Church of England went first to Protestant and then, under "Bloody Mary," to Catholic extremes, with persecutions and martyrdoms on both sides. Finally the Anglican Church straightened out upon a steady middle course during the long and glorious reign of Anne Boleyn's fiery, red-headed, able daughter, Elizabeth I (1558–1603). Under Elizabeth, the Church was given a theology more Protestant than it had had under her father, Henry VIII. Still, the Anglican worship was too "popish" to satisfy dissenters such as the Puritans, who hoped to purify it with the reforms of Calvin. On the other hand, it was anathema to Englishmen who retained the Roman Catholic faith. Yet, by law, all subjects had to conform to the ways of the established Church.

While losing many lands to Lutheranism, Calvinism, or Anglicanism, the Church of Rome undertook to reform itself and win back as much of the world as possible. This undertaking is known as the Catholic Reformation or the Counter Reformation. One of the agencies of the Counter Reformation was the Society of Jesus, founded by Ignatius Loyola in 1534. Its members, the Jesuits, who took an oath of allegiance directly to the pope, labored diligently to stop defections and to gain converts. Other agents of the Counter Reformation were the sovereigns of countries that remained within the Catholic fold.

So western Europe came to be divided between Catholic and Protestant and between one Protestant group and another. Many a nation was divided within itself.

These religious developments of the sixteenth century affected the colonization of America in several ways:

1. Minority groups opposing the state religion—such as the Puritans in England and the Mennonites and Moravians in Germany—looked to the New World as a place where they might worship God according to their lights. Thus the number of willing colonists was larger than it might otherwise have been.

2. Protestantism encouraged business enterprise by emphasizing the virtues of thrift and hard work, and permitting loans at interest, which in Catholic doctrine was usury, a sin. Overseas trading ventures often required loans and in many cases led to the founding of colonies. Colonization, from the point of view of many colonial promoters, was big business, and such business thrived as never before in a Protestant atmosphere.

3. The rise of national religions, in which the church was subordinate to the national sovereign, strengthened the nation-states. And the interests of the state, as well as the lure of private profit, provided a motive for the foundation of colonies.

4. Besides personal and national aggrandizement, the spread of religion was an object of colonization. The religious motive was sharpened by the contest between the forces of the Protestant Reformation and those of the Counter Reformation. The contest was extended from the Old World to the New. Catholics sought to keep America Catholic, and Protestants tried to frustrate Rome and win America, or at least a part of it, for their own particular faith.

England Against Spain

In the sixteenth century Spain acquired vast dominions in Europe as well as America, and her fate in the international politics and religious wars of the time, with England as her nemesis, had tremendous consequences for the future of the New World. Through a series of royal marriages a grandson of Ferdinand and Isabella inherited a large part of western Europe and was elected emperor of the Holy Roman Empire as Charles V. When Emperor Charles V retired (1556) his son King Philip II of Spain did not receive the emperorship of the Hapsburg possessions in Germany. But Philip II retained extensive territories, including the American colonies, parts of Italy, and the Netherlands, and (1580) he made himself King of Portugal as well as Spain. He also assumed the task of leading the Roman Catholic forces of the world against the Protestant Reformation.

The great power of the sixteenth-century world, Spain monopolized America, North and South. She denied to foreigners, with few exceptions, the right to trade or settle within her overseas domain. But other nations, too, had American claims. Eventually these nations—the French, Dutch, and English (and, much later, the Russians)—challenged the Spanish monopoly of North America.

An early challenge came from the Huguenots of France. Though a small minority in that country, they secured influence in the government when (1560) their leader Gaspar de Coligny was appointed Admiral, the head of the French navy. Coligny was interested in obtaining American bases from which the Huguenots might prey upon Spanish commerce. After a couple of unsuccessful colonization attempts, he sent out an expedition which established a Huguenot colony in Florida. An army from Spain fell upon the settlement (1565) and slaughtered most of the Huguenots. Soon France was distracted by religious strife at home, and not for half a century did Frenchmen again attempt to colonize in America.

Meanwhile (1568) the Dutch revolted against Philip II, their Spanish overlord. They fought, as Dutchmen, for national independence, and, as Calvinists, for religious freedom. They were an industrial and maritime people, noted for their linen and woolen cloth, their ships, their fisheries, and their trade. Holding an advantage upon the sea, they robbed the galleons bringing treasure from the New World to Spain. When Spain agreed to a truce (1609) the Dutch turned to planning American colonies of their own.

In their forays against Spanish shipping, both the Dutch and the French Protestants received encouragement and aid from England. Queen Elizabeth had to fend against the machinations of Philip II as he sought to enhance the power of Spain and win back to Rome the areas of Christendom that had been lost. English Catholics were ready to collaborate with a foreign king in forwarding this presumably holy work. With Phil-

ip's encouragement they plotted to get rid of Elizabeth and put Mary Stuart, "Queen of Scots," on the throne. Elizabeth, foiling them, had Mary executed.

In this undeclared war England did not remain on the defensive. During the Elizabethan age many Englishmen felt the call to national greatness which William Shakespeare expressed for them when he wrote of "this sceptred isle, this earth of majesty, this seat of Mars . . . this happy breed of men . . . this precious stone set in the silver sea . . . this England." The happy breed of men developed imperial aspirations of their own, and they were in no mood to respect the colonial monopoly claimed by Spain. Seamen loyal to the Queen—urged on by patriotism, piety, and the hope of plunder—struck at the colonial sources of Spanish strength in every way they could. Roving the waters of Spanish America, these "sea dogs" smuggled slaves, pirated treasure ships, and robbed unprotected towns. The greatest of them all, Francis Drake, followed Magellan's route into the Pacific, looted his way northward along the American coast, went on around the world, and returned a profit of several thousand per cent to the Queen, who secretly had backed his venture. When she knighted him, instead of rebuking him as the Spanish ambassador demanded, she indicated plainly enough that England was ready to challenge Spain upon the sea.

The decisive test soon came. After England had made an alliance with the rebels of the United Netherlands, Philip II declared war. Determining to invade and conquer England, he assembled an unprecedented fleet of his best and largest warships, an "Invincible Armada." But the Spaniards thought of themselves as soldiers more than sailors, and they applied their ideas of land warfare to naval combat, loading troops on their unwieldy vessels to board the enemy craft and grapple at close range with the latter's men. The English, islanders that they were, relied upon their navy and their privateers, not upon an army. They had fast, maneuverable ships which could sail into the Spanish fleet, fire destructive broadsides, and escape to return and fire again. When, in 1588, the Armada appeared in the English Channel, the new naval tactics did not have a chance to show fully their superiority, for a terrible storm helped to scatter the invaders and destroy most of their ships.

England, having become the world's foremost sea power, could not be kept from colonial enterprises of her own on the other side of the Atlantic. Already Englishmen had made their first, rather tentative efforts to start settlements in the New World. Soon the English were to people the Atlantic coast of North America with colonies which eventually would grow into a great continental nation. Thus, for the most part, the age-old cultural heritage of Europe was to be passed on to the United States by way of England, and American institutions were to develop out of English ones.

The English Heritage

In colonizing America, Englishmen brought to this continent not only their material things like tools and their manual skills, their preferences in clothing, their styles of housing, and their tastes in food. They brought also their familiar symbols of calculation and communication. They brought their weights and measures—foot, yard, rod, mile, acre, ounce, pound, ton, pint, quart, gallon, and so on—and also their money system of pounds, shillings, and pence. Above all, they brought their language.

With the English language came a rich though intangible body of thought and feeling. There came a mass of folklore, myths and superstitions, songs and ballads, unwritten stories, proverbs, sayings, and all the wisdom of unlearned people. There came

also the literary classics, the scientific works, the accumulated treasures of English genius. Even the classics of ancient Greece and Rome and those of Renaissance Europe reached America, as often as not, in the language of England. The first American newspapers, pamphlets, and broadsides imitated those with which Englishmen had been familiar at home. The early colonial schools and colleges were patterned on those of the motherland.

God spoke to Americans in English. They read the Bible in English translations, more particularly the stately King James version (1610). The religion of most Americans—Catholic, Anglican, Puritan, Quaker—was shaped and colored by the experiences of Englishmen. Calvinism, instead of going directly across the Atlantic from Geneva, usually was transmitted by way of England or Scotland, as English Puritanism or Scottish Presbyterianism.

From England the colonists derived their conceptions of the proper relationship of man to man in society. They accepted the English ideal of the gentleman as a person above but not apart from the rest of humanity, a person with special privileges but also special obligations, including the obligation of serving the public and helping the less fortunate. The colonists also accepted the standards of the English middle class with its emphasis upon working hard and getting ahead. Neither in England nor in the colonies did Englishmen believe in social equality, but they did believe in opportunity, in keeping the way open for rising from a lower to a higher class.

In dealing with public problems the English as a nation were more pragmatic than doctrinaire. They were inclined to meet issues as they arose, and to settle them by compromise. The English were not noted for long-range planning and consistent action. Rather, they were known for their propensity to "muddle through." They were conservative, slow to change their ways, yet amenable to new procedures if these could be disguised with old, familiar labels. Americans were much the same. They gained a similar reputation for being practical rather than theoretical. At the time of the American Revolution, they pretended to be fighting for nothing really new. They claimed to be fighting for the recovery of old rights which had belonged to them as Englishmen.

In economic affairs the Englishmen were somewhat more enterprising and self-reliant than most of their European contemporaries, such as the Frenchmen and the Spaniards. The English were less dependent upon their government and less inhibited by it. They were comparatively far advanced in carrying on business by voluntary cooperation, by means of companies in which a number of men combined their capital and shared the risks. And the English honored profit-seeking more highly than did the people of most other countries. Americans inherited the English attitudes toward private, cooperative enterprise.

One of the most distinctive legacies from England to America was law. By the end of the Middle Ages the legal traditions of England had advanced to a point where they provided considerable security of person and of property. The English common law, from which grew the Anglo-American common law, was judge-made. Harking back from precedent to precedent, the judges sought to protect the individual from arbitrary actions by either King or Parliament. By legal custom, the ordinary subject had other safeguards. He could be arrested, and his goods could be seized, only if a warrant were first sworn out. When arrested, he was entitled to a trial by a jury of his peers, that is, his equals. He was further protected by fairly well-developed rules of evidence.

The government of England was—or at least was widely believed to be—"a government of laws, not men." From this belief

there logically followed the idea of judicial supremacy, the idea (not always successfully maintained) that courts were superior even to kings. The government, furthermore, was constitutional. The legal rights of the subject, together with the limitations on the sovereign, were embodied in a constitution made up of unwritten customs and of written statements. One such statement was Magna Carta (1215). Historically, Magna Carta was simply a charter of privileges which certain barons had wrung from the King, but traditionally it had come to mean that the people as a whole had rights which the King could not violate. Magna Carta also implied that government depended upon a *contract* between the ruler and his subjects. In the minds of Americans, this contract theory of government was confirmed by the written charters which the colonial founders received from the King.

The King's subjects (or some of them at least) had acquired a share in government through their elected representatives in Parliament, with its House of Commons and House of Lords. The principle was well established that the King could not tax the people without their consent, given through Parliament. With the King's approval, Parliament could make laws. By custom, the King had no right to send strangers among the people to administer local affairs. He appointed justices of the peace, who were the chief officers of local government, but the justices were members of the gentry who lived in the communities they served. The towns and counties possessed a high degree of self-rule. They feared no far-flung bureaucracy or large standing army, for the King had neither at his command. For self-defense, the people relied largely upon themselves, upon their own militia. While respecting law and authority, they cherished the conviction that it was proper to resist authority when it was abused. Along with the fine principles of representation and local self-government, however, the English possessed a number of less attractive traits. Their criminal code, for instance, was brutally harsh. The death penalty was provided for about two hundred offenses, one of which was poaching on a gentleman's estate.

Nowadays some of the characteristics thought of as uniquely "American" are in reality English, at least in origin; the English heritage has been extremely important in the making of American civilization. Yet the importance of that heritage must not be exaggerated. At present there are significant differences, as well as similarities, between English and American ways, and some of these differences are noticeable even to the casual observer. Even in colonial times, when the English in America were only a generation or two removed from the homeland, differences began to be observed.

Three general reasons for this divergence are fairly clear. First, English society was not transplanted as a whole. The people who left for America were not entirely typical of England; usually they were the more discontented or the more adventurous; they were themselves in some degree "different." Second, a great many (though a minority) of the colonists in English America were not English. Many were not even British, did not come from any part of the British Isles. These non-British settlers originated in various countries of Europe. Hence, in America, there was a mixture of diverse European influences. Third, the New World presented a new environment with new challenges and opportunities. This environment brought about changes in Old World habits and outlooks. While certain English traits flourished in America, others withered or never took root at all.

One of the central themes of American history is the process by which a distinctive variant of European civilization was produced in the United States. "What then is the American, this new man?" a Frenchman residing in New York state, St. Jean de Crevecœur, asked at the end of the War for Independence. American history is largely concerned with explaining what "this new man" is like, and how he got to be that way.

>>>->>>->>>->>>-<<<-<<<-<<<-<<<

BIBLIOGRAPHY

ON THE "first Americans," the most accurate and up-to-date general study is C. T. Foreman, *Indians Abroad, 1493–1938* (1943). See also Ruth Underhill, *Red Man's America* (1953); Clark Wissler, *The American Indian* (rev. ed., 1938); Paul Radin, *The Story of the American Indian* (1927); and Livingston Farrand, *Basis of American History* (1904). A useful encyclopedia is Frederick W. Hodge, *Handbook of American Indians* (2 vols., 1907–1910).

A good brief introduction to the European background of American history is R. R. Palmer and Joel Colton, *A History of the Modern World* (rev. ed., 1956). A more extensive account is W. C. Abbott, *The Expansion of Europe* (1938). The older work by E. P. Cheyney, *The European Background of American History* (1904) is still of value.

For a comprehensive treatment of exploration, see J. E. Gillespie, *A History of Geographical Discovery, 1400–1800* (1933). The mysteries of Norse exploration are discussed by H. Hermannsson, *The Problem of Wineland* (1936), and by H. R. Holand, *The Kensington Stone* (1932) and *Westward from Vinland* (1940). Holand argues that the Norsemen traveled inland as far as Minnesota and accepts the authenticity of the rune-like inscriptions on the "Kensington stone" found in that state. His conclusions are not generally accepted by historical scholars. S. E. Morison, *Admiral of the Ocean Sea* (2 vols., 1942), is a classic biography of Columbus.

Roger B. Merriman, *The Rise of the Spanish Empire in the Old World and the New* (4 vols., 1914–1934), is a monumental study. Briefer accounts are provided by H. I. Priestley, *The Coming of the White Man, 1492–1848* (1929), and by E. G. Bourne, *Spain in America, 1450–1580* (1905). English "sea dogs" who preyed upon Spanish commerce are well treated by James A. Williamson in *Sir John Hawkins* (1927) and *The Age of Drake* (1938).

CHAPTER 2

Planting the English Colonies

THE ENGLISH COLONIES in America did not result from deliberate governmental planning. They originated in a variety of responses to the economic changes and religious and political struggles going on in England during the sixteenth and seventeenth centuries. After the death of Queen Elizabeth, the nation was disturbed by decades of conflict between Puritan and Anglican, Parliament and King. There was civil war, dictatorship, a return to the old royal line, and finally a peaceful revolution by which Parliament made itself supreme. Meanwhile England was advancing out of feudalism and into capitalism faster than any other country. Though influenced in some cases by outworn feudal notions, colonization was essentially a business enterprise, a product of the new age. But it was motivated by ideals as well as by profits. The genius of the English both as social dreamers and as practical businessmen is revealed in the founding of the thirteen main-

land colonies over the long period from 1607 to 1733.

King and Parliament

The successors of Queen Elizabeth were not able to control events so masterfully as she had done. As head of the Church of England, she had contended victoriously against the Roman Catholics. The Stuarts who followed her on the throne, and who leaned toward Catholicism, did not have equal luck or skill in dealing with the radical Protestants.

The great Tudors (Henry VII, Henry VIII, and Elizabeth I) had been rather despotic and yet generally popular, for they ruled with considerable tact and gave the people what was urgently needed: stability of government. Englishmen of the 1500's remembered the disorders of the previous century, when quarrels among the powerful families of the nobility led to the wasting and bloody Wars of the Roses. But English-

men of the 1600's no longer felt so much inclined to accept despotic rule, no matter
how able and agreeable the ruler might be.
And most of the Stuart kings proved to be
politically less able and astute than the Tudors had been.

James I began the Stuart dynasty in 1603.
A Scotsman, he was looked upon as a foreigner, and he continued as King of Scotland as well as England though the two
countries were not then united (as they
came to be in 1707). He was a learned man
but a poor politician—the "wisest fool in
Christendom," it was said. Convinced that
kings ruled by divine right, he let the English know at the outset that he intended to
govern as he pleased. Soon he was in trouble
with Parliament.

Strongly represented in Parliament were
the rising businessmen, most of whom were
Puritans. Though members of the Church
of England, they felt that it was still too
much like the Church of Rome. They
wished to simplify the ritual and reduce the
power of the bishops, who were appointed
by the King. The businessmen also objected
to high taxes. James I antagonized Parliament by resorting to illegal and arbitrary
taxation and also by favoring English Catholics and supporting "high church" forms of
elaborate ceremony.

James I died, in 1625, before actually coming to blows with Parliament, but his son
Charles I was even more extreme and eventually brought on violence. From 1629 to
1640, Charles I ruled as an absolute monarch,
refusing to call Parliament into session, imposing high-church forms upon the people,
and imprisoning Puritan leaders. Finally he
called Parliament because he needed money
and hoped the members would vote taxes for
him. This "Long Parliament" remained in
session almost twenty years.

During that time, civil war broke out between the adherents of the King and the
friends of Parliament. The King's follow-

ers, the Cavaliers, included landholding
nobles and others who disliked extreme
Protestantism and desired a strong monarchy. The Parliament men, the Roundheads, were largely Puritans, but these were
divided between Independents and Presbyterians, the latter favoring a centralized
church government. The Roundhead leader,
Oliver Cromwell, an Independent, was both
a religious zealot and a military genius. He
had a well-disciplined, praying army. Yet
for a time Charles I was able to hold his own
by playing the Presbyterians against the Independents and by getting aid from the
Scots. Finally he was defeated, tried, and
beheaded.

From 1649 to 1658 Cromwell, relying on
his Independent army, was practically dictator of England, with the title of Lord
Protector (after 1653). During his rule, shipping and overseas trade were encouraged by
governmental policy. The theater and other
amusements offensive to devout Puritans
were prohibited. Freedom of speech and of
the press was curtailed. When Cromwell
died, there was no strong man to succeed
him, and after his son had been Protector
for less than a year, the Protectorate came
to an end.

Weary of Cromwellian autocracy, the
English people in 1660 welcomed home the
exiled son of Charles I. Parliament accepted
Charles II as King on the condition that he
should rule in partnership with its members
and not in the high-handed way of his father
and grandfather. The handsome and debonair Charles II, tired of his travels, desired
above all to stay in England and keep his
throne. A clever politician, he managed to
do so, despite his favoritism to English Catholics and his secret intrigues with Catholic
France.

His brother James II, who succeeded him
in 1685, lacked his cleverness and ingratiat-
ing ways. James II appointed Catholics to
high office and attempted to dictate to Par-

liament and the courts. He so antagonized Englishmen that he lost all popular support. He fled to France, without resisting, when Parliament offered the throne to his Protestant daughter Mary and her husband William of Orange, ruler of the Netherlands and Protestant champion of Europe. William and Mary became joint sovereigns of England in 1688. By this "Glorious Revolution" the long struggle between King and Parliament finally was settled in Parliament's favor.

These events of seventeenth-century England form an essential part of American history. They help to explain the causes and course of English colonization. For instance, when James I and Charles I pursued their pro-Catholic and high-church policies, Puritans and other Protestants were impelled to look for new homes abroad. When Cromwell was dictator, Cavaliers had cause to migrate. After Charles II came to the throne, he rewarded his friends with generous colonial grants, as his Stuart predecessors had done before him. Then, after the Glorious Revolution, politics in England ran a smoother course, and dissenting Protestants were given the right to worship in their own way, though they still had few political rights. No longer were there overpowering political and religious motives for Englishmen to leave the land of their birth.

No longer were there strong economic motives, either. Previously, during a large part of the sixteenth and seventeenth centuries, there had been important economic and social reasons, as well as political and religious ones, for Englishmen to interest themselves in colonizing ventures on the other side of the Atlantic.

Englishmen Look Overseas

The dream of America as a place of unique opportunity—for liberty, abundance, security, and peace—appeared in England soon after Columbus' discovery. This dream found a classic expression in *Utopia*, a book written by Sir Thomas More and published in Latin in 1516 (translated, 1551), which described society on an imaginary island supposedly discovered by a companion of Americus Vespucius in the waters of the New World. Life in Utopia was as nearly perfect as human beings guided by reason and good will could make it. Though the Utopians lived comfortably enough, they scorned the mere accumulation of material things, and while all were expected to keep busy, none was oppressed or overworked. They enjoyed complete freedom of thought but were careful not to offend one another in the expression of their beliefs. True lovers of peace, they went to war only to defend their neighbors and thereby insure their own ultimate safety. In presenting such a picture of an ideal community, the book commented by indirection upon the social and economic evils of More's England.

The Tudor age, for all its literary glory and its swashbuckling spirit, was not a happy time for most of the common people, who suffered not only from war and religious strife but also from the effects of economic change. While the population of England grew steadily—from three million in 1485 to four million in 1603—the food supply did not increase proportionately. Landowners concentrated on the production of wool. Neither cotton nor silk being yet in general use, wool was in great demand for making cloth. Land tilled at one time by serfs and later by rent-paying tenants, much of it better suited to sheep-raising than to the production of crops, was steadily enclosed for sheep-runs and taken away from the farmers on it. Thousands of evicted tenants roamed the countryside in gangs, to the alarm of more fortunate householders, whose feelings are preserved in the nursery rime: "Hark, hark! The dogs do bark: the beggars are coming to town." The Elizabethan government passed rather ineffectual laws

enclosure

for halting enclosures, relieving the worthy poor, and compelling the able-bodied or "sturdy beggars" to work. Relatively few of these could find re-employment in raising or manufacturing wool. All the while the cost of living rose, mainly because of an increased money supply arising from the output of Spanish gold and silver mines in America. England, it seemed, contained either too many sheep or too many people.

Amid the widespread distress, a rising class of merchant-capitalists prospered from the expansion of foreign trade as they turned from the export of raw wool to the export of woolen cloth. These merchant-capitalists gathered up the raw material, put it out for spinning and weaving in individual households, and then sold the finished product both in England and abroad. At first each exporter did business on his own, though he might belong to the Company of Merchant Adventurers. This company regulated the activities of its members, secured trading privileges for them, and provided protection for their voyages. In time chartered companies sprang up, each with a monopoly from the sovereign of England for trading in a particular region, among them the Muscovy Company (1555), the Levant Company (1581), the Barbary Company (1585), the Guinea Company (1588), and the East India Company (1600). Some of these were regulated companies, similar to the Merchant Adventurers, each member doing business separately. Others were joint-stock companies, much like modern corporations, with stockholders sharing risk and profit either on single ventures or, as became more common, on a permanent basis. These investors often made fantastic profits from the exchange of English manufactures, especially woolens, for exotic goods, and they felt a powerful urge to continue with the expansion of their profitable trade.

To further this drive, spokesmen for the merchant-capitalists developed a set of ideas about the proper relation of government and business—ideas supporting the argument that (notwithstanding the sufferings of the dispossessed) the whole nation benefited from the activities of the overseas traders. The trade of England as a whole, it was said, was basically like that of any individual or firm: transactions were worthwhile if sales exceeded purchases in value. The difference in value would have to be paid in money (gold and silver), and the inflow of money into England would stimulate business and strengthen the national economy by raising commodity prices and lowering interest rates. Merchant-capitalists depended upon loans to carry on their business, and interest was considered now as a cost of production, whereas in medieval times it had been regarded as sinful usury. According to their theory, the government should act to encourage a "favorable" balance of trade —that is, an excess of exports over imports. This economic philosophy, restated by Thomas Mun in his book *England's Treasure by Forraign Trade* (1664), came to be known in the eighteenth century as "mercantilism." It guided the economic policies not only of England but also of Spain, France, and other nation-states.

Colonies would fit well into this mercantilistic program, would also alleviate poverty and unemployment, and would serve other useful purposes, or so it seemed to a number of thoughtful Englishmen in the late sixteenth and early seventeenth centuries. The Oxford clergyman Richard Hakluyt, who published a series of explorers' narratives and an essay (1584) on "western planting," made himself the outstanding propagandist for the establishment of colonies. He and others argued that colonies would provide an additional market for English manufactures, and that the colonial demand would give employment in the mother country to the poor who lived there "idly to the annoy of the whole state." Colonial commerce, while yielding profit for shipowners and customs duties for the government, would bring from the colonies products for which England previously had depended

The actual pioneers of English colonization were Sir Humphrey Gilbert and his half-brother Sir Walter Raleigh, both of whom were friends of Hakluyt and of the

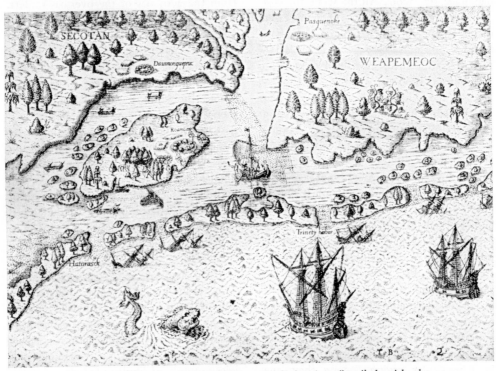

Arrival at Roanoke. *John White, a "skilful painter," sailed with the first colonizing expedition to Roanoke Island, in 1585. He recorded the country and its inhabitants in a series of pictures which Thomas Hariot, another member of the expedition, published in a* Briefe and True Report of the New Found Land of Virginia. *The illustration reproduced above was entitled "The Arrival of the Englishmen." It shows the sheltered position of Roanoke Island behind the Outer Banks of the North Carolina coast. After the failure of the first colonizing attempt, White went to Roanoke as governor of the second colony, in 1587. Returning to England for supplies, he was unable to get back to Roanoke again until 1590. He then could find no trace of the colonists, including his daughter and his granddaughter, Virginia Dare.*

upon foreigners—products such as tobacco, lumber, naval stores, and above all, silver and gold. Colonies might also serve as bases for finding and controlling a westward passage to Asia, attacking the Spanish Empire, and converting the Indians to Protestantism so that the Catholic revival, the Counter Reformation, would not spread to the New World.

Queen. Gilbert obtained from Elizabeth a patent conferring upon him the exclusive right "to inhabit and possess at his choice all remote and heathen lands not in the actual possession of any Christian prince." In 1583 Gilbert planted on Newfoundland an abortive colony, then was himself lost at sea. Raleigh, receiving a grant similar to Gilbert's, sent out in 1585 an expedition which left colonists on Roanoke Island, off the coast of what afterwards became North Carolina, but the entire group returned to England after only a year. After a second failure Raleigh in 1587 sponsored a third voyage, and against his orders the settlers, including women and children, disembarked at the same place. Here was born Virginia Dare, the first American-born child of English parents. A relief expedition, delayed till 1591 by the hostilities with Spain, found Roanoke Island utterly deserted. What became of the "lost colony" is still a mystery.

The colonizing efforts of Gilbert and Raleigh taught lessons and set examples for later and more successful promoters of colonization. After sending out his ill-fated settlers, Raleigh sought financial aid from merchants to whom he sold rights of trading with his proposed colony. He realized that the undertaking was too big for the purse of one man alone. Some of the colonizers after him raised funds for their ventures by forming companies and selling stock, but others as individuals or unincorporated groups depended on their own resources. After the accession of James I, Raleigh was accused of plotting against the King. Raleigh was deprived of his monopoly, imprisoned, and eventually executed. None of his successors received grants so vast and undefined as both his and Gilbert's had been. Thereafter the crown, in theory the owner as well as the sovereign of lands to be occupied by Englishmen, granted and regranted territory to companies or proprietors, on terms that imposed varying conditions, and with boundaries that had limits but often were conflicting and vague.

Virginia and Maryland

Virginia was the name that—in honor of herself, the Virgin Queen—Elizabeth gave to an indefinite stretch of the North American mainland bordering the Atlantic coast. Along these shores Raleigh's investors aimed to renew his colonizing efforts. There were two groups of interested merchants, the one residing mostly in Plymouth and the other in London. In 1606 the Londoners obtained from James I a charter giving them the exclusive right to colonize between the thirty-fourth and the thirty-eighth parallels. Taking the East India Company as their model, they intended to found not an agricultural settlement but a trading post. To it they expected to send English manufactures for barter with the Indians, and from it they hoped to bring back American commodities procured in exchange or produced by the labor of their own employees.

Their first expedition of three small ships (the *Goodspeed*, the *Discovery*, and the *Sarah Constant*) carrying 120 men sailed into Chesapeake Bay and up the James River in the spring of 1607. The colonists—too many of whom were adventurous gentlemen and too few of whom were willing laborers—ran into serious difficulties from the moment they landed and began to build the palisaded settlement of Jamestown. Though beautiful to look at, the site was low and swampy and unhealthful. It was surrounded by thick woods which were hard to clear for cultivation, and it was threatened by hostile Indians under the imperial chief Powhatan. The settlers faced an overwhelming task in trying to sustain themselves, and the promoters in London complicated the task by demanding a quick return on their investment. When the men in Jamestown should have been growing food, they were required to hunt for gold and to pile up lumber, tar, pitch, and iron ore for outgoing vessels. Inbound ships brought new colonists but insufficient supplies. Leadership in the colony was divided among the several members of a council, who quarreled continually until one of them managed to assert his will. This was Captain John Smith, hero of his own narratives of hairbreadth escapes from both

Turks and Indians but a sensible and capable leader nevertheless. After Smith returned to England for treatment of a serious powder burn, there ensued the horrible

money and gave to "planters" willing to migrate with private capital—that is, tools and other equipment. The company began to plan for an agricultural commu-

---

Suffering at Jamestown
1607–1608

An expedition under Captain Christopher Newport began the Jamestown settlement in May, 1607. In June, Captain Newport sailed for England, leaving behind 104 settlers. In September only 46 of these were still living. One of the survivors, George Percy, wrote an account of the terrible time at Jamestown:

"There were never Englishmen left in a foreign country in such misery as we were in this new discovered Virginia. We watched every three nights, lying on the bare cold ground, what weather soever came; and warded all the next day; which brought our men to be most feeble wretches. Our food was but a small can of barley, sodden in water, to five men a day. Our drink, cold water taken out of the river; which was at a flood very salt; at low tide full of slime and filth, which was the destruction of many of our men. Thus we lived for the space of five months [from August, 1607, to January, 1608] in this miserable distress, not having five able men to man our bulwarks upon any occasion. If it had not pleased God to put a terror in the savages' hearts, we had all perished by those wild and cruel pagans, being in that weak estate as we were; our men night and day groaning in every corner of the fort most pitiful to hear. . . .

"It pleased God after a while to send those people which were our mortal enemies, to relieve us with victuals, as bread, corn, fish, and flesh in great plenty, which was the setting up of our feeble men; otherwise we had all perished."

"starving time" in the winter of 1609–10, when famine and disease reduced the population of Jamestown from about five hundred to only sixty. The nearly crazy survivors were taken off on relief ships which arrived in the spring. Jamestown seemed about to be abandoned.

It was saved, however, by steps which the promoters in London already were taking. To add to their funds, they created the Virginia Company, the stock of which they sold to "adventurers" willing to hazard

nity as well as a trading post and, while continuing to send its own employees to Virginia as laborers, no longer tried to feed them from a common storehouse to which all contributed their crops. In a new charter (1609) the boundaries of Virginia were redefined to include a zone four hundred miles wide along the Atlantic coast and stretching westward and northwestward across the continent. In this charter and in a third one (1612) the company also acquired extensive powers of colonial government. Henceforth the directors appointed a governor who, together with a council having only advisory powers, was to oversee affairs in the colony.

The first governor, Lord Delaware, bringing supplies and immigrants, sailed up the James just in time to turn back the wretches fleeing Jamestown. He re-established the settlement, then went home on account of illness. His deputy, Thomas Dale, ruled for several years with the harshest of discipline, sentencing numerous offenders to be flogged, hanged, or broken on the wheel. Yet, during the Dale regime, the basis of

dians was cemented when Rolfe married Powhatan's daughter Pocahontas, who afterward was entertained as a princess on a visit to England, where she died. But Powhatan's brother and successor, Opechancanough, broke the peace with a massacre of more than three hundred and fifty unsuspecting Virginians.

The lack of adequate defenses in the colony, the general mismanagement of the company, and the bickerings among its directors led James I, in 1624, to revoke the charter and take the government of Virginia into his own hands. As a profit-mak-

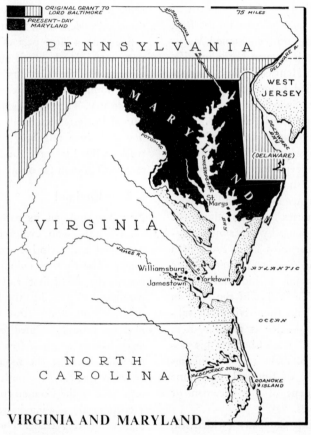

VIRGINIA AND MARYLAND

Virginia's future prosperity was laid when one of the planters, John Rolfe, experimented successfully with the growing and curing of tobacco. And a truce with the In-

ing venture the colony was a failure, yet in a larger sense it was a success, for it demonstrated that English men and women could survive and prosper in America.

One of the stockholders of the Virginia Company, George Calvert, Lord Baltimore, conceived the idea of undertaking a new colony on his own. Himself a convert to the Roman Catholic faith, Calvert had in mind primarily a gigantic speculation in real estate and incidentally the establishment of a refuge for Roman Catholics, victims of political discrimination in England. After getting a Newfoundland grant from James I and spending a winter on it, he looked over Virginia and decided to relocate his colony in the warmer climate to the south of his previous location. From Charles I he obtained a patent to a wedge of Virginia's territory which lay north of the Potomac and east of Chesapeake Bay, and which the King now christened Maryland in honor of his Roman Catholic wife, the Frenchwoman Henrietta Maria. George Calvert having died before the grant was made official, it was issued (1632) to his son Cecilius, the second Lord Baltimore.

The Maryland charter contained some curious provisions which revived in the colony a feudal concept long dead in the mother country. Calvert and his heirs were to hold their province as "true and absolute lords and proprietaries," acknowledging the suzerainty of the King by the annual payment of two Indian arrowheads and a fifth of all the gold and silver to be mined. The proprietor, occupying within Maryland a position comparable to that of the King in England, was to have the privilege of subinfeudating his land—that is, granting it in parcels to men who would become his vassals. But he was to make no laws incompatible with those of England, and none without the consent of the freemen or their representatives.

Since the Virginia Company (which still claimed its land rights) objected to the Calvert grant, Lord Baltimore remained at home to defend his interests at court while he sent two of his brothers, with one of

them, Leonard Calvert, as governor, to see to the settlement of the family's province. In March of 1634 the *Ark* and the *Dove*, bearing two or three hundred passengers, mostly Roman Catholics, entered the Potomac and turned into one of its eastern tributaries. On a high and dry bluff these first arrivals laid out the village of St. Mary's, while the neighboring Indians, already withdrawing to avoid native enemies, assisted by providing stocks of corn. The early Marylanders knew no massacres, no plagues, no starving time. Their most serious trouble arose from border disputes with the Virginians, disputes which provoked some bloodshed but finally were ended by the King's decision in favor of Maryland.

Spending a large part of the family fortune in the development of their American possessions, the Calverts had to attract many thousands of settlers if their venture was to pay. They encouraged the immigration of Protestants as well as Roman Catholics, and since relatively few of the latter were inclined to leave England, the Protestant settlers soon far outnumbered them.

New England

New England got its name from Captain John Smith, who explored its coast and published a descriptive account, including a map. The right to colonize this area, between the forty-first and the forty-fifth parallels, had passed to the Plymouth group of merchants at the same time (1606) the London group obtained colonizing privileges farther south. After an unsuccessful planting effort at the mouth of the Kennebec River, the Plymouth enterprisers reorganized as the Council for New England, a corporation dealing in real estate rather than promoting trade. The Council transferred its lands to individuals and companies in a series of overlapping and confusing grants. These, confirmed or altered by new grants directly from the King, provided the basis for all the colonies that emerged in New England—Massachusetts (including Plymouth and Maine), Connecticut, Rhode Island, and New Hampshire.

Many of the New England colonizers and almost all the colonists were Puritans, who had a religious as well as an economic interest in leaving England for settlements beyond the sea. The Puritans, influenced in varying degrees by the teachings of John Calvin, differed considerably among themselves, but most of them were alike in being mere Nonconformists, while a small minority were out-and-out Separatists. Detesting what they considered "popish" forms and practices, the Nonconformists aimed at first to "purify" the Church of England from within, though in America they were to break away completely. The Separatists, who were more radical, were determined from the beginning to worship as they pleased in their own independent congregations. Like all subjects of the King, however, they were forbidden by law to absent themselves from regular Anglican services, to hold unauthorized religious meetings, or to leave the realm without the King's consent.

Slipping away a few at a time, the members of a Separatist congregation from Scrooby, in Nottinghamshire, crossed the English Channel and began their lives anew in Holland. Here they were allowed to meet and worship freely, but, as aliens, they were not allowed to join the Dutch guilds of craftsmen, and so they had to work long and hard at unskilled and poorly paid jobs. Some of them decided to move again, this time across the Atlantic, where they might find opportunity for living more happily and also for propagating "the gospel of the Kingdom of Christ in those remote parts of the world." These Pilgrims made arrangements with English merchants for financing their venture, and they got permission from the Virginia Company to settle as an inde-

pendent community on its land. They tried, and failed, to get from James I a guarantee of religious freedom, but they learned "that he would . . . not molest them, provided they carried themselves peaceably." This was a historic concession on the part of the King, for it opened English America to settlement by dissenting Protestants.

From Plymouth, England, the *Mayflower* took its 102 passengers to Plymouth in New England, where on a bleak December day in 1620 they disembarked, though they had not reached their intended destination. During the first winter half of them died from scurvy and exposure, but the rest managed to put their colony on its feet. Among the Indians thereabout, who as a result of a recent plague had been decimated even worse than they, the Englishmen discovered friends—Squanto, Samoset, Massasoit—who showed them how to gather seafood and cultivate corn. On their sandy and marshy soil the settlers could not aspire to rich farms, but they developed a profitable trade in fish and furs. Taking over this trade, the great-hearted leader William Bradford and a group of "undertakers" arranged to pay off the colony's debt to its financiers in England, even though the latter had not lived up to their agreement to continue to send supplies.

Since Plymouth lay outside the Virginia Company's possessions, its legal status as a colony was dubious from the start. Before leaving the ship forty-one of the first arrivals, to deal with threats of disobedience, signed the Mayflower Compact. This Compact was like the church covenant by which the Separatists formed congregations, except that it bound its signers to observe the ordinances of a civil rather than a religious society, and it professed their allegiance to the King. The colonists soon cleared their land title with a patent from the Council for New England, but never secured a royal charter giving them indisputable rights of government. As citizens of a virtually independent republic they went their way for over seventy years, until Plymouth was annexed to the much larger colony of Massachusetts Bay.

prominent Puritans among the stockholders, desiring to create a refuge for their faith, expressed their willingness to go to America if they were given control of the company. By the Cambridge Agreement

---

The Mayflower Compact
1620

"In the name of God, Amen. We, whose names are underwritten, the Loyal Subjects of our dread Sovereign Lord King *James*, by the Grace of God, of *Great Britain, France*, and *Ireland*, King, *Defender of the Faith*, &c. Having undertaken for the Glory of God, and Advancement of the Christian Faith, and the Honour of our King and Country, a Voyage to plant the first colony in the northern Parts of Virginia; Do by these presents, solemnly and mutually in the Presence of God and one another, covenant and combine ourselves together into a civil Body Politick, for our better Ordering and Preservation, and Furtherance of the Ends aforesaid; And by Virtue hereof do enact, constitute, and frame, such just and equal Laws, Ordinances, Acts, Constitutions, and Offices, from time to time, as shall be thought most meet and convenient for the general Good of the Colony; unto which we promise all due Submission and Obedience."

Massachusetts had its earliest beginnings in the English fisheries along its coast. From these a plan developed for establishing a permanent fishing and trading station and then a missionary outpost at Salem. A corporation, formed to raise funds for putting the struggling colony on a sounder basis, was reorganized in 1629 as the Massachusetts Bay Company, with a royal charter which granted a strip of land lying between lines three miles south of the Charles River and three miles north of the Merrimack and extending westward to the Pacific. The Massachusetts Bay Company at first intended to maintain and develop the Salem settlement as a commercial enterprise, then changed its plans because of the stern High-Church policies of the new king, Charles I. Now a number of wealthy and

they were given such control, and the corporation's headquarters were transferred from Old to New England. The stockholders elected John Winthrop as governor of the company and hence of the colony also. A gentleman of means, with a university education, a deep but narrow piety, a cool and calculating temperament, and a remarkably forceful if stubborn character, Winthrop became the father of Massachusetts.

Under Governor Winthrop, the refounded Puritan colony got off to an auspicious start in 1630, when eleven ships and about a thousand settlers, many of them well-to-do, ventured across the Atlantic. They made Boston rather than Salem the nucleus and capital of their colony, but they soon established several outlying towns. After a few years Massachusetts grew so fast that its people had reason to think God smiled upon their project. To escape the tyranny of Charles I, while he ruled England without a Parliament, the Puritans migrated in such numbers that by 1643 their colony had a population of about 15,000, as many as all the rest of English America at that time. Then, during the war

Another outpouring from Massachusetts Bay, to various parts of New England (and to other places in English America), meanwhile had begun. This exodus was motivated generally by one or both of two considerations: the unproductiveness of the stony farms around Boston, and the oppressiveness of the Massachusetts government. Governor Winthrop and a handful of

Housing the First Settlers. *When the English first landed at Jamestown, Plymouth, and elsewhere in America, they had neither time nor facilities to build substantial frame or brick houses. Nor were these colonists familiar with the log cabin that later became typical of the American frontier. So they constructed temporary shelters of various kinds, including wigwams patterned after those of the Indians and cottages similar to those of some of the poorer folk in England. The Pioneer Village at Salem, Massachusetts, is a reconstruction of Salem village as it may have looked during its earliest years. The photograph shows, at the left, one of the reconstructed Salem cottages with a dirt floor, a thatched roof, and a chimney made of small logs daubed with plaster. Such houses were far from fireproof. In 1626, as a fire-prevention measure, Plymouth Colony adopted a law prohibiting thatched roofs.* (ESSEX INSTITUTE, SALEM, MASS.)

against King and Cavaliers, quite a few of the immigrants went back to aid the Puritan cause at home, and for a while those returning to England outnumbered those newly arriving in Massachusetts.

assistants and freemen (stockholders in the company) ruled as if they were agents of God. They were slow to yield to the popular demand for increasing the number of freemen and giving all of them law-making powers in the colonial legislature, called the General Court. Having broken with the Church of England, the Puritan leaders governed both a church and a state of their own, and they were no more inclined to brook dissenters than the King and the archbishop themselves had been. In such a theocracy as Massachusetts became, religion and politics were hard to tell apart, and theological heterodoxy seemed to those in authority very much like treason. Individualists—and Puritanism somehow bred them—had little choice but to give in or get out. Such individualists were responsible for new settlements north and south of Massachusetts Bay, in New Hampshire and Rhode Island. Farmers seeking richer lands as well as greater religious independence began new settlements to the west, in Connecticut.

The Connecticut Valley, a hundred miles beyond the settled frontier, had fertile meadows which invited pioneering despite the presence of warlike Indians and the claims of the already fortified Dutch. In 1635 and 1636 several entire Massachusetts congregations, impelled by the strong bent of their spirits, as the Reverend Thomas Hooker said, drove their cattle and hogs through the wilderness and established four towns along the Connecticut River. At the same time a fort was built at the river's mouth by agents of two Puritans in England who asserted a proprietary right to the whole region. Disregarding this claim, the valley towns united under a kind of constitution known as the Fundamental Orders of Connecticut. A separate colony, the project of a Puritan minister and a wealthy merchant from England, grew up around New Haven on the coast. Eventually (1662) the governor of Connecticut obtained a royal charter extending his colony's jurisdiction over the New Haven settlements.

Rhode Island was founded by Roger Williams, a sensitive and likeable but trouble-some young minister of Massachusetts Bay. Styling himself only a "seeker" after truth and salvation, Williams was free from the dogmatism and self-righteousness of the Puritans in power. He believed in a complete separation of church and state and in absolute freedom of conscience. What was even more shocking to the colonial authorities, he argued that the land belonged to the Indians and that the Massachusetts Bay Company had no valid title to it! Banished from the colony, he took refuge among the Narragansett Indians during a bitter winter, then with a few of his friends established the town of Providence, in 1636. Soon afterward Mrs. Anne Hutchinson, the Samaritan-minded wife of a substantial Bostonian, attracted many more followers than Williams with her heretical doctrine that the Holy Spirit dwelled within and guided every true believer. After a trial at which Governor Winthrop acted as both prosecutor and judge, Mrs. Hutchinson too was expelled, and she and some of her followers moved to Narragansett Bay, not far from Providence. In time other communities of dissidents arose in that vicinity and were combined under a royal charter (1663) as Rhode Island and Providence Plantations.

New Hampshire and Maine had become the separate possessions of two proprietors, Captain John Mason and Sir Ferdinando Gorges, when (1629) they divided along the Piscataqua River their grant from the Council for New England. Despite lavish promotional efforts, especially on the part of Gorges, few settlers were drawn to these northern regions until the religious disruption of Massachusetts Bay. In 1638 John Wheelwright, a disciple of Anne Hutchinson, led a party of his fellow-heretics to Exeter, in New Hampshire. Thereafter a number of towns in that province and in Maine were peopled by orthodox or unorthodox Puritans from Massachusetts or by Anglicans from across the sea. The Massachusetts Bay Company extended its authority to the whole territory to the north but ultimately lost its cases against the heirs of both Mason and Gorges in the highest

Eliot, a saintly missionary who translated the Bible into the Indian language, the Puritans viewed the redmen as "pernicious creatures" who deserved extermination unless

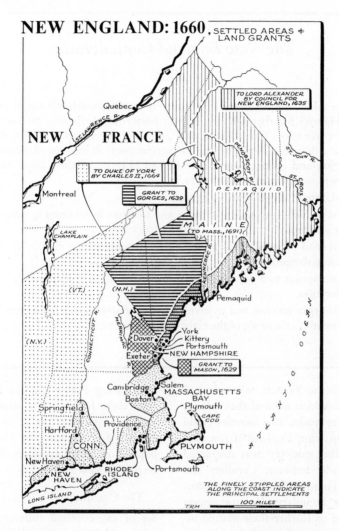

NEW ENGLAND: 1660, SETTLED AREAS + LAND GRANTS

courts of England. New Hampshire then (1679) was set up as a separate royal province. Maine, the Gorges family having sold their rights to it, remained a part of Massachusets from 1691 until admitted to the Union as a state in 1820.

As New England spread, the settlers ran into trouble with the Indians. With a few exceptions like Roger Williams and John

they would be willing to adopt the white man's ways. In 1637 the exasperated Pequots went on the warpath in the Connecticut Valley. The Connecticut frontiersmen marched against a palisaded Pequot stronghold and set it afire. About five hundred of the Pequots were burned to death or killed when trying to escape, and most of the survivors were hunted down, captured, and sold as slaves. The Pequot tribe was wiped out.

The New England colonies faced danger not only from the Indians but also from

By 1675, when King Philip's War began, the New England Confederation had deteriorated so much that it could no longer be relied upon for organizing frontier de-

---

The New England Confederation
1643

"The said United Colonies [Massachusetts, Plymouth, Connecticut, and New Haven] for themselves and their posterities do jointly and severally hereby enter into a firm and perpetual league of friendship and amity for offence and defence, mutual advice and succor upon all just occasions both for preserving and propagating the truth and liberties of the Gospel and for their own mutual safety and welfare."

The United Colonies further agreed:

1. To provide men and provisions and to share in all costs in proportion to their abilities.

2. To send immediate aid to any of their confederates that might be invaded or in danger.

3. To appoint two commissioners apiece for managing the affairs of the confederation.

4. To begin no war, and to involve the confederation in no war, without the consent of at least six of the eight commissioners.

---

the Dutch and the French, who claimed the territory on which some of the outlying settlements were made. The colonies could not expect help from England at the time when the mother country was distracted by the civil war between Cavaliers and Roundheads. To provide frontier protection, to adjust boundary disputes among themselves, and to further their mutual interests in other ways, four of the colonies joined (1643) in "The Confederation of the United Colonies of New England." These four were Massachusetts, Plymouth, Connecticut, and New Haven. The other settlements—those of Rhode Island, New Hampshire, and Maine—were excluded, since Massachusetts aspired to annex them and objected to recognizing them as equals.

fense. King Philip and the Wampanoags, with their Indian allies, destroyed or depopulated twenty towns and caused the deaths of a sixteenth of the white male population in three years of gloom and terror for New England.

The Carolinas

Six of the eventual thirteen colonies had originated before the political disturbances in England during the 1640's and 1650's, which temporarily halted colonizing activities from abroad. Then (1660) Charles II returned from his wandering exile to reign as the Merry Monarch and reward his faithful courtiers with truly regal gifts of land in the New World. He not only acknowledged with royal charters the various colonies which had broken off from the detestable (to him) Puritan commonwealth of Massachusetts, but he also gave rise within a quarter of a century to six additional colonies: North and South Carolina, New York, New Jersey, Pennsylvania, and Delaware.

Carolina (after the Latin *Carolinus*, meaning Charles), partly taken like Maryland from the Virginia domain, was awarded by Charles II to a group of eight of his favorites, all prominent politicians, of whom the most active in Carolina affairs was Anthony Cooper, Lord Ashley. In successive charters (1663, 1665) these eight received a joint title to the whole of the wide territory between the latitudes of 29° and 36° 30'. Like Lord Baltimore in Maryland, they were en-

development, selling or giving away the rest in smaller tracts, and collecting annual payments as quitrents from the owners. Though committed to the advancement of the Church of England, the Carolina proprietors welcomed customers whether Anglican or not.

These dealers in land made the mistake, however, of experimenting for a time with a bizarre scheme of society and government which tended to discourage immigration. To draw up their plan, they commissioned the philosopher John Locke, who afterwards became famous, though not for this piece of work. It looked well enough on paper—with its nobility bearing such titles as "landgrave" or "cacique" and its serflike class of "leet-men"—but it was too arti-

THE CAROLINAS AND GEORGIA

dowed with certain feudal privileges within their grant. Like him, they expected to profit as landlords and land speculators, reserving tremendous estates for their own

ficial and undemocratic ever to be carried out. The actual government developed, with some delay, along natural though different lines in the two widely separated areas of settlement, the one northeast and the other southwest of Cape Fear. After treating these areas for a while as parts of a single colony, with the same governor, from geographical handicaps, the coastal region being isolated by the Dismal Swamp, by the southeastwardly flow of the rivers, and by the lack of natural harbors usable

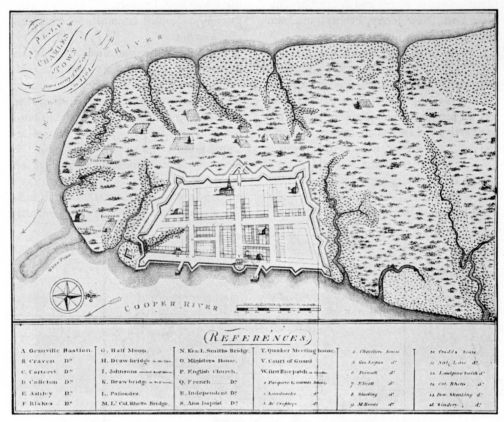

A City in the Wilderness: Charleston in 1704. *Lord Ashley, the most active of the Carolina proprietors, gave instructions to divide Charleston "into regular streets, for be the buildings never so mean and thin at first, yet as the town increases in riches and people, the void places will be filled up and the buildings will grow more beautiful." Thus, from the beginning, Charleston grew according to an orderly, rectangular plan. To hasten settlement, the proprietors in 1694 directed the Carolina governor to fortify the town. This map of 1704 shows Charleston (population, about 2,000) with its completed fortifications. Inside the walls were four churches, a few warehouses and shops, and several fine houses in addition to more modest dwellings. Outside were a Quaker meeting house and several rice plantations.*

the proprietors at last (1712) made them separate colonies, each with a governor of its own. North and South Carolina already possessed distinct characteristics and quite different histories.

North Carolina suffered in the early years for ocean-going ships. The first settlers came mostly from other mainland colonies —a few from New England, the majority from Virginia. They soon acquired a bad reputation among Virginians, who looked upon them as a lazy and immoral set of

runaway servants, debtors, thieves, and pirates. In fact, the early North Carolinians
were honest enough on the whole, but they
showed the marks of their primitive backwoods existence, with practically no towns,
churches, or schools, few roads or large
plantations, and more than their share of
trouble from both rebellious whites and re-
sentful Indians, culminating in the bloody
Tuscarora War (1711). These pioneers also
showed the marks of neglect by the proprietors, who gave most of their attention
to the southern half of their property.

South Carolina was favored with an excellent harbor at the point where the Ashley and Cooper rivers joined "to form the
Atlantic Ocean" (as later South Carolina
boosters said). Here the proprietors saw
to the founding of the city of Charleston,
with wharves, fortifications, fine houses,
and wide streets. Several of the colony's
early leaders and many of its first inhabitants came from the declining sugar plantations of the British West Indies, especially
Barbados. Prosperous plantations developed
on the mainland, and population grew much
faster here than north of Cape Fear, yet the
growth of South Carolina was limited by
the threat of the Spaniards on her southern
border.

New Netherland: New York

The year after making his Carolina grant
Charles II bestowed (1664) upon his
brother the Duke of York (afterwards King
James II) all the territory lying between
the Connecticut and Delaware rivers. A
large part of this land presumably belonged
to the Massachusetts Bay Company by virtue of the company's sea-to-sea grant. The
whole region was claimed by the Dutch,
who occupied strategic points within it.

The Dutch Republic, after winning independence from Spain, had launched upon
its own career of overseas trading and empire building in Asia, Africa, and America.

On the basis of Hudson's explorations the
Dutch staked an American claim and proceeded promptly to exploit it with a busy
trade in furs. To add permanence to the
business, the Dutch West India Company
began to encourage settlement, transporting
whole families on such voyages as that of
the *New Netherland* in 1624, and later offering vast feudal estates to "patroons" who
would bring over immigrants to work the
land. So developed the colony of New
Netherland. It centered around New Amsterdam with its blockhouse on Manhattan
Island, and included thinly scattered settlements on the Hudson, the Delaware, and
the Connecticut, with forts for their protection. In 1655 the Dutch extended their sway
over the few Swedes and Finns settled
along the lower Delaware. In the Connecticut Valley, however, they had to give in to
the superior numbers of the English moving out from Massachusetts Bay.

Three Anglo-Dutch wars arose from the
commercial and colonial rivalry of England
and The Netherlands throughout the world
and particularly in America, where the
English resented the foreign stronghold
which wedged apart their own northern
and southern colonies and provided smuggling bases for the Dutch. During the second of these wars, in 1664, troop-carrying
vessels of the English navy put in at New
Amsterdam and extracted a surrender from
the arbitrary and unpopular governor, the
peg-legged Peter Stuyvesant. During the
final conflict the Dutch reconquered and
briefly (1673-1674) held their old provincial capital, then lost it again for good.

New York, formerly New Netherland,
already the property of the Duke of York
and renamed by him, was his to rule as
virtually an absolute monarch. Instead of
going to America he delegated his powers
to a governor and a council. He confirmed
the Dutch patroonships already set up, the
most notable of them being Rensselaers-

wyck with its 700,000 acres around Albany, and he gave away comparable estates to Englishmen so as to create a class of influential landowners loyal to him. He was supposed to see to the establishment of the

mediate valley of the Hudson. In time New York became predominantly English in population and customs, yet Dutch traditions lingered on to leave a distinctive regional flavor.

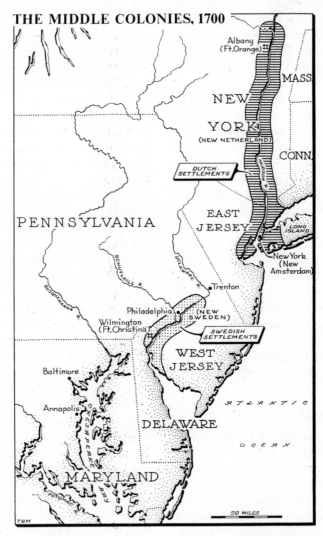

THE MIDDLE COLONIES, 1700

Church of England in his province, but since he was himself a Roman Catholic and the inhabitants included Calvinists (either Puritan or Dutch Reformed) as well as Anglicans, he found it expedient to be broadminded with regard to religion. The early settlements were confined to the im-

On the north and west the Duke's dominions were extended as far as Lake Ontario by means of a protectorate over the Iroquois. On the east, however, his territory was trimmed in a boundary compromise with Massachusetts and Connecticut. On the south it was enlarged somewhat by his claim (based on conquest from the Dutch) to land west of the lower Delaware, but was diminished even more by his generosity in parting with his possessions. He gave what became New Jersey to a couple of cronies, both Carolina proprietors, Sir George Carteret and Lord John Berkeley. The latter sold his half interest to two enterprising members of the Society of Friends, thus bringing the Quakers into the colonization business. And the Duke gave what became Delaware to another Quaker, the greatest of all the colonizers, William Penn.

The Quaker Colonies

The Society of Friends originated in mid-seventeenth-century England in response to the preachings of George Fox, a Nottingham shoemaker, whose followers came to be known as Quakers from his admonition to them to "tremble at the name of the Lord." The essence of Fox's teachings was the doctrine of the Inner Light, the illumination from God within each soul, the divine conscience which when rightly heeded could guide human beings along the paths of righteousness. Of all the Protestant sectarians of the time, the Quakers were the most anarchistic and the most democratic. They had no church government except for their monthly, quarterly, and annual meetings at which the congregations were represented on a local, regional, and national basis. They had no traditional church buildings—only meetinghouses. They had no paid clergy, and in their worship they spoke up one by one as the spirit moved them. Disregarding social distinctions such as those of sex and class, they treated women as equals and addressed one another with the "thee" and "thou" then commonly used in speaking to servants and inferiors. Defying other accepted conventions, they refused to participate in taking oaths or in fighting wars. The Quakers were unpopu-

lar enough as a result of these beliefs and practices, and they increased their unpopularity by occasionally breaking up other religious groups at worship. Many of them were jailed from time to time.

Naturally, like the Puritans earlier, George Fox and his followers looked to America for asylum. A few of them went to New England, but there (except in Rhode Island) they were greeted with fines, whippings, and orders to leave, and three men and a woman who persisted in staying were actually put to death. Many migrated to North Carolina, and there, as the first and fastest growing religious community, they soon predominated in colonial politics. Yet the Quakers desired a colony of their own, and Fox himself visited America (1671–1672) to look over the land. As the head of a sect despised in England, however, he could not get the necessary grant without the aid of someone influential at the court. Fortunately for his cause, his teachings had struck the hearts of a number of wealthy and prominent men, one of whom in particular made possible a large-scale effort to realize the Quaker dream.

William Penn—whose father was Sir William Penn, an admiral in the Royal Navy and a landlord of valuable Irish estates—received a gentleman's education at his father's expense but could not overcome his mystical inclinations despite his father's discipline. Converted to the doctrine of the Inner Light, the younger Penn took up evangelism and, though always moderate and soft-spoken, was repeatedly put in prison, where he wrote a powerful tract, *No Cross, No Crown*. With George Fox he visited the European continent and found Quakers there, as in the British Isles, who longed to emigrate.

New Jersey, half of which two of his fellow Quakers owned, received Penn's attention when he was asked to assist them with their debts. In their behalf he helped to see to the division of the province into East and West Jersey, Carteret as one of the original proprietors keeping the East, and the Quakers the West. West Jersey soon began to fill up with Friends from England while East Jersey was being populated mostly by Puritans from New England. Before long (1682) Penn together with other wealthy Quakers purchased the eastern property from Carteret, and eventually (1702) the two Jerseys were reunited as one colony, second in Quaker population only to Pennsylvania itself.

Pennsylvania—which Charles II insisted on naming for his old ally, the admiral—was based on the King's grant of 1681. Penn, reconciled with his father, had inherited the latter's Irish lands and also his claim to the equivalent of $80,000 owed by the King. Charles II, possessing more real estate than ready cash, paid the debt with a grant of territory, between New York and Maryland, which was larger than England and Wales combined and which (unknown to him) contained more value in soil and minerals than any other province of English America. Within this fabulous estate Penn was to have the rights of both landlord and ruler while acknowledging the feudal suzerainty of the King by the token payment of two beaver skins a year.

Like the Calverts, the Carolina proprietors, and the Duke of York, Penn intended to make money from land sales and quitrents and from private property to be worked for him. He promptly sold several large tracts to rich Quaker associates and one tract of 15,000 acres to a group of German immigrants led by Francis Daniel Pastorius. Through his informative and honest advertising, as in his pamphlet entitled *A Brief Account of the Province of Pennsylvania*, which was translated into several European languages, he made Pennsylvania the best known and most cosmopolitan of all the colonies. Like the rest of the colonial proprietors, however, he and his descendants were to find almost hopeless the task of collecting quitrents.

Much more than a mere real estate promoter, Penn was interested in Pennsylvania most of all as what he called a Holy Experiment. Colonies, he said, were the "seeds of nations," and he proposed to plant the seeds of brotherly love. Closely supervising the planting, he devised a liberal Frame of Government for his settlers, and he personally voyaged to Pennsylvania (1682) to oversee the laying out, between the Delaware and Schuylkill rivers, of the city he appropriately named Philadelphia ("Brotherly Love"), which with its rectangular streets set the pattern for most later cities in America. He believed, as had Roger Williams, that the land belonged to the Indians, and he was careful to see that they were reimbursed for it, as well as to see that they were not debauched by the fur traders' fire-water. With the Indians, who honored him as a rarity, an honest white man, his colony had no trouble during his lifetime. It prospered from the outset because of his thoughtful planning and also because of the mildness of the climate and the fertility of the soil, the well-to-do and well-equipped class of settlers he brought in, and the assistance they received from the people of other colonies and from the Hollanders and Swedes and Finns already on the ground—for Pennsylvania when Penn first saw it was no such wilderness as Virginia had been when John Smith arrived.

Delaware, after its transfer to Penn from the Duke of York (1682), was treated as a part of Pennsylvania (and was known as "the lower counties") but was given the privilege of setting up its own representative assembly. The three counties did so in 1703, and thereafter Delaware was considered a separate colony, though until the Revolution it continued to have the same governor as Pennsylvania.

Georgia

Georgia, the last of the mainland colonies, was unique in its origins. It was founded by neither a corporation nor a proprietorship, and its guiding purpose was neither to make profits nor to create a sectarian refuge. In the beginning Georgia was the work of trustees serving without pay. Their main purpose was twofold: to provide a new start in life for Englishmen imprisoned for debt, and to erect a military barrier against the Spaniards on the southern border of English America.

As claimants to the whole continent, the Spaniards had looked suspiciously upon the encroachment at Jamestown, and had taken one captive while giving up three of their own men in a halfhearted attempt to frighten the English away. In a treaty of 1676 Spain recognized England's title to lands already occupied by English subjects. Ten years later Spanish forces from Florida attacked and destroyed an outlying South Carolina settlement south of the treaty line. When Spain and England went to war in Europe (1701–1713) hostilities were renewed in America, and thereafter another European conflict with American repercussions was continually expected.

General James Oglethorpe, a hero of the late war with Spain, was much concerned about the need for a buffer colony between South Carolina and Florida. As head of a parliamentary committee investigating English prisons, Oglethorpe also knew at first hand the plight of honest debtors rotting in confinement. He conceived the idea of solving both problems at once by resettling such prisoners as farmer-soldiers on the faraway frontier.

The charter from George II (1732) transferred the land between the Savannah and Altamaha rivers to the administration of Oglethorpe and his fellow trustees for a period of twenty-one years. In their colonization policies they were to keep in mind the needs of military security. Landholdings were limited in size so as to make settlement compact. Negroes free or slave were excluded, and Roman Catholics also, to forestall the danger of wartime insurrection and of collusion with enemy coreligionists. And the Indian trade was strictly regulated, with rum prohibited, to lessen the risk of Indian complications.

Oglethorpe himself led the first expedition, building in 1733 a fortified town at the mouth of the Savannah, and later constructing additional forts south of the Altamaha. Debtors released from imprisonment in England and refugees from the religious conformity of Switzerland and Germany were brought to Georgia and outfitted at the expense of the trustees, who raised funds from charitable individuals as well as from Parliament. Temporarily, and partially, the trustees achieved both their military and their humanitarian objective. Thousands of former convicts, screened to eliminate real criminals, were socially and economically reborn in America. And after Oglethorpe, with regular troops, had chastised the Florida Spaniards, the border became relatively safe. Nevertheless, immigrants began to shy away, preferring South Carolina, where there were no laws against big plantations, slaves, and rum. Before the twenty-one years of the trusteeship were up, these restrictions were repealed, and after 1750 Georgia developed along lines similar to those of South Carolina.

The Island Colonies

In the study of American history we naturally focus our attention upon the thirteen British colonies that eventually became the original thirteen states of the United States. Yet, to see events in the perspective of their own time, we must bear in mind the fact that during the seventeenth century England laid the foundations of a global empire, not merely an American one. She acquired possessions in Africa and Asia as well as America. And in the American hemisphere she colonized a number of islands which, from her point of view, were as valuable as any of the continental settlements from Maine to Georgia, if not more so.

The Bermudas were the first of these islands to be settled, in 1612. For a time they were treated as a part of Virginia, and like Virginia they owed their prosperity to tobacco. Later, in the 1620's, a string of West Indian isles were colonized. These eventually were divided into two colonies, the one consisting of Barbados and the Windward Islands, the other consisting of the Leeward Islands. In 1655 Jamaica was seized from

Spain and began to be developed as a rich source of sugar. In 1670 the Bahamas were granted to the Carolina proprietors, who were interested in the islands not only as additions to the Carolina domain but also as bases for warding off possible Spanish threats to Charleston.

In general, the island colonies attracted the same kinds of settlers as did the mainland colonies. Of the approximately 75,000 Englishmen who crossed the Atlantic in the Great Migration of the 1620's and 1630's, about 50,000 disembarked in the West Indies or in other British possessions apart from the North American continent. More Puritans went to tiny Barbados than to all of Massachusetts.

->>>->>>->>>->>((-((-((-((

BIBLIOGRAPHY

ON THE English backgrounds of settlement in America, a charming and informative book is Wallace Notestein, *The English People on the Eve of Colonization, 1603–1630* (1954). Brief but perceptive is Alan Simpson, *Puritanism in Old and New England* (1955), which treats puritanism as a religious revival. Mercantilist ideas are explained by K. E. Knorr, *British Colonial Theories, 1570–1850* (1944). Economic backgrounds are profoundly studied in J. U. Nef, *Industry and Government in France and England, 1540–1640* (1940).

T. J. Wertenbaker has recounted the beginnings of settlement in a number of works. His *First Americans, 1607–1690* (1927) is comparatively brief and general. His *The Founding of American Civilization* is a trilogy consisting of *The Middle Colonies* (1938), *The Old South* (1942), and *The Puritan Oligarchy* (1947). New England beginnings are also well described in

C. M. Andrews, *The Fathers of New England* (1919), which is compact, colorful, and authoritative. J. T. Adams, *The Founding of New England* (1921), is prejudiced against the Puritans. The early South is expertly treated by W. F. Craven, *The Southern Colonies in the Seventeenth Century, 1607–1689* (1949), and by V. W. Crane, *The Southern Frontier, 1670–1732* (1929).

Each of the colonies is the subject of numerous books. On the settlement of Virginia, G. F. Willison's *Behold Virginia* (1951) is both readable and reliable. On Plymouth, the same author's *Saints and Strangers* (1945) is recommended. The beginnings of Massachusetts are well told by S. E. Morison in *Builders of the Bay Colony* (1930). Other noteworthy volumes are M. P. Andrews, *The Founding of Maryland* (1933); J. S. Bassett, *The Constitutional Beginnings of North Carolina* (1894); R. L. Meriwether, *The Expansion of South*

Carolina, 1729–1765 (1940); and S. G. Fisher, *The Making of Pennsylvania* (1932).

The founding of colonies may also be approached through biographies of leading founders. Bradford Smith, *Captain John Smith: His Life and Legend* (1953), shows the doughty captain to have been no such liar as his detractors have called him. S. H. Brockunier, *The Irrepressible Democrat: Roger Williams* (1940), and Edith Curtis, *Anne Hutchinson* (1930), reveal Rhode Island's beginnings in religious dissent. W. W. Comfort, *William Penn, 1644–1718* (1944), is one of the better of the many biographies of the great Quaker statesman. William Bradford tells his own story in his *History of Plymouth Plantation*, which is available in several editions.

On colonial beginnings and institutional development, a work of exhaustive scholarship is C. M. Andrews' *The Colonial Period of American History* (4 vols., 1934–1938).

CHAPTER 3

The Colonists and Their Work

I N THE SHAPING of the colonial economy —that is, in the determination of the ways the colonists made their living— three forces were especially important. One of these was the policy of the British government, which discouraged certain occupations and encouraged others, in accordance with mercantilist principles. Mercantilism required that the provinces supplement and strengthen rather than compete with the economy of the homeland. From 1650 on, Parliament enacted law after law to regulate the farm production, the manufacturing, and the money, shipping, and trade of the colonies. A second and more important influence upon economic life derived from the geographical conditions in America, which favored some lines of activity and made others impracticable. A third influence consisted of the aims and energies of the individual settlers, who brought with them from the British Isles and the European Continent (and, in the case of the slaves, from Africa) their own skills and habits

and aspirations for personal success. As a result of these diverse factors, there arose in the thirteen colonies a variety of agricultural, industrial, and commercial pursuits, not all of which conformed to the broad mercantilistic plan.

Geographical Influences

The geographical setting of the English colonies, along the Atlantic seaboard from Maine to Georgia, conditioned the economic life that developed in them. Three thousand miles and more from England, they were separated from the mother country, and yet connected with it, by the Atlantic Ocean. The overseas crossing took from four to eight weeks in close-packed and often disease-ridden ships which sailed at irregular intervals depending on wind and weather. The distance and the difficulty of ocean travel put the colonists very much upon their own resources once they had landed on the American shore. Nevertheless, the nature of the shoreline and of the terrain behind it inclined them toward the sea, and they kept in touch with the homeland by means of the same ocean they had crossed.

Along most of its extent the coast had been submerged and the rivers emptying into the ocean had been "drowned" by the prehistoric sinking of the continent's edge. So there was, and is, an indented coastline with a number of bays and harbors, into each of which flows one or more rivers giving access for varying distances to and from the interior. For instance, the Charles leads to Boston harbor at its mouth, the much longer Hudson to New York harbor, the Delaware to Delaware Bay, the Susquehanna and the Potomac and the York and the James (among others) to Chesapeake Bay, and the Ashley and the Cooper to Charleston harbor. At a time when travel and transportation by water was easier and more economical than by land, the rivers with their tributaries largely determined the lines of settlement and the course of trade. Running more or less at right angles to the coast, these rivers (with a few notable exceptions) tended to keep the colonies economically apart from one another and close to overseas markets and sources of supply.

The topography of the area in which the colonies were located divides it lengthwise into three belts at different levels: the coastal plain, the piedmont plateau, and the Appalachian highland. The plain, very narrow in New England but increasing southward from New York to a width of 200 miles in Georgia, is so low that the rivers traversing it flow backward with the incoming tides, and hence it is known (in the South) as the "tidewater" region. The piedmont, 150 miles across at its widest, is several hundred or more feet higher than the plain and is set off from it by the "fall line," an imaginary line drawn through the points at which the rivers descend to the

lowland over falls or rapids. From the piedmont the Appalachian mountains rise to elevations as high as 6,000 feet in New Hampshire and North Carolina, and from New England to Georgia the mountain barrier is unbroken except along the course of the Hudson and the Mohawk rivers, but between the various parallel ranges are valleys which allow fairly easy movement along the highland southwestward from Pennsylvania. Since these topographical belts cut across colonial boundaries, they made for economic differences within the same colony and, to some extent, for similarities between corresponding regions of different colonies.

Depending upon latitude, elevation, and distance from the sea, the climate in the area which was English America varies a great deal from place to place, providing most though not all kinds of weather to be found within the temperate zone. There is a remarkable contrast between the steamy summers of the South Carolina coast and the snowy winters of the New England interior, so well described by John Greenleaf Whittier in his poem "Snowbound." Yet the climate on the whole was fairly similar to what the colonists had known at home in the British Isles and western Europe, similar enough that they could easily adapt themselves to it. The unfamiliar features— the more dramatic weather changes, the more violent storms, the more brilliant and abundant sunshine—generally appealed to the newcomers and no doubt stimulated them to unwonted activity. Differences in agriculture between North and South resulted from the regional variations in length of the growing season, amount and distribution of rainfall, and extremes of heat and cold, together with regional variations in types of soil.

Soils in America resembled those in Europe enough to permit the growing of most of the familiar crops, in one place or another. But the soils varied considerably, from the silted river bottoms of the tidewater to the sandy pine barrens on the edge of the upcountry in the South, and from the rich lands of the Susquehanna Valley to the thin topsoil of glacier-scoured New England in the North. Subsoil minerals abounded, especially in the mountains, but most of them—coal, oil, gas—were left for later exploitation. Available in the colonial period were widely scattered deposits of iron ore, both in the mountains and in the lowland bogs. But at that time the most valuable natural resource, other than the soil itself, was the wood which grew upon it and which then served hundreds of industrial uses.

To the first colonists, America was trees. From the Atlantic to the Appalachians and beyond stretched a great forest, unbroken except for occasional small clearings made by the elements or by the Indians, and thick with tall pines, maples, oaks, and countless other varieties of trees as well as shrubs. Even before sighting land the early voyagers to America could sometimes smell the fresh and invigorating forest scent, and once they had disembarked they found themselves in a veritable Garden of Eden, full of birds and beasts for game; flowers, berries, and fruits; and infinite resources of wood. All this made a refreshing contrast with comparatively treeless England, rapidly being deforested to meet the needs of industry. And yet the friendly forest—so green and beautiful, so rich in materials for food and shelter and manufactures of many kinds—also had its uninviting and even hostile aspects. In its shadows lurked the wolves and panthers that devoured the settler's livestock, lurked also the redmen who often threatened his and his family's lives. It stood in the way of the frontiersman eager to cultivate the soil, and he had to convert forest into fields by the slow and laborious effort of girdling or else chopping down the trees, burning the dead or downed timber, and eventually uprooting the stumps. The song "Woodman, Spare That Tree," popular with a later generation of Americans, would have appealed to few of the first settlers or the frontiersmen who followed the receding forest. With them the object was to get rid of the trees, and unceasingly the ax resounded.

Apart from the great forest, the geographical fact that most distinguished the new from the old country and most influenced the economic development of the colonies was sheer space, the vast extent of land. Not that all the land was readily accessible. The need for clearing the forest, the presence of hostile tribes, the dependence upon water transport, and ultimately the difficulty of crossing the mountain barrier—all these considerations hindered the actual occupation of the land, and they operated more and more effectively in proportion to remoteness from the seaports. Hence the English settlements, scattered though they might seem, remained on the whole fairly compact throughout the colonial period, at least in comparison with the Spanish and French settlements in the New World, though not in comparison with the crowded towns and countryside of the Old World. There populations teemed and lacked sufficient room. Here land was plentiful and people relatively scarce.

The Labor Supply

If the colonies were to be a source of profit for proprietors and companies and a source of economic strength for England, ways must be found to bring over a part of the excess manpower of the Old World to exploit the natural riches of the New. As has been seen, the enterprisers of colonization encouraged settlement by means of advertising campaigns, religious tolerance, and generous grants of land.

Thus attracted, many of the early settlers

possessed sufficient wealth to pay their own way over and even to bring with them some capital (in the form of tools, supplies, or money), but others among the prospective emigrants from Europe and the British Isles were too poor to finance a voyage across the ocean and a new start in life on this side. To facilitate the immigration of people such as these, Virginia and some of the other colonies offered "headrights" —land grants of fifty acres or more per head—for each new laborer brought in from abroad. The person financing the laborer's voyage received not only the land grant but also the laborer's services for a period of years. In the colonies offering headrights, the labor rather than the land became the principal motive for settlers who paid the passage of new immigrants, and in other colonies the right to the immigrant's services was the object from the beginning.

This system of temporary servitude grew naturally out of existing practices in England, such as that of apprenticeship, by which a man bound himself to a master for

An Eighteenth-Century Indenture. *This contract, dated May 13, 1784, was made late in the history of indentured servitude and typifies the standardized form that developed. Note that it is printed, with spaces left blank to be filled in. In this particular case, the contract was made between the master and his servant before either of them sailed for America. Originally, a contract was written in two identical parts on a single sheet, which was torn in two, leaving an indented or indentured edge—hence the term "indenture."*

seven years to learn a trade. The men and women, English or foreign, who bound themselves to a master in America in return for their passage over were known as "indentured" servants because of the papers recording the contract, papers which were cut or torn with an indentured or indented edge so that the two copies, one going to the master and the other to the servant, would correspond. The period of service varied in the different colonies, ranging from four to seven years, and so did the conditions of work, which were regulated by colonial custom and law. Upon completing his term the servant was entitled to certain benefits—clothing, tools, occasionally land—in addition to his freedom and the privilege, if he could afford it, of acquiring indentured servants of his own.

Not all such servants came of their own free will: some were sent by force. From time to time, beginning as early as 1617, the English government dumped shiploads of convicts in America, though according to Captain John Smith "some did chuse to be hanged ere they would go thither, and were." The government also transported prisoners taken in battles with the Scots and with the Irish in the 1650's. Likewise it got rid of other groups deemed undesirable: orphans, vagrants, paupers, and those who were simply "lewd and dangerous." Still other involuntary emigrants were neither dangerous nor dependent but were victims of kidnaping or "impressment." In some cases the government itself paid for the transportation of its exiles. More commonly the authorities avoided this expense through arrangements with shipowners or captains who reimbursed themselves by selling the services of their passengers in America.

Unlike the exiles, most of the servants came willingly, eagerly. Some of them, before sailing, made contracts directly with their masters-to-be in the colonies. Others,

especially the numerous "free willers" or "redemptioners" from Europe, gave their indentures to the captain of the ship they boarded, and he auctioned off these contracts after putting in at an American port. Each buyer then claimed his servants.

They went in the largest numbers to Pennsylvania, after its founding late in the seventeenth century, for opportunities and working conditions were most attractive there, and they continued to go to Pennsylvania and New York, though in dwindling numbers, until long after the American Revolution. Relatively few landed in New England, where the economy was not such as to create much of a demand for them. In the seventeenth century they flocked to the tobacco colonies of Virginia and Maryland. Afterwards some continued to go there, but more and more the white servants were supplemented and replaced by Negro slaves.

The first Negroes in the English mainland colonies arrived in Jamestown in 1619. "About the last of August," the Jamestown planter John Rolfe noted, "came in a Dutch man of War that sold us twenty negars." The local planters bought these people not as slaves, it seems, but as servants to be held for a period of years and then freed, like the white servants with whom the planters already were familiar. Gradually permanent bondage for Negroes took the place of temporary servitude in Virginia, and the number of black slaves increased slowly—until about 1700. Then the importation of slaves began to rise very rapidly while the arrival of servants declined even more rapidly.

There were two main reasons for this change. In the first place, slavery gave the master a constant labor supply and practically complete control over it. Slaves, identifiable by their color, could not run away and merge themselves with the mass of free humanity so easily as white servants could. Slaves, moreover, could not rise out of their bondage to compete with their masters for wealth and political influence as the servants sometimes did. In the second place, slaves (considering the length of their service) were cheaper than servants, especially with the fall of slave prices after 1697, when the monopoly of the Royal African Company was broken and the slave trade was opened to English and colonial merchants on a competitive basis. While slaves in Virginia thus became more plentiful, indentured servants grew increasingly scarce, attracted as they were to such newer colonies as Pennsylvania.

Slavery in colonial times, of course, was not confined to Virginia, nor was it confined to Negroes. Numerous attempts were made to enslave the Indians, and while a few of them lived out their lives in bondage, they were in general rather difficult to catch and to hold. Negro slavery came to the rice country of South Carolina and Georgia from the West Indies and took the place of white servitude from the outset. Slaves labored as domestics and occasionally as farmhands for wealthy families in the North. As of 1763, there were in all the colonies about 230,000 Negroes, most of them slaves. About 16,000 lived in New England, 29,000 in the Middle Colonies, and the rest in the South.

Population Growth

Besides the Africans, other non-English peoples came in large numbers to the colonies after the end of the seventeenth century, while immigration from England itself fell off. Recovering from a prolonged depression in the 1630's, England thereafter began to develop more and more industries which demanded workmen, so that the talk of overpopulation ceased to be heard. Instead of encouraging emigration from its own shores, the government tried to check the loss of English manpower by prohibiting the departure of skilled artisans, while continuing to unload the unemployable or the undesirable upon the defenseless colonies. Although, during the eighteenth century, the colonies received relatively few newcomers from England, the populations of several of them were swelled by vast numbers of arrivals from France, Germany, Switzerland, Ireland, and Scotland.

Of these immigrants the earliest though not the most numerous were the French Calvinists, or Huguenots. Under the Edict of Nantes (1598) they had enjoyed liberties and privileges which enabled them to constitute practically a state within the state in Roman Catholic France. In 1685 the edict was revoked, and singly and in groups the Huguenots took the first opportunity to leave the country, until a total of about 300,000 had left for England, the Netherlands, America, and elsewhere, only a small minority of them going to the English colonies. These émigrés were mostly artisans, merchants, and men of letters and science who enriched their new homes with both their talents and their wealth. In America they settled in the towns along the coast from Charleston to Boston, to become the ancestors of Americans like Paul Revere (Rivoire).

Like the French Protestants, many German Protestants suffered from the arbitrary enactments of their rulers, and German Catholics as well as Protestants suffered even more from the devastating wars of the Sun King of France, Louis XIV. The Rhineland of southwestern Germany, the area known as the Palatinate, was especially exposed to the slaughter of its people and the ruin of its farms. For the Palatine Germans, the unusually cold winter of 1708-9 came as the last straw, and more than 12,-000 of them sought refuge in England. The Catholics among them were shipped back to Germany and the rest were resettled in England, Ireland, or the colonies. Arriving in New York, approximately 3,000 of them tried to make homes in the Mohawk Valley, only to be ousted by rapacious colonial landlords. Some of the Palatines moved farther up the Mohawk, but most of them made their way to Pennsylvania, where they received a hearty welcome. After that, the Quaker colony was the usual destination of Germans, who sailed for America in growing numbers, largely Moravians and Mennonites with religious views similar to those of the Quakers. But quite a few of the German Protestants went to North Carolina, especially after the founding (1710) of New Bern by a company of 600 German-speaking Swiss. All together, the Germans comprised the largest body of eighteenth-century white immigrants except for the Scotch-Irish.

The Scotch-Irish, the most numerous of the newcomers, were not Irishmen at all, though coming from Ireland, and they were distinct from the Scots who came to America directly from Scotland. In the early 1600's King James I, to further the conquest of Ireland, had seen to the peopling of the northern county of Ulster with his subjects from the Scottish Lowlands, who as good Presbyterians might be relied upon to hold their ground against the Irish Catholics. These Ulster colonists—the Scotch-Irish—eventually prospered despite the handicap of a barren soil and the necessity of border fighting with the Irish tribesmen. Then, after about a century, the English government destroyed their prosperity by prohibiting the export of their woolens and other products, and at the same time threatened their religion by virtually outlawing it and insisting upon conformity with the Anglican Church. As the long-term leases of the Scotch-Irish terminated, in the years after 1710, the English landlords doubled and even tripled the rents. Rather than sign new leases, thousands upon thousands of the ill-used tenants embarked in successive waves of emigration. Understandably a cantankerous and troublesome lot, these people often were coldly received at the colonial ports, and most of them pushed out to the edge of the American wilderness. There they occupied land with scant regard for ownership, believing that "it was against the laws of God and nature that so much land should be idle while so many Christians wanted it to labor on and to raise bread." There also they fought the Indians as earlier they had fought the Irish. Among their illustrious descendants was the characteristically Scotch-Irish Andrew Jackson.

The Scots and the Irish, as migrants to America, had no connection with the Scotch-Irish. Scottish Highlanders, some of them Roman Catholics frustrated in the rebellions of 1715 and 1745, went with their tartans and kilts and bagpipes to more than one of the colonies, but mostly to North Carolina. Presbyterian Lowlanders, afflicted with high rents in the country and unemployment in town, left in largest numbers shortly before the American Revolution. These Scots, Lowlanders and Highlanders alike, with few exceptions became loyalists after the outbreak of the Revolutionary War, but the Scotch-Irish were patriots almost to the man, as were the Irish. The Irish had migrated in trickles over a long period and yet, by the time of the Revolution, were about as numerous as the Scots, though less conspicuous, many of them having lost their Roman Catholic religion and their identity as Irishmen.

All these various immigrants contributed to the remarkable growth of the colonies. In 1700 the colonial population totaled a quarter of a million or less; by 1775 it was nearly ten times as large, more than two million. The number practically doubled every twenty-five years, as Benjamin Franklin observed, leading the English clergyman Thomas Malthus to his pessimistic conclusion (1798) that any population, if unchecked, would increase in a geometrical progression while the means of subsistence (except in a new and favored country like America) could not be increased nearly so fast. Important as the continuing immigration was, the rapid growth of the colonial population was mainly due to natural increase, to the excess of births over deaths. In the colonies, with their abundance of land and opportunity, large families were an asset rather than a liability, and husbands and wives heeded the Biblical advice: "Be ye fruitful and multiply."

Hence the colonists of English origin, those who had arrived earliest and had had the longest time to multiply, continued greatly to outnumber those of non-English origin. Yet the proportion of non-English ancestry increased year by year, from a tenth in 1700 to a third (including the people from Africa) in 1760. Much the most homogeneous and most purely English part of the colonies was New England. Much the most cosmopolitan part was the Middle Colonies, above all Pennsylvania. By the 1770's, the Pennsylvania population was in origin roughly a third English, a third German, and a third Scotch-Irish. These groups did not intermix very much but were concentrated in separate areas, the English around Philadelphia, the Germans to the north and west, and the Scotch-Irish still farther out on the frontier. The Germans continued to speak their native language, which eventually was corrupted into a German-English dialect known as "Pennsylvania Dutch." Nevertheless, in the colonies as a whole, there was a good deal of intermarriage between the different nationalities, and even before the Revolution thousands of Americans could trace their ancestry to two or more nations of the Old World.

As compared with the population of England, that of the colonies was not only mixed but also youthful and masculine, containing somewhat fewer old persons and women, especially along the frontier. And the colonial population was surprisingly mobile, New Englanders resettling in

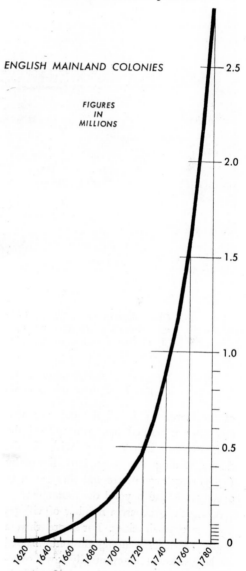

Estimated Colonial Population

ENGLISH MAINLAND COLONIES

FIGURES
IN
MILLIONS

New Jersey and other colonies to the south, Pennsylvanians (Scotch-Irish and Germans) swarming up the Shenandoah Valley to emerge upon and people the back country

Charleston in 1740. This painting by a Charlestonian shows the busy waterfront on the Cooper River. The prominent steeple is that of St. Philip's Church. At this time, with a population of nearly 7,000, Charleston was the fourth largest of the colonial towns. Its merchants prospered by trading in the South Carolina staples, deerskins and rice. These were carried away in English ships, which brought in cargoes of furniture, shoes, linen, hardware, and other manufactured goods.

of the Carolinas. In all the colonies men and women pushed upstream toward the unsettled wilderness, until with Daniel Boone leading the way into Kentucky (1769) they began here and there even to occupy the land beyond the mountains.

Along the seacoast a number of villages grew into small cities. For more than a century after its founding, Boston remained the largest town, but eventually it was overtaken by both Philadelphia and New York. In 1760 Philadelphia had more than 23,000 people, New York about 18,000, and Boston nearly 16,000. Next in order were Charleston, S.C., with approximately 8,000 and

Newport, R.I., with 7,500. After 1700 these colonial towns increased more rapidly than most English cities, yet not always so rapidly as the American population as a whole. Eight out of a hundred Americans lived in towns in 1720, and only about five or six out of a hundred in 1742. The rest of the people—the overwhelming majority throughout the colonial period—were scattered over the countryside and lived upon farms of one description or another.

Agriculture

Though there were regional differences, farming throughout the colonies had cer-

Flour and foodstuffs were imported from the North, chiefly from Philadelphia, but Charleston had more commerce with the West Indies than with the Northern colonies. It had far more trade with England than did any Northern port. The city had developed remarkably in a space of less than forty years. Compare this picture with the 1704 map of Charleston on page 42.

tain characteristics in common. In all the colonies it was a matter of adapting European plants and animals to American conditions or applying European techniques to the cultivation of native crops. The colonist's tools and methods were an improvement on those of the Indian but were extremely primitive. The ground was broken with hoe and mattock or with a crude wooden plow, usually drawn by oxen because of their slower and steadier pull than horses could provide, and often requiring two men to hold and guide it. Harvesting was a back-breaking work with sickle or scythe. Grain was threshed with a flail or by the trampling of oxen, and it was winnowed by being tossed in the air for the breeze to carry away the chaff. In George Washington's time these processes were not much advanced beyond what they had been in the day of the Pharaohs, and in colonial America there was even less care of the soil than there had been in ancient Egypt. Most of the colonists gave little thought to conserving their land by rotating crops, applying fertilizers, or checking erosion. Their attitude was reasonable enough in their circumstances: it paid them to economize on labor, not on land.

Near the frontier—that ever-expanding arc which, from Maine to Georgia, bounded the area of settlement—subsistence farming was the rule. The frontiersman planted his corn and beans amid the stumps in patches he had incompletely reclaimed from the forest, and with his crops and his catch of wild game he fed himself and his family. Eventually some of the backwoodsmen went in for cattle-raising on a fairly large scale, especially in Pennsylvania and the Carolinas. In these areas, long before the day of the cowboy on the Great Plains, herders let their branded cattle roam over an open range and, after the annual roundup, drove them to distant cities. The town of Cowpens, South Carolina, derived its name from its origin as a cattle-raising center. As the line of settlement moved outward, so also did the frontier kind of farm and ranch life. Within that line—in areas which, beginning with the seacoast itself, had shared most of the frontier characteristics at one time or another—arose patterns of agriculture increasingly more elaborate, more productive, and more diverse.

In New England the early settlers usually took up land in groups, each member receiving a village lot of his own, sharing the "common" as pasture and timberland, and tilling the strips assigned to him in the outlying fields. This township system was a relic of the manorial system, but here the town proprietors took the place of the feudal lord, and the farmers themselves planned their interdependent labors at their town meetings. After 1700 the commons were divided into private property and the strips were consolidated into separate farms. The typical farm became one that was small enough to be worked by the farmer, his sons, and perhaps an occasional hired hand, with the aid of neighbors at harvests and at house or barn raisings. It was bounded by fences made of stones that had been laboriously cleared off the fields. A

fairly self-sufficient unit, producing mainly for use rather than for sale, it contained a variety of scrawny livestock, apple and other orchards, and fields devoted chiefly to hay and corn, the prevalence of the "blast" or black-stem rust having discouraged the cultivation of wheat.

An exception to the usual New England farm scene was to be found on the shores and islands of Narragansett Bay. Here were rich and extensive farms on which were bred fine sheep, cattle, and horses, notably the Narragansett pacer. And here gangs of Negro slaves were used.

In New York, despite the abundance of excellent soil, agricultural productivity lagged because of the engrossment of the land in great estates, running to thousands and even hundreds of thousands of acres, on which few people were willing to work as tenants when they could get farms of their own in other colonies. The Dutch and their descendants set examples of careful tillage on the freeholds they had acquired at an early date. In Pennsylvania, of all the colonies the most favored by nature for farming, the Germans likewise applied the intensive cultivation they had learned in the old country. Their neat and substantial barns were their pride, but the work of their womenfolk in the fields was sometimes shocking to non-Germans. With fairly large holdings, these farmers needed all the labor they could get, and in addition to their wives and daughters they employed indentured servants, women as well as men. In New York and Pennsylvania the farmers concentrated upon the production of staples to be sold abroad and at home. After ceasing to produce enough food to feed all its own people, New England depended upon these "bread colonies" for its wheat. So, to some extent, did those Southern colonies that were preoccupied with the growing of tobacco.

Tobacco came into use in Europe and

Asia soon after Columbus's first return from the West Indies, where he had seen the Cuban natives smoking small cigars (*tabacos*) which they inserted in the nostril.

to Tobacco (1604), in which he urged his people not to imitate "the barbarous and beastly manners of the wild, godless, and slavish Indians, especially in so vile and

---

Virginia Tobacco Land
1686

In 1686 the Reverend John Clayton of Yorkshire, England, visited the Virginia tobacco country. Two years later he reported to the Royal Society of London (a society of Englishmen and colonials devoted to scientific inquiry):

"And yet in truth 'tis only the barrenest parts that they have cultivated, by tilling and planting only the highlands, leaving the richer vales unstirred, because they understand not anything of draining. So that the richest meadow lands, which is one third of the country, is boggy, marsh, and swamp, whereof they make little advantage, but lose in them abundance of their cattle, especially at the first of the spring, when the cattle are weak, and venture too far after young grass. Whereas vast improvements might be made thereof, for the generality of Virginia is sandy land with a shallow soil, so that after they have cleared a fresh piece of ground out of the woods, it will not bear tobacco past two or three years, unless cow-penned [and thus manured]. . . . Therefore every three or four years they must be for clearing a new piece of ground out of the woods, which requires much labour and toil, it being so thick grown all over with massy timber. Thus their plantations run over vast tracts of ground, each ambitious of engrossing as much as they can, that they may be sure to have enough to plant, and for their stocks and herds of cattle to range and to feed in. Plantations of 1,000, 2,000 or 3,000 acres are common, whereby the country is thinly inhabited, the living solitary and unsociable, trading confused and dispersed, besides other inconveniences. Whereas they might improve 200 or 300 acres to more advantage, and would make the country much more healthy. For those that have 3,000 acres have scarce cleared 600 acres thereof, which is peculiarly termed the plantation, being surrounded with the 2,400 acres of wood, so that there can be no free or even motion of the air."

In England Sir Walter Raleigh popularized the smoking habit, and the demand for tobacco grew despite the early objections of both moralists and mercantilists. Moralists denounced tobacco as a poisonous weed, the cause of many diseases. King James I himself led the attack with *A Counterblaste*

stinking a custom." Mercantilists at first were horrified because England's imports of tobacco came from the Spanish colonies and payment for them resulted in the loss of English gold.

Tobacco fitted well into the mercantilistic scheme of England, however, after

John Rolfe had succeeded (1612) in domesticating the plant in the English colonies, at Jamestown. The growing of tobacco was so profitable that it soon spread all around

methods of crop control. Both falling prices and soil exhaustion (tobacco being very hard on the soil) stimulated the formation of larger and larger plantations, so that

Tobacco Preparation: Eighteenth Century. *When tobacco was harvested, the stalks were hung in a well-ventilated barn to cure. After several months, in damp weather when the leaves were pliable, they were stripped from the stalks, sorted, and tied into "hands," then packed tightly in hogsheads. These were stored in public warehouses until examined by official inspectors. Eventually the hogsheads were carried by boat or wagon or were rolled to the nearest ship landing. Ships from England ascended the rivers of the tobacco country to pick up cargoes. From William Tatham,* An Historical and Practical Essay on the Culture and Commerce of Tobacco *(London, 1800).*

Chesapeake Bay and became the economic mainstay of Virginia, Maryland, and part of North Carolina. Overproduction ensued, and the price fell repeatedly during the eighteenth century. Again and again, without much success, the planters tried various

some of the economies of large-scale production could be gained and fresh lands could be continually brought into use. On these plantations slave labor was easily adapted to the simple and repetitive round of tasks which tobacco required—sowing, transplanting, weeding, worming, picking, curing, stripping, and packing.

Slave labor was fairly well suited also to rice culture along the Georgia and Carolina coasts. Here dikes and ditches leading from the tidal rivers permitted the necessary flooding and draining of the paddies, while care was taken to see that no salt water reached the rice with the incoming tides. To cultivate the growing rice, men had to stand knee-deep in mud, their bare backs exposed to malarial mosquitoes and to the broiling sun. Since white men could not be hired to do it, Negroes were compelled to perform this torturing and unhealthful work. But the rice plantations were smaller than the tobacco plantations and did not provide a similar year-round routine which would utilize slave labor to the full.

Indigo supplemented rice after the successful cultivation of the dye plant (1743) by Eliza Lucas, the daughter of a West Indian planter. Grown on high ground, the indigo did not get in the way of the rice on the river bottoms, and it occupied the slaves at times when they were not busy with the rice. They tended the indigo fields, cut the leaves, soaked them in vats, and extracted the residue as a blue powder. Glad for a chance to be freed from foreign sources of the dye, Parliament granted a bounty of sixpence a pound.

The British government tried to encourage the production of other crops which would meet the needs of mercantilism. It gave bounties for hemp, and a little was grown in the colonies, particularly in North Carolina, but not enough to make the experiment pay. The government also attempted to force the growth of grapes for wine and of mulberry trees for silk, but had even less success with these than with hemp. Too much skilled labor was required for such products. Obstinately the colonial farmers and planters stuck to those lines of production in which they had a comparative advantage over producers elsewhere in the world. In some cases, as with tobacco and indigo, the colonial products happened to supplement those grown in England and thus to fit the mercantilistic pattern. In other cases, as with wheat, the produce of the colonies competed with that of the mother country and was either irrelevant to the mercantile system or incompatible with it.

Industries

The early colonists were manufacturers as well as farmers. In the 1600's families produced nearly all their necessities within the household. To the end of the colonial period, household manufacturing continued to prevail on ordinary farms, though not in the rising towns. The farmer had to be a jack of all trades, and his wife and daughters had to be jills of many trades. The members of the family built their house and outbuildings, with neighborly cooperation, and made their own furniture and furnishings. They butchered and cured their meat, dried and preserved their fruit, ground their corn meal and flour, baked their cakes and bread, churned their butter, distilled their brandy, and brewed their beer. They prepared and spun their flax and wool, wove such cloths as the linen and woolen mixture known as linsey-woolsey, dyed them with homemade dyes or purchased indigo, and cut and sewed their clothes. They tanned their leather and cobbled their shoes. They boiled wood ashes and fats to produce soap, and they poured tallow or barberry wax into molds to make candles.

Specialists in various arts and crafts came to America in the seventeenth century but found it hard to make a living from their specialties. These men had to turn to farming, and their skills deteriorated from disuse. Even after 1700 there were few opportunities for craftsmen in rural areas, particularly in the South. On many a plantation, slaves were trained to produce the needed manufactures that it was not feasible to import from England.

In the rising towns of the North artisans of many kinds appeared—carpenters, chandlers (candlemakers), coopers (barrelmakers), cordwainers (shoemakers), weavers, tailors, wheelwrights, and dozens of others. Except in such lines as millinery and dressmaking, women artisans were rare, though now and then a widow took over her husband's work and succeeded as a cobbler, tinworker, or even blacksmith. By 1750 almost a third of the people of Philadelphia owed their living to a craft of some kind.

The craft usually was a family enterprise, and the shop was on the ground floor of the master craftsman's home. The master was assisted by his sons and by one or more journeymen and apprentices, who lived as members of his household, and who aspired eventually to become masters with shops of their own. In some ways the craftsman was like the small businessman of the present. He had to procure and train workers, provide materials, supervise the work (while taking an active part in it), and find a market. When possible, he made goods to order, or, as he called them, "bespoke" goods, but in slack times he might produce a stock of articles for general sale. In newspaper advertisements he sometimes made exaggerated and even fraudulent claims for his wares, while running down the wares of his competitors. He sold on credit or for barter, seldom for cash.

In America the guild, or association of craftsmen, which in England regulated each of the trades, did not take root. Regulations regarding apprenticeship, the quality of goods, and other matters were provided by the colonial and municipal governments. Despite the laws intended to maintain high standards, some of the products were shoddy and most of them were inferior to the machine-made goods of today. By 1750, however, American artisans were turning out some articles which compared with the best of that time or of any time. For instance, the gunsmiths of Lancaster, Pennsylvania, were justly famous for the Pennsylvania rifle (also known as the Kentucky rifle), and the wagon-makers of the same town for the Conestoga wagon (the original "covered wagon," with ends up-curved to hold the load securely on hills and rough roads). American silversmiths, such as Paul Revere, did work as fine as that of England or France and finer than that of the rest of Europe. The same was true of American cabinetmakers.

Colonial craftsmanship became notable for quantity as well as quality. As late as 1700, all but a tiny fraction of the manufactures which the colonists bought were made in England. Before the Revolution, more than half of the manufactures were made in America. The rise of the colonial craftsman was watched with concern by men in London who took seriously the doctrines of mercantilism.

When colonial merchants began to organize the work of shops and households on a larger and more efficient scale, there arose the "putting-out" system, which was a forerunner of the later factory system. The merchant supplied materials to workers in homes or shops, then gathered up and marketed the finished product. Before the Revolution, Lynn, Massachusetts, was already famous for shoemaking and Germantown, Pennsylvania, for producing knit goods. Under the putting-out system the workers were not drawn together as in post-Revolutionary factories.

Water power was widely used in various kinds of colonial mills. At the rapids of streams small enough to be easily dammed, grist and fulling mills were set up to take

some of the heavier labor out of the household, grinding grain and fulling cloth
(shrinking and tightening the weave by a
process of soaking and pounding) for the
farmers roundabout. The millowner was
usually a farmer himself in his spare time.
He frequently used his water wheel to
power a sawmill for cutting his neighbors'
logs. Other and busier sawmills accompanied the lumber industry which followed
the retreating forest. Circular saws were as
yet unknown, and the up-and-down powered saw, while it would do the work of
twenty men in cutting soft pine, was not
véry efficient in cutting hardwoods, particularly if the trees were large. So it had to be
supplemented by the large "pit saw" operated by two men, one down in a pit and the
other on the ground above, and also by the
ax and the adze, the hammer and the
wedge. Other forest industries yielded
pitch, tar, resin, turpentine, and potash for a
number of industrial uses.

Like lumbering, the fur trade and the
fisheries were extractive industries, depending closely upon the resources provided by
nature. Both fishing and fur trading became
big businesses employing what were, by
colonial standards, large amounts of capital.
It was expensive to provide fur traders with
goods for bartering with Indian trappers—
guns, knives, blankets, looking-glasses, and
beads to exchange for furs and hides—and
most of the business came to be controlled
by English merchants in London and colonial merchants in Albany, Philadelphia, and
Charleston. It was costly also to outfit fleets
for the fishing industry, which concentrated mainly in New England waters,
though almost every farmer near a stream
or pond was at least a part-time fisherman.

The fisheries led to shipbuilding, the first
colonial-built ships being put together on
the New England coast for the use of fishermen, and the abundance of timber and naval
stores enabled the industry in the colonies
to expand to the point of outdoing that of
England itself. So cheap and yet so sea-
worthy were the materials that, despite the
high wages of colonial labor, excellent ships
could be produced at as little as half the
cost of those built in English yards. Usually
a master shipwright contracted for the construction of a vessel, and he procured, paid,
and directed the laborers who did the work.
While New England kept its early lead in
shipbuilding, New York and Pennsylvania
also had their shipyards, and Virginia and
the Carolinas, with their fine supply of live-
oak timber, became important centers of
the industry in the latter half of the eighteenth century.

Some undertakings on a still larger scale
than ship construction were to be found in
the iron industry. From almost the very beginnings of Virginia and Massachusetts,
small bloomeries and forges were erected to
utilize the bog ores in those colonies, and
eventually sizeable furnaces were erected to
smelt either bog or rock ores in almost all
the colonies. The most extensive industrial
enterprise anywhere in English America
was that of the German ironmaster Peter
Hasenclever, in northern New Jersey. It
was founded in 1764 with British capital
and was operated thereafter with a labor
force of several hundred, many of whom
were brought over from ironworks in Germany. It included not only furnaces and
forges but also sawmills and a gristmill.

From the beginning of colonization, the
home government encouraged the colonial
production of iron in a crude form, as a raw
material for English mills and foundries.
When colonial ironmakers began to produce more than merely the crude metal,
their competitors in England induced Parliament to pass the Iron Act of 1750, which
removed the English duty on pig and bar
iron but forbade the colonists to engage in
the secondary processing of iron or steel.
This prohibition was in line with other acts

intended to prevent the rise of advanced manufactures in America. The Woolen Act (1699) prohibited the export of wool or woolens from a colony to any place outside its boundaries, and the Hat Act (1732) similarly prohibited the export of hats, which could be cheaply made in America because of the availability of beaver skins. But the colonists usually disregarded such legislation when it was to their interest to do so.

Thus, with industry as with agriculture, developments in the colonies depended more upon American conditions than upon British policy. The industries that flourished were those appropriate to a country in which certain resources were abundant, capital was scarce, skilled labor was highly paid, markets were widely scattered, and overland transportation was difficult. Most of the industries were relatively small in scale, even for their time; many were devoted to the processing of raw materials for further manufacture rather than the finishing of consumer goods. The crafts, however, steadily progressed. They held promise for the future industrial greatness of the United States.

Money and Commerce

Though the colonists produced most of what they consumed, they by no means achieved economic self-sufficiency. The colonies as a whole could not supply their entire wants from their own agriculture and industry. Neither could any of the separate colonies, nor could an individual household except at an extremely low level of living. To maintain and raise their living standards the mainland colonists had to have the benefits of trade with one another and with people overseas.

Intercolonial trade was fairly extensive and diversified. In the busy coastal traffic the surplus products of each region were exchanged—such products as the fish and rum of New England, the flour and meat of the Middle Colonies, and the tobacco and indigo of the South. The trade between the seaports and their hinterland involved some of these same products, besides many others, including the variety of small articles carried by the packhorse peddler. A large proportion of the commodities distributed upriver from the seaports had their origin abroad, and a large proportion of those gathered in the interior were destined for export. Much of the intercolonial and inland trade was thus a part of overseas commerce.

Foreign trade provided indispensable consumer and capital goods which the colonists could not manufacture for themselves in suitable quantity or quality. From abroad the millowner had to get his machinery, the shipwright his hardware and navigating instruments, the farmer his spades and other tools, the Indian trader most of his supplies. Even a modest home included kitchen utensils, tableware, needles and thread, lanterns, and other equipment of European make. Wealthier families bought additional imports, luxury items such as mirrors, paper, books, fine furniture, and fancy cloth. The more the colonists prospered, whether individually or collectively, the more they demanded goods of foreign manufacture.

The central problem in the overseas commerce of the colonies was to find the means of payment for these increasing imports. Money was scarce in the colonies. They did not mine their own gold or silver, and the mercantilist policy was intended to drain them of such specie as they might acquire. They did obtain a motley collection of Spanish and other European coins from their dealings with pirates and from certain routes of overseas trade. Massachusetts, alone among the colonies, coined its own money, the "pine-tree shilling," but only for about three decades (1652–1684). Generally, in their transactions with one another, the colonists resorted to barter or else used money substitutes, though always calculating in terms of pounds, shillings, and pence. Beaver skins circulated widely as a medium of exchange and so did tobacco, not the leaves but warehouse certificates representing tobacco in storage. All the colonies experimented at one time or another with paper currency, often securing it with land, but Parliament suppressed this expedient by legislating against the Massachusetts land bank in 1740 and by outlawing paper money in New England in 1751 and in the rest of the colonies later on. Anyhow this kind of paper was not acceptable in payment for imported goods and services, which had to be bought with specie or with bills of exchange arising from colonial exports. In short, the colonies had to sell abroad in order to buy from abroad, but British policy attempted to limit and control their selling opportunities.

Though the tobacco planters had an abundant staple for export, they were not allowed to dispose of it to the highest bidder in the markets of the world. According to a series of Trade Laws first enacted in 1660, tobacco was one of the "enumerated items" which must be exported only to the British Isles, whence more than half of it was re-exported to other places. The laws also prohibited the growing of tobacco in the British Isles, but protection against competition in the mother country did not quite offset the disadvantages of the colonial planter. He usually sold his annual crop to an English merchant (or after the mid-eighteenth century to a Scottish merchant) either directly or through a "factor" in the colonies, and the merchant credited him with its value, after deducting charges for shipping, insurance, and a merchant's commission. Through the merchant he bought slaves and manufactured goods, and the merchant deducted the cost of these from the planter's credit on the books. After tobacco prices had begun to fall, the planter

often found at the end of a year that his crop did not pay for all the goods he had ordered in return. The merchant then carried him until the next year and charged interest on the extension of credit. As the years went by, the planter went more and more deeply into debt, eventually leaving his indebtedness to his heirs.

The colonial merchant in such ports as Boston, New York, and Philadelphia did not have the same difficulties as the tobacco planter, though he had others of his own. He was favored by the Navigation Acts, passed in 1650 and after, which excluded foreign ships from practically all of the colonial carrying trade. And he found a market in England for the furs, timber, naval stores, and vessels produced in the Northern colonies. But, according to the Trade Laws, he could not export fish, flour, wheat, or meat to the mother country, for he would thereby compete with her own producers. He had to dispose of these prohibited items in other markets if he was to obtain adequate means of paying for his imports from England.

In the English island colonies of the Caribbean the Northern merchant found a ready outlet for mainland products. In the French, Dutch, and Spanish islands of the Caribbean he also got eager customers—and often better prices. Responding to pressure from English sugar planters, who wished to monopolize the mainland trade, Parliament in the Molasses Act of 1733 put a high duty on foreign sugar taken to the continental colonies. The molasses duty was intended to discourage commerce with the foreign islands. But the Northern merchant could evade the tax by smuggling, and he often did.

From the ports of New England and the Middle Colonies went cargo after cargo of lumber, horses, wheat, flour, biscuit, corn, peas, potatoes, beef, pork, bacon, and fish. From the West Indies were obtained sugar, molasses, rum, dyewoods, cotton, ginger, coffee, Spanish coins, and bills of exchange (these were drafts, drawn by planters in the West Indies, on merchants in England; they

bills of exchange, and then back home with manufactured goods.

The most famous or infamous of the triangular trades bypassed England itself.

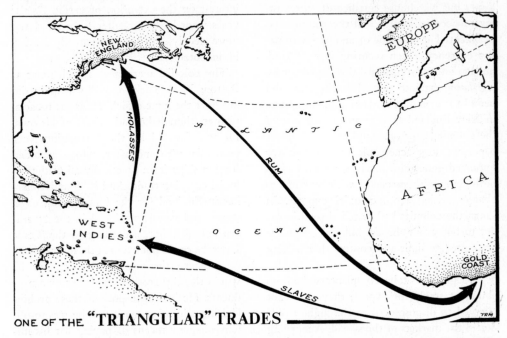

ONE OF THE "TRIANGULAR" TRADES

served much the same purpose as checks drawn on a bank). Sometimes West Indian products were carried directly to England; more commonly they were brought back to American ports, where part was sold in the domestic market and the rest exported to England. These exports, together with bills of exchange and Spanish money, helped to pay for the English goods imported into the thirteen colonies.

To and from England, to and from the West Indies—these were much the most important routes of trade for the Northern merchant. He also worked out a number of routes of indirect trade with the mother country, some of them complex and frequently changing, others fairly stable and somewhat "triangular" in their simplicity. Thus he might direct his ships to Catholic southern Europe with fish, then to England with wine and other proceeds in cash or

In this trade a ship took rum and other items from a New England port to the Guinea Coast of Africa, slaves from Africa to the West Indies, and sugar and molasses as well as specie and bills from the West Indies to the home port. There some of the cargo would be distilled into rum for another voyage of the same kind. On the African coast the slave marts were kept supplied by native chieftains who made a business of capturing enemy tribesmen in warfare and bringing them, tied together in long lines known as "coffles," out of the jungle. Then, after some haggling on the seashore, came the horrors of the "middle passage"—so-called because it was the second of the three legs of the voyage—during which the slaves were packed in the dark and stinking hold, with no sanitary facilities, no room to stand up, and scarcely air enough to breathe. Those who died en route were thrown overboard, and the losses from disease were generally high. Those who survived were "seasoned" for a time in the West Indies before being shipped on to the mainland. As the owner or captain of a slaver, many a Yankee made a fortune by thus supplying the Southern planters with labor for their fields. And some of the planters, like William Byrd I of Virginia, added to their own wealth by reselling slaves that Northern ships brought in.

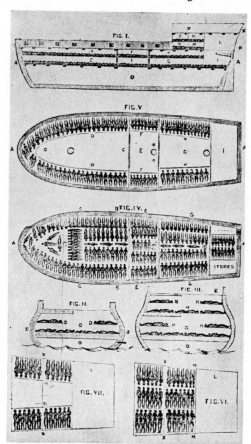

A Slave Ship. *This plan of the* Brookes, *an eighteenth-century vessel built especially for the slave trade, shows how little space was wasted. The slaves were packed in so tightly that they had no room to stand or even to sit. During part of the day (except in bad weather) they were allowed on deck to get food, air, and exercise. They usually were shackled. Their misery was intensified by seasickness and frequently by epidemics of dysentery and other diseases. Despite the high losses from death en route, more Negro than white colonists crossed the Atlantic before 1800. From first to last, five million or more slaves were shipped from Africa, though probably less than a tenth of them ultimately were landed on the North American continent.*

➤➤➤-➤➤➤-➤➤➤-➤➤➤⧉⧉⧉-⧉⧉⧉-⧉⧉⧉-⧉⧉⧉

BIBLIOGRAPHY

THE PEOPLE of the colonies are viewed statistically in S. H. Sutherland, *Population Distribution in Colonial America* (1936), and in E. B. Greene and V. D. Harrington, *American Population before the Federal Census of 1790* (1932).

Among studies of nationality groups coming to America, I. C. C. Graham's *Colonists from Scotland* (1956) is a model of objectivity and clarity. Other valuable studies include Fredric Klees, *The Pennsylvania Dutch* (1950); A. H. Hirsch, *The Huguenots of Colonial South Carolina* (1928);

H. J. Ford, *The Scotch-Irish in America* (1914); and A. B. Faust, *The German Element in the United States* (2 vols., 1909).

Authoritative general treatments of labor in the colonies are R. B. Morris's *Government and Labor in Early America* (1946) and M. W. Jernegan's *Laboring and Dependent Classes in Colonial America, 1607–1783* (1932). Aspects of Negro slavery are described, from very different points of view, in U. B. Phillips's *American Negro Slavery* (1918) and W. E. B. DuBois's *The Suppression of the African Slave Trade*

(1896). On the Negro, see also J. C. Ballagh, *A History of Slavery in Virginia* (1902), and L. J. Greene, *The Negro in Colonial New England* (1942). Studies of the indenture system in the two colonies where it was most strongly established are C. A. Herrick, *White Servitude in Pennsylvania* (1926), and Samuel McKee, *Labor in Colonial New York, 1664–1776* (1935).

Carl Bridenbaugh, *The Colonial Craftsman* (1950), the best work on the subject, is charmingly written. R. M. Tryon, *Household Manufactures in the United States, 1640–1880* (1917), is comprehensive enough. The production of iron is treated by the following: A. C. Bining, *British Regulation of the Colonial Iron Industry* (1933) and *Pennsylvania Iron Manufacture in the Eighteenth Century* (1938); Kathleen Bruce, *Virginia Iron Manufacture in the Slave Era* (1931); and E. N. Hartley, *Ironworks on the Saugus* (1957), a detailed history of a remarkably large-scale Massachusetts enterprise which was operating at its height in the 1650's. Lyman Carrier, *The Beginnings of Agriculture in America* (1923), is a good introduction to colonial farming. R. K. Akagi, *Town Proprietors of the New England Colonies* (1924), throws light on the New England system of land tenure. Important forest and sea industries are described by R. McFarland, *A History of the New England Fisheries* (1911), and by R. G. Albion, *Forests and Sea Power* (1926), a book both readable and solid.

L. H. Harper, *The English Navigation Laws* (1939), sets forth the legal patterns within which colonial commerce was supposed to operate. Bernard Bailyn, *The New England Merchants in the Seventeenth Century* (1955), concludes that the merchants during that period benefited from their position within the imperial system. F. B. Tolles describes the business of Philadelphia Quaker merchants in *Meeting House and Counting House* (1948). Problems of money are handled with profound scholarship in C. P. Nettels's *Money Supply of the American Colonies before 1720* (1924) and with a light and entertaining touch in Kenneth Scott's *Counterfeiting in Colonial America* (1957).

CHAPTER 4

Growth of American Ways

AT THE TIME of the discovery and settlement of America, the center of Western civilization was shifting from the Mediterranean to the North Atlantic. The people of the thirteen colonies, living as they did on the farther rim of that ocean, continued to participate in the growing Atlantic civilization and to be influenced by new currents of thought coming from abroad. Yet they did not remain merely European in their outlook, though they were representatives of a branch of European culture, nor did they remain purely English, though the great majority of them were of English stock. Wherever they came from, they clung at first to their accustomed ways, trying to make themselves feel at home in their new and strange environment. But that environment (including the wilderness surroundings, the generous economic basis of life, the presence of a variety of nationalities) led the colonists to depart from many of their customs. During the

century and a half from 1607 to 1763 they developed variations of their own from the social, intellectual, and political patterns of Europe in general and England in particular. By the end of that period they showed signs of becoming distinctively "American" —a term which had been applied to them even before 1700 but which did not come into general use till after 1750.

Provincial Society

In England, as in Europe, class lines were sharply marked during the seventeenth and eighteenth centuries. At the apex of English society were the relatively few but wealthy and influential members of the royal family and the titled aristocracy. Below them, yet also notable for their prosperity and prestige, were the country gentlemen and the rising merchants, two classes which became virtually one through intermarriage and through cross investments, the landowners in ships and the shipowners in land. Beneath them in the social scale were the middle classes of shopkeepers and artisans in the towns and landowning yeomen in the country. Lowest of all stood the masses of urban workers and farm tenants and laborers, who varied considerably among themselves in their individual shares of the national income. The chances for any Englishman to rise above the station of his father and grandfather were rather slim—unless he went to America.

In the colonies the English class arrangement was not reproduced. Few or none of the nobility became colonists, though some of them were colonial enterprisers. Many Virginians afterwards believed that their ancestors had been Cavaliers and hence aristocrats. Certain it is that many more Cavaliers went to Virginia than to Massachusetts, but the Cavaliers were simply the partisans of the King against the parliamentary Roundheads in the civil war and were not necessarily nobles. To Virginia, as to Massachusetts and other colonies, there migrated a relatively small number of untitled gentlemen and a great many members of the middling and lower orders. Some of these arrivals doubtless hoped to reconstruct in America something like the social system they had known in England, only here they hoped to occupy the higher levels themselves. A fortunate few did acquire extensive landholdings and proceeded to mimic the aristocrats back home, but no true aristocracy was transplanted to the colonies.

A colonial class system nevertheless grew up. Once social differentiation was well developed, as it was by the middle of the eighteenth century, the upper classes in the colonies consisted of the royal officials, the proprietary families, the great landholders in the North and the planters in the South, and the leading merchants with their investments mostly in forms of property other than land. The middle classes included most of the landowning farmers and, in the towns, the lesser merchants, shopkeepers, ship captains, professional men, and self-employed artisans. The lower classes comprised the indentured servants and the poorest farmers, together with the comparatively small number of wage earners, including farm hands, sailors, and fishermen. Forming a separate class or caste, though often working in the fields alongside white servants and even alongside men of the master class, were the Negro slaves, the lowliest of all.

Social mobility—the movement of individuals up and down the social scale—was much greater in colonial America than in contemporary England or in the twentieth-century United States. All except the slaves could aspire to a higher place for themselves or at least for their children. Once a man had made a fortune, he was accepted readily by those who theretofore had considered him their social inferior. The colonists, believing in enterprise and material success, honored the self-made man. Afterwards his descendants were inclined to forget the humble and even grubby origins of the family fortune and to think of themselves as thoroughgoing aristocrats.

The rise of rich colonial families may be illustrated by a few examples. In Virginia, in the seventeenth century, William Byrd I sold pots, pans, guns, and rum to the Indians in exchange for furs and hides, and he also dealt in Indian and Negro slaves. Inheriting his father's wealth, William Byrd II in the eighteenth century augmented it by continuing the same trades, by operating tobacco plantations, sawmills, and gristmills, and by speculating grandly in real estate. In South Carolina, the Huguenot craftsman Pierre Manigault arrived as a penniless refugee in 1695. At first he worked with his wife in the fields, then opened a tavern in Charleston and later branched out with a distillery and a barrelmaking shop. His son Gabriel, a planter, merchant, and slave trader, became the richest man in the colony. In New York the Scotsman Robert Livingston used his position as town clerk of Albany, after 1674, to further his trading and land-speculating schemes; in a few years he acquired a manor of 160,000 acres.

In Massachusetts John Hull, son of a blacksmith who arrived in 1634, helped his father on the family farm, was apprenticed to a goldsmith in Boston, rose to be a master craftsman, invested his earnings in the shipping business, and did well. His widow married William Phips, once a Maine frontiersman, then a Boston ship's carpenter. With the capital provided by his wife, Phips started his own shipbuilding business and also went into the West Indian trade. Already prosperous, he struck it fabulously rich when he discovered and salvaged a sunken Spanish treasure-ship. He was knighted, and Sir William and Lady Phips settled down in a Boston mansion appropriate to their new station in life.

Class consciousness and class distinctions were quite noticeable in colonial America. Usually a person's place in society was obvious from his appearance and dress. An ordinary farmer in his coarse linen homespun or a town craftsman in his leather apron made a sharp contrast with a planter or merchant in buckle shoes, knee breeches, colorful waistcoat, starched ruffles, and powdered wig. A farm girl, her face parched by winter fire or summer sun, her buxom figure clothed in homemade linsey-woolsey, was not likely to be mistaken for a planter's or merchant's daughter, whose delicate form was clad in imported silks and satins, and whose complexion was protected by a dainty parasol.

As if such marks of class were not enough, the colonists carefully discriminated among themselves in their use of etiquette. A man of considerable rank was addressed as "Esquire." A somewhat less distinguished person was called "Master" or "Mister." Ordinary people were referred to as "Goodman" Smith or "Goodwife" Jones. And a servant or slave was known simply by his first name or by a nickname. Pews in many churches were assigned, from front to back, according to the social standing of the parishioners. On the roll of Harvard College, students were listed not in alphabetical order but in the order of the supposed status of their parents. Judged by their insistence upon fine points of prestige, the well-to-do colonists seem to have been a little unsure of themselves and of their exact place in society.

As some of the rich grew richer, some of the poor became more impoverished. There was a widening of extremes. If many of the early indentured servants acquired valuable land and respectable status after completing their servitude, many of the later ones either took up subsistence farming on the frontier or sank to the level of the "poor whites" on worn-out lands in the neighborhood of the planters. Yet, especially in New England, the vast majority of the people came to form a self-respecting, property-owning middle class. Throughout colonial America the benefits of physical well-being were more widely diffused than anywhere else in the world.

Problems of poverty and human exploitation nevertheless appeared. The lot of the slave was a hard one, and the lot of the servant sometimes even worse, as long as his servitude lasted. A few humanitarians began to take note of what they considered the wrongs of the society they knew. Of these reformers the foremost was a New Jersey Quaker, John Woolman, who wrote appealingly and traveled widely in a patient effort to better the condition of workers, especially slaves. In *Some Considerations on the Keeping of Negroes* (Part I, 1754; Part II, 1762) he took up an antislavery crusade which had been preached before him, but never so earnestly, by other Quakers, by

Mennonites, and by a few Puritans, such as Samuel Sewall. In *A Plea for the Poor* (written in 1764 but not published till thirty years later) Woolman warned against

with them or sent for their families after first preparing the way.

From the beginning, the family shelters of the colonists were fairly close imitations

John Crump House. *This home in the colonial capital of Virginia, which has been reconstructed on its original foundations, was built in three stages in the 18th century.* (COLONIAL WILLIAMSBURG)

acquisitiveness as a source of oppression and war, and he reminded the wealthy that, in Christian doctrine, they were not owners but only trustees of their property. "The Creator of the earth," he wrote, "is the owner of it."

Home and Family

Domesticity was a keynote of life in the English colonies. They—unlike the Spanish and French colonies—were peopled predominantly by home makers, by married men who brought their wives and children

of those already familiar to them, yet houses (like almost everything else) were more or less altered by Americanizing trends. The first English pioneers built thatched huts rather than log cabins of the kind now considered peculiarly American. Introduced by the early Swedish settlers along the Delaware, the log cabin did not become the typical frontier dwelling until the eighteenth century. By that time a variety of building materials and architectural styles had appeared in the older settled areas. Though a higher proportion of colonial than of English houses were built of wood, a considerable number were built of stone or brick, some of which was imported. In New England a common type of farmhouse was the "salt-box," two stories high in front and one in back, and sided with unpainted clapboards. In the Middle

Georgian mansions, which as a rule were copies of English models, reduced in size and simplified in ornament.

Home conveniences and furnishings were few and simple by modern standards. For most families, even in the later colonial period, the fireplace provided light as well as

The John Ward House. *The left-hand portion of this house in Salem, Massachusetts, was built in 1684. The right-hand portion, with another gable, was added later, and the lean-to in the rear still later. Note the second-story overhang. This was characteristic of many seventeenth-century dwellings in New England. It was copied from medieval English houses, but its origin and purpose are uncertain. The most likely theories are these: (1) it was a technical matter of construction: separate, offset posts for the two stories made possible a stronger framing than did one long post; (2) it was a matter of aesthetics: people liked the way the overhang looked. Note too the casement windows with their diamond-shaped panes, also typical of the time.* (ESSEX INSTITUTE, SALEM, MASS.)

Colonies the red-brick house with a Dutch gambrel roof and the substantial farmhouse of native stone were characteristic. In the South the more prosperous planters erected

warmth, though it was commonly supplemented by the pine knot or the tallow dip. After about 1750 the Franklin stove was available for more efficient heating, and a variety of lamps and candles for better lighting, though the new and greatly superior spermaceti candles were too expensive for any except the well-to-do. In most

which was the scene of most of the family's activities.

Crowded into the generally small houses were comparatively large families. A family

The John Ward House: Kitchen. *In colonial New England the kitchen usually was located either in an ell of the house or in a lean-to at the rear (in the South, the kitchen often was located in a separate outbuilding). The kitchen, with its large fireplace, was used not only for the preparation of meals but also as a dining room, a general workroom, and to a considerable extent a living room. Its furniture included a trestle table, chairs, a wash-bench, meat tubs, a cheese press, a churn, a spinning wheel, often a loom, and sometimes a pallet bed for an indentured servant or an apprentice.* (ESSEX INSTITUTE, SALEM, MASS.)

houses the furniture was homemade and more or less crude, but mansions of the wealthy contained fine imported pieces. While the planter's or the merchant's dwelling had bed chambers with canopied beds, a parlor, and other rooms with specialized functions, the ordinary farmer's house had few bedrooms, perhaps only a loft where the entire family slept, and a large kitchen

as a rule included not only numerous children but also a varying number of dependent relatives, such as elderly grandparents or unmarried aunts. The household was further enlarged in many cases by the presence of servants, domestic slaves, or hired hands living under the same roof. In isolated places, especially in the South, strangers were usually welcomed and entertained, both because hospitality was deemed a virtue and because the visitors brought news and gossip from the outside world.

As head of the household, the father wielded strong authority over its members.

however, was somewhat higher in the colonies than in the homeland. Since they were relatively scarce, colonial women were proportionately valued for reasons of supply and demand. They were, for instance, more free than Englishwomen to travel about

The Powel House: Parlor. *Though rather plain on the outside, the Powel mansion had one of the most elegant interiors in Philadelphia. The house was built in 1768 and was bought the following year by the wealthy merchant Samuel Powel, who in 1770 became mayor of the city. Powel furnished the house with expensive articles he had collected on a grand tour of Europe. "It looks like the habitation of a Turkish bashaw," one of his friends admiringly wrote. The spacious parlor, extending the full width of the house, provided a graceful and impressive setting for the entertainment of Philadelphia high society. Note the delicate carving of the mantelpiece and the intricate plaster work on the walls and ceiling. Note also the rich imported furnishings—the Chippendale chest, tables, and chairs, the gilded Chinese Chippendale mirrors, the gilt-framed paintings, and the Oriental rug.* (PHILADELPHIA MUSEUM OF ART)

He was entitled to whatever property his wife had owned before her marriage to him, but he was responsible also for her debts and misdeeds. The position of women,

without male escorts or female chaperones, though Sarah Knight's journey from Boston to New York by herself (1704) was rather exceptional, at least in regard to distance.

Children, too, had economic as well as sentimental value in a land where a chronic manpower shortage existed and where idleness was commonly looked upon as a sin.

pected to work about the house and in the fields at an early age. As wealth increased and life as a whole became easier, the lot of the young improved. By the middle of the

Westover. *In 1688 William Byrd I began the construction of a house on land he had bought along the James River, not far from the place where Richmond, Virginia, later was to be located. His son, the brilliant William Byrd II, lived here during much of his life (when he was not in England). In 1749 the house burned down, and William Byrd III had it rebuilt. He failed, however, to maintain the fortune his father and grandfather had accumulated, and eventually the estate passed out of the family's possession. A French traveler, the Marquis de Chastellux, who was a guest at Westover in 1782, wrote: "There are magnificent houses at every view, for the banks of the James River form the garden of Virginia. That of Mrs. Byrd surpasses them all in the magnificence of the buildings, the beauty of its situation, and the pleasures of society." Westover is one of the finest examples of the Georgian style, as applied to domestic architecture, in America.* (PHOTOGRAPH BY THOMAS T. WATERMAN, LIBRARY OF CONGRESS)

Child care was rigorous and infant mortality high. Babies were baptized with water from an icy font, toddlers had to sit through long sermons in drafty church buildings, and—at least according to the teachings of presumed experts on child raising, such as the famous John Locke—youngsters were supposed to be hardened through exposure to outdoor cold and slush. Discipline was strict: children were expected to speak only when spoken to, and the rod was seldom spared. Childhood as a playtime was short, for the child was ex-

eighteenth century, numerous toys and playbooks were available, even for families of modest means, and many parents of the richer classes showed their parental pride and indulgence by having their children sit for portraits.

In the life of the colonial family there was much more than congeniality and companionship to hold a married couple together. The family as a unit performed many functions which, since that time, have been taken over by business enterprises or by the state. It had economic functions as the producer of most of what its members consumed. It performed educational services, many a child learning his A B C's at his mother's knee from the family Bible. The family served as a welfare agency in caring for the aged, the unemployable, and the sick. It was even a defense organization, at least on the frontier, where the lonely farmstead became a fortress to be manned by the whole family at the sound of the war-whoop. Having all these forces of cohesion, families were rarely broken, except by death. Divorces were seldom sought and, except in New England, were difficult or impossible to obtain. Occasionally, it is true, husbands deserted or wives absconded, as advertisements in contemporary newspapers reveal.

There was little place in colonial society for the unmarried man or woman, save in the growing cities at one extreme and in the unbroken wilderness at the other. Widows and widowers remarried promptly. Girls usually were wed while in their teens, and boys by the age of twenty. Unmarried women in their early twenties were thought of as old maids; unmarried men older than twenty-five, as bachelors. In Maryland bachelors at one time had to pay a special tax. When it came to choosing a mate, most young people were free to follow their own preferences, without dictation from their parents. By the 1750's matrimonial advertisements even began to appear in newspapers.

Immorality in colonial America would be hard to measure. Among their contemporaries in neighboring colonies, the country-folk of North Carolina had a reputation for loose morals, but as a whole these Carolinians were probably no worse than their critics. The church and court records of New England contain much evidence of premarital relations in that part of the country, but what the evidence most likely proves is that the Puritans were prone to confess their sins and to keep careful records, rather than that these people were especially given to fornication. Furthermore, the Puritan betrothal was itself such a solemn and binding ceremony that some New Englanders doubted whether intercourse between engaged couples was really wrong, and in the early eighteenth century Harvard students discussed that very question in public debate. Among indentured servants extramarital relations were a common evil, or so it was believed—and no doubt correctly, since servants usually were forbidden to marry during their servitude. As for the slaves, their marriages were not recognized in law, and few masters were as much concerned with the identity of a slave father as they were with the fecundity of a slave mother. The offspring of white fathers and black mothers, and vice versa, began to appear at an early date and, despite the intensification of race prejudice, became more numerous as time went on. Though indentured servants were blamed for the racial intermixture, men of the master class were responsible for some of it. In the rural South, as in the rural North, prostitutes were almost unheard of, but in the seaports commercialized vice grew with the growth of commerce itself.

Religion: Decline and Revival

Whether more virtuous or not, the colonists on the whole, at least in the seventeenth century, were more devout than Americans of today. In that age of faith, religion was no mere Sunday observance: it pervaded all the affairs of life. By 1700 there were signs that religiosity had begun to decline, but during the eighteenth century it was revived to a considerable extent.

Though originating abroad, religions developed a new and distinctive pattern in America. With the immigration of diverse sectarians from several countries, the colonies became an ecclesiastical patchwork made up of a great variety of churches. Toleration flourished to a degree remarkable for the time, not because it was deliberately sought but because conditions favored its growth. No single religious establishment predominated in the colonies as the Church of England did in the British Isles and as other state churches, Lutheran or Roman Catholic, did in western Europe.

By law, the Church of England was established in Virginia, Maryland, New York, the Carolinas, and Georgia. In these colonies everyone regardless of belief or affiliation was supposed to be taxed for the support of the church, and only Anglicans were supposed to vote or hold public office. Actually, except in Virginia and Maryland, the Church of England succeeded in maintaining its position as the established church only in certain localities.

Even in Virginia and Maryland, Anglicanism ceased to be quite the same thing that it was in England. To watch over the far-flung American parishes, the King and the Bishop of London depended upon the colonial governors. Most of the time the governors were preoccupied with political affairs, and the parishes worked out relatively democratic and independent church organizations of their own. Local vestries (governing boards of laymen) appointed pastors and provided for the payment of salaries. As tobacco prices fell, salaries were not increased. Hence not enough able and well-qualified men were attracted to the ministry. Some were further discouraged by the fact that they had to cross the ocean to be ordained by a bishop in England. Maryland became notorious for its idle and profligate "fox-hunting parsons." Even the most conscientious parsons in the South found it next to impossible to give adequate care to the souls of their parishioners, so far apart did the farmers and planters live and so extensive were the parish boundaries. Often the elaborate rituals of the church had to be simplified or omitted altogether.

To strengthen Anglicanism in America, the Bishop of London began in 1689 to delegate the supervision of the colonial churches to his personal representatives, or commissaries. When the first commissary, James Blair, was appointed in Virginia, more than half of the parishes in the colony had no minister. When Blair died in 1743, after more than fifty years of devoted labor, there were only two unsupplied parishes.

To further strengthen Anglicanism, in America and elsewhere, the Church of England in 1701 set up the Society for the Propagation of the Gospel in Foreign Parts. Missionaries of the S. P. G. founded a number of new Anglican communions in the colonies, especially in Massachusetts and Connecticut. Seeing that Anglicanism in America was handicapped by the lack of a bishop, the missionaries agitated for the appointment of one. But Congregationalists and Presbyterians opposed this as a step toward tyranny, and the Anglican clergy of Virginia and Maryland agreed with them. No bishop was appointed.

Neither in England nor in America were Anglicans and Puritans quite so different as has often been thought. The Puritan fathers of Massachusetts intended at first only to transplant a purified branch of the Church of England. They proceeded, however, to create a separate tax-supported church-state, with the congregation in each town managing its own ecclesiastical affairs under the leadership of its minister. Thus they became Separatists, much like the settlers at Plymouth. And the Puritan church came to be called the Congregational, because of the more or less independent, autonomous nature of each congregation. Yet the Puritans continued to feel that they had a kind of spiritual kinship with the Church of England.

In theology the Puritans were more rigid, more grim, than the Anglicans, yet less so than the Calvinists of Europe. The Puritans, developing their own brand of Calvinism, rational and less dogmatic than John Calvin himself had been.

Originally the New England Puritans believed that only God's elect should belong

---

Confession of a Witch

1692

Mrs. Mary Osgood, of Andover, Massachusetts, was examined for witchcraft, September 8, by a group of judges. They reported:

"She confesses that, about 11 years ago, when she was in a melancholy state and condition, she used to walk abroad in her orchard; and upon a certain time she saw the appearance of a cat, at the end of the house, which yet she thought was a real cat. However, at that time, it diverted her from praying to God, and instead thereof she prayed to the devil; about which time she made a covenant with the devil, who, as a black man, came to her and presented her a book, upon which she laid her finger, and that left a red spot: and that upon her signing, the devil told her he was her God, and that she should serve and worship him, and she believes she consented to it. She says, further, that about two years agone, she was carried through the air, in company with deacon Frye's wife, Ebenezer Baker's wife, and Goody Tyler, to five mile pond, where she was baptised by the devil, who dipped her face in the water and made her renounce her former baptism, and told her she must be his, soul and body, forever, and that she must serve him, which she promised to do."

About six weeks later, on October 19, she was visited by Increase Mather, who reported:

"Mrs. Osgood freely and relentingly said that the confession which she made upon her examination for witchcraft, and afterwards acknowledged before the honourable judges, was wholly false, and that she was brought to the said confession by the violent urging and unreasonable pressings that were used toward her; she asserted that she never signed the devil's book, was never baptised by the devil, never afflicted any of the accusers, or gave her consent for their being afflicted."

---

added the doctrine that, after the fall of man, God voluntarily agreed to a covenant or contract in which He laid down the terms of salvation and promised to abide by them. The Puritans believed that, once the Bible was accepted on faith, every word would appear perfectly reasonable in the light of this covenant. They were more to the church, but it was hard to know in every case exactly who was eligible for membership, exactly who had been chosen for eternal happiness. If a person underwent a religious experience in which he felt an infusion of God's grace, and if he thereafter led an upright life, that person probably was one of the elect. Many were confident that they had undergone a satisfactory experience, but many others could never be sure. So people searched their own hearts and consciences, and those of their neighbors as far as possible, to find a reassuring sign of the desperately needed grace of God.

The Puritans also strove to lead a useful, conscientious life of thrift and hard work.

They honored material success. As they prospered and life became a little easier, many lost the inner spirit of their religion and retained only the outward forms. Often the children of church members were unable to testify that they had experienced God's grace. To maintain church membership, a conference of ministers in 1662 approved a plan to admit as partial members,

with the right to vote but without the right to partake of communion, those members' children who merely professed a belief in Christian principles. Strict Puritans ridiculed this "Half-Way Covenant," and it did little to stop the growth of a worldly outlook. Sabbath after Sabbath the ministers preached sermons deploring the signs of waning piety. "Truely so it is," one minister declared in 1674, "the very heart of New-England is changed and exceedingly corrupted with the sins of the Times: there is a Spirit of Profaneness, a Spirit of Pride, a Spirit of Worldliness, a Spirit of Sensuality, a Spirit of Gainsaying and Rebellion, a Spirit of Libertinism, a Spirit of Carnality, Formality, Hypocrisie and a Spiritual Idolatry in the Worship of God."

None of the seventeenth-century ministers labored harder to keep up the old faith

Christ Church, Cambridge, Massachusetts. *Peter Harrison, who designed Christ Church, has been called "America's first professional architect." Born in England, Harrison became a ship captain when only twenty-three. He married an American woman with considerable property and prospered as a merchant of Newport, Rhode Island. In versatility though not in genius he rivaled Benjamin Franklin. He was not a jack of all trades, according to his biographer Carl Bridenbaugh, but was "rather a master of ten—ship-handling, navigation, shipbuilding, woodcarving, drafting, cartography, surveying, military engineering and construction, commerce, and the new agriculture," in addition to architecture. He acquired the largest and best selected architectural library in colonial America. Among the notable structures he designed were King's Chapel in Boston, Touro Synagogue in Newport, St. Michael's in Charleston, and Christ Church in Cambridge. The building committee for Christ Church insisted upon the most simple and inexpensive construction. Though he did not manage to keep within the cost limit, Harrison succeeded in creating a charmingly original design, in the spirit of the late Georgian style, at a remarkably low cost (see photograph on opposite page). On the interior, he produced an effect of considerable spaciousness for so small a church by leaving out the usual gallery, or balcony, on each side.* (LIBRARY OF CONGRESS)

than did Increase Mather and his son Cotton. Puritanism demanded a well-educated ministry, and the Mathers were intellectual giants. Like most scientists of the period, they believed in witches. In one of the many learned books he wrote, *Illustrious Providences* (1684), Increase Mather undertook to show that God had a special concern for New England and that the people should note carefully any evidence of "Witchcrafts, Diabolical Possessions, Remarkable Judgements upon noted Sinners," and the like. There later arose a widespread hysteria, which went to its greatest extremes in the Massachusetts town of Salem, where it was stimulated by the mumbo-jumbo of two West Indian slaves who were steeped in voodoo lore. Hundreds of people were accused as witches, many of them sentenced to die, and nineteen actually hanged before the witchcraft trials were stopped, in 1692. Afterwards almost all the witch-hunters publicly repented their part in the affair. The Mathers often were blamed for it, though in fact they had pled for moderation during the trials and had helped to bring them to an end.

Meanwhile, the Congregational Church received a blow when King Charles II annulled the original Massachusetts charter, which was restored with amendments in 1691. Thereafter Quakers, Baptists, and other sectarians were free to worship as they pleased in what once had been the exclusive land of the Puritans.

Not all the Puritans were Congregationalists: some of them became Presbyterians. In belief, these two groups were essentially the same, but they differed in ecclesiastical organization, the Presbyterians having a more highly centralized government, with a governing body of presbyters (made up of ministers and lay elders) for the churches of each district. In the early 1700's many of the Puritan churches of Connecticut, and most of those founded in other colonies by emigrants from New England, adopted the Presbyterian form of government. The number of Presbyterians in America was greatly increased by the immigration of the Scotch-Irish. At first, most of these people lacked churches and pastors. Francis Makemie, often called the father of Presbyterianism in America, organized the first American presbytery (1705) and for twenty years traveled up and down the coast from New York to South Carolina to set up churches for the churchless.

Another Calvinist group, numerous in parts of New York and New Jersey, was the Dutch Reformed. Originally the American Baptists, of whom Roger Williams is considered the first, were also Calvinistic in their theology. Then, in Rhode Island and in other colonies, a bewildering variety of Baptist sects sprang up. They had in common a belief that infant baptism did not suffice and that rebaptism, usually by total immersion, was necessary. Some remained Calvinists, believers in predestination, and others came to believe in salvation by man's free will.

Quite different from the Calvinists were the Quaker mystics and the German pietists, such as the Mennonites, Dunkers, and Moravians. The Quakers (Society of Friends) abandoned their early enthusiasm, which once had caused them to disturb other religious gatherings, at about the time they first settled in America. As their wealth increased, many of the Friends lost still more of their old-time fervor, the rich Philadelphia merchants dividing their allegiance between meetinghouse and countinghouse. Though politically dominant in Pennsylvania from the beginning, the Quakers did not use their power to compel conformity. Of all the colonies, Rhode Island and Pennsylvania were characterized by the greatest religious diversity and freedom. In Pennsylvania and other places where Germans settled, the Lutherans as well as the pietist sects added variety to the colonial religious scene.

Everywhere in America, Protestants extended toleration to one another somewhat more readily than to Roman Catholics. To strict Puritans the Pope seemed no less than Antichrist. Their border enemies in New France, being "papists," seemed agents of the Devil bent on frustrating the divine mission of the wilderness Zion in New England. In most of the English colonies, however, the Roman Catholics were far too small a minority to occasion serious conflict. They were most numerous in Maryland, and even there they numbered no more than 3,000. Ironically, they suffered their worst persecution in that colony, which had been founded as a refuge for them and had been distinguished by its Toleration Act of 1649. According to Maryland laws passed after 1691, Catholics not only were deprived of political rights but also were forbidden to hold religious services except in private houses.

Even fewer than the Catholics, the Jews in colonial America totaled no more than about 2,000 at any time. The largest community lived in New York City, smaller groups in Newport and Charleston, and dispersed families in all the colonies. There was no rabbi in America, none of the ghettos familiar in Europe, and relatively little social discrimination. In New England the Jews, unlike the Catholics, were widely esteemed, because of the Puritans' interest in the Old Testament and in Hebrew culture. The conditions of life in the colonies had much the same effect on Jews as on Christians: group ties tended to be loosened and religious observances to be relaxed.

During the late 1600's and the early 1700's, as has been seen, the piety so characteristic of the first settlers gave way more and more to a worldly view. This change was due to several influences. With the westward movement and the wide scattering of

the colonial population, many of the frontiersmen lost touch with organized religion. With the rise of towns and the multiplication of material comforts, the inhabitants of the more densely settled areas were inclined toward an increasingly secular outlook. With the appearance of numerous and diverse sects, some people were tempted to doubt whether any particular denomination, even their own, possessed a monopoly of truth and grace. And with the progress of science and free thought in Europe, culminating in the Enlightenment of the eighteenth century, at least a few Americans began to adopt a rational and skeptical philosophy.

For thousands of the colonists, the trend away from religion was reversed by a revival movement known as the Great Awakening, which reached a climax in the 1740's. Wandering exhorters from abroad did much to stimulate the revivalistic spirit. John and Charles Wesley, founders of Methodism, which began as a reform movement within the Church of England, visited Georgia and other colonies in the 1730's with the intention of revitalizing religion and converting Indians and Negroes. George Whitefield, a powerful open-air preacher from England and for a time an associate of the Wesleys, made several evangelizing tours through the colonies. Everywhere he went, Whitefield drew tremendous crowds, and it was said (with some exaggeration) that he could make his hearers weep merely by uttering, in his moving way, the word "Mesopotamia."

Though itinerants like Whitefield contributed to the rousing of religious excitement, the Great Awakening could hardly have occurred without the work of regular ministers with an evangelizing bent. One of the most important of these was Theodore J. Frelinghuysen, a youthful German-born pastor of three Dutch Reformed congregations in central New Jersey. Frelinghuysen preached the necessity of spiritual rebirth not only to the Dutch Reformed but also to the Scotch-Irish Presbyterian settlers of the Raritan Valley. His emo-

Among the errors was the prevalent idea that a person could be saved by his own efforts, through conversion. Among the disorders was the practice of uneducated men

"Sinners in the Hands of an Angry God"

Jonathan Edwards (1703–1758) was the most original and systematic theologian of colonial America. A mystic who counterposed the horror of eternal damnation against the joys of eternal paradise, Edwards argued that God's grace is the only way that any man can be redeemed from the original sin committed by Adam (although he sometimes implied, as in this sermon, that poor sinners could yield themselves up to God's grace if their hearts were "filled with love to him who has loved them"). Edwards's aim of purifying Calvinism was far less representative of his era than was the religious liberalism of his contemporary, Benjamin Franklin. But the extremes of terror and salvation that he posed were undeniably effective: when he preached this sermon at Enfield, Connecticut, in 1741, it produced great "breathing of distress, and weeping."

Your wickedness makes you as it were heavy as lead, and to tend downwards with great weight and pressure towards hell; and if God should let you go, you would immediately sink and swiftly descend and plunge into the bottomless gulf . . .

O sinner! Consider the fearful danger you are in: it is a great furnace of wrath, a wide and bottomless pit, full of the fire of wrath, that you are held over in the hand of God . . . You hang by a slender thread, with the flames of divine wrath flashing about it, and ready every moment to singe it, and burn it asunder . . .

And now you have an extraordinary opportunity, a day wherein Christ has thrown the door of mercy wide open, and stands in the door calling and crying with a loud voice to poor sinners . . .

And let every one that is yet out of Christ, and hanging over the pit of hell, . . . now hearken to the loud calls of God's word and providence. This acceptable year of the Lord, a day of such great favours to some, will doubtless be a day of as remarkable vengeance to others. . . .

tional preaching divided his own parishioners. The older and more well-to-do among them were scandalized; the young and the poor rallied to his support.

The Puritans of New England also were divided on the issue of revivalism. A majority of the Congregational ministers of Massachusetts denounced the "errors" and "disorders" arising from revival meetings.

"taking upon themselves to be preachers of the word of God," creating confusion and tumult, and leading members away from their regular churches.

Yet the outstanding preacher of the Great Awakening in New England was a Puritan of the Puritans and one of the most profound theologians in the history of American religious thought. This preacher was

Jonathan Edwards. From his pulpit in Northampton, Massachusetts, Edwards attacked the new doctrines of easy salvation for all. He called upon his people to return to the faith of their fathers. He preached afresh the old Puritan ideas of the absolute sovereignty of God, the depravity of man, predestination, the necessity of experiencing a sense of election, and election by God's grace alone. Describing hell as vividly as if he had been there, he brought his listeners to their knees in terror of divine wrath. Day after day the agonized sinners crowded his parsonage to seek his aid; at least one committed suicide. For all his effort, Edwards brought about little permanent and continuing increase in Congregational membership.

The Great Awakening spread over the colonies like a religious epidemic. It was most contagious in frontier areas and among the comparatively poor and uneducated folk, especially in the South. In the Southern back country it affected the largest number of people, prevailed the longest, and had the most lasting consequences. The Presbyterian Church was split by the formation of a large and rapidly growing group of revivalistic, "New Light" Presbyterians. New members flocked to various free-will Baptist sects; the Baptists were on the way to becoming eventually one of the two most numerous denominations in the United States.

At the end of the colonial period, despite the successful work of many revivalists, English America contained fewer church members for its population than did any other Christian country of the time, and fewer than does the United States today. Even in New England, which was better churched than either the Middle Colonies or the South, probably no more than twenty persons in a hundred belonged, in 1760, to any religious body. This low proportion of membership, however, is not necessarily a fair measure of the importance of religion to eighteenth-century Americans. Many of them failed to join a church simply because there was no acceptable one within reach.

Literature and Learning

As an American variant of English culture developed in the colonies, it was reflected in the partial Americanization of the English language. New words originated in borrowings from the Indians (such as *skunk* and *squash*), from the French (*portage*, *prairie*), and from the Dutch (*boss*, *cooky*). Americanisms also arose from the combining of words already in the English language (*bull-frog*, *snow-plow*), from the formation of new adjectives based on existing nouns (*handy*, *chunky*), from the adoption of unfamiliar uses for familiar words (*branch*, meaning *stream*; *fall*, meaning *autumn*), and from the retention of old English expressions which were being dropped in England (*cater-corner*; *bub*, for *boy*). After 1700 English travelers in America began to notice a strangeness in accent as well as vocabulary, and in 1756 the great lexicographer Dr. Samuel Johnson mentioned the existence of an "American dialect."

Dr. Johnson thought of Americans as barbarians, and some no doubt were, but from the beginning many were concerned lest civilization be lost in the wilderness. They took pains to provide schooling for their children. At no time, however, did any of the colonies possess a system of free public education in quite the modern sense of tax-supported, compulsory schools. Massachusetts came the closest to it. That colony had the advantages of fairly compact settlement, a comparatively large number of university graduates among the early settlers, and a religion that strongly emphasized the ability to read the Bible. By a Massachusetts law of 1647, designed to circumvent "that old deluder Satan," each town of 50 householders was required to hire a schoolmaster to teach reading and writing, and each town of 100 householders was required to set up a Latin grammar school (high school). This law was not always enforced, but other colonies did not even adopt such legislation. Instruction in reading and writing was generally left to "dame schools" conducted in private houses, to church schools operated by the Quakers and other sects, to privately endowed "old field" schools (on worn-out plantation lands), to private tutors in the mansions of merchants and planters, and above all to mothers and fathers at the family fireside.

Far more people learned to read than ever attended school, yet a great many never learned to read at all. The literacy rate, which is unknown, must have varied a good deal from place to place. It seems to have been very low in some of the thinly settled areas, especially in the South. It was highest in the towns, especially in New England. Nevertheless, the Connecticut legislature stated in 1690 that many people in Connecticut were "unable to read the English tongue," and of the thirteen town proprietors of Manchester, New Hampshire, in 1716, eight could not write. Colonial wills and other legal documents often were signed with a mark, by people who could not write even their own names. On the whole, literacy doubtless improved during the eighteenth century, and by the time of the Revolution probably a majority of Americans could read.

The urge to read grew with the improvement in lamps and candles, which made reading a feasible way to spend long winter evenings. Reading tastes, in books, ran mostly to the Bible and theological works but also to the classics of Greece and Rome and to contemporary scientific and practical treatises. Books were available in numerous collections. Several of the wealthy colonists owned hundreds of volumes apiece; William Byrd II had one of the largest private libraries, with more than 3,600 volumes, at Westover, his plantation home. A dozen or more subscription libraries were established, most of them in Pennsylvania, and a few small endowed public libraries, one of the earliest at Bath, North Carolina. Harvard College, in 1723, possessed 3,200 volumes. Much the larger proportion of all these books were printed abroad and imported, but the American towns of Cambridge and Boston were active book-publishing centers. Over two hundred titles came from their presses between 1640 (when the first edition of *The Whole Book of Psalms*, known as the "Bay Psalm Book," appeared) and 1700.

Periodical publications thereafter supplemented books and pamphlets as reading matter. Founded in 1704, the first regular newspaper in the colonies, though it was not very newsy, was the weekly Boston *News-Letter*, a small folded sheet of four pages with two columns to a page. By the 1760's one or more weekly papers were being published in each of the colonies except New Jersey and Delaware, both of which were well enough supplied by the presses of New York and Philadelphia. At first the papers contained much literary matter as well as news, the news being mostly of local interest. But more and more the journals concentrated upon public occurrences, and the coverage of a single paper was broadened to include the colonies as a whole through republication of items from exchange subscriptions. Several monthly magazines, notably the *American Magazine* of Philadelphia, were started after about 1750, with hopes of wide circulation. One after another they appeared for a year or two and then expired. More successful and more widely read were the yearly almanacs. Originally mere collections of weather data, these turned into small magazines of a sort, containing a great variety of literary fare. *Poor Richard's Almanac*, now well remembered, was only one of many, though a superior one.

Its publisher, Benjamin Franklin, was one of a few colonial-born men of letters who wrote works of lasting literary merit. His still widely read *Autobiography* was written after the colonial period (1770–1778), but before that he had a number of published essays to his credit, including *Advice to a Young Man on Choosing a Mistress* (1745), *Reflections on Courtship and Marriage* (1746), *Observations Concerning the Increase of Mankind* (1755), and *Advice to a Young Tradesman* (1762). These titles suggest the pragmatic and worldly-wise outlook of Franklin. Quite different was the sternly logical and other-worldly view of Jonathan Edwards, whose treatise *On the Freedom of the Will* (1754) is considered, by those who can understand it, as perhaps the most brilliant of American theological studies. John Woolman in his *Journal* (published in 1775, after his death) related a life as spiritual as Edwards's and as humanitarian as Franklin's but more humble and sensitive than either. A writer rivaling Franklin in charm, though not in productivity, was William Byrd II, whose breezy *History of the Dividing Line* (not published till 1841) recounted his experiences as one of the commissioners who in 1728 marked off the boundary between Virginia and North Carolina. The *History* is full of sly and sophisticated comments on the Carolina mores.

If early Americans did not produce much that is remembered as great literature, the reason is not that they wrote little or wrote poorly, but rather that they were most interested in kinds of writing which are not especially popular today. As a rule, colonial authors had no time for *belles lettres*, for fiction, poetry, drama, and the like. Writers concentrated upon sermons, religious tracts, and subjects of urgent, practical concern. When poets did take up the pen, as a few

able ones did in New England, they usually found their inspiration in religious themes. Anne Bradstreet, mother of eight children, reached a wide audience with the sweetly spiritual and didactic verse of her volume, *The Tenth Muse Lately Sprung Up in America* (1650). Michael Wigglesworth succeeded even better with his grim *Day of Doom* (1662). This, the first American "best-seller," must have terrified some of its contemporary readers; it shocks the modern reader with its rejoicing at the sufferings of the damned. Edward Taylor, recently "rediscovered" and now considered the finest poet of colonial New England, allowed very little of his verse to be published during his life, perhaps because he felt that its rich and sensuous imagery might seem unbecoming to him as a Puritan minister.

No native dramatists appeared in colonial America, and comparatively few plays were produced. The Puritans, Quakers, and many other Protestants condemned playacting as sinful. They found their drama in the church itself. The first theaters opened in the South, one at Williamsburg in 1718, and the famous Dock Street Theater at Charleston in 1736. By the middle of the century plays could be seen in all the larger seaport cities except Boston, where the Puritan ban remained. Apart from the legitimate stage, there were traveling shows, forerunners of the carnival and circus, with trapeze performers, Punch-and-Judy puppets, and wild-animal exhibits. There was also horse-racing as a widely attended spectator sport, especially in the South.

While there were singing societies among some of the German settlers from an early date, the colonists in general gave little attention to organized music, and musical instruments were for a long time taboo in Puritan, Quaker, and certain other churches. As for the fine arts, these were mainly folk arts. Carpenters, cabinetmakers, silversmiths, and other craftsmen made everyday objects that often were artistic as well as useful, and women expressed their artistic sense in needlework. Before the 1760's there was little painting except for the usually rather

conservative Congregationalists who were dissatisfied with the growing religious liberalism of Harvard. The College of New Jersey (1746), later known as Princeton, was set up by Presbyterians in response to

---

Puritan Poetry

Like their Anglican contemporaries in England, the Puritans of New England were friendly to the arts. But whereas Anglican poets celebrated this world and the flesh as well as God, Puritan poetry focused on things divine. These traditions are unified in the writing of Edward Taylor (1645–1729), who migrated from England to Boston when in his early twenties, graduated from Harvard College, and lived out his life as minister and physician on the western Massachusetts frontier. His "Huswifery" is distinguished for its fusion of religious zeal with a homely, striking, and brilliantly sustained metaphor.

> Make me, O Lord, thy Spinning Wheele compleat.
> Thy Holy Worde my Distaff make for mee.
> Make mine Affections thy Swift Flyers neate
> And make my Soule thy holy Spoole to bee
> My Conversation make to be thy Reele
> And reele the yarn thereon Spun of thy Wheele.

> Make me thy Loome then, knit therein this Twine:
> And make thy Holy Spirit, Lord, winde quills:
> Then weave the Web thyselfe. The yarn is fine.
> Thine Ordinances make my Fulling Mills.
> Then dy the Same in Heavenly Colours Choice,
> All pinkt with Varnisht Flowers of Paradise.

> Then cloath therewith mine Vnderstanding, Will,
> Affections, Judgment, Conscience, Memory
> My Words, and Actions, that their shine may fill
> My wayes with glory and thee glorify.
> Then mine apparell shall display before yee
> That I am Cloathd in Holy robes for glory.

---

stiff likenesses produced by self-trained portrait painters.

Of the six colleges in actual operation by 1763, all but two were founded by religious groups primarily for the training of preachers. Harvard (1636) was established by Congregationalists, William and Mary (1693) by Anglicans, and Yale (1701) by

the Great Awakening. At any of these institutions a student with secular interests could derive something of a liberal education from the prevailing curricula, which included logic, ethics, physics, geometry, astronomy, rhetoric, Latin, Hebrew, and Greek. From the beginning Harvard was intended not only to provide an educated

Harvard College, About 1740. *At the left is Harvard Hall, built in 1675; in the center Stoughton Hall, 1699; at the right Massachusetts Hall, 1720. In 1641 an anonymous writer put down the essential facts regarding the beginnings of higher education in America, as follows: "After God had carried us safe to New-England, and wee had builded our houses, provided necessaries for our liveli-hood, rear'd convenient places for Gods worship, and settled the Civill Government: One of the next things we longed for and looked after was to advance Learning and perpetuate it to Posterity; dreading to leave an illiterate Ministry to the Churches, when our present Ministers shall lie in the Dust. And as wee were thinking and consulting how to effect this great Work, it pleased God to stir up the heart of one Mr. Harvard (a godly Gentleman and a lover of Learning, there living amongst us) to give the one halfe of his Estate (it being in all about 1700. l.) towards the erecting of a Colledge, and all his Library: after him another gave 300. l. others after them cast in more, and the publique hand of the State added the rest: the Colledge was, by common consent, appointed to be at Cambridge (a place very pleasant and accommodate) and is called (according to the name of the first founder) Harvard Colledge."*

ministry but also to "advance learning and perpetuate it to posterity." King's College (1754), afterwards Columbia, had no theological faculty and was interdenominational from the start. The Academy and College of Philadelphia (1755), which grew into the University of Pennsylvania, was a completely secular institution, founded by a group of laymen under the inspiration of Benjamin Franklin. It offered courses in utilitarian subjects as well as the liberal arts—in mechanics, chemistry, agriculture, government, commerce, and modern languages. Though the colonies thus were well supplied with colleges, at least in comparison with other countries at the time, some Americans continued to go to English universities. But the great majority of colonial leaders, after 1700, received their entire education in America.

Until a medical school was opened in Philadelphia (1765) there was no opportunity for aspiring physicians to get academic training on this side of the Atlantic. Those who desired to attend a medical school had to go abroad, and usually they went to the University of Edinburgh. Most of the practicing physicians had no medical degrees. Some put in a sort of internship with an older practitioner, and others took up the healing art entirely on their own. Medical science, primitive and superstition-ridden in England and Europe, was little if any worse in America. Some of the colonial physicians and, surprising though it seems, churchmen like Cotton Mather and Jonathan Edwards advocated as earnestly as anyone in the world the most controversial medical innovation of their time—inoculation against smallpox. There was no law school in the colonies, and men prepared themselves for a legal career by independent study, by working with an established lawyer, or, in comparatively few cases, by attending one of the Inns of Court (law schools) in London.

In the colonial colleges, especially after 1700, considerable attention was given to scientific subjects. Chairs in "natural philosophy," or physical science, were endowed at William and Mary and at Harvard. The most advanced scientific thought of Europe —Copernican astronomy, Newtonian physics—eventually made its way into American teaching. But scientific speculation and experiment were not the exclusively aca-

demic, professional occupations that they later became.

Mather, Edwards, and many other ministers, merchants, and planters in America were active as amateur scientists. The Royal Society of London, founded in 1662 for the advancement of science, honored a number of them by electing them as fellows. To this society the American members and nonmember correspondents sent samples and descriptions of plants, animals, and remarkable phenomena. One member, William Byrd II, contributed "An Account of a Negro Boy That is Dappled in Several Places of His Body with White Spots." Most of the contributions were more significant, and by means of them the colonial amateurs added a good deal to the accumulation of data upon which later scientific progress was to be based. They also sent in plans for mechanical inventions and helped to start the reputation of Americans as a mechanically ingenious people.

The greatest of colonial scientists and inventors, Benjamin Franklin, gained world-wide fame with his kite experiment (1752) which demonstrated that lightning and electricity were one and the same. Showing their respect for experimental science, Harvard, Yale, and William and Mary honored themselves by honoring Franklin as a Master of Arts. The University of St. Andrews in Scotland and Oxford University in England conferred doctoral degrees upon him. Thereafter he took satisfaction in being known as "Dr. Franklin." He interested himself in countless subjects besides electricity, and he was a theoretical or "philosophical" scientist as well as a practical one. He also was a promoter of science. In 1727 he and his Philadelphia friends organized the Junto, a club for the discussion of intellectual and practical matters of mutual interest. In 1744 he led in the founding of the American Philosophical Society, the first learned society in America.

Benjamin Franklin, *by J. S. Duplessis.* (NEW YORK PUBLIC LIBRARY)

Not only a scientist, philosopher, and inventor, but also a craftsman, public-spirited citizen, humanitarian, essayist, and later a statesman and diplomat, Franklin did more things superbly well than any other American of his time, or any time. Prudent yet daring and original, genial and witty yet serious in his devotion to the truth, he was as likable as he was admirable. In his pragmatism he typified the emerging American, or at least one prominent American, ideal. Other ideals were well represented by some of his notable contemporaries—Puritanism by Jonathan Edwards, mysticism by John Woolman, gentlemanliness by William Byrd. All these have left their traces on the American mind, but none so conspicuously as the attitude of Franklin. Hence he seems always "modern," timeless in his appeal.

Law and Politics: Toward Self-Government

As with social and intellectual life, the legal and political institutions inherited from England also were more or less modified in their transmission to the colonies. Changes in the law resulted in part from the scarcity of English-trained lawyers, who were almost unknown in America before 1700. Not till a generation after that did the authorities in England make a deliberate effort to impose the common law and the statutes of the realm upon the provinces. By that time the legal standards on this side of the ocean had become pretty well fixed, and a confusion of thirteen variant legal systems had come into being through lack of acquaintance or sympathy with English law, though all these systems embodied many of its essentials, including such ancient rights as trial by jury.

Pleading and court procedure were simplified in America, and punishments were made less severe. Instead of the gallows or the prison, the colonists more commonly resorted to the whipping post, the branding iron, the stocks, and the ducking stool (for gossipy women). Crimes were redefined. In England a printed attack on a public official, whether true or false, was considered libelous. In the colonies, at the trial (1734) of the New York publisher John Peter Zenger, who was powerfully defended by the Philadelphia lawyer Andrew Hamilton, it was held that criticisms of the government were not libels if factually true—a verdict which meant a long stride toward freedom of the press. Legal philosophy itself was changed as colonists came to think of law as a reflection of the divine will or the natural order, not as an expression of the power of an earthly sovereign. Colonial lawyers, who became an influential class during the eighteenth century, were less closely attached to English tradition than the legal profession in the United States was afterward to be.

As for local government, the English pattern was reproduced more faithfully in Virginia and elsewhere in the South than in New England or the Middle Colonies. In the South the county was transplanted as the basic unit, with its court made up of justices of the peace and its sheriff appointed by the colonial governor. In New England the county did not take root, and instead the more autonomous town (township) became the most important unit, with its town meeting and its selectmen who executed the policies which the meeting decided upon. Both the county and the township appeared in the Middle Colonies, where local government was a kind of cross between that in New England and that in the South.

In all the colonies—royal, proprietary, and corporate—the colonial governments took the same general pattern. In each colony there were a governor and a two-house legislature, as in England there were a King and a two-house Parliament, though this rough similarity did not result from deliberate imitation. In England the title of "governor" originally was given to the executive head of a business corporation, and in America it came to have political significance when trading companies were transformed into political communities. The governor was appointed by the King in the royal colonies and by the proprietor in the proprietary colonies, and he was elected by the people in the corporate colonies, which after 1691 included only Connecticut and Rhode Island. A governor's council, its members chosen in the same way as the governor (except in Massachusetts, where they were elected by the assembly, known as the General Court), served as the upper chamber of the legislature. The lower house—known by different names, the Virginia House of Burgesses, first called in 1619, being the oldest—consisted of elected members. Executive, legislative, and judicial powers were somewhat mixed, for the governor and his council sat as the supreme court. Nevertheless, there was a separation of powers between the governor and the elected assembly, and the colonists took for granted the principle of separation which ultimately was to be embodied in the Federal Constitution. The very idea of a written constitution seemed natural to them because of their familiarity with colonial charters.

The colonial governments, as they had evolved by 1700, were not entirely democratic even with regard to the elected assemblies. The right to vote was limited by religious qualifications in some places and by property qualifications everywhere, the size of the property requirement varying from one colony to another. On the whole, since ownership of real estate was widely diffused, the electorate was fairly broad, considerably broader than in England. In Massachusetts and other New England colonies the great majority of adult males had the franchise, though they did not always bother to exercise it. In Virginia and other Southern colonies there was a much smaller proportion of voters, and the assemblies were more oligarchic than democratic. By law, an assemblyman had to own more property than a mere voter, and by custom (already in force by 1700) he had to reside in the district he represented. So arose the peculiarly American idea of geographical representation, as in the United States Congress, which is quite different from the British Parliament, whose members have always been allowed to represent any constituency in the country, no matter which one they might happen to live in.

Political parties, as they developed in England during the eighteenth century, did not arise in the colonies, yet there was "politics" in the sense of struggles for office and for control of government. The assemblies, conceiving of themselves as little parliaments, persistently contended against the governors, not only in the royal colonies, where the governors were agents of the King, but even in the corporate colonies, where the governors were elected.

On several occasions political conflict led to violence. In some cases relatively democratic elements, identified with the frontier, aligned themselves against the governing cliques of the seaboard, but there is no single pattern that fits all the colonial rebellions. In Virginia the frontier followers of Nathaniel Bacon, exasperated at the government's neglect of Indian defenses, in 1676 marched on Jamestown and defeated the troops of Governor William Berkeley. After Bacon died of fever, his rebellion came to a sudden end, and Berkeley took a bloody revenge, seeing to the execution of thirty-seven of the leading rebels. "That old fool has hanged more men in that naked country," remarked Charles II, "than I have done for the murder of my father." In New York, at the time of the bloodless revolution of 1688–1689 in England, Jacob Leisler led an uprising against the Stuart regime. With the backing of the common people, Leisler proclaimed himself lieutenant-governor, but his enemies among the colonial ruling classes put down his revolt and had him hanged. In Pennsylvania a band of frontiersmen known as the Paxton Boys descended on Philadelphia in 1763 to demand defense money and changes in the tax laws, and bloodshed was averted only by concessions from the government.

in 1711 it was extended to New Hampshire on the north, in 1732 to Virginia on the south, and ultimately all the way to Georgia. After 1753 Franklin as deputy postmaster improved the service, providing

The Albany Plan

1754

At the call of the British government, delegates from seven colonies met in Albany, New York, to consider ways of dealing with the perennial Indian danger. War with France was about to break out. Benjamin Franklin was interested in the overall problem of colonial unity and defense, and with the aid of other delegates he devised a plan for intercolonial government. This plan was not approved by the colonial assemblies, for they did not wish to give up any of their own powers, and so it never went into effect. But the plan is evidence of the serious thought that, even before the Revolution, some colonial leaders gave to the question of American federation. The main provisions were as follows:

1. Parliament was to set up "one general government" in America, including all the thirteen colonies, each of which was to "retain its present constitution" except for the powers to be given to the general government.

2. The King was to appoint a President-General for the general government, and the colonial assemblies were to elect representatives to a Grand Council.

3. The President-General, with the advice of the Grand Council, was to have the following powers: (a) to handle Indian relations, making treaties and deciding upon peace or war; (b) to raise troops, build forts, and provide warships; (c) to make such laws and levy such taxes as would be necessary for the foregoing purposes.

Such strife was a disruptive force within the colonies, but other factors offset it and made for intercolonial unity. The growth of population, producing an almost continuous line of settlement along the seacoast, brought the people of the various colonies into closer and closer contact, as did the gradual construction of roads, the rise of intercolonial trade, and the improvement of the colonial post office. In 1691 the postal service operated only between Massachusetts and New York and Pennsylvania;

weekly instead of biweekly posts and speeding them up so that, for example, mail was delivered from Boston to Philadelphia in about three weeks instead of six. Post riders carried newspapers as well as letters and thus enlarged and unified the colonial reading public. Still another influence toward cohesion among the colonists was the presence in the neighboring wilderness of dreaded enemies, the French and their Indian allies. By the middle of the eighteenth century the people of the various colonies had acquired a certain sense of belonging together, as was indicated by the fact that they were beginning to speak of English visitors as strangers and foreigners.

Not yet, however, did the colonists have a feeling of common destiny strong enough to prepare them for an intercolonial government. In 1754 delegates from Pennsylvania, Maryland, New York, and the New England colonies, meeting in Albany to negotiate a peace with the Iroquois, remained to discuss colonial federation. War with the French was imminent. Franklin proposed to his fellow delegates a plan for cooperation among the colonies to provide for the common defense. But this Albany Plan could not get the approval of the colonial assemblies. They were not ready for united action till after the French and Indian War.

The Need for Colonial Unity. *Probably the first American editorial cartoon, this sketch appeared in Benjamin Franklin's newspaper, the Pennsylvania Gazette of Philadelphia, for May 9, 1754. The cartoon was intended to illustrate the need for colonial unity and, in particular, for the adoption of Franklin's Albany Plan.*

BIBLIOGRAPHY

AMONG GENERAL discussions of colonial society and civilization, L. B. Wright's *The Cultural Life of the American Colonies, 1607–1763* (1957) is particularly good in dealing with the South. The same author's *The Atlantic Frontier: Colonial American Civilization* (1947) perceptively treats the colonies as a "frontier" of Europe, as does Michael Kraus's *The Atlantic Civilization* (1949). The continuing personal contacts between colonists and mother country are shown in W. L. Sachse's *The Colonial American in Britain* (1956). R. V. Coleman, *Liberty and Property* (1951), is a rather anecdotal account of the colonies from 1664 to 1763, with considerable information on social history. A good introduction is C. M. Andrews, *Colonial Folkways* (1919). J. T. Adams, *Provincial Society, 1690–1763* (1927), is not altogether reliable.

Carl Bridenbaugh has contributed a great deal to our understanding of colonial society, culture, and politics in *Cities in the Wilderness: The First Century of Urban Life in America, 1625–1742* (1938); *Seat of Empire: the Political Role of Eighteenth Century Williamsburg* (1950); *Myths and Realities: Societies of the Colonial South* (1952); and (with Jessica Bridenbaugh) *Rebels and Gentlemen: Philadelphia in the Age of Franklin* (1942). On Virginia society and politics, see also C. S. Sydnor, *Gentlemen Freeholders: Political Practices in Washington's Virginia* (1952).

W. W. Sweet, *Religion in Colonial America* (1942), summarizes the subject. The rise and decline of Puritanism is analyzed by Perry Miller in *The New England Mind: The Seventeenth Century* (1939) and *The New England Mind: from Colony to Province* (1953). The latter volume is good on Salem witchcraft, which is more fully treated by M. L. Starkey in *The Devil in Massachusetts* (1949). Perry Miller and T. H. Johnson, eds., *The Puritans* (1938), is a comprehensive anthology with a brilliant introduction. On the revival of religion, see E. C. Gaustad, *The Great Awakening in New England* (1957), Perry Miller, *Jonathan Edwards* (1949), and O. E. Winslow, *Jonathan Edwards, 1703–1758* (1940). Janet Whitney's *John Woolman, American Quaker* (1942) is a fine and sympathetic study. David de Sola Pool, *Portraits Etched in Stone: Early Jewish Settlers, 1682–1831* (1952), recounts the early years of what was to become the largest Jewish community in the world, in New York.

Brook Hindle, *The Pursuit of Science in Revolutionary America, 1735–1789* (1956), gives attention to technology as well as science. O. T. Beall, Jr., and R. H. Shryock, *Cotton Mather, First Significant Figure in American Medicine* (1954), depicts Mather's leading role in the movement for inoculation against smallpox and shows that the witch-hunter was also a remarkable scientist. John Duffy, *Epidemics in Colonial America* (1953), is good not only on medicine and public health but also on other aspects of social history. The most thorough biography of the greatest colonial scientist is Carl Van Doren, *Benjamin Franklin* (1938); but see also V. W. Crane, *Benjamin Franklin and a Rising People* (1954), for a compact and understanding treatment of the man as a whole. F. B. Tolles, *James Logan and the Culture of Provincial America* (1957), is a brief but perceptive life of William Penn's one-time secretary. Colonial education is surveyed in Paul Monroe, *The Founding of the American Public School System* (vol. 1, 1949).

On houses and public buildings, see Hugh Morrison, *Early American Architecture from the First Colonial Settlements to the National Period* (1952). Nathaniel Bacon is described as the leader of a democratic movement in J. T. Wertenbaker's *Torchbearer of the Revolution* (1940) and as a rather unprincipled troublemaker in W. E. Washburn's *The Governor and the Rebel: A History of Bacon's Rebellion in Virginia* (1958).

CHAPTER 5

The Empire: Success and Failure

During the sixteenth and seventeenth centuries the English had to contend with the Spaniards and the Dutch for room in North America. In the eighteenth century, however, the greatest threat to English America came from the French. By their final defeat of France in 1763, England and the English colonies gave new and convincing evidence of their capacity to survive and grow in international competition. For the moment the British Empire, victorious and prosperous, seemed an imposing success. Yet it was about to prove a failure, at least so far as its ability to hold the thirteen mainland colonies was concerned. After the great victory over the French, the empire builders in London undertook to bind the outlying provinces more closely than ever to the metropolitan center. In their determination to strengthen and reform the empire, these men were guided partly by the already well-developed philosophy of mercantilism and partly by a newly emerging concept of imperialism. But they overlooked certain contradictions inherent in their theories—contradictions which made their policies unworkable in the long run and unacceptable to the colonists even in the short run. Instead of consolidating the empire, its rulers unwittingly prepared the way for its early disruption.

The French in America

During the sixteenth century France had acquired claims to North America by virtue of Verrazano's and Cartier's explorations. Thereafter the French maintained contact with the New World through fishing and fur-trading expeditions which annually exploited the coasts and waters around New-

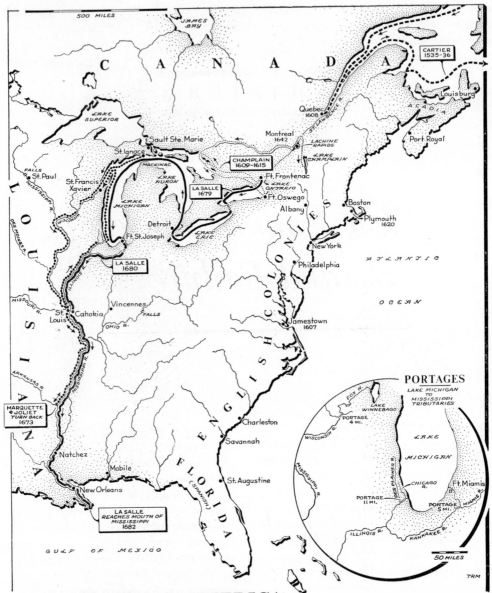

500 MILES

JAMES BAY

C A N A D A

CARTIER 1535-36

Louisburg

ACADIA

Quebec 1608

ST. LAWRENCE R.

LAKE SUPERIOR

Sault Ste. Marie

Montreal 1642

LACHINE RAPIDS

Port Royal

St. Ignace

MACKINAC

CHAMPLAIN 1609-1615

LAKE CHAMPLAIN

FALLS

St. Paul

St. Francis Xavier

LAKE HURON

LA SALLE 1679

Ft. Frontenac

LAKE ONTARIO

Ft. Oswego

Boston

MISSISSIPPI R.

WISCONSIN R.

LAKE MICHIGAN

Detroit

Albany

Plymouth 1620

L O U I S I A N A

DES MOINES R.

Ft. St. Joseph

LA SALLE 1680

LAKE ERIE

New York

A T L A N T I C

MISSOURI R.

ILLINOIS R.

Vincennes

FALLS

Philadelphia

O C E A N

St. Louis

Cahokia

OHIO R.

Jamestown 1607

E N G L I S H

C O L O N I E S

ARKANSAS R.

MARQUETTE + JOLIET TURN BACK 1673

Charleston

Savannah

Natchez

Mobile

St. Augustine

F L O R I D A (SPANISH)

New Orleans

LA SALLE REACHES MOUTH OF MISSISSIPPI 1682

G U L F   O F   M E X I C O

PORTAGES

LAKE MICHIGAN TO MISSISSIPPI TRIBUTARIES

FOX R.

LAKE WINNEBAGO

PORTAGE 4 MI.

WISCONSIN R.

L A K E

M I C H I G A N

MISSISSIPPI R.

DES PLAINES R.

CHICAGO R.

Ft. Miamis

PORTAGE 11 MI.

PORTAGE 5 MI.

ILLINOIS R.

KANKAKEE R.

50 MILES

TRM

THE FRENCH IN AMERICA: EXPLORATIONS & SETTLEMENTS

foundland and the Gulf of St. Lawrence. But the French were delayed longer than the Spaniards in undertaking colonization, because of religious divisions and civil wars which kept Frenchmen preoccupied at home. Near the end of the sixteenth century the country was reunited and reinvigorated under the leadership of Henry of Navarre, a Huguenot who accepted conversion to Catholicism in order to become King as Henry IV. Then France tried to make up for lost time as a colonizing power. She staked out imperial claims which by the middle of the eighteenth century extended over the whole of the North American heartland, from the mouth of the St. Lawrence to the mouth of the Mississippi, and from the Alleghenies to the Rockies.

during the starving time. The founder of Quebec, Samuel de Champlain, one of a series of truly heroic French agents of empire, aimed to establish a base for finding a

Champlain Fights the Iroquois. *Samuel de Champlain—a veteran of the French army and navy, a friend of King Henry IV, and a hardy navigator and explorer—is considered the founder of New France. In 1603 Champlain set out upon the first of several explorations of the New World. In 1608 he led the expedition which founded the settlement at Quebec. In 1609 he discovered the lake that is named for him. At Lake Champlain he met a band of Iroquois; some of his men fired, and the terrified Indians fled. Thus began a historic enmity between the Iroquois and the French. While the French were allied with the Hurons and other enemies of the Iroquois, the Dutch and later the English in New York cultivated Iroquois friendship and trade. After 1700 the Iroquois adopted a policy of neutrality as between the English and the French. The loss of the traditional Iroquois tie was a handicap to the English in the French and Indian War. The sketch of the first encounter with the Iroquois was made by Champlain himself and was published in his book about his voyages (1613).*

The French founded their first permanent settlement in America at Quebec in 1608, less than a year after the English had started their first at Jamestown. The earliest pioneers of New France, unprepared for the terrors of the Canadian winter, suffered losses comparable to those of the Virginians

waterway to the Orient, carrying on the fur trade, and converting the natives to Christianity. He made a beginning, but for many years New France grew in population very slowly. Few Roman Catholics felt any inclination to leave their beloved homeland, *la belle France,* and the discontented Protestants who desired to emigrate were excluded from the colony.

The French greatly extended their sway in America after the Grand Monarch, Louis XIV, took the government into his own hands (1661) and, with a program of centralization at home and expansion abroad, proceeded to live up to his supposed remark, "I am the state." His finance minister and economic planner, Jean Colbert, conceived of an integrated empire consisting of four parts: France itself as the center and the source of capital and manufactured goods; her West Indian islands (especially Martinique and Guadeloupe) as suppliers of sugar and other exotic products; posts along the African coast as aids in carrying on the slave trade; and the settlements in Canada as a market for exports from France and a granary for provisioning the West Indies. The colonies were to be governed directly from Paris, pretty much as if they were local subdivisions of France itself. New France was to have a governor, an intendant, and a bishop, each to be appointed by the King and each to serve as a check upon the other two. In practice this arrangement led to jealousies and cross-purposes which often frustrated the colonial administration —except when some individual official in America had the character and will to assert his pre-eminence. Such a man was Jean Talon, the first of the intendants, and even more outstanding was Count Frontenac, the greatest of the governors (1672–1698).

Though Colbert intended to make Canada a compactly settled agricultural province, the aspirations of Talon and Frontenac for the glory of France caused them to expand New France beyond Colbert's limits, and other forces also tended to disperse the colonial population. The lure of the forest and its furs drew immigrant peasants into the wilderness, where they often married Indian squaws and adopted tribal ways. Another group, the Jesuits, were impelled onward by their missionary zeal in the search for savage souls to save. And the bottom lands of the Mississippi attracted farmers discouraged by the short growing season in Canada.

The nature of the Illinois country had been made known by adventuresome explorers. In 1673 Louis Joliet and Father Marquette journeyed together by canoe from Green Bay along the Fox, Wisconsin, and Mississippi rivers as far as the mouth of the Arkansas, then returned with assurance that the Mississippi empties into the Gulf of Mexico, not the Gulf of California as previously thought. The next year René Robert Cavelier, Sieur de La Salle, a supremely romantic and at the same time a shrewdly practical man, began the explorations which finally, in 1682, took him to the delta of the Mississippi, where he took possession of the surrounding country for the King of France, naming it Louisiana in the King's honor. Subsequently traders and missionaries wandered to the southwest as far as the Rio Grande, and the explorer La Vérendrye (1743) pushed westward from Lake Superior to a point within sight of the Rocky Mountains. Eventually Frenchmen revealed the outlines of the whole continental interior and marked its boundaries with the cross and the fleur-de-lis.

To secure their hold upon the territory thus staked out, they founded a string of widely separated communities, strategically located fortresses, and far-flung missions and trading posts. On Cape Breton Island they established Fort Louisbourg, one of the most redoubtable strongholds in all the New World, to guard the approach to the Gulf of St. Lawrence. From both banks of the St. Lawrence River the strips of land ("seigneuries") of would-be feudal lords stretched away to the edge of the clearings. On a high bluff above the river stood Quebec, the pride of the French empire in America. Farther up the river was Montreal, even more "provincial" and less sophisticated than Quebec. Hundreds of miles to the northwest, near the juncture of Lake Superior with Lakes Michigan and Huron, was the tiny outpost of Sault Sainte Marie. Hundreds of miles to the southwest, at the juncture of Lakes Huron and Erie, was the well-fortified Detroit. Still farther in the same direction, along the Mississippi between the Missouri and the Ohio, was a cluster of hamlets—Cahokia, Kaskaskia, Fort Chartres, Sainte Genevieve—each with its outlying common-fields of black earth under cultivation. Over on the Wabash was the fifth tiny settlement of the Illinois country, Vincennes.

On the lower Mississippi were plantations much like those in the Southern colonies of English America, plantations worked by Negro slaves and supporting a race-conscious class of "creoles," who had far more pretensions to grandeur than did the comparatively poor and necessarily democratic seigneurs of Canada. Louisiana became relatively populous, especially after thousands of settlers had been brought in by the land-speculation schemes of John Law, whose "Mississippi Bubble" burst in 1721, to the ruin of investors in Europe and the disillusionment of recently arrived Louisianans. Founded in 1718, New Orleans soon grew into a city comparable in size with some of those on the Atlantic seaboard but quainter than most, with its houses built of cypress logs and bark roofs and set upon stilts above the swampy ground. To the east of New Orleans, along the Gulf of Mexico, were the towns of Biloxi (founded 1699) and Mobile, completing the string of mainland settlements which stretched all the way around from Fort Louisbourg.

Anglo-French Conflict

Spacious though it was, the continent of North America seemed too small to contain both the English and the French. The

Parlange, Pointe Coupée Parish, Louisiana. *This house was built in 1750; the widow of the original owner married a French naval officer named Charles Parlange. It is a classic example of French colonial architecture as it developed during the eighteenth century in Louisiana. The ground-floor walls are of brick, the upper-story walls of cypress timbers chinked with a mixture of clay and Spanish moss. The hipped roof is covered with cypress shingles. Encircling the entire house is a gallery, or upstairs porch, with a series of French doors opening upon it. The grounds are ornamented with various shrubs and with pecan, live-oak, and cedar trees.* (LIBRARY OF CONGRESS)

English, as Protestants, and the French, as Roman Catholics, eyed each other with suspicion and fear. As fishermen and fur traders they competed for the profits of the forest and the sea. Each national group began ultimately to feel that its very survival in America depended upon the elimination of the other's influence.

No serious warfare between the two sets of colonists occurred, however, so long as their homelands remained at peace. Charles II and James II of England persisted in their friendship for Louis XIV of France despite the fact that Louis, with his wars of French aggrandizement, ran directly counter to the traditional English policy of maintaining a balance of power on the European continent. In the Treaty of Whitehall (1686) James II and Louis XIV pledged themselves to refrain from hostilities in

America even if ("which God forbid") they should find themselves at war with one another in Europe. This was an early and interesting attempt to keep America out of

Queen Anne, with the aid of alliances he had formed before his death, carried on the struggle against France and its new-found ally, Spain.

Advantages of the French Threat
1748–1749

Peter Kalm, a university professor in Swedish Finland, toured some of the English colonies during 1748–1749. He concluded:

"It is . . . of great advantage to the crown of England that the North American colonies are near a country under the government of the French, like Canada. . . . For the English colonies in this part of the world have increased so much in their number of inhabitants, and in their riches, that they almost vie with Old England. Now in order to keep up the authority and trade of their mother country, and to answer several other purposes, they are forbidden to establish new manufactures which would turn to the disadvantage of the British commerce: they are not allowed to dig for any gold or silver, unless they send them to England immediately: they have not the liberty of trading to any parts that do not belong to the British dominions, excepting some settled places, and foreign traders are not allowed to send their ships to them. These and some other restrictions occasion the inhabitants of the English colonies to grow less tender for their mother country. . . .

"I have been told by Englishmen . . . that the English colonies in North America, in the space of thirty or fifty years, would be able to form a state by themselves, entirely independent of Old England. But as the whole country which lies along the sea-shore is unguarded, and on the land side is harassed by the French, in times of war these dangerous neighbors are sufficient to prevent the connection of the colonies with their mother country from being quite broken off. The English government has therefore sufficient reason to consider the French in North America as the best means of keeping their colonies in due submission."

Europe's wars, but in just a few years it was a dead letter. In the Glorious Revolution of 1689 James II was deposed and was replaced by Louis XIV's enemy, William III, who continued to be stadholder (chief magistrate) of the Netherlands as well as King of England, and who soon resumed his stubborn resistance to the European aggressions of the French. His successor,

These wars spread from Europe to America, where they were known to the English colonists as King William's War (1689–1697) and Queen Anne's War (1701–1713). The first, which involved few of the colonists except in northern New England, led to no decisive result. The second, which entailed border fighting with the Spaniards in the South as well as the French and their Indian allies in the North, ended in one of the great and far-reaching international settlements of modern history, the Treaty of Utrecht. At Utrecht the English were awarded some sizeable territorial gains in North America at the expense of the French: Acadia (Nova Scotia), Newfoundland, and the shores of Hudson's Bay.

After about a quarter of a century of European and American peace, England went to war with Spain over the question of English trading rights in the Spanish colonies, and the English in Georgia came to blows with the Spaniards in Florida. The Anglo-Spanish conflict soon merged in a general European war when Frederick the Great of Prussia seized some of the territory of Maria Theresa of Austria. Louis XV of France joined the Prussians against the Austrians in the hope of getting the Austrian Netherlands (Belgium), and George II of England came to the aid of Maria Theresa so as to keep the French out of the Low Countries. Again New England and New France were involved in the hostilities—in what the English colonists referred to as King George's War (1744–1748). New Englanders captured the French bastion at Louisbourg, on Cape Breton Island, but to their bitter disappointment they had to abandon it in accordance with the peace treaty, which provided for the mutual restoration of conquered territory.

This war and the two preceding it had arisen from European causes primarily, and only a small fraction of the people in the English colonies had taken any part. To the colonists these were foreign wars—King William's, Queen Anne's, King George's—rather than their own. But the next conflict was different. Known to the colonists as the French and Indian War, it recently has been renamed the "Great War for the Empire," which in fact it was. Unlike the preliminaries, this climactic struggle originated in the interior of North America.

The Great War for the Empire

Within the American wilderness a number of border disputes arose, but the most serious of them concerned the ownership of the Ohio Valley. The French, desiring to control this direct route between Canada and Louisiana, began to build a chain of fortifications to make good their claim. Pennsylvania fur traders and Virginia land speculators, the latter organized as the Ohio Company, looked to the country across the Alleghenies as a profitable field for their operations, and the British government, aroused to the defense of its territorial rights, gave instructions to the colonial governors to resist French encroachments. Acting on these instructions, the governor of Virginia sent George Washington, then only twenty-one, to protest to the commanders of the French forts newly built between Lake Erie and the Allegheny River, but these commanders politely replied that the land was French. While Washington was on his fruitless mission, a band of Virginians tried to forestall the French by erecting a fort of their own at the strategic key to the Ohio Valley— the forks of the Ohio, where the Allegheny and Monongahela rivers join. A stronger band of Canadians drove the Virginians away, completed the work, and named it Fort Duquesne. Arriving with the advance guard of a relief force from Virginia, Washington met a French detachment in a brief but bloody skirmish, then fell back to a hastily constructed stockade, Fort Necessity, where he was overwhelmed by troops from Fort Duquesne and compelled to surrender (July 4, 1754). The first shots of the French and Indian War had been fired.

For the English colonists, the war had begun inauspiciously, and it continued to go badly for them during the next few years. They received aid from the home government, but this aid was inefficiently and unintelligently applied. The British fleet failed to prevent the landing of large French reinforcements in Canada, and the newly appointed commander in chief of the British army in America, General Edward Brad-

from Pennsylvania to Virginia was left exposed to Indian raids, and many frontier settlers withdrew to the east of the Allegheny Mountains.

The French Claim the Ohio

1751

The French government sent the following instructions to its officials in New France:

"The River Ohio, otherwise called the Beautiful River, and its tributaries belong indisputably to France, by virtue of its discovery by Sieur de La Salle; of the trading posts the French have had there since, and of possession which is so much the more unquestionable as it constitutes the most frequent communication from Canada to Louisiana. It is only within a few years that the English have undertaken to trade there; and now they pretend to exclude us from it.

"They have not, up to the present time, however, maintained that these rivers belong to them; they pretend only that the Iroquois are masters of them, and being the sovereigns of these Indians, that they can exercise their rights. But 'tis certain that these Indians have none, and that, besides, the pretended sovereignty of the English over them is a chimera.

"Meanwhile 'tis of the greatest importance to arrest the progress of the pretensions and expeditions of the English in that quarter. Should they succeed there, they would cut off the communication between the two colonies of Canada and Louisiana, and would be in a position to trouble them, and to ruin both the one and the other, independent of the advantages they would at once experience in their trade to the prejudice of ours."

dock, failed to retake the forks of the Ohio. Brave but aged, wise in the ways of European warfare but unused to the American woods, Braddock wore out his men by having them cut a long military road through the forest toward Fort Duquesne, and he exposed them to attack from the tree-hidden enemy by marching them in the accepted European formation. Seven miles from the fort (July 9, 1755) he ran into a French and Indian ambush; he himself and large numbers of his men were killed, and the survivors fled all the way back to Fort Cumberland in Maryland. The frontier

After about two years of fighting in America, the governments of France and England finally declared hostilities, and a world war (known in Europe as the Seven Years' War, 1756–1763) began. France and England now changed partners, France allying herself with her former enemy, Austria, and England joining France's former ally, Prussia. Henceforth battles were fought not only on the American mainland but also in the West Indies, in Europe, and around the world in India.

In this global contest the British had the advantage of the mightiest navy on the seas and, with Frederick the Great on their side, the finest army in Europe. In America the people of the English colonies outnumbered those of the French colonies by approximately 15 to 1, but were by no means that much stronger militarily. The French had numerous and powerful Indian allies, many of them newly attracted to the French by the latter's early victories in the war. The English had few such allies; the Iroquois, traditionally friendly to the English and hostile to the French, now remained firmly neutral. Furthermore, the French government kept its colonists in a fairly good state of military discipline and readiness, and could count upon the loyal services of a high proportion of its colonial manpower. The British government, on the other hand, exercised much less control over its thirteen colonies, which often acted as if they were autonomous. Only where and when they were exposed to immediate danger did the English colonists wholeheartedly support the war effort.

At first the overall direction of British strategy was weak. Then (1757) William Pitt as prime minister was allowed to act as practically a wartime dictator of the empire (much as Winston Churchill was in 1940 and after). Pitt reformed the army and the navy, replacing bureaucratic deadwood with young and eager officers. He gave generous subsidies to Frederick the Great, who thus was enabled to keep the French fairly busy in Europe. And he turned from the defensive to the offensive in America, with a determination to drive the French out of the continent.

With Pitt as organizer, the British regulars in America, together with colonial troops, proceeded to take one French stronghold after another, including Fort Duquesne in 1758. The next year, after a siege of Quebec, supposedly impregnable atop its towering cliff, the army of General James Wolfe struggled up a hidden ravine,

surprised the larger forces of the Marquis de Montcalm, and defeated them in a battle in which both commanders were slain. The fall of Quebec marked the climax of the

START OF THE FRENCH & INDIAN WAR

American phase of the war, and the decisive battle was afterward remembered as a romantic and tragic encounter between two high-minded and able men.

Some other phases of the war were less romantic, less high-minded. In the course of it the British resorted to such expedients as population dispersal. Fearing trouble from the French inhabitants of Nova Scotia, the British uprooted several thousand of them and scattered them throughout the English colonies; some of these Acadians eventually made their way to Louisiana, where they became the ancestors of the present-day Cajuns. Meanwhile the French and their savage allies were committing worse atrocities, and hundreds of defenseless families along the English frontier fell before the hatchet and the scalping knife.

Peace finally came after the accession of

treaty signed at Paris in 1763. By its terms the French ceded to Great Britain some of their West Indian islands and all their colonies in India except two. The French also

The Taking of Quebec. *In 1759 the capture of Quebec was the main objective of the British campaign in America. General James Wolfe, only thirty-two, commanded an army that proceeded up the St. Lawrence River on navy transports. General Jeffrey Amherst, commander in chief of the British armies in America, was to take forts Crown Point and Ticonderoga, then join Wolfe before Quebec. Amherst was delayed, and Wolfe decided to go ahead alone, though his army was smaller than that of the French at Quebec, under the Marquis de Montcalm. The Quebec defenses were too strong for a direct attack from the river. After a few months' siege, Wolfe daringly landed his troops above the town, led them up an insufficiently guarded ravine, and reached the heights known as the Plains of Abraham. Now the cautious Montcalm had no choice but to fight. He attacked without waiting to assemble all his available forces, and in about fifteen minutes he was compelled to retreat. The contemporary English engraving portrays in the one scene a whole succession of events—the landings, the climb up the ravine, and the battle itself.* (LIBRARY OF CONGRESS)

the peace-minded George III and the resignation of Pitt, who disagreed with the new King and wished to continue hostilities. Yet Pitt's aims were pretty well realized in the

transferred Canada and all other French territory east of the Mississippi, except the island of New Orleans, to Great Britain, and New Orleans and the French claims west of the Mississippi to Spain. Thus the French gave up all their title to the mainland of North America.

The Old Colonial System

Until the end of the colonial wars with the French, the British government in its treatment of the colonies had been guided, at least roughly, by the long-standing ideas of mercantilism. The mercantilist philosophy valued colonies primarily for their trade. Supposedly the home country would be benefited if English merchants were given, so far as feasible, a monopoly of colonial commerce. To carry out this policy, Parliament from 1651 on passed the series of Navigation Acts and other laws designed to inhibit direct trading between the colonists and foreigners and to discourage the rise of colonial manufactures which might compete with those of England. For more than a century, however, the laws were not rigorously and consistently enforced. The

tionalize the administration of the colonies and to tighten the control of the home government over them.

As early as 1624 King James I took a

NORTH AMERICA AFTER 1713

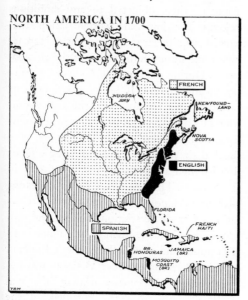

NORTH AMERICA IN 1700

NORTH AMERICA AFTER 1763

British Empire remained a rather vague concept in theory and a rather loose organization in practice, though from time to time attempts were made to centralize and ra-

step toward centralization when he deprived the Virginia Company of its powers of governance and himself assumed the management of Virginia as a royal province. Then the mid-seventeenth-century struggle between King and Parliament, culminating in civil war, checked the development of a systematic royal administration of the colonies. Left to themselves, they took advantage of the turmoil in England by flouting the kingly prerogatives. Massachusetts even went so far as to exercise the sovereign power of coining its own money, the pine-tree shilling. After the Restoration in England, Charles II was slow to discipline this worst offender, Massachusetts, even though an investigation showed a good deal of smuggling and a rather independent spirit there. Finally, in 1684, the King acted with determination, revoking the charter which had made Massachusetts a corporate, virtually self-governing colony.

Charles II did not intend to stop with that. Both he and his brother and successor, James II, admired the absolutist ways of Louis XIV, who in Canada had but one colony, which he ruled directly through his appointed officials, without having to contend with an elected assembly. Taking the Dominion of Canada as his model, James II set up a Dominion of New England which eventually included also New Jersey and New York. Over all these colonies, their legislatures having been abolished, ruled a single royal governor, the stern and unpopular Sir Edmund Andros. When James II was deposed in the English Revolution of 1689 the Andros regime collapsed, amid mob demonstrations in New England and Leisler's Rebellion in New York. So ended the first attempt at colonial unification from above.

But the trend toward increasing royal control of the colonies was resumed, though it did not go as far as some English officials desired. Despite the lobbying of Increase Mather and the protests of the Puritans, Massachusetts was not given back its old corporate charter but was made a royal colony (1691). So also were New York (1685), New Jersey (1702), the Carolinas (1719–1729), and Georgia (1752). Only Pennsylvania-Delaware and Maryland continued as proprietary colonies, and only Connecticut and Rhode Island as corporate ones. Some of the English experts in colonial affairs wished to see these colonies brought directly under the King's control like the others and a governor-general put in charge of all thirteen, with a deputy governor responsible to him in each one. But Parliament could not be persuaded to approve such a plan.

Though the colonies continued to be governed in the King's name, Parliament asserted its supremacy in colonial as well as domestic and foreign affairs after the Glorious Revolution of 1689. Theoretically Parliament represented the interests of the whole kingdom and indeed the whole empire. Actually it represented best the interests of the great merchants in England. Most of them objected to any ambitious scheme for imperial reorganization that would require large expenditures, increase taxes, and diminish the profit of the colonial trade. During the reigns of George I (1714–1727) and George II (1727–1760), both of whom were German-born, the real executive in England came to be the prime minister and his fellow cabinet ministers, who held their places not by the King's favor but by their ability to control a majority in Parliament. The first of the prime ministers, Robert Walpole, believed that a relaxation of trade restrictions against the colonies would enable them to buy more English goods and would thus benefit England and its merchants. Under Walpole was begun a policy of "salutary neglect" that was followed until after the outbreak of the French and Indian War.

Meanwhile the day-to-day administration of colonial affairs remained decentralized and inefficient. There was in England no separate and full-fledged colonial office. The officials of the various departments—treasury, admiralty, and so forth—had the responsibility of administering the laws overseas as well as at home. Among the departments there was much overlapping and confusion of authority, and within them there were few men or none who had visited America and obtained first-hand knowledge of American affairs. To provide information about colonial conditions and opinions, the assemblies in the colonies sent to London their own agents or lobbyists, among them Benjamin Franklin, who represented not only Pennsylvania but also Georgia, New Jersey, and Massachusetts. To coordinate the colonial business of the different government agencies in England was the function of two bodies, the Privy Council and the Board of Trade. Both were, however, essentially advisory groups with little power to take decisive action.

The conflicts of administrative authority in London, together with the deliberate ministerial policy of "salutary neglect," weakened the hold of England upon the colonies, and so did the character of the officials who were sent to America. These included the officials placed in charge of each royal colony—governor, councillors, secretary, attorney general, receiver general, surveyor general, supreme-court justices—and the agents of the London administrative departments, such as collectors of customs and naval officers, who were located in all the colonies. Some of these officeholders were able and devoted men, but the majority were not. There being no merit system, appointments often were made on the basis of bribery or favoritism rather than ability or integrity. Many an appointee remained in England and, with part of his salary, hired another man to take his place in America. Such a deputy, poorly paid as he was, found it hard to resist opportunities to augment his income with bribes. For example, a customs collector seldom hesitated, for a fee smaller than the duty itself, to pass the goods of a smuggling colonial merchant. Even honest and well-paid officials, desiring to get along with the people among whom they had to live, usually found it expedient to yield to popular resistance in the colonies.

This resistance to imperial authority centered in the colonial assemblies. By 1700 they had established the right to levy taxes, make appropriations, and pass laws for their respective colonies. Their legislation was subject to veto by the governor and to disallowance by the Privy Council, but they could force the governor to approve laws by withholding his salary and they could get around the Privy Council by repassing disallowed laws in slightly altered form. The assemblies came to look upon themselves as little parliaments, each practically as sovereign within its colony as Parliament itself was in England.

So strong had grown the colonial feeling against direct legislation by Parliament that, during the French and Indian War, the English government did not attempt to tax or draft the colonists directly but called upon the assemblies to provide quotas of soldiers and supplies. This requisition system, itself a concession to provincial prejudice, heightened the self-importance of the assemblies, and most of them further asserted their autonomy by complying in a slow and niggardly way. Some of them, unwilling to be taxed by Parliament, also refused to tax themselves; they issued paper money instead.

In Virginia the legislature not only issued paper money but, when the resulting inflation raised the price of tobacco, also passed a law to deprive the Anglican clergy (who were paid in tobacco) of the benefits of the price rise. When this law was disallowed (1760), one of the ministers sued his vestrymen for his full pay. At the trial of the "parson's cause" the young lawyer Patrick Henry, defending the vestrymen, denounced the Privy Council for its tyranny and told his fellow Virginians to ignore its action. Roused by Henry's oratory, the jurors awarded the parson damages of only one penny. Thus did they defy the authority of the British government.

In Massachusetts the merchants disregarded the laws of the empire even more flagrantly than did the planters in Virginia. Throughout the war these merchants persisted in trading with the enemy in Canada and in the French West Indies. British officials resorted to general search warrants—"writs of assistance"—for discovering smuggled goods and stamping out the illegal and unpatriotic trade. As attorney for the Massachusetts merchants, James Otis maintained that these searches violated the ancient rights of Englishmen and that the law of Parliament authorizing the warrants was therefore null and void. With eloquence as stirring as Henry's, Otis insisted that Parliament had only a limited power of legislating for the colonies.

As the war ended, the London policy makers faced a dilemma, though they were not fully aware of it. On the one hand, they could revert to the old colonial system with its half-hearted enforcement of the mercantilist program, but that would mean virtual independence for the colonies. On the other hand, the men in London could renew their efforts to reform the empire and enforce the laws, but that would lead to revolt and absolute independence.

The New Imperialism

The thirteen mainland colonies were only a part of the British possessions scattered throughout the Americas and the world, and before 1763 they were not considered (except in their own eyes) as the most valuable part. Some of them, such as

Virginia and Maryland with their tobacco production, fitted in fairly well with the aims of mercantilism, but on the whole the island colonies contributed a great deal more than those of the mainland to the profits of English merchants and the prosperity of the English homeland. The "sugar islands" in particular—Barbados and the Windward Islands, the Leeward Islands, Jamaica—yielded remarkable opportunities for the investment of English capital. They also complemented the economies of some of the mainland colonies by providing a market for the output of fisheries, farms, and forest industries.

Believing in a kind of commercial imperialism, most English merchants opposed the acquisition of territory for its own sake. But some Englishmen and Americans began to believe that land itself should be acquired for the empire because of the population the land would support, the taxes it would produce, and the sense of imperial greatness it would confer. Both William Pitt and Benjamin Franklin were among the advocates of this new territorial imperialism. Franklin wrote powerfully upon the future greatness of the British Empire in America, stressing the need for vast spaces to accommodate the rapid and limitless growth of the American people. Old-fashioned mercantilists, however, continued to think of trade as the essence of empire, and of island and coastal possessions as bases for trade. The issue came to a head with the peacemaking at the end of the French and Indian War. Commercial imperialists urged that Canada be returned to France in exchange for the most valuable of her sugar islands, Guadeloupe. Territorial imperialists, Franklin among them, argued in favor of keeping Canada. The decision to retain Canada marked a change in the emphasis of imperial policy.

With the acquisition of Canada and the other fruits of war in 1763, the area of the

British Empire was more than doubled and the problems of governing it were made many times more complex. The war had left the British government with a staggering burden of debt, and English landlords and merchants objected violently to increased taxes. The rather half-hearted war effort of the colonists had shown the cumulative evils of "salutary neglect." And, by giving Great Britain undisputed title to the transmontane West as well as Canada, the peace had brought new problems of administration and defense. British statesmen feared that France, by no means crushed, might soon launch an attack somewhere in America for the recovery of her lost territories and prestige.

Responsibility for the solution of these postwar problems fell to the young monarch George III, who had come to the throne in 1760. Unlike his father and his grandfather, George III was thoroughly British and proud of it, and he was determined to follow the advice of his mother to be a King in fact as well as name. Shrewdly, he took care not to upset the recently developed constitutional practice according to which the party controlling Parliament made and unmade ministries. Instead, becoming a politician himself, the King created a party of his own through patronage and bribes and thus took control of Parliament away from the Whigs. Though not at all the ogre he was once pictured in American schoolbooks, George III achieved his aim of personal government and therefore deserves much of the credit or blame for the acts that followed.

More immediately responsible was George Grenville, whom the King made prime minister in 1763. Grenville, a brother-in-law of William Pitt, did not share Pitt's sympathy with the colonial point of view. He agreed with the prevailing British opinion that the colonists should be compelled to obey the laws and to pay a part of the cost of defending and administering the empire. He fancied himself something of an efficiency expert, and he was indeed an able administrator. Furthermore, as Chancellor of the Exchequer and First Lord of the Treasury, he was well acquainted with matters of public finance. Promptly he undertook to impose system upon what had been a rather unsystematic aggregation of colonial possessions in America.

The Western problem was the most urgent. With the repulse of the French, frontiersmen from the English colonies had begun promptly to move over the mountains and into the upper Ohio Valley. Objecting to this intrusion, a federation of Indian tribes under the remarkable chieftain Pontiac raised the war cry. The British government issued, as an emergency measure, a proclamation forbidding settlers to advance beyond a line drawn along the mountain divide between the Atlantic and the interior. Though the emergency passed, the principle of the Proclamation Line of 1763 remained —the principle of controlling the westward movement of population. This was something new. Earlier the government had encouraged the rapid peopling of the frontier for reasons of both defense and trade. In time the official attitude had begun to change, because of a fear that the interior might draw away so many people as to weaken markets and investments nearer the coast, and because of a desire to reserve land-speculating and fur-trading opportunities for English rather than colonial enterprisers. Then, having tentatively announced a new policy in 1763, the government soon extended and elaborated it. A definite Indian boundary was to be located, and from time to time relocated, in agreement with the various tribes. Western lands were to be opened for occupation gradually, and settlement was to be carefully supervised to see that it proceeded in a compact and orderly way.

To provide further for the defense of the colonies, and to raise revenue and enforce imperial law within them, the Grenville ministry with the cooperation of Parliament meanwhile instituted a series of measures some of which were familiar in principle and others fairly novel. Regular troops were now to be stationed permanently in the provinces, and (by the Mutiny Act, 1765) the colonists were called upon to assist in provisioning and maintaining the army. Ships of the navy were assigned to patrol American waters and look out for smugglers. The customs service was reorganized and enlarged, and vice-admiralty courts were set up in America to try accused smugglers without the benefit of sympathetic local juries. Royal officials were ordered to take up their colonial posts in person instead of sending substitutes. The Sugar Act (1764), designed in part to eliminate the illegal trade between the continental colonies and the foreign West Indies, lowered the high molasses duty of the Molasses Act of 1733, but imposed new duties on a number of items and made provision for more effective collection. The Currency Act (1764) forbade the colonial assemblies to issue any more paper money and required them to retire on schedule all the paper money issued during the war. And, most momentous of all, the Stamp Act (1765) imposed a tax to be paid on every legal document in the colonies, every newspaper, almanac, or pamphlet, and every deck of cards or pair of dice.

Thus the new imperial program with its reapplication of old mercantilist principles began to be put into effect. In a sense it proved highly effective. British officials soon were collecting more than ten times as much annual revenue in America as before 1763. But the new policy was not a lasting success.

Inner Contradictions

It is doubtful whether mercantilism, carried to its logical extremes, could have been made to work. How could the colonists provide a growing market for English goods, as well as a source of cash and raw material, if they were to be deprived of the (illegal) trading and other activities which in the past had made it possible for them to pay? Mercantilism, it would seem in retrospect, would work at all only when it did not work very well, only when it was not pushed to extremes and its inner contradictions thereby exposed. Very likely, time would have shown the British leaders not only that their cause was exceedingly unwise, but that it was quite impracticable as well.

But most of the leading colonists were unwilling to wait patiently to find out whether the measures of the new imperialism were economically feasible. The experience of the French and Indian War, while convincing prominent Englishmen of the need for tighter imperial control, had exerted an opposite effect on the attitude of colonials. Rightly or wrongly, they had gained a heightened sense of self-confidence in their own military prowess, along with a certain contempt for British regulars and especially their officers, such as the unfortunate General Braddock. The French threat having been removed from the frontier forest, many of the colonists felt a new surge of expansive energy and daring. In short, they concluded that they needed not more but rather less of imperial guidance and protection than they had previously received.

Precisely through its different influences on the thinking of Englishmen and continental colonists, the grand victory of the empire was to lead directly to the empire's dismemberment in the American Revolution.

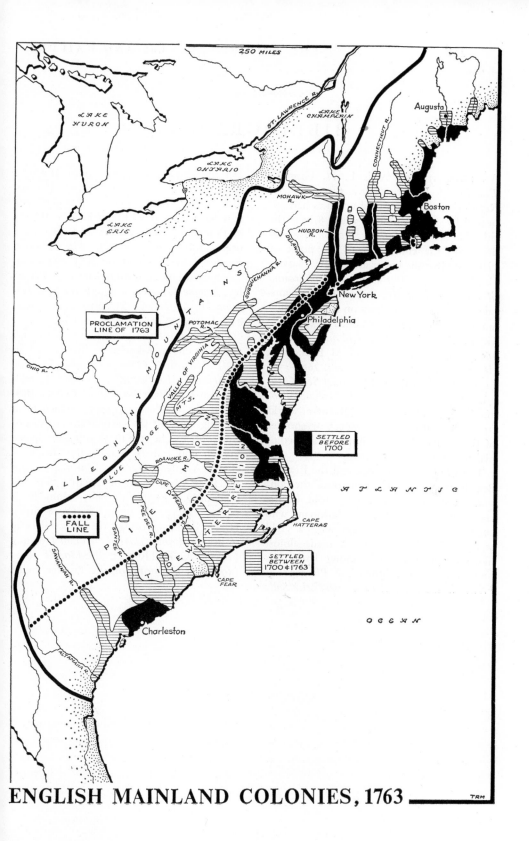

250 MILES

LAKE HURON

LAKE ONTARIO

ST. LAWRENCE R.

LAKE CHAMPLAIN

Augusta

CONNECTICUT R.

MOHAWK R.

Boston

LAKE ERIE

HUDSON R.

DELAWARE R.

New York

PROCLAMATION LINE OF 1763

SUSQUEHANNA R.

Philadelphia

POTOMAC R.

OHIO R.

ALLEGHANY MOUNTAINS

VALLEY OF VIRGINIA

MTS.

BLUE RIDGE

ROANOKE R.

CAPE FEAR R.

PEE DEE R.

SANTEE R.

SAVANNAH R.

FALL LINE

PIEDMONT REGION

SETTLED BEFORE 1700

ATLANTIC

CAPE HATTERAS

TIDEWATER REGION

SETTLED BETWEEN 1700 & 1763

CAPE FEAR

OCEAN

Charleston

ALTAMAHA R.

ENGLISH MAINLAND COLONIES, 1763

TRM

→»-→»-→»-→»-→»«-«‹-«‹-«‹-«‹

BIBLIOGRAPHY

AN EXHAUSTIVE STUDY is L. H. Gipson's *The British Empire before the American Revolution,* of which nine volumes had appeared by 1956. Volumes 7 and 8 bear the title *The Great War for the Empire* and deal with the conflict from the point of view of British imperial policy makers. C. M. Andrews, *The Colonial Background of the American Revolution* (1924), contains an enlightening essay on British policy and its problems. Earlier books of value are G. L. Beer, *The Old Colonial System, 1660–1754* (2 vols., 1912); O. M. Dickerson, *American Colonial Government, 1696–1765* (1912); C. M. Andrews, *Colonial Self-Government* (1904); and E. B. Greene, *Provincial America* (1905). All these works treat with authority one aspect or another of the conflict between imperial and colonial government.

The rise of New France and the Franco-British struggle for the control of the continent are most interestingly told in the classic writings of Francis Parkman, who combined sound scholarship with a vivid style—so vivid that it often reads almost like a movie scenario. Among Parkman's more important volumes are *Pioneers of France in the New World* (1865), *La Salle and the Discovery of the Great West* (2 vols., 1879), and *A Half Century of Conflict* (2 vols., 1892). These and other writings have been republished in *The Works of Francis Parkman* (1922), and some have been skillfully condensed in *The Parkman Reader* (1955), edited by S. E. Morison.

Important modern studies are H. I. Priestley, *France Overseas through the Old Regime* (1939); and G. M. Wrong, *The Rise and Fall of New France* (2 vols., 1928).

One phase of the clash between English and French in America is illuminated in A. T. Volwiler's *George Croghan and the Westward Movement, 1741–1782* (1926). See also J. E. Bakeless, *Daniel Boone, Master of the Wilderness* (1955), which is an exciting story of the early trans-Appalachian frontier. The role of Washington in the French and Indian War is the theme of C. H. Ambler's *George Washington and the West* (1936) and of the first two volumes of D. S. Freeman's multi-volume biography, *George Washington* (1948–1957). H. H. Peckham brings recent scholarship to bear in *Pontiac and the Indian Uprising* (1947). A. B. Hulbert, *Braddock's Road* (1903), is a history of the famous route.

CHAPTER 6

Getting Ready for Revolt

THE POLICY of George III's government, beginning with the measures of 1763–1765, provoked resistance in the colonies and led to a decade of discontent that culminated in armed revolt. First came the Stamp Act crisis (1765–1766), when tax collectors got a riotous reception in the colonies and the law was consequently repealed. When it was followed by new efforts to tax the colonists, disorders reappeared and reached a climax (1770) in the so-called "Boston Massacre." Finally (1773–1775), a dispute over tea brought on another outbreak of lawlessness, stern repressive measures, and the first battles of actual war.

War came in consequence of a real clash of interests, economic and political, between the groups dominant in England and those dominant in the colonies. This conflict was the end result of a century and a half of divergence in the development of English and American ways. As an outstanding historian (Charles M. Andrews) has said, "New soil had produced new wants, new desires, new points of view, and the colonists were demanding the right to live their own lives in their own way."

Colonial Self-Interest

Self-interest generally led the colonists to be loyal subjects before 1763, and even after that time they had much to gain from maintaining their imperial connection. They enjoyed access to the markets of the empire, bounties on the production of certain goods, the protection afforded by British naval and military forces, and the pride of belonging to the most powerful aggregation of peoples on the globe. In some respects the colonists had more in common with Englishmen than with one another.

Serious disputes continued to pit colonist against colonist. In 1771 a small-scale civil war broke out as a consequence of the Regulator movement in North Carolina. The

Regulators were farmers of the Carolina up-country who organized to oppose the extortionate taxes which the sheriffs collected. These sheriffs, along with other local offi-

mance, in which nine on each side were killed and many others wounded. Afterward, six Regulators were hanged for treason. Though such bloodshed was excep-

---

Disunity in the Colonies
1760

During the French and Indian War the Englishman Andrew Burnaby visited America. Afterwards he wrote a book entitled *Travels through the Middle Settlements in North America in the Years 1759-60*. The book was published in London in the critical year 1775. Burnaby's readers must have concluded that the colonists were in no condition to put up an effective resistance to British authority, for he wrote:

"Fire and water are not more heterogeneous than the different colonies in North America. Nothing can exceed the jealousy and emulation which they possess in regard to each other. The inhabitants of Pennsylvania and New York have an inexhaustible source of animosity, in their jealousy for the trade of the Jerseys. Massachusetts-Bay and Rhode Island are not less interested in that of Connecticut. The West Indies are a common subject of emulation to them all. Even the limits and boundaries of each colony are a constant source of litigation. In short, such is the difference of character, of manners, of religion, of interest of the different colonies that I think if I am not wholly ignorant of the human mind, were they left to themselves, there would even be a civil war, from one end of the colony to the other; while the Indians and Negroes would, with better reason, impatiently watch the opportunity of exterminating them all together."

---

cials, were appointed by the governor; there was no local self-government in the colony. At first the Regulators tried to redress their grievances peaceably, by electing their leaders to the colonial assembly. The western counties were badly underrepresented in the assembly, and the Regulators were unable to get control of it. They finally armed themselves and undertook to resist tax collections by force. To suppress the revolt, Governor William Tryon raised an army of militiamen, mostly from the eastern counties. The militiamen met and defeated the Regulators, some 2,000 strong, in the Battle of Ala-

tional, the people of the colonies were divided by numerous conflicts of interest.

After 1763, however, the policies of the British government increasingly offset the divisive tendencies within the colonies and caused Americans to look at the disadvantages of empire more closely than at its benefits. These policies threatened, in some degree or other, the well-being of nearly all classes in America.

Northern merchants would suffer from the various restraints upon their commerce, from the closing of the West to their ventures in land speculation and fur trading, from the denial of opportunities in manufacturing, and from the increased load of taxation. Southern planters, already burdened with debts to English merchants, would not only have to pay additional taxes but would also be deprived of the chance to lessen their debts by selling Western land, in which George Washington and others were much interested. Professional men—preachers, lawyers, and professors—considered the interests of merchants and planters to be identical with their own. Small farmers, much the most numerous group in the colonies, stood to lose as a result of reduced markets and hence lower prices for their crops, together with an increase in their taxes and other costs, not to mention the difficulty of getting paper-money loans. Town workers faced the prospect of narrowing opportunities, particularly because of the restraints on manufacturing and paper money.

Already, at the end of the French and Indian War, the colonists were beginning to feel the pinch of a postwar depression. Previously the British government, pouring money into their midst to finance the fighting, had stimulated a wartime boom. Now the government was going to take money out of the colonies instead of putting it in. If the government's measures should be strictly enforced, the immediate effect would be to aggravate the hard times. The long-run effect would be to confine the enterprising spirit of the colonists and condemn them to a fixed or even a declining level of living.

Grievous as were the economic consequences of George III's program, its political consequences would be as bad or worse. While colonial democracy was far from all-inclusive, the colonists were used to a remarkably wide latitude in self-government. Nowhere else in the world at that time did so large a proportion of the people take an active interest in public affairs. The chief centers of American political activity were the provincial assemblies, and here the people (through their elected representatives) were able to assert themselves because the assemblies had established the right to give or withhold appropriations for the costs of government within the colonies. If, now, the British authorities should succeed in raising extensive revenues directly from America, the colonial voters and their representatives would lose control over public finance, and without such control their participation in politics would be very nearly meaningless.

Home rule was not something new and different that these Americans were striving to get. It was something old and familiar that they desired to keep. They would lose it if the London authorities were allowed to carry out the program of raising revenues from colonial taxation and providing unconditional salaries for royal officials. The discontented Americans eventually prepared themselves to lay down their lives for a movement that was both democratic and conservative—a movement to conserve the liberties they already possessed.

The Stamp Act Crisis

If Prime Minister Grenville had wished deliberately to antagonize and unify some of the most influential groups in the colonies (which, of course, he did not) he could have chosen no means more effective than the Stamp Act. The tax fell upon all Americans, of whatever section, colony, or class. In particular, the stamps required for ship's papers and legal documents offended merchants and lawyers. Tavern owners, often the political oracles of their neighborhoods, now were supposed to buy stamps for their licenses; and printers, for their newspapers and other publications. Thus the tax antagonized those who could play most effectively upon public opinion.

Nevertheless, it occurred to few colonists

that they could do more than grumble and buy the stamps, until the Virginia House of Burgesses sounded a "trumpet of sedition" that aroused Americans to action almost

Virginians should pay no taxes except those voted by the Virginia assembly, and that anyone advocating the right of Parliament to tax Virginians should be deemed an en-

---

The Stamp Act Congress: Resolutions

"I. That His Majesty's subjects in these colonies owe the same allegiance to the Crown of Great Britain that is owing from his subjects born within the realm, and all due subordination to that august body the Parliament of Great Britain.

"II. That His Majesty's liege subjects in these colonies are intitled to all the inherent rights and liberties of his natural born subjects within the kingdom of Great Britain.

"III. That it is inseparably essential to the freedom of a people, and the undoubted right of Englishmen, that no taxes be imposed on them but with their own consent, given personally or by their representatives.

"IV. That the people of these colonies are not, and from their local circumstances cannot be, represented in the House of Commons in Great Britain.

"V. That the only representatives of the people of these colonies are persons chosen therein by themselves, and that no taxes ever have been, or can be constitutionally imposed on them, but by their respective legislatures. . . ."

---

everywhere. In the House of Burgesses a group of young aristocrats aspired to exert themselves against the oligarchy of tidewater planters who, with the royal governor, dominated Virginia politics. Foremost among these young malcontents was Patrick Henry, who was ambitious to enlarge the fame he had gained in the "parson's cause." Henry made a fiery speech in the House (May, 1765), concluding with a hint that George III like earlier tyrants might lose his head, and to shocked cries of "Treason!" Henry is said to have replied: "If *this* be treason, make the most of it." Then he introduced a set of resolutions declaring that Americans possessed all the rights of Englishmen, especially the right to be taxed only by their own representatives; moreover, that

emy of the colony. The House of Burgesses defeated the most extreme of Henry's resolutions, but all of them were printed and circulated as the "Virginia Resolves," thus giving the impression in other colonies that the people of Virginia were both more daring and better unified than was the fact.

Stirred by the Virginia Resolves, mobs in various places began to take the law into their own hands, and during the summer of 1765 riots broke out in various places, the worst of them in Boston. Men belonging to the newly organized "Sons of Liberty" went about terrorizing stamp agents and burning the stamps. The agents, themselves Americans, hastily resigned to save their skins, and very few stamps were sold in the continental colonies. In Boston the mob got out of hand and proceeded to harry pro-British "aristocrats" such as the lieutenant governor, Thomas Hutchinson, wrecking his house even though he had opposed the passage of the Stamp Act.

At about the time that Patrick Henry presented his resolutions to the Virginia assembly, James Otis proposed to his fellow legislators in Massachusetts that they call an intercolonial congress for concerted action against the new tax. In October, 1765, the Stamp Act Congress met in New York with delegates from nine of the colonies present.

lonial rights. But the moderates were in the majority, and the congress petitioned both the King and the two houses of Parliament. Though admitting that Americans owed to Parliament "all due subordination," the congress denied that they could rightfully be taxed except by their provincial assemblies.

If the British government had tried to enforce the Stamp Act, possibly the Revolutionary War would have begun ten years earlier than it actually did. The government was not deterred by resolves, riots, and pe-

The Declaratory Act
1766

While repealing the Stamp Act, Parliament denied the arguments put forth by Americans at the meeting of the Stamp Act Congress and on other occasions. The constitutional issue was sharply drawn, as may be seen by comparing the resolutions of the Stamp Act Congress with these words of Parliament's "declaratory" act:

"Whereas several of the houses of representatives in his Majesty's colonies and plantations in America have of late, against law, claimed to themselves, or to the general assemblies of the same, the sole and exclusive right of imposing duties or taxes upon his Majesty's subjects in the said colonies and plantations; and have, in pursuance of such claim, passed certain votes, resolutions, and orders, derogatory to the legislative authority of parliament, and inconsistent with the dependency of said colonies and plantations upon the crown of Great Britain: . . . be it declared . . . That the said colonies and plantations in America have been, are, and of right ought to be subordinate unto and dependent upon the imperial crown and parliament of Great Britain; and that the King's majesty, by and with the advice and consent of the lords spiritual and temporal and commons of Great Britain in parliament assembled, had, hath, and of right ought to have full power and authority to make laws and statutes of sufficient force and validity to bind the colonies and people of America, subjects of the crown of Great Britain, in all cases whatsoever."

They divided into moderates and extremists. The extremists argued that a petition should be addressed only to the King, on the ground that Parliament had nothing to do with co-

titions, but the Americans also used something more persuasive than any of these. That was economic pressure. Already, in response to the Sugar Act of 1764, many

New Englanders had quit buying English goods. Now the colonial boycott spread, and the Sons of Liberty intimidated those colonists who were reluctant to participate in it. The merchants of England, feeling the loss of much of their colonial market, begged Parliament to repeal the Stamp Act, while stories of unemployment, poverty, and discontent arose from English seaports and manufacturing towns.

Having succeeded Grenville as prime minister, the Marquis of Rockingham used his influence in favor of appeasing both the English merchants and the American colonists, and King George III himself finally was convinced that the act must be repealed. Opponents of repeal, and they were strong and vociferous, insisted that unless the colonists were compelled to obey the Stamp Act, they would soon cease to obey any laws of Parliament. So Parliament passed the Declaratory Act, asserting parliamentary authority over the colonies in "all cases whatsoever," and then repealed the Stamp Act (1766). In their rejoicing over the repeal, most Americans paid little attention to the sweeping declaration of Parliament's power.

The Townshend Program

The appeasement policy of the Rockingham government was not so well received in England as in America. English landlords protested that the government had "sacrificed the landed gentlemen to the interests of traders and colonists." Soon the King dismissed the unpopular Rockingham and called upon William Pitt to form a new ministry. A critic of the Stamp Act, Pitt had a reputation in America as the colonists' friend, though his reputation suffered somewhat when he accepted a peerage as Lord Chatham. He continued as prime minister after gout and mental illness had laid him low, and the actual leadership of his administration fell to the Chancellor of the Exchequer, Charles Townshend, "Champagne Charlie," a brilliant man but a sort of playboy of British politics.

Townshend had to deal with imperial problems and colonial grievances still left over from the Grenville ministry. Now that the Stamp Act was gone, the worst of these grievances was the Mutiny Act of 1765, which required the colonists to provide quarters and supplies for the British troops in America. The Massachusetts assembly, refusing to vote the supplies, was the first to defy the Mutiny Act, but the New York assembly, when it did the same thing, presented a more serious challenge to imperial authorities, since the army headquarters were in New York.

To enforce the Mutiny Act and raise a revenue in the colonies, Townshend proposed two measures to Parliament. First, New York was to be punished by the suspension of its assembly until the law was obeyed there. By thus singling out New York, Townshend thought he would avoid Grenville's mistake of arousing all the colonies at once. Second, duties were to be laid upon colonial imports of glass, lead, paint, paper, and tea. Townshend reasoned that the colonists could not logically object to taxation of this kind. At the time of the Stamp Act, some Americans had made a distinction between "internal" and "external" taxes and had denounced the stamp duties as internal taxation. While Townshend laughed at this distinction he took the colonists at their word and proposed duties which, without question, were to be collected externally. Parliament (1767) approved the Townshend duties and suspended the New York assembly.

To the colonists, however, the Townshend duties were scarcely more acceptable than the stamp tax, and the suspension of the one assembly threatened the annihilation of all. Taking up New York's cause as well as its own, the Massachusetts assembly sent out a circular letter urging all the rest to stand up against every tax, external or internal, imposed by Parliament. At first the Massachusetts circular evoked little response in some of the legislatures and ran into strong opposition in at least one of them, that of Pennsylvania. Then Lord Hillsborough, in the new office of Secretary of State for the Colonies, issued a circular letter of his own in which he warned that assemblies endorsing the Massachusetts letter would be dissolved. Promptly the other colonies, even Pennsylvania, rallied to the support of Massachusetts.

Besides inducing Parliament to lay import duties and suspend the New York assembly, Townshend also took steps to enforce commercial regulations in the colonies more effectively than ever. The most fateful of these steps was the establishment of a board of customs commissioners in America. Again, Townshend was giving the colonists what they had said they wanted, but they had been interested only in avoiding delays arising from the referral of important decisions to London, while he intended to stop the leaks in the colonial customhouses. His commissioners, with headquarters in Boston, virtually ended the smuggling at that place, though smugglers continued to carry on a busy trade in other colonial seaports.

Naturally the Boston merchants were the most indignant, and they took the lead in organizing another boycott. In 1768 the merchants of Philadelphia and New York joined those of Boston in a nonimportation agreement, and later some of the Southern merchants and planters also agreed to cooperate. Throughout the colonies, crude American homespun became suddenly fashionable, while English luxuries were frowned upon. Some enthusiasts, advocating the development of colonial manufactures of all kinds, looked forward to the creation of a self-sufficient America, with an economy independent of the Empire's.

Before the consequences of his program were fully apparent, Townshend himself died, leaving the question of revising his import duties to his successor, Lord North.

Samuel Adams. *In 1771, the year after the Boston Massacre, the wealthy John Hancock commissioned John Singleton Copley to paint a portrait of Hancock and another of Samuel Adams. Then a widower of forty-nine, Adams was prematurely old and was afflicted with palsy. Careless of his clothes, he usually wore a badly worn, rusty suit. Dressed up for his portrait, he is shown protesting to the lieutenant-governor of Massachusetts against the presence of the British troops in Boston, before the Massacre. At the time of this painting, Copley, of Boston, was an outstandingly busy and successful American portraitist. He was, for a while, a Patriot and an admirer of Adams; indeed, he testified against the British soldiers at the Massacre trial. Later Copley became a Loyalist and in 1774 he left America, to continue his artistic career in England for the rest of his life.* (COURTESY, MUSEUM OF FINE ARTS, BOSTON)

Hoping to break the nonimportation agreement and divide the colonists, Lord North secured (1770) the repeal of all the Townshend duties except the tea tax.

Meanwhile the presence of the customs commissioners in Boston led to violence.

The Boston mob had the most aggressive leader of all, Samuel Adams. The impoverished son of a once wealthy brewer, Adams had taken to politics after he himself had failed in business. As a rabble-rouser he had no equal in the colonies, and from the time of the Stamp Act troubles he was the guiding spirit of Massachusetts radicalism, even outdoing James Otis. Adams's success as a politician depended upon his finding suitable topics for agitation, and the British government, having repeatedly supplied him with topics, obliged him again by locating the customs commissioners in Boston and then stationing troops there.

To the Boston "liberty boys," the presence of the customs commissioners was a standing invitation to violence, and before long the terrified officials were driven to take refuge in Castle William, out in the harbor. So that they could return safely to their duties, the British government placed four regiments (afterwards reduced to two) within the city. The presence of the redcoats antagonized Samuel Adams and his followers more than ever. While his men ragged the soldiers and engaged them in brawls, Adams filled the newspapers with imaginary stories of rapes and other atrocities committed by the troops, and he spread throughout Boston a rumor that the soldiers were preparing for a concerted attack upon the citizens. On the night of March 5, 1770, a mob of dockworkers and other "liberty boys" fell upon the sentry at the customhouse. Hastily Captain Preston lined up his regiment in front of the building to protect it. There was some scuffling, and one of the soldiers was knocked down. Other soldiers then fired into the crowd, killing five of its members.

These events quickly became known as the "Boston Massacre" through the efforts of Samuel Adams and his adherents, who published an account bearing the title *Innocent Blood Crying to God from the Streets of Boston* and giving the impression that the dead were victims of a deliberate plot. The soldiers, tried before a jury of Bostonians and defended by Samuel Adams's cousin John Adams, were found guilty of no more than manslaughter and were given only a token punishment. Nevertheless, through newspapers and pamphlets, Samuel Adams convicted the redcoats of murder in the minds of many contemporary Americans, and year after year on March 5 he revived the people's memory with orations recalling the events of 1770. Later generations accepted his version of the "massacre" and thus, without knowing it, honored his skill as the foremost propagandist of the pre-Revolutionary decade.

The Philosophy of Revolt

Though America quieted down for a while after 1770, Americans did not abandon their principles, and these principles were revolutionary, at least in implication. "The Revolution was effected before the war commenced," one of the greatest of the Revolutionary leaders, John Adams, afterwards remarked. "The Revolution was in the minds and hearts of the people." Of course, very few of the people thought of outright independence till after the war had begun, and even those few (among them Samuel Adams) considered it best not to admit that independence was their ultimate aim. For the time being, most politically conscious Americans desired no more, and no less, than autonomy within the Empire. They argued that the English Constitution, correctly interpreted, supported their claims to individual liberty and colonial self-rule, and that the laws of nature and of God justified them in resisting infringements upon their rights.

In the course of the argument the Americans came to the conclusion that they were better Englishmen than the English themselves, better acquainted with the Constitu-

The "Bloody Massacre." *This broadside, "Engrav'd Printed & Sold by Paul Revere, Boston," pictures the Patriot version of the Boston incident of March 5, 1770. At the extreme right, Captain Thomas Preston, in command of the Custom-House guards, leers as he orders his grinning men to fire on the unarmed citizens. The Custom House, Preston's headquarters, is sarcastically labeled "Butcher's Hall." Accompanying the picture were the names of the dead and eighteen lines of verse, beginning:*

Unhappy Boston! see thy Sons deplore
Thy hallow'd Walks besmear'd with guiltless Gore:
While faithless P --- n and his savage Bands
With murd'rous Rancour stretch their bloody Hands;
Like fierce Barbarians grinning o'er their Prey,
Approve the Carnage, and enjoy the Day.

tion and more devoted to the liberties it guaranteed. Some of the Whig politicians in England, such as William Pitt and above all Edmund Burke, who spoke eloquently in favor of conciliation, were more or less inclined to agree. But other Englishmen, like the famous lexicographer and literary critic Samuel Johnson, looked upon the Americans as a deluded and indeed a barbarized offshoot of the English people. The majority in England were outraged rather than convinced by all the speechmaking and pamphleteering on the other side of the Atlantic.

To Englishmen the Constitution, though worthy of the highest respect, was an assortment of laws and usages that had developed through many centuries and that were rather elastic and vague. To Americans, on the other hand, it was a fixed and definite body of principles, which ought to be written down so as to avoid disagreements. Americans believed the colonies did have written constitutions—the colonial charters, which supposedly guaranteed to Americans all the traditional rights of Englishmen.

Of these rights the most fundamental, according to the colonists, was the right to be taxed only with their own consent. But the colonists were not consistent in all things, nor were they in this matter of taxation. At first some of them objected only to "internal" taxes such as those imposed by the Stamp Act. Most colonists hesitated to assert that all imperial taxation was unconstitutional, since they long had been taxed at least indirectly by the various trade laws. When Townshend levied his "external" duties, the Philadelphia lawyer John Dickinson maintained in the *Letters of a Pennsylvania Farmer* that even external taxation was legal only when designed to regulate trade and not to raise a revenue. But Americans did not like trade regulations, either, when the regulations began to be enforced.

Eventually the discontented colonists took an unqualified stand upon the slogan "No taxation without representation."

This clamor about "representation" made little sense to Englishmen. Only about one in twenty-five of them was entitled to vote for members of Parliament, and many populous parts of England had no representatives at all. According to the prevailing English theory, however, Parliament did not represent individuals or geographical areas. Instead, it represented the interests of the whole nation and indeed the whole Empire, no matter where the members happened to come from. The unenfranchised boroughs of England, the whole of Ireland, and the colonies 3,000 miles away—all were represented in the Parliament at London. That was the theory of "virtual" representation, but Americans believed in actual representation. They felt they could be represented in Parliament only if they sent their quota of members to it. For a time some of them, even James Otis, considered proposals for electing American representatives, but most of the colonists realized that if they should participate in the action of Parliament they would be bound by that action, even though they were outnumbered and outvoted. So they fell back upon the argument that they could be fairly and properly represented only in their own colonial assemblies.

According to the American view of the Empire, and according to actual fact, these assemblies were little parliaments, as competent to legislate for their respective colonies as Parliament was for England. The Empire was a sort of federation of commonwealths, each with its own legislative body, all tied together by common loyalty to the King (much as in the British Commonwealth of Nations today). This being their conception of the Empire, the Americans protested bitterly against the pretensions of Parliament but had nothing except kind words for George III—until they decided to cut their imperial ties completely and declare for independence. According to the English view, the Empire was a single, undivided unit, and everywhere within it the King and Parliament together were supreme.

The American doctrine of resistance to unconstitutional and tyrannical laws was based chiefly upon the Bible and the writings of John Locke. For generations the preachers of New England had taught that no man need obey a government when it violated the will of God as set forth in the Scriptures. Now, to show that rebellion against tyranny was lawful in God's sight, they retold such Bible stories as the one about a King of Israel who burdened his people with unjust taxes and was overthrown.

John Locke (1632–1704) had much the same relation to the American Revolution as Karl Marx later had to the Communist Revolution in Russia, though Locke (a conservative rather than a revolutionist like Marx) would probably have been shocked if he had lived to see the use that Americans made of his doctrines. In his *Two Treatises of Government* (1690) Locke attempted to justify a revolution that had already occurred, the English revolution of 1688–1689 by which Parliament had won supremacy over the King. According to Locke's theory, men originally lived in a state of nature and enjoyed complete liberty, then agreed to a "compact" by which they set up a government to protect their "natural rights," especially their right to the ownership and enjoyment of private property. The government was limited by the terms of the compact and by "natural law." It was contrary to natural law for a government to take property without the consent of the owners, Locke wrote, and Americans noted in particular his sentence: "If any one shall claim a power to lay and levy taxes on the people

by his own authority, and without such consent of the people, he thereby invades the fundamental law of property, and subverts the end of government." To Americans of the 1760's and 1770's it was clear that the British government was flouting the law of nature as well as the will of God. And, according to Locke, if a government should persist in exceeding its rightful powers, men would be released from their obligation to obey it. What was more, they would have the right to make a new compact and establish another government.

The Tea Excitement

From time to time after 1770 Americans resisting British law broke the comparative stillness in America with such deeds as the seizure of a revenue ship on the lower Delaware, the burning of another (the *Gaspee*) in Narragansett Bay, and the tarring and feathering of a customs officer on the streets of Boston. Not till 1773, however, did Americans reassert their revolutionary principles with anything approaching the unity and vigor of former years.

Tea revived the dispute. The East India Company, with a large stock of unsalable tea on hand, was nearly bankrupt, and Lord North induced Parliament to go to the company's relief with the Tea Act of 1773. This law permitted the company to retail its product in America without paying any of the usual taxes except the tea tax still remaining from the original Townshend duties. With these privileges the company could bypass the middlemen and sell directly to colonial consumers at a price so low that even smugglers could not compete.

Lord North, like others in his office before him, was surprised by the reaction of the Americans. Not that he expected the tea-importing merchants in the colonies to like the new law, for it threatened to drive them out of business and replace them with a giant monopoly. But the colonists—especially the women—were excessively fond of tea. Lord North thought they would be so glad to get it cheap that they would swallow the hated tea tax along with it. In-

heaved them into the water. As the electrifying news of the Boston "tea party" spread, other seaports followed the example and held tea parties of their own.

Some Unpopular British Measures
1763–1773

Proclamation of 1763. Prohibited land purchase or settlement west of the Appalachian Mountains.

Sugar Act, 1764. Cut in half the import duty on foreign (non-British) molasses but provided for strict enforcement.

Stamp Act, 1765. Required tax stamps for newspapers, legal documents, playing cards, and other items. (Repealed, 1766.)

Mutiny Act (Supplemented by *Quartering Act*), **1765.** Provided for the maintenance of British troops in America and for the use of various kinds of buildings, including uninhabited private houses, as barracks.

Townshend Act, 1767. Levied duties on imports of glass, lead, paint, paper, and tea. (Repealed, 1770, except for the tea tax.)

Tea Act, 1773. Gave financial aid to the East India Company and allowed the company to export tea to America without paying any duties except the existing tea tax.

---

stead, they renounced their beloved beverage and turned for the time being to substitutes such as coffee and chocolate.

Meanwhile, with strong popular support, leaders in various colonies made plans to prevent the East India Company from landing its cargoes in colonial ports. In Philadelphia and New York determined men kept the tea from leaving the company's ships, and in Charleston they stored it away in a public warehouse. In Boston, having failed to turn back the three ships in the harbor, the followers of Samuel Adams staged a spectacular drama. On the evening of December 16, 1773, three companies of fifty men each, masquerading as "Mohawks," passed between the protecting lines of a tremendous crowd of spectators, went aboard, broke open the tea chests, and

When the Bostonians refused to pay for the property they had destroyed, George III and Lord North decided upon a policy of coercion, to be applied not against all the colonies but only against one, the chief center of resistance, Massachusetts. In four acts of 1774 Parliament proceeded to put this policy into effect. One of the laws closed the port of Boston, another drastically reduced the local and provincial powers of self-government in Massachusetts, still another permitted royal officers to be tried in other colonies or in England when accused of crimes, and the last provided for the quartering of troops in the colonists' barns and empty houses.

These Coercive Acts were followed by the Quebec Act, which was separate from them in origin and quite different in pur-

Taking the Pledge. *This British caricature, entitled "A Society of Patriotic Ladies, at Edenton in North Carolina," was published in London in March, 1775. It ridicules the American buy-at-home movement. The women are emptying their tea canisters and signing a pledge, which reads: "We the Ladies of Edenton do hereby Solemnly Engage not to Conform to that Pernicious Custom of Drinking Tea, or that we the aforesaid Ladies will not promote the Wear of any Manufacture from England untill such time that all Acts which tend to Enslave this our Native Country shall be Repealed."* (COURTESY OF THE METROPOLITAN MUSEUM OF ART)

pose. Its object was to provide a civil government for the French-speaking, Roman Catholic inhabitants of Canada and the Illinois country. The law extended the bound-

gerously thin. When Catholics ceased to be actively persecuted in the mother country, alarmists in the colonies began to fear that Catholicism and Anglicanism were about to

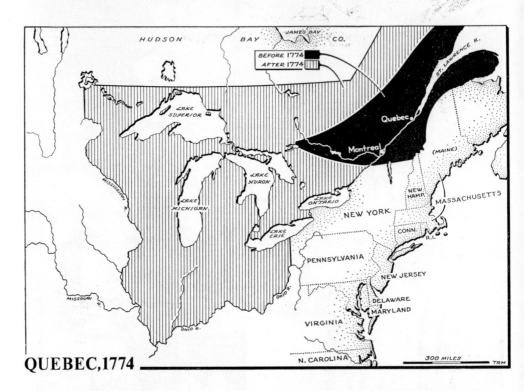

QUEBEC, 1774

aries of Quebec to include the French communities between the Ohio and Mississippi rivers. It also granted political rights to Roman Catholics and recognized the legality of the Roman Catholic Church within the enlarged province. In many ways it was a liberal and much-needed piece of legislation.

To the Protestants in the thirteen colonies, however, the Quebec Act was anathema. They were already alarmed by rumors that the Church of England schemed to appoint a bishop for America with the intention of enforcing Anglican authority upon all the various sects. To them the line between the Church of England and the Church of Rome always had seemed dan-

merge, and at the passage of the Quebec Act they became convinced that a plot was afoot in London for subjecting Americans to the tyranny of the Pope. Moreover, those interested in Western lands believed that the act, by extending the boundaries of Quebec, would reinforce the land policy of the Proclamation Line of 1763 and put an additional obstacle in the way of westward progress.

Had it not been for the Quebec Act, Lord North might have come close to succeeding in his effort to divide and rule the colonies by isolating Massachusetts. As it was, the colonists generally lumped the Quebec law with the Massachusetts measures as the fifth in a set of "Intolerable

Acts." From New Hampshire to South Carolina the people prepared to take a united stand.

The Continental Congress

Revolutions do not just happen: they must be led and organized. From 1765 on, colonial leaders provided a variety of organizations for converting popular discontent into action, organizations which in time formed the basis for an independent government.

Some of these organizations were local, some colony-wide, and some intercolonial. In many cases the provincial assemblies themselves served as centers of resistance, and sometimes they were replaced or supplemented by extralegal meetings, as when (in 1768) Sam Adams called a convention

as Sons of Liberty, and also set up committees of prominent citizens for a number of specific objects. The most famous and most effective were the committees of correspondence. Massachusetts took the lead (1772) with such committees on the local level, a network of them connecting Boston with the rural towns, but Virginia was the first to establish committees of correspondence on an intercolonial basis. These made possible cooperation among the colonies in a more continuous way than had the Stamp Act Congress, the first effort at intercolonial union for resistance against imperial authority. Virginia took the greatest step of all toward united action in 1774 when, the governor having dissolved the assembly, a rump session met in the Raleigh Tavern at

---

The "Intolerable" Acts

1774

1. **Boston Port Act.** Removed the British custom-house from Boston and closed the port to all shipping.

2. **Massachusetts Government Act.** Concentrated power in the royal governor by giving him the appointment of members of the council (previously elected by the General Assembly), requiring his permission for the holding of town meetings, and providing that sheriffs (appointed by him) should select juries.

3. **Administration of Justice Act.** Allowed British soldiers and officials to be tried in England or in another colony than the one in which they were accused of offenses.

4. **Quartering Act.** Extended the provisions of the existing Mutiny and Quartering Acts and directed the local authorities of Boston to find quarters for troops inside the town itself.

5. **Quebec Act.** Greatly enlarged the boundaries of Quebec and granted religious freedom to the Roman Catholic inhabitants of the province.

---

of delegates from the Massachusetts towns to sit in place of the General Court, which the royal governor had dissolved. Adams and others in various places organized mobs

Williamsburg, declared that the Intolerable Acts menaced the liberties of every colony, and issued a call for a Continental Congress.

Variously elected by the assemblies or by

extralegal meetings, delegates from all the thirteen colonies except Georgia were present when, in September, 1774, the Continental Congress convened in Philadelphia. The

in a very close vote, they defeated the plan of Joseph Galloway for a colonial union under British authority, a plan which included a legislative council made up of rep-

---

Declaration and Resolves
(First Continental Congress)

1774

". . . That the foundation of English liberty, and of all free government, is a right in the people to participate in their legislative council: and as the English colonists are not represented, and from their local and other circumstances cannot properly be represented, in the British parliament, they are entitled to a free and exclusive power of legislation in their several provincial legislatures, where their right of representation can alone be preserved, in all cases of taxation and internal polity, subject only to the negative of their sovereign, in such manner as has been heretofore used and accustomed. But, from the necessity of the case, and a regard to the mutual interest of both countries, we cheerfully consent to the operation of such acts of the British parliament as are bona fide restrained to the regulation of our external commerce, for the purpose of securing the commercial advantages of the whole empire to the mother country, and the commercial benefits of its respective members excluding every idea of taxation, internal or external, for raising a revenue on the subjects of America without their consent. . . ."

---

delegates divided into moderates and extremists, as those at the Stamp Act Congress nine years earlier had done, but this time the more extreme members seized the upper hand. At the outset they showed their strength by designating Carpenters' Hall as the meeting place. This was the headquarters of the Philadelphia Carpenters' Company, and some members complained that its selection was an unseemly attempt to curry favor with the city's artisans. In the ensuing sessions of the Congress, however, the extremists were unable to carry through a program quite so thorough as some of them would have liked.

A majority of the delegates in Carpenter's Hall agreed upon five major decisions. First,

resentatives from the colonial assemblies and a president general to be appointed by the King. Second, they drew up a somewhat self-contradictory statement of grievances, conceding to Parliament the right to regulate colonial trade but demanding the elimination of all oppressive legislation passed since 1763, and they addressed a petition to George III as their "Most Gracious Sovereign." Third, they approved a series of resolutions from a Suffolk County (Massachusetts) convention recommending, among other things, that military preparations be made for defense against possible attack by the British troops in Boston. Fourth, they agreed to nonimportation, nonexportation, and nonconsumption as means of stopping all trade with Great Britain, and they formed a "Continental Association" to see that these agreements were carried out. Fifth, the delegates adjourned to meet again the next spring, thus indicating that they conceived of the Continental Congress as a continuing organization.

Through their representatives in Philadelphia the colonies had, in effect, reaffirmed their autonomous status within the empire and declared economic war to maintain that position. The more optimistic of the Americans supposed that economic warfare alone would win a quick and bloodless victory, but the more pessimistic had their doubts. "I expect no redress, but, on the contrary, increased resentment and double vengeance," John Adams said to Patrick Henry; "we must fight." And Henry replied, "By God, I am of your opinion." During the winter of 1774–1775 the enforcement of the nonimportation, nonexportation, and nonconsumption agreements proved increasingly difficult as people in the Middle Colonies and in the South, viewing the Continental Association as more tyrannical than the British government, began to complain against the sacrifices they were compelled to make—all for the sake of those troublemakers in Massachusetts!

During the winter the Parliament in London debated proposals for conciliating the colonists. Lord Chatham (William Pitt) urged the withdrawal of troops from America, Edmund Burke urged the repeal of the Coercive Acts, but in vain; and not even Chatham and Burke thought of renouncing parliamentary authority over the colonies. Lord North, conceding less than Burke or Chatham, introduced a set of proposals of his own, and Parliament approved them early in 1775. The essence of these so-called Conciliatory Propositions was that the colonies, instead of being taxed directly by Parliament, should tax themselves at Parliament's demand. With this offer Lord North

intended to redivide Americans by appealing to the disgruntled moderates. But his offer was too grudging, and it came too late. It did not reach America till after the first shots of war had been fired.

Lexington and Concord

For months the farmers and townspeople of Massachusetts had been gathering arms and ammunition and training as "minutemen," ready to fight on a minute's notice. The Continental Congress had approved preparations for a defensive war, and these citizen-soldiers only waited for an aggressive move by the British regulars in Boston.

In Boston, General Thomas Gage, commanding the British garrison, knew of the warlike bustle throughout the countryside but thought his army too small to do anything until reinforcements should arrive, though some of his less cautious officers assured him that Americans were cowards, and Major John Pitcairn insisted that a single "small action" with the burning of a few towns would "set everything to rights." When General Gage received orders to arrest the rebel leaders Sam Adams and John Hancock, known to be in the vicinity of Lexington, he still hesitated, but when he heard that the minutemen had stored a large supply of gunpowder in Concord (eighteen miles from Boston) he at last decided to act. On the night of April 18, 1775, he sent a detachment of about 1,000 men out from Boston on the road to Lexington and Concord. He intended to surprise the colonials with a bloodless coup.

But during the night the hard-riding horsemen William Dawes and Paul Revere warned the villages and farms, and when the redcoats arrived in Lexington the next day, several dozen minutemen awaited them on the common. Shots were fired and some of the minutemen fell, eight of them killed and ten more wounded. Advancing to Concord, the British burned what was left of the powder supply after the Americans hastily had removed most of it to safety. On the road from Concord back to Boston the 1,000 troops, along with 1,500 more who

garded he had given the order to fire. According to the British officers and soldiers, one of the American guns had flashed first. The truth is still unknown, but the fact re-

The Battle of Lexington. *A contemporary engraving by Amos Doolittle. It pictures the American version of the affair of April 19, 1775, at Lexington. In the center is shown "the party who fired first," at the command of Major Pitcairn, on horseback. In the foreground are some of the fallen and the fleeing members of the "Provincial Company of Lexington" (minutemen). The more prominent buildings on the edge of the square, or green, are the Public Inn at the left of the large tree and the Meetinghouse at the right of it. Behind the Meetinghouse are companies of British regulars marching along the road to Concord.* (COURTESY OF THE NEW YORK PUBLIC LIBRARY, STOKES COLLECTION)

met them at Lexington, were harassed by the continual gunfire of farmers hiding behind trees, rocks, and stone fences. Before the day was over, the British had lost almost three times as many men as the Americans.

The first shots had been fired, but who had fired the first shot? According to the Lexington minutemen, Major Pitcairn upon his arrival had shouted, "Disperse, ye rebels!" and when this command was disre-

mains that the rebels succeeded in circulating their account well ahead of the British version, and they adorned it with horrible tales of redcoat atrocities. The effect was to rally to the rebel cause thousands of colonists, North and South, who previously had been lukewarm in its support. A war was on, and most Americans believed the enemy had started it.

➤➤-➤➤-➤➤-➤➤≻≺≺≺-≺≺≺-≺≺≺-≺≺≺

BIBLIOGRAPHY

A RECENT SURVEY is L. H. Gipson, *The Coming of the Revolution, 1763–1775* (1954), which explains and justifies British policies. Readable and reliable accounts are C. L. Becker, *The Eve of the Revolution* (1921); and, with the advantage of twenty additional years of historical scholarship, J. C. Miller, *Origins of the American Revolution* (1943). Also valuable is C. H. Van Tyne, *The Causes of the War of Independence* (1922). Opposing views of the Empire are revealed in C. H. McIlwain's *The American Revolution: A Constitutional Interpretation* (1923), which defends the American case. The validity of the colonists' position is questioned, however, by R. L. Schuyler in *Parliament and the British Empire* (1929). The political background in England is clarified by G. H. Guttridge in *English Whiggism and the American Revolution* (1942). See also Sir Lewis Namier's *Structure of Politics at the Accession of George III* (1929) and his *England in the Age of the American Revolution* (1930).

Becker and others view the Revolution as a kind of civil war—a struggle for power between radicals and conservatives in America—as well as a war for independence from Great Britain. This interpretation long has prevailed, but recently it has been sharply challenged. The most forceful attack comes from R. E. Brown, whose *Middle-Class Democracy and the Revolution in Massachusetts, 1691–1780* (1955) argues that, at least in Massachusetts and probably elsewhere, the aim of the Revolutionary leaders was to preserve the democracy they already had. The internal-conflict idea, with respect to other colonies, is questioned by various studies. See Theodore Thayer, *Pennsylvania Politics and the Growth of Democracy, 1740–1776* (1953); R. P. McCormick, *The History of Voting in New Jersey* (1953); C. A. Barker, *The Background of the Revolution in Maryland* (1940); and Oscar Zeichner, *Connecticut's Years of Controversy, 1750–1776* (1949). These books show unique patterns in each state. E. S. Morgan finds basic agreement among most Americans in his bold and concise reinterpretation, *The Birth of the Republic, 1763–1789* (1956). On the other hand, E. P. Douglass upholds and elaborates upon the traditional view in his *Rebels and Democrats: The Struggle for Equal Political Rights and Majority Rule during the American Revolution* (1955).

There also has been much debate on the question whether British policy changed in 1763 or merely was more strictly enforced after that time. O. M. Dickerson, *The Navigation Acts and the American Revolution* (1951), points to an increasingly exploitative British policy as a cause of the revolt.

A. M. Schlesinger, *The Colonial Merchants and the American Revolution, 1763–1776* (1917), is a classic. E. S. and H. M. Morgan, *The Stamp Act Crisis* (1953), maintains that American leaders were more consistent in their stand against taxes than has usually been supposed. Taking the Stamp Act as a turning point, Clinton Rossiter's *Seedtime of the Republic* (1953) traces the origin and development of the American tradition of political liberty. Carl Bridenbaugh, *Cities in Revolt: Urban Life in America, 1743–1776* (1955), treats the rebellion as largely an urban phenomenon.

Agitation that whipped up a revolutionary spirit is well handled in the following: A. M. Schlesinger, *Prelude to Independence: The Newspaper War on Britain, 1764–1776* (1958); Philip Davidson, *Propaganda and the American Revolution, 1763–*

1783 (1941); J. C. Miller, *Sam Adams, Pioneer in Propaganda* (1936); and Jacob Axelrad, *Patrick Henry, The Voice of Freedom* (1947). A conservative who advocated independence is portrayed in C. D. Bowen's *John Adams and the American Revolution* (1950). The dilemmas of a typical "moderate" are revealed in J. F. Roche's *Joseph Reed: A Moderate in the American Revolution* (1957).

Birth of the United States

IN THE AMERICAN REVOLUTION a war for autonomy on the part of the united colonies soon turned into a war for independence on the part of the United States. This new nation, with a population less than a third as large as the nine million of Great Britain, and with military and economic resources proportionally still smaller, finally secured not only the recognition of its independence but also the title to a vast territory in the West. The Americans had the advantage of fighting on their home terrain, far from the centers of British might. They profited from the mistakes of an enemy, long afterward famous for "muddling through," who at this time only muddled his campaigns and did not see them through. Above all, they had the benefit of tremendous foreign aid, especially after the American war merged with a world contest in which Great Britain faced the strongest powers of Europe as actual or potential foes. But the success of the Americans was due also to their own patriotic effort. Effectively, if imperfectly, they rallied their resources, human and material, in response to the inspiration of civilian leaders like Thomas Jefferson and Thomas Paine. Though losing battle after battle, they avoided catastrophes and gained at least a few decisive victories through the exertions of thousands of armed men under the majestic generalship of George Washington. And, having held their own in war, they won the peace because their diplomats—Benjamin Franklin, John Adams, John Jay—shrewdly made the most of the opportunities that the world situation offered.

War Aims: Independence

When, three weeks after the battles of Lexington and Concord, the Second Continental Congress met in the State House in Philadelphia, the delegates (again from every colony except Georgia, which was not represented until the following autumn) agreed in their determination to support the war but disagreed about its objects. At one extreme the Adams cousins, John and Samuel, leaned toward independence though

grievances within the British Empire, not for independence. During that year, however, many of them began to change their minds, for various reasons. For one thing,

---

Declaration of the Causes and Necessity of Taking up Arms

1775

". . . Lest this declaration should disquiet the minds of our friends and fellow-subjects in any part of the empire, we assure them that we mean not to dissolve that union which has so long and so happily subsisted between us, and which we sincerely wish to see restored. Necessity has not yet driven us into that desperate measure, or induced us to excite any other nation to war against them. We have not raised armies with ambitious designs of separating from Great Britain, and establishing independent states. . . .

"In our own native land, in defence of the freedom that is our birth-right, and which we ever enjoyed till the late violation of it—for the protection of our property, acquired solely by the honest industry of our fore-fathers and ourselves, against violence actually offered, we have taken up arms. We shall lay them down when hostilities shall cease on the part of the aggressors, and all danger of their being renewed shall be removed, and not before. . . ."

---

they did not yet avow it, and at the other extreme John Dickinson hoped for an early reconciliation with Great Britain. Most of the delegates, holding views that ranged between those of Dickinson and the Adamses, disregarded Lord North's Conciliatory Propositions as insincere but voted reluctantly for one last appeal to the King in the Olive Branch Petition. Then, July 6, 1775, they adopted a Declaration of the Causes and Necessity of Taking up Arms, announcing that the British government had left the American people with only two alternatives, "unconditional submission to the tyranny of irritated ministers or resistance by force," and that the people had decided to resist.

So, for the first year of the war, the Americans were fighting for a redress of

they were making sacrifices so great, as in the Battle of Bunker Hill, the bloodiest engagement of the entire war and one of the most sanguinary anywhere in the eighteenth century, that their original war aims seemed incommensurate with the cost. For another thing, they lost much of their lingering affection for the mother country when she made ready to use savage Indians, Negro slaves, and foreign mercenaries (the hated "Hessians") against them. And, most important of all, they felt that they were being forced into independence when the British government replied to the Olive Branch Petition with the Prohibitory Act, which closed the colonies to all overseas trade and made no concession except an offer of pardon to repentant rebels. The Americans desperately needed military supplies to con-

COMMON SENSE;

ADDRESSED TO THE

INHABITANTS

OF

AMERICA,

On the following interesting

SUBJECTS.

I. Of the Origin and Design of Government in general,
with concise Remarks on the English Constitution.

II. Of Monarchy and Hereditary Succession.

III. Thoughts on the present State of American Affairs.

IV. Of the present Ability of America, with some miscellaneous Reflections.

Man knows no Master save creating HEAVEN,
Or those whom choice and common good ordain.

THOMSON.

PHILADELPHIA;

Printed, and Sold, by R. BELL, in Third-Street.

MDCCLXXVI.

Common Sense. Title page of the first edition of Thomas Paine's pamphlet advocating American independence. It was published anonymously in Philadelphia on January 10, 1776. Many other editions appeared during the next several months; estimates of the total number of copies sold vary from 120,000 to 500,000. After the publication of Common Sense *Paine enlisted as a soldier and accompanied Washington's army on its retreat across New Jersey. During that time he wrote a series of essays under the collective title of* The Crisis, *to arouse support for the Patriot cause. The first of the* Crisis *papers contains the sentence: "These are the times that try men's souls." After the American Revolution Paine went to France and took an active part in the French Revolution, which began in 1789. In support of the French Revolutionary cause he wrote* The Rights of Man *(1791–1792). He also wrote* The Age of Reason, *in which he attacked some aspects of conventional Christianity and*

tinue the war, and now they could get them from abroad in adequate amounts only if they broke completely with Great Britain and proceeded to behave in all respects as if they comprised a sovereign nation.

These feelings in America were not caused, but were clarified and crystallized, by the publication in January, 1776, of the pamphlet *Common Sense.* Its author, unmentioned on the title page, was Thomas Paine, who with letters of introduction from Benjamin Franklin had emigrated from England to America less than two years before. Though long a failure in various trades, Paine now proved a brilliant success as a revolutionary propagandist. In his pamphlet he argued with flashing phrases that it was plain common sense for Americans to separate from an England rotten with the corrupt monarchy of George III, brutal as an unnatural parent towards her colonies, responsible for dragging them in to fight her wars in the past, and no more fit as an island kingdom to rule the American Continent than a satellite was fit to rule the sun. "O! ye that love mankind! ye that dare oppose not only the tyranny but the tyrant, stand forth!" Month after month the pamphlet was reprinted until several hundred thousand copies were in circulation, passing from hand to hand and being read and reread.

Despite the persuasions of *Common Sense,* the American people were far from unanimous, and they entered upon a bitter debate over the merits of dependence and independence. While the debate raged, the Continental Congress advanced step by step toward a final break. Congress opened the ports of America to all the world except Great Britain, entered into communication with foreign powers, and recommended to

expounded his own rationalistic beliefs. Returning to America in 1802, he spent his last years as a lonely, obscure man. (LIBRARY OF CONGRESS)

the various colonies that they establish governments without the authority of the Empire, as in fact they already were doing. Congress also appointed a committee to draft a formal declaration and, on July 2, 1776, before approving the declaration, adopted a resolution "That these United Colonies are, and, of right, ought to be, free and independent states; that they are absolved from all allegiance to the British crown, and that all political connexion between them and the state of Great Britain is, and ought to be, totally dissolved." Two days later Congress approved the Declaration of Independence, which gave reasons for the action already taken.

The 33-year-old Virginian Thomas Jefferson wrote the Declaration of Independence, his fellow committeemen Benjamin Franklin and John Adams revised the wording a little, and Congress made more drastic changes, striking out passages which condemned the British people and the slave trade. As the jealous Adams afterward complained, Jefferson said nothing new in composing the document. Its very virtue, in fact, lay in his noble phrasing of beliefs already widespread in America. He planned the document in two parts. In the first he restated the familiar compact theory of John Locke, who had held that governments were formed to protect the rights of life, liberty, and property, but Jefferson gave the theory a more humane twist by referring instead to the rights of "life, liberty and the pursuit of happiness." In the second part he listed the alleged crimes of the King who, with the backing of Parliament, had violated his compact with the colonists and thus had forfeited all claim to their loyalty.

Once adopted, the Declaration of Independence exerted an incalculable influence upon later history. With its democratic principle that "all men are created equal," it stimulated humanitarian movements of various kinds in the United States, and abroad it helped to inspire the French Revolution with its Declaration of the Rights of Man.

Declaration of Independence
1776

Major Premise: "We hold these truths to be self-evident, that all men are created equal, that they are endowed by their Creator with certain unalienable Rights, that among these are Life, Liberty and the pursuit of Happiness. That to secure these rights, Governments are instituted among Men, deriving their just powers from the consent of the governed, That whenever any Form of Government becomes destructive of these ends, it is the Right of the People to alter or abolish it. . . ."

Minor Premise: "The history of the present King of Great Britain is a history of repeated injuries and usurpations, all having in direct object the establishment of an absolute tyranny over these States."

Conclusion: "We, therefore, . . . solemnly publish and declare, That these United Colonies are, and of Right ought to be Free and Independent States. . . ."

The Declaration of Independence. *This is part of the original draft, showing some of the changes and corrections.* (LIBRARY OF CONGRESS)

More immediately, it led to increased foreign aid for the struggling rebels and prepared the way for France's all-out intervention on their side. It steeled American patriots to carry on without regard to offers of a peace short of the stated goal. And at the same time it divided Americans more cruelly and more extensively than they ever had been divided before.

At the news of the Declaration of Independence, crowds gathered to cheer, fire guns and cannon, and ring church bells in Philadelphia, Boston, and other places, but there were many people in America who did not rejoice. Some had disapproved of the war from the beginning, and others had been willing to support it only so long as its aims did not conflict with their basic loyalty to the King. These people, numerous but in the minority, refused to cross the new line that had been drawn. Either openly or secretly they remained Loyalists, as they chose to call themselves, or Tories, as they were known to the Whig or Patriot majority. Among the Loyalists were rich families and poor ones, highly educated men (like the scientist Benjamin Thompson) and illiterates, townspeople and backwoodsmen. Among the Loyalist leaders were royal officials and Anglican clergymen who had sided with the British government throughout the prewar decade of controversy, plus a few of the wealthy merchants and large planters who earlier had belonged to the Patriot party but who seceded from it after the Declaration of Independence.

The remaining Patriots continued to be divided among themselves. On the one hand were men like John Adams and George Washington who wished to see independence achieved with comparatively little social change in America, but whose ranks were thinned by the loss of their former allies, now Loyalists. On the other hand were men like Thomas Jefferson who desired to accomplish democratic and humanitarian reforms along with independence. Thus (as in other wars, including World War II) patriotic Americans held different as well as common aims, some intending only to smite the foreign enemy, others aspiring also to lead a popular crusade at home.

The New States and the Confederation

While waging war, the Patriots also busied themselves with providing government for the new nation. With the outbreak of war they set up provisional governments based upon existing assemblies or emergency conventions as the royal officials fled from their positions in one colony after another. When the colonies became states, the Patriots formed permanent governments with written constitutions. The constitution-making procedure varied from state to state. In Rhode Island and Connecticut the legislatures merely revised the old colonial charters, and in most of the other states the legislatures, though not elected for that purpose, took it upon themselves to draft new constitutions. Thomas Jefferson, for one, insisted that the fundamental law should come from the people of each state, who should elect constitutional conventions and then vote on ratification. Actually, conventions were held in only three states, referendums in only five, and both a convention and a referendum in only one—Massachusetts.

The new constitutions, all pretty much alike in general outline though different in detail, were both conservative and democratic. They were conservative in retaining essentially the same structure as the old colonial governments. Except in Georgia and Pennsylvania, both of which experimented with a unicameral legislature, each constitution provided for a two-house legislature, with an elected senate taking the place of the former governor's council. All the constitutions continued the office of governor, though most of them denied the holder of this position the bulk of the executive powers he had enjoyed in colonial days. All of the new documents confirmed and extended the ideas of popular rule which long had been put into practice; every one of them included a bill of rights, and some had preambles stating that sovereignty (the ultimate power of government) resided in the people. To vote in any state a man had to own only a modest amount of property, in some states just enough so that he could qualify as a taxpayer. To hold office he had to meet a somewhat higher property requirement, essentially as in pre-Revolutionary times. Only in New Jersey were women allowed to vote, and eventually they were deprived of the suffrage even there. But, considering the widespread ownership of property, something approaching universal manhood suffrage existed from the beginning in all the states.

Once in operation, the new states proceeded to make advances in social as well as political democracy. In one way or another they multiplied opportunities for land ownership and thus enlarged the voting population. For instance, they eliminated the legal rights of primogeniture and entail, which before the war had helped to maintain a landed aristocracy by transferring an entire estate to the oldest son (when a man died without a will) and by keeping the estate intact from generation to generation (when a man by entailment willed that the property never be sold). The new states also made considerable progress toward religious freedom, though some retained religious tests for officeholding. New York and the Southern states, in which the Church of England had been tax-supported, soon saw to its complete disestablishment, and the New England states stripped the Congregational Church of some of its privileges. Virginia, in its Declaration of Rights, boldly announced the principle of complete toleration and, under the leadership of Jefferson as governor, enacted the principle in the Statute of Religious Liberty (1786). And the new states took steps toward personal as well as religious freedom. All of them except South Carolina and Georgia prohibited the importation of slaves, and even South

Carolina laid temporary wartime bans on the slave trade. After the first antislavery society in America (founded in 1775) began its agitation, and prominent Southerners including Jefferson and Washington declared their opposition to slavery, Virginia and other Southern states changed their laws so as to encourage manumission, Pennsylvania passed a gradual-emancipation act (1780), and Massachusetts through a decision of its highest court (1783) held that the state's Bill of Rights outlawed the ownership of slaves. Besides all this, five of the new states put provisions into their constitutions for the establishment of public schools, and all soon began to revise their criminal codes so as to make the punishment more nearly fit the crime.

While the separate states were fashioning constitutions and recasting their legal systems, the Second Continental Congress tried to create a written form of government for the states as a whole. No sooner had the Congress appointed a committee to draft a declaration of independence than it appointed another to draft a plan of union, and after much debate and many revisions the Congress, in November, 1777, adopted the committee's plan, the Articles of Confederation.

The Articles of Confederation provided for a central government very similar to the one already in actual operation, though it increased the powers of Congress somewhat. Congress was to have the powers of conducting war, carrying on foreign relations, and appropriating, borrowing, and issuing money, but not the powers of regulating trade, levying taxes, or drafting troops. For troops and taxes it would have to make requisitions upon the states. There was to be no separate, single, strong executive (the "President of the United States" was to be merely the presiding officer at the sessions of Congress), but Congress itself was to see to the execution of the laws through an executive committee of thirteen, made up of one member from each state, through *ad hoc* and standing committees for specific functions, and through such administrative de-

---

The End of Slavery in Massachusetts
(Decision of the State's Chief Justice)

1783

"As to the doctrine of slavery and the right of Christians to hold Africans in perpetual servitude, and sell and treat them as we do our horses and cattle, that (it is true) has been heretofore countenanced by the Province Laws formerly, but nowhere is it expressly enacted or established. It has been a usage—a usage which took its origin from the practice of some of the European nations, and the regulations of British government respecting the then Colonies, for the benefit of trade and wealth. But whatever sentiments have formerly prevailed in this particular or slid in upon us by the example of others, a different idea has taken place with the people of America, more favorable to the natural rights of mankind, and to that natural, innate desire of Liberty, which with Heaven (without regard to color, complexion, or shape of noses) has inspired all the human race. And upon this ground our Constitution of Government, by which the people of this Commonwealth have solemnly bound themselves, sets out with declaring that all men are born free and equal—and that every subject is entitled to liberty, and to have it guarded by the laws, as well as life and property—and in short is totally repugnant to the idea of being born slaves. This being the case, I think the idea of slavery is inconsistent with our own conduct and Constitution; and there can be no such thing as perpetual servitude of a rational creature, unless his liberty is forfeited by some criminal conduct or given up by personal consent or contract."

---

partments as it might choose to create. There were to be no Confederation courts, but disputes between the states were to be settled by a complicated system of arbitration. The states were to retain their individual sovereignty, each of the legislatures electing and paying the salaries of two to seven delegates to Congress, and each delegation having only one vote no matter how numerous. At least nine of the states (through their legislatures) would have to approve any important measure, such as a

treaty, before Congress could pass it, and all thirteen would have to approve before the Articles could be ratified or amended.

Ratification was delayed by differences of opinion about the proposed plan. Some Americans were willing enough to accept a relatively weak central government, but others preferred to see it strengthened. The people of the small states insisted upon equal state representation, but those of the large states thought they should be represented in proportion to their population. Above all, the states claiming Western lands wished to keep them, but the rest of the states demanded that the whole territory be turned over to the Confederation government. The "landed" states, among which Virginia had the largest and best claim, founded their claims upon colonial charters, with the exception of New York, which based its rights upon a protectorate over the Iroquois Indians. The "landless" states, particularly Maryland, maintained that as the fruit of common sacrifices in war the West-

schemed to secure the cancellation or confirmation of private grants already made. At last New York gave up its rather hazy claim, and Virginia made a qualified offer to cede its lands to Congress. Then Maryland, the only state still holding out against ratification, approved the Articles of Confederation, and they went into effect in 1781.

The Articles of Confederation
1781

1. [Article II] "Each state retains its sovereignty, freedom and independence, and every Power, Jurisdiction and right, which is not by this confederation expressly delegated to the United States, in Congress assembled."

2. [Article IV] The free inhabitants of each state "shall be entitled to all privileges and immunities of free citizens in the several states," and "full faith and credit" shall be given by each state to the judicial and other official proceedings of other states.

3. [Article V] Each state shall be represented in Congress by no less than two and no more than seven members, shall pay its own delegates, and shall have one vote (regardless of the number of members).

4. [Article VI] No state, without the consent of Congress, shall enter into diplomatic relations or make treaties with other states or with foreign nations, or engage in war except in case of actual invasion.

5. [Article VIII] A "common treasury" shall be supplied by the states in proportion to the value of their land and improvements; the states shall levy taxes to raise their quotas of revenue.

6. [Article IX] Congress shall have power to decide on peace and war, conduct foreign affairs, settle disputes between states, regulate the Indian trade, maintain post offices, make appropriations, borrow money, emit bills of credit, build a navy, requisition soldiers from the states, etc.—but nine states must agree before Congress can take any important action.

7. [Article X] A "Committee of the States," consisting of one delegate from each state, shall act in the place of Congress when Congress is not in session.

8. [Article XIII] No change shall be made in these Articles unless agreed to by Congress and "afterwards confirmed by the legislatures of every state."

---

ern land had become the rightful property of all the states. In this dispute selfish interests as well as high principles were involved, for rival groups of land speculators

The Confederation government came into being in time to conclude the war and make the peace. Meanwhile, during the years of fighting from 1775 to 1781, the Second Continental Congress served as the agency for directing and coordinating the war effort of the people of the thirteen states.

Mobilizing for War

Congress and the states faced overwhelming tasks in raising and organizing armies, providing the necessary supplies and equipment, and paying the costs of war.

Supplies of most kinds were scarce at the outset, and shortages persisted to the end. Though America, being a land of hunters, contained numerous gunsmiths, they were not able to meet the wartime demand for guns and ammunition, nor were they able to produce heavy arms. Some of the states offered bounties for the encouragement of manufactures, especially for the production of guns and powder, and Congress in 1777 established a government arsenal at Springfield, Massachusetts. Even so, the Americans themselves managed to manufacture only a small fraction of the equipment they used. They supplemented their own manufactures with matériel which fell into their hands upon the seizure of forts like Crown Point and Ticonderoga (in 1775), the surrender of British armies, and the capture of supply ships by American privateers. But they got most of their war materials through importations from Europe, particularly from France.

In trying to meet the expenses of war, Congress had no power to tax the people, and the states had little inclination to do so. Indeed, cash was scarce in the country, as it always had been. When Congress requisitioned the states for money, none of them contributed more than a tiny part of its share. At first Congress hesitated to requisition goods directly from the people, but finally allowed army purchasing agents to take supplies from farmers and pay with certificates of indebtedness. Congress could not raise much money by floating long-

terms loans at home, since few Americans could afford war bonds and those few usually preferred to invest their funds in more profitable ventures, such as privateering. So

Continental Currency. *This forty-dollar bill, issued in 1778, was, like most of the Continental currency, of rather small dimensions—only three inches by four. From 1775 to 1779 the Continental Congress issued more than $240 million in paper money. Prices rose to fantastic heights, and the money became almost worthless. In 1780 Congress undertook to call in and cancel as much of the currency as possible. It was accepted from the states as part of their tax requisitions, and it was received from citizens at a ratio of forty paper dollars to one silver dollar. In 1790, after the adoption of the Constitution, the new Congress provided that the Continental notes still outstanding be accepted for United States bonds at a ratio of 100 to 1. During the Revolution the various states also issued paper money—a total of nearly $210 million. Both the Congress and the state legislatures felt it necessary to resort to such money because of the scarcity of coin and the popular opposition to high taxes.* (THE CHASE MANHATTAN BANK MUSEUM OF MONEYS OF THE WORLD)

Congress had no choice but to issue paper money, and Continental currency came from the printing presses in large and repeated batches. The states added sizeable currency issues of their own.

With goods and coin so scarce and paper money so plentiful, prices rose to fantastic heights and the value of the paper money fell proportionately. There quickly appeared all the usual evils of wartime profit-eering, and more too. One reason why Washington's men suffered from shortages of food and clothing at Valley Forge during the terrible winter of 1777-1778 was that American farmers and merchants preferred to do business with the British forces oc-cupying near-by Philadelphia, since the British could pay in gold or silver coin. To check the inflationary trend, Congress ad-vised the states to pass laws for price con-trol, but soon saw the futility of such meas-ures and recommended that they be dropped. Eventually, in 1780, Congress de-cided that the states should accept Continen-tal currency from taxpayers at the rate of forty paper dollars to one silver dollar, then send it to Congress to be destroyed. If the currency was not turned in for taxes at a fortieth of its face value, it became utterly worthless; hence the expression, "Not worth a Continental." By this time Congress was able to meet the most pressing of its financial needs by borrowing from abroad.

The states added to their financial re-sources by seizing lands belonging to the Crown and to colonial proprietors. In 1777 Congress recommended that the states also confiscate and sell the property of Loyalists active in the British cause, then lend the proceeds to the central government. The states were eager enough to expropriate the Loyalists, though not to make the requested loan. Already Patriots were punishing Tories in various ways, taking from them the rights of citizenship, barring them from certain occupations, and imposing special taxes and heavy fines upon them. The sei-zure and sale of Loyalist property, resulting incidentally in a widened distribution of land ownership among the buyers, netted the states a total of several million pounds, in value if not in actual cash. Around 100,-000 of the Loyalists themselves, either vol-untarily or because of banishment, left the

country during the course of the war, the most numerous group going to Quebec and laying the foundations of English-speaking Canada. If the sorrows of the expropriated and the exiled seem heart-rending, it must be remembered that the Patriots were engaged in a life-and-death struggle with Great Brit-ain and that the Loyalists, comprising what in later years would be called a "fifth col-umn," were eager to aid the enemy when-ever they got the chance.

While thousands of Tories enlisted and fought in the British ranks, only a small pro-portion of the Patriots were willing to vol-unteer for the American armies, once the first surge of patriotism at the start of the war had passed. The states had to resort to persuasion and force, to bounties and the draft, the bounties being commonly in the form of land scrip, since land was an asset with which the states were well supplied. Thus recruited, militiamen remained under the control of their respective states. The recruits were, many of them, expert marks-men and on the average they were physi-cally bigger and stronger than the British regulars, yet man for man they were no match for the redcoats in battle since they lacked the regulars' fine training, discipline, and *esprit de corps.*

Foreseeing some of the disadvantages of separately organized militias, Congress early called upon the states (while they were still colonies) to raise troops for a reg-ular force, the Continental army, and agreed that it should have a single com-mander in chief. George Washington, forty-three years old, sober and responsible by nature, possessed more command experience than any other American-born officer avail-able. And he had political as well as military qualifications. An early advocate of inde-pendence, he was admired and trusted by nearly all the Patriots. A Virginian, he had the support not only of Southerners but also

Steuben at Valley Forge. *Many foreigners served as officers in the Continental army—too many, it seemed to General Washington. Most of them received their commissions from Congress, not from the commander in chief. Once he referred to the foreigners as "hungry adventurers." But he deeply appreciated the assistance of a few of the volunteers from abroad, especially the Marquis de Lafayette and the Baron von Steuben. A veteran of the Prussian army, Steuben came to the United States in 1777, and Washington appointed him inspector general, with overall charge of military discipline, instruction, and supply. Steuben reorganized the Continental army, provided for improved training and drill of soldiers, and wrote a manual of army regulations. The painting by Edwin A. Abbey, which hangs in the Pennsylvania House of Representatives, shows Steuben instructing troops in Washington's camp at Valley Forge, near Philadelphia, during the winter of 1777–1778. After the war he settled in New York.* (COURTESY OF THE PENNSYLVANIA DEPARTMENT OF COMMERCE)

of Northerners who feared that the appointment of a New Englander might jeopardize sectional harmony. As the unanimous choice of the delegates, he took command in June, 1775.

Congress chose well. Throughout the war Washington kept faithfully at his task, despite difficulties and discouragements that would have daunted a lesser man. With the aid of foreign military experts such as the

George Washington. [OPPOSITE] *From 1772 to 1795 the Maryland-born artist and taxidermist Charles Willson Peale painted from life more than a dozen portraits of George Washington, under whom he served as a soldier during the Revolutionary War. This portrait, which conveys something of the moral as well as the physical grandeur of Washington, shows him in the uniform of commander in chief at his Princeton headquarters in 1776. Here is a more realistic likeness of Washington than the far more familiar unfinished portrait by Gilbert Stuart. Peale founded the Pennsylvania Academy of the Fine Arts and also the Peale Museum in Philadelphia. In the museum were displayed stuffed animals against a realistically painted background, skeletons of prehistoric monsters, objects brought from the West by the Lewis and Clark expedition (1804–1806), and scientific curiosities of various kinds.* (THE PENNSYLVANIA ACADEMY OF THE FINE ARTS)

Marquis de Lafayette and the Baron von Steuben he succeeded in building and holding together the Continental army, though at no time did it number as many as 10,000

THE WAR IN THE NORTH, 1775

CANADA

Quebec

MONTGOMERY

Montreal

RICHELIEU R.

LAKE CHAMPLAIN

CROWN Point

Ft. Ticonderoga

NEW YORK
(VERMONT)

LAKE GEORGE

CONNECTICUT R.

NEW HAMP.

MAINE (MASS.)

ARNOLD

KENNEBEC R.

Falmouth (Portland)

Albany

HUDSON R.

MASS.

Concord
Lexington
BUNKER HILL
Boston

Newburyport

50 MILES

TRH

men (not counting the militia of the separate states). The morale of the soldiers, who were getting short rations and low pay, became so bad that mutinies broke out (in 1781) among the Pennsylvania and New Jersey troops. Meanwhile, during the dark winter of Valley Forge, some congressmen and army officers, conspiring together in the so-called Conway cabal, hinted at replacing Washington as commander in chief. He, on the other hand, complained often and bitterly against his employers, the delegates in Congress, who seemed to do too little in supplying him with manpower and equip-

ment, and too much in interfering with his conduct of military operations. The faults were not all on the side of Congress, which had its difficulties too. Washington had his shortcomings as a military commander and he lost more battles than he won. Yet he was a great war leader. For all his faults and failures, he led the army and the nation to ultimate victory with his supreme steadiness and courage, his sacrificial devotion to the cause of independence.

The Fighting, to 1777

For about the first year of the fighting (1775–1776) the colonial armed forces took the offensive. After the British retreat from Concord and Lexington, the Americans besieged the army of General Gage in Boston, and though suffering severe casualties in the Battle of Bunker Hill (actually fought on Breed's Hill, June 17, 1775), they inflicted even greater losses upon the enemy and thereafter they continued to tighten the siege. Far to the south, at Moore's Creek Bridge in North Carolina, a band of Patriots crushed an uprising of Tories (February 27, 1776) and thereby discouraged British plans for invading the Southern states with Loyalist aid. Far to the north the Americans themselves undertook an invasion of Canada. The fearless Benedict Arnold, assuming command on the death of Richard Montgomery, threatened Quebec after a winter march of incredible hardship, but in the end met frustration and defeat. In the spring a civilian commission headed by the seventy-year-old Franklin returned from the north without success in its efforts to secure the allegiance of Canada as the fourteenth state. Already, however, General Gage had given up his attempt to hold Boston and had departed with his troops and with hundreds of Loyalist refugees (March 17, 1776) for Halifax. Within a year from the firing of the first shots, the enemy had been driven from American soil.

The enemy soon returned, to put the Americans on the strategic defensive for the remainder of the war. During the summer of 1776, in the weeks immediately following the Declaration of Independence, the waters around the city of New York became filled with the most formidable military force Great Britain ever had sent abroad. Here were hundreds of men-of-war and troop-ships and a host of 32,000 disciplined soldiers under the command of the tall and affable Sir William Howe. Having no grudge against the Americans, Howe would rather awe them into submission than shoot them, and he believed that most of them, if given a chance, would show that they were at heart loyal to the King. In a parley with commissioners from Congress he offered the alternatives of submission with royal pardon or battle against overwhelming odds. To oppose Howe's awesome array, Washington could muster only about 19,000 poorly armed and trained soldiers, including both Continentals and state troops, and he had no navy at all. Yet without hesitation the Americans chose continued war, which meant inevitably a succession of defeats. The British pushed the defenders off Long Island, compelled them to abandon Manhattan Island, and drove them in slow retreat over the plains of New Jersey, across the Delaware River, and into Pennsylvania.

Warfare being for eighteenth-century Europeans a seasonal activity, the British settled down for the winter with occupation forces at various points in New Jersey and with an outpost of Hessians at Trenton on the Delaware. But Washington did not content himself with sitting still. On Christmas night, 1776, he daringly recrossed the icy river, surprised and scattered the Hessians, and occupied the town. Then he advanced and drove off a force of redcoats at Princeton. Unable to hold either Princeton or Trenton, he finally took refuge for the rest of the winter in the hills around Morris-

town. As the campaign of 1776 came to an end, the Americans could console themselves with the thought that they had won two minor victories, that their main army was still intact, and that the invaders were really no nearer than ever to the decisive triumph which Howe so confidently had anticipated.

For the campaign of 1777 the British devised a strategy which, if Howe had stuck to it, might have cut the United States in two and prepared the way for final victory by Great Britain. According to this plan, Howe would move from New York up the Hudson to Albany while another force, in a gigantic pincers movement, would come down from Canada to meet him. One of Howe's ambitious younger officers, the dashing John Burgoyne, "Gentleman Johnny," secured command of this northern force and elaborated upon the plan by preparing for a two-pronged attack along both

WASHINGTON'S RETREAT, 1776

the Mohawk and the upper Hudson approaches to Albany.

Then, fortunately for the United States, Howe adopted a different plan for himself, intending to dispirit the Patriots and rally the Loyalists by seizing the rebel capital, Philadelphia. Taking the bulk of his forces away from New York by sea, Howe landed

BRITISH CAMPAIGNS, 1777

at the head of Chesapeake Bay, brushed Washington aside at the Battle of Brandywine (September 11), and proceeded to occupy Philadelphia, while Washington after an unsuccessful attack at Germantown (October 4) went into winter quarters at Val-

ley Forge, and the scattered Congress resumed its sittings in York, Pennsylvania.

Up north, Burgoyne was left to carry out his twofold campaign without aid from Howe. Sending Colonel Barry St. Leger with a fast-moving force up the St. Lawrence River toward Lake Ontario and the headwaters of the Mohawk, Burgoyne with his own army advanced directly down the upper Hudson Valley. He got off to a flying start, easily taking Fort Ticonderoga and an enormous store of powder and supplies, and causing such consternation that Congress removed General Philip Schuyler from command in the north and replaced him with Horatio Gates, in response to the demands of New Englanders. By the time Gates took command, Burgoyne already faced a sudden reversal of his military fortunes in consequence of two staggering defeats. In one of them, at Oriskany, New York (August 6), Nicholas Herkimer with his German farmers checked a force of St. Leger's Indians and Tories, so that Benedict Arnold had time to go to the relief of Fort Stanwix and close off the Mohawk Valley to St. Leger's advance. In the other battle, at Bennington, Vermont (August 16), the Bunker Hill veteran John Stark with his New England militiamen severely mauled a detachment that Burgoyne had sent out to seek supplies. Short of materials, with all help cut off, Burgoyne fought a couple of costly engagements and then withdrew to Saratoga, where Gates surrounded him. Burgoyne was through, and he knew it. On October 17, 1777, he ordered what was left of his army, nearly 5,000 men, to lay down their arms.

Not only the United States but also Europe took note of the amazing news from the woods of upstate New York, and France in particular was impressed. The British surrender at Saratoga, a great turning point in the war, led directly to an alliance between the United States and France.

Foreign Friends

Shortly after the fighting had begun, Congress appointed a secret committee with Franklin as chairman for the purpose of corresponding with "our friends" in Great Britain and, more significantly, in "other parts of the world." Later Congress replaced this agency with a Committee for Foreign Affairs and then (1781) with a Department of Foreign Affairs, the immediate ancestor of the State Department. As far as possible, however, Congress as a whole conducted foreign relations, often overruling or bypassing the agencies it created.

Even before the Declaration of Independence, Congress drew up a treaty plan for liberal commercial arrangements with other countries and prepared to send representatives to the capitals of Europe for negotiating treaties—which necessarily would mean European recognition of the United States as one of the sovereign nations of the world. "Militia diplomats," John Adams called the early American representatives abroad, and unlike the diplomatic regulars of Europe they knew little of the formal art and etiquette of Old World diplomacy. Yet most of them were well acquainted with certain fundamentals, for they had gained much diplomatic experience through their dealings with one another in intercolonial affairs, with the Indian tribes in war and peace, and with the British government as colonial agents in London. Since overseas communication was slow and uncertain (it took from one to three months to cross the Atlantic), these representatives abroad sometimes had to interpret the instructions of Congress very freely and make crucial decisions entirely on their own.

Of all the possible foreign friends of the United States, the most promising and most powerful was France, who still resented her defeat at the hands of Great Britain in 1763. France, under King Louis XVI, who came to the throne in 1774, had an astute and determined foreign minister in the Count de Vergennes, an expert practitioner of Machiavellian principles, thoroughly trained in the cutthroat diplomacy of eighteenth-century Europe. Vergennes soon saw that France had a vital interest in the outcome of the American war. If the colonies should assert and maintain their independence, the power of Great Britain would be seriously weakened by the loss of a good part of her empire, and the power of France would be correspondingly increased. But Vergennes was too shrewd to talk to Americans about the interests of France. As he once had said regarding French relations with the Turks, "Let us enlighten them as to their true interests; let us appear to be occupied only with what concerns them, without reference to ourselves."

From the start of the troubles between England and her colonies, the French had maintained observers in America to report the course of events, and after the shooting began both Americans and Frenchmen put out diplomatic feelers. In London the Massachusetts colonial agent Arthur Lee met the French dramatist and political genius Caron de Beaumarchais, and the two discussed the possibilities of secret assistance to the colonies. Beaumarchais reported to Vergennes, and Vergennes dispatched an army officer to America to encourage the rebellion, urge independence, and promise supplies. After several meetings with Vergennes's spokesman, Franklin's committee of secret correspondence sent Silas Deane to France as a "merchant" to make "commercial" arrangements. In consequence of these arrangements Beaumarchais shipped large quantities of munitions to America through a fictitious trading firm which he had rigged up to disguise the fact that most of the shipments were financed by the King of France and the King of Spain. Whether this sort of lend-lease was a gift or a loan became later a question of bitter dispute between Congress and Beaumarchais.

After the Declaration of Independence Franklin himself went to France to get fur-

Paris on December 4, 1777. In London the knowledge of Burgoyne's surrender caused Lord North to decide in favor of a peace offensive, an offer of complete home rule

---

Treaty of Alliance with France

1778

1. If war should break out between France and Great Britain, France and the United States will make "common cause" against Great Britain.

2. The aim of this alliance is to maintain the independence of the United States.

3. France "renounces forever" all claim to Canada or other one-time British possessions in North America.

4. "Neither of the two parties shall conclude either truce or peace with Great Britain without the formal consent of the other first obtained."

5. The two parties guarantee "forever against all other powers" the possessions of one another in the Western Hemisphere.

---

ther aid and outright recognition of the United States. A natural diplomat, the equal if not the superior of the world's best at that time, Franklin immediately captivated Frenchmen of all classes—and Frenchwomen too. But Vergennes hesitated. At the first news of the American Declaration, he was inclined to make a treaty recognizing United States independence, but he did not wish to act without Spain, and when reports came of Washington's defeat on Long Island he decided to wait and watch the military developments in America. If and when the Americans should show that they had a real chance of winning, then France would intervene. Meanwhile Vergennes was willing to go on financing the American war. He initiated a series of subsidies which in time amounted to nearly $2 million and a series of loans which totaled over $6 million.

The news that Vergennes and Franklin were waiting for—the news from Saratoga —arrived in London on December 2 and in

within the Empire for Americans if they would quit the war. In Paris, learning of Lord North's intentions from a British spy, Franklin let the word get out for Vergennes to hear. Vergennes worried. If the Americans should accept the British offer, his opportunity to weaken France's traditional enemy would be gone, and if they could not get what they wanted from France, they might accept. Without waiting for Spain to go along with France, Vergennes on February 6, 1778, signed two treaties with Franklin and Deane, one a treaty of commerce and amity, and the other, which was supposed to be secret, a treaty of conditional and defensive alliance, to take effect if Great Britain should go to war with France. Congress and the King quickly ratified the treaties, and Congress received and banqueted a minister from France while the King welcomed Franklin as minister from the United States.

France soon drifted into war with Great

Britain, and in 1779 Spain, with objectives of her own, declared war as an ally of France though not of the United States; Spain refused even to receive officially the American representative in Madrid, John Jay. A year later the Netherlands, persisting in its profitable trade with both the French and the Americans, found itself also at war with Britain and agreed to a treaty with the United States. The League of Armed Neutrals—Russia, Denmark, Sweden—assumed a defiant attitude toward Britain, but refrained from considering war and refused to have any official dealings with the upstart nation in America.

Indirectly all the countries arrayed in hostility to Britain contributed to the ultimate success of the United States by complicating the task of the latter's foe. Directly, the Netherlands provided loans to the Americans but was powerless to give military or naval support, and Spain gave unofficial subsidies but confined her military and naval activities to strictly Spanish ob-

also provided a navy and an expeditionary force that, with Washington's army, made possible the decisive victory at Yorktown.

Victory at Yorktown

During the first two years of the war the important campaigns and battles had taken place in the North, but after Saratoga the fighting in that part of the country developed into a stalemate. Replacing General Howe, Sir Henry Clinton withdrew from Philadelphia and took what had been Howe's army back to New York. Washington used most of his army to keep watch around New York while (1778-1779) sending part of it to chastise the Indians along the frontier for their horrible massacres in the Cherry Valley (New York) and the Wyoming Valley (Pennsylvania). During that same winter George Rogers Clark, with orders from the state of Virginia and not from Washington or Congress, led a heroic expedition over the mountains and redeemed the settlements of the Illinois country from

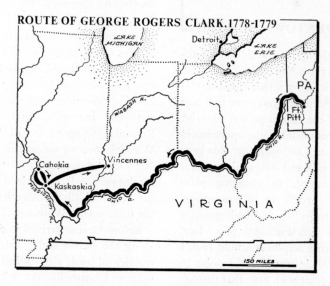

ROUTE OF GEORGE ROGERS CLARK, 1778-1779

jects. France (for her own reasons, of course) was the true friend in need of the Americans. Not only did she furnish them most of their money and munitions but she

the British and their Indian allies. In 1779 the treason of Benedict Arnold shocked Washington and Patriots everywhere but did little military damage except for the transfer of Arnold's services to the British, since his scheme for betraying the Hudson River stronghold of West Point was frustrated in the nick of time. During the final

ROAD TO YORKTOWN, 1780-1781

two years of fighting, all the significant action occurred in the South.

Sir Henry Clinton, a rather timid strategist, planned a Southern offensive that was supposed to end the American will to resist, but he put the command of the operation in the hands of Lord Cornwallis, an able general but one as rash as Clinton himself was cautious, and capable of changing plans and disobeying orders in mid-campaign. Clinton and Cornwallis based their strategy on assumption which was not to prove fact. They assumed that seapower would enable them to move their troops from point to point along the coast with ease, that the difficulties of overland travel would make American counteraction ineffectual, and that Loyalists would rise *en masse* to welcome and assist the redcoats as liberators.

With the conquered South as a base, Clinton and Cornwallis thought they could dispose of the rest of the country at their leisure. While it was true that in Georgia and the Carolinas there were numerous Tories, some of them disgruntled veterans of the Regulator movement, it was also true that in Virginia as in Massachusetts the mass of the people were fiercely patriotic and that even in the lower South the Loyalist strength was grossly overestimated. Actually, having the support of most of the countryside, the Patriot forces were to be better off than the British in matters of logistics and supply. And the French, while far from able to maintain consistent control of the coastal waters, were finally to have a fleet in the right place at the right time.

The British succeeded in taking Savannah (December 29, 1778) and Charleston (May 20, 1779), inspiring many Loyalists to take up arms, and advancing far into the interior. At every turn they were harassed, however, by Patriot guerrillas led by such resourceful fighters as Thomas Sumter, Andrew Pickens, and Francis Marion, the "Swamp Fox." Penetrating to Camden, well up the Wateree River in South Carolina, Cornwallis met and crushed (August 16, 1780) a combined force of militiamen and Continentals under Horatio Gates, who did not quite deserve his fame as the hero of Saratoga. Congress recalled Gates, and Washington gave the southern command to Nathanael Greene, an erstwhile Quaker blacksmith of Rhode Island and probably the ablest of all the American generals of the time, next to Washington himself.

Before Greene arrived in the war theater along the North and South Carolina line, the tide of battle already had begun to turn against Cornwallis. At King's Mountain (October 7, 1780) a band of Patriot riflemen from the backwoods killed, wounded, or captured an entire force of 1,100 New York and South Carolina Tories, upon whom

Cornwallis had depended as auxiliaries. Once arrived, Greene confused and exasperated Cornwallis by dividing the American forces into fast-moving contingents while refraining from a showdown in open battle. One of the contingents inflicted what Cornwallis admitted was "a very unexpected and severe blow" at Cowpens (January 17, 1781). At last, having received the reinforcements he awaited, Greene combined all his forces and arranged to meet the British on ground of his own choosing at Guilford Court House, North Carolina. After a hard-fought battle (March 15, 1781) Greene was driven from the field, but Cornwallis lost so many men that he decided at last to abandon the Carolina campaign.

For a while Cornwallis thought of joining with the forces of Benedict Arnold, now in command of British raiders in Virginia, and undertaking the conquest of that state. In Virginia he sent out new raiding parties, drove off a Patriot army under Lafayette, and then—despite the expostulations of his superior officer, General Clinton—retreated to the peninsula between the York and James rivers and began to build fortifications at Yorktown. While Clinton worried about Cornwallis's moves, Washington made plans with the Count de Rochambeau, commander of the French expeditionary force in America, and with Admiral de Grasse, commander of a French fleet in American waters, for trapping Cornwallis. Washington and Rochambeau marched a Franco-American army from the New York vicinity to join Lafayette in Virginia while Grasse sailed with additional troops for Chesapeake Bay and the York River. These joint operations, perfectly timed and executed, caught Cornwallis between land and sea. After a few shows of resistance, he asked for terms on October 17, 1781, four years to the day after the capitulation of Burgoyne, and two days later he surrendered his whole army of more than 7,000.

The fighting was over, but the war was not quite won. The United States continued to be something of an occupied country, with British forces holding the seaports of Savannah, Charleston, Wilmington, and New York. Before long a British fleet met and defeated Admiral de Grasse's fleet in the West Indies, ending Washington's hopes for further seapower assistance. So far as the naval and military situation was concerned, the British still held the upper hand in America. And peace was yet to be made.

Winning the Peace

Until Yorktown, peace had been for Americans an illusory and at times a dangerous proposition, and the prospects even after that victory, though improved, were not ideal. The trouble was with Spain. She entered the war solely to recover lost territories in America and Europe, above all the island of Gibraltar, and she had an alliance binding France to make no separate peace. The United States had promised in its treaty of alliance to conclude no peace without France. Now, if Spain should fight on till she won Gibraltar back, and if France should stick by Spain, and the United States by France, the Americans might be at war forever. That, however, was not the real danger to American interests. The danger was that Spain, to get Gibraltar or American territory, might enter into a deal with Great Britain at the expense of the United States, and that France might feel compelled to go along with Spain. In making peace, the United States had as much to fear from its ally as from its enemy.

When, in 1779, Spain in the role of mediator proposed a peace conference, Congress promptly named John Adams as the American delegate and sent him instructions to enter into no negotiations unless Great Britain first recognized the United States as "sovereign, free, and independent." Adams, already abroad as a militia diplomat, proceeded to Paris and remained there waiting for new peace opportunities after the Spanish proposal had been forgotten. The blustery

men and playing up to the Secretary for Foreign Affairs, La Luzerne secured the replacement of the single delegate with a whole delegation, including Franklin and

The Peacemakers of 1783. *Only John Jay, John Adams, and Benjamin Franklin actually took part in the peace negotiations, though two other commissioners (Henry Laurens and Thomas Jefferson) were appointed. Jay, Adams, and Franklin are pictured in that order, from left to right, in Benjamin West's unfinished painting. West, born in Pennsylvania, had studied art in Italy and, in 1763, had settled in England, where he became one of the leading artists. His "grand historic style" was highly esteemed by English patrons of art, including King George III, who appointed him a court painter. In his historical paintings West exhibited considerable realism despite his grand manner. He left his mark upon all of the first generation of notable American painters—John Singleton Copley, Gilbert Stuart, Charles Willson Peale, John Trumbull, Washington Allston, and others who studied under him.* (COURTESY OF THE H. F. DU PONT WINTERTHUR MUSEUM)

Adams did not get along with Vergennes as well as the soft-spoken Franklin did. Vergennes sent to America a new minister, La Luzerne, to do something about the Adams nuisance. Lobbying with congress-

John Jay as well as Adams, and La Luzerne virtually dictated the delegation's instructions. These instructions told the prospective peacemakers to keep in close touch with the French government, tell it everything, follow its advice. Thus the United States was put into the hands of Vergennes by the time (1781) Austria and Russia made their joint mediation offer that led eventually to a general peace settlement.

Then Yorktown, by giving the Americans new bargaining power, rescued them from the worst of their dependence upon Vergennes. In England, Cornwallis's defeat provoked outcries against continuing the war and demands for cultivating American friendship as an asset in international politics. Lord North resigned and Lord Shel-

essary" terms of peace, including independence and the establishment of the Mississippi as the western boundary of the United States, and "desirable" terms including the cession of Canada for the purpose of "reconciliation," a "sweet word," as he said. But John Jay, recently arrived from his fruitless mission to Spain, where he had acquired reason to be suspicious of Spaniards and all Europeans, objected to continuing the negotiations on the grounds that the Americans were addressed not as plenipotentiaries of a sovereign nation but as "persons" from

---

Treaty of Paris
1783

1. "His Britannic Majesty acknowledges the said United States . . . to be free, sovereign and independent States."

2. Boundaries shall run, as described in some detail, from Nova Scotia to and through the Great Lakes and the Lake of the Woods, "thence on a due west course to the river Mississippi," down the Mississippi to the thirty-first parallel, and then east to the Atlantic Ocean.

3. The people of the United States shall have fishing rights and liberties in the waters of British North America.

4. Creditors on either side "shall meet with no lawful impediment to the recovery of the full value, in sterling money, of all *bona fide* debts heretofore contracted."

5. Congress "shall earnestly recommend to the legislatures of the respective States" that they make restitution for confiscated Loyalist property.

6. There shall be no future confiscations or prosecutions on account of the part that anyone may have taken in the war.

7. Hostilities shall cease, and "His Britannic Majesty shall, with all convenient speed, and without causing any destruction, or carrying away any negroes or other property of the American inhabitants, withdraw all his armies, garrisons and fleets from the said United States, and from every post, place and harbour within the same."

---

burne emerged from the political wreckage as prime minister. British emissaries appeared in France to talk informally with Franklin. He suggested what he called "nec-

"colonies or plantations." The negotiations were delayed until Jay was satisfied.

All along Franklin and Jay and Adams had kept Vergennes informed of their conversations with British agents, in accordance with the instructions from Congress. Then, one day, Jay learned that Vergennes's private secretary was off on a secret mission to England. Jay feared that Vergennes was going to leave the United States in the lurch and make a separate peace by which Great Britain and Spain would divide between themselves the territory west of the Alleghenies and east of the Mississippi. Such a deal, as Franklin exclaimed, would have "cooped us up within the Allegheny Mountains." Though Jay was mistaken as to the details of the secret mission, he was right in thinking that Vergennes was suggesting separate negotiations which were to be kept from the American peacemakers and which might have proved disadvantageous to the United States. From that day on, Franklin and Jay and Adams ceased to inform Vergennes of their diplomacy but went ahead on their own and soon drew up a preliminary treaty with Great Britain. In doing so, they may have violated the spirit but they did not violate the letter of the Franco-American alliance, since they were not making a separate final peace. Of course, they disregarded their instructions from Congress, but those instructions had come originally from Vergennes himself.

After the preliminary articles were signed (November 30, 1782), Jay and Adams left to Franklin the delicate task of telling Vergennes what had been done. Franklin admitted to Vergennes that the Americans perhaps had violated etiquette in failing to keep the French informed, but he trusted that the incident would cause no rift in the Franco-American alliance. Cleverly Frank-

lin observed: "The English, I just now learn, flatter themselves they have already divided us. I hope this little misunderstanding will therefore be kept a secret, and that they will find themselves totally mistaken." Vergennes, dealing with a fellow master of diplomacy, could not say much and was doubtless glad to have an excuse for ending the war regardless of the wishes of his Spanish ally. Franklin coolly asked for another loan from France—and got it!

The preliminary treaty became effective on January 20, 1783, when Spain as well as France agreed to end hostilities. It included a number of provisions that Franklin and Jay and Adams had opposed, and some of these were to lead to serious friction with Great Britain and with Spain in the years ahead. Yet it also included essentially the "necessary" terms which Franklin originally had indicated, though not his "desirable" ones such as the cession of Canada. On the whole the peace was remarkably favorable to the United States in granting a clear-cut recognition of independence and a generous, though ambiguous, delimitation of territory —from the southern boundary of Canada to the northern boundary of Florida and from the Atlantic to the Mississippi. Indeed, by playing off the powers of Europe against one another, Franklin and his colleagues had achieved the greatest diplomatic success in the history of the United States. With good reason the American people celebrated as the last of the British occupation forces embarked from New York and General Washington at the head of his troops rode triumphantly in.

->>>->>>->>>->>((<-(((-(((-(((

BIBLIOGRAPHY

AN UP-TO-DATE synthesis is J. R. Alden's *The American Revolution, 1775–1783* (1954), which is especially good on military events. A popularly written survey is J. C. Miller's *Triumph of Freedom, 1775–1783* (1949). E. B. Greene, *The Revolutionary Generation, 1763–1790* (1943), emphasizes social changes. These changes, resulting from the "stream of revolution," are also stressed—and perhaps overstressed—in J. F. Jameson's influential interpretive essay, *The American Revolution Considered as a Social Movement* (1926).

For wartime as well as prewar development of political ideas, see C. L. Becker's *The Declaration of Independence* (1922) and R. G. Adams's *The Political Ideas of the American Revolution* (1922). Both of these authors see a progression of ideas culminating in the concept of a federated empire and finally of a separate and sovereign nation. See also the more recent study by Edward Dumbauld, *The Declaration of Independence and What It Means Today* (1950). Americans who opposed the idea of independence are sympathetically treated by C. H. Van Tyne in *The Loyalists in the American Revolution* (1905).

Government during the Revolution is the subject of E. C. Burnett's *The Continental Congress* (1941) and Lynn Montross's *The Reluctant Rebels: The Story of the Continental Congress, 1774–1789* (1950). In *The Articles of Confederation* (1948) Merrill Jensen interprets the Articles as a democratic and workable constitution. For state governments, see the thorough study by Allan Nevins, *The American States during and after the Revolution* (1924), and Douglass, *Rebels and Democrats.*

For campaigns and battles, the most complete modern account is Christopher Ward, *The War of the Revolution* (2 vols., 1952). W. M. Wallace, *Appeal to Arms* (1951), is briefer but also contains precise military details. Lynn Montross, *Rag, Tag, and Bobtail* (1952), is a readable story of the Continental army. G. F. Scheer and H. F. Rankin, *Rebels and Redcoats* (1957), fights the battles mainly in the words of the officers and soldiers themselves.

The central figure of the period is fully portrayed in Freeman's *George Washington.* C. P. Nettels, *George Washington and American Independence* (1951), reveals the forces leading Washington to favor a break with Great Britain. See also Bernard Knollenberg, *Washington and the Revolution* (1940). Louis Gottschalk does justice to the Marquis de Lafayette in three excellent volumes: *Lafayette Comes to America* (1935), *Lafayette Joins the American Army* (1937), and *Lafayette and the Close of the American Revolution* (1942). C. L. Ver Steeg, *Robert Morris, Revolutionary Financier* (1954), is a fresh, scholarly appraisal that clarifies Morris's career. Aspects of Benjamin Franklin's wartime career are well treated in A. O. Aldridge's *Franklin and His French Contemporaries* (1957), a judicious study of Franco-American political and cultural relations, and in W. B. Clark's *Ben Franklin's Privateers* (1956), which reads like fiction though solidly grounded on fact. Gerald Stourzh, *Benjamin Franklin and American Foreign Policy* (1954), analyzes the diplomatic thinking of America's greatest diplomat.

On foreign relations, S. F. Bemis's *The Diplomacy of the American Revolution* (1935) is indispensable.

CHAPTER 8

A More Perfect Union

A S USUALLY HAPPENS at the end of a long
and hard-fought war, peace in 1783
brought to the American people
tasks almost as trying as those of the war itself. Congress, with the inadequate powers
granted to it in the Articles of Confederation, did not quite succeed in solving its
postwar problems of diplomacy and public
finance, though it made a good beginning
toward organizing its territories in the West.
The states, too, had difficulties with debts
and taxes and, in the case of Massachusetts,
with an armed uprising. Concentrating upon
the shortcomings of the Confederation, historians used to refer to the 1780's as the
"Critical Period" of American history—a
period supposedly of impending chaos and
collapse from which the nation was rescued
only by the timely adoption of a new Constitution. Actually the 1780's were years of
hopeful striving rather than black despair,
of economic recovery and not merely depression, of governmental progress under

the Articles of Confederation despite temporary failures. Possibly the Articles with
suitable revisions might still be serving as
our twentieth-century frame of government,
and serving reasonably well, if a group of
determined and impatient men had not managed to bring about a drastic change in 1787–
1788. Certainly the new Constitution created
a "more perfect union" than was otherwise
possible at that time, and it provided a fundamental law capable of growth and adap-
tation to meet the needs of the nation for
centuries to come.

Failures in Foreign Affairs

The peace treaty of 1783 recognized the independence of the United States and
granted the new nation a vast domain—on
paper—but Americans found it hard to exercise their full sovereignty in fact. At once
they ran into serious conflict with both
Great Britain and Spain, yet they could not
count upon the support of France even

though France remained technically America's ally.

Despite the treaty provision calling upon the British to evacuate American soil, British forces continued to occupy a string of frontier posts along the Great Lakes within the United States. Secret orders to hold these forts went from the Colonial Office in London to the Governor-General of Canada on April 8, 1784, just one day before King George III proclaimed the peace treaty as being in final effect and called upon all his subjects to obey its terms! The real reason for the secret orders was the Canadian and British desire to maintain points of contact with Indian tribes in the Northwest for the conduct of the fur trade and the continuance of defensive alliances with them. The avowed reason, which was an afterthought, was the alleged failure of the United States to carry out its treaty obligations, particularly in regard to private debts.

These debts, dating from pre-Revolutionary days, were owed by American citizens, mostly Southern planters, to merchants and other creditors in England. The American debtors had no intention of paying—many of them had supported the Revolution in order to gain independence and thus throw off their old obligations. The treaty provided only that the United States should place no obstacle in the way of the collection of the debts, and the United States did place no obstacle in the way. True, the individual states interfered with debt collections, through the passage of debtor stay laws, the issuance of paper money as legal tender, and the rulings of courts sympathetic with local debtors.

According to the ill-founded British complaints, the United States was violating not only the article regarding private debts but also the one regarding Loyalist property. On this point the treaty said merely that Congress should recommend to the various states that they make restitution to certain categories of Loyalists whose possessions had been confiscated during the war. Congress did recommend, but the states did not respond. The British had not really expected them to. The article was put into the treaty as a gesture of the King's concern for the fate of his faithful subjects. Anticipating that the states would do little or nothing for Loyalist refugees, Parliament itself appropriated money for their relief.

To British allegations of bad faith, Americans countered with the charge that Great Britain, besides refusing to abandon the frontier posts, was disregarding the treaty provision which obligated her to compensate American slaveowners whose slaves had been carried off by the British armies at the end of the war. And the two countries disputed the meaning and application of still another article, the one defining the northeastern boundary of the United States. Over part of its course the boundary was supposed to follow the St. Croix River, but unfortunately the river had two major branches, and the treaty did not specify which of the two was meant.

The peace arrangements led also to a boundary dispute between the United States and Spain. In her settlement with Spain, Great Britain gave back Florida (which had been British from 1763 to 1783) with the Atlantic and the Mississippi specified as its eastern and western limits but with no precise definition of its northern border. In the preliminary treaty with the United States, however, Great Britain had agreed secretly that, if she herself were to keep Florida, its boundary would be set at latitude 32° 28′ and that, if she ceded it to Spain, its boundary would be located farther south, at the thirty-first parallel. Afterwards the United States insisted upon the more southerly of these lines, but Spain demanded the additional northern strip as rightfully a part of Florida. Spain also claimed extensive territory even north of that, as belonging to her by virtue of her (rather small-scale) military operations in the American West during the Revolutionary War.

There was another conflict between Anglo-American arrangements and the claims of Spain. In their treaty of peace Great Britain and the United States recognized the right of subjects and citizens of both countries to navigate the Mississippi River to its mouth. But Spain, possessing Louisiana as well as Florida and thus occupying both banks of the lower Mississippi, denied that Great Britain had any rights there to grant to the United States. In 1784 Spain exercised her lawful power over her territorial waters by closing the lower Mississippi to American navigation.

Thus several provisions of the peace with Great Britain failed to give Americans the benefits they desired and expected, and the treaty omitted entirely still other provisions they had hoped for. Above all, American shippers and traders wanted commercial arrangements that would give them privileges of trading and shipping on equal terms with British subjects in all parts of the British Empire. No longer colonists, these businessmen, it is true, now had opportunities for exploiting world-wide routes of trade which, before the war, had been legally closed to them. Congress proceeded to make satisfactory commercial treaties with the nations of Europe—with France (1778), the Netherlands (1782), Sweden (1783), and Prussia (1785). Congress also agreed to pay protection money to the Sultan of Morocco (1786) so that American merchantmen in the Mediterranean would be free from the depredations of at least some of the Barbary pirates. Without benefit of treaty, American enterprisers opened fabulously profitable trade routes to the Orient, beginning with the voyage of the *Empress of China* in 1784–1785. Yet, though commerce flourished in new directions, most American

trade persisted as much as possible in the old, prewar patterns. In the United States the bulk of imports continued to come from British sources, for Americans were used to British goods, and British merchants knew and catered to American tastes, offered attractive prices, and extended long and easy credit. To earn the British funds needed to pay for these imports, Americans desired free access to more British markets than were open to them after the war.

In 1784 Congress sent John Adams as minister to London with instructions to get a commercial treaty and speed up the evacuation of the frontier posts. Taunted by the query whether he represented one nation or thirteen, Minister Adams made no headway in England, partly because Congress had no power to retaliate against the kind of commercial warfare which Great Britain was pursuing against the United States. Throughout the 1780's the British government refused even to return the courtesy of sending a minister to the American capital.

The Spanish government, by contrast, was willing to negotiate its differences with the United States, and in 1785 its representative, Don Diego de Gardoqui, arrived in New York (whither Congress had moved from Philadelphia) to deal with the Secretary for Foreign Affairs, John Jay. After months of the most friendly conversations, Jay and Gardoqui initialed a treaty (1786). By its terms, the Spanish government would have granted Americans the right to trade with Spain but not with her colonies; would have conceded the American interpretation of the Florida boundary; and (in a secret article) would have joined in an alliance to protect American soil from British encroachments. The United States, besides guaranteeing Spanish possessions in America, would have agreed to "forbear" the navigation of the Mississippi for twenty years, though not to abandon the right of navigation. Jay found it hopeless, however, to secure the necessary nine state votes for the ratification of his treaty by Congress, since the delegates from the five Southern states objected bitterly and correctly that the interests of Southerners in Mississippi navigation were being sacrificed to the interests of Northerners in Spanish trade.

Planning for the West

Into the areas of postwar border conflict with Great Britain and Spain moved an unprecedented horde of American settlers during and after the Revolution. When the war began, only a few thousand lived west of the Appalachian divide; by 1790 their numbers had increased to 120,000. Most of the migrants made the mountain crossing under the auspices of able and far-seeing land promoters. James Robertson and John Sevier led pioneers from North Carolina to the Watauga settlements (1770) and later to the Cumberland Valley (1779), thus laying the foundations for the future state of Tennessee. Richard Henderson, promoter of the Transylvania Company and employer of Daniel Boone, stimulated the growth of Kentucky by selling lands, organizing a provisional government (1776), and having the Wilderness Road hewn out. The managers of the Vandalia Company encouraged migration to what eventually became West Virginia. And the Allen brothers—Ethan, Ira, and Levi—attracted purchasers for their regal holdings of real estate in the Green Mountains of Vermont. Upon such speculators the frontiersman usually had to depend for his land title and for other favors, yet he was characteristically an individualist determined to make a future for himself. He and his family, together with the thousands of others like him, comprised what was potentially the strongest single factor for redeeming the West for the United States.

But the United States could realize this potentiality only if the government were able to meet the needs of the frontier settler and keep him loyal to its distant authority. The settler needed protection from the Indians, access to outside markets for his surplus crops, and courts with orderly processes of law. In dealing with the West, Congress inherited responsibilities which formerly had baffled King and Parliament.

At first Congress lacked clear-cut jurisdiction over the trans-Appalachian region, and for several years conflicts of authority persisted among Congress, the states, and the frontier settlements themselves. Of course, with Virginia's cession in 1781, the landed states had begun to yield their Western claims to the Confederation. But Virginia had ceded her territory on the condition that private grants within it be canceled, and for a few years the grantees lobbied successfully to keep Congress from accepting the territory with that stipulation. North Carolina temporarily took back its ceded land, other states postponed their cessions, and not till 1802 did the last of them, Georgia, give up its claim. Meanwhile these states transferred the actual ownership of most of the land south of the Ohio River to private individuals and companies, and impatient settlers proceeded to set up their own state governments for Frankland or Franklin (Tennessee) and for Kentucky, while North Carolina attempted to incorporate the one and Virginia the other as mere counties.

In 1784, having persuaded Virginia to make a new cession without specific restrictions, Congress accepted Virginia's Western lands and began to make policy for the national domain. The most momentous decision, already resolved upon, was that settlements in the territory should not be held in permanent subjection as colonies but should be transformed ultimately into states equal with the original thirteen. In the Ordinance of 1784 Congress temporarily adopted Thomas Jefferson's very democratic plan

for the transition to statehood of the territory between the Ohio River and the Great
Lakes. This territory was to have been divided into ten districts, each to be self-gov-

ber of free inhabitants of the smallest existing state.

Having thus prepared a scheme of territorial government, Congress in the Ordi-

STATE CLAIMS TO WESTERN LANDS, 1781

erning from the start, to be represented by
a delegate in Congress as soon as its population reached 20,000, and to be admitted as a
state when its population equaled the num-

nance of 1785 provided a system of land
survey and sale. The land to the north of
the Ohio was to be surveyed and marked
off in a rectangular pattern before any of it

was sold. This program derived from the practice of New England towns rather than from that of the South, where the settler located a choice plot and afterwards determined its boundaries, usually following topographical irregularities. The land ordinance of Congress provided for east-west base lines, north-south "ranges," and townships with sides paralleling the ranges and base lines. Each township was to contain thirty-six square-mile sections. In every township four sections were to be set aside for the United States and one for a public school. The rest of the sections were to be sold at auction for not less than a dollar an acre. Since there were 640 acres in a section, the prospective buyer of government land had to have at least $640 in ready cash or in United States certificates of indebtedness.

These terms favored the large speculators too much and the ordinary frontiersmen too little to suit Jefferson, who believed that the West ought to belong to actual settlers on the ground. But the large speculators desired still further advantages, and Congress, in a hurry to realize returns from its domain, soon gave in to lobbying groups composed of some of its own members and various former army officers. To the Ohio and Scioto companies and the associates of John Cleves Symmes, Congress disposed of several million acres at only a few cents an acre. Millions of acres besides had been reserved at the time of cession by Virginia and Connecticut as bounty lands for their Revolutionary soldiers. Thus, before the government surveys had been well started, most of the choicest land north of the Ohio River was already spoken for (as was all the land south of the Ohio, to which the ordinances of Congress did not apply).

To protect their interests in the Northwest, the directors of the Ohio and Scioto companies demanded a territorial government that would give less influence to the inhabitants than would the one outlined in Jefferson's Ordinance of 1784, and the companies' skillful lobbyist Manasseh Cutler carried their case to Congress. Some of the congressmen themselves disliked Jefferson's idea of creating as many as ten new states north of the Ohio, since these states in time

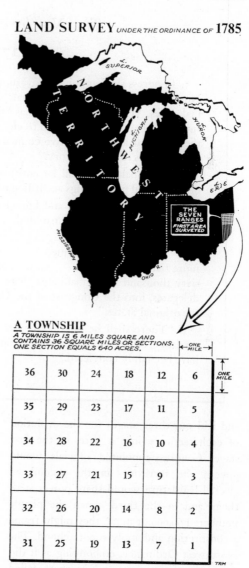

LAND SURVEY *UNDER THE ORDINANCE OF* **1785**

A TOWNSHIP
A TOWNSHIP IS 6 MILES SQUARE AND CONTAINS 36 SQUARE MILES OR SECTIONS. ONE SECTION EQUALS 640 ACRES.

36	30	24	18	12	6
35	29	23	17	11	5
34	28	22	16	10	4
33	27	21	15	9	3
32	26	20	14	8	2
31	25	19	13	7	1

might gain political ascendancy. Soon Congress replaced the original law—which had never gone into actual effect—with the Ordinance of 1787. This famous "Northwest

Ordinance" established one Northwest Territory for the time being, provided for its subsequent division into several territories, not fewer than three nor more than five,

well as of frontier settlers. In 1785 and 1786 congressional commissioners made treaties with representatives of the Iroquois and other tribes, who thereby surrendered their

---

The Northwest Ordinance

1787

1. Congress shall appoint a governor, a secretary, and three judges for the Northwest Territory. These officials shall adopt suitable laws from the original states. When the territory has "five thousand free male inhabitants of full age," they shall be allowed to elect representatives. These, together with the governor and a legislative council of five, shall form a general assembly to make laws for the territory.

2. The inhabitants shall be entitled to the benefits of trial by jury and other judicial proceedings according to the common law.

3. "Religion, morality, and knowledge being necessary to good government and the happiness of mankind, schools and the means of education shall forever be encouraged."

4. "There shall be formed in the said territory not less than three nor more than five States. . . . And, whenever any of the said States shall have sixty thousand free inhabitants therein, such State shall be admitted, by its delegates, into the Congress of the United States, on an equal footing with the original States."

5. "There shall be neither slavery nor involuntary servitude in the said territory, otherwise than in the punishment of crimes whereof the party shall have been duly convicted."

---

and laid out three stages for the evolution of each territory into a state. In the first stage, Congress-appointed officials would govern the territory, in the second an elected legislature would share power with them, and in the third, when the people numbered 60,000 or more, they might frame a constitution and apply for statehood. The Northwest Ordinance, embodying as it did the views of conservative Easterners, failed to satisfy the restless inhabitants of the Ohio country.

The Indian policy of Congress fell short of the requirements of land speculators as

claims to a stretch of land north of the Ohio in return for comparatively worthless trinkets. Repudiating the treaties, many of the tribesmen went on the warpath. Congress vainly instructed Colonel Josiah Harmar, commanding the federal troops in the Ohio country, to drive the Indians back, then in desperation called upon the aging hero George Rogers Clark to save the frontier. While the campaign against the Indians in the Northwest faltered, a new threat arose in the Southwest, where the Creeks under the half-breed Alexander McGillivray not only repudiated their treaties ceding land but also formed an alliance with the Spaniards to resist the advance of American frontiersmen.

Some of the frontier leaders in the Southwest, instead of fighting the Spaniards, turned to collaborating with them. These leaders and their followers thought for a time that they saw advantages for themselves in the possible creation of a Southwestern confederacy under Spanish tutelage. They might thus get what the United States seemed unable to give them—protection from the Indians, cheap or free land, and an outlet to Eastern and foreign markets through the navigation of the Mississippi. After the collapse of the Jay-Gardoqui negotiations, the "Spanish Conspiracy" began to hum, attracting not only unscrupulous adventurers like General James Wilkinson but also prominent politicians such as William Blount of Kentucky and John Sevier of Tennessee. At the same time another underground separatist movement was afoot on the far northern frontier. The aspirations of Vermont for statehood having been frustrated by the rival claims of New York and New Hampshire to its soil, the Allen brothers intrigued with British agents for returning the Green Mountain country to the British Empire.

Debts, Taxes, and Daniel Shays

At the end of the war foreign ships crowded into American seaports with cargoes of all kinds, and the American people bought extravagantly with cash or credit. In consequence the wartime accumulations of specie were drained out of the country, consumer indebtedness to importing merchants was multiplied, and a postwar depression lasting from 1784 to 1787 was made worse than it might otherwise have been. The depression, with its money scarcity, bore heavily upon debtors both public and private, complicating the financial problems of many

citizens and of the Confederation and state governments.

The Confederation government had canceled most of its war debt to Americans by repudiating hundreds of millions of dollars in Continental currency. Yet it still owed a domestic debt estimated at about $34 million in 1783, and through continued borrowings from abroad, mostly from the Netherlands, its foreign debt increased to more than $10 million by 1788. During the 1780's Congress received a sizeable annual income, though a fluctuating and inadequate one, chiefly from the proceeds of foreign loans and from requisitions upon the states. Promptly making interest payments on these loans, Congress maintained an excellent credit rating with Dutch and other foreign bankers, but could not keep up with its domestic obligations and lost credit at home. At a fraction of the face value, shrewd speculators bought up Confederation certificates of indebtedness from former Revolutionary soldiers and others who despaired of payment from Congress and who needed ready cash.

The states, too, came out of the war with large debts, and one by one they added to their obligations by taking over parts of the Confederation debt owed to their respective citizens. Taxable resources varied a good deal from state to state. The chief reliance everywhere was upon the direct tax on land and its improvements, income taxes then being unthought of. The states supplemented their revenues by means of customs duties and harbor fees, though these tariff and navigation laws served also to protect the states' manufacturers and shippers from foreign competition. To some extent the tariffs interfered with trade between states, but with a few exceptions they were designed to limit importations of foreign and not American goods. Actually there were fewer barriers to interstate trade in the 1780's than there are today.

Suffering seriously from the postwar deflation and from the tax burden upon their land, the debtor farmers of the country demanded relief in the form of paper money, and seven of the states responded by issuing such currency. Of these seven, Rhode Island went to the greatest extremes, not only designating its paper as legal tender but compelling creditors to accept it or lose the right to collect their debts. While creditors fled from debtors eager to pay in Rhode Island currency, the highest court of the state, in the case of *Trevett* v. *Weeden* (1786), held that the monetary legislation was unconstitutional, and the legislature summoned the judges before it and censured them for their action.

The other six states refused to yield to the advocates of inflation and pursued policies of unrelieved taxation to support their public debts. To the state creditors—that is, the bondholders—all this was sound and honest public finance. But it seemed like robbery and tyranny to many of the poverty-stricken farmers, especially in New England, who felt that money was being extorted from them to swell the riches of the wealthy bondholders in Boston and other towns. At a time when cash was not to be had, these farmers were called upon to pay in specie not only state tax collectors but also mortgage holders and other private creditors. When debtors failed to pay they found their mortgages foreclosed and their property seized, and sometimes they found themselves in jail.

Mobs of distressed farmers rioted in various parts of New England but caused the most serious trouble in Massachusetts. There the malcontents of the Connecticut Valley and the Berkshire Hills, many of them Revolutionary veterans, found a leader in Daniel Shays, himself a former captain in the Continental army. Organizing and drilling his followers, Shays put forth a program of demands including paper money, tax relief, a

moratorium on debts, the removal of the state capital from Boston to the interior, and the abolition of imprisonment for debt. During the summer of 1786 the Shaysites concentrated upon the immediate task of preventing the collection of debts, private or public, and went in armed bands from place to place to break up court sittings and sheriff's sales. In Boston, members of the legislature, including Samuel Adams, denounced Shays and his men as rebels and traitors. When winter came these rebels, instead of laying down their arms, advanced upon Springfield to get more of them from the arsenal there. From Boston approached an army of state militiamen financed by a loan from wealthy merchants who feared a new revolution. In January, 1787, this army met the ragged troops of Shays, killed several of them, captured many more, and scattered the rest to the hills in a blinding snowstorm.

As a military enterprise, Shays's Rebellion was a fiasco, yet it had important consequences for the future of the United States. In Massachusetts it resulted in a few immediate gains for the discontented groups. Shays and his lieutenants, at first sentenced to death, were soon pardoned, and some concessions to his earlier demands were granted in the way of tax relief and the postponement of debt payments. Far more significant, the rebellion also affected the country as a whole by giving added urgency to the movement for a new Constitution.

A New Government Needed?

Before 1787 the Confederation government, for all its unfinished business, was already a going and a growing concern. Though it did not rest directly upon the people, it supported and was supported by a bureaucracy of reasonably faithful employees. Though it lacked sufficient immediate revenues, it possessed a resource in the public lands, which, once sales were well under way, could be expected to provide a plentiful independent income. Though it had no judicial system of its own, the state courts served well enough for most purposes, and the states settled disputes among themselves either through arbitration under the auspices of Congress or through the deliberations of interstate commissioners. Though it had no single, separately elected executive, the Confederation administered its laws through departments with secretaries responsible to Congress. If the procedures had been left to go on developing, with only a few amendments, most likely the secretaries in time would have formed a cabinet with one of their number functioning as a sort of prime minister—so that today the United States would have a modified parliamentary system of government.

True, the government under the Articles of Confederation was "weak," and deliberately so. Having just fought a war to avert the danger of remote and tyrannical authority, many Americans desired to keep the centers of political power close to the people in the thirteen states. Others, however, either disliked the Confederation plan from the outset or came eventually to desire something different. Disgruntled at the refusal of Congress to grant them half pay for life, some of the military men through their exclusive and hereditary Society of the Cincinnati hoped to control and to invigorate the government, some of them even aspiring to a kind of army dictatorship. Artisans or "mechanics," the manufacturers of the time, preferred a uniformly high national tariff to the varying state tariffs. Merchants and shippers preferred a single and effective commercial policy to thirteen different and ineffective ones. Land speculators wished to see the Indian menace finally removed from their Western tracts, and creditors desired to stop the state issues of paper money. Investors in Confederation securities hoped to have the Confederation debt made good and the value of their securities enhanced. Large property owners in general looked for a reliable means of safety from the threat of mobs.

So, during the 1780's, the country was divided between the proponents of a new, more highly centralized government and the friends of the existing loose Confederation. Some of these state-rights men were opposed to change because they did not wish to lose the authority and prestige they enjoyed in the existing state governments. Such men preferred local and individual liberties to centralization. On the other hand, the advocates of a new central government valued national freedom and efficiency more than individual or local liberties.

The issue was not whether the Confederation should be changed but how drastic the changes should be. Even its defenders came reluctantly to agree that the government needed strengthening at its weakest point, its lack of power to tax. To save the Articles of Confederation, its friends backed the impost amendment of 1783, which would have authorized Congress to levy customs duties, and all the states ratified the amendment except Rhode Island, whose single veto was of course enough to kill it. Later the state-rights advocates proposed that the states make to Congress a temporary and qualified grant of taxing authority (not an amendment to the Articles), but most of the centralizers had begun to lose interest in such remedies. These critics no longer wanted the Confederation to succeed: they hoped it would fail, so that they could get the country behind them in seeking a thorough change.

The most resourceful of them was the political genius, New York lawyer, one-time military aide to General Washington, and illegitimate son of a Scottish merchant in the West Indies—Alexander Hamilton. From the beginning he had been dissatisfied with

the Articles of Confederation, had seen little to be gained by piecemeal amendments,
and had urged the holding of a national
convention to overhaul the entire document.
To achieve his aim he took advantage of a
movement for interstate cooperation which
began in 1785 when a group of Marylanders
and Virginians met in Alexandria to settle
differences between their two states over the
use of the Potomac River and the Chesapeake Bay. As the owner of thousands of
acres beyond the mountains, Washington
was much interested in the development of
the upper Potomac as a waterway, and he
invited the conferees to his home at Mount
Vernon. There they decided to invite the
other states to send delegates to a larger
conference on commercial questions to
meet at Annapolis in 1786. Hamilton was
present at the Annapolis meeting as a delegate from New York, and he found the
turnout disappointing, for only five of the
states were represented. Yet he took satisfaction in seeing the conference adopt his
report and send copies to the state legislatures and to Congress. His report forcefully
criticized the Articles of Confederation and
recommended that Congress call a convention of special delegates from all the states
to foregather in Philadelphia the next year
and consider ways to "render the constitution of the federal government adequate to
the exigencies of the union."

At the moment, in 1786, there seemed little possibility that the Philadelphia convention would be any better attended or would
accomplish any more than the previous
meeting at Annapolis. The leadership of
Washington would be essential for success,
and Washington appeared to be well satisfied with the condition of the country as it
was. He wrote privately that, despite the
states' refusal to grant Congress the power
to tax, the "internal governments" were
"daily acquiring strength," the laws were
well enforced and crime was rare, the peo-

ple were more industrious than ever, the
"ravages of war" were already repaired,
and the "foundations of a great empire"
were firmly laid. One of the wealthiest men
in the country, but temporarily short of
cash, Washington doubted whether he
would undertake the trouble and expense
of a trip to Philadelphia.

Then, early in 1787, the news of commotion and bloodshed in Massachusetts spread
throughout the country and the world, news
which seemed to foretell other and more
dangerous insurrections than that of Shays.
In Paris the American minister, Thomas Jefferson, was not alarmed. "I hold," he con-
fided in a letter to his Virginia friend James
Madison, "that a little rebellion, now and
then, is a good thing, and as necessary in the
political world as storms in the physical."
At Mount Vernon, however, Washington
did not take the news so calmly. "There
are combustibles in every State which a
spark might set fire to," he exclaimed. "I
feel infinitely more than I can express for
the disorders which have arisen. Good
God!" Washington refused to listen to renewed suggestions that he make himself a
military dictator, but after Congress had issued its call for a constitutional convention
he borrowed money for the journey and, in
May, left Mount Vernon for Philadelphia.

The Constitutional Convention

Fifty-five men, representing all the states except Rhode Island, attended one or more
sessions of the convention which from May
to September, 1787, sat in the Philadelphia
State House. Never before or since has there
been a more distinguished gathering in
America. These "Founding Fathers," instead
of being graybearded ancients as the term
implies, were on the whole relatively young
men, many of them in their twenties and
thirties and only one (Benjamin Franklin)
extremely old; his 81 years raised the average age from 43 to 44. Despite their com-

parative youth, the delegates were men of vast practical experience in business, plantation management, and politics, and they were well educated for their time, more the Revolutionary leaders—for example, Patrick Henry, Thomas Paine, and Thomas Jefferson—were conspicuously absent from the constitutional convention.

The Philadelphia State House (Independence Hall). *Here, in the building at the right, the Second Continental Congress held its meetings, and here the Declaration of Independence was signed. Here also the constitutional convention met, in 1787. This view, from an engraving made in the 1790's, shows the Chestnut Street approach. Construction of the State House was begun in 1732. The near-by building, with the cupola, is the City Hall, which was built between 1789 and 1792. This building housed the United States Supreme Court during the 1790's, while Philadelphia was the national capital. Note the stone-paved street and sidewalk and the pump (between the sidewalk and the State House).*

than a third of them being college graduates. Practically all of them represented, both directly and indirectly, the great property interests of the country. Most of the delegates desired a strong government and feared what one of them called the "turbulence and follies" of democracy. Certain of

At the outset the nationalist or strong-government majority, better prepared than the state-rights minority, took the initiative. One of the majority members nominated Washington to preside and easily secured his election. Another introduced and carried a motion that the proceedings be absolutely secret. And Edmund Randolph, of the Virginia delegation, proposed a resolution, passed by the convention, that "a *national* government ought to be estab-

But the call of Congress and the commissions from the states to their "deputies" in Philadelphia had authorized only a *revision* of the Articles, and some delegates now

---

The Virginia Plan
1787

The following branches of government were recommended in the Virginia Plan:

    1. A "National Legislature," with the states represented in proportion either to their "quotas of contribution" or to "the number of free inhabitants." Two branches, the members of the first to be elected by the people, the members of the second to be nominated by the state legislatures and elected by the first. Powers: to "legislate in all cases to which the separate states are incompetent," to "negative all laws passed by the several states, contravening in the opinion of the National Legislature the articles of Union," and to use force against recalcitrant states.

    2. A single "National Executive" to be chosen by the National Legislature.

    3. A "National Judiciary" to be chosen by the National Legislature.

    4. A "Council of Revision," consisting of the National Executive and part of the National Judiciary, with power to "examine" and reject state and national laws before they went into effect.

---

lished, consisting of a *supreme* Legislative, Executive and Judiciary." Then Randolph submitted a plan for such a government, a plan the Virginians already had worked out. This scheme embraced a "National Legislature" with two branches, the first to be elected by the people of the states and the second to be elected by the first; a "National Executive" to be chosen by the legislature; and a "National Judiciary" to be chosen likewise and to form, together with the executive and members of the legislature, a "Council of Revision" with power to review legislative acts and void them. To proceed along these lines would be to abandon the Articles of Confederation and build the government anew.

raised doubts whether the convention properly could entertain such proposals as were embodied in the Virginia plan. A debate went on for weeks, with the state-rights men compelled to take the negative, since they had not been ready with a plan of their own. Finally William Paterson of New Jersey introduced an alternative scheme which left "the United States in Congress" as the nucleus of the government, as in the existing Articles, but gave Congress the power to pass acts for raising revenue and regulating trade, and added a "federal Executive" (not a "national" one) to be elected by Congress and a "federal Judiciary" to be chosen by the executive.

Along with other nationalists, Hamilton

denounced Paterson's plan, but unlike most of them he was not satisfied with Randolph's either. He explained that, personally, he would like to see the state governments "extinguished" entirely, or at least reduced to the status of mere administrative units, and a single "General Government" substituted for them. Expatiating upon the beauties of the British Constitution, he urged his fellow delegates to imitate it as closely as, in the circumstances, they could. Not that the United States should have a King and a House of Lords but, according to him, it should have a lifetime "elective monarch" and Senators that also would hold office for life. He submitted a sketch of his ideas—not, he said, as a substitute for the Randolph plan but as a proposal for amendments to it. Hamilton's suggestions did not affect the actual shaping of the Constitution, nor did they help to break the deadlock which, after

plished. If this should happen, the men at Philadelphia would "become a reproach and by-word down to future ages," said the venerable Franklin, the voice of calmness and conciliation throughout the summer. "And what is worse, mankind may hereafter, from this unfortunate instance, despair of establishing governments by human wisdom, and leave it to chance, war and conquest." Franklin moved that the convention thereafter open its daily sessions with prayer, and though Hamilton objected, the motion was carried without a vote.

Through the calming influence of Franklin and others, especially Oliver Ellsworth of Connecticut, the delegates managed to compromise the most serious of their differences and go on with their work. To the men from the small states, the worst feature of the Virginia plan was its system of representation in the proposed two-house legisla-

---

The New Jersey Plan

1787

The main features of the New Jersey Plan were:

1. The continuance of the existing one-house Congress, with one vote for each state, but with the following additional powers: to raise a revenue from import duties, stamp taxes, and postage; to regulate interstate and foreign commerce; and to provide for the collection of taxes within any state failing to pay its share of the requisitions upon the states.

2. A plural "Federal Executive" to be elected by Congress.

3. A "Federal Judiciary" to be appointed by the Executive.

4. The establishment of acts of Congress and federal treaties as the "supreme law" of the states, and the authorization of the Federal Executive to "call forth the power of the Confederated States . . . to enforce and compel an obedience."

---

a month of bickering, had arisen in the convention.

By the end of June the convention seemed in danger of dissolving, with nothing accom-

ture. In the lower house, which was to be popularly elected, the states were to be represented in proportion to their population, and thus the largest would have several

times as many representatives as the smallest. In the upper house, which was to be
elected by the lower, some of the smaller
states at any given time might have no representatives at all! To the small-state delegates the Congress of the Articles of Confederation, as well as the Congress of the
New Jersey plan, at least had the merit of
equal representation for all the states, regardless of size. These delegates were ap-
peased when Ellsworth proposed and the
convention accepted the "Connecticut Compromise" or "Great Compromise," by which
the states were to be represented in the
House of Representatives proportionately
to their populations and in the Senate (to be
elected by the state legislatures) equally,
with two Senators apiece.

After the settlement of the issue between
large and small states, there remained troublesome differences between the North and
the South. Northerners thought the new
Congress should have power to impose tariffs and regulate trade. They also thought
that slaves, most numerous of course in the
Southern states, should be counted in determining a state's share of direct taxes (to be
levied on the state in proportion to its population) but not in determining its representation in the House. Southerners, on the
other hand, believed that slaves should be
included in computing representation but
not direct taxation. Southerners also feared
that Congress might impose export duties
on their crops, interfere with the slave trade,
and agree to commercial treaties (like the
one recently signed between Jay and Gardoqui) which would sacrifice the interests of
the South to those of the North.

Eventually the sectional differences were
adjusted by means of several constitutional
provisions. According to an arbitrary but
satisfying formula, three fifths of the slaves
were to be counted in the apportionment of
both representatives and direct taxes among
the states. By other provisions Congress was

permitted to regulate commerce but not to
levy export duties nor, for twenty years, to
prohibit the importation of slaves. And the
executive was allowed to make treaties, including treaties of commerce, but these
were to require the approval of a two-thirds
majority rather than a simple majority of
the Senate, and hence the South could exercise a veto over them.

The Constitution as it finally took form
at the end of summer in 1787, with James
Madison responsible for most of the actual
drafting, was an outgrowth of the Virginia
plan, though incorporating a few significant
features from the New Jersey plan and the
Articles of Confederation. The Constitution outlined an original and ingenious form
of government, derived from diverse forms
ancient and contemporary but copying
none of them. Though both federal and national, the proposed government was to be
more national than federal. The Constitution and all laws and treaties made under it
were to be the "supreme law" of the land,
regardless of anything in the constitution or
laws of any state to the contrary. Broad
powers were granted to the central government, including the congressional powers of
taxation, regulation of commerce, control
of money, and the passage of laws "necessary and proper" for carrying out its specific powers. Within the allotted sphere of
its powers, the new government was authorized to act directly upon the people of the
United States. At the same time the individual states were deprived of a number of
the powers—such as the issuance of money
and the passage of laws "impairing the obligation of contracts," that is, debtor stay
laws and the like—which the states had been
free to exercise under the Articles of Confederation. And nowhere in the Constitution as written in 1787 were the former
claims of the states to individual sovereignty
recognized.

The Constitution was designed to prevent

any single group from gaining absolute and unchecked power. This was the purpose of the separation of powers and the checks and balances set up among the legislative, executive, and judicial branches of the new government. The government was deliberately divided against itself so as to frustrate tyranny from whatever source. When the Founding Fathers spoke of tyranny, they usually had in mind the rule of mobs and demagogues. Under the Constitution an aspiring dictator with the populace behind him might gain influence in the House of Representatives, the only part of the government directly responsible to the voters, but he could get no laws enacted without the consent of the Senate and the signature of the President. The Senate was one step and the Presidency two steps removed from demagogic influence, or so the makers of the Constitution intended. The Senators were to be elected not by the people but by the state legislatures, and the President was to be chosen by special electors who were to be appointed in whatever manner the separate legislatures might designate. Even assuming the unlikely event that a powerful faction of malcontents should get control of the Presidency and both houses of Congress, the friends of the *status quo* could still rely upon the Supreme Court, which was one step further removed from the voters, since the President with the consent of the Senate was to appoint the judges for life. And some members of the Constitutional Convention assumed that the Supreme Court would in practice veto laws it deemed unconstitutional. These men did not insist on saying so in the Constitution itself, since strong objections had arisen in the convention against anything like a "council of revision" as proposed at first in the Virginia plan.

In respect to judicial review and in other respects the Constitution doubtless would have been less ambiguous if the nationalists

in the convention had not been obliged to consider the feelings of the state-rights element at the Philadelphia convention and in the country at large. None of the delegates was quite satisfied with the completed Constitution, such a patchwork of compromises had it become, and several including Randolph himself refused to sign it, while Hamilton and thirty-eight others signed. Since the delegates had exceeded their instructions from Congress and the states, they had reason to doubt whether the Constitution would ever be ratified if they followed the procedures laid down in the Articles of Confederation, which required the state *legislatures,* and *all* of them, to approve alterations in the form of the government. So the convention changed the rules, specifying in the Constitution that the new government should go into effect among the ratifying states when only *nine* of the thirteen had ratified, and recommending to Congress that the Constitution be submitted to specially called state *conventions* rather than to the legislatures of the states.

Ratification: "Federalists" v. "Antifederalists"

The Congress in New York, completely overshadowed by the convention in Philadelphia, accepted the latter's work and submitted it to the states for their approval or disapproval. The state legislatures, again with the exception of Rhode Island, arranged for the election of delegates to ratifying conventions, and sooner or later each of these conventions got down to business. Meanwhile, from the fall of 1787 to the summer of 1788, the merits and demerits of the new Constitution were debated in the legislatures, in mass meetings, and in the columns of newspapers, as well as in the convention halls. For the most part the struggle, though intense, was peaceful and deliberative, yet the opposing factions sometimes came to blows, and death and injury resulted in at least one place (Albany, New York).

Despite the reference of its preamble to "We the people," the Constitution was not

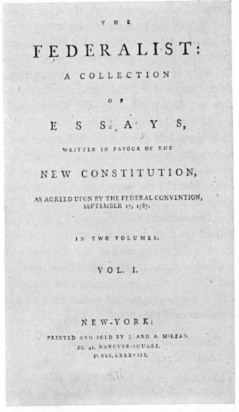

THE

FEDERALIST:

A COLLECTION

O F

E S S A Y S,

WRITTEN IN FAVOUR OF THE

NEW CONSTITUTION,

AS AGREED UPON BY THE FEDERAL CONVENTION,
SEPTEMBER 17, 1787.

IN TWO VOLUMES.

VOL. I.

NEW-YORK:

PRINTED AND SOLD BY J. AND A. M'LEAN,
No. 41, HANOVER-SQUARE.
M.DCC.LXXXVIII.

The Federalist: Title Page. *From October, 1787, to April, 1788, a series of seventy-eight articles appeared in the New York* Independent Journal *under the pen name "Publius" (at first it was "A Citizen of New York"). Defending the new Constitution against the criticisms of Antifederalists like George Clinton and Robert Yates, the essays argued cogently for prompt ratification. The articles were published in book form, May 28, 1788, with the title* The Federalist. *From June to August, 1788, there appeared seven more newspaper essays by "Publius," bringing the total to eighty-five. Most of these were written by Alexander Hamilton, and the rest by James Madison and John Jay.*

in literal fact ordained and established by the whole people of the United States. As is shown by the elections for the state conventions, something like three fourths of the adult white males in the country as a whole failed to vote for delegates, mainly because of indifference, and therefore exercised no real influence upon the outcome. Of those who did vote, a large majority favored ratification. The voters, however, did not have a clear-cut choice between a "federal" and a "national" government. The issues were confused by the terminology which was employed. Since the idea of a strongly national government was thought to be unpopular, the advocates of the new Constitution (which was strongly national as written in 1787) chose to call themselves "Federalists" and to call their opponents "Antifederalists." These misnomers stuck, despite the insistence of opponents of ratification that they were "Federal Republicans," the true federalists of the time.

In the contest over ratification the so-called Federalists who favored the Constitution had a number of advantages. They possessed a positive program and an appealing name, while the so-called Antifederalists by that very word were made to stand for nothing constructive, for chaos itself. The Federalists were the better organized group and had the weight of fame and superior leadership on their side. They could point to the support of the two most eminent men in America, Franklin and Washington. And Washington himself declared that the choice lay between the Constitution and disunion. The Federalists included also some of the most profound political philosophers of any period or place in Hamilton, Madison, and Jay, who under the joint pseudonym "Publius" wrote a long series of newspaper essays expounding the meaning and virtues of the Constitution. Afterwards published in book form as *The Federalist*, these papers have been considered as the most authoritative of all constitutional commentaries and, indeed, as one of the greatest of all treatises on political science.

The opponents of ratification produced

no comparable set of Antifederalist papers, yet these men too were able and sincere and they made a vigorous case for themselves in their own speeches and newspaper propaganda. Among the outstanding Antifederalists were George Clinton, governor of New York and bitter foe of Hamilton; Luther Martin of Maryland, one of the most powerful as well as wordy lawyers in the entire country; and the redoubtable and eloquent Patrick Henry. In the nature of the case the Antifederalists necessarily resorted mainly to negative argument. The Constitution, they protested, was illegal—as indeed it was if judged by the Articles of Confederation, put an end to individual liberty, the Antifederalists added. Of all their specific criticisms the most compelling was this: the Constitution lacked a bill of rights.

For all the efforts of the Antifederalists, ratification proceeded apace during the winter of 1787–1788. Delaware, the first to act, did so unanimously, as also did two others of the smallest states, New Jersey and Georgia. In the large states of Pennsylvania and Massachusetts the Antifederalists put up a determined struggle but lost in the final vote. By June of 1788, when the New Hampshire convention at last made up its mind, nine of the states had ratified and thus

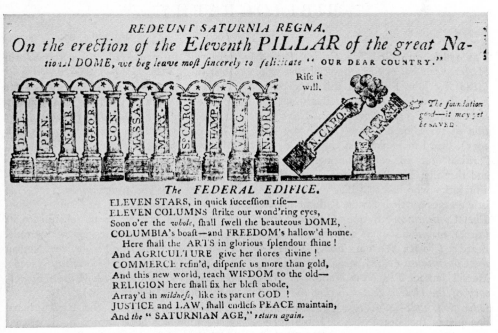

A Federalist Cartoon. *The* Massachusetts Centinel *of Boston, in its issue for August 2, 1788, thus commented on New York's ratification of the new Constitution. Only two of the thirteen states have yet to ratify. A hand is shown lifting the North Carolina "pillar" into place, and the optimistic caption says, "Rise it will." The Rhode Island pillar is broken, but "The foundation [is] good—it may yet be SAVED."* (COURTESY OF THE NEW-YORK HISTORICAL SOCIETY, NEW YORK CITY)

the existing fundamental law. The new government would increase taxes, obliterate the states, wield dictatorial powers, favor the "well-born" over the common people, and had made it possible for the Constitution to go into effect among themselves. A new government could hardly hope to succeed, however, without the participation of Virginia and New York, whose conventions remained closely divided. Before the end of the month Virginia and then New York consented to the Constitution by rather narrow votes. The New York convention yielded to expediency, even some of the most staunchly Antifederalist delegates fearing that the state's commercial interests would suffer if, once the other states had got together under the "New Roof," New York were to remain outside. Massachusetts,

Virginia, and New York all ratified on the assumption, though not on the express condition, that certain desired amendments would be added to the Constitution, above all a bill of rights. Deciding to wait and see what became of these hopes for amendment, the North Carolina convention adjourned without taking action. Rhode Island, for the time being, did not even call a convention to consider ratification.

-»>-»>-»>-»>«-«<-«<-«<

BIBLIOGRAPHY

THE 1780's are called *The Critical Period of American History* in a book of that title (1888) by John Fiske, but this conception is challenged by Charles A. Beard in *An Economic Interpretation of the Constitution of the United States* (1913; new ed., 1935). Beard maintains that the period was "critical" only for certain business interests, and that the Constitution was the work of a minority who had selfish as well as idealistic reasons for their action. R. L. Schuyler, *The Constitution of the United States* (1923), elaborates upon a thesis similar to Beard's. Charles Warren, *The Making of the Constitution* (1928), strongly disagrees. Merrill Jensen, *The New Nation: A History of the United States during the Confederation, 1781–1789* (1950), fills out and documents the Beard thesis. Jensen contends, moreover, that the so-called "Federalists" were really nationalists, and that the "Antifederalists" were the true federalists of the time. R. E. Brown, *Charles Beard and the Constitution* (1956), undertakes to traverse the Beard thesis point by point.

Carl Van Doren, *The Great Rehearsal* (1948), gives a straightforward account of the making and adoption of the Constitution and implies that the American experience of the 1780's was, or could be, a "great

rehearsal" for world federation after World War II.

The constitutional thought of one of the foremost Founding Fathers is succinctly analyzed in E. M. Burns's *James Madison: Philosopher of the Constitution* (1938). Madison's career is meticulously recounted in Irving Brant's *James Madison: The Nationalist, 1780–1787* (1948) and *James Madison: Father of the Constitution, 1787–1800* (1950), two volumes of an extensive biography which undertakes to rehabilitate its subject as a leading statesman of his time. On another Founding Father, see Nathan Schachner's *Alexander Hamilton* (1946). See also C. P. Smith's *James Wilson: Founding Father, 1742–1798* (1956).

The inside story of the constitutional convention was little known to Americans until the publication of Madison's notes in 1840, now available in *James Madison's Journal of the Federal Convention* (1893), edited by E. H. Scott. A comprehensive edition of Madison's notes and other original sources is *Records of the Federal Constitution* (4 vols., 1911–1937), edited by Max Farrand. Another original source is *The Federalist*, available in many editions.

There is no readily available collection of Antifederalist papers comparable to *The*

Federalist. There are, however, several good biographies of Antifederalist leaders, among them E. W. Spaulding's *His Excellency George Clinton: Critic of the Constitution* (1939) and Helen Hill's *George Mason: Constitutionalist* (1938).

Some problems of the Confederation government and phases of life in the 1780's are made clear in the following: R. A. East, *Business Enterprise in the American Revolutionary Era* (1938); B. W. Bond, Jr., *The Civilization of the Old Northwest* (1938); A. P. Whitaker, *The Spanish-American Frontier, 1783–1795* (1927); and M. L. Starkey, *A Little Rebellion* (1955), which brings Daniel Shays and his followers convincingly to life.

CHAPTER 9

Beginnings Under the Constitution

UPON THE MEN elected to the new government, who took office in 1789, fell the tasks of breathing life into the Constitution, filling in some of the gaps in the document, and solving the problems of diplomacy, the frontier, and public finance that the old government of the Confederation scarcely had begun to deal with. The new government had certain fortuitous advantages over the old one, since conditions both at home and abroad were more favorable to its success. At home the nearly 4,000,000 people, having recovered from the postwar depression, were on the whole extremely prosperous. Abroad there were disturbances—with the beginning of the French Revolution and then the outbreak of a European war—that contributed to the security as well as the prosperity of the United States even though causing se-

rious difficulties for it. The American people differed among themselves on both domestic and foreign policies, and political parties soon arose to give expression to these differences. Yet, despite the rise of political opposition, the new government got off to a remarkably good start. The Constitution was made a going concern, the public credit placed upon a sound basis, the frontier areas were attached firmly to the Union, and the dangers from Great Britain and Spain were considerably reduced.

Elaborating upon the Constitution

When the first elections under the Constitution were held, in the early months of 1789, the results showed that the new government was to be in the hands of its friends. Few if any of the newly elected congressmen and Senators had been extreme Antifederalists; almost all had favored ratification, and many had served as delegates to the Philadelphia convention. The President-elect, George Washington, had presided at

For the time being the seat of government was to continue to be the city of New York, and thus the sensibilities of the geographical sections were neatly balanced, the President

Federal Hall, New York. *Here George Washington was inaugurated as President on April 30, 1789, taking his oath of office on the balcony that overlooks Wall Street. The building was originally constructed as the City Hall in 1699–1700. It was extensively remodeled and enlarged after the Revolution, and was renamed Federal Hall when it served as the temporary capitol of the United States, in 1789–1790. At the end of Wall Street is the Gothic-styled Trinity Church (Anglican). It was built in 1688, destroyed in a great fire following the British occupation of the city in 1776, and rebuilt in 1788. Behind the church was a meadow sloping down to the Hudson River.*

the convention; many who had favored ratification did so because they expected him to preside over the new government also. He received the votes of all the presidential electors whom the states, either by legislative action or by popular election, had named. John Adams, a firm Federalist though not a member of the convention, received the next highest number of electoral votes and hence was to be Vice President.

being from the South, the Vice President from New England, and the capital in the Middle States. Congressmen were so slow to reach New York that not until April was a quorum on hand to make an official count of the electoral vote and send a messenger to notify General Washington of his election. After a journey from Mount Vernon marked by elaborate celebrations along the way, Washington was inaugurated on April

30, taking the oath of office on a balcony of Federal Hall at Broad and Wall Streets, in full view of the cheering crowd below, then stepping back inside to read his inaugural

specific situations as they arose. It left many questions unanswered. What, for example, should be the rules of the two houses for the conduct of their business? What code

Washington's First Inauguration
1789

The temporary capitol of the new government was the City Hall in New York. Here George Washington was inaugurated as President on April 30, 1789. William Maclay, a diary-keeping Senator from Pennsylvania, recorded the ceremonies thus:

"The President was conducted out of the middle window into the gallery [overlooking Wall Street], and the oath was administered by the Chancellor [the highest judicial officer of the state of New York]. Notice that the business [was] done was communicated to the crowd by proclamation, etc., who gave three cheers, and repeated it on the President's bowing to them.

"As the company returned into the Senate chamber, the President took the chair and the Senators and Representatives their seats. He rose, and all arose also, and [he] addressed them. This great man was agitated and embarrassed more than ever he was by the leveled cannon or pointed musket. He trembled, and several times could scarce make out to read, though it must be supposed he had often read it before. . . . When he came to the words *all the world*, he made a flourish with his right hand, which left rather an ungainly impression. I sincerely, for my part, wished all set ceremony in the hands of the dancing-masters, and that this first of men had read off his address in the plainest manner, without ever taking his eyes from the paper, for I felt hurt that he was not first in everything. He was dressed in deep brown, with metal buttons, with an eagle on them, white stockings, a bag [for his back hair], and sword."

address to the assembled members of the House and the Senate. In his remarks he impressed upon his hearers the seriousness of the governmental experiment upon which they were embarking.

Indeed, the responsibilities facing the first President and the first Congress were in some ways greater than those facing any President or Congress to follow. Though these men of 1789 had the Constitution as a guide, that document provided only a general plan which had yet to be applied to

of etiquette should govern the relations between the President on the one hand and Congress and the people on the other? Should he have some high-sounding title, such as "His Highness the President of the United States and Protector of Their Liberties"? (John Adams, who would have been horrified at the thought of a later Vice President being called "The Veep," thought both he and the President ought to have dignified forms of address.) What was the true meaning of various ambiguous phrases in the Constitution? In answering these and other questions, Washington and his colleagues knew they were setting precedents that, in many cases, would give lasting direction to the development of the Constitution in actual practice.

By filling certain gaps in the Constitution, the first Congress served almost as a continuation of the constitutional convention itself. The work of the convention had been incomplete in various respects, especially in that it had omitted a bill of rights. Dozens of amendments, intended to make good this lack, had been proposed in the state ratifying conventions, and Congress now undertook the task of sorting these, reducing them to a manageable number, and sending them to the states for ratification. Of the twelve sent out, ten were ratified, and these took effect in 1791. The first nine of them were intended to guarantee to the people certain basic rights, such as freedom of religion, of speech, and of the press, immunity from arbitrary arrest, and trial by jury. The tenth amendment, reserving to the states all powers except those specifically withheld from them or delegated to the federal government, bolstered state rights and changed the emphasis of the Constitution from nationalism to federalism.

In regard to the structure of the federal courts, the Constitution had only this to say: "The judicial power of the United States shall be vested in one Supreme Court, and in such inferior courts as the Congress may from time to time ordain and establish." Thus the convention had left up to Congress the number of Supreme Court judges to be appointed and the kinds of lower courts to be organized. In the Judiciary Act of 1789 Congress provided for a Supreme Court of six members, one chief justice and five associate justices, for thirteen district courts with one judge apiece, and for three circuit courts, each to consist of one of the district judges sitting with two of the Su-

preme Court justices. In the same act Congress gave the Supreme Court the power to make the final decision in cases involving the constitutionality of state laws. If the Constitution was in fact to be the "supreme law of the land," the various state courts could not

Alexander Hamilton. *Hamilton was not a big man, physically. He stood about five feet, six inches. Yet he had an imposing and commanding presence. His dignity was enhanced by his handsome, clean-cut features and his piercing look. Something of his energy, will, and personal force is suggested in John Trumbull's portrait of him. Trumbull, born in Connecticut, served as a soldier in the Revolutionary War, studied under Benjamin West in London, and (in 1804) opened a studio in New York. His father, Jonathan Trumbull, governor of Connecticut during the Revolution, had been a friend and adviser of General Washington. The general called him "Brother Jonathan," and this became a nickname for New Englanders and then for the American people as a whole. Not till about 1850 did "Uncle Sam" replace "Brother Jonathan" as the popular symbol of the United States.* (COURTESY, MUSEUM OF FINE ARTS, BOSTON)

be left to decide for themselves whether the state legislatures were violating that supreme law.

As for executive departments, the Constitution referred indirectly to them but did not specify what or how many they should be. The first Congress created three such departments—State, Treasury, and War—

tary of State another Virginian, Thomas Jefferson, who had not opposed the Constitution though he had had nothing to do with its framing or adoption, having been away

---

Jefferson Characterizes Washington, 1814

"His mind was great and powerful, without being of the very first order; his penetration strong, though not so acute as that of a Newton, Bacon, or Locke; and as far as he saw, no judgment was ever sounder. It was slow in operation, being little aided by invention or imagination, but sure in conclusion. . . . He was incapable of fear, meeting personal dangers with the calmest unconcern. Perhaps the strongest feature in his character was prudence, never acting until every circumstance, every consideration, was maturely weighed; refraining if he saw a doubt, but, when once decided, going through with his purpose, whatever obstacles opposed. His integrity was most pure, his justice the most inflexible I have ever known, no motives of interest or consanguinity, of friendship or hatred, being able to bias his decision. . . . His time was employed in action chiefly, reading little . . . On the whole his character was, in its mass, perfect, in nothing bad, in few points indifferent . . ."

---

and also the offices of Attorney General and Postmaster General.

In appointing department heads and other high officials, President Washington determined to select men who were qualified by character and experience, who were well disposed toward the Constitution (no Antifederalists need apply), and who as a group would provide a balanced representation of the different sections of the country. To the office of Secretary of the Treasury he appointed Alexander Hamilton, of New York, who had taken the lead in the calling of the constitutional convention and who, though only thirty-two, was an expert in public finance. For Secretary of War he chose the Massachusetts Federalist, General Henry Knox. As Attorney General he named Edmund Randolph, of Virginia, author of the plan upon which the Constitution had been based. He picked as his Secre-

from the country as minister to France.

From time to time Washington called upon these four men for advice, usually as individuals. They did not form a cabinet in the sense of a group of presidential counselors holding regular meetings (the cabinet in this sense began to develop during the Presidency of Jefferson). When Washington took office he supposed, as did many others, that the Senate would act for certain purposes as an advisory council, since according to the Constitution the Senate was to give its advice and consent for the appointment of high officials and for the ratification of treaties. With only 22 members in the beginning, the Senate was small enough so that Washington could expect to consult personally with it. He changed his mind, however, after taking a treaty draft to the Senators for their advice. They demanded that he leave the document for them to inspect and change at their leisure, and he refused, resolving never again to submit a treaty to the Senators until it had been completed and signed. Thus he set a precedent in treaty-making which for the most part his successors have followed.

As President, Washington thought it was his duty to see that the laws of Congress, if constitutional, were faithfully carried out. A man of strong will, he was the master of his own administration, but he did not conceive of himself as a popular leader (as did, for example, Andrew Jackson and Franklin D. Roosevelt in after years) who should find out the will of the people and then see that Congress enacted it into law. One of his department heads, Secretary of the Treasury Hamilton, undertook to provide the legislative leadership which Washington himself did not. According to the act creating the Treasury Department, its head was to report directly to Congress. Hence Hamilton concluded that his position gave him a special relationship with the law-making body, that his position made him, indeed, a kind of prime minister. Though his conception of the Treasury Secretary's role did not establish an enduring precedent, Hamilton exerted a greater positive influence than anyone else upon both domestic and foreign policies during Washington's Presidency, continuing to be influential even after his resignation in 1794.

Hamilton's Economic Planning

Of all the leading men of his time, Hamilton was one of the most aristocratic in his personal tastes and in his political philosophy. He distrusted the common people. An admirer of the British political system, with its rule by King and upper classes, he wished to adapt its principles as closely as he could to government in the United States. What the country most needed, he thought, was order and stability; the people already had enough liberty, indeed too much of it. He

thought the new government could be strengthened and made to succeed if the support of the wealthy men of the country could be brought to it. And, believing that all men were motivated by self-interest, he assumed that the way to gain the support of the wealthy was to give them a stake in the success of the new government. He therefore planned a program of financial legislation which, among other things, was intended to cause the propertied classes to look to the federal government for profitable investments and for the protection and promotion of their property interests.

If men of means were to have faith in the government, then it must keep faith with them by making good its debts and establishing its credit on a sound basis. So, first of all, Hamilton proposed that the existing public debt be "funded," or in other words that the miscellaneous, uncertain, depreciated certificates of indebtedness, which the old Congress had issued during and since the Revolution, be called in and exchanged for uniform, interest-bearing bonds, payable at definite dates. Next he recommended that the Revolutionary state debts be "assumed" or taken over by the United States, his object being to cause the state as well as the federal bondholders to look to the central government for eventual payment. His plan was not to pay off and thus eliminate the debt, either state or federal, but just the opposite: to create a large and permanent public debt, new bonds being issued as old ones were paid off. He believed, and rightly, that such a permanent debt would not only attach the government's creditors to the new government but would also stimulate business enterprise by making bonds available as liquid capital, that is, as safe and easily negotiable forms of property for the investment of businessmen's surplus funds.

Besides arranging for the funding of the federal debt and the assumption of the state debts, Hamilton also planned the establishment of a national bank. At the time, there were only a few banks in the country, located in Boston, Philadelphia, and New York. A new, national bank would serve several purposes. It would aid business by providing loans and also currency—in the form of banknotes, which in those days were used instead of checks. It would aid the government by making available a safe place for the deposit of federal funds, by facilitating the collection of taxes and the disbursement of the government's expenditures, and by keeping up the price of government bonds through judicious bond purchases. The kind of institution that Hamilton had in mind was to be "national" in the sense that it was to be chartered by the federal government, was to have a monopoly of the government's own banking business, and was to be government-controlled to some degree, one fifth of the directors being appointed by the government.

The funding and assumption of the debts, together with the payment of regular interest on them, would cost a great deal of money, and so Hamilton had to find adequate sources of revenue. He thought the government should depend mainly upon two kinds of taxes (in addition to the receipts to be anticipated from the sales of public land). One of these was an excise to be paid by distillers of alcoholic liquors. This tax would fall to some extent upon the rum manufacturers of New England seaports, but the rum industry was declining, and the tax would hit most heavily the whiskey distillers of the back country, especially in Pennsylvania, Virginia, and North Carolina. These distillers were not big businessmen; they were small farmers who converted part of their corn and rye crop into whiskey, so as to have a concentrated and valuable product that they could conveniently take to market by horseback or muleback over poor mountain roads.

Hamilton knew perfectly well what the incidence of the excise tax would be, and he deliberately intended for it to fall upon the frontier farmers, so that they would feel and know the power of the new government.

The other tax upon which Hamilton relied was the tax on imports, that is, the tariff. Such a tax would serve not only to raise a revenue, but also to protect and encourage American manufactures by raising the price of competing manufactured goods brought in from abroad. In the old Articles of Confederation, according to its defenders as well as its critics, the worst defect had been Congress's lack of power to levy customs duties. One of the first acts of the new Congress, in 1789, was the passage of a tariff law designed to foster industries while raising a revenue, but the average level of duties under this law was extremely low. Hamilton advocated a higher and more decidedly protective tariff. In his Report on Manufactures he glowingly set forth the advantages, as he saw them, of stimulating the growth of industry in the United States. Factories, he said, would make the nation more nearly self-sufficient in wartime, would increase prosperity by creating a home market for the produce of the farms, and would make possible the fuller utilization of all kinds of labor, including the labor of women and children, even those (to quote Hamilton himself) of "tender years."

Between 1789 and 1792 Hamilton succeeded in persuading Congress to pass the necessary laws for erecting his financial system—but only after a bitter struggle with a rising opposition group.

As for the funding of the public debt, very few of the congressmen objected to the plan itself, for they agreed with Hamilton that the government must make its credit good. Many of them disagreed, however, with his proposal to fund the debt *at par*, that is, to exchange new bonds for old certificates of indebtedness on a dollar-for-dollar basis. These old certificates, as has been seen, originally had been issued to merchants and farmers in payment for war

Hamilton insisted that such a plan was impracticable and that the honor of the government required a literal fulfillment of its earlier promises to pay. Congress finally

---

Constitutionality of the Bank: Hamilton

"It is conceded that *implied powers* are to be considered as delegated equally with *express ones*. Then it follows, that as a power of erecting a corporation may as well be *implied* as any other thing, it may as well be employed as an *instrument* or *mean* of carrying into execution any of the specified powers, as any other *instrument* or *mean* whatever. . . .

"It is objected that none but necessary and proper means are to be employed; and the Secretary of State maintains that no means are to be considered as *necessary* but those without which the grant of the power would be *nugatory*. . . .

"It is certain that neither the grammatical nor popular sense of the term requires that construction. According to both, *necessary* often means no more than *needful, requisite, incidental, useful,* or *conducive to.* . . .

"If the *end* be clearly comprehended within any of the specified powers, and if the measure have an obvious relation to that *end*, and is not forbidden by any particular provision of the Constitution, it may safely be deemed to come within the compass of the national authority. . . .

"A bank has a natural relation to the power of collecting taxes—to that of regulating trade—to that of providing for the common defence. . . . [Therefore] the incorporation of a bank is a constitutional measure. . . ."

---

supplies during the Revolution, or to officers and soldiers of the Revolutionary army in payment for their services. Many of these original holders had been forced to sell at a sacrifice during the hard times of the 1780's, to speculators who bought up the securities at a fraction of their face value. Admitting that the government should arrange to pay every cent it owed, to *whom* should it arrange to pay? Many congressmen believed that the original holders deserved some consideration, and James Madison, a representative from Virginia, argued for a plan by which the new bonds would be divided between the original holders and the later purchasers. But the friends of

passed the funding bill in the form that Hamilton desired.

His assumption bill ran into even greater difficulty. Its opponents had a very good case, for if the federal government took over the state debts, the people of one state would have to pay federal taxes for servicing the debts of other states, and some of these debts, such as that of Massachusetts, were much larger than others, such as that of Virginia. Naturally, Virginians did not think it fair for them to have to pay a share of the large Massachusetts debt, and their representatives in Congress balked at the assumption bill. Finally the bill got the support of some of them and so managed to pass, but only because of a logrolling deal. The Virginians wanted the national capital to be permanently located near them in the South. Hamilton having appealed to Jeffer-

visers for written opinions on the subject. In Hamilton's opinion the establishment of a bank was a fitting exercise of the powers of Congress. Though the Constitution no-

---

Constitutionality of the Bank: Jefferson

"The incorporation of a bank, and the powers assumed by this bill, have not, in my opinion, been delegated to the United States by the Constitution.

"I. They are not among the powers specially enumerated. . . .

"II. Nor are they within either of the general phrases, which are the two following:—

"1. 'To lay taxes to provide for the general welfare of the United States.' . . . They [Congress] are not *to do anything they please*, to provide for the general welfare, but only *to lay taxes* for that purpose. . . . It was intended to lace them up straitly within the enumerated powers, and those without which, as means, these powers could not be carried into effect. . . .

"2. The second general phrase is, 'to make all laws *necessary* and proper for carrying into execution the enumerated powers.' But they can all be carried into execution without a bank. A bank, therefore, is not *necessary*, and consequently not authorized by this phrase.

"It has been much urged that a bank will give great facility or convenience in the collection of taxes. Suppose this were true; yet the Constitution allows only the means which are 'necessary,' not those which are merely 'convenient,' for effecting the enumerated powers."

---

son, shortly after the latter's return from France, Jefferson held a dinner at which arrangements were made to barter Virginia votes for the assumption bill in return for Northern votes for a Southern location of the capital. In 1790 the capital was changed back to Philadelphia for a ten-year period, and after that a new capital city was to be built on the banks of the Potomac River, on land to be selected by Washington himself.

When Hamilton's bank bill was introduced into Congress, Madison and others opposed it on the grounds that it was unconstitutional, and though a majority voted for it, President Washington himself had his doubts. He therefore asked his official ad-

where gave Congress the right in so many words, it did give Congress a general grant of powers "necessary and proper" for carrying out its specified powers, and among the specified powers were those of borrowing money, making appropriations, and levying taxes. A bank, said Hamilton, was necessary and proper in the sense of being useful and convenient for these purposes. It was therefore constitutional. But Jefferson, with the support of his fellow Virginian, Randolph, argued that the Constitution should be construed in a strict sense and that Congress should be allowed no powers not clearly given to it. A bank, he insisted, was not necessary and proper unless it was absolutely indispensable, and the bank was not indispensable since Congress could borrow, appropriate, tax, and exercise all its specified powers without it. Washington found Hamilton's case the more convincing, and he signed the bank bill when it came to him. The Bank of the United States began operations in 1791, under a charter which granted it the right to continue in business for twenty years.

the smaller distillers. He did not succeed in getting from Congress a tariff as highly protective as he had hoped for, yet the tariff law of 1792 did raise the rates somewhat.

Once enacted, Hamilton's program worked as he had intended. The public credit quickly was restored; the bonds of the United States were soon selling at home and abroad at prices even above their par value. The national prosperity rose to new

The First Bank of the United States. *The headquarters of the Bank of the United States, which was founded through Alexander Hamilton's efforts, were in Philadelphia. The Bank building on Third Street was completed in 1795. It is a good example of Early Republican architecture, with its rather box-like shape, its balustrade along the roof edge, its quoins at the angle of the walls, and its Roman pediment and columns in front. From a drawing and engraving by W. Birch & Son of Philadelphia, published in 1799.*

Hamilton also had his way with the excise tax, though after its passage the law was altered somewhat, in response to protests from farmers, so as to bear less heavily on

heights. The future of the national government was made secure.

At the same time, speculators got rich and corruption was rife. Not that Hamilton himself profited by his program: he was careful to protect his reputation for public honesty even if, to do so, he had to sacrifice his reputation for private morality. When he was accused of giving money to a Mr. Reynolds to engage in securities speculations for him, he denied the charge, and to disprove it he publicly confessed the fact that he had been having an affair with Mrs. Reynolds; the money, he explained, was blackmail. But some of Hamilton's associates, including his Assistant Secretary William Duer, who eventually landed in jail, did take advantage of their inside knowledge for improper speculation schemes. Moreover, many congressmen had bought up large amounts of the old certificates of indebtedness, and these men profited by their own legislation in funding the debt at par. Directly or indirectly, properly or improperly, thousands of wealthy merchants in the seaports also gained from the Hamilton program.

The mass of the people, the farmers scattered over the countryside, profited much less. While these people shared some of the benefit of national strength and prosperity, they bore most of the burden of paying for it. The financial program required taxes, and these came mostly from the farmers, who had to pay not only land taxes to their state governments but also the excise and, indirectly, the tariff to the federal government. The feeling grew that the Washington administration was not treating all the people fairly, and out of this feeling an organized political opposition arose.

Rise of Political Parties

The Constitution made no reference to political parties, and the Founding Fathers, George Washington in particular, believed that such organizations were evil and should be avoided. Yet parties soon arose, and today it is hard to see how the government could be successfully operated without

them. Even at the time of ratification they seemed inevitable to some observers, as for example James Madison, who hoped, however, that the federal system under the Constitution would have the effect of mitigating the worst of the evils. In the tenth number of the *Federalist* papers Madison explained that factions, or parties, were bound to arise because of differences in the amount and kind of property that people owned. The propertied and the propertyless, the debtors and the creditors, the landed, the manufacturing, and the mercantile interests—these and other groups could be expected to hold different views about the operations of the government and to organize for the furtherance of policies they considered favorable to themselves. So Madison said, and during the early 1790's the different economic groups did disagree about government policies. In those years the American two-party system originated in a division between the followers of Hamilton and those of Madison and Jefferson.

Jefferson and Madison were such close collaborators that it is sometimes difficult to separate the contributions of the two. Jefferson has generally been considered the more original and influential, though Madison has risen greatly in the esteem of historians in recent years. To describe the political philosophy of one is, in the main, to describe the political philosophy of both. Jefferson, himself a farmer, believed that farmers were God's chosen people and that an ideal republic would consist of sturdy citizens each tilling his own soil. Though an aristocrat by birth, his mother belonging to one of the first families of Virginia, the Randolphs, he had faith in the good intentions of such farmer-citizens and thought that, if properly educated, they could be trusted to govern themselves through the election of able and qualified men. But, in the 1790's, he feared city mobs as "sores upon the body politic." He then opposed the development of extensive manufactures because they would lead to the growth of cities packed with propertyless workers. While Hamilton emphasized the need for order and stability, Jefferson stressed the importance of individual freedom.

As a member of President Washington's official circle, Jefferson differed so strongly with his colleague Hamilton on particular issues such as the Bank that he soon offered to resign. But Washington preferred to keep both men in office so as to preserve national unity if possible. His became a coalition government, though he himself agreed more often with Hamilton than with Jefferson. The two Secretaries continued to work against each other, and each began to organize a following in Congress and in the country at large. After Hamilton had encouraged the journalist John Fenno to found an administration paper, the *Gazette of the United States,* Jefferson hired Madison's Princeton classmate, the poet Philip Freneau, as a clerk in the State Department so that Freneau could afford to publish a rival sheet, the *National Gazette.* Jeffersonians in different states formed committees of correspondence, based on the Revolutionary model, to coordinate their plans. The Virginia leaders, Jefferson and Madison, joined forces with the heads of three discontented factions in New York, George Clinton, Robert R. Livingston, and Aaron Burr. This combination became the nucleus of a political party which called itself Republican. The followers of Hamilton meanwhile became known as the Federalist party.

The Federalists of the 1790's were not entirely the same men as the Federalists of 1787–1788 who had campaigned for the ratification of the Constitution, nor were the Republicans exactly the same men as the old Antifederalists. There were numerous exceptions, the most noteworthy being Madison, who had played a leading role at the constitutional convention and in the

ratification effort, then had broken with Hamilton on the questions of funding and the bank, and had become one of the founders of the Republican party. Both of the parties contained members in all sections of the country, but the Federalists were most numerous in the commercial centers of the Northeast, though also strong in such Southern seaports as Charleston, while the Republicans were most numerous in the rural areas of the South and the West.

Unlike the old Antifederalists, the new Republicans did not denounce the Constitution. On the contrary, they professed to be its special friends and accused their opponents of violating it. The Republicans were, at the outset, strict constructionists. That is, they maintained, as in the debate on the Bank of the United States, that the Constitution should be construed in a strict and literal sense so as to allow Congress only those powers specifically granted to it. The Republicans were also the party of state rights as guaranteed in the Tenth Amendment. The Federalists, on the other hand, favored a loose or liberal interpretation of the fundamental law and were little concerned about the rights of states.

Republicans and Federalists differed in their social philosophies as well as in their economic interests and their constitutional views. Their differences in social outlook are seen in their reactions to the progress of the revolution in France. When that revolution first began, as a rather mild movement in favor of constitutional monarchy and the rights of man, practically all Americans hailed it as a step in the right direction. But when the revolution went to radical extremes, with attacks on organized religion, the overthrow of the monarchy, and eventually the guillotining of the King and Queen, Americans adopted different views about the events in France, the Federalists denouncing and the Republicans applauding them. Indeed, many of the Republicans imitated the French radicals (the Jacobins) by cutting their hair short, wearing pantaloons, and addressing one another as "Citizen" Smith or "Citizeness" Jones. Thus, for a time, it was possible to tell a man's party by his manners and appearance, for the Federalists kept the old-fashioned long hair or powdered wig, knee breeches, and traditional etiquette of the gentleman. Republicans accused the Federalists of being aristocratic and even "monarchical." Federalists referred to the Republicans, in horrified tones, as "Jacobins" and as "Jacobinical rabble"—terms which then had much the same implication as the word "Communist" many years later was to have.

The two parties had quite different leanings in foreign affairs. Both were pro-American, but Jefferson and the Republicans believed that American interests would best be served by maintaining close relations with France, while Hamilton and the Federalists believed that friendship with Great Britain was essential for the success of the United States.

When the time came for the election of 1792, the Republicans had no candidate to put up against Washington. Jefferson as well as Hamilton urged Washington to run for a second term, and the President consented for the good of the country, though he would have preferred to retire to Mount Vernon. But the Republicans did nominate a man to oppose Adams for the Vice Presidency. They were disappointed when their candidate, George Clinton, received only 50 electoral votes to Adams's 77. Yet they could take consolation in the fact that, in the congressional elections, they outdid the Federalists and won a majority in the House of Representatives.

Problems of the Frontier

While, during the early 1790's the American people began to be divided between two political parties, they became more strongly united than ever in their loyalty to the government itself. Previously, during the 1780's, the old Congress had been powerless to tie the outlying parts of the country firmly to the United States, as farmers in western Massachusetts rose in revolt and settlers in Vermont, Kentucky, and Tennessee toyed with the idea of separating these territories from the Union. Now, however, the Washington administration made the power of the federal government felt even on the farthest reaches of the frontier.

The federal authority was challenged when, in 1794, the farmers of western Penn-

Fashions in Dress, 1776–1812. [OPPOSITE] *Before the Revolutionary War, American clothing styles were borrowed from England; afterwards, from France. In 1776 the American gentleman, when dressed up, wore a three-cornered cocked hat, a wig with a queue, a ruffled shirt, a waistcoat, a brightly colored outer coat, knee breeches, stockings, and low buckled shoes. In 1800, wigless, he had a round hat with a low crown and wore tight-fitting pantaloons tucked inside high boots; in 1812 his hat had a higher crown. Loose-fitting trousers did not become fashionable until after the War of 1812. As for the well-dressed woman, in the 1780's she had a high-piled hair-do, a high-necked and low-waisted gown with a tight bodice and a full skirt, which was supported by numerous undergarments and sometimes by hoops or stays. She wore shoes with extremely high heels. During the 1790's and early 1800's her headdress, her neckline, and her heels became lower and her waist much higher, sometimes reaching as high as her bosom, which was now accentuated. Her skirt grew narrower and sometimes rather tight—becoming almost a hobble-skirt. She discarded most of her underclothes (this seemed shocking to later generations in the nineteenth century, when piles of underclothing again were decreed by fashion, as well as by Victorian modesty).*

1776.   EVENING DRESS. 1780.   1780.   1785.

EVENING DRESS. 1795.   EVENING DRESS. 1797.   1800.   1805.

1805.   1812.   1812.   1812.

sylvania refused to pay the whiskey excise and terrorized the would-be tax collectors, much as the colonists had done throughout America at the time of the Stamp Act. The so-called Whiskey Rebellion was not left to the authorities of Pennsylvania as Shays's Rebellion had been left to the authorities of Massachusetts. Urged on by Hamilton, Washington took drastic steps. Calling out the militia of three states, he raised an army of nearly 15,000, a larger force than he had commanded against the British during most of the Revolution, and he personally accompanied this army as far as the town of Bedford. At the approach of the militiamen, the farmers around Pittsburgh, where the rebellion centered, either ran for cover or stayed home and professed to be law-abiding citizens. The rebellion quickly collapsed. Though the Republicans made political capital by denouncing the administration, the whiskey distillers began to pay the tax. They no longer doubted the government's power to compel obedience to its laws.

While the whiskey rebels were intimidated into obedience, other frontiersmen were made loyal to the government by its acceptance of new states as members of the Union. First to be admitted were two of the original thirteen, North Carolina (1789) and Rhode Island (1790), both of which had ratified the Constitution when they found that a bill of rights was definitely to be added and that they could not conveniently go on as independent commonwealths. Then Vermont, which had had its own state government since the Revolution, was accepted as the fourteenth state (1791) after New York and New Hampshire finally agreed to give up their claims to sovereignty over the Green Mountain country. Next came Kentucky (1792) with the consent of Virginia, which previously had governed the Kentucky counties as its own. After North Carolina finally ceded its western lands to the Union, these were given a territorial government similar to that of the Northwest Territory and after six years became the state of Tennessee (1796). With the admission of these frontier states, the schemes for separating Vermont, Kentucky, and Tennessee from the Union soon came to an end.

In the more remote areas of the Northwest and the Southwest, meanwhile, the government had to contend with the Indians and their foreign allies, British and Spanish, in order to get a firm grasp upon all the territory belonging to the United States. The Indians of the Southwest—Cherokees, Creeks, Choctaws, and Chickasaws—were led by the colorful and vengeful Alexander McGillivray, a half-breed Creek chieftain who had fought as a Tory during the Revolution and who continued to hate Americans. In his efforts to resist the advance of American frontiersmen into the lower Mississippi Valley, McGillivray received the support and encouragement of Spain. In 1790 President Washington tried to buy peace with the Southwestern Indians by inviting McGillivray to New York and agreeing to pay him $100,000. Despite McGillivray's treaty with the United States, the Indians continued to accept subsidies from the Spaniards and to raid American settlements along the border. At last, in 1793-1794, the Tennesseans went on the warpath themselves, their militia invading Indian country and chastising several of the tribes. Thus the Southwestern frontier was made safe for the time being, though not through the efforts of the Washington administration, which refrained from forceful measures because it was engaged in delicate and long-drawn-out negotiations with Spain.

In the Northwest the government pursued a policy of force against the Indians, even at some risk of becoming involved in hostilities with their protector and ally,

Great Britain. Two expeditions failed before a third one finally succeeded in the conquest of the Ohio country. In 1790 the governor of the Northwest Territory, Arthur St. Clair, from the territorial capital at Marietta sent General Josiah Harmar with a tiny army to destroy the villages and the crops of the Indians along the Maumee River. Harmar and his men, their mission not fully accomplished, were driven back. The next year, after Washington had appealed to Congress for more recruits, St. Clair himself set out with an enlarged force, and his army was practically destroyed in a surprise attack. Desperately hoping to re-establish the prestige of the new government, Washington then gave the frontier command to General Wayne, who, despite his nickname "Mad Anthony," was a careful planner as well as a dashing soldier. With over 4,000 men, including a large contingent of Kentucky sharpshooters, Wayne moved cautiously toward the Maumee, building forts as he went. The British officials in Canada, who were providing the Indians with supplies, themselves ordered the construction of a fort about twenty miles from the mouth of the river, well within the boundary of the United States. Near the British fort, at a place where trees had been blown over by a windstorm, Wayne in the summer of 1794 met and decisively defeated the Indians in the Battle of Fallen Timbers, the British garrison prudently keeping out of the fight. Next summer the Indians agreed in the Treaty of Greenville to abandon to the white men most of what afterwards became the state of Ohio.

While the administration's Indian policy favored the growth of the Northwest, its land policy had an opposite effect. Some members of Congress advocated the sale of government lands on easy terms, so as to speed the settlement of the frontier. But Hamilton thought the lands should be sold at fairly high prices, so as to provide an abundant source of government revenue. In the Land Act of 1796, which re-enacted the provisions of the Ordinance of 1785 regarding the procedures of survey and sale, the minimum price was raised to two dollars an acre. Since a purchaser had to buy at least 640 acres at a time, few ordinary settlers could afford government land, even though they were allowed to pay in two installments a year apart. The law neither hastened the settlement of the Northwest nor brought in much revenue.

Before the government could be sure of its hold upon the border areas, it had to bring to terms the foreign powers which persisted in exerting influence there—Great Britain and Spain. In its diplomacy the Washington administration, by taking advantage of the opportunities that arose from the accidents of international politics, managed to reassert American independence and redeem the West.

Neutrality and Jay's Treaty

When Washington became President, Great Britain had not yet deigned to send a minister to the United States, though all the other powers of Europe (except Russia) had entered into normal diplomatic relations with the young republic. The British government did send a succession of observers, or spies, and one of them, Major George Beckwith, kept in close touch with Hamilton. He was impressed by Hamilton's advice that the British ought to appoint a regular minister and so head off a movement in Congress for discriminatory legislation against British trade. In Congress Madison and the Republicans argued that Great Britain, in refusing to make a commercial treaty with the United States, was waging a kind of economic warfare against this country, and that the United States should retaliate by imposing special customs duties and harbor dues, in excess of the regular rates, upon her goods and ships. Though this legislation did not pass, the threat of it induced the British government finally, in 1791, to dispatch a regular minister to America—the young and supercilious George Hammond, who soon began to court a Philadelphia girl.

Hammond had instructions to forestall hostile economic legislation by pretending to discuss American grievances, without actually conceding anything. The worst of these grievances, besides the lack of a commercial treaty, was the continued British occupation of frontier posts upon American soil. In an exchange of notes with Hammond, Jefferson most effectively presented the American case, but Hamilton at once weakened Jefferson's argument by assuring Hammond confidentially that Jefferson did not have the backing either of the Washington administration or of the American people. This was but one of many instances in which the Secretary of the Treasury interfered in the affairs of the Secretary of State. In consequence, Jefferson made little headway in his efforts to secure satisfaction from Great Britain for her persisting violations of the treaty of 1783. Yet Hamilton could easily justify his interference, at least to himself. Despite the lack of a commercial treaty, Americans carried on a tremendous trade with Great Britain, about nine tenths of American imports being of British origin. The customs duties on these imports provided much the largest share of the government's revenue, and this revenue was indispensable for the maintenance of Hamilton's financial system and, in his belief, for the preservation of the government itself. Hence he opposed any action that, by jeopardizing good relations with Great Britain, might interrupt in the slightest the flow of revenue-producing and life-giving commerce.

A new crisis in foreign affairs faced the Washington administration when the French revolutionary government, after guillotining King Louis XVI, went to war in 1793 with Great Britain and her allies. Should the United States recognize the radical government of France by accepting a diplomatic representative from it? Was the United States obligated by the alliance of 1778 to go to war on the side of France? These questions Washington put to his official advisers, and both Hamilton and Jefferson recommended a policy of neutrality, though they presented quite different arguments for it. Hamilton said the treaty of 1778 had been made with the French government of that time, that is, the monarchy; now that the King had been executed and the monarchy terminated, the treaty no longer was in effect. Jefferson insisted that the treaty had been made with the French nation and was still binding upon the United States, regardless of any change in the French form of government. Jefferson believed, however, that the terms of the treaty did not necessarily obligate the United States to give military aid. After considering Hamilton's and Jefferson's advice, Washington decided to recognize the French government and to issue a proclamation announcing the determination of the United States to remain at peace. The proclamation (1793), though it did not mention the word "neutrality," was generally interpreted as a neutrality statement, which it actually was. Next year Congress passed a Neutrality Act, forbidding American citizens to participate in the war and prohibiting the use of American soil as a base of operations for either side. Of course, neutrality did not rule out ordinary trade with the belligerents. It meant that the United States, while antagonizing neither, should enjoy the benefits of commerce with both.

The first challenge to American neutrality came from France. Not that the French revolutionaries asked for a declaration of war: they did not, for they supposed that the United States would be of more use to them as a nonbelligerent. Their purposes became apparent when their first minister to this country arrived. Instead of landing at Philadelphia and presenting himself immediately to the President, the youthful and brash Citizen Edmond Genêt disembarked at Charleston. There he made plans for using American ports to outfit French warships, issued letters of marque and reprisal authorizing American shipowners to serve as French privateers, and commissioned the aging George Rogers Clark to undertake an overland expedition against the possessions of Spain, which at the moment was an ally of Great Britain and an enemy of France. In all these steps, Genêt brazenly disregarded Washington's proclamation and flagrantly violated the Neutrality Act. When he finally reached Philadelphia, after being acclaimed by pro-French crowds on a tour through the interior, he got a stony reception from the President. He then assumed that the people were behind him, and he repeatedly appealed to them over the President's head. His conduct not only infuriated Washington and the Federalists but also embarrassed all except the most ardent Francophiles among the Republicans. At last Washington demanded that the French government recall him, but by that time Genêt's party, the Girondins, were out of power in France and the still more extreme Jacobins in control, so it would not have been safe for him to return. Generously the President granted him political asylum in the United States, and he settled down to live to a ripe old age with his American wife on a Long Island farm. Meanwhile the neutrality policy had survived its first great test.

The second challenge, an even greater one, came from Great Britain. Early in 1794 the Royal Navy suddenly seized hundreds of American ships engaged in trade in the French West Indies. The pretext for these seizures was a British interpretation of international law—known as the Rule of 1756

—which held that a trade prohibited in peacetime (as American trade between France and the French overseas possessions had been) could not be legally opened in time of war. At the news of the seizures, the prevalent opinion in the United States became as strongly anti-British as it had recently been anti-French, and the anti-British feeling rose still higher at the report that the Governor-General of Canada had delivered a rousing and warlike speech to the Indians on the northwestern frontier. With peace thus endangered, Hamilton grew more concerned than ever about the necessity, from his point of view, of maintaining good relations with Great Britain.

To him and to other Federalists it seemed that this was no time for ordinary diplomacy. Jefferson had resigned in 1793 to devote himself to organizing a political opposition, and the State Department was now in the hands of an even more ardently pro-French Virginian, Edmund Randolph. Bypassing the State Department, Washington named as a special commissioner to England the staunch New York Federalist, former Secretary for Foreign Affairs under the old Confederation, and current Chief Justice of the Supreme Court, John Jay. Jay was instructed to secure damages for the recent spoliations, withdrawal of British forces from the frontier posts, and a satisfactory commercial treaty, without violating the terms of the existing treaty of amity and commerce with France, signed at the time of the alliance in 1778. While Jay was in England, Hamilton weakened Jay's bargaining power by assuring Hammond in Philadelphia that under no circumstances would the United States consider fighting Great Britain or even aligning itself with nations hostile to Great Britain.

The treaty that Jay negotiated (1794) was a long and complex document, dealing with frontier posts, boundaries, debts, commerce, ship seizures, and neutral rights. It yielded more to Great Britain and obtained less for the United States than Jay had been authorized to give or instructed to get. When the terms were published in the

aided them and cheered them on. The American minister to France, James Monroe, and even the Secretary of State, Edmund Randolph, cooperated closely with

---

Jay's Treaty

1794

Frontier Posts. "His Majesty will withdraw all his troops and garrisons from all posts and places within the boundary lines assigned by the treaty of peace to the United States."

Boundaries. Joint surveys will be made to locate the U.S.-Canadian boundary west of the Lake of the Woods and at the northeast, between Maine and New Brunswick.

Debts. The United States "will make full and complete compensation" for uncollectible debts owed by Americans to British creditors.

Commerce. There shall be freedom of commerce and navigation between the United States and Great Britain and the British East Indies. (Article XII, permitting the United States to trade with the British West Indies also, but only in ships too small to cross the ocean, was stricken out before ratification.)

Ship Seizures. The British government will compensate Americans for ships and cargoes illegally captured in the past, the amount of payment to be determined by arbitration.

Neutral Rights. American ships carrying enemy (French) property, when captured by the British, shall be taken to British ports and the enemy property removed. (This was inconsistent with the usual American principle that "free ships make free goods.")

United States, the treaty was denounced as no treaty before or since, and Jay himself was burned in effigy in various parts of the country. The Republicans were unanimous in decrying it; they said it was a departure from neutrality, favoring Great Britain and unfair to France. Even some of the Federalists were outraged by its terms, those in the South objecting to the payment of the pre-Revolutionary debts, and those in the North condemning Article XII. Opponents of the treaty went to extraordinary lengths to defeat it in the Senate, and French agents

the French in a desperate attempt to prevent ratification. Nevertheless, after amending the treaty by striking out Article XII, the Senate gave its consent.

There was much to be said for Jay's Treaty, despite its very real shortcomings. By means of it the United States gained valuable time for continued peaceful development, obtained undisputed sovereignty over all the Northwest, and secured a reasonably satisfactory commercial agreement with the nation whose trade was most important. More than that, the treaty led immediately to a settlement of the worst of the outstanding differences with Spain.

In Madrid the Spanish foreign minister feared that the understanding between Great Britain and the United States might prove a prelude to joint operations between those two countries against Spain's possessions in North America. Spain was about to change sides in the European war, abandoning Great Britain for France, and it was therefore to Spain's interest to appease the United States. The relentless pressure of American frontiersmen advancing toward the Southwest made it doubtful whether Spain could long hold her borderlands in any event. And so, when Thomas Pinckney arrived in Spain as a special negotiator, he

had no difficulty in gaining practically everything that the United States had sought from the Spaniards for over a decade. Pinckney's Treaty (1795) recognized the right of Americans to navigate the Mississippi to its mouth and to deposit goods at New Orleans for reloading on ocean-going ships; fixed the northern boundary of Florida where Americans always had insisted it should be, along the thirty-first parallel; and bound the Spanish authorities to prevent the Indians in Florida from raiding across the border.

Thus, before Washington had completed his second term in office, the United States had freed itself from the encroachments of both Great Britain and Spain.

>>>->>>->>>->>>-<<<-<<<-<<<-<<<

BIBLIOGRAPHY

For an intimate glimpse of the first President and the first Congress, see the *Journal of William Maclay, United States Senator from Pennsylvania, 1789–1791* (1890; new ed., 1928). Senator Maclay was a staunch republican who admired George Washington but feared the "monarchical" tendencies of the time. How well grounded the Senator's fears were, L. B. Dunbar shows in *A Study of the "Monarchical" Tendencies in the United States from 1776 to 1801* (1923). A sound, brief introduction to the men and measures of the first administration is H. J. Ford's *Washington and His Colleagues* (1921). The administrative organization and policies are more thoroughly discussed by L. D. White in *The Federalists* (1948). See also L. K. Caldwell, *The Administrative Theories of Hamilton and Jefferson* (1944).

The origin of political parties—like the origin of the Constitution—was given an economic interpretation by Charles A. Beard. His *Economic Origins of Jeffersonian Democracy* (1915; new ed., 1949) has had an

influence second only to that of his *Economic Interpretation of the Constitution*. In *The Origins of the American Party System* (1956) Joseph Charles analyzes afresh the views and actions of Hamilton, Jefferson, Washington, and John Adams. C. G. Bowers, *Jefferson and Hamilton* (1925), is vivid, dramatic, and partial to Jefferson. L. M. Hacker more than redresses the balance in Hamilton's favor in *Alexander Hamilton in the American Tradition* (1957), which praises Hamilton as a "real conservative" and fully elaborates his economic ideas. Adrienne Koch, *The Philosophy of Thomas Jefferson* (1943), is a lucid analysis. The growth of parties in one commonwealth is expertly told in H. M. Tinkcom's *The Republicans and Federalists in Pennsylvania, 1790–1801* (1950).

On foreign affairs, two standard references, both by S. F. Bemis, are *Jay's Treaty* (1923) and *Pinckney's Treaty* (1926). Bemis emphasizes the European situation —"Europe's distresses"—as the factor making possible American diplomatic successes in the 1790's. A. P. Whitaker, in *The Spanish-American Frontier, 1783–1795* and a sequel, *The Mississippi Question, 1795–1803* (1934), gives more weight to conditions on the American continent, especially the growing strength of the United States along its borders with Spanish territory.

See also Frank Monaghan, *John Jay* (1935). An important new study is Alexander De Conde, *Entangling Alliance: Politics and Diplomacy under George Washington* (1958).

The Whiskey Rebellion is interestingly and authoritatively described in L. D. Baldwin's *Whiskey Rebels: The Story of a Frontier Uprising* (1939).

CHAPTER 10

Downfall of the Federalists

For the first dozen years under the Constitution, while the Federalists controlled the Presidency, they accomplished much. Under President Washington they infused vigor into the government (the *national* government, as he always called it) and set the nation upon a path of neutrality and diplomatic independence. Under his successor, John Adams, they maintained the rights and the self-respect of the republic in international affairs, and though in consequence they brought on hostilities with France and thus departed from neutrality, the President steered away from all-out war and finally made a satisfactory peace. In their grasp for power, however, the Federalists overreached themselves. They faced the dilemma of all rulers in a government that depends upon the will of the people—that is, the dilemma of choosing between governmental strength and individual freedom —and they made their choice in favor of strong government at the expense of popular liberty and popular support. After the

Federalists used troops against the whiskey rebels in 1794, the Republicans allowed no one to forget how the government had intimidated its citizens by a show of military might. In 1798, during the undeclared war with France, the Federalists violated civil liberties with their drastic Alien and Sedition Acts. At the next election, enough of the voters heeded the protests of Jefferson and Madison to give the Republicans control of the executive and legislative branches of the federal government, though not the judicial branch. The Federalists never won another presidential election, yet their main achievements endured and, in one form or another, still endure. We of today owe much to the party of Washington, Hamilton, and Adams for having launched the constitutional experiment so successfully.

Election of 1796

As the time approached for the election of 1796, some of the party friends of Washington urged him to run again. Already twice elected without a single vote cast against him in the electoral college, he could be counted upon to hold the Federalist party together and carry it to a third great vic-

---

Washington's Farewell Address
1796

"Against the insidious wiles of foreign influence (I conjure you to believe me, fellow-citizens) the jealousy of a free people ought to be *constantly* awake, since history and experience prove that foreign influence is one of the most baneful foes of republican government. But that jealousy, to be useful, must be impartial, else it becomes the instrument of the very influence to be avoided, instead of a defense against it. Excessive partiality for one foreign nation and excessive dislike of another cause those whom they actuate to see danger only on one side, and serve to veil and even second the arts of influence on the other. . . .

"The great rule of conduct for us in regard to foreign nations is, in extending our commercial relations, to have with them as little *political* connection as possible. . . .

"It is our true policy to steer clear of permanent alliances with any portion of the foreign world, so far, I mean, as we are now at liberty to do it; for let me not be understood as capable of patronizing infidelity to existing engagements. . . .

"Taking care always to keep ourselves by suitable establishments on a respectable defensive posture, we may safely trust to temporary alliances for extraordinary emergencies."

---

tory. But Washington, weary of the burdens of the presidential office, disgusted with the partisan abuse which was being heaped upon him, longed to retire to his beloved home, Mount Vernon. Though he did not object to a third term in principle, he did not desire one for himself. To make his determination clear, he composed, with Hamilton's assistance, a long letter to the American people and had it published in a Philadelphia newspaper.

In this "Farewell Address" the retiring President offered his fellow countrymen some advice so sound that his letter is still regarded as one of the greatest of all Amer-

ican state papers. First, with regard to domestic politics, he admonished the citizens of every part of the country to think always in terms of the national rather than a local or sectional interest. "The name of AMERICAN, which belongs to you, in your national capacity," he wrote, "must always exalt the just pride of patriotism more than any appellation derived from local discriminations." The North and the South, the East and the West, depended upon one another for their prosperity and happiness. Political parties were bad enough at best, and they would be far worse if they ever should be organized upon a geographical basis. The result, Washington warned, might be the disruption of the Union.

Having cautioned against the evils of party spirit, Washington turned to foreign affairs and emphasized the need for an independent diplomacy. "Observe good faith and justice toward all nations. Cultivate peace and harmony with all," he counseled. "The great rule of conduct for us in regard to foreign nations is, in extending our commercial relations, to have with them as little *political* connection as possible." We should "steer clear of permanent alliances" and rely upon temporary alliances in times of emergency. And we should see to it that foreign powers did not meddle in our own domestic politics. "Against the insidious wiles of foreign influence (I conjure you to believe me, fellow-citizens) the jealousy of a free people ought to be *constantly* awake, since history and experience prove that foreign influence is one of the most baneful foes of republican government."

When Washington thus referred to the "insidious wiles of foreign influence," he was not writing merely for rhetorical effect. He had certain real and definite evils in mind. Lately he had dismissed the Secretary of State, Edmund Randolph, and had recalled the minister to France, James Monroe, for working hand in hand with the French to defeat Jay's Treaty. The French were still interfering in American politics with the hope of defeating the Federalists in the forthcoming presidential election. As the election came near, the government of France broke off diplomatic relations with the United States, ordered the seizure of American ships on the high seas, and threatened war so as to be able to put the Republicans in power. The French supposed that, with Thomas Jefferson in the Presidency, they would be able to bend the United States to their will, though the French minister in Philadelphia assured his government that Jefferson was first of all an American and, once in office, would be guided by American interests.

There was no doubt that Jefferson would be the candidate of the Republicans, and he chose as his running mate the New York Republican leader, Aaron Burr. With Washington out of the running, there was some question as to who the Federalist candidate would be. Hamilton, the very personification of Federalism, was not "available" because he had aroused too many enemies with his forthright views. John Jay was too closely identified with his unpopular treaty, and Thomas Pinckney, though *his* treaty had been enthusiastically received, had the handicap of being a South Carolinian at a time when party leaders thought the next candidate should be a Northerner. John Adams, who as Vice President was directly associated with none of the Federalist measures, finally got the nomination for President at a caucus of the Federalists in Congress, and Pinckney the nomination for Vice President. Of course, the Constituion at that time did not distinguish between presidential and vice-presidential candidates. It merely provided that each elector should vote for two men, one of whom should not be from the same state as himself, and that the candidate with the highest number of electoral votes, if a majority, should be President, and the candidate with the next highest number Vice President.

With Washington stepping aside, the Federalist party lost much of its coherence and became torn by fierce factional rivalries. Hamilton disliked Adams and preferred Pinckney, as did many other Federalists, especially in the South. New Englanders, on the other hand, had no particular liking for Pinckney and feared a plot to make him President instead of Adams. Already the evils of political sectionalism, against which Washington so recently had warned, were making themselves felt within his own party. The result was a near disaster for the Federalists. They elected a majority of their presidential electors, despite the electioneering tactics of the French government, whose efforts may have boomeranged and helped the Federalists. But when the electors balloted in the various states, some of the Pinckney men declined to vote for Adams, and a still larger number of the Adams men

John Adams. *When elected to the Presidency, Adams was almost thirty years younger than the man depicted in this portrait, painted when he was past eighty. The artist was Samuel F. B. Morse. Afterwards best known as the inventor of the magnetic telegraph, Morse did not give up painting for invention until he was in his forties. He was born in Massachusetts, the son of Jedidiah Morse, who was America's foremost geographer of the late eighteenth and early nineteenth century. The younger Morse graduated from Yale, studied art under Benjamin West and Washington Allston in England, and in 1823 opened a studio in New York. He helped to found and was the first president of the National Academy of Design.* (IN THE BROOKLYN MUSEUM COLLECTION)

declined to vote for Pinckney. So Pinckney received fewer votes than Jefferson, and Adams only three more than Jefferson. The next President was to be a Federalist, but the Vice President was to be a Republican!

By virtue of his diplomatic services dur-

ing the Revolution, his writings as a conservative political philosopher, and his devotion to the public weal as he saw it, "Honest John" Adams ranks as one of the greatest of American statesmen. He had his human failings, however. For one thing, he seemed to be overly concerned with his own importance and dignity, at least in the eyes of his political opponents, who sometimes thought his posturings, round and fat as he was, a bit ridiculous. More important, like most prominent members of the illustrious Adams family afterwards, he lacked the politician's touch which is essential for successful leadership in a republican society. Even Washington, remote and austere as he sometimes seems to have been, was fairly adept at conciliating factions and maintaining party harmony.

As President, Adams was in a position requiring unusual political skill. Not only was his administration divided between a President of one party and a Vice President of another; it was also divided between the followers of Hamilton and those of Adams. Unwisely, the new President chose to continue Washington's department heads in office. Most of them were friends of Hamilton, and they looked to him for advice, though he held no official post. Many of the Congressmen also looked to Hamilton rather than the President. With the government as well as the people badly divided, Adams faced foreign problems as trying as those with which Washington had had to contend.

X. Y. Z. and Hostilities with France

As American relations with Great Britain and Spain improved in consequence of Jay's and Pinckney's treaties, relations with France, now under the government of the Directory, went from bad to worse. Despite the victory of the Federalists in the election of 1796, the leaders of the Directory assumed that France had the sympathy and support of the mass of the American people and could undermine the Adams administration by frustrating it in foreign affairs. Therefore the French, asserting that they were applying the same principles of neutral rights as the United States and Great Britain had adopted in Jay's Treaty, continued to capture American ships on the high seas and, in many cases, to imprison the crews. When Minister Monroe left France after his recall, the French went out of their way to show their affection for him and for the Republican party. When the South Carolina Federalist Charles Cotesworth Pinckney, a brother of Thomas Pinckney, arrived in France to replace Monroe, the Directory considered him *persona non grata* and refused to receive him as the official representative of the United States.

War seemed likely unless the Adams ad-

othy Pickering, favored war. Others urged a special effort for peace, and even Alexander Hamilton approved the idea of appointing commissioners to approach the Directory. Adams, himself a peace man, appointed a bipartisan commission of three: C. C. Pinckney, the recently rejected minister; John Marshall, a Virginia Federalist, afterwards famous as the great Chief Justice of the Supreme Court; and Elbridge Gerry, a Massachusetts Republican but a personal friend of the President's. In France, in 1787, the three Americans were met by three agents of the Directory's foreign minister, Prince Talleyrand, who had a reputation as the wizard of European diplomacy but who did not understand the psychology of Americans, even though he had lived for a time in the United States. Talleyrand's agents demanded a loan for France and a bribe for French officials before they would

Jefferson and Adams Describe Each Other

In 1787 Jefferson wrote to James Madison about John Adams, one of God's stewards on earth: "He is vain, irritable, and a bad calculator of the force and probable effect of the motives which govern men. This is all the ill which can possibly be said of him. He is as disinterested as the being who made him: he is profound in his views; and accurate in his judgment, except where knowledge of the world is necessary to form a judgment." Adams was in turn inclined to be rather patronizing toward Jefferson, eight years his junior. In 1809, after the vigorous disputes about policy between the Yankee and the Virginian, Adams wrote to Benjamin Rush: "There has never been the smallest interruption of the personal friendship between me and Mr. Jefferson that I know of. You should remember that Jefferson was but a boy to me. . . . I am bold to say I was his preceptor in politicks and taught him everything that has been good and solid in his whole political conduct."

ministration could settle the difficulties with France. Some of the President's advisers, in particular his Secretary of State, the stiff-backed New England Francophobe Tim-

deal with Adams's commissioners. According to legend, one of the Americans replied: "Millions for defense but not one cent for tribute!" Actually, the response of the com-

Building the Navy. *After the Revolutionary War the United States abandoned the warships it had accumulated, and from 1783 to 1798 there was no American navy. Then, with the outbreak of undeclared hostilities with France, the Navy Department was established and a naval building program begun. In that age of wooden sailing ships, there were three main categories of war vessels: (1) ships of the line, or line-of-battle ships, which were the largest and most heavily armed (roughly corresponding to twentieth-century battleships or dreadnoughts); (2) frigates, which were smaller and faster and had fewer guns (comparable to modern cruisers); (3) corvettes, sloops of war, and other relatively small craft (somewhat like the light cruisers, destroyers, and gunboats of the present). At the outset the United States navy eschewed line-of-battle ships and placed its chief reliance on specially designed frigates which were faster, more maneuverable, and more heavily gunned than their European counterparts. In 1798 the frigates United States, Constitution, and Constellation, already partly built, were completed, and the Philadelphia and several others were started. The illustration shows work in progress on the Philadelphia in a Philadelphia shipyard. This frigate was not finished in time to be used against the French, but it saw plenty of action later (1803) in the war with Tripoli. Tripolitan pirates captured the ship, and Americans in a daring raid destroyed her to prevent the enemy's using her against them.* (THE HISTORICAL SOCIETY OF PENNSYLVANIA)

missioners was summed up in Pinckney's laconic words: "No! No! Not a sixpence!"

When Adams received the commissioners' report, he sent a message to Congress in which he urged readiness for war, denounced the French for their insulting treat-

ment of the United States, and vowed he would not appoint another minister to France until he knew the minister would be "received, respected and honored as the representative of a great, free, powerful and independent nation." The Republicans, doubting the President's charge that the United States had been insulted, asked for proof. Adams then turned the commissioners' report over to Congress, after deleting the names of the three Frenchmen and designating them only as Messrs. X., Y., and Z. When the report was published, the "X. Y. Z. Affair" provoked even more of a reaction than Adams had bargained for. It aroused the martial spirit of most Americans, made the Federalists more popular than ever as the party of patriotism, and led to a limited and undeclared war with France, 1798–1800.

With the cooperation of Congress, which quickly passed the necessary laws, Adams cut off all trade with France, abrogated the treaties of 1778, and authorized public and private vessels of the United States to capture French armed ships on the high seas. Congress set up a Department of the Navy (1798) and appropriated money for the construction of warships to supplement the hundreds of privateers and the small number of government vessels already built for the protection of American shipping in the Mediterranean against the Barbary pirates. The new United States navy soon gave a good account of itself. Its warships won a number of duels with French vessels of their own class, the most spectacular performance being that of the *Constellation*, which under the command of Thomas Truxton defeated the *Insurgente* and then the *Vengeance*. In the space of about three years American men-of-war captured a total of eighty-five prizes, including armed merchantmen as well as vessels of the French navy. Of course, the French navy could not concentrate its efforts upon the American marauders, for it was mainly preoccupied with the European war and with the necessity of protecting itself from the British fleet.

Having abandoned neutrality, the United States now was cooperating so closely with Great Britain as to be virtually a cobelligerent, though technically at peace. When the British offered to lend a part of their fleet to the United States, President Adams declined to borrow, since he preferred to build up a navy of his own. Nevertheless, the British provided shot and shell to make up the deficient American supplies, furnished officers to help with the training and direction of American crews, and exchanged signaling information so that British and American ships could communicate readily with one another. Thus the United States was involved in the world war as a kind of associate member of the coalition against France.

The Adams administration did not go far enough, however, to suit the more violently pro-British and anti-French faction of the Federalist party. Once hostilities had begun, Hamilton advocated all-out war as his friend Secretary Pickering had done all along. But Adams hesitated. He feared that he might eventually have to call for a declaration of war and for the use of land troops as well as naval forces, so he requested Washington to emerge from his retirement and lead the army again, if the time should come. Washington agreed to serve on the condition that Hamilton be made second in command. War, complete and declared, would have given the Federalist party a chance to strengthen further its hold upon the national government, and it would have given Hamilton an opportunity to gain military glory and thus revive his waning political fortunes. Possibly it also would have assured the re-election of Adams in 1800, yet Adams preferred peace if it could be had on honorable terms.

The French foreign minister, Talleyrand, finally began to see the wisdom of an accommodation with the Americans. He took notice of the rapprochement between the United States and Great Britain, the successes of the American navy, and the failure of the American people to show the expected enthusiasm for the cause of France. He was enlightened in regard to American public opinion by George Logan, a Philadelphia Quaker who, with no official authorization but with a letter of introduction from Vice President Jefferson, visited France to work for peace in the midst of the undeclared war. After Logan returned, President Adams gave him a sympathetic hearing, though the Federalists in Congress passed a law, the so-called Logan Act, to prohibit citizens from engaging in private and unofficial diplomacy with foreign governments in the future. Adams now appointed a new minister to France, William Vans Murray, who was acceptable to the French and who as minister to the Netherlands had heard from Talleyrand and reported to Adams that the French government was at last ready to welcome a representative from the United States. But the Hamilton-Pickering faction of the Federalists objected to a prompt and easy re-establishment of relations with the hated French. To satisfy this group in his own party, Adams dispatched another commission of three to arrange a settlement with France before the arrival of the new minister. He finally had to dismiss Pickering as Secretary of State because of Pickering's continued efforts to obstruct the administration's peace plans.

When, in 1800, Adams's new three-man commission arrived in France, Napoleon Bonaparte was in power as First Consul. The Americans requested that France terminate the treaties of 1778 and pay damages for seizures of American ships. Napoleon replied that, if the United States had any claim to damages, the claim must rest upon the treaties, and if the treaties were ended, the claim must be abandoned. Napoleon had his way. The Americans agreed to a new treaty which canceled the old ones, arranged for reciprocity in commerce, and

ignored the question of damages. When Adams submitted this treaty to the Senate, the extreme Federalists raised so many objections that its final ratification was delayed until after he had left office. Nevertheless, the "quasi-war" had come to an honorable end, and the United States at last had freed itself from the entanglements and embarrassments of the "perpetual" alliance with France.

Repression and Protest

The outbreak of hostilities in 1798 had given the Federalists an advantage over the political opposition, and in the congressional elections of that year they increased their majorities in both houses. Meanwhile their new-found power went to their heads. Some of them schemed to go on winning elections by passing laws to weaken and to silence the opposition. They had as an excuse the necessity or the supposed necessity of protecting the nation from dangerous foreign influence in the midst of the undeclared war. By persecuting their critics, the Federalists produced a crop of Republican martyrs, gave rise to protests against their disregard of the Constitution, and provoked a reaction which helped to bring their party to defeat.

Since many Republican critics of the administration were foreigners by birth, especially Irish or French, the Federalists in Congress thought it desirable to limit the political rights of aliens and make it more difficult for them to become citizens of the United States. The first of three drastic laws of 1798, the Naturalization Act, lengthened from five to fourteen years the period during which a foreigner must reside in this country in order to become eligible for citizenship. The second, the Alien Act, authorized the President to order the deportation of any foreigner he considered dangerous. The third, the Sedition Act, was the most extreme of all, and it applied to native Americans as well as the foreign-born. It provided for the punishment—by a fine as high as $2,000 and by imprisonment for as long as two years—of anyone who should write, utter, or publish any words disre-

that, when a salute was fired in honor of the President, the wadding of the cannon had "struck him in the rear bulge of the breeches."

Alien and Sedition Acts
1798

Naturalization Act. No alien shall be admitted to citizenship unless he has resided within the United States for at least fourteen years. No native, citizen, subject, or resident of a country with which the United States is at war shall be admitted to citizenship.

Alien Act. The President may "order all such aliens as he shall judge dangerous to the peace and safety of the United States" to depart.

Alien Enemies Act. When war is declared or invasion threatened, "all natives, citizens, denizens, or subjects of the hostile nation or government, being males of the age of fourteen years and upwards, who shall be within the United States, and not actually naturalized, shall be liable to be apprehended, restrained, secured and removed, as alien enemies."

Sedition Act. Any persons combining or conspiring "with intent to oppose any measure or measures of the government of the United States" shall be liable to fines up to $5,000 and imprisonment up to five years. Any person writing, uttering, or publishing "any false, scandalous and malicious writing or writings" against the government, the Congress, or the President shall be liable to a fine up to $2,000 and imprisonment up to two years.

---

spectful of Congress or the President or any words calculated to stir up sedition (that is, resistance to the government).

President Adams did not invoke the Alien Act nor deport any aliens, but this law together with the Naturalization Act doubtless had some effect in discouraging immigration and encouraging many foreigners already here to leave. The administration did enforce the Sedition Act, arresting about two dozen men and convicting ten of them. Most of these were Republican newspaper editors whose writings, while tending to bring the Federalists into disrepute, were not truly seditious at all. One of the editors merely had expressed the wish

Worse than the jailing of mere newspapermen was the imprisonment of Matthew Lyon, a Republican member of Congress from Vermont and publisher of a small periodical called the *Scourge of Aristocracy*. The Irish-born Lyon, who had been in the habit of saying what he thought about the President, persisted in the habit even after the passage of the new law. In the President he saw "every consideration of public welfare swallowed up in a continual grasp for power, an unbounded thirst for ridiculous pomp, foolish adulation and selfish avarice." For expressing this opinion he was tried and found guilty of "deceitfully, wickedly and maliciously contriving to defame the Government of the United States" and also "John Adams, Esq." Lyon was sentenced to four months' imprisonment and a fine of $1,000. While in prison he was

by a citizen of another state. This amendment had been demanded by Republicans (it was favored also by many Federalists) after the Supreme Court had decided other-

---

Kentucky Resolutions
1798

"*Resolved,* that the several States composing the United States of America are not united on the principle of unlimited submission to their general government; but that by compact under the style and title of a Constitution for the United States and of amendments thereto, they constituted a general government for special purposes, delegating to that government certain definite powers, reserving each State to itself the residuary mass of rights to their own self-government; and that whensoever the general government assumes undelegated powers, its acts are unauthoritative, void, and of no force: That to this compact each State acceded as a State, and is an integral party, its co-States forming, as to itself, the other party: That the government created by this compact was not made the exclusive or final judge of the extent of the powers delegated to itself; since that would have made its discretion, and not the Constitution, the measure of its powers; but that as in all other cases of compact among parties having no common Judge, *each party has an equal right to judge for itself, as well of infractions as of the mode and measure of redress.*"

---

overwhelmingly re-elected to Congress, and after his release he was cheered as a hero, a group of Vermont schoolgirls, for example, carrying a banner which read: "Our brave Representative, who has been suffering for us under an unjust sentence and the tyranny of a detested understrapper of despotism, this day rises superior to despotism." (The little girls were not arrested, though they too violated the Sedition Act.)

With such martyrs as Lyon, the Republicans had what they considered living proof that the Federalists were trampling upon constitutional liberties and the reserved rights of the states. Early in 1798 state rights were strengthened in the Constitution by the addition of the Eleventh Amendment, which provided that no state could be sued

wise in the case of *Chisholm v. Georgia* (1793). That decision aroused Republican feeling against the Court, and, after the passage of the Alien and Sedition Acts, the Republicans had no reason to look to the Court for relief. Indeed, the Court never yet had declared an act of Congress unconstitutional, and the Republicans denied that it had the power to do so. They believed that the recent Federalist legislation, particularly the Sedition Act, was unconstitutional, for the First Amendment stated that Congress should pass no law abridging freedom of speech or of the press.

What agency of government should decide the question of constitutionality? The Republican leaders Jefferson and Madison concluded that the state legislatures should decide, and they ably expressed their view in two sets of resolutions, one written (anonymously) by Jefferson and adopted by the Kentucky legislature (1798, 1799), and the other drafted by Madison and approved by the Virginia legislature (1798). These Kentucky and Virginia resolutions asserted the following doctrines. The federal government had been formed by a "compact" or contract among the states. It was a limited government, possessing only certain delegated powers. Whenever it exercised any additional and undelegated powers, its acts were "unauthoritative, void, and of no force." The parties to the contract, the states, must decide for themselves when and whether the central government exceeded its powers. And "nullification" by the states was the "rightful remedy" whenever the general government went too far. The resolutions urged all the states to join in declaring the Alien and Sedition Acts null and void and in requesting their repeal at the next session of Congress, but none of the others went along with Virginia and Kentucky.

Nevertheless, these resolutions were of great historical significance, both immediately and in the long run. They were echoed and re-echoed down to the time of the Civil War. The New England Federalists invoked the same state-rights arguments in opposition to the policies of Jefferson himself, while he was President (1801–1809). Later these arguments were elaborated by the nullificationists of the South, led by John C. Calhoun, who harked back again and again to the "principles of '98 and '99." Meanwhile, in 1800, the resolutions served as a kind of political platform for the Republicans in their successful campaign to turn the Federalists out of office.

Election of 1800

In the election of 1800 Jefferson and Burr, representing the alliance of Virginia and New York, were again the Republican candidates. Adams was running for re-election on the Federalist ticket, and his running mate was C. C. Pinckney, brother of the Thomas Pinckney who had been the Federalist vice-presidential candidate in 1796. If Adams had been willing to continue and enlarge the war with France, he most likely could have reunited his party and gained another presidential term for himself. As it was, the Federalist leaders were divided worse than ever, and the party without its wartime halo of patriotism had less support than previously among the mass of the people.

During the nearly twelve years of Federalist rule, the party had created numerous political enemies in consequence of Hamilton's financial program, the suppression of the Whiskey Rebellion, Jay's Treaty, and the Alien and Sedition Acts. Denouncing these measures, and especially the last of them, the Republicans made state rights and constitutional liberties the main issues of their campaign in 1800. They pictured Adams as a tyrant and a man who wanted to be King. The Federalists, on the other hand, described Jefferson as a dangerous radical and his followers as wild men who, if they got into power, would bring on a reign of terror comparable to that of the French Revolution at its worst. Nothing that was sacred would be safe. If Jefferson should be elected, said the good Federalist and president of Yale College, Timothy Dwight, "the Bible would be cast into a bonfire, our holy worship changed into a dance of Jacobin phrensy, our wives and daughters dishonored, and our sons converted into disciples of Voltaire and the dragoons of Marat." Thousands of the respectable, the pious, and the propertied trembled at the prospect.

The contest was close, and the outcome in the electoral college depended upon the voting in one state, New York. In New

York City the vice-presidential candidate, Burr, was the organizer of Republican victory. The Revolutionary veterans of the city had formed the Tammany Society to

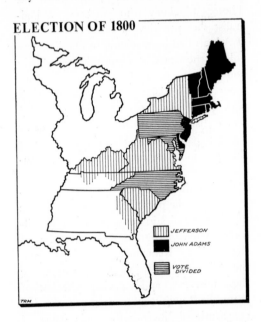

ELECTION OF 1800

JEFFERSON
JOHN ADAMS
VOTE DIVIDED

TRM

maintain their wartime fellowship and to combat the pretensions of the Society of the Cincinnati, the exclusive and aristocratic organization of Revolutionary officers. Though not himself a member of Tammany, Burr converted it into a political machine and, with its aid, carried the city for the Republicans by such a large majority as to carry the state also. The Republicans gained control of the legislature, and since New York was one of the states in which the legislature cast the electoral vote, the Republicans could count upon that vote in the presidential election.

But Alexander Hamilton had other ideas. During and after the election he was busy with a twofold intrigue. By one of his schemes he intended to snatch victory from defeat for the Federalists by changing the New York rules in the middle of the game. He planned to induce the legislature, before the Republicans took over, to pass a law re-

quiring the popular election of presidential electors, and then he hoped to rig this election in such a way that the Federalists would win it. By his other scheme he intended, while winning a majority for the Federalist ticket, to defeat Adams himself by persuading some of the Federalist electors to throw away their Adams votes, thus making C. C. Pinckney the next President —as, indeed, Hamilton had hoped to do with Thomas Pinckney in 1796. But Hamilton was frustrated in both of his plots.

When the electors of the several states cast their votes, Adams received a total of 65 and Pinckney 64. Jefferson got 73, and so did Burr. To avoid such a tie, Republican leaders had meant for at least one of their electors to refrain from giving Burr his vote. But through a misunderstanding—some said that Burr himself was secretly responsible—the plan went awry. And so the election was not yet over: in accordance with the Constitution the decision between the two highest, between Burr and Jefferson, was up to the House of Representatives, with the delegation from each state casting a single vote.

Since the Federalists controlled a majority of the states' votes in the existing Congress, they had the privilege of deciding which of their opponents was to be the next President, though the Republicans, in making their nominations, had clearly intended for Jefferson to have the first place on their ticket. Some of the more extreme of the Federalists now hoped to postpone or to prevent any breaking of the tie and, instead, to make new arrangements for the presidential succession so that the highest office in the land would yet fall to a Federalist. Others, fearing chaos and possible civil war if no election were made, thought it would be better to come to an understanding with Burr and elect him. Hamilton disapproved both proposals. Though he had a low opinion of Jefferson, he had a still lower one of

Burr, his bitter rival in law and politics in New York. Hamilton considered Burr an unprincipled and untrustworthy schemer, which he doubtless was—though, considering Hamilton's own recent electoral intrigues, this was certainly a case of the pot calling the kettle black. Burr himself remained strangely silent, neither electioneering openly for himself nor refusing publicly to accept office at the hands of the Federalists.

During the winter of 1800–1801 the House balloted again and again without mustering a majority for either candidate. Finally, only a few weeks before inauguration day, some of the Federalist die-hards gave in, the tie was broken, and Jefferson was named as President. Afterwards one of the Federalists claimed that he had given in because Jefferson's friends had assured him that Jefferson, if elected, would appoint him to a government job and would preserve the main Federalist policies with respect to commerce, the navy, and the public debt, while making no wholesale removals of Federalists from the lower offices of the government.

Packing the Courts

In addition to a majority of the presidential electors in 1800, the Republicans also won a majority of the seats in both houses of the next Congress. The only branch of the government left in Federalist hands was the judiciary, and Adams and his fellow partisans during his last months in office took steps to make their hold upon the courts secure.

By the Judiciary Act of 1801 the Federalists succeeded in reducing the number of Supreme Court justiceships by one but at the same time greatly increasing the number of federal judgeships as a whole. The act created a separate system of circuit courts of appeal, between the federal district courts and the Supreme Court. Formerly (in accordance with the Judiciary Act of 1789) a district judge had sat with two Supreme Court justices to hear appeals on the circuit. The new law also provided for ten additional district judgeships.

To these newly created positions Adams proceeded to appoint deserving Federalists. It was said that he stayed up until midnight on his last day in office, March 3, 1801, in order to complete the signing of the judge's commissions, and so these officeholders were known as his "midnight appointments." Since federal judges held office for life—that is, with good behavior—Jefferson as the incoming President would be powerless to remove Adams's appointees. Or so the Federalists assumed.

Much the most important of the Adams appointments, though not one of the midnight variety, was the naming of John Marshall as Chief Justice of the Supreme Court. Marshall, a leading Virginia Federalist, had served with Washington's army during the Revolution, and from first-hand observation of the sufferings at Valley Forge he had been impressed by the evils of a weak, divided, and inefficient form of government. Studying law on his own and at the College of William and Mary, he became one of the foremost lawyers in the country. He helped to win the bitter struggle in Virginia for ratification of the Constitution in 1788. As a member of the diplomatic commission involved in the X. Y. Z. Affair, he stood firmly for the national honor and the national pride. After Pickering's dismissal he served as Adams's Secretary of State, and after his appointment to the Supreme Court he held both positions until the end of Adams's term.

→»-→»-→»-→»(((-(((-(((-(((

BIBLIOGRAPHY

GILBERT CHINARD, *Honest John Adams* (1933), is an excellent biography. The Adams point of view is well illustrated in *The Selected Writings of John and John Quincy Adams* (1946), edited by Adrienne Koch and William Peden. M. J. Dauer, *The Adams Federalists* (1953), is especially good on the machinations of Alexander Hamilton against President Adams.

For a general account of the undeclared hostilities from 1798 to 1800, see G. W. Allen, *Our Naval War with France* (1909). A good biography of the hero of that war is E. S. Ferguson's *Truxtun of the Constellation* (1956), which throws light on the beginnings of the United States navy. F. B.

Tolles, *George Logan of Philadelphia* (1953), is a sympathetic life of the man who undertook, singlehanded, to bring peace. Bradford Perkins, *The First Rapprochement: England and the United States, 1795–1805* (1955), shows the wartime cooperation of the two countries.

The Joseph McCarthy excitement of the early 1950's gave a timely interest to two studies of an early threat to civil liberties in the United States: J. C. Miller, *Crisis in Freedom: The Alien and Sedition Acts* (1951), and J. M. Smith, *Freedom's Fetters: The Alien and Sedition Laws and American Civil Liberties* (1956), the more thorough of the two books.

CHAPTER 11

Life in the Young Republic

T HE AMERICAN PEOPLE won political independence in the Revolutionary War, and they were to win commercial independence in the War of 1812. Meanwhile they aspired to a kind of cultural independence also. They looked forward to a time when the United States would be uniquely great in science, art, and technology as well as government. This "happy land" was to be the "seat of empire" and the "final stage" of civilization, with "glorious works of high invention and of wond'rous art." So Philip Freneau and Hugh H. Brackenridge proclaimed in their *Poem on the Rising Glory of America* (1772). Later Freneau became an ardent Jeffersonian in politics, but his Federalist contemporaries sang the same theme. Joel Barlow, in his *Vision of Columbus* (1787), saw America as "the last and greatest theatre for the improvement of mankind."

By the early 1800's the United States had not yet fulfilled the promise of its poets, but beginnings had been made which suggested that the promise, or much of it, might eventually be fulfilled.

Education and the Professions

In certain respects the War of the Revolution temporarily handicapped American intellectual life. Some learned men turned from science and scholarship to military or political service. The noted astronomer David Rittenhouse, for example, left his telescopes and devoted himself to a Revolutionary committee, the Pennsylvania Council of Safety, while advising his countrymen to abandon schools and concentrate on defense. Many schools did close, especially in rural areas, and most of the colleges were disrupted. Harvard buildings were used as American army barracks; Nassau Hall at Princeton was damaged during Washington's New Jersey campaign; and the William and Mary campus became the military headquarters of Cornwallis before the Battle of Yorktown.

But the Revolution also stimulated intellectual activity and brought forth ideas that were to have lasting consequences. Through military service thousands of young men got better acquainted with their own country, and by reading patriotic pamphlets, or at least hearing them discussed, these soldiers received something of a political education. With the French alliance there came from France not only troops and supplies but also ideas—the skeptical, experimental, scientific notions of the Enlightenment. And, with independence as a war aim and finally as an accomplished fact, it seemed to thoughtful Americans that widespread literacy and learning were absolutely essential to the success of the new republic. Thomas Jefferson, for one, called for a "crusade against ignorance."

The friends of learning advocated not merely education as such but a special kind of education, one that would fill the minds of youth with patriotic, republican thoughts. The Massachusetts geographer Jedidiah Morse, author of *Geography Made Easy* (1784), said the country must have its own textbooks so that the people would not be infected with the monarchical and aristocratic ideas of England. The Connecticut schoolmaster and lawyer Noah Webster likewise contended that the American schoolboy should be educated as a patriot. "As soon as he opens his lips," Webster wrote, "he should rehearse the history of his own country; he should lisp the praise of liberty, and of those illustrious heroes and statesmen who have wrought a revolution in her favor."

To foster a distinctive culture and unify the nation, Webster insisted upon a simplified and Americanized spelling—*honor* instead of *honour*, for example. His *American Spelling Book* (1783), commonly known as the "blue-backed speller," eventually sold over 100 million copies, to become the best-selling book (except for the Bible) in the entire history of American publish-

ing. Webster also wrote grammars and other schoolbooks. His school dictionary (1806) was republished in many editions and eventually was much enlarged to form *An American Dictionary of the English Language* (1828). By means of his speller and his dictionary he succeeded in establishing a national standard of words and usages for the United States.

In their first constitutions, several of the states endorsed the principle of public education, but none actually required the establishment of free schools. A Massachusetts law of 1789 reaffirmed the colonial laws providing for the support of schools by the various towns. Jedidiah Morse observed later that the enforcement of the law was lax in many places. Even in Boston only seven public schools existed in 1790, and most of these were poorly housed; more than twice as many private schools were in operation. In Virginia, Jefferson as wartime governor proposed a plan by which the elements of reading and writing should be provided for all children, and secondary and higher education for the gifted, with state scholarships for the needy. The plan was not enacted into law. As late as 1815 none of the states (not even Massachusetts) had in actual operation a comprehensive public school system.

Outside of New England, schooling continued to be viewed as the responsibility of the family and the church rather than the state. In the Middle Atlantic region and the South, most schools were run by religious groups, by proprietary schoolmasters, or by philanthropic societies. Though requiring tuition from parents who could afford it, many schools accepted the poor without pay. In the cities, special organizations were formed for the education of the poor. One of these, the New York Free School Society, introduced from England (1806) the Lancastrian method, to economize on instruction costs: the teacher taught a lesson to several superior pupils, and then these "monitors" drilled groups of their fellow pupils.

During and after the Revolution, private

Academy, established in 1772 by North Carolina Moravians, was one of the earliest.

At the outbreak of the Revolution there had been a total of nine colleges in all the

A School in Session About 1800. *In such a one-room school, children of practically all ages were brought together. While one group recited, the rest learned their lessons—or were supposed to. Paper and ink were scarce; a slate and a slate pencil were commonly used instead. There was little in the way of furnishings except for backless benches and a few desks, usually placed under the windows, where the light was best. The teacher had to look out for the fire and perform the other chores of a janitor. Often the teacher was a college student, earning money during the long winter vacation from his own studies, or he was a recent college graduate supporting himself while he prepared for the law and politics. Daniel Webster and Thaddeus Stevens once taught school, and so did many another young man who afterwards became prominent in public life.* (LIBRARY OF CONGRESS)

academies sprang up in increasing numbers. Many were patterned after the academies founded by the Phillips family at Andover, Massachusetts (1778), and at Exeter, New Hampshire (1781). By 1815 there were 30 private secondary schools in Massachusetts, 37 in New York, and more than 100 in the country as a whole. Most of these admitted only boys, but a few academies or seminaries were provided for girls. Salem Female

colonies; in 1800 there were twenty-two in the various states, and the number continued steadily to increase thereafter. Whereas all but two of the colonial colleges were sectarian in origin and spirit, a majority of those founded during the first three decades of independence were nondenominational. Especially significant, in foreshadowing the future pattern of higher education, was the fact that five were state institutions: the universities of Georgia (1785), North Carolina (1789), Vermont (1791), Ohio (1804), and South Carolina (1805). For the time being, none of these was either quite public or a university in the modern sense. Their offerings were limited, and their financial support was derived mainly from private endowments, gifts, and tuition fees rather than appropriations of the rather niggardly legislatures.

All together, more than twenty colleges, public and private, were in operation during the first decade of the nineteenth century. The largest of them had an enrollment of no more than a few hundred students, and the total endowment of all the institutions amounted to little more than $500,000. Equipment was poor and libraries small— the Harvard library, with 15,000 volumes in 1812, was exceptional. Standards generally were low, and complaints were often heard that serious scholars were not being produced. As of 1775, only about one in a thousand men (and no women at all) had the benefit of such college education as was available; by 1815, the proportion had not risen a great deal.

Jefferson, John Adams, and a few other statesmen nourished the ideal of a true university, providing the best of training in the professions as well as the liberal arts. Nothing came of Jefferson's hope that a national university might be established. As wartime governor of Virginia, he managed to expand the work of William and Mary by adding professorships of law, medicine, and modern languages. George Wythe, the first law professor at the college, taught a remarkable number of youths who afterwards became distinguished lawyers and statesmen. Before 1800 the University of Pennsylvania and Columbia College instituted law courses, and Judge Tapping Reeve opened a private law school in Litchfield, Connecticut. As a rule, lawyers got their training, as in colonial times, by "reading law" in the office of a practicing attorney.

Most physicians likewise still studied medicine and gained experience by working with an established practitioner, but several medical schools were in existence by the early 1800's. The oldest of these, at the University of Pennsylvania, was founded in 1765. Its most distinguished professor, and the outstanding physician in America, was Benjamin Rush, who had received his medical degree at Edinburgh. As an army surgeon during the Revolutionary War, Dr. Rush protested against improper sanitation and medical care, which caused many more soldiers to die of camp diseases than of battle wounds. Afterwards he interested himself in the effects of diet and drink upon health, and he also made pioneering studies of psychosomatic and psychiatric disorders. As educators, Rush and other physicians had to struggle against age-old superstitions and against popular hostility to the dissection of corpses. In 1788 a riot was provoked when a human limb was hung out of a New York hospital window to dry, and from time to time medical students got into trouble for body-snatching, since cadavers seldom were available by legal means.

The science of public as well as private health remained in its infancy. In the summer of 1793 an epidemic of yellow fever raged unchecked in Philadelphia, bringing death to a tenth of the population in one of the worst disasters ever to befall an American city. The physicians were helpless, though Dr. Rush came near to guessing the cause of the epidemic when he explained it as being due to the miasma arising from decomposed matter. The Philadelphia experience stimulated programs for improving sanitation and making cities cleaner, and thus unwittingly the number of breeding places for the mosquito that transmits yellow fever were reduced. In many cases the prevailing medical practices hastened death instead of prolonging life. George Washington need not have died from a throat infection in 1799, but his physicians, doing their best according to their lights, bled and purged him so thoroughly as to impair his resistance to the disease.

As in colonial America, so also in the young republic scientific investigation (except in medical science) was largely the work of amateurs. But it was becoming more and more specialized, and scientists were growing increasingly conscious of their common professional interests. In 1780 the American Academy of Arts and Sciences was formed in Boston, its announced object being "to cultivate every art and science which may tend to advance the interest, honor, dignity, and happiness of a free, independent, and virtuous people." At meetings of the Academy the members read papers on scientific subjects, and eventually these began to be published in a regular series. The founding of this Academy in the midst of the Revolution indicates that the war did not completely distract Americans from scientific effort. Throughout the war years and afterward the noted botanist William Bartram persisted in collecting specimens and observing the plants and wild life of the South and West. His *Travels* (1791), translated into French, German, and other languages, was acclaimed abroad as well as at home.

On the whole, the republican atmosphere of America was favorable to scientific inquiry. To this country came Dr. Joseph Priestley in 1794, as a refugee from the reactionary spirit then prevailing in England. Already famous as the discoverer of oxygen, Priestley continued his researches in Pennsylvania, discovering carbon monoxide and the possibility of liberating air from water. He stimulated interest in chemistry, though some Americans disagreed with him when he maintained that fire consisted of a material substance, known as "phlogiston."

Painting had become a busy profession, and the young republic produced several artists of unusual talent. The first of the notable American-born painters, Benjamin West, did not make his career in the United States. After studying in Rome, West settled in England (1763) and rose to prominence in artistic circles there. His ideal, in art, was the "noble simplicity and quiet grandeur" of republican Rome, rather than strict realism on the one hand or baroque elaborateness on the other. West left his influence upon a whole generation of American artists—John Singleton Copley, Gilbert Stuart, Charles Willson Peale, and many others—who went to England to study under him. Most of them (Copley was a notable exception) returned to their native country and set up studios, to make a living from commissions to paint historical scenes and portraits of wealthy and notable Americans. Peale (1806) founded the Pennsylvania Academy of Fine Arts as a center for the encouragement of American painting, but aspiring artists continued to seek their training abroad, especially in England.

Despite the high hopes and the best efforts of the advocates of republican learning and cultural independence, American arts and sciences remained essentially derivative and provincial for a long time after political independence had become a fact. The same was true of American literature.

Letters, Drama, and Music

During the first forty years of independence, the most widely read of American writings—and some of the greatest ones (such as *The Federalist*)—were polemical and political, not belletristic. In pamphlet and newspaper the literate American followed the arguments about British colonial policy, the aims of the Revolution, the question of a new Constitution, and the party contests of the young republic. He became a "newspaper-reading animal," as an English visitor observed. This preoccupation with the news of the day drew attention away from literature of a more artistic and permanent kind. Thus, in one way, the published, or to get it sold after it was in print. Until well into the nineteenth century, there were in America no book publishers in the modern sense, no firms that

Brooklyn, New York, in the Early 1800's. *Settled by the Dutch, Brooklyn was not incorporated as a city until almost two centuries later, in 1834. It became a part of New York City in 1898. During the early 1800's, Brooklyn, on the tip of Long Island, retained a village atmosphere, though separated only by the East River from the bustling city of New York on Manhattan Island. Note the village pump—the water supply of the surrounding householders. From "Winter Scene in Brooklyn," a contemporary painting by Francis Guy.* (IN THE BROOKLYN MUSEUM COLLECTION)

newspapers handicapped literary development. Yet, in another way, the newspapers helped it, for they created a reading public and produced a potential market for literary works.

There was a more serious handicap to the rise of American authorship. An aspiring author found it hard to get his manuscript would bear the cost and take the risk of publishing. The author himself had to pay all or at least the larger part of the expenses. He could find few printers willing to share the burden with him, for they could reprint the works of popular English authors without paying a royalty. No author in the young republic could support himself by means of his writing alone. The first to try it was the novelist Charles Brockden Brown. He produced a series of well-written horror stories but had to take a job as magazine editor in order to eke out his income.

The American author, if he looked to periodicals or the theater for a market, did little if any better than with books. In the late eighteenth century, several magazines were published in the United States, the most important being the *Columbian*, the *American Museum*, the *Massachusetts Magazine*, and the *New-York Magazine*. All of these filled their pages chiefly by clipping material from English publications. Meanwhile the theater had grown into an accepted, permanent institution in American cities, with substantial buildings and regular schedules of performances. George Washington himself attended plays, and opposition to the theater as "the house of the devil" declined, though it by no means disappeared. But the American dramatist, like the writer of books and the contributor to magazines, had to compete with English authors, who did not have to be paid royalties.

Under the circumstances, it is surprising that the young republic contained so many able and active poets, essayists, novelists, and playwrights as it did. Among the most active poets and essayists were the "Hartford Wits," a group of Connecticut writers who met together for sociability and mutual encouragement. The leaders were Joel Barlow, Timothy Dwight, and John Trumbull (not to be confused with the contemporary painter of the same name). These men wrote epics on American greatness and satires on American foibles—as seen from a solid, Federalist, New England point of view. Barlow eventually went over to the Jeffersonian side, but the ablest and most thoroughgoing Jeffersonian poet, a hardy foe of the Hartford Wits, was Philip Freneau of New Jersey.

Novels became the rage in England during the last half of the eighteenth century, and their popularity spread to the United States, where the latest English successes were promptly imported and reprinted, and eagerly read. The most fashionable themes were sex and sentimentality, satire, and terror. When novelists finally appeared in America, they hoped to produce a native, original kind of fiction, but they had to appeal to the prevailing taste. They used essentially the same themes as the English novelists, though substituting American scenes and situations for English ones. The first American novel, William Hill Brown's *The Power of Sympathy* (1789), was intended, the author said, "to expose the fatal consequences" of immorality; it is a story (based on fact) of seduction, incestuous love, rape, and suicide. Hugh Henry Brackenridge's *Modern Chivalry*, an interminable tale published in installments (1792–1815), satirizes certain excesses and errors of democracy. Charles Brockden Brown's *Wieland* (1798), the best work of the greatest of the early American novelists, gives a terrifying account of a man who goes crazy and kills his wife and children.

The first play to be written and professionally performed in America, Thomas Godfrey's *The Prince of Parthia*, was produced in 1767 at the New Theater in Philadelphia. This melodrama of passion and violence in ancient Parthia, though borrowing some elements from Shakespeare and other English playwrights, demonstrated that an American could make original and interesting use of inherited dramatic traditions. So did the first comedy to be written and performed in this country—Royall Tyler's *The Contrast*. An excellent acting-play, on the theme of city versus country manners, *The Contrast* began a long and highly successful run in 1787, at the John Street Theater in New York. During the next twenty years and more, a number of other popular plays came from the pen of Tyler, the ablest native playwright of his time. A more versatile figure, the most influential in the early development of the American drama, was William Dunlap, who not only wrote and adapted plays but also produced them, designed and managed theaters, and made himself the defender and finally the historian of the American stage. No crusader for uniquely American productions, Dunlap questioned "how far we ought to wish for a national drama, distinct from that of our English forefathers." He presented what the public wanted—Shakespearian and other English plays, translations and adaptations of the latest European hits, and the works of Americans, including himself.

Most of the songs popular during and after the Revolution consisted of new and patriotic words set to familiar English tunes. "Yankee Doodle" was written, during the French and Indian War, by a British army surgeon with the intention of poking fun at the ragged colonial troops. It became a favorite with the Yankees themselves, and during the Revolution they added many variations, some of them unsuitable for polite company. Other popular music was written by Francis Hopkinson, the first notable American composer and a man of amazing versatility. The first student to be graduated from the College of Philadelphia, Hopkinson practiced law, served in the first Continental Congress and signed the Declaration of Independence, wrote verse, essays, and Revolutionary pamphlets, painted, gave public performances on the harpsichord, and sat as a judge in Pennsylvania

and federal courts, besides composing music. A collection of his best work was published under the title of *Seven Songs* (1788). His son, the eminent lawyer Joseph Hopkinson, wrote the words for "Hail, Columbia" during the undeclared war with France (1798); for many years, this stirring song remained the nearest equivalent to a national anthem.

The Churches and Religion

Americans of the young republic might have been patriotic enough but, from the point of view of many a religious leader, they were insufficiently pious. The religious excitement of the Great Awakening had passed, and sermons of the Revolutionary era lamented the "decay of vital piety," the "degeneracy of manners," and the luxurious growth of "vice."

Certainly large numbers of the people were turning away from familiar faiths. Many interested themselves in deism, the rational religion of Enlightenment philosophers, especially those in France. The deists believed in God but considered Him a rather remote being who had created the universe, not an intimate presence who was concerned with human individuals and their sins. Franklin, Jefferson, and others among the Founding Fathers held deistic views. Such views, at first confined to the well-educated, finally spread among the people at large. By 1800, books and articles attacking religious "superstitions" found eager readers all over the country. The most influential of such writings, Thomas Paine's *The Age of Reason* (1794-1796), was discussed in homes, colleges, taverns, stage-

Farm Life About 1800. [OPPOSITE] *The seasonal round of farm activities is illustrated in a contemporary engraving, which incidentally reveals the rather crude state of the engravers' art in the United States. The scenes at the left, from top to bottom, show plowing, harvesting (with sickles), threshing (with flails), spinning and knitting, and fence-mending. The scenes at the right show haying, flower-watering, corn-picking, cider-making, and sheep-shearing. Young boys enjoyed such recreations as hoop-rolling (top right) and fishing (bottom right).*

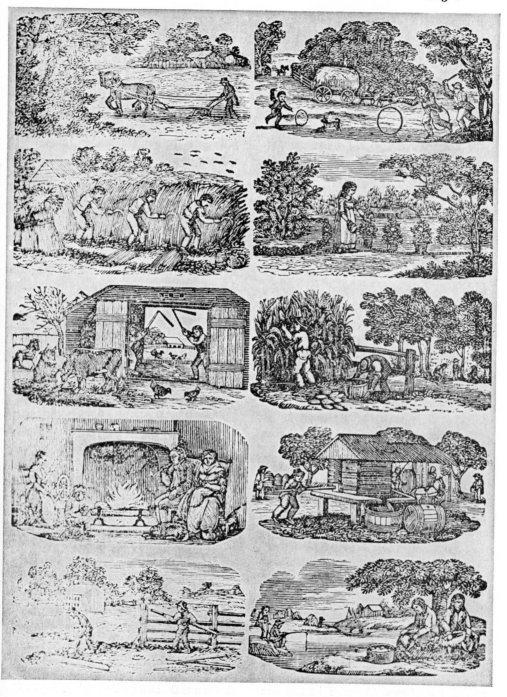

coaches, everywhere. Paine once declared that Christianity was the "strangest religion ever set up," for "it committed a murder upon Jesus in order to redeem mankind from the sin of eating an apple." No wonder the preachers regularly denounced Paine and deism and called for a new revival of religious faith.

While resisting the spread of free thought, the churches also had to deal with other problems. After the Declaration of Independence the groups with foreign ties had to reconsider their position, and even those without such ties faced the task of reorganizing on a national basis. As population moved westward, the churches had to follow the frontier if they were to grow with the country's growth. In responding to the challenges of the time—revitalization, reorganization, and expansion—some denominations succeeded much better than others. Old sects developed faster than ever, or they lagged behind as never before. New sects arose. The grim doctrines of Calvinism gave way to more optimistic faiths, and the religious pattern of the young republic became even more variegated than that of colonial America had been.

The Congregationalists, who led in numbers and influence at the close of the colonial period, soon lost their pre-eminence. They continued to be tax-supported in Massachusetts, Connecticut, and New Hampshire even after those colonies were transformed into states. But the Congregationalists lacked the missionary zeal, appealing theology, and strong, centralized organization that were essential for winning and holding converts.

In New England, its home ground, the Congregational Church was weakened by the growing popularity of universalist and unitarian doctrines. Many of its members rejected not only the idea of predestination but also the idea of the Trinity. They believed that salvation was available to all,

and that God was one (not three), Jesus being only a great religious teacher and not the son of God. The Universalist Church came into existence (1779) when believers in universal salvation began to hold meetings in Gloucester, Massachusetts. A little later (1782) the Unitarian Church was founded in Boston. The Universalists appealed to the poor and the Unitarians to the well-to-do, but both groups held essentially the same beliefs. The Universalists, it has been said, thought God was too good to damn man, while the Unitarians thought man was too good to be damned by God.

In the West the Congregationalists lost ground to the Presbyterians after agreeing to the Plan of Union of 1801. By this plan, members of the two denominations combined and chose either a Congregational or a Presbyterian minister in newly settled areas where neither group was numerous enough to justify a separate church. Eventually most of the united "Presbygational" congregations became Presbyterian.

American Presbyterians had adopted a constitution (1789) by which the whole country was divided into sixteen presbyteries and four synods, with a general assembly that served as the highest ecclesiastical court. Already well entrenched on the frontier, where so many of the Scotch-Irish had settled before the Revolution, the Church expanded with the expanding nation. Indeed, it grew too fast for the maintenance of internal harmony. Bickering reappeared between Old and New Lights, between traditional Calvinists and believers in salvation for all. New sects splintered off, as did the followers of Thomas and Alexander Campbell, who in the early 1800's rejected the Calvinist dogma of limited election. Later the Campbellites formed a separate church known as the Disciples of Christ.

Among the Baptists, as among the Presbyterians, there were disputes about the question of predestination or free will, but theological differences did not prevent the Baptists from growing more rapidly than any other denomination except one (the Methodist) during the late eighteenth and early nineteenth century. Scattered over the whole country, they were especially numerous in Virginia and the Carolinas. Long the most militant advocates of the separation of church and state, they ceased to impress others as dangerous radicals after this principle was adopted in the Virginia statute of religious liberty and in the federal Bill of Rights. Like the Congregationalists, the Baptists had a loose organization, but unlike the Congregationalists they did not rely on an educated and salaried ministry. They depended on zealous but unlearned farmer-preachers who carried the gospel to the common people in language that the common people could understand.

More than the Baptists or any other religious group, the Roman Catholics gained in prestige (though not in numbers) as a consequence of the Revolution. On the advice of Charles Carroll of Carrollton, Maryland statesman and Catholic lay leader, most of the Catholics in America supported the Patriot cause during the war. The French alliance brought Catholic troops and chaplains to this country. In such times as these, Catholic Americans no longer seemed, as in colonial days, like agents of the devil. After the war the Vatican provided for the United States a church government separate from that of England. In 1784 Father John Carroll was appointed head of Catholic missions in this country, and with the elaboration of the American hierarchy he was made the first American bishop (1789) and finally Archbishop of Baltimore (1808).

The Anglicans suffered more than any other religious group as a result of the Revolution. They were badly divided on the issues of the war, the clergy being mostly Loyalist in the states where Anglicans were few, and partly Loyalist in Virginia and Maryland. In these two states the Anglican Church had benefited from tax support, which was lost when the Church was disestablished. In other states the Church had depended upon aid from the mother country, and that aid was withdrawn. By the end of the war a large proportion of the parishes lacked clergymen, for there were few recruits to take the places of those who had died or had left the country as Loyalist refugees. Since there never had been an American bishop or an intercolonial organization of the Church, postwar Anglican leaders had to start from scratch in setting up an independent, national hierarchy. By 1789 they had succeeded in organizing the Protestant Episcopal Church. Till after the War of 1812 the Church remained weak, gaining few members, and losing many with the departure of the Methodists.

John Wesley, the founder of Methodism, did not set up a new church in England, nor did he intend to do so in America. In 1776, ten years after his lay ministers had begun to organize Methodist "classes" in the colonies, American Methodists insisted that they were not "common dissenters" but "a religious society in communion with the Church of England." But the war changed their attitude. When peace came, the greatest of Wesley's agents in America, Francis Asbury, concluded that American conditions required the formation of a separate body. In 1784, Asbury called a meeting of Methodist preachers, at Baltimore, and launched the Methodist Protestant Church, with himself as the first bishop.

The Methodists had a unique and effective organization. It was authoritarian, with power concentrated at the top, in the hands of the bishops. The preachers were itinerants: each of them had charge of several widely scattered congregations and rode the rounds from one to another. Every year the preachers met in a conference (by 1796 there were six annual conferences in different parts of the country) where a bishop conferred with them, ordained new ministers, and assigned all the riders to their circuits, making frequent changes. This system was well adapted to a growing, moving, frontier society. As the historian W. W. Sweet has said, the Presbyterian minister in the West "was called by the people," the Baptist farmer-preacher "came with the people," and the Methodist circuit-rider "was sent to the people." The circuit-rider brought a message of individual responsibility for eternal happiness. It was a welcome message. The Methodist Protestant Church, within sixty years after its foundation, became the largest in the United States.

Along with the Baptists and the Presbyterians, the Methodists gained many converts in the Second Awakening, a new wave of revivalism that swept the country at the turn of the century. This revivalism had two distinct phases. It began among the Presbyterians in certain colleges of the East and South, reaching its height at Yale under the leadership of President Timothy Dwight (1797–1817). Then, with zealous graduates carrying the evangelical spirit to the West, it went to even greater extremes on the frontier. In 1800, in Kentucky, the Presbyterians held the first camp meeting, an outdoor revival that lasted several days. The Methodists soon took up the camp-meeting technique, and the circuit-rider Peter Cartwright won fame as the most effective soul-saver of all backwoods revivalists. The camp meeting was a Methodist "harvest time," as Bishop Asbury said. It became increasingly popular, the bishop noting with satisfaction in 1811 that 400 camp meetings were to be held that year. Crowds of sinners as well as salvation seekers attended these open-air get-togethers, and the atmosphere sometimes was far from church-like. Many Presbyterians, especially Campbellites, came to frown on the camp meeting. Even Cartwright deplored the

worst outbreaks of frenzy, when men and women had fits, rolled in the dust, and lay twitching with the "holy jerks."

After 1800 the devil and the deists were on the run. Freethinkers by no means disappeared (the young Abraham Lincoln took up free thought in frontier Illinois) but they were put upon the defensive. The great majority of Americans subscribed to some variant of revealed Christianity, though it usually was not quite the same as the predominant faith of their forefathers. The churches in the nineteenth century placed more emphasis on the New Testament and the saving grace of Jesus—and less emphasis on the Old Testament and the stern decrees of Jehovah—than those of the seventeenth or even the eighteenth century had done.

Technology and Industry

While religious patterns were changing, so were industrial techniques, even more fundamentally. A new technology was developing, which was to have profound effects upon the future of the United States.

In part, the new technology came from England, where the Industrial Revolution was beginning at the time the American Revolution occurred. The essence of the Industrial Revolution was simply this: more rapidly and extensively than ever before, power-driven machines were taking the place of hand-operated tools. To tend the machines, workers were brought together in factories or mills located at the sources of power. New factory towns arose, with a new class of dependent laborers and another of millowners or industrial capitalists. The factory system was adapted most readily to the manufacture of cotton thread and cloth. In textile making, invention called forth invention. Improvements in weaving made necessary improvements in spinning, so that the spinners could keep up with the weavers, and these improvements required new devices for carding, that is, combing

A Camp Meeting. *Originating in 1800, the camp meeting soon became a popular American religious institution in rural areas, especially in the South and West. By 1820, about 1,000 meetings a year were held. The painting reproduced here was made in the 1830's. A typical camp meeting (in Maryland, in 1806) was described by a participant who wrote of the tents, the wagons, the plank seats, the covered stand for the preacher, and the daily schedule. "At day break the trumpets were blown round the camp for the people to rise 20 minutes afterward for family prayer at the door of every tent—if fair weather—at sunrise they blew at the stand for public prayer, and then breakfasted. At 10 oclock they blew for preaching—by 2 ocl. dinner was to be over in every tent. At 3 ocl. preaching again, and again at night." After several days of this, "hundreds were prostrate upon the earth before the Lord. . . . Will I ever see anything more like the day of Judgment on this side of eternity—to see the people running, yes, running, from every direction to the stand, weeping, shouting, and shouting for joy. Prayer was then made—and every Brother fell upon the neck of his Brother, and the Sisters did likewise. Then we parted. O! glorious day they went home singing and shouting."* (COURTESY OF THE NEW-YORK HISTORICAL SOCIETY, NEW YORK CITY)

and straightening the fibers for the spinner. Water, wind, and animal power continued to be used but began to be supplemented and replaced by steam. Especially was this true after the appearance of James Watt's steam engine (patented in 1769), which, though cumbersome and inefficient, was a great improvement upon Thomas New-comen's earlier "atmospheric" engine.

Though Americans copied all they could from England, the Industrial Revolution in the United States was largely an indigenous growth, with roots extending far back into the colonial period. In colonial America, though no factories existed, there were countless homes and workshops where craftsmen developed mechanical skills. Along many a creek stood water-power mills for grinding grain, sawing wood, and fulling cloth, and even for manufacturing iron, with trip-hammers and rolling and slitting machinery. Before 1776, America was well supplied with mechanics and inventors who could, and did, adapt their knowledge eventually to the production and operation of machines that became more and more complex.

When English imports were cut off by the prewar boycott and then by the Revolutionary War, desperate efforts were made to stimulate the manufacture of certain necessities in America. Homespun became both patriotic and fashionable, and to speed up the output of linens and woolens a few of the states gave loans or bounties for the making of wire for card teeth. Several of the states offered loans or bounties for the production of cannon, gunpowder, camp kettles, and other war material. Public efforts to encourage industry continued after the war, and to these a bit of tariff protection was added after the adoption of the Constitution. Private companies were formed, and one of these with Alexander Hamilton as a sponsor founded (1791) the town of Paterson, New Jersey, to exploit the available water power for manufacturing.

Still, the American textile industry lagged behind that of England. Capital was scarce in the United States, even after certain American shipowners began to invest some of their shipping profits in textile mills. For years, prospects of profit were dim because of the abundance of cheap English imports, and the machinery available remained inferior to the steadily progressing English inventions. To protect England's superior position as a manufacturing nation, the British government tried to prevent the export of textile machinery and

the emigration of skilled mechanics. Nevertheless, a number of mechanics and millwrights made their way to the United States, the most important of them being Samuel Slater. In 1790, with the aid of American mechanics, Slater built a spinning mill for the Quaker merchant Moses Brown at Pawtucket, Rhode Island. Though a few inferior spinning mills already were in operation, Slater's work is generally considered as the beginning of the factory system in America.

Despite the success of the Slater mill, the American textile industry grew rather slowly until English imports were checked by Jefferson's Embargo of 1807 and then by the War of 1812. The first census of manufacturing, in 1810, counted 269 cotton and 24 woolen mills in the country. From 1807 to 1815 the total number of cotton spindles increased from 8,000 to 130,000. Most of the factories were located in New England. Until 1814 they produced only yarn and thread: the weaving of cloth was left to families operating hand looms at home. Then the Boston merchant Francis C. Lowell, after examining textile machinery in England, perfected a power loom that was an improvement on its English counterpart. Lowell organized the Boston Manufacturing Company and founded at Waltham, Massachusetts, the first mill in America to carry on the processes of spinning and weaving under a single roof.

In textiles and in some other manufactured goods the young republic did not measure up to England. Americans generally produced the coarser kinds of yarn and cloth, and though they supplied their own needs in common metalware, they still imported the finer grades of cutlery and other metal products. Yet in certain respects American industry was neither imitative nor inferior, and some American inventors and engineers were equal to the greatest in the world. They were especially advanced in certain new techniques of mass production.

One of the most ingenious mechanics of his time was Oliver Evans, a Delaware farmer's son. Evans invented a card-making machine, constructed an automatic flour mill, improved upon the steam engine, and combined theory and practice in America's first textbook of mechanical engineering, *The Young Mill-Wright's and Miller's Guide* (1795). He put his flour mill into operation the same year the constitutional convention met, in 1787. Before that time, in the typical flour mill, men had to carry bags of wheat to an upper loft where a "hopper boy" emptied them. The grain fell down through the turning millstones to be cracked and ground. Then the men carried the meal back upstairs in tubs, raked it out to dry, and finally sifted it by hand. In Evans's mill, all this work was done by a variety of machines geared to the same water wheel. Vertical conveyors—endless belts with buckets attached—lifted the grain and later the meal, which was raked and sifted by machinery. Horizontal conveyors—large screws turning within tubes—moved material back and forth. Only two workers were needed. At one end of the mill a man emptied bags of wheat, and at the other end a man closed and rolled away barrels full of flour. Here was probably history's first continuous automatic production line, the beginning of automation.

Another pioneer in mass production was the Massachusetts-born, Yale-educated Eli Whitney. He is best known for the cotton gin, but he is even more important for the revolution he accomplished in the manufacture of guns.

The rise of the textile industry in England and America had created a tremendous demand for the cotton which planters had begun to grow in the American South.

But the planters were faced with the problem of separating the seeds from the cotton fast enough to meet the demand. There was a variety of cotton with smooth black seeds and long fibers that were easily cleaned, but this "long-staple" or "sea-island" variety could be grown successfully only along the coast or on the offshore islands of Georgia and South Carolina. There was also a short-staple cotton which could be raised almost anywhere in the South, but its sticky green seeds were very difficult to remove, a skilled slave being able to clean no more than a few pounds a day by hand. The planters were casting about for a machine or "gin" (that is, an engine) to clean the short-staple cotton when Whitney, then serving as a tutor on the Georgia plantation of General Nathanael Greene's widow, made his famous invention in 1793.

The gin was quite simple. A toothed roller caught the fibers of the cotton boll and pulled them between the wires of a grating, which held back the seeds, and a revolving brush removed the lint from the roller's teeth. But the gin had momentous consequences. With it, one slave could clean cotton as fast as several could by hand. Soon cotton growing spread into the upland South, and within a decade the total crop increased eightfold. Slavery, which with the decline of tobacco production had become a dying institution, was now revived, expanded, and firmly fixed upon the South.

During the undeclared war with France (1798–1800) all-out war was expected, and so the army needed many thousands of muskets in a hurry. Muskets then were made one at a time, and no two of them exactly alike, by skilled gunsmiths. There were not enough gunsmiths, and there was not enough time, to meet the army's anticipated need. But Whitney had a plan. He made a contract with the government for the delivery of 10,000 muskets within two years. Months passed, and not a single gun appeared. When government officials began to worry, Whitney reassured them with a demonstra-

according to a pattern. Then all he had to do was to assemble the guns.

This was the beginning of standardized quantity production through the manufac-

Whitney's Gun Factory. *The factory, construction of which began in 1798, was well located on Mill River and on the new turnpike from New Haven to Hartford, in Connecticut. At the right of the picture is a covered wooden truss bridge by which the turnpike crossed the river. At the left of the bridge are two large buildings (with a flume for water power) which housed the machine shops. Farther to the left, on the opposite side of the road, is a row of stone dwellings for the workmen. In the right foreground are the forging shop and a group of storehouses. From a painting made about 1825 by William Giles Munson, a resident of New Haven.* (COURTESY OF YALE UNIVERSITY ART GALLERY)

tion such as they never had seen before. From piles of assorted pieces he put together a complete and well-made weapon. He had been waiting while he "tooled up" his Connecticut factory. He had designed a machine to make each of the parts exactly

ture of interchangeable parts. Before long, the same system was used for making clocks, and eventually it was applied to sewing machines and many other complicated products.

By fastening cotton and slavery upon the

South, Whitney's gin contributed to the coming of the Civil War. His techniques of mass production, by building up the industrial strength of the North, helped the Union to win the war that the gin did so much to bring on. Such were some of the aftereffects of the industrial developments in the period of the young republic. There were also other political and social consequences of the changes then just getting under way. In America as in England, though somewhat more slowly, the Industrial Revolution created new classes and class conflicts, hastened the growth of crowded manufacturing towns, and gave rise to troublesome political issues, such as the perennial issue of the protective tariff.

Transportation and Trade

Before the full potential of the Industrial Revolution could be realized in the United States, transportation had to be improved. What was needed was a system of roads and waterways which would connect all parts of the country and create a market extensive enough to justify production on a reasonably large scale. In the late eighteenth and early nineteenth century goods still moved far more cheaply by water than by land. For the Atlantic seaports, ocean commerce with other continents was more easily carried on than overland trade with American settlements west of the Appalachian range. As Charles and Mary Beard have written, "the streets of London, the quays of Lisbon, and the Hong of Canton were more familiar sights to the merchants of the coast than were the somber forests and stump-studded clearings of Western America."

Temporarily, the Revolutionary War unsettled merchant shipping, as the British navy drove American merchantmen and fishing vessels from the seas. But, before the war was over, Americans learned to evade the enemy with light, fast, maneuverable ships. Indeed, the Yankees began to prey upon British commerce with hundreds of privateers. For many a shipowner, privateering proved to be more profitable than ordinary peacetime trade.

After the war the most important routes of the old colonial commerce were legally closed. The British government imposed severe restrictions on American trade and shipping to the West Indies and to the British Isles themselves. Before long, American shippers nevertheless managed to develop a prosperous business, partly by getting around the restrictions on the old routes and partly by working out new patterns of commerce. Especially important was the opening of the China trade. In 1784 the *Empress of China* sailed from New York to Canton and, the next year, brought back a cargo of silk and tea, which yielded a fabulous profit. Within five years Yankee ships were trading regularly with the Far East. Generally these ships carried various manufactured goods to the Pacific coast, exchanged them for hides and furs, and with these proceeded on across the Pacific, to barter them in China.

Not only in China but also in Europe and the Near East enterprising Yankees from Salem and other ports sought out every possible opportunity for commerce. These Yankees were aided by two acts of the new Congress (1789) giving preference in tariff rates and port duties to home-owned ships. American shipping was greatly stimulated (despite the loss of ships and cargoes seized by the belligerents) by the outbreak of European war in the 1790's. Yankee vessels took over most of the carrying trade between Europe and the European colonies in the Western Hemisphere. Eventually (as will be seen) this profitable business was brought to an end by the shipping laws of the American government and by the War of 1812.

Meanwhile, as early as 1793, the young

republic had come to possess a merchant marine and a foreign trade larger than those of any other country except England. In proportion to its population, the United

Transportation and trade within the United States labored under handicaps, but improvements were steadily being made. Difficulties were presented by the natural

Fulton's *Clermont* in 1810. *Robert Fulton, born (in 1765) in Lancaster County, Pennsylvania, became interested in water transportation as a youth. In 1786 he went to England, where he worked as an engineer and got acquainted with James Watt and Watt's steam engine. While in England, he began to experiment with steam-powered boats, and he continued his experiments in France until, in 1806, he returned to the United States, where the Clermont was under construction. This boat was 133 feet long and 18 feet wide, with a draft of seven feet. After its first successful run it continued to operate, in regular commercial service, on the Hudson River. From a contemporary French print.*
(COURTESY OF THE NEW YORK PUBLIC LIBRARY, STOKES COLLECTION)

States had more ships and commerce than any other nation in the world. And the shipping business was growing fast. Between 1789 and 1810 the total tonnage of American vessels engaged in overseas traffic rose from less than 125,000 to nearly 1,000,000. The percentage of the country's exports carried in American ships increased from 30 to 90, and imports from 17.5 to 93. As these figures indicate, ocean transportation thrived.

features of the country. Along the Atlantic seaboard the rivers, most of them running in a southeasterly direction, carried traffic from the back country to the sea, but there was no easy way of going overland from Maine southwestward to Georgia and Louisiana, though to some extent coastwise shipping made up for this lack. At the west of the mountains, the Mississippi River and its tributaries furnished a fairly good water route southward to New Orleans, but of course there existed no such natural route eastward to the Atlantic ports. The transportation problem was intensified with the movement of population into the Mississippi Valley, and this problem could not be fully solved until, somehow, the mountain barrier was overcome.

In river transportation a new era began with the development of the steamboat.

eventually the locomotive. Even before the high-pressure engine was available, a number of inventors experimented with steam-powered craft, and John Fitch exhibited to some of the delegates at the constitutional convention a 45-foot vessel with paddles operated by steam. The perfecting of the steamboat was chiefly the work of the inventor Robert Fulton and the promoter

Fulton's Famous Voyage
1807

In August, 1807, Robert Fulton wrote this letter to his friend Joel Barlow, a diplomat and poet, one of the group of authors known as the "Hartford Wits":

"My steamboat voyage to Albany and back has turned out rather more favourable than I had calculated. The distance from New York to Albany is 150 miles; I ran it up in thirty-two hours, and down in thirty hours; the latter is just five miles an hour. I had a light breeze against me the whole way going and coming, so that no use was made of my sails, and the voyage has been performed wholly by the power of the steam engine. I overtook many sloops and schooners beating to windward, and passed them as if they had been at anchor.

"The power of propelling boats by steam is now fully proved. The morning I left New York, there were not perhaps thirty persons in the city who believed that the boat would ever move one mile an hour, or be of the least utility; and while we were putting off from the wharf, which was crowded with spectators, I heard a number of sarcastic remarks. This is the way, you know, in which ignorant men compliment what they call philosophers and projectors.

"Having employed much time, and money and zeal, in accomplishing this work, it gives me, as it will you, great pleasure to see it so fully answer my expectations. It will give a cheap and quick conveyance to merchandise on the Mississippi and Missouri, and other great rivers, which are now laying open their treasures to the enterprise of our countrymen. And although the prospect of personal emolument has been some inducement to me, yet I feel infinitely more pleasure in reflecting with you on the immense advantage that my country will derive from the invention."

Oliver Evans's high-pressure engine, lighter and more efficient than James Watt's, made steam more feasible than before for powering boats as well as mill machinery and

Robert R. Livingston. Their *Clermont*, equipped with paddle wheels and an English-built engine, voyaged up the Hudson in the summer of 1807, demonstrating the practicability of steam navigation even though taking 30 hours to go 150 miles. In 1811 a partner of Livingston's, Nicholas J. Roosevelt, introduced the steamboat to the

STATES AND TERRITORIES IN 1802

West by sending the *New Orleans* from Pittsburgh down the Ohio and Mississippi. The next year this vessel entered upon a profitable career of fairly regular service between New Orleans and Natchez. Then the coming of the War of 1812 delayed the extension of steamboat lines on both eastern and western waters. Not till 1816 did a river steamer, the *Washington*, make a successful voyage upstream as far as Louisville, at the falls of the Ohio. Within a few years steamboats were carrying far more cargo on the Mississippi than all the flatboats, barges, and other primitive craft combined.

Though the steamboat made navigable rivers more useful, it of course did nothing to change the basic pattern of inland water transportation. The difficulty of getting over the mountains remained. Before 1800, when canals began to crisscross England, these appealed to forward-looking Ameri-

cans as a means of improving transportation in the United States, though in this country the rugged terrain complicated canal-building. George Washington interested himself in a project for canalizing the upper Potomac, so as to make a water connection with the West. This work was left unfinished, though short canals in Connecticut, Massachusetts, and the Carolinas were completed and in operation during the early 1800's. The canal age was yet to come to the United States.

Meanwhile the turnpike era began. In 1792 a corporation constructed a toll road the sixty miles from Philadelphia to Lancaster, with a hard-packed surface of crushed rock. This venture proved so successful that similar turnpikes (so named from the kind of tollgate frequently used) were laid out from other cities to neighboring towns. The invention of the wooden truss bridge made it possible for these roads to cross streams which previously had to be forded or else spanned by an expensive stone bridge. Since the turnpikes were built and operated for private profit, construction costs had to be low enough and the prospective traffic heavy enough to assure an early and ample return. So these roads, radiating from Eastern cities, ran for comparatively short distances and through rather thickly settled areas. If similar highways were to be extended over the mountains, the state governments or the federal government would have to finance the construction, at least in part.

When Ohio was admitted as a state (1802) the federal government agreed that part of the proceeds from the sale of public lands there should be used for building roads. In 1807 Jefferson's Secretary of the Treasury, Albert Gallatin, proposed that a national road, financed partly by Ohio land sales, be built from the Potomac to the Ohio, and both Congress and the President approved. The next year Gallatin presented a comprehensive plan of internal improvements, requiring an appropriation of $20 million, but Jefferson doubted the constitutionality of such an expenditure, and the plan was shelved. Finally, in 1811, construction of the national road began, at Cumberland, Maryland, on the Potomac. By 1818 this highway, with a crushed stone surface and massive stone bridges, was completed to Wheeling, Virginia, on the Ohio. Meanwhile the state of Pennsylvania contributed $100,000 to a private company which extended the Lancaster pike westward to Pittsburgh.

Over both of these roads, once they had

freight rates across the mountains now were lower than ever before. They were not low enough to permit the long-distance hauling of bulky loads like wheat or flour. But commodities with a high value in proportion to their weight, especially manufactures, moved from the Atlantic seaboard to the Ohio Valley in unprecedented quantities.

City and Country

The young republic was a land of remarkable diversity—in learning, in literary tastes, in religion, and in economic and social development. Much of the country remained a wilderness, yet its leading cities ranked in

On the National Road. *A scene at Fairview Inn, near the eastern terminus of the road, in Maryland. From its opening, in 1818, the road was heavily traveled by stagecoaches, Conestoga wagons, and other vehicles, besides droves of cattle, sheep, and hogs. Note, at the left, the zigzag rail fence (known as a "worm" or "snake" fence) which was common in the early nineteenth century. The workmen, at the side of the highway, are crushing stones for repairing the road's surface. From a painting (1889) by Thomas Ruckle.* (MARYLAND HISTORICAL SOCIETY)

been opened, there rolled a heavy traffic of stagecoaches, Conestoga wagons, private carriages, and other vehicles, as well as droves of cattle. Despite the high tolls,

size and urban sophistication with the largest of England and Europe, except for such national capitals as London and Paris. The United States had no comparable capital of politics, science, literature, and art. The total population, by the second census (1800), was nearly five and a half million. Only three people in a hundred lived in

taining no more than 3,200 people. With its broad but unpaved avenues radiating from the uncompleted Capitol and the President's House, in accordance with the elaborate

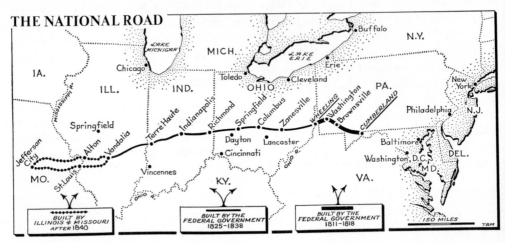

THE NATIONAL ROAD

towns of more than 8,000. Ten in a hundred lived at the west of the Appalachian mountains. Though Virginia was the most populous of the states, it contained none of the largest cities. Philadelphia (70,000) ranked first; New York (60,000) was close behind; and next in order were Baltimore (26,000), Boston (24,000), and Charleston (20,000). Washington City, the newly founded national capital, was only a raw and straggling village, the entire District of Columbia con-

plan of the French architect, P. C. L'Enfant, this small town nevertheless provided a new focus for the growing nationalism of Americans, and it symbolized their grand hopes for the future of their country. Hither President Adams and his wife Abigail, sacrificing the comforts and attractions of Philadelphia, moved in 1800. And here President-elect Jefferson was inaugurated the following year.

≫≫-≫≫-≫≫-≫≫-≪≪-≪≪-≪≪-≪≪

BIBLIOGRAPHY

A SURVEY of economic, social, and cultural developments in the late eighteenth and early nineteenth century is provided by J. A. Krout and D. R. Fox in *The Completion of Independence, 1790–1830* (1944). For the American scene in 1800, see the brilliant opening chapter in Henry Adams's *History of the United States* (9 vols., 1889–1891). The cultural nationalism of the time

and the career of its leading exponent are revealed in Harry Warfel's *Noah Webster: Schoolmaster to America* (1936) and in E. C. Shoemaker's *Noah Webster* (1936).

Aspects of religion in the young republic are treated by the following: G. A. Koch, *Republican Religion: The American Revolution and the Cult of Reason* (1938); H. E. Luccock and Paul Hutchinson, *The Story of Methodism* (1926); W. W. Sweet, ed., *Religion on the American Frontier: The Presbyterians, 1783–1840* (1936); R. G. Torbet, *A History of the Baptists* (1950); Conrad Wright, *The Beginnings of Unitarianism in America* (1955); J. T. Ellis, *American Catholicism* (1956), which compresses the story of more than 300 years into fewer than 300 pages; and A. M. Melville, *John Carroll of Baltimore* (1955), a biography of the founder of the American Catholic hierarchy.

Medical progress is shown in N. G. Goodman's biography of the leading physician of the young republic, *Benjamin Rush* (1934), who had his theories about the cause of yellow fever. A fine essay by R. H. Shryock on the yellow-fever epidemic of 1793 in Philadelphia is contained in *America in Crisis* (1952), edited by Daniel Aaron.

Jeannette Mirsky and Allan Nevins, *The World of Eli Whitney* (1952), tells the story of Whitney's inventions largely in his own words. A brief, readable, and valuable supplement is C. M. Green, *Eli Whitney and the Birth of American Technology* (1956). C. F. Ware, *The Early New England Cotton Manufacture* (1931), is excellent on the beginnings of the American textile industry.

A. B. Hulbert, *Paths of Inland Commerce* (1920), gives a short and readable account of transportation developments. Phases of land travel in the late eighteenth and early nineteenth century form the subjects of the following: P. D. Jordan, *The National Road* (1948); J. A. Durrenburger, *Turnpikes: A Study of the Toll Road Movement in the Middle Atlantic States and Maryland* (1931); and F. J. Wood, *Turnpikes of New England* (1919). River travel is treated by Thomas Boyd, *Poor John Fitch: Inventor of the Steamboat* (1935); T. J. Flexner, *Steamboats Come True* (1944); L. D. Baldwin, *The Keelboat on Western Waters* (1941); and L. C. Hunter, *Steamboats on the Western Rivers* (1949).

CHAPTER 12

Jeffersonian Principles in Practice

J EFFERSON AND THE REPUBLICANS, while out of power, had championed the rights of the states against the powers of the federal government. They had denounced the Federalists for stretching those powers too far and interpreting the Constitution too loosely. But, once they were themselves in control of the government, the new President and his party followers went even further, in some respects, than the Federalists had gone in the exercise of federal authority. If Jefferson seemed inconsistent, so did many of his opponents, for they now adopted the theory of state rights and used his own earlier arguments against him. Thus it was to be throughout American history: one party and then the other (usually the one out of power) claimed to be the special protector of the Constitution and of the rights of the states.

But the idea of state rights was not the essence of the Jeffersonian political philosophy. Jefferson stood primarily for the interests of the majority as he conceived them. As President, he did much to advance those interests, his greatest accomplishment being to double the territory of the United States.

President and Party Leader

Long afterwards Jefferson referred to his party's victory as "the revolution of 1800," but in his inaugural address of 1801, trying to sweeten the bitterness of the recent campaign, he emphasized the common principles of the two parties while restating the principles of his own. "We are all Republicans, we are all Federalists," he declared. "If there be any among us who would wish to dissolve this Union or to change its republican form, let them stand undisturbed as monuments of the safety with which error of opinion may be tolerated where reason is left free to combat it." Noting that

respect to domestic affairs, Jefferson proposed a "wise and frugal government" such as would leave men free to "regulate their own pursuits of industry." Yet he also fa-

The Unfinished Capitol, 1800. *When Jefferson was inaugurated as President, the magnificent plan for the federal city of Washington still remained for the most part on paper. Two white edifices had appeared in the Maryland woods—the President's "palace" and the new Capitol, with one wing completed. These two centers of government, about a mile and a half apart, were connected by Pennsylvania Avenue, a muddy road cut through swamps, and by a stone sidewalk bordering the avenue. Stonecutters were still busy at the Capitol. (Before it was finished, it was destroyed by the British, during the War of 1812.) This view of the east front is from a contemporary watercolor.* (LIBRARY OF CONGRESS)

the country was separated by a wide ocean from the "devastating havoc" of the European war, he recommended a foreign policy of "peace, commerce, and honest friendship with all nations, entangling alliances with none"—much as George Washington had done in the Farewell Address. With

vored the "encouragement of agriculture and of commerce as its handmaid."

From the outset Jefferson acted in a spirit of democratic simplicity, which was quite in keeping with the frontier-like character of the raw city of Washington, but which was very different from the ceremonial splendor of former Federalist administrations in the metropolis of Philadelphia. He walked like an ordinary citizen to and from his inauguration at the Capitol, instead of bling gait. Yet, though a rather ineffective public speaker, he charmed his guests in conversation and he wrote with greater literary skill than any President before or

---

Jefferson's First Inaugural

1801

"We are all Republicans, we are all Federalists. If there be any among us who would wish to dissolve this Union or to change its republican form, let them stand undisturbed as monuments of the safety with which error of opinion may be tolerated where reason is left free to combat it. I know, indeed, that some honest men fear that a republican government can not be strong, that this Government is not strong enough; but would the honest patriot, in the full tide of successful experiment, abandon a government which has so far kept us free and firm on the theoretic and visionary fear that this Government, the world's best hope, may by possibility want energy to preserve itself? I trust not. I believe this, on the contrary, the strongest Government on earth. I believe it the only one where every man, at the call of the law, would fly to the standard of the law, and would meet invasions of the public order as his own personal concern. Sometimes it is said that man can not be trusted with the government of himself. Can he, then, be trusted with the government of others? Or have we found angels in the forms of kings to govern him? Let history answer this question."

---

riding in a coach at the head of a procession. In the presidential mansion he disregarded the courtly etiquette of his predecessors, widower that he was, without a First Lady to take charge of social affairs. At state dinners, adopting the "rule of pell-mell," he let his guests scramble for places at the table. He did not always bother to dress up, and the fastidious minister from Great Britain complained of being received by the President in slippers which were down at the heels and coat and pantaloons which were "indicative of utter slovenliness and indifference to appearances."

Even at his best, the tall, freckle-faced, sandy-haired Jefferson did not make a very impressive appearance, what with his shyness, his awkward posture, and his sham-

since, with the possible exceptions of Abraham Lincoln and Woodrow Wilson. More than that, he was a genius with a wider diversity of talents than any other President, without exception. Besides being a politician and a diplomat, he was an architect, educator, inventor, scientific farmer, and philosopher-scientist, who in the presidential mansion diverted himself with such pastimes as sorting the bones of prehistoric animals. As a shrewd and practical politician, he was excelled by no other President, though he was equaled by Lincoln and by Franklin D. Roosevelt.

Jefferson was a strong executive, but neither his principles nor his nature inclined him to dictate to Congress. To avoid even the semblance of dictation, and to indulge

Thomas Jefferson. *Jefferson was 62 years old when this portrait was painted, in 1805, at the President's mansion in Washington, by Rembrandt Peale, son of Charles Willson Peale.* (COURTESY OF THE NEW-YORK HISTORICAL SOCIETY, NEW YORK CITY)

John Randolph of Roanoke. *Randolph added "of Roanoke" (his plantation) to his name so as to distinguish himself from relatives of the same name whom he disliked. A distant cousin of Jefferson's, he began his political career as a Jeffersonian, then disagreed with Jefferson and became a critic of both Republicans and Federalists. As a Virginia congressman (off and on from 1799 to 1829) he made himself an extreme defender of Southern rights. Often he filibustered with interminable, rambling speeches, which were lit with occasional flashes of brilliance. A master of invective, he once referred to an opposing politician as "this being, so brilliant yet so corrupt, which, like a rotten mackerel by moonlight, shined and stunk." Randolph had a freakish appearance— he was tall and skinny, with a small head and a wrinkled, parchment-like skin. When in his forties and fifties, he looked boyish from a distance but incredibly aged from close up. From a rotogravure after a painting by Chester Harding.*

his distaste for public speaking, he decided not to deliver his messages to Congress in person as Presidents Washington and Adams had done. Instead, he submitted his messages in writing, thus setting a precedent which was followed for more than a century, until President Wilson revived the

practice of addressing Congress in person. Yet Jefferson, as party leader, gave direction to his fellow partisans among the Senators and Representatives, by quiet and sometimes by rather devious means.

To his cabinet he appointed a group of Republicans who were like-minded with him but were more than mere yes-men. Two of the ablest were the Secretary of State, James Madison, and the Secretary of the Treasury, Albert Gallatin. Madison, Jefferson's long-time neighbor and friend, continued to be so close a collaborator that, throughout Jefferson's Presidency, it is hard to tell how much of the impetus to policy came from the President himself and how much from the Secretary of State, particularly in foreign affairs. Gallatin, born in Switzerland, his speech marked by a French accent, was as able a public financier as the great Hamilton had been and was in addition a thoroughgoing democrat, who at the time of the Whiskey Rebellion had used his talents as a lawyer to defend the oppressed farmers of the Pennsylvania frontier.

Jefferson used the patronage as a political weapon. Like Washington before him, he believed that federal offices should be filled with men loyal to the principles and policies of the administration. True, he did not attempt a sudden and drastic removal of Federalist officeholders, possibly because of assurances to the contrary which had been given in his name when Federalist votes in Congress were needed to break the tie with Burr. Yet, at every convenient opportunity, he replaced the holdovers from the Adams administration with his own trusted followers. By the end of his first term about half the government jobs, and by the end of his second term practically all of them, were held by good Republicans. The President punished Burr and the Burrites by withholding patronage from them; he never forgave the man whom he believed guilty of plotting to frustrate the intentions of the party and the ambitions of its rightful candidate.

A tie vote between the presidential and vice-presidential candidates of the same party could not occur again. The Twelfth Amendment, added to the Constitution in 1804 before the election of that year, by implication recognized the function of political parties; it stipulated that the electors should vote for President and Vice-President as separate and distinct candidates. Burr had no chance to run on the ticket with Jefferson a second time. In place of Burr, the congressional caucus of Republicans nominated his New York factional foe, George Clinton. The Federalist nominee, C. C. Pinckney, made a poor showing against the popular Jefferson, who carried even the New England states except Connecticut and was re-elected by the overwhelming electoral majority of 162 to 14, while the Republican membership of both houses of Congress was increased.

During his second term Jefferson lost some of his popularity, and he had to deal with a revolt within the party ranks. His brilliant but erratic relative John Randolph of Roanoke, the House leader, turned against him, accused him of acting like a Federalist instead of a state-rights Republican, and mustered a handful of anti-Jefferson factionalists who called themselves "Quids." Randolph became a fanatic on the subject of the Yazoo land claims. These arose from the action of the Georgia legislature, which, before ceding its territorial rights to the federal government, had made and then canceled a grant of millions of acres along the Mississippi to the Yazoo Land Companies. Jefferson favored a compromise settlement which would have satisfied both the state of Georgia and the Yazoo investors, many of whom were Northern Republicans whose support he needed. But Randolph, insisting that the claims were fraudulent, charged the President and the President's friends with complicity in corruption. A number of Randolph's colleagues in Congress were investors in the land companies or supporters of their claims, and time and again the tall, skinny Virginian would point his bony finger at one or another of these men and shriek "Yazoo!" He prevented the government from making any settlement of the question until after both he and Jefferson were out of office.

Randolph had a special antipathy toward Madison, whom he considered as one of the worst of the Yazoo men. He did all he could, which was not enough, to prevent Madison's nomination for the Presidency in 1808. Jefferson refused to consider a third term for himself, for he was opposed to it in principle, unlike Washington, who had declined to run again in 1796 only because he was weary of public office. Jefferson's refusal established a tradition against a third term for any President, a tradition which remained unbroken until Franklin D. Roosevelt was elected for a third time in 1940 (and then for a fourth time in 1944). Though unwilling himself to be a candidate in 1808, Jefferson was determined that his *alter ego*, Madison, should succeed him and carry on his policies without a break.

The Jeffersonians and the Judges

The Federalists had used the courts as a means of strengthening their party and persecuting the opposition, or so it seemed to the Republicans, and soon after Jefferson's first inauguration his followers in Congress launched a counterattack against the Federalist-dominated judiciary. They repealed the Naturalization Act, changing the residence period for citizenship of foreigners from fourteen to five years, and they allowed the hated Alien and Sedition Acts to expire. Then they repealed the Judiciary Act of 1801, abolishing the new circuit courts and arranging for each of the Supreme Court justices to sit with a district judge on circuit duty. As President, Jefferson did not have the power to remove Adams's "midnight" appointees from their newly created jobs, but Congress achieved

tional. (Not for more than half a century, in the Dred Scott case of 1857, did the Court do so a second time.)

William Marbury, one of President

Marbury v. Madison

1803

Chief Justice Marshall: "It is emphatically the province and duty of the judicial department to say what the law is. Those who apply the rule to particular cases must of necessity expound and interpret that rule. If two laws conflict with each other, the courts must decide on the operation of each.

"So if a law be in opposition to the constitution; if both the law and the constitution apply to a particular case, so that the court must either decide that case conformably to the law, disregarding the constitution, or conformably to the constitution, disregarding the law, the court must determine which of these conflicting rules governs the case. This is of the very essence of judicial duty.

"If, then, the courts are to regard the constitution, and the constitution is superior to any ordinary act of the legislature, the constitution, and not such ordinary act, must govern the case to which they both apply."

---

the same object by pulling their benches out from under them, despite Federalist protests that the repeal violated the constitutional provision that judges should hold office during good behavior, that is, for life.

In the debate on the question of the Judiciary Act of 1801 the Federalists maintained that the Supreme Court had the power of reviewing acts of Congress and disallowing those that conflicted with the Constitution. The Constitution itself said nothing about such a power of judicial review, but Hamilton in one of the *Federalist* papers had argued that the Supreme Court should have the power, and the Court actually had exercised it as early as 1796, though upholding the law of Congress then in question. In 1803, in the case of *Marbury v. Madison*, the Court for the first time declared a congressional act, or part of one, unconstitu-

Adams's "midnight appointments," had been named as a justice of the peace in the District of Columbia, but his commission, though duly signed and sealed, had not been delivered to him at the time Adams left the Presidency. Madison, as Jefferson's Secretary of State, refused to hand over the commission, and so Marbury applied to the Supreme Court for an order (writ of mandamus) directing Madison to perform his official duty. In the case of *Marbury v. Madison*, Chief Justice Marshall decided that Marbury had a right to the commission but that the Court had no power to issue the order. True, the original Judiciary Act of 1789 had conferred such a power upon the Court, but, said Marshall, the powers of the Court had been defined in the Constitution itself, and Congress could not rightfully enlarge them. Marshall did not claim, however, that only the federal judges could decide what the Constitution meant; he implied that each of the three branches of the federal government could decide for itself. In delivering his opinion, he went out of his way to discredit the Jefferson administration, yet shrewdly avoided an open conflict. Since he decided the immediate question (whether Madison should be ordered to deliver Marbury's commission) in Madison's favor, the administration had no opportunity to defy the decision by disobeying it.

While the case of *Marbury* v. *Madison* was still pending, President Jefferson prepared for a renewed assault upon that Federalist stronghold, the judiciary. If he could not remove the most obnoxious of the judges directly, perhaps he could do so indirectly through the process of impeachment. According to the Constitution, the House of Representatives was empowered to bring impeachment charges against any civil officer for "high crimes and misdemeanors," and the Senate sitting as a court was authorized to try the officer on the charges. Jefferson sent evidence to the House to show that one of the district judges, John Pickering of New Hampshire, was unfit for his position. The House accordingly impeached him, and the Senate, despite his obvious insanity, found him guilty of high crimes and misdemeanors. He was removed.

Later the Republicans went after bigger game, after one of the justices of the Supreme Court itself. Justice Samuel Chase, a rabidly partisan Federalist, had applied the Sedition Act with seeming brutality and had delivered political speeches from the bench, insulting President Jefferson and denouncing the Jeffersonian doctrine of equal liberty and equal rights. In doing so, Chase of course was guilty of no high crime or misdemeanor in the constitutional sense, and he was only saying what thousands of Federalists believed. Some of the Republicans came to the conclusion, however, that impeachment should not be viewed merely as a criminal proceeding, and that a judge could properly be impeached for political reasons—for obstructing the other branches of the government and disregarding the will of the people. As for Justice Chase, he could easily be shown to be out of step with Congress, the President, and public opinion, especially after the overwhelming victory of the Republicans in the election of 1804.

At Jefferson's own suggestion, the House of Representatives set up a committee to investigate Chase's conduct. Impeached on the basis of the committee's findings, the justice was brought to trial before the Senate early in 1805. Jefferson did his best, or his worst, to secure a conviction, even temporarily cultivating the friendship of Aaron Burr, who as Vice President presided over the trial. But Burr performed his duties with aloof impartiality, and John Randolph as the impeachment manager bungled the prosecution for the House of Representatives. A majority of the Senators finally voted for conviction, but not the necessary two-thirds majority. Chase was acquitted.

From the Republican point of view, the Pickering and Chase impeachments, though only half successful, did considerable good, for they caused the federal judges as a whole to be more discreet and less partisan in statements from the bench. If the Republicans had succeeded in getting rid of Chase, they might have been emboldened to take action against the Chief Justice himself. As things stood, Marshall remained secure in his position, and the political duel between the Chief Justice and the President continued.

Dollars and Ships

According to the Republicans, the administrations of Washington and Adams had been extravagant. Yearly expenditures had risen so much that by 1800 they were almost three times as high as they had been in 1793, and the public debt also had grown, though not so fast, since revenues had increased considerably. A part of these revenues came from internal taxation, including the hated whiskey excise. In 1802 the Republicans in Congress abolished the whole system of internal taxes, leaving customs duties and land sales as practically the only sources of revenue. Despite the tax cut, the new administration was determined to reduce the public debt by economizing on federal expenses. Secretary of the Treasury Gallatin proceeded to carry out a drastic retrenchment plan, scrimping as much as possible on expenditures for the ordinary operations of the government and effecting what Jefferson called a "chaste reformation" in the army and the navy. The tiny army of 4,000 men was reduced to only 2,500. The navy was pared down from twenty-five ships in commission to seven, and the number of officers and men was cut accordingly.

These reductions in the armed forces reflected other Jeffersonian principles as well as the desire for government economy. Jefferson feared that anything except the smallest of standing armies might become a menace to civil liberties and to civilian control of government. He believed that the navy, while no such threat to the principle of civilian supremacy, was likely to be misused as a means of forcing the expansion of overseas commerce, which he thought should be kept subordinate to agriculture. Yet, though he once said "peace is our passion," Jefferson was far from a pacifist fanatic. He desired an efficient if small military force, and his administration deserves credit for founding the United States Military Academy at West Point (1802). He also contributed to the efficiency of the navy, even while reducing the size of it, for most of the decommissioned ships were outmoded, and many of the discharged officers were deadwood. And, in spite of himself,

he was compelled to reverse his small-navy policy and build up the fleet because of trouble with pirates in the Mediterranean.

For years the Barbary states of North Africa—Morocco, Algiers, Tunis, and Tripoli—had made piracy a national enterprise. They demanded protection money from all nations whose ships sailed the Mediterranean, and even the mistress of the seas, Great Britain, gave regular contributions (she did not particularly desire to eliminate the racket, since it hurt her naval rivals and maritime competitors more seriously than it did her). During the 1780's and 1790's the United States agreed to treaties providing for annual tribute to Morocco and the rest, and from time to time the Adams administration ransomed American sailors who had been captured by the corsairs and were being held as slaves. Jefferson doubted the wisdom of continuing the appeasement policy. "Tribute or war is the usual alternative of these Barbary pirates," he said. "Why not build a navy and decide on war?"

The decision was not left to Jefferson. In 1801 the Pasha of Tripoli, dissatisfied by the American response to his extortionate demands, had the flagpole of the American consulate chopped down, that being his way of declaring war on the United States. Jefferson concluded that, as President, he had a constitutional right to defend the United States without a war declaration by Congress, and he sent a squadron to the relief of the ships already at the scene. Not till 1803, however, was the fleet in the Mediterranean strong enough to take effective action, under Commodores Edward Preble and Samuel Barron. In 1805 the Pasha, by threatening to kill captive Americans, compelled Barron to agree to a peace which ended the payment of tribute but exacted a large ransom ($60,000) for the release of the prisoners. This was hardly a resounding victory for the United States. While the navy, as a whole, had not acquitted itself very well, certain individual officers such as Lieutenant Stephen Decatur gained fame for their heroic exploits, and several of "Preble's boys" acquired experience and spirit which were to be of inestimable value later, during the War of 1812. Meanwhile, in 1807, the fleet was brought home because of a crisis with Great Britain, leaving unfinished the task of wiping out piracy in the Mediterranean.

Though the Tripolitan war cost money, Secretary Gallatin pressed on with his plan for diminishing the public debt. He was aided by an unexpected increase in tariff revenues. By the time Jefferson left office, the debt had been cut almost in half (from $83 million to $45 million), despite the expenditure of $15 million to buy Louisiana from Napoleon Bonaparte.

Jefferson and Napoleon

In the year that Jefferson was elected President of the United States, Napoleon made himself dictator of France with the title of First Consul, and in the year that Jefferson was re-elected, Napoleon assumed the name and authority of Emperor. These two men, the democrat and the dictator, had little in common except that both were revolutionary leaders. Yet they were good friends in international politics until Napoleon's ambitions leaped from Europe to America and brought about an estrangement.

Napoleon failed in a grandiose plan to seize the British Empire in India, though he succeeded in the conquest of Italy. Then he was reminded that France at one time had possessed a vast empire of her own in North America. In 1763 her possessions east of the Mississippi had gone to Great Britain, and those west of it to Spain. The former were lost for good, but the latter might be recovered. In 1800 (on the very day after the signing of the peace settlement with the United States) Napoleon arranged for Spain to cede these possessions to him in the secret treaty of San Ildefonso. Thus he got title to Louisiana, which included roughly the whole of the Mississippi Valley to the west of the river, plus New Orleans to the east of the river near its mouth. He intended Louisiana to form the continental heartland of his proposed empire.

Other essential parts of his empire-to-be were the sugar-rich and strategically valuable West Indian islands which still belonged to France—Guadeloupe, Martinique, and above all Santo Domingo. Unfortunately for his plans, the slaves on Santo Domingo had been inspired by the French Revolution to rise in revolt and create a republic of their own, under the leadership of the remarkable Negro, Toussaint L'Ouverture. Taking advantage of a truce in his war with England, Napoleon sent to the West Indies an army under his brother-in-law, Charles Leclerc, to put down the insurrection and restore French authority.

Meanwhile, unaware of Napoleon's ultimate aim, Jefferson pursued the kind of foreign policy that was to be expected of such a well-known friend of France. He appointed as the American minister to Paris the ardently pro-French Robert R. Livingston. Continuing and hastening the peace policy of Adams, he carried through the ratification of the Franco-American settlement of 1800 and put it into effect even before it was ratified. With respect to Santo Domingo, however, he did not continue the policy of Adams, who had cooperated with the British in recognizing and supporting the rebel regime of Toussaint. Jefferson assured the French minister in Washington that the American people, especially those of the slaveholding states, did not approve of the Negro revolutionary who was setting a bad example for their own slaves. He even gave the French minister to believe that the United States would join with France in putting down the rebellion.

But Jefferson began to reappraise the

whole subject of American relations with France when he heard rumors of the secret retrocession of Louisiana. "It completely reverses all the political relations of the U.S.," he wrote to Minister Livingston (April 18, 1802). Always before, we had looked to France as our "natural friend." But there was on the earth "one single spot" the possessor of which was "our natural and habitual enemy." That spot was New Orleans, the outlet through which the produce of the fast-growing West was shipped to the markets of the world. If France should actually take and hold New Orleans, Jefferson said, then "we must marry ourselves to the British fleet and nation."

Jefferson was even more alarmed when, in the fall of 1802, he learned the news that the Spanish intendant in charge at New Orleans had prohibited Americans from continuing to deposit their goods at that port, for transshipment from river craft to ocean-going vessels. By the Pinckney Treaty (of 1795) Spain had guaranteed to Americans the right of deposit either at New Orleans or at some other suitable place; without such a right of deposit, the use of the lower Mississippi was of little value to the United States. With the Mississippi thus practically closed off, the men of the "Western waters" (there were already a quarter of a million people in Kentucky alone) faced economic ruin, for there was no feasible route by which they could carry their crops directly over the mountains to the ports and markets of the East. These frontiersmen suspected, as did Jefferson himself, that Napoleon had procured the closing of the river for sinister purposes of his own. They demanded that something be done to reopen the river, and some of the more extreme among them clamored for war with France, the supposed source of all their troubles. The Federalists of the Northeast, though they had no real concern for the welfare of the West, played upon the discontent of the frontiersmen and encouraged the war cry for political reasons. The more the Federalists could arouse the West, the more they could embarrass the Jefferson administration. The President faced a dilemma. If he yielded to the frontier clamor and sought satisfaction through force, he would run the risk of war with France. If, on the other hand, he disregarded the clamor, he would stand to lose the political support of the West.

There was possibly a way out of the dilemma, and that was to purchase from Napoleon the port so indispensable to the United States. Or, assuming that the First Consul should prove unwilling to sell New Orleans, and assuming also that he had acquired East and West Florida along with Louisiana in the secret treaty with Spain, it might be possible to obtain from him all or part of the Floridas, or at least the rights of navigation and deposit on some river flowing into the Gulf of Mexico to the east of New Orleans. Jefferson did not think of trying to buy any part of Louisiana to the west of the Mississippi; he was content, for the time being, to let that river form the boundary between the French empire and the United States. Soon, after hearing rumors of the Louisiana retrocession, he instructed Livingston in Paris to negotiate for the purchase of New Orleans, and Livingston on his own authority proceeded to suggest to the French that they might be glad to be rid of the upper part of Louisiana as well.

Jefferson also induced Congress to provide an army and a river fleet, and he allowed the impression to get out that American forces, despite his own desire for peace, might soon descend upon New Orleans. Then he sent a special envoy to work with Livingston in persuading the French to sell. For this extraordinary mission he chose an ideally suited man, James Monroe, who was well remembered in France and who, at the same time, had the confidence of the American frontiersmen; his appointment would reassure them that the President was looking after their interests. Jefferson told Monroe that if he and Livingston could not obtain even the minimum needs of the United States—even the use of the Mississippi or some other river emptying into the Gulf—they were to cross the Channel to England and there discuss some kind of understanding with the British government. Whether Jefferson, in his hints at an attack on New Orleans and an alliance with Great Britain, merely meant to bluff the French, he had no chance to show. While Monroe's coach was still rumbling on its way to Paris, Napoleon suddenly made up his mind to dispose of the entire Louisiana Territory.

Startling though this decision seemed to some of his advisers, Napoleon had good reasons for it. His plans for an American empire had gone awry partly because of certain mischances, which might be summarized in two words—*mosquitoes* and *ice*. The mosquitoes brought yellow fever and death to General Leclerc and to thousands of the soldiers whom Napoleon had sent to reconquer Santo Domingo. The ice, forming earlier than expected in a Dutch harbor as winter came in 1802, delayed the departure of an expeditionary force that Napoleon was readying to reinforce Leclerc's army and also to take possession of Louisiana. By the spring of 1803 it was too late. Napoleon then was expecting a renewal of the European war, and he feared that he would not be able to hold Louisiana if the British, with their superior naval power, should attempt to take it. He realized also that, quite apart from the British danger, there was danger also from the United States: he could not prevent the Americans, who were pushing steadily into the Mississippi Valley, from sooner or later overrunning Louisiana.

The Louisiana Purchase

Napoleon left the negotiations over Louisiana to his finance minister, Barbé-Marbois, rather than his foreign minister, Talleyrand, since Talleyrand was remembered for the X. Y. Z. Affair and was distrusted by Americans, while Barbé-Marbois had their respect, having lived for some time in the United States and having married an American girl. Livingston and Monroe, after the latter's arrival in Paris, had to decide first of all whether they should even consider making a treaty for the purchase of the entire Louisiana Territory, since they had not been authorized by their government to do so. They dared not wait until they could get new instructions from home, for Napoleon in the meantime might change his mind as suddenly as he had made it up. They decided to go ahead, realizing that Jefferson could reject their treaty if he disapproved what they had done. After a little haggling over the price that Barbé-Marbois asked—and he asked and got somewhat more than Napoleon's minimum—Livingston and Monroe put their signatures to the treaty, on April 30, 1803.

By the terms of the purchase arrangement, the United States was to pay 60 million francs directly to the French government and up to 20 million more to American citizens who held claims against France for ship seizures in the past—or a total of approximately $15 million. The United States was also to give France certain commercial privileges in the port of New Orleans, privileges not extended to other countries. Moreover, the United States was to incorporate the people of Louisiana into the Union and grant them as soon as possible the same rights and privileges as other citizens. This seemed to imply that the Louisiana inhabitants were to have the benefits of statehood in the near future. The boundaries were not defined, Louisiana being transferred to the United States simply with the "same extent" as when owned by France and earlier by Spain. When Livingston and Monroe appealed to Talleyrand for his opinion about the boundary, he merely replied: "You have made a noble bargain for yourselves, and I suppose you will make the most of it."

In Washington, the President was both pleased and embarrassed when he received the treaty. He was glad to get such a "noble bargain," but, according to his oft-repeated views on the Constitution, the United States lacked the constitutional power to accept the bargain. In the past he had always insisted that the federal government could rightfully exercise only those powers assigned to it in so many words, and nowhere did the Constitution say anything about the acquisition of new territory. Now he thought, at first, that an amendment should be adopted so as to give the government the specific right to buy additional land; he even went so far as to draft a suitable amendment. But his advisers cautioned him that ratification might be long delayed or possibly defeated, and they assured him that he already possessed all the constitutional power he needed: the President with the consent of the Senate obviously could make treaties, and the treaty-making power would justify the purchase of Louisiana. Years afterward (in 1828) the Supreme Court upheld this view, but Jefferson—strict constructionist that he had been—continued to have doubts about it. Finally he gave in, trusting, as he said, "that the good sense of our country will correct the evil of loose construction when it shall produce ill effects." Thus, by implication, he left the question of constitutional interpretation to public opinion, and he cut the ground from under his doctrine of state rights.

When Jefferson called Congress into special session, a few of the die-hard Federalists of New England raised constitutional and other objections to the treaty, but the Senate promptly gave its consent and the House soon passed the necessary appropriation bill. The Spanish minister in Washington protested to Secretary Madison that the transaction was illegal, since Napoleon when acquiring Louisiana had promised never to part with it and also had agreed to provide an Italian kingdom for the son of the Spanish king but had never done so. Madison easily disposed of the protest by reminding the Spanish minister that the latter once had advised the United States to apply to France, not Spain, in response to a query whether Spain would be willing to sell a part of Louisiana.

Though Madison and Jefferson had a good case for the American title to Louisiana itself, they had considerably less justification when, taking advantage of the vagueness of the boundaries, they also claimed part of West Florida as American by virtue of the treaty with France. The Spaniards denied that any of Florida was included in Louisiana, and indeed the two provinces had had separate histories and had been separately administered. To persuade the Spaniards to give up Florida, Jefferson tried both promises of money and threats of force. Despite John Randolph's outraged opposition, he obtained from Congress an appropriation for secret uses, one of which was to bribe France to bring pressure upon Spain. It was no use. All of Florida remained in Spanish hands until after Jefferson left the Presidency.

When the United States concluded the purchase treaty with France, Spain was still administering Louisiana, the French never having taken actual possession. They did not take possession until late in 1803, and then only to turn the territory over to General James Wilkinson, the commissioner of the United States and the commander of a small occupation force. In New Orleans, beneath a bright December sun, the recently raised French tricolor was brought down and the Stars and Stripes was run up. For the time being, Louisiana Territory was before Napoleon's offer to sell Louisiana, Jefferson planned an expedition which was to cross all the way to the Pacific Ocean and gather not only geographical facts but

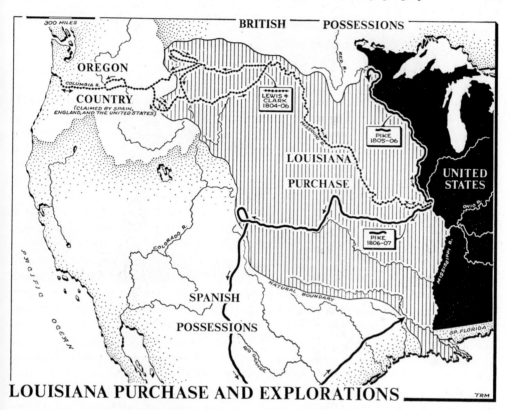

LOUISIANA PURCHASE AND EXPLORATIONS

given a semi-military government with officials appointed by the President; later it was organized on the general pattern of the Northwest Territory, with the assumption that it would be divided into states. The first of these was admitted to the Union as the state of Louisiana in 1812.

Meanwhile the geography of the far-flung territory was revealed by a series of explorations. Even before he became President, Jefferson as a scientist had been interested in finding out all he could about the nature and extent of the North American continent, and he had encouraged explorers interested in the Far West. After becoming President he renewed his efforts. In 1803,

also information about the prospects for Indian trade. Congress having secretly provided the necessary funds, Jefferson named as leader of the expedition his private secretary and Virginia neighbor, the 32-year-old Meriwether Lewis, who as a veteran of Indian wars was skilled in wilderness ways. Lewis chose as his colleague the 28-year-old William Clark, who like his older brother George Rogers Clark and like Lewis himself was an experienced frontiersman and Indian fighter.

Lewis and Clark, with a picked company of four dozen hardy men, set up winter quarters in St. Louis at about the time the United States took formal possession of

Louisiana. In the spring of 1804 they started up the Missouri River, and with the Shoshoni squaw Sacajawea as their guide, her papoose on her back, they eventually

of 1806 Pike was sent out again, this time by Wilkinson instead of Jefferson, to proceed up the valley of the Arkansas. He discovered, but failed in his attempt to climb, the

The Lewis and Clark Expedition, 1804–1806. *Patrick Cass, one of the men who accompanied Lewis and Clark, wrote* A Journal of the Voyages and Travels of a Corps of Discovery *(1811), which was the first account of the expedition to be published. This book was illustrated with crude drawings. The one here reproduced was captioned* "Captain Lewis & Clark holding a Council with the Indians."

crossed the Rocky Mountains, descended the Snake and the Columbia rivers, and in the late autumn of 1805 encamped on the Pacific coast. In September, 1806, they were back again in St. Louis, bringing with them carefully kept records of what they had observed along the way. No longer was the Far West a completely unknown country.

While Lewis and Clark were on their epic journey, Jefferson sent out other explorers to fill in the picture of the Louisiana Territory. The most important of these was Lieutenant Zebulon Montgomery Pike. In the fall of 1805, then only 26, Pike led an expedition from St. Louis up the Mississippi River in search of its source, and though he did not find it he learned a good deal about the upper Mississippi Valley. In the summer

peak that now bears his name. Then he turned southward into Mexico and ran into a Spanish army; he was compelled to surrender his maps and papers and return to the United States. His account of his Western travels left the impression that the land between the Missouri and the Rockies was a desert which American farmers could never cultivate and which ought to be left forever to the nomadic Indian tribes.

The Burr Conspiracy

In the long run the Louisiana Purchase prepared the way for the growth of the United States as a great continental power. Immediately, however, the Purchase provoked reactions which threatened or seemed to threaten the very existence of the Union. From both the Northeast and the Southwest there soon arose rumors of secession plots.

Most of the American people heartily approved the acquisition of the new territory, as they indicated by their presidential votes in 1804, but some of the New England Federalists raged against it. Their feelings are understandable enough. Both their party and their section stood to lose in importance with the growth of the West. From their point of view the existence of the Northwest Territory was bad enough, for they would soon be outnumbered in national politics with the creation of new states, the first of which in that area was admitted to the Union as the state of Ohio in 1803. The addition of Louisiana Territory, with its potential for still more new states, only made the evil worse in the minds of New England Federalists. A group of the most extreme of these men, known as the Essex Junto, concluded that the only recourse for New England was to secede from the Union and form a separate "Northern Confederacy." They justified such action by means of state-rights arguments similar to those Jefferson had used only about five years earlier in opposition to the Alien and Sedition Acts.

If a Northern Confederacy was to have any hope for lasting success as a separate nation, it would have to include New York as well as New England, or so the prospective seceders believed. But the prominent New York Federalist Alexander Hamilton had no sympathy with the secessionist scheme. He wrote: "Dismemberment of our empire will be a clear sacrifice of great positive advantages without any counterbalancing good, administering no relief to our real disease, which is *democracy*." He feared that disorders like those of the French Revolution were about to sweep over the United States. Then, he thought, the country would need a military dictator,

a sort of American Napoleon, to bring order out of chaos, and he imagined that he himself would emerge as the man of the hour. He had no future so far as ordinary politics was concerned.

His New York Republican rival, Aaron

Aaron Burr. *For many years the name of Aaron Burr was bracketed with that of Benedict Arnold as a synonym for traitor. Yet Burr never was proved guilty of treason, and historians still differ about his guilt. Among his contemporaries he was loved and admired by those who knew him best, especially by his daughter Theodosia, whom he raised to be one of the best educated women of her time. "I had rather not live than not be the daughter of such a man," she once wrote. She married Joseph Alston, a prominent politician and riceplanter of South Carolina. In 1812, with her young son, she embarked from South Carolina for a visit with Burr in New York. She never arrived: her ship disappeared without a trace. Of all the blows that fate dealt Burr, the loss of his beloved daughter grieved him the most. From a contemporary sketch by James Sharples.* (LIBRARY OF CONGRESS)

Burr, was another politician without prospects, at least within the party of the vengeful Jefferson. When some of the Federalists approached Burr, he agreed to run with their support for governor in 1804. Rumor had it that he was implicated in the disunion plot and that, if elected, he would lead the state into secession along with New England, but the rumor lacked proof and the plot itself was fantastic, an impossible dream. Nevertheless, Hamilton accused Burr of plotting treason and cast slurs upon his personal character. Burr lost the election, then challenged Hamilton to a duel. Hamilton dared not refuse; if he did, he would sacrifice his reputation for honor and manliness, a reputation that would be indispensable to the career supposedly awaiting him as the savior of his country. And so the two men with their seconds met at Weehawken, New Jersey, across the Hudson River from New York City, on a July morning in 1804. Hamilton was mortally wounded, and died the next day.

Burr, indicted for murder in both New Jersey and New York, presided over the United States Senate the following winter and then, at the end of his term as Vice President, faced a political outlook more hopeless than ever. He was ambitious and resourceful, with almost magical powers of attracting men (and women) to him. What could he do? During the next year he busied himself with mysterious goings and comings in the Southwest. He talked and corresponded with prominent men of the region, especially with General James Wilkinson, now governor of Louisiana Territory. Burr was up to something, and Wilkinson was his partner in it, but no one except Burr and Wilkinson themselves knew just what it was, and Burr told different stories. Some people believed (and some historians still believe) that he intended to separate the Southwest from the Union and rule it as an empire of his own. Very likely he did have imperial notions, for such notions were much in the air: Bonaparte had just become the Emperor Napoleon I of France, and Burr doubtless envisaged himself as the Emperor Aaron I—of Mexico. His ultimate aim most probably was the conquest of Spanish territory beyond the boundaries of Louisiana and not the division of the United States.

In the fall of 1806 the armed followers of Burr, with Blennerhassett's Island as their rendezvous, started by boat down the Ohio River, Burr himself joining them after they were well under way. Wilkinson, suddenly turning against Burr, sent a messenger to tell Jefferson that treason was afoot and that an attack upon New Orleans was expected. So Jefferson issued a proclamation calling for the arrest of Burr and his men as traitors. Eventually Burr was captured and brought to Richmond for trial.

The Burr trial (1807–1808) was one of the most dramatic in all American history, with its horrendous charge of treason and its colorful cast of characters: Burr himself, as charming as always; a galaxy of brilliant lawyers on both sides; the eccentric John Randolph as foreman of the grand jury; the stern Chief Justice, John Marshall, presiding over the trial on circuit duty; and the President of the United States, Thomas Jefferson, not present in Richmond but managing the prosecution by remote control, from Washington. Jefferson was determined to convict his one-time running mate, and the prosecution relied hopefully upon its star witness, General Wilkinson, though Wilkinson was a despicable character who accepted pay as a spy for the Spaniards and who demanded extra money from them on the grounds that, in heading off the Burr expedition, he had saved their territory from attack! Marshall, on the other hand, for political as well as judicial reasons, was determined that Burr should have a fair trial. As the presiding judge, Marshall applied quite literally the clause of the Constitution which provides that no one shall be convicted of treason except upon the testimony of at least two witnesses to the same "overt act." He excluded all evidence not bearing directly upon such an act, and so the jury had little choice but to acquit Burr, since not even one witness had actually seen him waging war against the United States or giving aid and comfort to its enemies.

Though freed, Burr gained lasting notoriety as a traitor; after exiling himself abroad for a few years, he returned and lived long enough to hail the Texas revolution (1836) as the fruition of much the same sort of movement as he had hoped to start. The trial had given the Chief Justice another chance to frustrate the President. It had set a precedent which made it almost impossible to convict anyone of treason against the United States. And the loyalty of the Southwestern frontiersmen had been proved beyond a doubt by their patriotic reaction to the cry of treason in their midst.

➤➤-➤➤-➤➤-➤➤≪-≪≪-≪≪-≪≪

BIBLIOGRAPHY

A WORK of historical genius is Henry Adams's *History of the United States during the Administrations of Jefferson and Madison* (9 vols., 1889–1891). This work is also available in a two-volume abridgment edited by Herbert Agar (1947). Henry Adams had one serious weakness as a historian: he was maliciously biased against his two leading characters, the one-time political foes of his great-grandfather. C. G. Bowers, without Adams's genius but with a flair for colorful writing, is violently prejudiced in Jefferson's favor in *Jefferson in Power* (1936). Irving Brant, *James Madison: Secretary of State, 1800–1809* (1953), with careful research corrects some of Adams's errors and portrays Jefferson as a great man and Madison as a man equally great. Adrienne Koch, *Jefferson and Madison: The Great Collaboration* (1950), in a more graceful style also depicts Madison as much more than a yes-man to Jefferson. L. D. White, *The Jeffersonians: A Study in Administrative History, 1801–1829* (1951), continues the high standards set in his *The Federalists*. A work of enduring value is Edward Channing's *The Jeffersonian System* (1906). Allen Johnson presents a brief and readable survey in *Jefferson and His Colleagues* (1920). D. J. Boorstin, *The Lost World of Thomas Jefferson* (1948), recaptures the intellectual atmosphere of Jefferson's time.

On the Louisiana Purchase, see E. W. Lyon's *Louisiana in French Diplomacy, 1789–1804* (1934) and his *The Man Who Sold Louisiana: The Life of François Barbé-Marbois* (1942). Oscar Handlin, *Chance or Destiny: Turning Points in American History* (1955), has an interesting chapter on the accidents that led up to the Purchase. On Jefferson's troubles with Mediterranean pirates, see G. W. Allen's *Our Navy and the Barbary Corsairs* (1905). See also Fletcher Pratt, *The Navy: A History* (1938), an impressionistic account.

Henry Adams did not like John Randolph any better than he did Jefferson or Madison, and Adams's *John Randolph* (1882) is brilliant but unfair. More superficial but also more sympathetic is G. W. Johnson's *Randolph of Roanoke: A Political Fantastic* (1929). Randolph's ideas form the subject of Russell Kirk, *Randolph of Roanoke: A Study in Conservative Thought* (1951).

Historians generally have condemned Aaron Burr, while most of his many biographers have sided with him. W. F. McCaleb acquits him of treason in *The Aaron Burr Conspiracy* (1903), and so does Nathan Schachner in *Aaron Burr: A Biography*

(1937). But T. P. Abernethy, *The Burr Conspiracy* (1954), is convinced of Burr's guilt.

On the Far West explorations, see John Bakeless, *Lewis and Clark: Partners in Dis-*covery (1947); Bernard De Voto, ed., *The Journals of Lewis and Clark* (1953), a highly readable edition; and S. H. Hart and A. B. Hulbert, eds., *Zebulon Pike's Arkansaw Journal* (1937).

CHAPTER 13

Free Seas and the Frontier

THE EUROPEAN WAR, renewed in 1803, was both a blessing and a curse for the United States. The continual conflict abroad enabled Americans to develop a profitable trade with the belligerents on both sides and at times to play them off against each other to the diplomatic advantage of this country, as in the cases of the Pinckney Treaty with Spain and the Louisiana treaty with France. Yet the war in Europe jeopardized the policy proclaimed by Washington and endorsed by Jefferson—the policy of neutrality and peace. Twice the United States became involved in the European struggle, the first time (1798) in opposition to France, the second time (1812) in opposition to Great Britain. The causes of the War of 1812 were debated by politicians at the time and have been disputed by historians ever since. It has been called a war of "agricultural imperialism," motivated by the desire of frontiersmen to gain additional territory; it has also been called a war for the freedom of the seas. Which of these considerations, the agrarian or the maritime, really accounted for the so-called "Second War of Independence"? The answer is that the questions of free commerce and frontier security were interrelated, and both must be taken into account if the background of the War of 1812 is to be satisfactorily explained.

Neutral Trade and Neutral Rights

In the early 1800's the warring nations of Europe found it impossible to take care of their own shipping needs. The merchant ships of France and Spain seldom ventured far upon the ocean, dominated as it was by the sea power of Great Britain, and the merchant marine of Britain herself was too busy in the waters of Europe and Asia to devote much attention to those of America. To some degree or other, all the belligerents had to depend upon the neutrals of the world for cargoes essential to effective war-making, and in the size and activity of its merchant marine the United States was much the most important of the neutrals. American shipowners prospered as, year after year, they engrossed a larger and larger proportion of the carrying trade between Europe and the West Indies. Farmers shared in the prosperity, for exports from the United States to the West Indies and Europe also increased prodigiously.

Each of the belligerents, while enjoying the benefits of neutral trade, would have liked to prevent neutrals from trading with its enemies. The nations at peace, on the other hand, desired to keep all shipping lanes open. With her vastly superior navy, Great Britain had the most to say about what the neutrals could or could not do. At one time, in her Rule of '56, she had asserted, as a principle of international law, that routes of trade prohibited in time of peace could not be permitted in time of war. In peace the French had closed the traffic between their West Indies and France to all foreigners, but during the war the French opened it to neutrals, and American shippers in large numbers took advantage of it. For several years the British government did not object—provided that the Americans first took their cargoes to the United States and then reshipped them to France. In the case of the *Essex* (1805), however, a British court held that goods destined for a particular nation, even though unloaded and reloaded along the way, should be viewed as going in a "continuous voyage" to that nation. (Long afterward this question of "continuous voyage" was to come up again, to plague Anglo-American relations during the Civil War and then during World War I.) Now that the Rule of '56 was reapplied to the carrying trade between the French West Indies and France, American shipowners ran the risk of losing their ships and cargoes to the British navy if they persisted in that profita-

ble business. And the hazards of neutral trade soon were multiplied.

In the battle of Trafalgar (1805) a British fleet practically destroyed what was left of the French navy. Thereafter the supremacy of Great Britain upon the seas was unchallenged, while Napoleon proceeded to extend his domination over the continent of Europe. Powerless to invade the British Isles, Napoleon devised a scheme, known as the Continental System, which he hoped would bring the enemy to terms. The British, he reasoned, were a nation of shopkeepers who depended for their existence upon buying and selling in the rest of the world, especially in Europe. If he could close the Continent to their trade, he thought, they ultimately would have to give in. So, in a series of decrees beginning with those of Berlin (1806) and Milan (1807), he proclaimed that British ships and neutral ships touching at British ports were not to land their cargoes at any European port controlled by France or her allies.

The British government replied to Napoleon's decrees with a succession of orders-in-council. These announced an unusual kind of blockade of the European coast. The blockade was intended not to keep goods out of Napoleon's Europe but only to see that the goods were carried either in British vessels or in neutral vessels stopping at a British port and paying for a special license. Thus, while frustrating the Continental System, Britain would compel the neutrals to contribute toward financing her war effort, and she would limit the growth of her maritime rivals, above all the United States. Her primary aim was to win the war, but a secondary purpose was to protect her dominant position in world shipping and trade. In other words, her orders-in-council were directed at the United States as well as France.

Caught between Napoleon's decrees and Britain's orders, American vessels clearing directly for Europe took the chance of capture by the British, and those going by way of a British port ran the risk of seizure by the French. Both of the warring powers disregarded American rights and sensibilities, yet to most Americans the British seas and taking sailors off the decks as victims of impressment.

Impressment

The British navy—with its floggings, its low pay, and its dirty and dangerous condi-

---

Commercial Warfare
1806–1810

Napoleon's Berlin Decree, 1806. No vessel coming from or touching at a British port shall be received in any European port of France or her allies.

British Orders in Council, 1807. All vessels trading to or from enemy ports shall be subject to capture unless they first put in at a British port, pay a fee, and obtain a certificate.

Napoleon's Milan Decree, 1807. Any vessel submitting to search by an English ship, or paying any fee to the English government, shall be considered as an English vessel and shall be liable to seizure.

The U.S. Embargo Act, 1807. No ship shall clear from the United States for any foreign port. No ship shall depart even for another American port without first giving bond, of twice the value of ship and cargo, that the goods will be relanded within the United States.

The U.S. Non-Intercourse Law, 1809. All shipping and trade between the United States and British- or French-controlled ports (but not the rest of the world) are prohibited. If either Great Britain or France "shall cease to violate the neutral commerce of the United States," trade and shipping will be resumed with the nation so doing.

Macon's Bill No. 2, 1810. Intercourse with France and Great Britain is renewed, but if either nation ceases its violations of American rights, and the other refuses to do so, the provisions of the Non-Intercourse Law will be reimposed against the nation thus refusing.

---

seemed like the worse offender of the two. Possessing effective sea power, they pounced upon Yankee merchantmen all over the wide ocean; the French could do so only in European ports. True, Napoleon's officials sometimes imprisoned and brutally mistreated the crews of confiscated ships, but the British navy far more often infringed upon personal liberty and national sovereignty, stopping American ships on the high tions on shipboard—was a "floating hell" to its sailors. They had to be impressed (forced) into the service and at every good opportunity they deserted, many of them joining the merchant marine of the United States and even its navy. To check this loss of vital manpower, the British claimed the right to stop and search American merchantmen, though not naval vessels, and reimpress deserters. They did not claim the right to take native-born Americans, but they did seize naturalized Americans born on British soil, for according to the laws of England a true-born subject could never give up his allegiance to the King: once an Englishman, always an Englishman. In actual practice the British often impressed native as well as naturalized Americans, and thousands upon thousands of sailors claiming the protection of the Stars and Stripes were thus kidnapped. To these hapless men, impressment was little better than slavery. To their shipowning employers it was at least a serious nuisance. And to millions of proud and patriotic Americans, even those living far from the ocean, it was an intolerable affront to the national honor.

To President Jefferson and Secretary Madison, impressment was likewise intolerable, and in their diplomacy with Great Britain they never forgot it. When they sent James Monroe to England, to make a new commercial arrangement replacing Jay's Treaty (which was to expire in 1807), they instructed him to insist that Great Britain abandon the principle as well as the practice. When they dispatched William Pinkney to assist Monroe and speed up the lagging negotiations, the President and the Secretary repeated their stern instructions regarding impressment. But the British officials would not hear of giving up the principle, so essential did they consider their searches and seizures for the successful prosecution of the European war. The most they would agree to was a slight modification of the practice. They gave Monroe and Pinkney a written promise that they would be careful in the future to protect Americans from "any molestation or injury" and would give "prompt redress" in case of any complaint. Monroe and Pinkney decided to accept this pledge, disregard their instructions, and go ahead with a commercial arrangement even though it said nothing about impressment. The ensuing Monroe-Pinkney treaty (De-

cember 31, 1806) was never ratified. Jefferson refused to submit it to the Senate; he agreed with Madison that public opinion would disapprove any treaty failing to offer complete satisfaction on the question of respect for American liberties and the American flag on the high seas.

Since no agreement had been reached, not even a temporary and partial one, the British continued to impress American seamen as before. In the summer of 1807, in the *Chesapeake-Leopard* incident, the British went to more outrageous extremes than ever. The *Chesapeake* was a public and not a private vessel, a frigate of the United States navy and not an ordinary merchantman. Sailing from Norfolk, with several alleged deserters from the British navy among the crew, the *Chesapeake* was hailed by His Majesty's ship *Leopard*, which had been lying in wait off Cape Henry, at the entrance to Chesapeake Bay. Commodore James Barron refused to allow the *Chesapeake* to be searched, and so the *Leopard* opened fire and compelled him, unprepared for action as he was, to strike his colors. A boarding party from the *Leopard* dragged four men off the American frigate.

This was an attack upon the United States! When news of the outrage got around the country, most of the people cried for a way of revenge. Not since the days of Lexington and Concord had Americans been so strongly aroused; never again were they to be so solidly united in opposition to Great Britain. Even the "most temperate people and those most attached to England," the British minister reported home, "say that they are bound as a people and that they must assert their honor on the first attack upon it." If Congress had been in session, or if President Jefferson had called a special session, as he was urged to do, the country might have stampeded into war. But, as the French minister in Washington informed Talleyrand, "the President

United States of America.

No. *3160*

I **William R. Lee,** *Collector for the District of* **Salem** and **Beverly,** *do hereby certify, that John Wallis an American Seaman, aged Nineteen years or thereabouts, of the height of Five feet two½ inches, and of a Dark complexion,* Was born in Salem in the State of Massachusetts

has this day produced to me proof, in the manner directed in the Act entitled, **"An Act for the Relief and Protection of American Seamen,"** *and pursuant to the said Act, I do hereby Certify, that the said John Wallis is a* **Citizen of the United States of America.**

In **Witness whereof,** *I have hereunto set my Hand and Seal of Office, this nineteenth day of January in the year of our Lord one thousand eight hundred and Eleven*

William Lee *Collector.*

Seaman's Protection Paper. *To protect American sailors from British impressment, Congress authorized the issuance of certificates of American citizenship, which came to be known as "protection" papers. These papers were not always respected by British naval officers. To them a certificate of naturalization was meaningless, for the British government claimed the allegiance of all British subjects for life. A certificate of American birth was not dependable, for it could be obtained by fraud. Some Americans made a business of selling forged documents. One woman, it is said, had an oversized cradle built, for British deserters to climb into, so that she could honestly swear that she had known them from the cradle.* (ESSEX INSTITUTE, SALEM, MASS.)

does not want war," and "Mr. Madison dreads it now still more."

Instead of assembling Congress and demanding a war declaration, Jefferson made a determined effort to maintain the national honor with peace. First, he issued an order expelling all British warships from American waters, so as to lessen the likelihood of future incidents. Then he sent to Minister Monroe, by the aptly named United States schooner *Revenge*, instructions to get satisfaction from the British government and to insist again upon the complete renunciation of impressment. On the whole the British government was conciliatory enough. It disavowed the action of Admiral Berkeley, the officer primarily responsible for the *Chesapeake-Leopard* affair, recalled him, and offered to indemnify the wounded and the families of the killed and to return the captured sailors (only three were left; one had been hanged). But the British cabinet refused to concede anything to Jefferson's main point; instead, the cabinet issued a proclamation reasserting the right of search to recover deserting seamen.

Thus the impressment issue stood between the British and American governments and prevented a compromise that might have led away from war. Though by 1812 the British had made a money settlement, the *Chesapeake* outrage meanwhile remained an open sore in Anglo-American relations. This incident, together with the impressment issue involved in it, was probably the most important single cause of the War of 1812, even though its final effect was delayed for five years.

"Peaceable Coercion"

Even at the height of the excitement over the *Chesapeake*, Jefferson made no preparations for a possible war. He and Madison believed that, if worst came to worst, the United States could bring Great Britain to terms, and France as well, through the use of economic pressure instead of military or naval force. Americans had made effective use of such pressure on earlier occasions in their history, as at the time of the Stamp Act. Madison, as a congressman in the 1790's and then as Secretary of State, had become the foremost champion of the idea of coercing Great Britain with economic measures. During the unsuccessful negotiations of Monroe and Pinkney in England, Congress authorized the President to forbid trading with Britain and thus strengthen the bargaining power of his diplomats. But in 1807 Jefferson concluded that something more drastic than this nonimportation and nonexportation law was needed, for Napoleon with his decrees was still interfering with American shipping, and pressure ought to be brought to bear against France as well as Great Britain. Dependent as both nations were upon the Yankee carrying trade, they presumably would mend their ways if they were completely deprived of it.

So, when Congress met for its regular session, Jefferson hastily drafted an embargo bill, Madison revised it, and both the House and the Senate promptly enacted it into law. The embargo prohibited American ships from leaving this country for any port in the world; if it had specified only British and French ports it could have been evaded by means of false clearance papers. Congress also passed a force act to make the embargo effective.

Though the law was nevertheless evaded in various ways, it was effective enough to be felt in France, much more in Great Britain, and still more in the United States itself. The embargo was, on the whole, an advantage to Napoleon, since it had the effect of supplementing his Continental System. While he was trying to keep British goods out of Europe, the American government was trying to keep them out of North America. Throughout the United States—except in the frontier areas of Vermont and

New York, which soon doubled their overland exports to Canada—the embargo brought on a serious depression. The planters of the South and the farmers of the West, though deprived of foreign markets for their crops, were willing to suffer in comparative silence, devoted Jeffersonian Republicans that most of them were. But the Federalist merchants and shipowners of the Northeast, still harder hit by the depression, made no secret of their rabid discontent.

Though the Northeastern merchants disliked impressment, the orders-in-council, and Napoleon's decrees, they hated Jefferson's embargo much more. Previously, in spite of risks, they had kept up their business with excellent and even fabulous returns; now they lost money every day their ships idled at the wharves. Again, as at the time of the Louisiana Purchase, they concluded that Jefferson had violated the Constitution (as indeed he had—if judged by the principles he had advocated before becoming President). "The Government of the United States is a delegated, *limited* Government," exclaimed the young New Hampshire lawyer Daniel Webster, then an advocate of state rights though afterwards to be famous as the champion of a strong Union. The Constitution, Webster said, had given Congress the power only to regulate commerce, not to destroy it as in the recent law. "This, it would seem, is not regulating commerce by an Embargo. It is, in effect, carrying on war, at the expense of one class of the community." Some of the more extreme Federalists, going further than Webster, talked of the secession of New England, as they had done after the purchase of Louisiana.

In the midst of the embargo-induced depression came the election of 1808. The Federalists, with C. C. Pinckney again their candidate, made the most of the embargo's unpopularity and won a far larger proportion of the popular and electoral votes than in 1804, yet Madison was safely elected as Jefferson's successor. The Federalists also gained a number of seats in the House and the Senate, though the Republicans continued to hold a majority in both houses. To Jefferson and Madison the returns indicated plainly enough that the embargo was a great and growing liability in politics. A few days before going out of office, Jefferson approved a bill terminating his and Madison's first experiment with what he called "peaceable coercion." But Jefferson's succession by Madison meant no basic change in policy, and other experiments with measures short of war were soon to be tried.

By the time he entered upon his presidential duties, James Madison already had behind him a career that would assure him immortality in history books. He was not only well experienced in affairs of government; he was also a more profound and original thinker than he was credited with being by his contemporaries and by later generations who have assumed that he was merely Jefferson's echo. Unfortunately for his reputation, he was not an impressive figure of a man, but was small and wizened, with a scholarly frown. Nor was he equipped with the personal charm or politician's skill needed for strong presidential leadership. What he lacked in personality, his wife more than supplied. Dolley Madison, North Carolina–born, was as gay and gracious a First Lady as ever adorned the White House.

Soon after Madison's inauguration, Congress passed and he signed a modified embargo bill known as the Non-Intercourse Act. By this act American ships were allowed to clear for any part of the world not under the jurisdiction of Great Britain or France, and they were to be allowed to go to Great Britain if and when she repealed her orders-in-council, and to France if and when Napoleon withdrew his decrees. Here was an inducement better calculated than the former, nondiscriminatory embargo to appeal to the belligerents. A prompt response came from the British through their young and personable minister to the United States, David Erskine (who, incidentally, had an American wife). In the so-called Erskine Agreement it was understood that the United States would be exempted from the orders-in-council and hence would reopen trade and shipping with Great Britain. Madison, pleased with the apparent success of his coercion policy, hastened to proclaim the reopening of this trade, and most Americans rejoiced in the belief that peace with honor was secure. But the happy dream lasted only three months. The President and the people were shocked when the news arrived that the British Foreign Minister, George Canning, for reasons best known to himself, had recalled Erskine and repudiated the agreement. Madison had no choice but to renew nonintercourse with Britain.

The Non-Intercourse Act, thus somewhat discredited, was replaced (1810) by another expedient commonly called Macon's Bill No. 2, which looked like the old law turned inside out. Macon's Bill freed commercial relations with the whole world, including Great Britain and France, but authorized the President to prohibit intercourse with either belligerent if it should continue its violations after the other had stopped. The freeing of American trade was more to the advantage of the British than the French, since it fitted in with the efforts of the former to pierce and weaken the Continental System. Napoleon had every incentive to induce the United States to reimpose the embargo against his enemy. He succeeded in doing so by means of a trick, the Cadore letter, which pretended to revoke the Berlin and Milan decrees as far as they interfered with American commerce. Madison, more desperate than ever in his eagerness to show results, accepted the Cadore letter as evidence of Napoleon's change of policy, even though the French continued to confiscate American ships. He announced that early in 1811, an embargo against Great Britain alone would automatically go into effect, in accordance with Macon's Bill, unless Britain meanwhile rescinded her orders-in-council. She refused to rescind them, and once again the United States, by cutting off trade with her, reinforced the policy of her imperial foe.

In time the new embargo, though less well enforced than the earlier, all-inclusive one had been, hurt the economy of England enough to cause influential Englishmen to petition their government for repeal of the orders-in-council. Eventually the orders were repealed—too late to prevent war, even if they had been the only grievance giving rise to the martial spirit in the United States. But they were not the only grievance. There was also impressment, and there was, besides, a border conflict between the British Empire and the expanding American frontier.

Red Men and Redcoats

Ever since the days of the Revolution the Indians generally had looked to their old "white father," the King of England, for protection against the relentlessly advancing Americans. And the British in Canada had relied upon Indian friendship to keep up their fur trade, even within the territory of the United States, and to maintain potentially useful allies. At one time, in 1794, this country nearly went to war with Great Britain because of her Indian policy, but Wayne's victory over the tribes at Fallen Timbers and the conclusion of Jay's Treaty dispelled the war danger and brought on a period of comparative peace. Then, in 1807, the border quiet was disturbed by an event occurring far away—the British assault upon the *Chesapeake*. The ensuing war crisis had repercussions that, as will be seen, terribly aggravated the frontier troubles already brewing in consequence of the growing conflict between tribesmen and settlers. Much of this conflict of red men and white was personified in the two opposing leaders, Tecumseh and William Henry Harrison.

The Virginia-born Harrison, already a veteran Indian fighter at 26, went to Washington as the congressional delegate from the Northwest Territory in 1799. He was largely responsible for the passage (1800) of the Harrison Land Law, which enabled settlers to acquire farms from the public domain on much easier terms than before. The buyer still had to pay a minimum price of $2 an acre, but he could take a tract of only 320 acres (instead of 640), and he could buy on credit, paying a fourth of the price down and the balance within four years. In 1804 the law was changed so that he could purchase as little as 160 acres at a time. Thereafter a man could begin buying himself a farm with only $80 in cash, and land in the Northwest Territory soon was selling fast. The growth of population led to a division of the area into the state of Ohio and the territories of Indiana, Michigan, and Illinois. By 1812, Ohio contained 250,000 people and was beginning to look like an Eastern state, as paths widened into roads, villages sprang up and in some cases grew into cities, and the forests receded before the spreading cornfields. By 1812, Michigan had few settlers, but Illinois contained a scattered population of about 13,000 and Indiana 25,000.

Receiving from Jefferson an appointment as governor of Indiana Territory, Harrison devoted himself to carrying out Jefferson's policy of Indian removal. According to the Jeffersonian program, the Indians must give up their claims to tribal lands and either convert themselves into settled farmers or migrate to the west of the Mississippi. Playing off one tribe against another, and using whatever tactics suited the occasion—threats, bribes, trickery—Harrison made treaty after treaty with the separate tribes of the Northwest. By 1807 the United States claimed treaty rights to eastern Michigan, southern Indiana, and most of Illinois. Meanwhile, in the Southwest, millions of acres were taken from other tribes in the states of Georgia and Tennessee and in Mississippi Territory. Having been forced off their traditional hunting grounds, the Indians throughout the Mississippi Valley seethed with discontent. But the separate tribes, helpless by themselves against the power of the United States, probably would have quieted down and accepted their fate if two complicating factors had not arisen.

One complication was the policy of the British authorities in Canada. For years they had neglected their Indian friends across the border to the south. Then came the *Chesapeake* incident and the surge of anti-British feeling throughout the United States. Now the Canadian authorities, expecting war and an attempted invasion of Canada, began to take desperate measures for their own defense. "Are the Indians to be employed in case of a rupture with the United States?" asked the lieutenant governor of Upper Canada (December 1, 1807). And Sir James Craig, the governor general of the entire province, replied: "If we do not employ them, there cannot exist a moment's doubt that they will be employed against us." Craig at once took steps to renew friendship with the savages and provide them with increased supplies. Thus the trouble on the sea, over the question of impressment, intensified the border conflict hundreds of miles inland.

The second factor intensifying this conflict was the rise of a remarkable native leader, one of the most admirable and heroic in Indian history. Tecumseh, "The Shooting Star," chief of the Shawnees, aimed to unite all the tribes of the Mississippi Valley, resist the advance of white

BATTLE OF TIPPECANOE, 1811

settlement, and recover the whole of the Northwest, making the Ohio River the boundary between the United States and the Indian country. He maintained that Harrison and others, by negotiating with individual tribes, had obtained no real title to land in the various treaties, since the land belonged to all the tribes and none of them could rightfully cede any of it without the consent of the rest. "The Great Spirit gave this great island to his red children. He placed the whites on the other side of the big water." So Tecumseh eloquently told Harrison. "They were not contented with their own, but came to take ours from us. They have driven us from the sea to the lakes—we can go no farther."

In his plans for a united front, Tecumseh was aided by his brother, a one-eyed, epileptic medicine-man known as the Prophet. The Prophet, visiting the Great Spirit from time to time in trances, inspired a religious revival which spread through numerous tribes and helped bring them together. Few savages doubted his supernatural powers after, having secretly learned from Canadian traders of a forthcoming eclipse, he commanded the sun to be dark on the appointed day. The Prophet's town, at the confluence of Tippecanoe Creek and the Wabash River, became the sacred place of the new religion as well as the headquarters of Tecumseh's confederacy. Leaving his brother there after instructing him to avoid war for the time being, Tecumseh journeyed down the Mississippi in 1811 to bring the Indians of the South into his alliance. At that time a great earthquake occurred centering at New Madrid, Missouri, and rumbling up and down the Mississippi Valley, causing much of the river to change its course. To many of the Indians, this seemed another awesome sign that a new era was at hand for them.

During Tecumseh's absence, Governor Harrison saw a chance to destroy the growing influence of the two Indian leaders. With 1,000 soldiers he camped near the Prophet's town, provoked an attack (November 7, 1811), and though suffering losses as heavy as those of the enemy, succeeded in driving off the Indians and burning the town. This, the Battle of Tippecanoe, disillusioned many of the Prophet's followers, for they had been led to believe that his magic would protect them from the white man's bullets. Tecumseh returned to find his confederacy shattered, yet there were still plenty of warriors eager for the warpath, and by the spring of 1812 they were busy with hatchet and scalping knife all along the frontier, from Michigan to Mississippi.

Westerners blamed Great Britain for the bloodshed along the border. Her agents in

Canada encouraged Tecumseh, used the Prophet as a "vile instrument," as Harrison put it, and provided the guns and supplies that enabled the savages to attack. To Harrison and to most of the frontiersmen, there seemed only one way to make the West safe for Americans. That was to drive the British out of Canada and annex that province to the United States.

While frontiersmen in the North demanded the conquest of Canada, those in the South looked to the acquisition of Florida. In Spanish hands, that territory was a perpetual nuisance, with slaves escaping across the line in one direction and Indians raiding across it in the other. Through Florida ran rivers like the Alabama, the Apalachicola, and others which in American possession would give access to the Gulf of Mexico and the markets of the world. In 1810 American settlers in West Florida took matters into their own hands, fell upon the Spanish fort at Baton Rouge, and requested that the territory be annexed to the United States. President Madison unhesitatingly proclaimed its annexation, then schemed to get the rest of Florida too. With Madison's connivance, the one-time Georgia governor George Mathews attempted (1811) to foment a revolt in East Florida. Spain protested, and Madison backed down, but the desire of Southern frontiersmen for all of Florida did not abate. Spain was Britain's ally, and a war with Britain would give these frontiersmen an excuse for taking Spanish territory as well as British.

Thus the war fever was raging on both the Northern and the Southern frontiers by 1812. The denizens of these outlying regions were not numerous as compared with the population of the country as a whole, and for the most part they were not directly represented in Congress, except by a few territorial delegates. Nevertheless they had able and determined spokesmen at the national capital after the arrival there of a group of young congressmen who, with good reason, soon gained the name of "war hawks."

The War Hawks

Three days before the Battle of Tippecanoe a new Congress met in Washington for the session of 1811–1812. In the congressional elections of 1810, most of the voters had indicated their disgust with such expedients as Macon's Bill No. 2 by turning out of office large numbers of Republican advocates of measures short of war, as well as Federalist advocates of continued peace. Of the newly elected congressmen and Senators, the great majority were warlike Republicans, and after the news of Tippecanoe they became more eager than ever for a showdown with the power which seemed to threaten both the security of the frontier and the freedom of the seas.

A new generation had arrived upon the political scene, a group of daring young men of whom the most influential came from the new states in the West or from the back country of the old states in the South. Two of the natural leaders were Henry Clay and John C. Calhoun, whose careers were to provide much of the drama of American politics for the next four decades. The tall, magnetic Clay, barely 34, was a Virginian by birth but had made Kentucky his home. Already, while still under the legal age for a Senator, he had appeared briefly in the United States Senate. As handsome as Clay though less appealing, the 29-year-old Calhoun was the son of Scotch-Irish pioneers in the South Carolina hills.

When Congress organized in 1811, the war faction of young Republicans got control of both the House and the Senate. As speaker of the House, Clay held a position of influence then second only to that of the President himself. Clay filled the committees with the friends of force, appointing Calhoun to the crucial Committee on For-

James Madison. *Madison was rather small of stature, reserved, and shy. His Federalist opponents pictured him as a weak President who yielded to the "war hawks" in Congress and came out for war in 1812 in order to gain their support for his renomination. For many years, historians accepted this view, but recent studies show Madison to have been a fairly strong President, the dominant figure in the making of foreign policy during his two terms. He insisted that American rights be respected by both Great Britain and France and early decided that the United States should go to war, if necessary, to preserve these rights. He chose war with Great Britain because he concluded that her offenses were more serious than Napoleon's, since her policies were deliberately designed to limit the independence and the commercial growth of the United States. The portrait reproduced here was painted by Asher B. Durand from an original by Gilbert Stuart. Stuart's painting was done in 1804 when Madison—then Secretary of State—was 53 years old.* (COURTESY OF THE NEW-YORK HISTORICAL SOCIETY, NEW YORK CITY)

eign Affairs, and launched a drive toward war for the conquest of Canada. This would bring Great Britain to terms and avenge the wrongs which Clay recited eloquently and at length. Or at least he sup-

posed it would, and he imagined further that the conquest would be quick and easy. The Kentucky militiamen, he declared, could take the whole province by themselves. Other Southern and Western representatives expressed similar views. "Sir," Calhoun said, "I believe that in four weeks from the time a declaration of war is heard on our frontier, the whole of Upper Canada and a part of Lower Canada will be in our power."

The Federalists in Congress, representing the commercial interests of the Northeast, deprecated the clamor for Canada and war. But they were powerless to stem the drive toward hostilities, even with the aid of dissident Republicans like the eccentric "Quid," John Randolph of Roanoke. Dubbing the Clay men "war hawks," Randolph ridiculed their cry as being like that of the whippoorwill, "one eternal monotonous tone—Canada! Canada! Canada!" He also argued that the real interests of Americans lay in friendship with Great Britain, the champion of constitutional liberty, and not in a war which would place the United States on the side of France and Napoleon, the tyrant of Europe. The main motive for war, Randolph charged, was "agrarian cupidity," the desire of American frontiersmen for additional land.

While Congress debated, President Madison moved reluctantly toward the conclusion that war was necessary. Diplomacy and economic pressure seemed unavailing. Already diplomatic relations were partially broken off, the United States no longer having a minister in England. The British government had a minister in this country, the able and well-disposed Augustus Foster, but he lacked authority to give satisfaction in regard to the orders-in-council or impressment. His government could not act fast enough to meet the crisis, for early in 1812 the government was in a state of confusion, with old King George III insane and the prime minister a victim of assassination. In deciding for war, Madison had to take into account political as well as diplomatic developments: only war could assure his remaining at the head of his party and the government. In May the war faction took the lead in the caucus of Republican congressmen who renominated him for the Presidency, and on June 1 he sent his war message to Congress.

In his message the President maintained that Great Britain—by impressing American citizens, interfering with American trade, and inciting the Indians along the frontier—was already waging war against the United States. He recommended that Congress declare war in return. Congress responded with a declaration of hostilities on June 18, two days after a new ministry had announced in Parliament that the orders-in-council were to be suspended, but before the news could reach Washington. The close vote on the declaration, 19 to 13 in the Senate and 79 to 49 in the House, showed how badly the American people were divided. Some members of the President's own party voted in the negative, and others abstained from voting. Almost all the congressmen and Senators from the West favored war, and so did a majority of those from the South, but most of those from the Northeast were opposed to it.

The division of public opinion was again revealed in the election of 1812. Opposing Madison and the war, a peace faction of the Republicans nominated a rival candidate, De Witt Clinton of New York, and the Federalists gave their support to him. Most of the electors in the Northeast voted for Clinton and peace, but all of those in the South and the West sustained Madison and the war, the President being re-elected by 128 to 89.

With the people thus divided, the country as a whole was not psychologically prepared for war, nor was it financially or militarily prepared. Congress had adjourned without increasing the army and navy, voting war taxes, or renewing the charter of the government's indispensable financial

ELECTION OF 1812

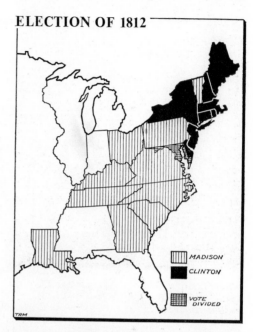

MADISON

CLINTON

VOTE DIVIDED

agency, the Bank of the United States, which expired in 1811. The war hawks, however, were not worried. On to Canada!

The Course of Battle

At first Great Britain, preoccupied with her mighty struggle against Napoleon, paid little attention to the American war, a mere annoyance to her. Then, in the fall of 1812, Napoleon launched the Russian campaign which, before the winter was over, was to bring him disaster and prepare the way for his ultimate defeat. As the months passed, Great Britain was able to divert more and more of her military and naval power to America. Only for about a year did the United States undertake the offensive; thereafter this country was forced to fight a defensive war, a war to protect its own territory.

The conquest of Canada, supposedly a

"mere matter of marching," as Jefferson himself put it, soon proved to be an exercise in frustration. Doubtless the best strategy for the United States would have been been in a vulnerable position, cut off from supplies or reinforcements. But the actual strategy had to depend upon political as well as military considerations. The war

Victory at Sea. *As of 1812, in the Napoleonic War, the British navy had fought 200 battles and won 200 victories, in engagements between single ships or whole fleets. Great Britain seemed invincible on the ocean. Then, on August 19, 1812, in the North Atlantic, the U.S. frigate* Constitution *boldly challenged and decisively defeated His Majesty's Ship* Guerrière. *On October 25, 1812, off the Canary Islands, the frigate* United States *met and destroyed H. M. S.* Macedonian. *This engagement is pictured in the painting by Thomas Birch, reproduced here. Commanding the* United States *was Stephen Decatur, a hero of the naval wars with Tripoli (1803) and Algiers (1815) as well as the War of 1812. Afterwards Decatur made the famous toast: "Our country! In her intercourse with foreign nations may she always be in the right; but our country, right or wrong." In 1812 the score, in naval duels on the high seas, was five American and three British victories; by the end of the war the score was approximately even.*
(COURTESY OF THE NEW-YORK HISTORICAL SOCIETY, NEW YORK CITY)

to mass all its strength behind a single spearhead movement upon Montreal. If the St. Lawrence thus had been blocked, the small force of British regulars, together with their Indian auxiliaries, would have was more popular and better supported in the West than in the East, and so the main effort had to be made in the West. A three-pronged invasion was planned to strike into Canada by way of Detroit, the Niagara

River, and Lake Champlain, with the greatest concentration of force at Detroit. At Detroit, however, after marching into Canada, the elderly General William Hull, Governor of Michigan Territory, retreated and surrendered the fort (August, 1812). The other invasion efforts also failed, and Fort Dearborn (Chicago) fell before an Indian attack.

During the year of disaster and defeat on land, the Madison administration and its supporters took what consolation they could in the news of successes on the sea. American frigates engaged British warships in a series of duels and won some spectacular victories, one of the most renowned being the victory of the *Constitution* over the *Guerrière*. American privateers destroyed or captured one British merchant ship after another, occasionally braving the coastal waters of the British Isles and burning vessels within sight of the shore. After that first year, however, the score was evened and more than evened by the British navy, which not only drove the American frigates to cover but also instituted a close blockade of the United States and harried the coastal settlements from Virginia to Maine.

While British seapower dominated the ocean, American fleets arose to control the Great Lakes. First, the Americans took command of Lake Ontario, enabling troops to cross over to York (Toronto), the capital of Canada. At York (April 27, 1813) the invaders ran upon a cunningly contrived land mine, the explosion of which killed more than fifty, including General Zebulon M. Pike. Some of the enraged survivors, without authorization, set fire to the capital's public buildings, which burned to the ground. After destroying also some ships and military stores, the Americans returned across the lake.

Next, Lake Erie was redeemed for American use, mainly through the work of the youthful Oliver Hazard Perry. Having constructed a fleet at Presqu' Isle (Erie, Pennsylvania), Perry took up a position at Put-in-Bay, near a group of islands off the mouth of the Maumee River. With the banner "Don't Give Up the Ship" flying on his flagship, he awaited the British fleet, whose intentions he had learned from a spy. He smashed the fleet upon its arrival (September 10, 1813) and established American control of the lake.

This made possible, at last, an invasion of Canada by way of Detroit. The post had been hard to reach overland, for supply wagons either had to struggle through the almost impassable Black Swamp of the Maumee Valley or had to make a long detour around it. After Perry's victory at Put-in-Bay, supplies as well as men could be quickly and easily transported by water. William Henry Harrison, who had replaced Hull in the Western command, now pushed up the river Thames into Upper Canada and won a victory (October 5, 1813) notable for the death of Tecumseh, who had been commissioned a brigadier general in the British army. The Battle of the Thames resulted in no lasting occupation of Canadian soil, but it disheartened the Indians of the Northwest and eliminated the worst of the danger they had offered to the frontier.

While Harrison was chastising the tribes of the Northwest, another Indian fighter was striking an even harder blow at the Creeks in the Southwest. The Creeks, aroused by Tecumseh on his Southern visit, were supplied by the Spaniards in Florida. These Indians had fallen upon Fort Mims, on the Alabama River just north of the Florida border, and had massacred the frontier families taking shelter within its stockade. Andrew Jackson, Tennessee planter and militia general, turning from his plans for invading Florida, tracked down the Creeks. In the Battle of Horseshoe

THE WAR OF 1812

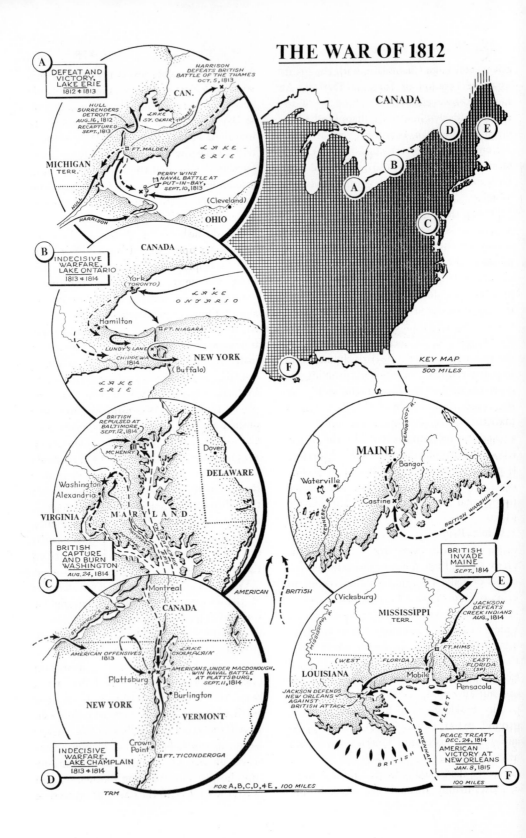

A — DEFEAT AND VICTORY, LAKE ERIE, 1812 & 1813

HARRISON DEFEATS BRITISH, BATTLE OF THE THAMES, OCT. 5, 1813

CAN.

LAKE ST. CLAIR

THAMES R.

HULL SURRENDERS DETROIT, AUG. 16, 1812. RECAPTURED SEPT. 1813

FT. MALDEN

LAKE ERIE

MICHIGAN TERR.

HULL

HARRISON

PERRY WINS NAVAL BATTLE AT PUT-IN-BAY, SEPT. 10, 1813

(Cleveland)

OHIO

CANADA

B — INDECISIVE WARFARE, LAKE ONTARIO, 1813 & 1814

York (TORONTO)

LAKE ONTARIO

Hamilton

FT. NIAGARA

LUNDY'S LANE

CHIPPEWA 1814

NEW YORK

(Buffalo)

LAKE ERIE

BRITISH REPULSED AT BALTIMORE, SEPT. 12, 1814

FT. McHENRY

Dover

DELAWARE

Washington
Alexandria

VIRGINIA

MARYLAND

C — BRITISH CAPTURE AND BURN WASHINGTON, AUG. 24, 1814

Montreal

CANADA

ST. LAWRENCE R.

AMERICAN OFFENSIVES, 1813

AMERICAN   BRITISH

LAKE CHAMPLAIN

AMERICANS, UNDER MACDONOUGH, WIN NAVAL BATTLE AT PLATTSBURG, SEPT. 11, 1814

Plattsburg

Burlington

NEW YORK

VERMONT

Crown Point

FT. TICONDEROGA

D — INDECISIVE WARFARE, LAKE CHAMPLAIN, 1813 & 1814

TRM

MAINE

Bangor

Waterville

KENNEBEC R.

PENOBSCOT R.

Castine

BRITISH WARSHIPS

E — BRITISH INVADE MAINE, SEPT. 1814

(Vicksburg)

MISSISSIPPI TERR.

JACKSON DEFEATS CREEK INDIANS, AUG., 1814

MISSISSIPPI R.

FT. MIMS

(WEST FLORIDA)

EAST FLORIDA (SP.)

LOUISIANA

Mobile

Pensacola

JACKSON DEFENDS NEW ORLEANS AGAINST BRITISH ATTACK

PAKENHAM

FLEET

BRITISH

F — PEACE TREATY DEC. 24, 1814. AMERICAN VICTORY AT NEW ORLEANS, JAN. 8, 1815

FOR A, B, C, D, & E, 100 MILES

100 MILES

CANADA

KEY MAP
500 MILES

Bend (March 27, 1814) Jackson's men took frightful vengeance, slaughtering squaws and children along with warriors. Then Jackson went into Florida and seized the Spanish fort at Pensacola.

After the battles of the Thames and Horseshoe Bend, the Indians were of little use to the British. But, with the surrender of Napoleon in Europe, the British could send their veterans of the European war to dispose of the "dirty shirts," the unkempt Americans. In 1814 the British prepared to invade the United States by three approaches—Chesapeake Bay, Lake Champlain (the historic route of Burgoyne), and the mouth of the Mississippi.

An armada under Admiral Sir George Cockburn, a hard-bitten old sea-dog, sailed up the Patuxent River from Chesapeake Bay and landed an army which marched a short distance overland to Bladensburg, on the outskirts of the District of Columbia. Hastily drawn up to oppose this army was a much more numerous force of poorly trained militiamen. When the firing started they gave more than they received, but they were unnerved by the repeated assaults of the well-disciplined redcoats and finally broke and ran. The British marched on into Washington (August 24, 1814), putting the government to flight. Then they deliberately burned the public buildings, including the White House, in retaliation for the earlier unauthorized incendiarism at York. The sack of Washington marked the low point of American fortunes in the war; better days were coming.

Leaving Washington in partial ruins, the invading army re-embarked and proceeded up the bay, toward Baltimore. But Baltimore, guarded by Fort McHenry, was ready. To block the river approach, the garrison had stretched a chain across the Patapsco and had sunk several boats in the river. From a distance the British bombarded the fort (September 13, 1814), while

through the night an American, Francis Scott Key, watched from one of the enemy ships where he had gone to secure the release of a prisoner. At the "dawn's early light," as Key wrote the next day, the flag on the fort was still flying "o'er the land of the free and the home of the brave." The British withdrew, and Key's words, set to the tune of an old drinking song, quickly became popular.

Meanwhile another invasion force was descending upon northern New York. On Lake Champlain the British mustered a fleet about the size of the American fleet drawn up to oppose it, and near by they had an army three times as large as the mixed force of regulars and militia facing it. Yet, in the Battle of Plattsburg (September 11, 1814), the defenders destroyed the invading fleet, and the invading army then retreated to Canada. The northern border was safe.

Far to the south the most serious threat of all soon materialized. In December, 1814, a formidable array of battle-hardened veterans, fresh from the Duke of Wellington's Peninsular campaign against the French in Spain, landed below New Orleans. On Christmas, Wellington's brother-in-law Sir Edward Pakenham arrived to take command. Neither he nor anyone else in America knew that, the day before, a treaty of peace between the British and American governments had been signed in faraway Belgium. Awaiting Pakenham's advance up the Mississippi was Andrew Jackson with a motley collection of Tennesseans, Kentuckians, creoles, Negroes, and pirates drawn up behind breastworks. For all their drill and bravery, the redcoats advancing through the open (January 8, 1815) were no match for Jackson's well-protected men. Making good use of artillery as well as rifles, the Americans held their fire as each wave of attackers approached, then sent out deadly volleys at close range. Finally the British retreated while an American

band struck up "Hail Columbia!" Left behind were 700 dead, including Pakenham himself, 1,400 wounded, and 500 other prisoners. Jackson's losses: 8 killed, 13 wounded.

New England Objections

With notable exceptions, such as the Battle of New Orleans, the military operations of the United States, 1812–1815, were rather badly bungled. This should cause little surprise. What is surprising is the fact that American arms succeeded as well as they did. After all, the government was woefully unprepared for the war at the outset and faced increasing popular opposition as the contest dragged on. The opposition centered in New England, and it went to remarkable extremes. Some of the Federalists there celebrated British victories, sabotaged their own country's war effort, and even plotted disunion and a separate peace.

The slogan "Free seas and sailors' rights" seemed like a mockery to the shipowners who made their living from overseas commerce, for the actions of Jefferson and Madison—embargoes, war, wartime restrictions on trade—interfered more seriously with New England commerce than did the policies of Great Britain or France. The shipowners wanted freedom of the seas, real and absolute freedom, and during most of the war some of them managed to exercise it despite the British blockade and the laws of the United States. The blockade, until 1814, did not extend north of Newport, Rhode Island, the British government deliberately cultivating the New England trade. Goods carried in Yankee ships helped to feed British troops in Canada as well as Spain, and for a time many a shipowner grew rich by trading with the enemy while denouncing Madison and the war, though eventually the business of the shipowners as a whole fell far below the level of the prosperous prewar years.

Though most of the money in the nation was concentrated in New England, only a small part of the government's war bonds could be sold there. One of the Treasury loans, desperately needed to keep soldiers in the field, almost fell through because of the refusal of the New England banks to lend. Secretary of the Treasury Gallatin had to turn to his friend John Jacob Astor of New York and two foreign-born bankers of Philadelphia for the necessary funds. On several occasions the governors of New England states refused to allow the state militia to take orders from the President or to fight outside the country. New Englanders were accused of collaborating with the enemy by placing blue lights on the coast to inform the British of American ship movements, and members of the extreme antiwar faction of the Federalist party came to be known as "Blue Light" Federalists.

In Congress the Republicans had continual trouble with the Federalist opposition. The leadership of the administration party fell to Calhoun, who devoted himself to justifying the war and raising men and money with which to fight it. At every step he ran against the obstructionists, foremost among them the young congressman from New Hampshire, Daniel Webster. In-

The Battle of New Orleans, January 8, 1815. [OPPOSITE] *This sketch, drawn at the battle by H. Laclotte, one of Jackson's men, shows Sir Edward Pakenham's army advancing in open formation against Jackson's well-protected militia (left of center) on Chalmette Plain, on the east bank of the Mississippi River about five miles below New Orleans. In the left foreground may be seen some of Jackson's heavy guns in action, as well as hand-to-hand combat between the guns' defenders and the attacking redcoats.* (COURTESY OF THE NEW-YORK HISTORICAL SOCIETY, NEW YORK CITY)

troducing resolution after resolution to embarrass the administration, Webster demanded reasons for the war and intimated that Napoleon had tricked the President cided to draft men into the regular army from the state militia. Helping to defeat the conscription bill, Webster warned that no such law could be enforced in his part of

The Hartford Convention
1815

New England opponents of the war, meeting at Hartford, Connecticut, late in 1814, demanded the following amendments to the Federal Constitution in their report, published early in the following year:

1. "Representatives and direct taxes shall be apportioned among the several states . . . according to their respective numbers of free persons. . . ."

2. "No new state shall be admitted into the Union by Congress . . . without the concurrence of two thirds of both houses."

3. "Congress shall not have power to lay any embargo . . . for more than sixty days."

4. "Congress shall not have power, without the concurrence of two thirds of both houses, to interdict the commercial intercourse between the United States and any foreign nation. . . ."

5. "Congress shall not make or declare war, or authorize acts of hostility against any foreign nation, without the concurrence of two thirds of both houses, except such acts of hostility be in defence of the territories of the United States when actually invaded."

6. "No person who shall hereafter be naturalized, shall be eligible as a member of the senate or house of representatives of the United States, nor capable of holding any civil office under the authority of the United States."

7. "The same person shall not be elected president of the United States a second time; nor shall the president be elected from the same state two terms in succession."

into antagonizing England, as in fact Napoleon had. Every measure to finance the fighting—by loans, taxes, tariffs, or a national bank—Webster and his Federalist allies vehemently denounced. At a time when volunteering lagged and the army was seriously undermanned, he opposed a bill to encourage enlistments. Privately he rejoiced at the frustration of the Republicans. "They are in a sad pickle," he wrote. "Who cares?"

In its extremity the administration decided the country. "The operation of measures thus unconstitutional and illegal ought to be prevented by a resort to other measures which are both constitutional and legal," he declared (December 9, 1814). "It will be the solemn duty of the state governments to protect their own authority over their own militia and to interpose between their citizens and arbitrary power." Here Webster, echoing the 1798–1799 doctrines of Jefferson and Madison, hinted at a kind of nullification.

To a few of the Federalist die-hards, nullification was not enough. For nearly twenty years their party had not won a national election. As new states in the South and West, strongly Republican, were added to the Union, the Federalists had become more and more hopelessly a minority party in the country as a whole. But they were the majority in New England. If it were to become a separate confederacy, they could control its destinies and escape the dictation of slaveholders and backwoodsmen. The talk of secession, heard before at the time of the Louisiana Purchase and again at the time of Jefferson's embargo, was revived during the war and reached a climax in the winter of 1814–1815, when the republic appeared to be on the verge of ruin.

On December 15, 1814, while the British were beginning their invasion by way of New Orleans, delegates from the New England states met in Hartford, Connecticut, to consider the grievances of their section against the Madison administration. The meeting was secret, so the rest of the country expected the worst. The Richmond, Virginia, *Inquirer* declared that nullification or secession was treason and that the respectable gentlemen assembled at Hartford, if they attempted either course, should be dealt with as traitors. New England was threatening to secede, and the South was upholding the Union, or so it seemed to the newspaper readers of the time.

Actually the would-be seceders were overruled by the comparatively moderate men who were in the overwhelming majority at the Hartford convention. The convention's report, when published, proved to be much milder than the public had expected, though ominous enough. It reasserted the right of nullification but only hinted at secession, observing that "the severance of the Union by one or more States, against the will of the rest, and especially in time of war, can be justified only by absolute necessity." But the report proposed seven essential amendments to the Constitution, presumably as the condition of New England's remaining in the Union. These amendments were intended to protect New England from the growing influence of the South and the West.

The Federalists, apparently in a strong bargaining position, assumed that the Republicans would have to give in to the Hartford convention terms, since the government was in such dire extremity. Soon after the convention adjourned, however, the news of Jackson's smashing victory at New Orleans reached the cities of the Northeast. While most Americans rejoiced, the Federalists were plunged into gloom. A day or two later came tidings from abroad concerning the conclusion of a treaty of peace. Of course, the treaty had been signed before the Battle of New Orleans, but the people heard of the battle first. They got the impression that the United States had won the war. "Peace is signed in the arms of victory!" *Niles's Register* exclaimed. The Hartford convention and the Federalist party were discredited as not only treasonable but also futile.

The Peace Settlement

During the War of 1812 peace talks began before the battles did. President Madison, reluctant to ask for a declaration of war and "regretting the necessity which produced it," looked hopefully toward an early end to hostilities. Soon after the declaration the British government, wishing to liquidate a minor war and concentrate upon the major one, against Napoleon, sent an admiral to Washington with armistice proposals, but negotiations failed to develop because of Madison's continued insistence upon the renunciation of impressment. Britain's ally Russia, eager to get supplies from America as well as unhampered military aid from England, twice offered to mediate, the first time on the day before Napoleon's invading forces entered Moscow (September 13, 1812). The British politely declined both of the Czar's offers but finally agreed to meet the Americans in direct negotiations on neutral ground. After prolonged delays the peacemakers got together in Ghent, Belgium, on August 8, 1814.

At that time the fortunes of battle in America certainly did not favor the United States, with its very capital exposed to capture by the enemy. Yet, after nearly four months of negotiation, a treaty was made which spared the United States from the loss of any of its territory. Though this was hardly a success as measured by the early ambitions of the war hawks, it was something of an achievement in view of the military realities as they were at the time the negotiations began. There were three reasons why American diplomacy at Ghent succeeded as well as it did. In the first place, the military situation in America improved somewhat, with the successful defense of Baltimore and the victory at Plattsburg. Second, the British had to give more attention to European than to American affairs, and the revival of Bonapartism in France, after Napoleon's defeat in 1814, presaged a renewal of the European war. Third, the American peace delegation at Ghent happened to be composed of men of exceptional ability, men who were more than a match for their opposite numbers around the peace table.

The delegation included men of both parties and all sections. At the head of it was John Quincy Adams, a one-time Federalist who had broken with his party to support Jefferson's embargo, and a diplomat of varied experience who recently had been minister to Russia. One of his colleagues was Henry Clay, once a war hawk, now a peace dove. Others were the lead-

ing Federalist of Delaware, James A. Bayard; the former chargé d'affaires in London, Jonathan Russell; and the Secretary of the Treasury in both Jefferson's and Madison's administrations, Albert Gallatin. A natural diplomat, Gallatin held the delegation together by moderating the disputes of Adams and Clay. These two, Adams the self-righteous puritan and Clay the sportsman and gambler, had frequent personality clashes as well as disagreements over the interests of their respective sections, New England and the West.

To deal with the Americans, Great Britain sent an undistinguished admiral, an undistinguished lawyer, and an undistinguished bureaucrat. She had outstanding statesmen, but they could not be spared for negotiations so comparatively trivial to her as those at Ghent. Lord Castlereagh, minister of foreign affairs, and the Duke of Wellington were busy with preparations for the European peace conference to be held at Vienna, which they attended in person.

At Ghent the two sets of peacemakers at first presented fantastically extreme demands, then gradually backed down and finally agreed to a compromise. The Americans, in accordance with their instructions, originally demanded the renunciation of impressment as a necessary condition to peace, and they also asked for all or part of Canada and for British aid in acquiring Florida from Spain. The Englishmen, contrary to their instructions, presented an ultimatum requiring the United States to cede territory in the Northwest for the formation of an Indian buffer state. Then, when their home government refused to sustain them in the ultimatum, they withdrew it and proposed that peace be made on the principle of *uti possidetis*. This meant that each of the belligerents should keep the territory it actually held whenever the fighting stopped. Expecting large territorial gains from the invasion of America, the Englishmen at Ghent tried to delay negotiations so as to maximize the gains. But the government in London, becoming more and more alarmed by developments in Europe, decided to hasten the settlement with the United States and recommended peace on the basis of the *status quo ante bellum,* which meant a return to things as they had been before the war began. Already President Madison had advised his delegation that they need no longer make an issue of impressment. A treaty providing for the *status quo,* hastily drawn up, was signed on Christmas Eve, 1814.

According to the Treaty of Ghent, the war was to end not immediately, but when the document had been ratified and proclaimed on both sides (hence it is not exactly true, as is sometimes said, that the Battle of New Orleans was fought after the war was over). Each of the belligerents was to restore its wartime conquests to the other. Four commissions with both American and British members were to be appointed to agree upon disputed or undetermined segments of the boundary between Canada and the United States.

The Treaty of Ghent was followed by other settlements which contributed to the improvement of Anglo-American relations. A separate commercial treaty (1815) gave Americans the right to trade freely with England and the British Empire except for the West Indies. A fisheries convention (1818) renewed the privileges of Americans to catch and dry fish at specified places along the shores of British North America. The Rush-Bagot agreement (1817) provided for mutual disarmament on the Great Lakes. Gradually disarmament was extended to the land, and eventually (though not till 1872) the Canadian-American boundary became the longest "unguarded frontier" in the world.

Though the British had not renounced impressment in principle, they ceased to apply it in practice after 1815. With the final end of the Napoleonic wars after the Battle of Waterloo, the nations of Europe entered upon a century of comparative peace, broken only by wars of limited scale. So the British no longer had occasion to violate American sovereignty on the high seas, and the government and people of the United States could afford to devote their energies primarily to affairs at home.

Despite the postwar settlements and the end of impressment, the War of 1812 left a legacy of hatred which complicated Anglo-American relations for many years to come. The memory of wartime atrocities persisted in the United States—atrocities such as the Raisin River massacre, in which the Indian allies of Great Britain slaughtered American captives, or the affair at Dartmoor prison in England, when American prisoners of war, held after the fighting was over, were shot down as they sought to escape. Decade after decade, anti-British politicians in the United States were always ready to refresh the memories of citizens who otherwise might have been inclined to forget these things.

The War of 1812 was anomalous in many ways. Though avowedly waged for free seas and sailors' rights, it was opposed by the group most directly interested in seagoing commerce, the New England merchants, who sneeringly referred to it as "Mr. Madison's war," not theirs. Peace overtures began before the fighting did, and the peace treaty was signed before the last and greatest of the battles had been fought. The treaty did not even mention the most important of the war aims—the conquest of Canada and the elimination of impressment. Indeed, the war was at best a draw, and the United States was lucky to avoid surrendering some of its own territory. Yet the war had important consequences. It broke the Indian barriers that had stood in the way of the northwestward and southwestward expansion of settlement. It gave rise to a spirit of nationalism which discredited the antiwar party and helped to overcome the divisive forces of postwar sectionalism. Perhaps most important of all, it stimulated the growth of manufactures, thus accelerating the progress of the nation toward industrial greatness.

The year the war ended, 1815, marks a turning point in the relations of the United States with the rest of the world. Previously, this country had become involved again and again in the broils of Europe, and much of the time the requirements of diplomacy had dictated domestic policies. Afterwards, for most of a century, domestic politics held a clear priority over foreign affairs as the country entered upon a period of comparative "isolation."

Free Seas Again

No sooner had peace come in 1815 than Congress declared war again, this time against Algiers, which had taken advantage of the War of 1812 to loose its pirates once more against American shipping in the Mediterranean. Two American squadrons now proceeded to North African waters. One of the two, under the command of Stephen Decatur, a naval hero of the late war with England, captured a number of corsair ships, blockaded the coast of Algiers, and forced the Dey to accept a treaty which not only ended the payment of tribute by the United States but required the Dey to pay reparations to this country. Going on to Tunis and Tripoli, Decatur collected additional indemnities in both of those places. This naval action in the Mediterranean brought a more clear-cut victory for the freedom of the seas than had the War of 1812 itself. Of course, the victory was made possible by the growth in naval strength and national spirit which the war with England had occasioned. After 1816, when the Dey of Algiers began to make trouble again, only to have his entire fleet destroyed by combined British and Dutch forces, the United States had no further difficulties with the Barbary pirates.

-->>>-->>>-->>>-->>>-<<<--<<<--<<<--<<<-

BIBLIOGRAPHY

ON THE ORIGINS of the War of 1812, the long-standing view was that the freedom of the seas was all-important. J. W. Pratt challenges this view in his *Expansionists of 1812* (1925). Pratt concludes that border considerations—the desire of Northwestern frontiersmen to get Canada, and of Southwestern frontiersmen to get Florida, so as to eliminate the Indian menace—were also highly significant. This interpretation is attacked by A. L. Burt in *The United States, Great Britain, and British North America from the Revolution to the Peace after the War of 1812* (1940). Burt denies that the frontier conflict was a prime cause of war and insists that maritime difficulties, particularly impressment, were as important as they have appeared to be in the traditional view.

J. F. Zimmerman, *Impressment of American Seamen* (1925), gives plenty of instances and figures to show the extent of the British practice. L. M. Sears, *Jefferson and the Embargo* (1927), is a good study of the American attempt at economic coercion.

Glenn Tucker, *Tecumseh: Vision of Glory* (1956), provides a realistic and dramatic life of an impressive Indian. The "hero" of Tippecanoe is portrayed in D. B. Goebel, *William Henry Harrison* (1926), and in Freeman Cleves, *Old Tippecanoe* (1939).

The leading war hawk and his times receive scholarly and colorful treatment in Bernard Mayo's *Henry Clay: Spokesman of the New West* (1937). A concise and readable biography covering Clay's entire career is Clement Eaton, *Henry Clay and the Art of American Politics* (1957). The war-hawk phase of Calhoun's life is ably presented by C. M. Wiltse in *John C. Calhoun: Nationalist, 1782–1828* (1944), the first volume of a thorough three-volume biography.

Irving Brant, *James Madison: The President, 1809–1812* (1956), the fifth volume of a monumental biography, continues to defend Madison's statesmanship against the charges of Henry Adams. The opposition of his Federalist foes and the workings of the Hartford convention are revealed in *The Life and Letters of Harrison Gray Otis* (2 vols., 1913), edited by S. E. Morison.

An up-to-date general account is F. F. Beirne, *The War of 1812* (1949). The chap-

ters on the war from Henry Adams's 9-volume history have been republished as *The War of 1812* (1944). The enemy's side is presented in C. P. Lucas, *The Canadian War of 1812* (1906), and in William Wood's *The War with the United States* (1915). Marquis James, *Andrew Jackson: The Border Captain* (1933), stirringly recounts Jackson's campaigns. C. F. Adams, *Studies Military and Diplomatic, 1775–1865* (1911), includes an essay analyzing the Battle of New Orleans. A. T. Mahan, *Sea Power in Its Relation to the War of 1812* (2 vols., 1919), is a classic by the influential big-navy advocate.

The state of military preparedness at the start of the war can be seen in J. R. Jacobs's *The Beginning of the United States Army, 1783–1812* (1947). C. C. Alden and Allan Westcott, *The United States Navy: A History* (1943), gives a good summary of the navy's role both in the War of 1812 and in the fighting with the Mediterranean pirates. A more extensive and more colorful account of the Barbary War is provided by Fletcher Pratt in *Preble's Boys: Commodore Preble and the Birth of American Sea Power* (1950).

CHAPTER 14

The West and the Sectional Balance

SECTIONALISM—the rivalry of one part of the country against another—had roots that went deep in American history. Even in colonial times there were three well-recognized sections (New England, the Middle Colonies, and the South) and occasionally the inhabitants of one expressed their dislike for those of another. During the Revolutionary era the Patriots sometimes were divided by sectional jealousies, and during the early years of independence sectional feeling flared up again and again. It was provoked by the Jay-Gardoqui negotiations, the questions of slavery and commerce at the constitutional convention, Hamilton's economic program, the Alien and Sedition Acts, the Louisiana Purchase, the embargo, and the War of 1812. Immediately after the war, broad, national views seemed to prevail, but between

1819 and 1821 there arose a sectional crisis more ominous than any before. The specific question was whether Missouri should be admitted as a slave state. Also involved was the larger question of whether the North or the South should control the rising West. The Missouri controversy, which ended in a compromise, provided a kind of dress rehearsal for a still greater crisis which, more than a generation later, was to culminate in civil war.

Postwar Economic Issues

The War of 1812 led to chaos in shipping and banking, stimulated the growth of manufactures, and exposed dramatically the inadequacy of the existing transportation system. Hence arose the postwar issues of re-establishing the Bank of the United States, protecting the new industries, and providing a nationwide network of roads and waterways. On these issues the former war hawks Clay and Calhoun became the leading advocates of the national as opposed to the local or sectional point of view. The party of Jefferson now sponsored measures of a kind once championed by the party of Hamilton. In regard to the bank and the tariff the new nationalists were completely successful; in regard to internal improvements, only partly so.

The wartime experience seemed to make necessary another national bank. After the first Bank's charter expired (1811), a large number of state banks sprang up. These issued vast quantities of banknotes (promises to pay, which then served much the same purpose as bank checks were later to do) and did not always bother to keep a large enough reserve of gold or silver to redeem the notes on demand. The notes passed from hand to hand more or less as money, but their actual value depended upon the reputation of the bank that issued them, and the variety of issues was so confusing as to make honest business difficult and counterfeiting easy. This bank money was not legal tender, and it was not issued directly by the state governments, yet its issuance hardly conformed with the clause of the Constitution giving Congress the exclusive power to regulate the currency and forbidding the states to emit bills of credit.

Congress struck at the currency evil not by prohibiting state banknotes but by chartering a second Bank of the United States, in 1816. Except that it was allowed a larger capital, this institution was essentially the same as the one founded under Hamilton's leadership in 1791; the government, as before, owned a fifth of the stock, appointed a fifth of the directors, and deposited public funds in the bank. In return for the charter, the bank had to pay a "bonus" of $1,-500,000 to the government. Though its potentialities were not fully realized during the first few years of its existence, this national bank possessed the power of controlling the state banks by presenting their notes from time to time and demanding payment either in cash or in its own notes, which were as good as gold. Once the Bank of the United States began to exercise its power, the state banks had to stay on a specie-paying basis or risk being forced out of business.

The war had a disastrous effect upon American shipping, especially after the British blockade was extended to include the New England coast. Between 1811 and 1814 exports dropped from $61,000,000 to $7,000,000 and imports from $53,000,000 to $13,000,000. The total tonnage of American vessels engaged in foreign trade declined from about 950,000 to less than 60,000 tons. Some ships managed to escape the blockade but others were caught and confiscated, altogether about 1,300 of them.

Farmers, unable to get their produce out to the markets of the world, suffered from the ruin of the carrying trade, but manufacturers prospered as foreign competition almost disappeared in consequence of the embargoes and the blockade. Much of the capital and labor formerly employed in commerce and shipbuilding was diverted to manufacturing. Goods were so scarce that, even with comparatively unskilled labor and poor management, new factories could be started with an assurance of quick profits.

By the end of the war, cotton mills were most numerous in New England, but they were not confined to that region, nor were they yet its dominant economic interest, for the carrying trade retained first place. In the middle states, especially New Jersey and Pennsylvania, there were a number of small spinning mills. In the South, in Georgia and the Carolinas, spinning mills also had arisen, though no power looms were in operation, and production was limited to the demands of local markets. The South —with its abundance of raw cotton, water power, and idle labor—seemed to have a promising future as a manufacturing region; it also had its enthusiastic advocates of industry.

As the war came to an end, the manufacturing prospects of the United States, both North and South, were suddenly dimmed. British ships swarmed alongside American wharves and began to unload their cargoes of manufactured goods at cut prices, even selling below cost. As Lord Brougham explained to Parliament, it was "well worth while to incur a loss upon the first exportation, in order, by the glut, to stifle in the cradle those rising manufactures in the United States, which war had forced into existence, contrary to the natural course of things." Thus, though the war was over, Great Britain persisted in a kind of economic warfare against the United States.

The "infant industries" needed protection if they were to survive and grow strong enough to stand upon their own feet against foreign competition. So the friends of industry maintained, reviving the old arguments of Hamilton. In 1816 the protectionists brought about the passage of a tariff law with rates high enough to be definitely protective, especially on cotton cloth. The vote in Congress indicated that the tariff, as yet, was neither a strictly partisan nor a strictly sectional issue. The vote of the Federalists was divided, and so was the vote of the Republicans. While the Representatives from the middle states were almost unanimously in favor of protection, New Englanders and Southerners voted on both sides of the question. Webster, of New Hampshire, opposed the bill; he was a spokesman for the shipping interests, which would be harmed by it, and for the Boston Manufacturing Company, which was big and efficient enough to have no need of it.

Calhoun, of South Carolina, favored the bill. In later years both Webster and Calhoun reversed their positions, after the economic interests of their respective sections had undergone a further transformation.

The second Bank of the United States, by providing credit and currency, and the tariff of 1816, by lessening the competition of foreign goods, contributed to the growth of manufactures. But something else was needed to promote the nation's business and also its security in case of another war. What was needed was better transportation. Despite the progress being made with steamboats and turnpikes, there remained serious gaps in the transportation network of the country, as experience during the War of 1812 had shown. Once the coastwise shipping had been cut off by the British blockade, the coastal roads became choked by the unaccustomed volume of north-south traffic. At the river ferries, long lines of wagons waited for a chance to cross. Oxcarts, pressed into emergency service, took six or seven weeks to go from Philadelphia to Charleston. In various localities there appeared serious shortages of goods normally carried by sea, and prices rose to new heights, rice costing three times as much in New York as in Charleston, flour three times as much in Boston as in Richmond. On the northern and western frontiers the military campaigns of the United States were partly frustrated by the absence of good roads.

With this wartime experience in mind, President Madison in 1815 called the attention of Congress to the "great importance of establishing throughout our country the roads and canals which can be best executed under the national authority," and he suggested that a constitutional amendment would resolve any doubts about the authority of Congress to provide for the construction of canals and roads. Representative Calhoun promptly espoused a bill by which the moneys due the government from the Bank of the United States—both the "bonus" and the government's share of the annual profits—would be devoted to internal improvements. "Let us, then, bind the republic together with a perfect system of roads and canals," Calhoun urged. "Let us conquer space." He hoped, as had Gallatin earlier, that eventually the Atlantic cities would be connected with the West, the Hudson with the Great Lakes, and Maine with Louisiana.

Calhoun considered internal improvements as a broad, national question, but many of his colleagues, by their votes on the so-called "bonus bill," revealed that it was a sectional question as well. Those from New England were almost solidly opposed to the bill; those from the South nearly evenly divided; those from the West mostly in favor of it, though far from unanimous; and those from the middle states of Delaware, Maryland, and New Jersey about two to one against it. Those from New York and Pennsylvania gave it their overwhelming support. The New Yorkers looked to the federal government for aid in the building of a canal between the Hudson River and Lake Erie; this project would give New York City the best of all routes to the West. The Pennsylvanians sought for Philadelphia a gateway to the South by way of a proposed canal between Delaware Bay and Chesapeake Bay, and they sought for Pittsburgh an improved outlet to the Mississippi Valley, by making navigable the falls of the Ohio (near Louisville).

Congress passed the bonus bill, but President Madison, on his last day in office (March 3, 1817), returned it with his veto. While he approved its purpose, he still believed that a constitutional amendment was necessary. And so, with some exceptions, the tremendous task of internal improve-

James Monroe. *When Monroe was governor of Virginia (1799-1802) an acquaintance said of him: "To be plain, there is often in his manner an inartificial and even an awkward simplicity, which, while it provokes the smile of a more polished person, forces him to the opinion that Mr. Monroe is a man of most sincere and artless soul." In 1825, when Monroe was in his last year as President, a Virginia lady gave her impression of him after attending a New Year's reception at the White House: "From the frank, honest expression of his eye . . . I think he well deserves the encomium passed upon him by the great Jefferson, who said, 'Monroe is so honest that if you turned his soul inside out there would not be a spot on it.'" The portrait here reproduced was done by Gilbert Stuart, who painted portraits of all the men who served as Presidents during his lifetime—Washington, Adams, Jefferson, Madison, Monroe, and John Quincy Adams.* (THE PENNSYLVANIA ACADEMY OF THE FINE ARTS)

ments was left to the state governments and to private enterprise.

"Era of Good Feelings"

After 1800 the Presidency seemed to have become the special possession of Virginians, who passed it from one to another in unvarying sequence. After two terms in office

Jefferson named his Secretary of State, James Madison, to succeed him, and after two more terms Madison secured the nomination of *his* Secretary of State, James Monroe. Against this succession of Virginians, the so-called "Virginia Dynasty," many in the North already were muttering, yet the Republicans had no difficulty in electing their candidate in the remarkably listless campaign of 1816. Monroe received 183 ballots in the electoral college; his opponent, Rufus King of New York, only 34, from the states of Massachusetts, Connecticut, and Delaware.

At the time he became President, Monroe was 61 years old. Tall and dignified, he wore the old-fashioned garb of his youthful days, including knee-length pantaloons and white-topped boots. He had reached the peak of a long and varied career as Revolutionary soldier, diplomat, and cabinet officer. Although when young he had been regarded as impulsive and changeable, he now was noted for his caution and patience. He was neither so subtle nor so original as his gifted predecessors from Virginia, Jefferson and Madison, yet he was more able than posterity generally has considered him. He had a mind of his own, and he was the master of his administration, even though he picked a group of exceptionally strong men for his advisers.

In choosing his cabinet, Monroe intended to recognize and harmonize the major interests of the country. Though he declined Andrew Jackson's suggestion that he appoint Federalists as well as Republicans, he tried to see that every section was adequately represented. For the first and most important position, that of Secretary of State, he selected the New Englander and one-time Federalist, John Quincy Adams. This choice was significant in view of the well-established custom which made the State Department a steppingstone to the

Presidency: Monroe appeared to be announcing that he would be the last of the Virginia Dynasty and that the next President (after a second term for Monroe) would be a Massachusetts man. For Secretary of War, Monroe chose the forceful South Carolinian, John C. Calhoun, after Henry Clay had declined the office, preferring to continue as speaker of the House. Clay's refusal left the cabinet without an adequate representative from the West, and various circumstances resulted in an over-representation of the South, despite Monroe's good intentions.

The new President was inaugurated on a bright March day which seemed to reflect the optimism of a nation recovering from war and wartime disunity. Throughout the country, business was good and getting better. In Washington a new and more graceful Capitol was rising from the ashes of the old one, and the damaged White House was being rebuilt. "The present happy state," the opening words of Monroe's inaugural address, gave expression to the national mood. The sober-minded Monroe, welcoming the "increased harmony of opinion," declared, "Discord does not belong to our system." Soon after his inauguration he did what no other President since Washington had done: he made a goodwill tour through the country, eastward to New England, westward as far as Detroit. In New England, so recently the scene of rabid Federalist discontent, he was greeted everywhere with enthusiastic demonstrations. The *Columbian Centinel*, a Federalist newspaper of Boston, commenting on the "Presidential Jubilee" in that city, observed that an "era of good feelings" had arrived. This phrase soon became popular; it spread throughout the country, and eventually it came to be almost synonymous with the Presidency of Monroe.

There was a good deal of hidden irony

in this phrase of 1817, for the "good feelings" did not last long, and the period over
which Monroe presided turned into one of
very bad feelings indeed. During his first
term a crisis in foreign affairs was precipitated by the Florida question. A business
depression fell like a blight after the Panic
of 1819. And the very existence of the
Union was threatened by the controversy
over Missouri.

Yet, surprising though it may seem, Monroe was re-elected in 1820 with the nearest
thing to a unanimous electoral vote that
any presidential candidate, with the exception of George Washington, has ever had.
Indeed, all but one of the electors cast their
ballots for Monroe. The lone dissenter, a
strong-minded Yankee from New Hampshire who thought Monroe unfit for the
Presidency, voted for John Quincy Adams.
The Federalists had not even bothered to
put up an opposing candidate.

By that time the Federalist party had
ceased to exist as a national organization,
though it lingered on as a political force in
some localities, especially in New England.
The party had been discredited by its ob-
structionist activities against what, in the
end, had proved to be a popular war. No
longer could the Federalists stand as the
champions of broad, national policies, since
the Republicans on the whole had gone so
far beyond the old Federalists in the advocacy of national measures. One by one
the majority of the Federalists joined the
party of Jefferson, Madison, and Monroe
until finally the two-party system all but
disappeared for a time. The decline of organized party opposition to the Monroe administration was one reason why good feelings seemed so evident in politics. But this
state of affairs did not please all the Federalist politicians. Some of them, in particular
their last presidential candidate, Rufus King,
hoped to find an issue which would enable

them to revive the party and regain control of the federal government.

Florida and the Far West

The first big problem facing John Quincy
Adams as Secretary of State was that of
Florida. Already the United States had annexed West Florida, but Spain still claimed
the whole of the province, East and West,
and actually held most of it, though with
a grasp too feeble to stop the abuses against
which Americans long had complained—
the escape of slaves across the border in
one direction, the marauding of Indians
across it in the other. In 1817 Adams began
negotiations with the Spanish minister, Don
Diego de Onís, for acquiring all of Florida
(or rather for acquiring that part of it
which the United States did not already
claim). Talks between the cantankerous
puritan and the wily don progressed haltingly, then were broken off when the hot-
tempered Andrew Jackson took matters
forcefully into his own hands.

Jackson, in command of American troops
along the Florida frontier, had orders from
Secretary of War Calhoun to "adopt the
necessary measures" to end the border troubles. Jackson also had an unofficial hint—
or so he afterwards claimed—that the administration would not mind if he undertook a punitive expedition into Spanish territory. At any rate he invaded Florida,
seized the Spanish forts at St. Marks and
Pensacola, and ordered the hanging of two
British subjects on the charge of supplying
the Indians and inciting them to hostilities.
News of these events provoked a sharp discussion behind the scenes in Monroe's cabinet. Calhoun and others insisted that the
general should be punished or at least repri-
manded for exceeding his authority, but
Adams defended Jackson so ably as to prevent any action against him.

Instead of blaming Jackson or disavowing the raid, Adams wished the government to assume complete responsibility for it, for he saw in it a chance to further his Florida diplomacy. Rejecting a Spanish protest, he demanded reparations from Spain to pay the cost of the expedition, though he did not press this demand. He pointed out that Spain had promised in Pinckney's Treaty to restrain the Indians in her territory but had failed to live up to her treaty obligations. The United States, he argued, was justified by international law in taking drastic measures for self-defense. He implied that this country would be justified in going even farther than it had done.

Jackson's raid demonstrated that the United States, if it tried, could easily take Florida by force, unless Spain could get aid from some other power. The only power to which she could look was Great Britain. The British foreign minister, Lord Castlereagh, was not inclined to intervene. In the "existing state of the world," he informed the Spaniards, the "avowed and true" policy of his government was to "appease controversy" and to "secure, if possible, for all states a long interval of repose." He advised Spain to yield Florida in the interests of world peace. Even Jackson's execution of the two British subjects in Florida did not change the policy of Castlereagh, who concluded that these men had been engaged in shady activities and were unworthy of their government's protection.

Unable to obtain British support, Spain had little choice but to come to terms with the United States, though the resourceful Onís made the most of a bad situation for his country. In the treaty of 1819 it was agreed that the King of Spain should cede "all the territories which belong to him situated to the eastward of the Mississippi and known by the name of East and West Florida." This ambiguous wording was used so as to evade the troublesome question whether Spain was ceding both East and West Florida or whether West Florida already belonged to the United States. In return the United States assumed the claims of its citizens against the Spanish government to the amount of $5,000,000. This money was to be paid to American citizens, not to the Spanish government: we did not "purchase" Florida, as is sometimes said. The United States also gave up its claims to Texas, and Spain her claims to territory north of the forty-second parallel from the Rockies to the Pacific. Thus a line was drawn from the Gulf of Mexico northwestward across the continent delimiting the Spanish empire and transferring to the United States the Spanish title to the West Coast north of California. Adams and Onís had concluded something more than a Florida agreement: it was a "transcontinental treaty."

President Monroe, with the approval of the Senate, promptly ratified the treaty, but the coming of a revolution delayed ratification by Spain. The treaty finally went into effect in 1821. Thereafter the whole of Florida was, without question, territory belonging to the United States. And for the first time the area of the Louisiana Purchase had a definite southwestern boundary.

At the time of his negotiations with Onís, Adams showed much more interest in the Far West than did most of his fellow countrymen. Few Americans were familiar with the Oregon coast except for New Englanders engaged in Pacific whaling or in the China trade. Only the fur traders and trappers knew intimately any of the land between the Missouri and the Pacific. Before the War of 1812 John Jacob Astor's American Fur Company had established Astoria as a trading post at the mouth of the Columbia River, but when war came Astor sold his interests to the Northwestern Fur Company, a British concern operating from Canada, and after the war he centered his own operations in the Great Lakes area, from which he eventually extended them westward to the Rockies. Manuel Lisa's Missouri Fur Company, founded in 1809, with headquarters in St. Louis, sent traders

structions from the War Department to find the sources of the Red River, Long with nineteen soldiers ascended the Platte and South Platte rivers, discovered the peak

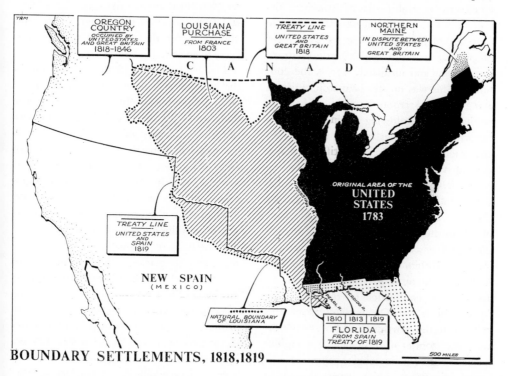

BOUNDARY SETTLEMENTS, 1818, 1819

and supplies up the Missouri and its tributaries and brought back peltries obtained from the Indians. The Rocky Mountain Fur Company, which Andrew Henry and William Henry Ashley organized in 1822, pushed the trade farther north and west and revolutionized the business by sending out white trappers who procured their furs directly and brought them to an annual "rendezvous" in the mountains to be sold to the company's agents.

The trappers or "mountain men," notably Jedediah S. Smith, explored the Far West and gained an intimate knowledge of it, but they did not write books. General information about the region was increased in consequence of the explorations of Major Stephen H. Long. In 1819 and 1820, with in-

named for him, and returned eastward by way of the Arkansas River, but failed to find the headwaters of the Red. "In regard to this extensive section of country between the Missouri River and the Rocky Mountains," Long said in his report, "we do not hesitate in giving the opinion that it is almost wholly unfit for cultivation, and of course uninhabitable by a people depending upon agriculture for their subsistence." On the published map of his expedition the Great Plains were marked as the "Great American Desert." Thus he gave increased currency to the idea earlier put forth by Pike that the farming frontier would run against a great natural barrier beyond the Missouri. Meanwhile the vacant lands to the east, between the Appalachians and the Mississippi, were rapidly being converted into plantations and farms.

The Great Migration

One of the central themes of American history, for nearly three centuries after the founding of Jamestown, was the movement of population from the Atlantic coast to the interior and ultimately across the continent. This was no steady march, uniform along a broad front. It proceeded in irregular waves, following the lines of greatest attraction and least resistance, and accelerating in times of prosperity and peace. A sudden surge, greater than any preceding it, swept westward during the boom years which followed the War of 1812. Before the war thousands of settlers had made homes to the west of the Appalachians, but most of the settled area would have been included within a triangle drawn so that its base lay along the Atlantic coast and its apex at the confluence of the Ohio and Mississippi rivers. On both sides of this triangle, to the Northwest and to the Southwest, the frontier of settlement was rapidly pushed outward in consequence of the "great migration" which began as soon as Indian resistance had been weakened by the Battles of the Thames and Horseshoe Bend.

Weakened though it had been, the Indian threat still had to be taken into account. In a series of treaties forced upon the tribes after 1815, the federal government resumed the policy of compelling the red men to choose between settling down as civilized farmers and migrating beyond the Mississippi. Along the Great Lakes and the upper Mississippi a chain of stockaded forts was erected to protect the frontier. A "factory" system, by which government factors or agents traded with the Indians, supplying them with goods at cost, was instituted in an effort to drive out of business the Canadian traders who persisted in carrying on their activities on American soil. After

several years the government factories were abandoned because of the opposition of American fur companies, which objected to government competition with private enterprise. By that time the Canadian traders had retreated across the border, and foreign influence over the American tribes finally came to an end.

The land abandoned by the Indians in the Northwest had been richly favored by nature, though its qualities were not entirely understood by the early pioneers. In prehistoric times most of the Mississippi Valley had lain beneath the ocean, then had risen in a geologic upheaval to form a level lowland, which eventually received some topographical variety from erosion and glaciation. A glacier extending as far south as southern Illinois smoothed the terrain and left a deposit of unusually rich soil. Below the line the glacier reached, the terrain was rougher and the soil less fertile, except on the bottom lands along the rivers. Over most of the Northwest extended the great primeval forest, but in central Illinois the forest gave way to a grand prairie billowing with wild grass as tall as six feet. The first settlers avoided this treeless stretch, for they saw unfamiliar problems in its tough sod and scarcity of wood, and they little knew the productivity of its black loam. They sought out the bottom lands and even the unglaciated, though wooded hills, since these areas were the most accessible to them, coming as they usually did by way of the Ohio.

They swarmed as never before. "Old America seems to be breaking up and moving westward," remarked an Englishman who joined the throng. Some were Kentucky and Tennessee frontiersmen, restless spirits who had begun to feel crowded as their states became increasingly populous. Others were small farmers from the back country of Virginia and the Carolinas who fled the encroachment of slavery and the plantation system. Still others came from the middle states, New England, and foreign countries, but the great majority were Southerners. Whatever the starting point, the Ohio River was for most of the migrants the main route, the "grand track," until the completion of the Erie Canal in 1825. They took the turnpike to Pittsburgh or the national road to Wheeling and thus reached the river, or they took one of its tributaries such as the Kanawha, the Cumberland, or the Tennessee. Downstream they floated on flatboats bearing all their worldly goods. Then, leaving the Ohio at Cincinnati or at some place farther down, they pressed on overland with wagons, handcarts, packhorses, cattle, hogs.

Once having arrived at his destination, preferably in the spring or early summer, the settler built a lean-to or cabin for his family, then hewed a clearing out of the forest and put in a crop of corn to supplement the wild game he caught and the domestic animals he had brought with him. His livestock shifted for themselves; the frontier hog became so thin on its diet of acorns that it was commonly referred to as a "wind-splitter." Reverting for the time being to a near-primitive existence, the family became almost self-sufficient, in homespun garments, fur caps, and deerskin moccasins. Besides doing most of the household chores, the women helped with the planting, hoeing, and harvesting; almost invariably they milked the cows if there were cows to milk. These frontier folk knew loneliness and poverty and dirt, suffered much from the forest fevers and from malnutrition, commonly had a lean and sallow look. Yet they were on the whole remarkably proud, bold, and independent. They were "half wild and wholly free."

One phase of the migration to the Northwest can be illustrated by the story of the Lincoln family. In 1816 the Lincolns rode and walked from Kentucky into southern Indiana, where they remained about fifteen years before going on to Illinois. During the first year in Indiana they lived in a three-sided cabin with an open face looking south, where a log fire burned day and night. Then they moved into a more pretentious cabin, with a dirt floor, no windows, and a tiny loft where the young Abraham slept on a pile of leaves.

In Kentucky surroundings similar to those of Lincoln's birth, Jefferson Davis was born less than a year before Lincoln and only about a hundred miles away. As a small boy, Davis departed from Kentucky with his family shortly before the War of 1812. The Davises went to Louisiana and then to Mississippi, joining the forerunners of the great migration that, after 1815, set out for the Southwest. The later careers of Lincoln and Davis reflected the division of the nation that already was in the making.

To the Southwest moved people like the Davises from Kentucky, others from Tennessee, and some from as far away as New England. Most numerous among the settlers on the Southern frontier, however, were farmers and planters from the South Atlantic states, especially from the piedmont of Georgia and the Carolinas. Their motive for migrating was, in a word, cotton. With the spread of cotton cultivation throughout the uplands of the older South, the soil there lost much of its natural fertility from repeated croppings, or washed away as torrential rains gullied the hillsides. Seeking fresh soil with a climate suitable for cotton, the planters naturally looked to the Southwest, around the end of the Appalachian range, where there stretched a broad zone within which cotton could thrive. Included in this zone was the Black Belt of central Alabama and Mississippi, a prairie with a fabulously productive soil of rotted limestone.

The advance of the Southern frontier meant the spread of cotton and slavery.

Usually the first arrivals were ordinary frontiersmen like those farther north, small farmers who made rough clearings in the forest. Then came planters who bought up the cleared or partially cleared land, while the original settlers moved on west and started over again. As a rule the planters made the westward journey in a style quite different from that of the other pioneers. Over the alternately dusty and muddy roads came great caravans consisting of herds of livestock, wagonloads of house-

[a]

[b]

[c]

[d]

From Forest to Farm. *First [a], a clearing is begun and a rude cabin is built. The stream remains unbridged and has to be forded. Second [b], the cabin is fenced in (note the "worm" fence), more trees are cut, stumps are burned, a small crop is put in, and the stream is spanned by a log bridge. Third [c], the cabin is enlarged, a barn is built, the fencing is improved, fields are widened, and a bridge is erected. Finally [d], all trace of the wilderness is gone, an imposing house has replaced the cabin, a village has grown up near by, and an arched stone bridge has been built. These illustrations are from O. Turner,* Pioneer History of the Holland Land Purchase of Western New York *(1850).*

hold goods, long lines of slaves, and, bringing up the rear, the planter and his family riding in carriages. Soon the clearings expanded into vast fields white with cotton, and the cabins of the pioneers gave way to more sumptuous log dwellings and ultimately to imposing mansions which demonstrated the rise of a class of the newly rich.

Though by 1819 settlers already were pushing beyond the Mississippi, much of the area to the east of the river, around the Great Lakes and along the Gulf of Mexico, was yet to be occupied. Despite the gaps in settlement, the population of the Mississippi Valley had increased far more rapidly than that of the nation as a whole. The census of 1810 indicated that only one American in seven lived to the west of the Appalachian mountains; the census of 1820, almost one in four. During the immediate postwar years four new states were erected in this region—Indiana (1816), Mississippi (1817), Illinois (1818), and Alabama (1819). Meanwhile Missouri had grown populous enough for statehood, and the struggle over her admission indicated how important, politically and otherwise, the West was becoming in the eyes of the rest of the nation. For the time being, however, the westward movement was slowed down by the onset of the depression following the Panic of 1819.

The Panic of 1819

The modern business cycle—prosperity, collapse, depression, recovery—had its beginnings in the nineteenth century. The first of the modern depressions began with the Panic of 1819. Thereafter, throughout the century, major depressions came at intervals of approximately twenty years: 1837, 1857, 1873, 1893.

Of course, even in the colonial era there had been occasional periods of hard times. These were usually due to crop failures or to low prices for some staple such as to-bacco and were local or regional in extent. After the French and Indian War and again after the Revolution there were depressions of a fairly general nature, and still another was caused by Jefferson's embargo in 1808.

The subsequent depressions, however, were more complex in their causation, more far-reaching in their consequences, and more rhythmic in their occurrence. New causes had appeared. The rise of banking and the use of bank credit as money made for increased fluctuation and uncertainty in prices: invariably the nineteenth-century depressions were touched off by bank failures and a collapse of credit. The widening of the market and the growth of specialization meant that people in every occupation and in every part of the country were more dependent on one another: more and more they produced goods for sale rather than for their own use, and they were inclined to produce greater quantities than could be profitably sold. The development of the factory system, with the increased use of machinery, made it still harder for producers to keep supply in adjustment with demand, since the productive process was lengthened and a longer time elapsed between the planning of the output and the sale to the final consumer. Thus economic activity became more speculative than ever. Speculation of various kinds, especially in land and in corporation stocks, was characteristic of the predepression booms. While the depressions of the nineteenth century had certain features in common, each also had distinctive characteristics of its own.

In part the Panic of 1819 was a delayed reaction to the War of 1812 and to the preceding years of warfare in Europe. Since 1793 the continual fighting had drawn manpower from European fields, disrupted business as well as agriculture, and created an abnormal demand for the produce of American plantations and farms. The whole period was one of exceptionally high prices for American producers, and though some prices fell with the decline of trade in 1814, they recovered with the resumption of exports to Europe after the war. The price of cotton, for example, rose from 15 cents a pound in 1813 to 29 cents in 1815 and 33 cents in 1817.

Rising prices for farm products stimulated a land boom in the United States, particularly in the West. After the war the government land offices did a bigger business than ever before; not for twenty years were they to do as good a business again. In 1815 sales totaled about a million acres and in 1819 more than five million. Many settlers bought on credit: under the land laws of 1800 and 1804 they could pay as little as $80 down, and they hoped to raise the remaining three installments within four years from the proceeds of their farming. Speculators bought large tracts of choice land, hoping to resell it at a profit to incoming settlers. At the land-office auctions, bidding became so spirited that much of the public land sold for prices far above the minimum of $2 an acre, some in the Black Belt of Alabama and Mississippi going for $100 and more. Still higher prices sometimes were paid by optimistic real-estate promoters who laid out town sites, even in swamps, and expected to make fortunes through the sale of city lots. Until 1817 neither the settlers nor the speculators needed hard cash to buy government land: they could borrow from the state banks and pay the government with banknotes.

Even after the founding of the Bank of the United States in 1817, wildcat banks continued to provide easy credit for a couple of years. Indeed, the U.S. Bank itself at first offered easy loans. Then in 1819, under new management, it suddenly began to tighten up. It called in loans and foreclosed mortgages, acquiring thousands of acres of mortgaged land in the West. It gathered up state banknotes and presented them to the state banks for payment in cash. Having little money on hand, many of these banks closed their doors. Most of the rest soon had to follow suit, for they were beset by depositors with notes to be cashed. The panic was on.

Six years of depression followed. Prices rapidly fell. Within a few months cotton dropped from 33 cents a pound to 15 and eventually to 10, wheat from $2 a bushel to $1 and then in some places to 25 cents, and corn from 90 cents to 50 cents and finally to as little as 10. The value of land declined to a half or less of what it had been before the crash. Factories closed down, leaving more men and women unemployed than ever before, as many as a half million according to one estimate. In New York City a tenth of the population went on relief, provided by local charity.

But the depression was worst and lasted the longest in the West. With the prices of farm products so low, those settlers buying land on credit could not hope to keep up their payments. Some stood to lose everything—their land, their improvements on it, their homes. They demanded relief from their congressmen, and Congress responded with the land law of 1820 and the relief act of 1821. By the new land law the credit system was abolished but the minimum price was lowered from $2.00 to $1.25 and the minimum tract from 160 to 80 acres. Hereafter a purchaser would have to buy his farm outright, but he could get one for as little as $100. The relief act allowed a previous buyer to pay off his debt at the reduced price, to accept the reduced acreage and apply the payments to it, and to have an extension of time in meeting his installments.

The depression had lasting effects upon the political attitudes of Westerners. Already hostile to the Bank of the United States, most of these people became even more so, for they blamed it for their misfortunes. Having been disillusioned by the loss of the foreign market for their produce, many of them also became ripe for plans to develop a home market in this

proximately 60,000 people resided in Missouri Territory, of whom about 10,000 were slaves. In that year, while Missouri's application for statehood was being considered

---

Public Lands: Terms of Sale
1785–1820

Ordinance of 1785. Allowed a minimum purchase of 640 acres and set a minimum price of $1 an acre. Made no provision for credit.

Act of 1796. Raised the minimum price to $2 an acre but allowed a year's credit on half of the amount due.

Act of 1800. Reduced the minimum purchase from 640 to 320 acres and extended credit to four years, with a down payment of one fourth of the whole amount and three later installments.

Act of 1804. Further reduced the minimum purchase to 160 acres. (Now a man with as little as $80 on hand could obtain a farm from the government, although he would still owe $240 to be paid within four years.)

Act of 1820. Reduced the minimum purchase still further, to 80 acres, and the minimum price to $1.25 an acre, but abolished the credit system.

Note: Under each of these laws, the land was first offered for sale at auction, and much of it sold for more than the minimum price.

---

country through the promotion of manufactures and the development of improved roads and waterways. Very likely, economic distress made the people of Missouri even more disgruntled than they otherwise would have been when their application for statehood was denied.

The Missouri Compromise

When Missouri applied for admission as a state, slavery already was well established there. The French and Spanish inhabitants of the Louisiana country (including what became Missouri) had owned slaves, and in the Louisiana Purchase treaty of 1803 the American government promised to maintain and protect the inhabitants in the free enjoyment of their property as well as their liberty and religion. By 1819, ap-

in Congress, Representative James Tallmadge, Jr., of New York, moved to amend the enabling bill so as to prohibit the further introduction of slaves into Missouri and to provide for the gradual emancipation of those already there. This Tallmadge amendment provoked a controversy that was to rage for the next two years.

Though the issue arose suddenly, waking and terrifying Thomas Jefferson like "a fire bell in the night," as he said, sectional jealousies that produced it had been accumulating for a long time. Already the concept of a balance of power between the Northern and Southern states was well developed. From the beginning, partly by chance and partly by design, new states had come into the Union more or less in pairs, one from the North, another from the South. With the admission of Alabama in 1819, the Union contained an equal number of free and slave states, eleven of each. Thus the free and slave states were evenly balanced in the Senate, though the free states with their more rapidly growing population had a majority in the House.

Up to this time the Ohio River had formed a sort of natural boundary between slavery and freedom in the West. Above the river, in the Northwest Territory, slavery was prohibited "forever" by the famous Ordinance of 1787. Yet a kind of slavery existed in the state of Illinois and continued to exist there as late as the 1840's. Though the state constitution of 1818 prohibited the ownership of slaves, they were nevertheless employed on Illinois farms under the guise of indentured servants. Only by a narrow margin did antislavery voters in Illinois manage, in 1824, to defeat a movement to amend the constitution so as to permit outright slavery in the state. Meanwhile abundant space was available for the expansion of slavery in the Louisiana Purchase territory and in the Florida territory which was being acquired from Spain. If Missouri should be admitted as a slave state, not only would the existing sectional balance be upset but also a precedent would be established which, in the future, would still further increase the political power of the South.

In the North the most active antislavery people were well-to-do philanthropists and reformers who generally supported the Federalist party. They opposed the extension of slavery on both humanitarian and political grounds. On the eve of the dispute over Missouri the Manumission Society of New York was busy with attempts to rescue runaway slaves, and the Quakers were conducting a campaign to strengthen the laws against the African slave trade and to protect free Negroes from kidnappers who sold them into slavery. In the South there

were still a large number of critics of slavery and its abuses, but here the humanitarian impulse was not reinforced by political interest as it was in the North. Northerners, in particular the Federalists, never tired in their denunciations of the Virginia Dynasty and the three-fifths clause which, they charged, gave the Southern states a disproportionate weight in national politics.

Once the Missouri controversy had arisen, it provided the opportunity, which Federalist leaders such as Rufus King had awaited, to attempt a revival and reinvigoration of their party. By appealing to the Northern people on the issue of slavery extension, the Federalists could hope to win many of the Northern Republicans away from their allegiance to the Republican party's Southern leadership. In New York the De Witt Clinton faction of the Republicans, who had joined with the Federalists in opposition to the War of 1812, and who were outspoken in their hostility to "Virginia influence" and "Southern rule," were more than willing to cooperate with the Federalists again. The cry against slavery in Missouri, Thomas Jefferson wrote, was "a mere party trick." He explained: "King is ready to risk the union for any chance of restoring his party to power and wriggling himself to the head of it, nor is Clinton without his hopes nor scrupulous as to the means of fulfilling them." Though Jefferson himself took a biased, partisan view of the subject, there seems little reason to doubt that some of the Federalists desired to use the Missouri controversy for creating a new, sectional alignment of parties, the North against the South. Certainly Senator King was the foremost of the "anti-Missourians" who insisted upon the exclusion of slavery.

The Missouri question soon was complicated by the application of Maine for admission as a state. Massachusetts had consented to the separation of the northern part of the Commonwealth but only on the condition that Maine be granted statehood before March 4, 1820. The speaker of the House, Henry Clay, informed Northerners that if they refused to consent to Missouri's becoming a slave state Southerners would deny the application of Maine. In the House the Northern majority nevertheless insisted on the principle of the Tallmadge amendment, but in the Senate a few of the Northerners sided with the Southerners and prevented its passage.

While the House and the Senate thus were deadlocked, members of both chambers engaged in wordy debate, though most of the people of the country, except in Missouri and Maine, showed surprisingly little interest in the excitement at Washington. In Congress the advocates of Missouri as a slave state insisted that an antislavery restriction was unconstitutional, since each state when it entered the Union became the equal of all the others and could regulate its own "domestic" institutions as it pleased. The restrictionists or "anti-Missourians" replied that Congress could impose conditions upon the admission of a state and, indeed, had done so in the past. Threats of disunion and civil war were heard on both sides. As the debate dragged on, it grew repetitious and boring, almost every congressman apparently having determined to say something to impress his constituents. Finally the House refused to listen when a representative from Buncombe County, North Carolina, rose to have his say. He insisted that he was bound to "make a speech for Buncombe," and thus (according to tradition) the word "bunkum" or "bunk" was added to the American language.

A way out of the impasse opened when the Senate combined the Maine and Missouri bills, without prohibiting slavery in Missouri. Then, to make the package more acceptable to the House, Senator Jesse B. Thomas of Illinois proposed an amendment prohibiting slavery in all the rest of the Louisiana Purchase territory north of the southern boundary of Missouri (latitude 36' 30°). The Senate adopted the Thomas amendment, and Speaker Clay undertook to guide the amended Maine-Missouri bill through the House. Eventually, after the measure had been broken up into three separate bills, he succeeded. A group of Northern Republicans, some of them suspecting the political designs of the Federalists, voted with the Southerners to make the compromise possible. Through the misinterpretation of a remark by John Randolph, the pro-compromise Northerners came to be known as "doughfaces," which thereafter gained currency as a term of reproach applied to Northern politicians who were accused of having Southern principles.

This first Missouri Compromise (1820) did not end the dispute; a second compromise was necessary. In 1820 Maine was actually admitted as a state, but Missouri was only authorized to form a constitution and a government. When the Missouri constitution was completed, it contained a clause forbidding free Negroes or mulattoes to enter the state. Several of the existing states, denying the right of citizenship to free persons of color, already had laws against their immigration. Other states, among them New York, recognized colored persons as citizens. According to the federal Constitution, "The citizens of each State shall be entitled to all privileges and immunities of citizens in the several States." This meant that a citizen of such a state as New York, whether he was white or black, was entitled to all the privileges of a citizen of Missouri, including of course the privilege of traveling or residing in the state. The anti-Negro clause was clearly unconstitutional, and a majority in the House of Representatives threatened to exclude Missouri until it was eliminated. Finally Clay offered a resolution that Missouri should be admitted to the Union on the condition that the clause should never be construed in such a way as to deny to any citizen of any state the privileges and immunities to which he was entitled under the Constitution of the United

"that the present question is a mere preamble—a title-page to a great tragic volume." And Thomas Jefferson observed: "A geographical line, coinciding with a marked

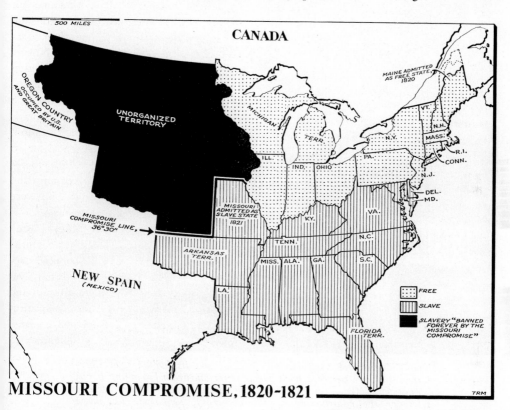

MISSOURI COMPROMISE, 1820-1821

States. In the circumstances, this resolution was meaningless, yet Clay secured its passage and enhanced his reputation as the "Great Pacificator," a reputation he was again and again to confirm during his long career. Clay's resolution made possible the admission of Missouri as a state, in 1821.

Sectional Feelings

The Missouri Compromise, by balancing a free state against a slave state and drawing a line between free and slave territory, satisfied most of the people of the country, both North and South. But far-seeing men feared that this solution would not last. "I take it for granted," wrote John Quincy Adams,

principle, moral and political, once conceived and held up to the angry passions of men, will never be obliterated; and every new irritation will mark it deeper and deeper."

While the Missouri question was being debated, a heightened spirit of sectionalism affected the discussion of other matters of national politics. The tariff and internal improvements suddenly became more definitely sectional issues than they had been in 1816 and 1817. Suffering from the depression, Northern manufacturers in increasing numbers looked to the federal government for relief in the form of tariff protection, while Southern planters and politicians lost most of the protectionist sentiment they lately had had. The tariff bill of 1820 was defeated by Southern votes in Congress. Meanwhile bills for improving roads and

Though the Missouri controversy did not unite the North, as some of the Federalists hoped it would, it made at least a beginning toward the creation of a solid South.

The University of Virginia. *The campus and its buildings, at Charlottesville, were designed by Thomas Jefferson. From his hilltop home, "Monticello" (right of center, in the distance), he watched with a telescope the construction of the university, 1819–1825. The large building, the "Rotunda," contained the library and classrooms. On both sides of the "Lawn," fronting the Rotunda, are rows of dwellings for professors and students. In planning a curriculum for the university, Jefferson was concerned lest the "poison" of improper political doctrines be diffused among the students. He undertook to prevent this, not by proscribing books and ideas he disliked, but by prescribing certain works that he considered basic to an understanding of American government—essays on government by the Englishmen John Locke and Algernon Sidney; and the Declaration of Independence, The Federalist, the Virginia Resolutions of 1799, and George Washington's Farewell Address.* (COURTESY OF HENRY SHAW NEWMAN, THE OLD PRINT SHOP, NEW YORK)

waterways also were defeated by Southern votes. Even the Florida treaty became an issue of sectional politics, some Northerners opposing it because it increased slave territory, some Southerners objecting because it did not add Texas as well as Florida for the future creation of slave states.

At that time the most disaffected of the Southern states was Virginia and not, as later on, South Carolina. The Carolinian Calhoun hailed the compromise as a means of preserving the Union. The Virginian Jefferson looked to the fateful day when the South might have to defend itself in a civil war. In this perspective the subject of education, always one of his chief concerns, became even more crucial. He was afraid that Southern youths attending Northern colleges might be indoctrinated with "lessons of anti-Missourianism." Already the University of Virginia, the favorite project of his old age, was under construction. He hoped that this university, devoting itself to sound Southern doctrines, would attract from Virginia and other Southern states a large number of students who otherwise would have pursued their studies in the North. For him, education once had been a means of liberating the human mind; now it became also a means of enabling slaveholders to protect their interests. Henceforth, in the South, the liberal and equalitarian philosophy which we think of as Jeffersonian declined in popularity and respect. Jefferson himself, in response to the Missouri controversy, had done much toward launching the new conservative trend.

➤➤➤➤➤➤➤➤⫸⫷⫷⫷⫷⫷⫷⫷⫷

BIBLIOGRAPHY

F. J. Turner, *Rise of the New West* (1906), stresses the frontier but deals with the whole of American history from 1819 to 1829. George Dangerfield, *The Era of Good Feelings* (1952), is a well-written synthesis and interpretation of the period from the end of the War of 1812 to the beginning of Andrew Jackson's Presidency. President Monroe's career may be followed in the up-to-date biography by W. P. Cresson, *James Monroe* (1946).

A masterly account of John Quincy Adams's Florida negotiations as well as his entire diplomatic career may be found in S. F. Bemis, *John Quincy Adams and the Foundations of American Foreign Policy* (1949). The Florida negotiations receive a definitive treatment in P. C. Brooks, *Diplomacy and the Borderlands: The Adams-Onís Treaty of 1819* (1939).

L. K. Mathews, *The Expansion of New England* (1909), traces the movement of New Englanders into the Middle West. The flight from one New England state is the well-handled theme of L. D. Stilwell, *Migration from Vermont, 1776–1860* (1937), a book that deserves to be much more widely known than it is.

On the early settlement of the Middle West, see A. L. Kohlmeier, *The Old Northwest as the Keystone of the Arch of the American Federal Union* (1938). Excellent studies of the beginnings of civilization on the prairie are S. J. Buck, *Illinois in 1818* (1917), and T. C. Pease, *The Frontier State, 1818–1848* (1918). J. D. Barnhart, *Valley of Democracy* (1953), discusses democratic trends in the West from 1775 to 1818 and explains them in terms of the "frontier thesis." R. C. Buley, *The Old Northwest: Pioneer Period, 1815–1840* (2 vols., 1950), contains interesting details of social history.

On the Far West, see R. A. Billington, *The Far Western Frontier, 1830–1860* (1956), for a fast-moving narrative. See also Cardinal Goodwin, *The Trans-Mississippi West, 1803–1853* (1922). On the frontier in the South, see S. W. Martin, *Florida in the Territorial Days* (1944), and Everett Dick, *The Dixie Frontier* (1948).

Protection against the Indians is treated ably by E. B. Wesley, *Guarding the Frontier: A Study of Frontier Defense from 1818 to 1825* (1935), and H. P. Beers, *The Western Military Frontier, 1815–1846* (1935).

A full and clear exposition of the complex events culminating in the Missouri

Compromise is provided in Glover Moore's *The Missouri Controversy, 1819–1821* (1953), which abounds in new information and new insights. Still useful also is F. C. Shoemaker, *Missouri's Struggle for State-* *hood* (1916). For the antislavery background of the Missouri question, see A. D. Adams, *The Neglected Period of Anti-Slavery in America, 1808–1831* (1908).

CHAPTER 15

Reassertion of Nationalism

WHILE THE DIVISIVE spirit of sectionalism came to a head in the Missouri controversy, the national pride inspired by Andrew Jackson's glorious victory at the close of the War of 1812 did not entirely disappear. The ideals of nationalism were not dead, and they were vigorously reasserted both by the Supreme Court under the Federalist John Marshall and by the administration of the Republican James Monroe. In a series of his greatest decisions, most of them announced during the postwar decade, Marshall vindicated and strengthened the national sovereignty against the rights of states. With an assertive policy in foreign affairs, culminating in the announcement of what was afterwards known as the Monroe Doctrine, the President and his advisers, in particular his Secretary of State John Quincy Adams, proclaimed United States leadership of the Western Hemisphere as against the pretensions of European powers. The Monroe-Adams policies were far more popular than were the Marshall decisions, which were widely attacked, especially in the South. Still, with the revival of Revolutionary memories as an additional bond of patriotism and union, for the time being the forces of nationality prevailed over the wedges of separation.

Marshall and the Court

Marshall remained as Chief Justice for almost thirty-five years, from 1801 to 1835. During these years Republican Presidents filled vacancies with Republican justices, one after another, and yet Marshall continued to carry a majority with him in most of the Court's decisions. He was a man of practical and penetrating mind, of persuasive and winning personality, and of strong will. The members of the Court boarded together, without their families, during the winter months when the Court was in session, and Marshall had abundant opportu-

John Marshall. "*Marshall is of a tall, slender figure, not graceful or imposing, but erect and steady. . . . I love his laugh, it is too hearty for an intriguer; and his good temper and unwearied patience are equally agreeable on the bench and in the study.*" *Thus, about 1810, wrote the young lawyer Joseph Story, who later was to be an associate justice of the Supreme Court, the author of* Commentaries on the Constitution of the United States *(3 volumes, 1833), and an outstanding American authority on jurisprudence. In his appraisal of Marshall, the young Story added:* "*He examines the intricacies of a subject with calm and persevering circumspection and unravels its mysteries with irresistible acuteness.*" *The portrait was done by Chester Harding, who began as a self-taught, itinerant painter and rose to become one of the most successful American artists of the first half of the nineteenth century.* (BOSTON ATHENAEUM)

nity to bring his talents to bear upon his younger associates. He not only influenced their ways of thinking; he also molded the development of the Constitution itself. The net effect of the hundreds of opinions delivered by the Marshall Court was to strengthen the judicial branch at the expense of the other two branches of the

government; increase the power of the United States and lessen that of the states themselves; and advance the interests of the propertied classes, especially those engaged in commerce, while giving only incidental attention, if any, to the interests of the mass of farmers in moderate circumstances. So long as Marshall lived, the principles of Federalism had a powerful advocate, even after the Federalist party had ceased to exist.

Marshall and the majority of his colleagues stood for conservatism as well as nationalism. During the postwar boom and then the depression following the Panic of 1819, the conservative, propertied, creditor interests of the country frequently turned to the Supreme Court for protection against state laws that interfered with the collection of debts or otherwise threatened property rights. Wealthy individuals and the directors of rising corporations in banking or manufactures usually were able to hire the most skillful and persuasive of the nation's lawyers, men like Daniel Webster, who while still in his thirties rose to the top of the American bar. Though a state-rightist during the War of 1812, Webster became a nationalist afterward, preaching most of the doctrines of Alexander Hamilton. Marshall owed much to lawyers like Webster and time and again incorporated their arguments in his opinions.

In almost all the cases involving a conflict between state and federal powers, Marshall decided against the states. He expanded and gave new meaning to the Constitution by stretching the powers granted to the federal government and emphasizing the limitations placed upon the state governments. The cases fall into four main groups according to the provisions of the Constitution involved—the contract clause, the clause regarding appellate jurisdiction of the Supreme Court, the "necessary and proper" clause, and the commerce clause.

No state, the Constitution says, shall pass

any law "impairing the obligation of contracts." The first Supreme Court case involving this provision was that of *Fletcher v. Peck* (1810), which arose out of the notorious Yazoo land frauds. The Court had to decide the question whether the Georgia legislature of 1796 could rightfully repeal the act of the previous legislature granting lands under shady circumstances to the Yazoo Land Companies. In the decision, which was unanimous, Marshall held that a land grant was a contract and therefore, regardless of any corruption involved, the repeal was invalid. This was the first time the Supreme Court had voided a state law on the ground that it conflicted with a provision of the United States Constitution, though the Court previously had declared state laws unconstitutional because they were inconsistent with federal laws or treaties.

Dartmouth College v. *Woodward* (1819) was an even more famous case concerning the contract clause. The case had originated in a quarrel between the trustees and the president of the college, and it became a hot political issue in New Hampshire when the Republicans championed the president, and the Federalists took the side of the trustees. Getting control of the state government, the Republicans undertook to revise Dartmouth's charter (granted by King George III in 1769) so as to convert the private college into a state university. Webster, himself a Dartmouth graduate, represented the trustees when the case came before the Supreme Court in Washington. The Court, he reminded the judges, had decided in *Fletcher* v. *Peck* that "a *grant* is a contract." The Dartmouth charter, he went on, "is embraced within the very terms of that decision," since "a grant of corporate powers and privileges is as much a *contract* as a grant of land." Then, according to a later story, he brought tears to the eyes of the justices with an irrelevant peroration

concluding: "It is, sir, as I have said, a small college. And yet there are those who love it—" After delaying a year, while some of the justices made up their minds, the Court gave its decision in favor of Webster and the trustees. While the importance of the case often has been exaggerated, it had a significant bearing upon the development of business corporations. It proclaimed the principle that corporation charters were contracts and contracts were inviolable; thereafter the states had to contend against this doctrine in their efforts to control corporate activity.

Did the Supreme Court rightfully have the power to hear appeals from the state courts, as in the Dartmouth College case? The Judiciary Act of 1789 provided that whenever the highest state court decided against a person claiming rights under the federal Constitution, laws, or treaties, the judgment could be reviewed and possibly reversed by the Supreme Court. But Virginia state-rightists denied the constitutionality of the Judiciary Act. They insisted that the federal government, of which the Supreme Court was a branch, could not be the final judge of its own powers, for, they said, it would then be a consolidated government instead of a true federal one such as the Constitution had intended. In the case of *Cohens* v. *Virginia* (1821) Marshall gave the Court's reply to the dissident Virginians. A Virginia court had convicted the Cohens of selling lottery tickets in violation of a state law, and the Cohens had appealed their case under the disputed provision of the Judiciary Act. Though Marshall decided against the Cohens, he did not satisfy the state of Virginia. He affirmed the constitutionality of the Judiciary Act, explaining that the states no longer were sovereign in all respects, since they had given up part of their sovereignty in ratifying the Constitution. The state courts, he insisted, must submit to federal jurisdiction; otherwise the government would be prostrated "at the feet of every state in the Union."

Meanwhile, in *McCulloch* v. *Maryland* (1819), Marshall had confirmed the "im-

of such an institution came well within the "necessary and proper" clause. Then, to dispose of the tax issue, Webster added an ingenious argument of his own. The power to

---

McCulloch v. Maryland

1819

Chief Justice Marshall used the following argument in his decision that a state, such as Maryland, could not constitutionally tax a branch of the United States Bank:

"That the power to tax involves the power to destroy; that the power to destroy may defeat and render useless the power to create; that there is a plain repugnance in conferring on one government a power to control the constitutional measures of another, which other, with respect to those very measures, is declared to be supreme over that which exerts the control, are propositions not to be denied. . . .

"If the States may tax one instrument, employed by the [federal] government in the execution of its powers, they may tax any and every other instrument. They may tax the mail; they may tax the mint; they may tax patent rights; they may tax the papers of the customhouse; they may tax judicial processes; they may tax all the means employed by the government, to an excess which would defeat all the ends of government. This was not intended by the American people. They did not design to make their government dependent on the States."

---

plied powers" of Congress by upholding the constitutionality of the Bank of the United States. The Bank, with headquarters in Philadelphia and branches in various cities throughout the country, became so unpopular in the South and the West that several of the states tried to drive the branches out of business by outright prohibition or by prohibitory taxes. Maryland, for one, laid a heavy tax on the Baltimore branch of the Bank. This case presented two constitutional questions to the Supreme Court: could Congress charter a bank and, if so, could one of the states thus tax it? As one of the Bank's attorneys, Webster first repeated the arguments used originally by Hamilton to prove that the establishment

tax, he said, involved a "power to destroy," and if the states could tax the Bank at all, they could tax it to death. But the Bank with its branches was an agency of the federal government: no state could take an action tending to destroy the United States itself. Marshall adopted Webster's words in deciding for the Bank.

This verdict, however, did not quite settle the issue. Ohio, which had put a tax of $50,000 on each of the Bank's branches in the state, disregarded the McCulloch decision. The Bank obtained a federal injunction forbidding the state auditor, Ralph Osborn, to collect the tax. Ignoring the injunction, Osborn and his aides seized the specie and notes of the Bank. In *Osborn* v.

The Bank of the United States (1824) the Supreme Court confirmed the McCulloch decision and held that state agents, such as Osborn, were individually responsible for their illegal actions. Thereafter state officials were deterred from enforcing state laws against the Bank through fear of arrest and punishment.

The case of *Gibbons* v. *Ogden* (1824) brought up the question of the powers of Congress, as against the powers of the states, in regulating interstate commerce. The state of New York had granted Robert Fulton's and Robert Livingston's steamboat company the exclusive right to carry passengers on the Hudson River to New York City. From this monopoly Aaron Ogden obtained the business of navigation across the river between New York and New Jersey. Thomas Gibbons, with a license granted under an act of Congress, went into competition with Ogden, who brought suit against him and was sustained by the New York courts. When Gibbons appealed to the Supreme Court, the justices faced the twofold question whether "commerce" included navigation and whether Congress alone or Congress and the states together could regulate interstate commerce. Marshall replied that "commerce" was a broad term embracing navigation as well as the buying and selling of goods. Though he did not exactly say that the states had no authority whatever regarding interstate commerce, he asserted that the power of Congress in regard thereto was "complete in itself" and might be "exercised to its utmost extent." He concluded that the state-granted monopoly was void.

Here was a grant which neither Marshall nor Webster, Gibbons's attorney, considered as sacred. The decision, the last of Marshall's great pronouncements, was the first conspicuous one in which the Marshall Court appeared to be on the popular side. Most people, then as always, hated monopolies, and he had declared a monopoly unconstitutional! The lasting significance of *Gibbons* v. *Ogden* was that it freed internal transportation from restraints by the states, and thus prepared the way for the unfettered economic development of the nation. More immediately, it had the effect of helping to head off a movement which was under way for hamstringing the Supreme Court.

For some time Virginia Republicans like Thomas Jefferson, Spencer Roane, and John Taylor of Caroline (a Virginia county) had protested against the views of their fellow Virginian John Marshall. In *Construction Construed and Constitutions Vindicated* (1820) Taylor argued that Marshall and his colleagues were not merely interpreting but were actually changing the nature of the Constitution, which should properly be changed only by the amending process, requiring the approval of three fourths of the states. In Congress some critics of the Court, mostly from the South and the West, proposed various means of curbing what they called judicial tyranny. A Kentucky Senator suggested making the Senate, not the Court, the agency to decide the constitutionality of state laws and to settle interstate disputes. Other Senators and congressmen introduced bills to increase the membership of the Court (from seven to ten) and to require more than a mere majority to declare a state law unconstitutional. The Court reformers did not succeed, however, in passing any of their various panaceas, and after the *Gibbons* v. *Ogden* decision the hostility to the judicial branch of the government gradually died down, to be revived in later years.

Latin American Independence

To most people in the United States, South and Central America had been "dark continents" before the War of 1812. Suddenly they emerged into the light, and Americans looking southward beheld a gigantic spectacle: the Spanish empire struggling in its death throes, a whole continent and more in revolt, new nations in the making with a future no man could foresee. Spain, occupied with the French during the Napoleonic wars, had been unable to keep her colonies under control, and after the downfall of Napoleon she was too weak to reassert her authority, at least by herself. She must look to the powers of Europe for aid.

What should be the policy of the United States? Should we actively assist the emerging nations of Latin America? Should we at least recognize their independence?

Already a profitable trade had developed between the ports of the United States and those of the Río de la Plata in South America, of Chile, and above all of Cuba, with flour and other staples being exported in return for sugar and specie. This trade was small in comparison with that of Great Britain, whose exports to Latin America were several times as large as those of the United States, but the trade was growing steadily and during the depression after 1819 it held up better than business in general did. Presumably the trade would increase much faster once the United States had established regular diplomatic and commercial relations with the countries in revolt.

Commercial interests did not alone account for American sympathies with the Latin American cause: there were also strategic and ideological interests. Jefferson as President had proposed a "large policy" which would eliminate European influence from this hemisphere and make the United States the leader of a group of New World republics. The coming of the War of 1812 prevented the execution of any such large policy, and for several years after 1815 the actual policy was cautious and unheroic, though favorable to the cause of independence.

In 1815 the United States proclaimed its neutrality in the wars then raging between Spain and her rebellious colonies. This neutrality in itself was advantageous to the rebels, since it implied a recognition of them as belligerents, as nations for the purposes of waging war, though not as nations for all purposes. It meant, for example, that their warships would be treated as bona-fide belligerent vessels, not as pirate ships. Moreover, even though the neutrality law was revised and strengthened in 1817 and 1818, it still permitted the revolutionists to obtain unarmed ships and supplies in the United States. It prohibited the purchase of arms or armed vessels and the enlistment of men in this country, but these prohibitions could be evaded and often were. In short, the United States was not a strict and impartial neutral but a nonbelligerent whose policy, though cautious, was intended to help the insurgents and actually did so.

This policy did not go far enough to please the more enthusiastic champions of Latin American liberty in the United States, foremost of whom was Henry Clay, the speaker of the House. Clay held an interesting view of neutrality. He said it required treating both sides alike: since we exchanged diplomatic representatives with Spain, we should do the same with her enemies! He opposed a reduction of the army, arguing that, while it was no longer needed for war against Great Britain, it might eventually be needed for war against Spain. He tried to force the administration's hand by proposing an appropriation for sending an American minister to Buenos Aires. In speech after eloquent speech he maintained that the Latin American cause was our own, the cause of the Americas against the despotism of the Old World. Mingling patriotism with profits, he also insisted that recognition of Latin American independence would lead to increased exports from the United States. But he converted neither Congress nor the administration to his views.

John Quincy Adams, the Secretary of State, was no such flaming admirer of Latin Americans as was Clay. Adams denied the existence of any real similarity between the American Revolution and the Spanish American revolutions, denied that the United States and Latin America had much in common. He feared that Clay's ideas, if put into effect, might involve the United States in war. In a Fourth-of-July address, pretending to speak as a private citizen and not as a government official, he warned of "the inevitable tendency of a direct interference in foreign wars, even wars for freedom, to change the very foundation of our own government from *liberty* to *power.*"

Adams and President Monroe hesitated to take the risky step of recognition unless Great Britain would agree to do so at the same time. In 1818 and 1819 the United States made two bids for British cooperation, and both were rejected. Foreign Minister Castlereagh replied for his government that the British and American views of the matter were by no means identical, as the Americans appeared to assume. The purpose of Great Britain, Castlereagh explained, was the "restoration of the supremacy of Spain, on an improved plan of government indeed, especially as regarded the commercial interests of the colonies, but still her entire supremacy." That is, Great Britain favored the re-establishment of the Spanish empire with a liberalized commercial policy which would give the British a preference in trade. Commercially, independence for the Spanish colonies would be to the disadvantage of the British, since it would give Americans at least an even chance to compete in Latin American markets.

Adams and Monroe hesitated for other reasons besides their comparative lack of enthusiasm about Latin America, their fear of war, and the refusal of Great Britain to go along with the United States. While Adams believed that *de facto* governments (governments actually in power) should be recognized, he doubted at first whether any of the new regimes to the south had established its position beyond the possibility of overthrow from within or reconquest from without. Besides, Adams was disinclined to offend Spain by recognizing her revolted provinces so long as he was engaged in the delicate negotiations with her representative, Onís, in regard to Florida. By 1822 the scene had changed. The Florida treaty finally had been ratified, and at least five of the Spanish American nations seemed to have become going concerns. Spain, recovering from a revolution at home, appeared to be more powerless than ever to make trouble. And the European powers, losing their last hope of support from Great Britain, were not likely to intervene.

In 1822 President Monroe informed Congress that five nations—La Plata (Argentina), Chile, Peru, Colombia, and Mexico—were ready for recognition, and he requested an appropriation for sending ministers to them. In itself this was a bold stroke: the United States was going ahead alone as the first country to recognize the new governments, in defiance of the rest of the world. Yet, in the way he went about it, the President was extremely cautious. Instead of sending and receiving diplomatic representatives on his own responsibility, he waited for Congress to act. And he intended to send the first minister to Mexico because Mexico was an "empire" and not a republic; recognition of an empire presumably would not arouse so much antagonism in Europe. In fact, after Congress had provided the requested appropriation, Colombia was the first of the new nations to be recognized, her agent in Washington being accepted as the Colombian minister. Within a few years, diplomatic relations were established with the others.

Origin of the Monroe Doctrine

In 1823 President Monroe stood forth as a much bolder champion of America against Europe than he had done in 1822. Presenting to Congress his annual message on the state of the Union, he announced a policy which afterwards—though not for thirty years—was to be known as the "Monroe Doctrine." One phase of this policy had to do with the relationship of Europe to America. "The American continents," Monroe declared, ". . . are henceforth not to be considered as subjects for future colonization by any European powers." Furthermore, "We should consider any attempt on their part to extend their system to any portion of this hemisphere as dangerous to our peace and safety." And we should consider any "interposition" against the sovereignty of existing American nations as an unfriendly act. A second aspect of the President's pronouncement had to do with the relationship of the United States to Europe. "Our policy in regard to Europe," said Monroe, ". . . is not to interfere in the internal concerns of any of its powers."

How did the President happen to make these statements at the time he did? What specific dangers, if any, did he have in mind? Against what powers in particular was his warning directed? To answer these questions, it may be well to consider first the relations of the United States with the European powers as of 1823, and then the main steps in the decision of the Monroe administration to make an announcement to Congress and the world.

After Napoleon's defeat the powers of Europe combined in a "concert" to uphold the principle of "legitimacy" in government and prevent the overthrow of existing regimes from within or without. When Great Britain withdrew from the concert, it became a quadruple alliance with Russia and France as the strongest of its four members. Tsar Alexander I of Russia also sponsored the "Holy Alliance," which eventually was joined by all the European sovereigns except the Pope and the King of England, and which was supposed to put into practice the Tsar's rather fuzzy ideal of peace and justice based upon Christian principles. Though the quadruple alliance and the Holy Alliance were separate, most Americans made no distinction between them, commonly referring to the European concert as the "Holy Alliance." In 1823, after assisting in the suppression of other revolts in Europe, the European allies authorized France to intervene in Spain to restore the Bourbon dynasty that revolutionists had overthrown. Some observers in England and the Americas wondered whether the allies next would back France in an attempt to retake by force the lost Spanish empire in America.

Actually, France was still a relatively weak power, not yet recovered from the long and exhausting Napoleonic wars. Though France disliked Latin American independence, she was willing to accept it as one of the realities of the world, especially if it should result in the creation of monarchies instead of republics. France endeavored to bring about the establishment of pro-French kingdoms in Latin America by means of intrigue, but dared not challenge British seapower with an expedition to subvert the new governments by force.

Russia, the great land power of Europe, lacked naval strength. She desired the friendship of the United States because of her world-wide conflicts with Great Britain. When the Tsar expressed his wish that the United States become a member of the Holy Alliance, Secretary Adams politely let him know that this country could best serve the exalted purpose of the alliance by remaining apart from it. While American pacifists admired the Tsar as a friend of brotherhood and peace, Adams grew sarcastic about the supposedly peace-loving Tsar who sold warships to Spain to assist her war against her revolting colonies. Besides the vague threat Russia offered to Latin American independence, there were other causes of friction between her and the United States. Russia owned Alaska, and Russian fur traders ranged as far south as California. In 1821 the Tsar issued a ukase (imperial order) requiring foreign ships to keep approximately 100 miles from the Northwest coast above the fifty-first parallel. This order perturbed Adams not only because it interfered with the activities of American traders and whalers in the North Pacific but also because it implied a Russian territorial claim which would enlarge the area of Russian America. Adams protested strongly to the Russians. Instead of taking offense, they agreed to negotiate regarding the southern boundary of their possessions. The settlement was not completed until 1824, when the Russians abandoned their claims south of 54° 40', but already in 1823 the negotiations were under way and Russian-American relations were reasonably good.

In the minds of most Americans, certainly in the mind of their Secretary of State, Great Britain at that time seemed a serious threat to American interests. Adams was much concerned about supposed British designs upon Cuba. Like Jefferson and others before him, Adams opposed the transfer of Cuba from a weak power like Spain, its owner, to a strong power like Great Britain. He thought Cuba eventually should belong to the United States, for the "Pearl of the Antilles" had great economic and strategic value and, because of its location, was virtually a part of the American coastline. Adams did not desire to seize the island; he wanted only to keep it in Spanish hands until, by a kind of political gravitation, it should fall naturally to the United States. Despite his worries over the sup-

posed British threat to Cuba, he and other American leaders were pleased to see the rift between Great Britain and the concert of Europe. He was willing to cooperate with her, but only to the extent that her policies and his own coincided in regard to this hemisphere.

These policies did not exactly coincide, however, as was shown by Castlereagh's rejection of the American overtures for joint recognition of Latin American independence in 1818 and 1819, and as was shown again by the American reaction to a British proposal for a joint statement in 1823. That summer, Castlereagh's rival and successor, George Canning, suggested to the American minister in London, Richard Rush, that Great Britain and the United States should combine in announcing to the world their opposition to any European movement against Latin America. Though Rush lacked instructions to act, he was ready to go ahead with Canning on one condition—that Great Britain agree to recognize the Latin American nations as the United States already had done. When Canning declined to promise recognition, Rush wrote home for instructions. During the summer Canning remained eager for Rush's cooperation, but in the fall, having been assured by the French minister that France had no intention of "acting against the colonies by force of arms," Canning suddenly lost interest in his idea of a joint statement with the United States.

Meanwhile the Monroe administration was considering the proposal that Canning earlier had made. Monroe sent the Rush correspondence to former Presidents Madison and Jefferson for their advice, and both of them recommended that Rush be authorized to sign a joint statement with Canning. Adams objected. For one thing, he did not like the statement that Canning had proposed: it included a pledge by Great Britain and the United States that neither of the two would seek further territory in this hemisphere, and Adams did not wish to estop this country from future territorial acquisitions. For another thing, he believed

west. He also was responsible for the inclusion of the phrase renouncing American interference in European affairs. Indirectly, George Washington, Thomas Jefferson,

---

Monroe Doctrine

1823

". . . The American continents, by the free and independent condition which they have assumed and maintain, are henceforth not to be considered as subjects for future colonization by any European powers. . . .

"In the wars of the European powers in matters relating to themselves we have never taken any part, nor does it comport with our policy to do so. . . . We should consider any attempt on their part to extend their system to any portion of this hemisphere as dangerous to our peace and safety. With the existing colonies or dependencies of the European powers we have not interfered and shall not interfere. But with the Governments who have declared their independence and maintained it, and whose independence we have, on great consideration and on just principles, acknowledged, we could not view any interposition for the purpose of oppressing them, or controlling in any other manner their destiny, by any European power, in any other light than as the manifestation of an unfriendly disposition toward the United States."

---

it would be more honorable for the American government to speak out on its own instead of following along like a "cockboat in the wake of the British man-of-war." Actually, when the time arrived for Monroe's message to Congress, the President no longer faced a question of acting with Great Britain or alone. He had the choice of acting alone or not at all, since Canning had changed his mind about cooperation with the United States.

Monroe himself deserves the credit for the form his message finally took: the ultimate responsibility was his. The authorship of his famous doctrine, however, is complex. Adams contributed the no-colonization clause, which was almost word for word the same as his recent protests to Russia against her encroachments in the North-

Henry Clay, and others helped to formulate the message, for they had long advocated the notion of a world divided into two spheres, in one of which the United States must predominate, in the other of which Europe might be left to go her way. Indeed, the basic ideas of Monroe's message were old and familiar. Like the Declaration of Independence and Washington's Farewell Address, the Monroe Doctrine was noteworthy because it gave effective expression to ideas already widely held.

Though Canning's overture led to Monroe's announcement, the message was directed against all the powers of Europe, including Great Britain, which seemed at least as likely as Russia to undertake further colonizing ventures in America. The message was intended to head off the threat of

European schemes against Latin American independence, but the most serious threat was one of undermining that independence by subtle influences rather than overt military action. The message aimed to rally the people of Latin America to look to their own security. It also aimed to stir the people of the United States. In issuing his challenge to Europe, Monroe had in mind the domestic situation as well as the international scene. At home the people were bogged down in a business depression, were divided by sectional politics, were apathetic toward the rather lackluster administration of Monroe. In the rumors of European aggression against this hemisphere lay an opportunity for him to arouse and unite the people with an appeal to national pride.

Consequences of Monroe's Message

On the whole the American people responded favorably to Monroe's appeal, most of the newspapers approving it. But the people were divided about the meaning of that part of his message which said the United States would not "interfere in the internal concerns" of European countries. Should Americans confine their political interests to their own hemisphere, or should they give at least moral support to the cause of human freedom throughout the world? Monroe's message touched off a congressional debate on this question of isolation or intervention, the specific issue being American policy in regard to the Greek war for independence.

The Greeks, having revolted against the Ottoman Empire in 1821, aroused the sympathy and admiration of liberal-minded folk in Europe and America. The Turks, it was said, gathered ears by the bushel and sold into slavery the wives and children of slaughtered rebels. Pro-Hellenic enthusiasts in the United States collected money to aid the revolution, and some even enlisted in the Greek armies. People petitioned Congress and appealed to the President for action by the American government in behalf of Greece. When Monroe asked Madison for advice regarding Canning's proposal to Rush, Madison urged that Monroe make a declaration in favor of Greek as well as Latin American independence. But Adams insisted that we should keep out of European affairs if we expected European nations to keep out of American affairs. So in his famous message, while committing the United States not to interfere in Europe, Monroe included only a comparatively mild expression of sympathy with the struggling Greeks.

Within a week after the message had been delivered, Daniel Webster introduced into the House a resolution calling upon the President to send an American commissioner to Greece to look into the advisability of recognizing the country's independence. Early in the new year, 1824, Webster brought his massive oratory to bear in favor of his resolution and in favor of the Greeks. Their cause, he said, was ours. It was civilization against the brute, Christianity against the infidel, international law against the lawless. It was a world-wide issue, with the Holy Alliance and all the reactionary forces of Europe on the side of the scarcely human Turks. "Does it not become us, then, is it not a duty imposed on us," Webster asked, "to give our weight to the side of liberty and justice, to let mankind know that we are not tired of our own institutions, and to protest against the asserted power of altering at pleasure the law of the civilized world?" But Adams, in charge of American diplomacy, was even less inclined to risk involvement in a war for independence in Greece than he had been when it was a question of independence in Latin America. He steered the administration men in Congress against Webster, and they soon killed his resolution with an indefinite postponement. Not till 1833, after other powers already had welcomed Greece into the international community, did the United States establish diplomatic relations with her.

Americas.) So far as Adams was concerned, the United States ought to avoid involvements with Latin American as well as European countries.

The United States Capitol, 1824. *After the original Capitol had been burned by the British in 1814, a new building was begun by Benjamin H. Latrobe and completed, in 1830, by Charles Bulfinch. Later it was extensively enlarged and modified. The English-born Latrobe, an engineer as well as an architect, designed many important buildings and engineering works in Richmond, Philadelphia, and Baltimore. The Boston-born Bulfinch, the most influential American architect of his time, designed the Boston State House (completed in 1800) and many other public buildings and private dwellings in New England. Characteristic of Bulfinch's style are the dome and west front (shown here) of the Capitol in Washington. From a watercolor by Charles Burton.* (COURTESY OF THE METROPOLITAN MUSEUM OF ART)

While nothing came of the House debate, it was significant in revealing the isolationist implications of the Monroe and Adams policies, and it foreshadowed later debates on essentially the same issue at the time of World Wars I and II. (Isolation used to be considered as part of the Monroe Doctrine; in recent years it usually has been treated as a separate policy, applying specifically to Europe in contrast to the Monroe Doctrine proper, a statement of policy regarding the

The press and people of Latin America, like those of the United States, generally applauded Monroe's bold statement of 1823. But Latin Americans wondered precisely what it meant for them. From Adams they soon learned at least what it did not mean. Six months after the delivery of the message, the Colombian minister in Washington asked Adams for an explanation of it. The Colombian feared that France was scheming to set up Bourbon kingdoms in Buenos

Aires and elsewhere; he was worried in particular about the future of Colombia as an independent republic; he raised the question whether the United States would agree to an alliance for the guarantee of Colombian independence. Adams replied rather evasively, praising Colombia for her determination to defend herself, discounting the supposed danger from France, and avoiding any definite commitment as to what his own government would do if a clear threat to Colombia or her neighbors should arise. Brazil also inquired about an alliance with the United States and got no more satisfaction than Colombia had received.

In Europe, Monroe's message was hailed with ridicule instead of enthusiasm. It was looked upon as the empty bluff of an upstart republic. It frightened off no European government from aggressive ventures in this hemisphere. For the time being, the rivalries among the European powers and the refusal of Great Britain to cooperate with Russia and France prevented any of them from contemplating such ventures. The United States, alone, could not have enforced against a combination of hostile powers the policy that Monroe had announced. Before long his words were forgotten, to be revived by President James K. Polk in 1845, though the phrase "Monroe Doctrine" did not appear until 1853. Eventually the United States grew strong enough to put teeth into the doctrine. Today this country would resist attempts by hostile powers to gain territory or political influence in the Americas even if Monroe had never delivered his famous message. But the nation would resist more spontaneously and more wholeheartedly because of the Monroe Doctrine with its long history and its distinctive name. Like the Declaration of Independence, the Constitution of the United States, and the national flag, it has become one of the symbols that unify and inspirit the American people.

The Heritage of Patriotism

In Monroe's own time the Fourth of July, another of the symbols of American patriotism, was a far more important holiday than it has since become, and a much stronger bond of union than was his doctrine. Annually recalled with fife and drum and flamboyant speeches, the American Revolution gave the nation a common heritage of heroic memories. The War of 1812 was too recent for the unpatriotic factionalism it had engendered to be entirely forgotten, but the earlier war with Great Britain, as it receded into the past, was more and more surrounded by a haze of heroic legend.

When General Lafayette revisited the United States in 1824–1825, the glorious past was revived as never before. Not only was Lafayette a hero of the Revolution; he was also a leading European liberal and a foe of the Holy Alliance, and recently had congratulated Monroe and Adams for causing the United States to stand forth boldly "as the protecting genius of America." The beloved general toured the East, the South, and the West. Everywhere, without distinction of faction or party, crowds cheered him in frenzied celebrations. He appeared in Congress as an official guest, and Congress voted him $200,000 and a whole township of public lands. The honors done the distinguished visitor, as Jefferson observed, seemed for the moment to overshadow all questions of politics.

Lafayette graced with his presence the Bunker Hill ceremonies at which, on the fiftieth anniversary of the battle, a monument was dedicated to the soldiers who had fallen there. The orator of the day, Daniel Webster, thrilled the vast audience when he suddenly spoke directly to the aging Revolutionary veterans assembled on the slope before him: "Venerable men!" But his theme was more the American fu-

ture than the American past. Upon the success of the political experiment in the
United States, he averred, the fate of popular government throughout the earth would

ferson, the author of the Declaration of
Independence, and Adams, "its ablest advocate and defender" (as Jefferson said),
who at one time were bitter political rivals,

Fourth of July, 1819. *This public celebration, in Center Square, Philadelphia, was typical of celebrations held annually throughout the
country on Independence Day. The painting by J. L. Krimmel shows
gaily clad militiamen parading, small boys firing off toy guns, women
preparing picnic lunches, and some of the men getting drunk. Over the
tent at the left is a portrait of George Washington and a print of the
engagement between the* Chesapeake *and the* Shannon *in the War of
1812, with the famous words of the* Chesapeake's *captain, James Lawrence: "Don't give up the ship."* (THE HISTORICAL SOCIETY OF PENNSYL-
VANIA)

depend. "The last hopes of mankind, therefore, rest with us"—with the Union. "Let
us cultivate a true spirit of union and harmony," he concluded. "Let us act under a
settled conviction, and an habitual feeling,
that these twenty-four states are one country."

The Revolutionary heritage was most
dramatically brought home to the American people by news of the deaths of
Thomas Jefferson and John Adams. Jef-

had become friendly correspondents in their
old age. They died on the same day, and
that day was July 4, 1826, exactly half a
century after the signing of the Declaration
of Independence. To some, this appeared
to be more than a coincidence, perhaps a
sign from God instructing the American
people to cherish the nationality their ancestors had so dearly won. In another of his
orations Webster praised both of the great
men, the Virginia Republican and the Mas-

sachusetts Federalist. "With America, and in America, a new era commences in human affairs," he announced, turning once more

from things gone by to things ahead. "America, America, our country, fellow-citizens, our own dear and native land. . . ."

->>>->>>->>>->><<<-<<<-<<<-<<<

BIBLIOGRAPHY

ON LATIN AMERICAN diplomacy and the Monroe Doctrine, see again the previously cited biography of John Quincy Adams by S. F. Bemis. A standard work is Dexter Perkins's *The Monroe Doctrine, 1823–1826* (1927). It may well be supplemented by E. H. Tatum, *The United States and Europe, 1815–1823* (1936), which maintains that the Monroe Doctrine was directed against England even more than against Russia or the "Holy Alliance." A. P. Whitaker, *The United States and the Independence of Latin America, 1800–1830* (1941), is the best single work on the origins of the Monroe Doctrine as well as on the recognition of Latin American independence. Also extremely valuable is C. C. Griffin, *The United States and the Disruption of the Spanish Empire* (1937). J. H. Powell, *Richard Rush: Republican Diplomat, 1780–1859* (1942), is a fine biography of the man who served as go-between in the Anglo-American conversations that led up to Monroe's famous pronouncement.

The most complete account of the great Chief Justice and his decisions is A. J. Beveridge's *The Life of John Marshall* (4 vols., 1916–1919). E. S. Corwin, *John Marshall and the Constitution* (1919), is a readable introduction written by an outstanding constitutional historian. A. C. McLaughlin, *A Constitutional History of the United States* (1935), contains a fairly detailed treatment of Marshall and his great cases. A leading contemporary critic of Marshall is presented along with his anti-nationalist ideas in E. T. Mudge's *The Social Philosophy of John Taylor of Caroline: A Study in Jeffersonian Democracy* (1939).

Merle Curti, *The Roots of American Loyalty* (1946), discusses the origin, growth, and changing form of patriotism in the United States. Patriotism as manifested by the activities of former soldiers of the Revolution and the War of 1812 is discussed in W. E. Davies, *Patriotism on Parade: The Story of Veterans' and Hereditary Organizations in America, 1783–1900* (1955). Further light is thrown on the development of patriotic traditions in W. F. Craven, *The Legend of the Founding Fathers* (1956).

CHAPTER 16

Material Progress: The Canal Age

AMERICANS of the generation following the War of 1812 acquired a basis for national unity more solid than mere pride in the past. Engineers and laborers advanced toward a solution of the transportation problem by building canals and eventually railroads to link the coastal cities with the interior, the East with the West. Merchants widened the scope of their activities till business came to be conducted on a scale more nearly nation-wide than ever before. With the continued growth of industry, some workers began to show at least faint signs of self-consciousness as members of a distinct class, with common interests transcending those of their separate localities. The people as a whole, benefiting from the new developments in transportation and production, were able to raise their living standards while steadily increasing in num-

bers. Material progress prepared the way for their ultimate unification, politically as well as economically (though, as late as 1860, this unifying process had not gone far enough to overcome the divisive forces within the nation).

The People, 1820–1840

During the 1820's and 1830's, as during the whole of American history, three trends of population were fairly obvious: rapid increase, migration to the West, and movement to towns and cities.

Americans continued to multiply almost as fast as in the colonial period, the population still doubling every twenty-five years or so. The total figure, lower than 4 million in 1790, approached 10 by 1820 and rose to nearly 13 in 1830 and to about 17 million in 1840. The United States was growing much more rapidly in population than the British Isles or Europe: by 1860 it had gone ahead of the United Kingdom and had nearly overtaken Germany and France.

birth rate, which more than offset the death rate.

Immigration accounted for little of the population growth before the 1840's. The

---

Life Expectancy

	At Birth		At Age 20	
	Male	Female	Male	Female
	Massachusetts			
1789	34.5	36.5	54.2	54.3
1850	38.3	40.5	60.1	60.2
	U.S. (White)			
1945	64.4	69.5	68.6	72.9

Note: Figures for the United States as a whole are not available for the earlier years. The U.S. figures for 1945 are given for purposes of comparison. The much greater rise in life expectancy at birth than at age twenty reflects the fact that infant mortality was reduced much more than the death rate for those who survived infancy.

The Negro population increased more slowly than the white. After 1808, when the importation of slaves was made illegal, the proportion of Negroes to whites in the nation as a whole steadily declined. In 1820 there was one colored person to every four whites; in 1840, one to every five. The slower increase of Negroes was due to their comparatively high death rate, not to a low birth rate. Slave mothers had large families, but life was shorter for both slaves and free Negroes than for whites.

The mortality rate for whites slowly declined. Public health improved a little, though epidemics continued to take their periodic toll, among them a cholera epidemic which swept the country in 1832. On the average, people lived somewhat longer than in earlier generations. The population increase, however, was due less to lengthened life than to the maintenance of a high

long years of war in Europe, from 1793 to 1815, had kept the number of newcomers to America down to not more than a few thousand a year, and then the Panic of 1819 checked the immigrant tide which had risen

Population Growth, 1790–1840

after Waterloo. During the 1820's arrivals from abroad averaged about 14,000 annually. Of the total population of nearly 13 million in 1830, the foreign-born numbered less than half a million, mostly naturalized citizens. Soon immigration began to grow to new heights, reaching a total of 60,000 for 1832 and nearly 80,000 for 1837. Then, after a decline due to economic depression, the annual numbers rose still higher, an unprecedented flood of foreigners arriving in the 1840's and 1850's.

Since the United States exported more goods than it imported, returning ships often had vacant space and filled it with immigrants as ballast, so to speak. Competition among shipping lines reduced fares so that, by the 1830's, the immigrant could get passage across the Atlantic for as little as $20 or $30. No longer did he need to sell his services to a temporary master in America in order to pay for the voyage. And so the system of indentured servitude, which had dwindled steadily after the Revolution, disappeared entirely after the Panic of 1819.

Until the 1830's most of the new arrivals came from the same sources as had come the bulk of the colonial population—from England and Northern Ireland. In the 1830's, however, the number arriving from Ireland proper began to grow, anticipating the tremendous influx of Irishmen which was to occur in the next two decades. Generally the newcomers, the Irish as well as others, were welcomed in the United States. They were needed to provide labor for building canals and railroads, manning ships and docks, and performing other heavy work essential to the expanding economic system. But the Irish, as Roman Catholics, excited Protestant prejudices in some communities. In 1834 an anti-Catholic mob set fire to a convent in Charlestown, Massachusetts, and the next year Samuel F. B. Morse (who is better remembered as a portrait painter and as the inventor of the telegraph)

published his *Foreign Conspiracy*, which served thereafter as a textbook for nativists crusading against what they imagined was a popish plot to gain control of the United States. Still, the federal government did nothing to check immigration, and shipowners, employers, and some of the states took measures to encourage it.

While most of the Irish remained in the seaports and factory towns of the Northeast, many immigrants joined the throng of home-seekers continually moving to the West. Usually, though not always, the pioneers found homes on the frontier in approximately the same latitudes as they had left in the older states. That is to say, for the most part Northerners settled the Northern frontier and Southerners the Southern. Thus the early arrivals in southern Ohio, Indiana, and Illinois came largely from Virginia, North Carolina, and Kentucky. Later arrivals, who in the 1830's were peopling northern Ohio, Indiana, and Illinois, came largely from New England and New York. Southerners predominated in the population of Arkansas, which became a state in 1836. New Englanders and New Yorkers were most numerous in Michigan, which compensated for Arkansas in the sectional balance when admitted to the Union the following year.

The West (including both Northwest and Southwest) continued to grow much more rapidly than the rest of the country. By 1830 more than a fourth of the American people lived to the west of the Appalachians; by 1850, nearly a half. Some of the seaboard states suffered serious losses of manpower and womanpower, not to mention the personal property that departing migrants took away. Year after year the Carolinas gave up nearly as much in human resources as they gained by natural increase; their populations remained almost stationary. The same was true of Vermont and New Hampshire. Many a village in these two states was completely depopulated, its houses and barns left to rot, as its people scattered over the country in search of an easier life than the granite hills afforded.

number of city dwellers increased remarkably. In 1790 one person in thirty lived in a community of 8,000 or more; in 1820, one in twenty; and in 1840, one in twelve. The

---

Chicago and Its Prospects
1837

H. L. Ellsworth's *A Sketch of the State of Illinois* (1837), a guidebook for migrants to the West, described Chicago thus:

"The city of Chicago is the largest place in the state of Illinois, and has grown up almost entirely within the last seven years. Its growth, even for western cities, has been unexampled. In Dr. Beck's Gazetteer, published in 1823, Chicago is described as a village of 10 or 12 houses, and 60 or 70 inhabitants. In 1832, it contained five small stores, and 250 inhabitants; and now (1837) the population amounts to 8000, with 120 stores, besides a number of groceries; of the former, twenty sell by wholesale. It has also twelve public houses [hotels], three newspapers, near fifty lawyers, and upwards of thirty physicians.

"Chicago is connected by means of the numerous steamboats, ships, brigs, schooners, etc., that navigate the great fresh water seas of the north, with all the different trading ports on lakes Michigan, Huron, and Erie, and especially with Buffalo, to and from which various lines of regular packets are constantly arriving and departing. Some of the steamboats are of great power and burthen. . . .

"The care which the original surveyors took to give the prairie winds a full sweep through the city, has distinguished it as the most healthful place in the western country, and has made it the resort of a large number of people during the sickly season. The natural advantages of the place, and the enterprise and capital that will concentrate here, with the favourable prospects for health, must soon make this the emporium of trade and business for all the northern country."

Not all the migrating villagers and farmers sought the unsettled frontier: some moved instead to increasingly crowded population centers. Cities (considered as communities of 8,000 or more) grew faster than the nation as a whole. In 1820 there were more than twice as many cities, and in 1840 more than seven times as many, as there had been in 1790. While the vast majority of Americans continued to reside in the open country or in small towns, the

proportion of urbanites varied not only from time to time but also from region to region. In the West and in the South, cities were few and comparatively small; in the South, towns of any size were relatively rare. The metropolis of the West was Cincinnati (25,000 in 1830), which was larger than its nearest rivals, Pittsburgh and Louisville, put together. Chicago was not even incorporated as a town until 1833. The South had no cities except New Orleans

(45,000 in 1830) and Charleston (30,000), though Baltimore (80,000), more a border city than a Southern one, was the third largest in the nation. The Northeast was

increased its lead in both population and trade. Its growth was based on the possession of a superior natural harbor and on several historical developments after the

New York Port, 1828. *A view of South Street, from the intersection with Maiden Lane, which got its name from the fact that Dutch washer-maidens in New Amsterdam used to come here to do their laundry in a brook outside of town. The East River docks lined South Street; there were other docks along the Hudson River on the opposite side of Manhattan Island. Below Maiden Lane, the city by 1828 was almost solidly built up. Above the Lane, there were gardens around the houses, and there were vacant lots which in some cases ran out into open fields. Nude boys swam in the East River in summers. The population of the city was approaching 150,000. Note the cobblestone pavement. From a contemporary print.* (COURTESY OF THE NEW YORK PUBLIC LIBRARY, STOKES COLLECTION)

much the most highly urbanized section, with New York (200,000 in 1830), Philadelphia (175,000), Boston (60,000), Albany (25,000), and a number of lesser cities.

The rise of New York City was phenomenal. By 1810 it had surpassed Philadelphia, which earlier had replaced Boston as the largest city in America. New York steadily

War of 1812. After the war the British chose New York as the chief place to "dump" their manufactured goods, and thus helped make it an import center. State laws, which were liberal with regard to auction sales, encouraged inland merchants to do their buying in New York. The first packet line, with regularly scheduled monthly sail-ings between England and the United States, made New York its American terminus (1816) and hence a more important center of overseas commerce than ever. And the Erie Canal (completed in 1825) gave the city unrivaled access to the interior.

New Waterways

Despite the road improvements of the turnpike era (1790's–1820's) Americans continued as in colonial times to depend wherever possible on water routes for travel and transportation. The larger rivers, especially the Mississippi and the Ohio, became increasingly useful as steamboats grew in number and improved in design.

A special kind of steamboat evolved to meet the problems of navigation on the Mississippi and its tributaries. These waters were shallow, with strong and tricky currents, shifting bars of sand and mud, and submerged logs and trees. So the boat had to have a flat bottom, paddle wheels rather than screw propellers, and a powerful, high-pressure engine, which meant a dangerously explosive one. To accommodate as much cargo and as many passengers as possible, the boat was triple-decked, its superstructure rising high in the air. Such a "floating palace" at its best was an impressive sight, elaborately ornamented with gilt and "gingerbread." More and more steamboats plied the Western waters every year, a couple of hundred in 1830, three times as many in 1850. They grew in size until they averaged about 500 tons. So keen was competition that passenger fares and freight rates were steadily lowered and schedules speeded up. Races were common, and so were accidents. Even if a boat managed to escape burning up or running aground, its life was short— not more than five or six years.

River boats carried to New Orleans the corn and other crops of Northwestern farmers, the cotton and tobacco of Southwestern planters. From New Orleans, ships took the cargoes on to Eastern ports. Neither the farmers of the West nor the merchants of the East were completely satisfied with this pattern of trade. Farmers could get better prices for their crops if the alternative existed of sending them directly eastward to market, and merchants could sell larger quantities of their manufactured goods if these could be transported more directly and more economically to the West. The old problem of east-west transportation still existed.

True, the highways across the mountains, such as the Philadelphia-Pittsburgh turnpike and the National Road, provided a partial solution to the problem. But the costs of hauling goods overland, though lower than before these roads were built, were too high for anything except the most compact

THE OHIO-MISSISSIPPI OUTLET

and valuable merchandise. Waterways were needed instead of highways. It was calculated that four horses could pull a wagon weight of one ton 12 miles a day over an ordinary road and one and a half tons 18 miles a day over a turnpike. On the other hand, four horses could draw a boatload of a hundred tons 24 miles a day on a canal.

to be dug, the job would be up to the various states.

New York was the first to act. It had the natural advantage of a comparatively level

The Erie Canal. *The junction of the Erie and the Northern canals, near the eastern terminus of the Erie, north of Albany. Note the double set of locks and, at the right, the tandem team of horses on the towpath. From an aquatint by John Hill.* (COURTESY OF THE NEW-YORK HISTORICAL SOCIETY, NEW YORK CITY)

Since the late eighteenth century, when canals began to prove their worth in England, they had appealed to forward-looking Americans, and in the early 1800's a few fairly short canals were built and maintained by private companies in the United States. In his notable report on internal improvements (1808) Albert Gallatin recommended the construction of a number of waterways, but sectional jealousies and constitutional scruples stood in the way of action by the federal government, and the necessary expenditures were too great for private enterprise. If extensive canals were

route between the Hudson River and Lake Erie, through the only break in the entire Appalachian chain. Yet the engineering tasks were imposing. The distance was more than 350 miles, several times as long as any of the existing canals in America, and there were ridges to cross and a wilderness of woods and swamps to penetrate. For many years New Yorkers debated whether the scheme was practical. The canal advocates finally won the debate after De Witt Clinton, a late but ardent convert to the cause, was elected governor. Digging began on the Fourth of July, 1817.

This, the Erie Canal, was by far the greatest construction job that Americans ever had undertaken, and it was the work of self-made engineers. Though one of them made a careful study of English canals, he and his associates did more than merely copy what he saw abroad. They devised ingenious arrangements of cables, pulleys, and gears for bringing down trees and uprooting stumps. Instead of the usual shovel and wheelbarrow, they used specially designed plows and scrapers for moving earth. To make watertight locks they produced an ideal cement from native limestone. The canal itself was

used: the churning of a paddle wheel or propeller would cave in the earthen banks.) Cuts and fills, some of them enormous, enabled the canal to pass through hills and over valleys; stone aqueducts carried it across streams; and 88 locks, of heavy masonry, with great wooden gates, took care of the necessary ascents and descents.

Not only was the Erie Canal an engineering triumph; it quickly proved a financial success as well. It was opened for through traffic in October, 1825, with fitting ceremonies. Governor Clinton at the head of a parade of canal boats made the trip from

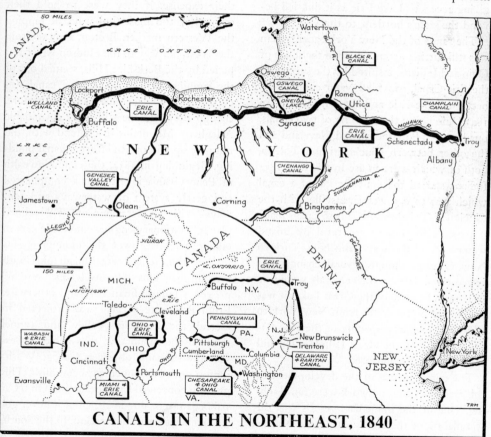

CANALS IN THE NORTHEAST, 1840

simply a big ditch, forty feet wide and four feet deep, with towpaths along the banks for the horses or mules which were to draw the canal boats. (Steamboats were not to be

Buffalo to the Hudson and then downriver to New York City, where he emptied a keg of Erie water into the Atlantic to symbolize the wedding of the lake and the ocean.

Soon traffic was so heavy that, within about seven years, the tolls brought in enough to repay the whole construction cost. The prosperity of the Erie encouraged the state to enlarge its canal system by building several branches. An important part of the system was the Champlain Canal, begun at about the same time as the Erie and completed in 1822, which connected Lake Champlain with the Hudson River. Though some of the branches did not pay for themselves, they provided useful water connections between New York City and the larger towns of the state. The main line, giving access to Lake Erie as it did, led beyond the state's borders, to the West.

The range of the New York canal system was still further extended when the states of Ohio and Indiana, inspired by the success of the Erie Canal, provided water connections between Lake Erie and the Ohio River. In 1825 Ohio began the building of two canals, one between Portsmouth and Cleveland and the other between Cincinnati and Toledo, both of which were in use by 1833. In 1832 Indiana started the construction of a canal which was to connect Evansville with the Cincinnati-Toledo route. These canals made it possible to ship or to travel by inland waterways all the way from New York to New Orleans, though several changes between canal, lake, and river craft would be necessary. By way of the Great Lakes it was possible to go by water from New York to Chicago. After the opening of the Erie Canal, shipping on the Great Lakes by sail and by steam rapidly increased.

The consequences of the development of this transportation network were far-reaching. One of the immediate results was the stimulation of the settlement of the Northwest, not only because it had become easier for migrants to make the westward journey but also, and more important, because it had become easier for them, after taking up their farms, to ship their produce to markets.

Towns boomed along the Erie and other canals, New York City benefiting the most of all. Though much of the Western produce, especially corn, continued to go downriver to New Orleans, an increasing proportion of it and most of the wheat of the Northwest went in the direction of New York. And manufactured goods now went in growing volume from New York by the comparatively direct and economical new routes to the West.

Rival cities along the Atlantic seaboard took alarm at the prospect of New York's acquiring so vast a hinterland, largely at their expense. If they were to hold their own, they too must find ways of tapping the Western market. Boston, remote from the West, her way to the Hudson River impeded by the Berkshire Hills, seemed out of the running, at least so far as a canal was concerned. Philadelphia and Baltimore, though they had the still more formidable Allegheny Mountains to contend with, did not give up without an effort at canal building. Beginning in 1834, the commonwealth of Pennsylvania invested in a complicated and costly system of waterways and railways—with an arrangement of "inclined planes," stationary engines, and cable cars to take canal boats over the mountains—intending thus to connect Philadelphia with Pittsburgh. This "Pennsylvania system" proved a failure, financially and otherwise. From Baltimore a canal was projected to ascend the Potomac Valley and tunnel through the mountains, thus achieving essentially the same object as George Washington once had hoped to accomplish. This grandly conceived Chesapeake and Ohio Canal began to be dug in 1828, but it never got farther west than Cumberland. In the South, Richmond and Charleston also aspired to reach the Ohio Valley; Richmond, planning at first to join the James and the Kanawha, eventually saw a canal built as far as Lynchburg.

For none of these rivals of New York did canals provide a satisfactory way to the West. Some cities, however, saw their opportunity in a different and newer means of transportation. Before the canal age had reached its height, the era of the railroad already was beginning.

The First Railroads

It is hard to date the beginning of railroads, since they resulted from a combination of different elements, each of which had a separate history. One of these was the use of rails, wooden or iron, laid on a prepared roadbed to make a fairly straight and level track. Another was the employment of steam-powered locomotives, and a third was the operation of trains as public carriers of passengers and freight. For nearly two hundred years before the nineteenth century opened, railways with cars pulled by men (and women) or by animals had been used to haul coal from English mines, and in the early 1800's similar railways appeared in the United States. By 1804 both English and American inventors had experimented with steam engines for propelling land vehicles as well as boats. In 1820 John Stevens ran a locomotive and cars around a circular track on his New Jersey estate. Finally, in 1825, the Stockton and Darlington Railroad in England began to operate with steam power over a short length of track and to carry general traffic.

This news quickly aroused the interest of American businessmen, especially in those seaboard cities that sought better communications with the West. First to organize a railroad company was a group of New Yorkers, who in 1826 obtained a charter for the Mohawk and Hudson and five years later began running trains the 16 miles between Schenectady and Albany. First to begin actual operations was the Baltimore and Ohio; the only living signer of the Declaration of Independence, Charles Carroll of

Carrollton, dug a spadeful of earth in ceremonies to start the work on July 4, 1828, and a 13-mile stretch opened for business in 1830. In that same year the Charleston and Hamburg ran trains over a segment of its track in South Carolina; when this line was completed, in 1833, it was the longest in the world (136 miles). The next year the commonwealth of Pennsylvania finished its line from Philadelphia to the Susquehanna River as part of the "Pennsylvania system" of rail and waterways. Meanwhile, in Massachusetts, three companies received charters for routes radiating out from Boston, the most important of these being the Western Railroad which reached Worcester in 1836. Not only the seaboard but also the Mississippi Valley became the scene of railroad building. By 1836 a total of more than 1,000 miles of track had been laid in eleven states.

There did not yet exist what could be called a railroad system. Even the longest of the lines was comparatively short, and most of them served mainly to connect water routes and supplement water transportation. But there was no lack of railroad enthusiasts and grandiose railroad plans, some of which were eventually to be realized. Charleston was never to get its direct, through route over the mountains to the Ohio Valley. Boston, however, was reaching westward to tap the trade of the Erie Canal. The Mohawk and Hudson (nucleus of the New York Central), the Baltimore and Ohio, and the Pennsylvania were ultimately to become through lines from New York to St. Louis and Chicago. With a few exceptions, as in Pennsylvania, these early railroads were built and operated by private corporations, though they received financial aid from state and local governments (the commonwealth of Pennsylvania soon sold its railroad interests to the Pennsylvania Railroad, a private company). In the beginning, railroad promoters were motivated not only by the private profit to be gained from the railroad business but also by the community benefits to be derived from improved transportation.

During the 1830's the railroad underwent

and engines of the one might not fit on the tracks of the other. In the early years experiments were made with various forms of motive power—horses, sails, and stationary

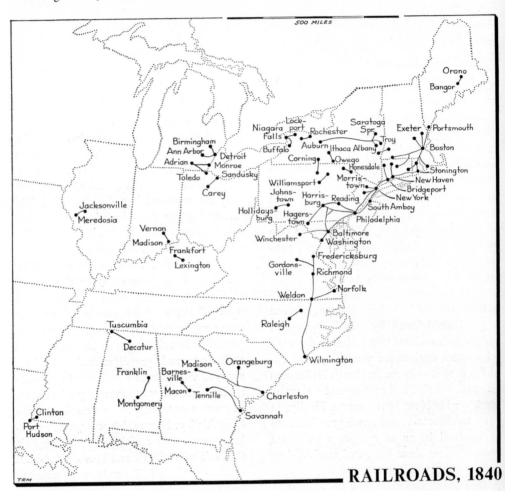

RAILROADS, 1840

a rapid technological development. At first the track consisted of strap-iron rails laid on wooden stringers which were anchored to granite blocks set in the ground, but this kind of track proved too rigid to absorb the shocks of actual use and was soon replaced by heavier iron rails on wooden ties ballasted with crushed rock. The tracks of different companies varied in width, so that when two different lines connected, the cars

steam engines with windlasses and cables (for steep grades), as well as steam locomotives. The very first locomotives were imported from England, but as early as 1830 engines of American manufacture like the Charleston and Hamburg's *Best Friend of Charleston* were put into use, and before long only American locomotives were used on American roads; some were even exported. Since railroads in this country were built with sharper curves and steeper grades, the locomotives had to be both more flexible and more powerful than in England. Passenger cars, originally mere stagecoaches adapted to rails, took the form of a large elongated wooden box with two rows of reversible seats and a center aisle soon after 1840. Schedules were erratic and wrecks frequent, most of the roadbeds and bridges being hastily and poorly constructed.

tive frightened their chickens and cows and that the sparks set fire to their hay. The pious thought trains contrary to the will of God, and others thought it a serious strain on the human constitution to move along at such high speeds as 15 or 20 miles an hour. The most determined opposition came from those who had a vested interest in forms of transportation which the railroad threatened—turnpikes and canals.

An Early Locomotive. *Built about 1834 for the Natchez and Hamburg Railroad (now a part of the Illinois Central) in the state of Mississippi, the "Mississippi" was advanced in design for its time. Note that the boiler is horizontal (not vertical, as on earlier locomotives), the smokestack is in front, and there are four drive-wheels. There are no pilot wheels, however, and no cow-catcher. All the early locomotives were individually named—like ships.* (ILLINOIS CENTRAL RAILROAD)

The dangers and disasters were only one reason for the popular hostility which the first railroads aroused. Farmers complained that the roaring and puffing of the locomo-

From the outset railroads and canals were bitter competitors. For a time the Chesapeake and Ohio Canal Company blocked the advance of the Baltimore and Ohio Railroad through the narrow gorge of the upper Potomac, and the state of New York prohibited railroads from hauling freight in competition with the Erie Canal and its branches. Canal partisans and railroad advocates furiously debated the relative merits

not to those that continued to depend exclusively upon waterways.

Broadening of Business

Developments in transportation steadily broadened the scope of business enterprise

---

Traveling by Railroad
1835

In her widely read work on *Society in America* (1836) the scholarly Englishwoman Harriet Martineau recalled railroad trips she had taken in South Carolina and Pennsylvania:

"My journeys on the Charleston and Augusta railroad were by far the most fatiguing of any I underwent in the country. The motion and the noise are distracting. Whether this is owing to its being on piles in many places, whether the fault is in the ground or the construction, I do not know. Almost all the railroad traveling in America is very fatiguing and noisy. . . .

"One great inconvenience of the American railroads is that, from wood being used for fuel, there is an incessant shower of large sparks, destructive to dress and comfort, unless all the windows are shut, which is impossible in warm weather. Some serious accidents from fire have happened in this way; and during my last trip on the Columbia and Philadelphia railroad, a lady in the car had a shawl burned to destruction on her shoulders; and I found that my own gown had thirteen holes in it; and my veil, with which I saved my eyes, more than could be counted."

---

of the two methods of transportation. Canals, the canal men argued, could accommodate heavier loads and operate at lower costs; even some of the railroad advocates conceded that canals probably would always carry most of the bulky traffic. Railroads, on the other hand, had the advantages of speed and year-round operation (canals closed down for the winter freeze) and could be located almost anywhere, regardless of terrain and the availability of water. Where free competition existed, railroads took most of the passenger traffic and the light freight.

The future, in fact, belonged to the towns and cities along the path of the "iron horse."

while bringing about a greater degree of geographical specialization in economic activity. More than ever, a particular locality could concentrate upon the production of a certain kind of goods, since it could depend on other parts of the country to buy its surplus and supply its needs. While such specialization intensified differences of economic interest and thus accounted for much of the growing sectionalism in politics, it also made the East and the West, the North and the South, increasingly interdependent.

The Northwest, though it had its rising industrial towns, became pre-eminently the source of the great agricultural staples, corn and wheat. In the South many planters who once had raised their own foodstuffs began to import grain and meat from the Northwest and devote themselves exclusively to their cotton crop. Though small farmers producing corn and hogs as well as cotton continued to be numerous—indeed, the most numerous class in the South—this section came to be increasingly dominated by the cotton and slave economy. In the Northeast the farmers lost their former advantage of nearness to the market, once the produce of the Northwest could be brought cheaply to Eastern consumers by canal. New Englanders with their stony acres found it especially difficult to compete with the frontier farmers, who year by year brought new and rich fields under cultivation, and those Yankees who remained on their farms turned more and more to dairying, fruit-growing, and truck-farming. Despite Western competition, the farmers of New York and Pennsylvania carried on profitably a diversified agriculture. But the Northeast as a whole, to a greater extent than any other section, was given over to industry and commerce.

While mills and factories multiplied, the household and the workshop declined but slowly as producers of manufactured goods. In the textile industry the use of machinery and the dependence on water power (occasionally steam power) made it necessary to bring operations together under a single roof. Yet a good deal of spinning and weaving continued to be done in the home, either for sale or for home use. Though shoes were still made by hand and not by machines, shoe manufacture was increasingly the work of men and women who, in a careful division of labor, specialized in one or another of the various tasks. Mass-produced shoes, in ungraded sizes and without distinction as to rights or lefts, came in the 1830's chiefly from eastern Massachusetts and were bought mostly by frontier emigrants, sailors, and Southern planters, who used them for their slaves. Other people still made their own

shoes or had them made to order by a cobbler. Iron came largely from Pennsylvania, where it was produced in furnaces using local sources of ore, limestone, and charcoal. Other furnaces were scattered over the country, however, and finished iron products were wrought in thousands of local blacksmith shops. Sizeable wagon and carriage factories appeared in cities like New York, but smaller towns almost everywhere had their own wheelwrights and carriage-makers, though some of these were beginning merely to assemble vehicles from spokes, fellies, and other parts which came ready-made from the big-city manufacturers.

The expansion of business was not simply a more or less automatic result of transportation improvements or other technological changes. It was also the result of daring and imagination on the part of businessmen and their employees. Two industries, one old and one new, illustrate the capacities of Yankee enterprise. One was the whaling industry, which was reaching its heyday in the 1830's. From New Bedford and other New England ports, bold skippers and their crews, having driven most of the whales from the Atlantic, voyaged far into the Pacific in their hazardous tracking of the source of spermaceti for candles, whale oil for lamps, and whalebone for corset stays and other uses. Another example of Yankee enterprise was the ice industry. Though for years Northeastern farmers had harvested winter ice from ponds and stored it for the summer, the large-scale transportation and sale of ice as a commodity began in the 1830's. The New England ice harvest then found a ready market in Northern cities, on Southern plantations, and around the world in India, whither it was carried in fast sailing ships; a voyage was considered highly successful if no more than half the cargo melted on the way.

American ships and shipping entered

upon a golden age. With their advantages in natural resources and with two centuries of experience behind them, Yankee shipbuilders produced vessels unmatched for econ-

on the way to becoming, for a time, the largest in the world.

Overseas commerce thrived. True, with the rise of the home market, exports and im-

The Whale Fishery. *Whaling was a hazardous occupation. The whalemen had to leave their ship in small boats to harpoon their prey. Before the middle of the nineteenth century, Yankee ships were pursuing whales far into the North Atlantic, the North Pacific, and the Arctic oceans. Note the iceberg at the right in this drawing.*

omy, speed, and beauty of design. Many of these ships were sold abroad; most remained in American hands, though their crews were increasingly made up of foreigners of every seagoing nationality. So efficient were the ships and crews, and so enterprising the shipowners and captains, that eventually vessels flying the Stars and Stripes carried nine tenths of this country's exports and imports and much of the business of other nations besides (by law they had a monopoly of American coastal shipping). The American merchant marine was

ports (though increasing) became a smaller and smaller part of the nation's total business. Yet, for the prosperity of Americans in general and some of them in particular, foreign trade was extremely important. Most of the cotton crop and a large part of the wheat crop, for example, were sold abroad. So was much of the output of American textile mills—coarse and cheap fabrics, for which there was more demand in China than in the United States. On the other hand, finer clothes were regularly imported, as were countless other items, necessities as well as luxuries. Exports annually exceeded imports in value, so that the United States had what the old mercantilists had considered a "favorable" balance of trade, the difference being made up largely by the shipment of specie to this country.

The distribution of goods, whether of foreign or of domestic origin, continued to be rather haphazard by present-day standards, though it was becoming more and more systematic. Stores specializing in groceries, dry goods, hardware, or other lines appeared in the larger cities, but smaller towns and villages depended on the general store, like the one where Abraham Lincoln

barter, taking country eggs and other produce in exchange for such things as pins and needles, sugar, and coffee. Many customers, living remote from any store, welcomed the occasional visits of the peddler, who came afoot or by horse, with his pack or with his peddler's wagon equipped with sloping sides which opened to reveal his racks of wares. A special variety of peddler, the Connecticut Yankee, toured the West and the South as a factory agent to sell clocks, at one time made of wood (including the works) but in the 1830's and after usually made of brass.

The organization of business was undergoing a gradual change. Most of it was, and

The Ice Industry. *Harvesting natural ice became a big business in New York State as well as New England. This lithograph of 1845 pictures the cutting and storing of ice at Rockland Lake in New York.*
(COURTESY OF THE NEW-YORK HISTORICAL SOCIETY, NEW YORK CITY)

once clerked in New Salem, Illinois. The typical general store was crammed with a bewildering variety of merchandise. The storekeeper did much of his business by

continued to be, operated by individuals or partnerships operating on a small scale. The dominating figure was the great merchant capitalist, who owned and directed much of the big business of the time. He owned his own ships, and he organized certain industries, as for example that of shoe manufacturing, on the putting-out system, according to which he provided the materials, directed the work, and sold the finished product. In the larger enterprises, however, the individual merchant capitalist was giving way before the advance of the corporation. Corporations had the advantage of combining the resources of a large number of shareholders, but their development was long held back by handicapping laws. A corporation had to have a charter, granted by the state, and at first a special act of the legislature was required. By the 1830's the states were beginning to pass general incorporation laws according to which any group meeting certain requirements could secure a charter merely by paying a fee. Moreover, the laws began to grant the privilege of limited liability, which meant that the individual stockholder was liable only to the extent of losing the value of his stock if the corporation should fail.

Corporations made possible the accumulation of larger and larger amounts of capital for manufacturing enterprises as well as for banks, turnpikes, and railroad companies. Some of this capital came from the profits of wealthy merchants who turned from shipping to newer ventures, some from the savings of men of only moderate means, and some from tax collections, since state governments often bought shares in turnpike, canal, and railroad companies. A considerable part was supplied by foreign, especially English, investors. From all these sources too little was derived to meet the demands of promoters with ambitious schemes of personal profit or community improvement. Hence the banks, which should have confined their long-term lending to the limit of their savings deposits, often were induced to issue excessive amounts of banknotes as a means of providing capital for expanding business ventures. As a result of this practice, bank failures were more frequent and bank deposits less secure than they might otherwise have been.

Workers and Unions

The growth of industry required labor as well as capital. From the colonial beginnings, labor had been scarce in America. At the opening of the nineteenth century nearly 90 of every 100 Americans still lived and worked on the land: they were farmers. City workers were comparatively few, and many of them were skilled artisans who owned and managed their shops: they were small businessmen, not employees. There were also some unskilled laborers—longshoremen and the like—but there was no sizeable reservoir of manpower for new industries to draw upon. In response to the needs of industry a considerable class of wage-earners finally began to form. Its members came mostly from the marginal farms of the East (those farms least able to compete with the fertile fields of the West) and somewhat later from the British Isles and Europe.

In the textile mills two different methods of labor recruitment were used. One of these, which prevailed in the middle states and parts of New England, brought whole families to the mill. Father, mother, and children, even those no more than four or five years old, worked together in tending the looms. The second, the Waltham or Lowell system, which was common in Massachusetts, enlisted young women in their late 'teens and early twenties. These unmarried girls went from farms to factories to work for only a few years and then returned with their savings, to settle down as housewives. They did not form a permanent working class.

Labor conditions in American mills seemed very good in comparison with conditions in English factories and mines. Child labor, indispensable for eking out the manpower supply, entailed fewer evils in the United States, where the working children

who worked in British mines. A parliamentary investigation revealed that some of these unfortunates, naked and filthy, crawled on their hands and knees to pull

Cotton Mills, Lowell, Massachusetts. *Lowell was incorporated as a town in 1826 and chartered as a city ten years later. It was located near the falls of the Merrimack River, where a drop of 31 feet produced tremendous water power. Canals carried the water to the mills. In the central building of the Boott Cotton Mills, shown here, there were about 900 looms, all tended by girls, one girl to every four looms. Altogether about 1,200 "operatives," mostly girls, were employed in the Boott Mills as of 1850. "Visitors," is was said, "will be agreeably surprised with the neat and respectable appearance of the operatives of this industrious city; and equally so with their moral condition. One third of the entire population of this city is connected with the Sunday schools established by the various religious societies; and there is less intemperance and crime than in most other places of its size in New England."* (LIBRARY OF CONGRESS)

remained under the control of their parents, than in England, where asylum authorities hired out orphans to factory employers. The lot of the working woman in mills like those of Lowell appeared idyllic in contrast with the plight of contemporary women

coal carts through narrow tunnels. No wonder that English visitors considered Lowell a female paradise. The Lowell girls lived in pleasant boardinghouses (much like college residence halls) where their morals were carefully supervised. They were well paid by the standards of the period. They found time to write and publish a monthly magazine, the *Lowell Offering*, even though working hours were long—from sunup to

maintain a family at what was generally considered a decent living standard; many of them lived in the most unhealthful of shanties. After about 1840 Irish men and

---

The Big Strike in Philadelphia
1835

John Ferral, a leader of the Philadelphia General Trades' Union, told a "brother" labor leader in Boston how "the workies" of Philadelphia had won the ten-hour day by a general strike in the summer of 1835:

"Fortunately, at this crisis, the Cordwainers [shoemakers] of the Ladies' Branch struck for wages; the Handloom Weavers had already declared their intentions, and the Laborers on the wharves of Schuylkill were out on strike several days previous. The Cordwainers, with that sympathy of feeling which pervades all intelligent working men, marched out to meet the laborers. Addresses were then delivered, calling upon all day workmen to strike for the hours; and nobly the call was responded to. Bricklayers, plasterers, house carpenters, stone masons, laborers, &c., vied with each other in this generous rivalry of action. . . .

"The recognition and adoption of the ten hour system by the public servants of Philadelphia city and county could not with safety have been longer deferred; each day added thousands to our ranks. We marched to the public works, and the workmen joined in with us; when the procession passed, employment ceased, business was at a stand still, shirt sleeves were rolled up, aprons on, working tools in hand were the orders of the day. Had the cannon of an invading enemy belched forth its challenge on our soil, the freemen of Philadelphia could not have shown a greater ardor for the contest; the blood-sucking aristocracy, they alone stood aghast; terror-stricken, they thought the day of retribution was come, but no vengeance was sought or inflicted by the people for the wrongs they had suffered from their enemies."

---

sundown six days a week. In the early days of the factory these hours seemed natural enough to people who were used to the day-long labor of the farm.

Much worse off were the construction gangs who performed the heavy, unskilled work on turnpikes, railroads, and canals. A large and growing number of these men were Irish immigrants. They received low pay and, since their work was seasonal and uncertain, did not make enough in a year to

women began to be employed in textile mills. As these newcomers replaced the native farm girls, the earlier paternalistic system broke down and working conditions deteriorated somewhat. Piece rates were paid instead of a daily wage; these and other devices were used to speed up production and exploit the labor force more efficiently.

Neither ditch-diggers nor millhands, however, were the first to organize and act collectively to improve the conditions of their work. Skilled artisans formed the earliest labor unions and arranged the first strikes (shortly before 1800). From the 1790's on, the printers and cordwainers took the lead. The cordwainers—makers of high-quality boots and shoes, each man fashioning his entire product—suffered from the competition of merchant capitalists who put out work to be performed in separate tasks. These artisans sensed a loss of security and status with the development of mass-production methods, and so did members of other skilled trades, such as carpenters, joiners, masons, plasterers, hatters, and shipbuilders. In cities like Philadelphia, Baltimore, Boston, and New York, the skilled workers of each craft formed societies for mutual aid. During the 1820's and 1830's the craft societies began to combine on a city-wide basis and set up central organizations known as trade unions. Since, with the widening of the market, workers of one city competed with those at a distance, the next step was to federate the trade unions or to establish craft unions of national scope. In 1834 delegates from six cities founded the National Trades' Union, and in 1836 the printers and the cordwainers set up their own national craft unions.

This labor movement soon collapsed. Labor leaders struggled against the handicap of hostile laws and hostile courts. By the common law, as interpreted by judges in the industrial states, a combination among workers was viewed as, in itself, an illegal conspiracy. But adverse court decisions did not halt, though they handicapped, the rising unions. The death blow came from the Panic of 1837 and the ensuing depression.

Increasing Comfort

For most Americans the march of technology and enterprise brought added comforts to daily life. But not all the people found themselves better off year after year, and some actually suffered a worsening of their material condition. During periods of depression, as after the panics of 1819 and 1837, want and misery spread. Nor did those who gained from the general trend of economic progress share equally in the benefits. The income disparity between the poor and the rich steadily widened. City dwellers —at least the more well-to-do among them —enjoyed the use of labor-saving and comfort-giving inventions sooner and more extensively than did the people on farms and in small towns.

True, life and labor on the farm became somewhat easier with the introduction of new tools, though not all such advantages were readily accepted. The spring wagon (1825) seemed to some a useless luxury, and the cast-iron plow (1819) gained acceptance slowly among farmers who, believing that iron poisoned the soil, preferred the older wooden plow. But by 1830 iron plows were in such great demand that they were mass produced, two factories in Pittsburgh alone turning out nearly 35,000 a year. Before long, steel plows came into use, especially in the prairie country, where the sod was too tough for cast-iron implements, to say nothing of wooden ones. Harvesting was still backbreaking work, though the addition of the cradle to the scythe had made it possible to cut and shock a field of grain faster than before. As early as 1831 Cyrus Hall McCormick demonstrated his horse-drawn mechanical reaper on a Virginia wheatfield. Not till after 1840 did horse-powered mowers, reapers, hay-rakes, and other such farm machinery begin to come into fairly general use.

While, during hard times, countryfolk were less likely to experience downright want than were the unemployed in towns and cities, many urbanites were beginning to enjoy conveniences unknown to the farm. By the 1820's New York and Philadelphia had municipal waterworks, and some houses even had water piped indoors.

Though in summer this water was tepid and tasteless in comparison with that from a rural well or a spring, it could be improved by the addition of ice, regularly supplied to householders for their iceboxes. Streets be-

means, these styles became simpler and more chaste. Altogether, the range in housing was extreme—from the city mansion or the plantation house to the slum hovel and the frontier lean-to.

Important Social and Scientific Events
1835–1847

First steamer crossed ocean, from England to New York, 1835.

First photograph in the United States taken, 1839.

First use of anesthesia, 1842.

First telegraph line completed, 1844.

Sewing machine patented by Elias Howe, 1845.

First postage stamps issued by government, 1847.

---

gan to be lighted by gas, the New York Gas Company being chartered in 1823, and other cities acquiring gasworks in subsequent years. Urban sanitation still left much to be desired—scavenging pigs rooted in New York streets as late as the 1830's—yet on the whole cities were taking on a cleaner and more civilized appearance.

No longer did the well-to-do have their houses built in the Classical or Early Republican style, which had succeeded the colonial Georgian. New fashions were appearing in the 1820's and 1830's. Greek Revival architecture called for dwellings that resembled or at least were reminiscent of the temples of ancient Athens. The Gothic style was inspired by visions of medieval castles, and the Italian was supposed to recall the villas of Florentine merchant princes. The wealthier the home-owner, the more stylishly elaborate his house, particularly if it was located in the city. New styles were slow to reach rural areas and small towns, and, as applied by carpenters serving buyers of modest

As yet, central heating in residences was rare. Hot-air furnaces had been installed here and there for some time, but not till 1840 did improvements make such furnaces practical and safe. Meanwhile stoves for heating and ranges for cooking were becoming common. The Franklin stove, invented by the great scientist, prepared the way, though it burned only wood and was not very efficient except in comparison with the fireplace. Numerous inventors turned their talents to designing better and better coal stoves after 1820. The fireplace, though vastly more charming in retrospect, grew unfashionable in the eyes of up-and-coming families; often it was blocked off and one of the modern heaters placed in front of it. Lighting the fire was easier after the phosphorus match (first American patent, 1836) made it unnecessary to use flint, steel, and tinder or to hoard coals from bedtime to morning.

Though kerosene was not yet available, continual improvements were made in lamps burning whale oil or camphine, the latter a rather hazardous combustible. A majority of families, though a steadily declining majority, continued to burn candles which they dipped or molded at home.

The list of new household conveniences could be lengthened, but such a dry recital would give a wholly inadequate notion of what material progress meant to Americans of the time. To most of them it was almost a religion. As invention followed invention they were confirmed in the faith that they lived in a wondrous age of infinitely increasing ease and plenty. Some assumed that progress in material things led automatically to progress in society and government as well. Others came to the conclusion that active effort would be needed if they were to keep social and political improvement abreast of technological advance.

>>>->>>->>>->>>-<<<-<<<-<<<-<<<

BIBLIOGRAPHY

C. R. Fish, *The Rise of the Common Man, 1830–1850* (1927), contains much information on improvements in the material conditions of life. A. A. Ekirch, *The Idea of Progress in America, 1815–1860* (1944), analyzes attitudes regarding the possibility, if not the inevitability, of further improvement in material things and in human relationships.

G. R. Taylor, *The Transportation Revolution, 1815–1860* (1951), deals with roads, bridges, canals, steamboats, railroads, and ocean shipping. A. F. Harlow, *Old Towpaths: The Story of the American Canal Era* (1926), is a popularly written general account. W. S. Sanderlin, *The Great National Project* (1947), is a scholarly study of the Chesapeake and Ohio Canal.

On railroads, see A. D. Turnbull's *John Stevens: An American Record* (1928), which is a biography of the pioneer railroad man in the United States. See also Edward Hungerford, *The Story of the Baltimore and Ohio Railroad, 1827–1927* (2 vols., 1928); F. W. Stevens, *The Beginnings of the New York Central Railroad* (1926); and S. M. Derrick, *Centennial History of the South Carolina Railroad* (1930). These are histories of the three original railroads in this country.

S. E. Morison, *The Maritime History of Massachusetts, 1783–1860* (1921), is a fascinating story of ships and shipping, merchants and trade. F. R. Dulles, *The Old China Trade* (1930), is a readable survey. R. G. Albion, *Square-Riggers on Schedule* (1938), tells of the first regularly scheduled ocean shipping. E. P. Holman, *The American Whalemen* (1928), deals with a colorful aspect of the fisheries.

Good studies of manufacturing in the 1820's and 1830's are scarce. Two able ones which touch upon the period are A. H. Cole, *The American Wool Manufacture* (2 vols., 1926), and Ware, *The Early New England Cotton Manufacture*.

Among the best of the urban histories, though not treating all aspects of city life, is R. G. Albion's *The Rise of New York Port, 1815–1860* (1939), which describes and explains the remarkable growth of the Manhattan metropolis. Ralph Weld, *Brooklyn Village, 1816–1834* (1938), deals with New York's neighbor in a period when it was a boom town. Blake McKelvey, *Rochester, the Water-Power City, 1812–1854* (1945), shows the effects of the Erie Canal upon one of the leading canal ports. L. D. Baldwin, *Pittsburgh: The Story of a City* (1938), relates Pittsburgh's rise to the increase in Ohio River traffic. N. M. Blake, *Water for the Cities* (1956), traces the development of municipal water systems in Philadelphia, New York, Boston, and Baltimore between 1790 and 1860. Not only city growth but also business and transportation developments make up the theme of J. W. Livingood's *The Philadelphia-Baltimore Trade Rivalry, 1780–1860* (1947).

CHAPTER 17

The Coming of Mass Politics

T HE FEDERALIST PARTY having all but disappeared, the presidential election of 1824 became a kind of free-for-all among rival Republicans, the choice finally going to John Quincy Adams. The followers of Andrew Jackson, one of the defeated candidates, succeeded in frustrating Adams during his Presidency and in electing their hero in 1828; the Republican party, having split, thus produced a two-party system once again. Jackson's admirers (both at that time and in after years) thought that his victory signified a rather sudden arrival of democracy in the United States. This was not quite the case, since essential elements of democracy had been present in this country for a long time. True, certain extensions of democratic thought and practice preceded, accompanied, and followed Jackson's rise to power, and the Jacksonians rather than their party foes endorsed and aided these changes. True, also, the rise of Jackson was both a cause and a consequence of an unprecedented effort to arouse and or-

ganize the citizens and bring them out to vote—and to vote "right." In Jackson's day the people began as never before to participate in their own government, as politicians developed new techniques of mass manipulation, and politics took on a modern look.

Democracy Old and New

There never existed in the United States an aristocracy of the European sort—a hereditary ruling class. From the colonial beginnings the English idea of representative government had been free to grow without the encumbrance of the English tradition of family privilege. Of course, some Americans became wealthier than others and acquired more than an equal share of influence in government. Occasionally—from Bacon's to Shays's Rebellion—less favored groups even resorted to violence against their fellow Americans within a colony or state. Most of the time, however, the people as a whole were well content with the amount of self-government they possessed, so well content that many eligible voters seldom if ever bothered to go to the polls. When Great Britain undertook to change the existing arrangements, Americans resisted the new laws and fought the Revolutionary War so as to preserve their democratic liberties. Then, in the state constitutions and in the federal Constitution, the people through their representatives put down in writing their conception of political democracy.

American democracy in those days was less broadly based than today. As we have seen, women could not vote or hold office, nor could men who were too poor to meet the property requirements. Yet, since the vast majority of men were farmers living on their own farms, and since women were highly esteemed by the community and no doubt were generally heeded by their husbands, comparatively few Americans (excepting slaves) suffered any serious or irremediable deprivation of political rights during the early years of national independence. The fate of the Federalists, when they attempted to suppress freedom of speech in the Sedition Act, shows that the people, as voters, were far from helpless.

Though John Adams and Thomas Jefferson differed in their political theories as well as in their practical policies, the two rival leaders agreed that the men with a material stake in society should govern. True, Jefferson advocated government by "the people," but he had in mind those people who owned at least a little plot of ground: he shrank from the prospect of propertyless city mobs ever gaining political power in America. Moreover, he trusted the people to elect their betters to office and allow an aristocracy of talent (not necessarily of birth or wealth) to run public affairs. Adams was somewhat more conservative than Jefferson, and Alexander Hamilton somewhat more than Adams. Hamilton believed that the "rich and well-born" alone should govern. Some Federalists agreed with Hamilton and feared that democracy already had gone to dangerous extremes. Some Republicans, on the other hand, were beginning to question whether democracy had been carried far enough. Still, most members of both parties considered the American constitutional system as very nearly ideal.

With the opening of the nineteenth century, Americans ceased to be so nearly unanimous in the belief that the United States was democratic enough. Many began to wonder whether the facts of economic and political life would long continue to fit the prevailing conception of popular rule. According to the Declaration of Independence, all men are created equal, at least in political rights. By existing laws, however, not quite all men were in fact equal when it came to voting or holding office. In a community where practically everyone was the owner of at least a little real estate, the matter of inequality was not serious or disturbing. But, with the growth of industry, a time might come when a large proportion if not a majority of the people in some areas would consist of virtually propertyless workers and their families crowded into factory towns. By the early 1800's a sizeable proletariat (that is, a class of laborers with little or no property) already had appeared in England. People of this class were still extremely rare in the United States, most American town workers being independent artisans who possessed their own shops and tools and, in some cases, their own farms.

With the continued growth of factories, there might eventually arise a large class of dependent workingmen and a small class of new aristocrats—an industrial plutocracy—in the United States. So it seemed to Alexis de Tocqueville, a perspicacious young Frenchman who visited this country in 1831–1832 to study the influence of the idea of equality in actual practice. In his book *Democracy in America* Tocqueville wrote:

"In proportion as the principle of the division of labor is more extensively applied, the workman becomes more weak, more narrow-minded, and more dependent. The art advances, the artisan recedes. On the other hand, in proportion as it becomes more manifest that the productions of manufactures are by so much the cheaper and better as the manufacture is larger and the amount of capital employed more considerable, wealthy and educated men come forward to embark in manufactures which were heretofore abandoned to poor or ignorant handicraftsmen. The magnitude of the efforts required, and the importance of the results to be obtained, attracts them. Thus at the very moment at which the science of manufactures lowers the class of workmen, it raises the class of masters." Tocqueville thus concluded that factory owners would dominate their employees. "What is this but aristocracy?" he asked. The "friends of democracy," he advised, should watch out for this possible danger.

This prospect of widening class differences seemed pertinent to the question of widening the suffrage and making government more democratic. Some politicians favored giving every white man the vote, because they hoped to get the gratitude and support of the newly enfranchised voter, or because they believed in the principle of general manhood suffrage. They had persuasive arguments, based on the Christian doctrine of universal brotherhood and the Revolutionary postulate of the equality of man. Other politicians held to the long-accepted principle that only property owners should share in government; otherwise, these politicians argued, property eventually would be unsafe from those who coveted it and who, once in control of government, could take it.

The conservative democrats, the defenders of the old way, lost ground as the advocates of broad-based democracy made fairly steady progress toward reforming the various state governments during the early nineteenth century. Reformers in America made more headway than did reformers of similar mind abroad. In England and other countries the friends of democracy were busy; in fact, Americans and Europeans shared ideas and encouraged one another in what amounted to an international movement for government by the people. But the Americans had certain advantages which enabled them to move ahead farther and faster. For one thing, of course, democracy in the United States was considerably more advanced and more widely accepted to start with. For another thing, this country's internal geographical conditions and its geographical position in the world favored democratic experiments. Here was abundant room for population to expand, and people moved about a good deal (in comparison with the peoples of other nations), seeking and finding opportunities to begin life anew. On the newly settled frontier a rough equality between man and man generally prevailed. Very likely the fact of widespread economic opportunity and economic equality led many Americans to expect political opportunity and political equality as well. Since a wide ocean stood between Americans and any strong potential enemy, they could afford to experiment with popular rule during the peaceful years after 1815. If the powers of Europe had been close to this country's borders, the requirements of self-defense and military preparedness might have necessitated a powerfully centralized national government and left little leeway for the states to put democratic theories into practice to the extent that most of them did.

Changes in State Government

When Ohio and other new states in the West joined the Union, they adopted constitutions which gave the vote to all adult white males and allowed all voters the right to hold public office. Thus the new states set an example for the older ones. These older states became concerned about the loss of their population to the West, and they began slowly and haltingly to grant additional political rights to their people so as to encourage them to stay at home. Even before the War of 1812 a few of the Eastern states permitted white men to vote whether or not they owned property or paid a tax. After 1815 the states began to revise their constitutions by calling conventions that served as grand committees of the people to draw up new documents and submit them for public approval. Eventually all the states (some of them not till after the Civil War) changed their constitutions in the direction of increased democracy.

Change was resisted, and at times the democratic trend was stopped short of the aims of the more radical reformers, as, for example, when Massachusetts held its convention in 1820. The reform-minded delegates complained that in the Massachusetts government the rich were better represented than the poor, both because of the restrictions on voting and officeholding and because of the peculiar system of property representation in the state senate. The number of senators from each district of the state depended not upon the number of people in the district but upon the amount of its taxable wealth. The reformers urged an amendment apportioning senators according to population alone. Daniel Webster, one of the conservative delegates, opposed the change on the grounds that "power *naturally* and *necessarily* follows property" and that "property as such should have its weight and influence in political arrangement." Webster and the rest of the conservatives could not prevent the reform of senate representation, nor could they pre-

vent elimination of the property requirement for voting. But, to the disgust of the radicals, the new constitution required that every voter be a taxpayer and that the governor be the owner of considerable real estate.

In the New York convention of 1821 the conservatives, led by Chancellor James Kent, insisted that a taxpaying requirement for the suffrage was not enough and that, at least in the election of state senators, the property qualification should be retained. Kent argued that society "is an association for the protection of property as well as of life" and that "the individual who contributes only one cent to the common stock ought not to have the same power and influence in directing the property concerns of the partnership as he who contributes his thousands." The reformers, appealing to the Declaration of Independence, maintained that life, liberty, and the pursuit of happiness, not property, were the main concerns of society and government. The property qualification was abolished in New York.

Other states proceeded more slowly in the broadening of democracy, none of them going to radical extremes. Progress was peaceful, except in Rhode Island. There the constitution was the old colonial charter, little changed, and it disqualified as voters more than half of the adult males of the state. Thomas L. Dorr and his suffragist followers, despairing of reform by legal processes, held a convention of their own, drew up a new constitution, and tried to set up an administration with Dorr as governor. When the existing state government began to imprison his followers he led a band of his men in an attack upon the Providence arsenal (1842). The Dorr Rebellion quickly was put down, yet it hastened the reforms which afterward came in Rhode Island.

In the South reformers criticized the overrepresentation of the tidewater areas and the underrepresentation of the back country in the legislatures. When the Virginia constitutional convention met, in 1829, the delegates from the western counties

after the Civil War, the legislature keeping to itself the choice of presidential electors. With few exceptions, free Negroes could not vote anywhere in the South.

An Argument Against Universal Suffrage
1821

According to the original constitution of New York, the state senate was elected by owners of land worth at least $250, and the assembly by owners of land worth at least $50. At the constitutional convention of 1821 the radicals proposed to abolish all property qualifications for voting. A conservative delegate, James Kent, objected. Then chancellor of the state chancery court, Kent was one of the nation's foremost legal authorities. Later he wrote a classic four-volume work entitled *Commentaries on American Law* (1826–1830). In 1821 he was willing to abolish the property qualification for assembly elections, but he wished to "preserve our Senate as the representative of the landed interest." He told his fellow delegates:

"By the report before us, we propose to annihilate, at one stroke, all those property distinctions and to bow before the idol of universal suffrage. That extreme democratic principle, when applied to the legislative and executive departments of the government, has been regarded with terror, by the wise men of every age, because in every European republic, ancient and modern, in which it has been tried, it has terminated disastrously, and been productive of corruption, injustice, violence, and tyranny. . . .

"The apprehended danger from the experiment of universal suffrage applied to the whole legislative department, is no dream of the imagination. It is too mighty an excitement for the moral constitution of men to endure. The tendency of universal suffrage is to jeopardize the rights of property and the principles of liberty. There is a constant tendency . . . in the poor to covet a share in the plunder of the rich; in the debtor to relax or avoid the obligation of contracts; in the majority to tyrannize over the minority, and trample down their rights; in the indolent and profligate to cast the whole burthens of society upon the industrious and the virtuous; and *there is a tendency in ambitious and wicked men to inflame these combustible materials.*"

gained some slight concessions but not enough to satisfy them. Elsewhere in the Southeast the planters and politicians of the older counties continued to dominate the state governments. In South Carolina there was no popular vote for President until

Nor could Negroes vote in most of the Northern states. Pennsylvania at one time allowed Negro suffrage but eventually (1837) amended the constitution so as to prohibit it. In North and South, women continued to be denied the vote, regardless of the amount of property they might own. Everywhere the ballot was open, not secret, and often it was cast as a spoken vote rather than a written one. The lack of secrecy

The multiplication of voters was due only in part to the widening of the electorate. It was due in greater measure to a heightening of interest in politics and a strengthening

Election Day. *Neither sobriety nor secrecy was required at nineteenth-century polling places. Here one citizen takes a drink, while another staggers drunkenly. A voter, sitting on the steps, marks his ballot while another looks over his shoulder. Other voters hand their ballots—which were furnished by the political parties—to a polling official on the porch. From the painting, "The County Election," by George Caleb Bingham. After studying at the Pennsylvania Academy of the Fine Arts and in Germany, Bingham began his career in Missouri, setting up a studio in Jefferson City, then in St. Louis, and finally in Kansas City. His paintings of real-life scenes are noted for their honesty and humor.*
(COURTESY OF THE CITY ART MUSEUM, ST. LOUIS)

meant that voters could be, and sometimes were, bribed or intimidated.

Despite the persisting limitations, the number of voters increased far more rapidly than did the population as a whole. Before the 1820's fewer than 5 persons in 100 usually voted; by 1840, about 17 in 100 or nearly half of the free male population did.

of party organization. Citizens now were aroused and brought out to vote who in former times had seldom bothered with elections.

Not only did the number of voters increase: so did the number of elective offices in the states. The very first state constitutions had provided for the appointment of high state officials by the governor or by the legislature. The newer constitutions put the election of these officials, including judges in some cases, into the hands of the people. Supposedly the people thus were to have increased control over government. Actually, with authority so divided and diffused, it was harder than ever for the people to locate and hold to account the officials responsible for particular policies.

Political parties became more important as both the electorate and the elections grew in number and complexity. Parties were necessary for bringing together voters of diverse interests and providing common goals so that the will of the people could express itself in a united and meaningful way. Parties were necessary also to give central direction to governments made up of independently elected officials. Hence, as the states became more democratic, political organizations within them became more tightly knit. Political machines and party bosses appeared in states which, like New York and Pennsylvania, had large and heterogeneous electorates with a variety of conflicting interests. In New York and Pennsylvania the spoils system was introduced before it was transplanted to the federal government. State jobs were awarded to loyal workers of the victorious party, and job-seeking came to be the motive which held together and inspirited the core of the party membership.

Free-for-All of 1824

The rising spirit of democratic politics found expression in the presidential election of 1824. Previously, from 1796 to 1816, presidential candidates had been nominated by caucuses of the members of each of the two parties in Congress. In 1820, when the Federalists declined to oppose his candidacy, Monroe ran as the Republican nominee without the necessity of a caucus nomination. If the caucus system should be revived

and followed in 1824, it would mean that the nominee of the Republicans in Congress would run unopposed, as Monroe had done, for the Federalist party had ceased to exist as a national organization. Several men aspired to the Presidency, however, and they and their followers were unwilling to let a small group of congressmen and Senators decide the question. After all, these congressmen and Senators had not been elected with a view to making a presidential nomination: they did not speak for the people.

In 1824 "King Caucus" was overthrown. Fewer than a third of the Republicans in Congress bothered to attend the gathering which went through the motions of nominating a candidate (William H. Crawford) and he found the caucus nomination as much a handicap as a help in the campaign. The rest of the candidates received nominations from state legislatures and endorsements from irregular mass meetings throughout the country.

Three of the presidential hopefuls were members of Monroe's cabinet. Of these, John Quincy Adams had the best-founded claim. As Secretary of State for two terms he had made a distinguished record in his conduct of foreign affairs, and he held the office that had become traditionally the steppingstone to the Presidency. But, as he himself ruefully realized, he was a man of cold and forbidding manners: he was not a candidate with strong popular appeal. Contending against Adams was the Secretary of the Treasury, William H. Crawford of Georgia, an impressive giant of a man who seemed to have a promising future in national politics. The caucus candidate, Crawford had the backing of the extreme state-rights faction of the Republican party. In mid-campaign, however, he was stricken by a paralyzing illness. While Crawford was still in good health and apparently a formidable candidate, another of his colleagues, Secretary of War John C. Calhoun, entered the lists in a desperate effort to head him off. When the chances for Calhoun as a presidential aspirant grew dim, he restrained his ambition and turned to seeking the Vice Presidency.

Challenging the cabinet contenders was Henry Clay, the speaker of the House. This tall, black-haired Kentuckian, with his broad smile and his ready handshake, had a "magnetic" personality that gained him a devoted following. He also stood for a definite and coherent program, which he called the "American System." His plan, a familiar one but attractive to citizens just recovering from a business depression, was to create a great home market for factory and farm producers by means of a protective tariff to stimulate industry, a national bank to facilitate credit and exchange, and internal improvements at federal expense to provide transportation between the cities and the farms. In the midst of the campaign, Congress raised protective duties somewhat in the tariff of 1824 and made some provision for internal improvements in the General Survey Act (1824), which President Monroe signed. Despite this legislation (and the existence of the Bank of the United States, chartered in 1816) much more needed to be done before Clay's "American System" could be fully realized.

Andrew Jackson offered no such clear-cut program as did "Harry of the West." Though Jackson had served briefly as a representative in Congress and was a member of the United States Senate, he had no legislative record to run on. Nevertheless, he had the inestimable advantages of a military hero's reputation and a campaign shrewdly managed by the Tennessee politician friends who had put him forward as a candidate. To some of his contemporaries he seemed a crude, hot-tempered frontiersman and Indian-fighter. Actually, though arising from humble backgrounds as an orphan in the Carolinas, he had become a well-to-do planter who lived in an elegant mansion ("The Hermitage") near Nashville and was, at least by his own lights and the standards of the West, a gentleman. To Daniel Webster, who was well acquainted with the rich and well-born of Boston, Jackson with his dignified and soldierly bearing appeared to be "more presidential" than any of the other candidates (though Webster eventually favored Adams).

At election time these four men were in the field: Adams, Crawford (despite his illness), Clay, and Jackson. All belonged to the same party, the Republican, but they represented different factions and, to some extent, different sections. Adams, the candidate of the Northeast, had little following in the rest of the country. Crawford, of the Southeast, had considerable support in the North, including the support of the New York party machine. Though coming from Kentucky, Clay was more nearly identified with the interests of the Northwest than with those of the Southwest, and with his American System he thought he represented also the interests of the Northeast. Jackson, the personification of the Southwest, attracted Eastern city workers as well as Western frontiersmen, most of the newly enfranchised voters favoring him. Issues were not clearly drawn among the four candidates. While Clay had his nationalistic platform and Crawford stood for state rights, Adams was best known for his role in diplomacy, and Jackson was presented simply as a great patriot and a friend of the common man. The election was decided on the basis of personalities as well as sectional interests.

Once the returns were counted, there was no doubt that the next Vice President was to be Calhoun, who ran on both the Adams and the Jackson tickets. But there was considerable doubt as to who the next President would be. In those states where the people chose the presidential electors, Jackson led all the rest at the polls. In the electoral college also he came out ahead, with 99 votes to Adams's 84, Crawford's 41, and Clay's 37. He lacked the necessary majority, however. So, in accordance with the Twelfth Amendment, the final decision was left to the House of Representatives, which was to choose among the three candidates with the highest electoral vote. Clay, for all his charm, was out of the running.

"Corrupt Bargain!"

If Clay, in 1825, could not be President, he could at least be president-maker, and perhaps he could lay the ground for his own election later on. As speaker, he was in a strategic position for influencing the decision of the House of Representatives. In deciding among the three leading candidates, the House was to vote by states, the delegation from each state casting one vote. Clay, as the winner of the recent election in Kentucky, Ohio, and Missouri, could swing the congressional delegations of those three states at least.

Before Congress got around to making the decision, the friends of Jackson, Crawford, and Adams approached Clay in behalf of their respective candidates. To which of the three should he give his support? Jackson's followers insisted that Jackson, with his popular and electoral pluralities, was really the people's choice and that Congress had no rightful alternative but to ratify the people's will. But Jackson was Clay's most dangerous rival for the political affections of the West, and he could not be depended upon to champion Clay's legislative program. Crawford was out of the question, for he was now a paralytic, incapable of discharging the duties of the Presidency. Only Adams was left. Personally, he was no friend of Clay and had clashed with him repeatedly, when both were peace delegates at Ghent, and afterward. Politically, however, Adams was similar to Clay in cherishing na-

tionalistic principles such as those of the "American System." Finally Clay gave his support to Adams, and the House elected him.

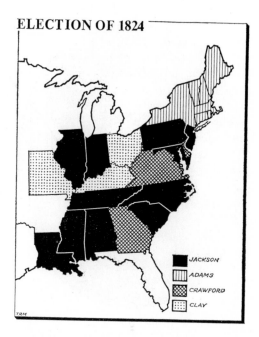

ELECTION OF 1824

JACKSON
ADAMS
CRAWFORD
CLAY

The Jacksonians were angry enough at this, but they became far angrier when the new President made known his appointments. Clay was to be the Secretary of State! The State Department being the well-established route to the Presidency, Adams thus appeared to be naming Clay as his own successor. The two must have agreed to make each other President—Adams now, Clay next—or so the Jacksonians exclaimed, and they pretended to be horrified by this "corrupt bargain." Very likely there had been some sort of understanding, and though there was nothing improper in it, it proved to be politically unwise for both Adams and Clay.

When John Randolph referred sarcastically to the Adams-Clay coalition as a combination of "the Puritan and the blackleg," the new Secretary of State was so exasperated that he challenged Randolph to a duel, though Clay was in principle opposed to dueling. The affair turned out to be bloodless, Clay being in earnest but a poor shot, and Randolph magnanimously firing into

John Quincy Adams. *Adams was a handsome youth of about twenty-eight when John Singleton Copley painted this portrait of him, in 1795. By the time he became President, Adams was a balding, watery-eyed, rather unprepossessing though highly intelligent man of nearly sixty. A hard, conscientious worker, he rose at four in the morning and built a fire before the White House servants were up. Then he made a long entry in his diary for the previous day. He wrote so much that he suffered from paralyzing writer's cramps; finally he taught himself to use his left hand so as to relieve his right. Occasionally, in the early morning, he swam, nude, in the Potomac River. Once his boat overturned with his clothes, and he hid in the shrubbery along the bank while his servant fetched a dry outfit.* (COURTESY, MUSEUM OF FINE ARTS, BOSTON)

the air. The only effect was to dramatize further the strange bargain between two men as unlike as Adams and Clay. Already Clay had gained the undying enmity of that good hater, Jackson, whose hostility stood in the way of Clay's future advancement. Soon after Adams's inauguration as Presi-

dent, Jackson resigned from the Senate to accept a renomination for the Presidency from the Tennessee legislature and to begin a three-year campaign for election in 1828. Politics now overshadowed everything else. Throughout his term in the White House, Adams and his policies were to be thoroughly frustrated by the political bitterness arising from the "corrupt bargain."

The Second President Adams

The career of John Quincy Adams divides naturally into three parts. In the first part, as befitted the son of John Adams, he made a brilliant record in diplomacy, serving as the American minister in one foreign capital after another and then as one of the most successful of all Secretaries of State. In the second phase of his career, as President (1825–1829), he endured four ineffectual years which amounted to a mere interlude between the periods of his greatness. In the third, as a congressman from Massachusetts, he served his constituents and the nation with high distinction, gaining fame as "Old Man Eloquent," the foremost congressional champion of free speech. His frustration in the White House shows that the Presidency demands more than exceptional ability and high-mindedness, for John Quincy Adams possessed both. The Presidency also requires political skill and political luck, and these he did not have.

In his inaugural address and in his first message to Congress he boldly stated a broad conception of the powers and duties of the federal government. He recommended "laws promoting the improvement of agriculture, commerce, and manufactures, the cultivation of the mechanic and of the elegant arts, the advancement of literature, and the progress of the sciences, ornamental and profound." To refrain from exercising the powers of government for the benefit of the people, he declared, "would be to hide in the earth the talent committed to our charge." He had more in mind than the mere dredging of rivers and the building of roads and canals. He spoke of scientific expeditions, astronomical observatories, and a national university. Thus he went considerably beyond the "American System" of Clay.

These views of Adams, though they seem reasonable enough today, struck many of his contemporaries as dangerous and unconstitutional. He had no chance of getting an appropriation from Congress to improve the minds of his countrymen. The most he could get was a few million dollars for improving rivers and harbors and for extending the National Road westward from Wheeling. This amount was more than Congress had appropriated for internal improvements under all his predecessors together, but it was far less than he hoped for.

Even in the field of diplomacy, where Adams had more experience than any other President before or since, he failed in the major efforts of his administration. Yielding to Secretary of State Clay's wish for cooperation with the Latin American governments, Adams appointed two delegates to attend an international conference which the Venezuelan liberator, Simon Bolívar, had called to meet at Panama in 1826. Objections arose in Congress for two reasons. One was that Southerners hated to think of white Americans mingling in Panama with colored delegates from Haiti, the independence of which the United States refused to recognize. The other reason for obstruction was simply politics—the determination of Jacksonians to discredit the administration. They charged that Adams aimed to sacrifice American interests and involve the nation in an entangling alliance. While the Jacksonians filibustered, Congress delayed the Panama mission so long that it became futile. One of the American delegates died on the way to the conference, and the other arrived after it was over. The United States had accomplished nothing to offset British influence, which prevailed in Latin America.

To this extent, the Panama fiasco marked a diplomatic defeat for Adams and Clay and a victory for George Canning, the British foreign secretary. The President soon suffered another defeat at Canning's hands. Adams demanded the complete opening of the British West Indies to American trade as a "right" rather than a "privilege." Refusing to accept the limited freedom of West Indian trade that the British government allowed, he instituted reprisals by discriminating against British shipping in American ports. To this policy of demands and reprisals, Great Britain responded not by welcoming Americans to equal commerce but by excluding their ships from the islands. Not content with half a loaf, Adams lost even that.

He was worsted not only in his struggle with Great Britain but also in a contest with the state of Georgia. That state attempted to remove the remaining Creek and Cherokee Indians so as to gain additional soil for cotton planters. The Creeks, however, had a treaty with the United States (1791) which guaranteed them the possession of the land they occupied. A new treaty (1825) ceded the land to the state, but Adams refused to enforce this treaty, believing that it had been obtained by fraud. The Georgia governor defied the President of the United States and went ahead with plans for Indian removal. At last (1827) the Creeks agreed to still another treaty in which they yielded their claims. Adams's stand had been honorable but unpopular. Southerners condemned him for encroaching upon state rights, and Westerners as well as Southerners disapproved of his interfering with efforts to get rid of the Indians.

Southerners again denounced the administration and its supporters on account of the tariff of 1828. This measure originated in the demands of Massachusetts and Rhode Island woolen manufacturers, who complained that the British were dumping woolens on the American market at prices with which the domestic millowners could not compete. Petitioning Congress, the distressed millowners expected relief from the Woolens Bill of 1827. It passed the House but was defeated in the Senate when Vice President Calhoun cast his negative vote to break a tie. Thus frustrated, the protectionists of New England combined with those of the Middle and Western states to bring further pressure upon Congress, after getting together in a grand tariff convention at Harrisburg, Pennsylvania.

The bill of 1828 contained high duties not only on woolens but also on a number of other items, such as flax, hemp, iron, lead, molasses, and raw wool. Thus it displeased New England manufacturers, for it would raise the cost of their raw materials as well as the price of their manufactured goods. A story arose that the bill had taken its shape from a Jacksonian plot to embarrass New Englanders and discredit Adams. The bill related to "manufactures of no sort or kind but the manufacture of a President of the United States," John Randolph said. Supposedly it was intended to put Adams in a dilemma that would lose him friends whether he signed or vetoed it. While some politicians did see the measure as an electioneering device, others intended it seriously as a means of benefiting the farmers and manufacturers of the middle states and the West.

When the bill was considered item by item, Southerners voted against reductions in the hope that some of its outrageous duties would so antagonize New Englanders that they would help defeat it. But when it came to a final test, Daniel Webster voted for it despite its duties on raw materials, and he carried with him enough New England votes to enable it to pass. Adams signed it. The Southerners, whose tactics had backfired, cursed it as the "tariff of abominations."

Jackson Vindicated

The prospects for Adams's re-election in 1828 were never good, and they got worse as the fateful day approached. In the midterm congressional elections of 1826 his opponents gained control of both the House and the Senate—the first time an administration had been repudiated so early at the polls. Clay and Webster advised the President to use the patronage ruthlessly to save himself. Adams allowed a few of the Jackson men to be turned out of office and some of the Jackson newspapers to be deprived of their public printing contracts. But he refused to make wholesale dismissals, even though he felt sure that "the influence of almost every officer, both of the custom-house and of the post-offices," had been "violently hostile" to him. He even retained his Postmaster General, John McLean, who used the vast patronage of the Post Office as a means of weakening the administration and strengthening the opposition. Of course, Adams had no way of removing the Vice President, Calhoun, who was running for re-election on the Jackson ticket. Adams was beset by enemies not only in Congress but also within his own official family.

By 1828, the Republican party having split completely, there were again two parties in the campaign—the Adamsites, who called themselves National Republicans, and the Jacksonians, who took the name of Democratic Republicans. Adams himself once had been a Federalist, and most of the old Federalists joined his party, though some became followers of Jackson. The Democratic Republican organization was essentially a continuation of the original Jeffersonian party. Both National Republicans and Democratic Republicans included men of all sections and classes, but the former were most numerous in the Northeast, the latter in the South and West; the former among the business class, the latter among the farmers and city workers. The Democratic Republican party gained strength with the shifting of the New York party machine from Crawford to Jackson. The Jacksonians also had the support of the state-righters of the South, while the National Republicans, as their name implied, were advocates of the active use of the powers of the national government.

Issues, however, figured little in the campaign of 1828, though much was said about the "corrupt bargain" and something was said about the West Indian trade and the "tariff of abominations." Regarding the tariff, Adams was on record, having signed the abominations bill, but nobody knew exactly where Jackson stood. Again, as in 1824, more was made of personalities than of policies, and this time there was far worse mudslinging than ever before. Indeed, one would have thought that two criminals were running for the highest office in the land.

As for Adams, the Jacksonians charged that as President he had been guilty of gross waste and extravagance, using public funds to buy gambling devices (a chess set and a billiard table) for the White House. But that was not the worst of Adams's alleged crimes. Once, as minister to Russia, he had tried to procure a beautiful American girl for the sinful pleasures of the Tzar, or so the Jacksonians said. Of course, these charges were wholly false. Indeed, they were fantastic things to say about a man as conscientious and puritanical as John Quincy Adams.

As for Jackson, the Adamsites had accusations even worse. He was a murderer and an adulterer, according to the speeches, handbills, and pamphlets of his party foes. A "coffin handbill" listed within coffin-shaped outlines the names of militiamen whom Jackson was said to have shot in cold blood during the War of 1812. Actually,

these men had been deserters who were executed after due sentence by a court-martial. It was also rumored that Jackson knowingly had lived in sin with the wife of an-

ELECTION OF 1828

JACKSON
ADAMS
VOTE DIVIDED

other man. Actually, he had married the woman, his beloved Rachel, at a time when the pair honestly though mistakenly supposed her first husband had divorced her.

Never before had there been such an unedifying campaign, but never before had there been so many voters to be reached. Apparently the party managers on both sides thought it necessary to appeal to the lowest common denominator of popular interest. Certainly the excitement brought the people out on election day, some of them but recently enfranchised. More than three times as many Americans voted in 1828 as in 1824.

Though the majority voted for Jackson, a large minority (44 per cent) favored Adams, who received all but one of the electoral votes from New England, all from New Jersey and Delaware, and some from New York and Maryland. These totaled only 83, however, as compared with 178 for Jackson, who carried the rest of the country. His victory was decisive enough, even though not quite so sweeping as it seemed.

toral triumph and embittered him against his party foes. Adams, too, was slow to forget the campaign slanders of which he had been the target. His father had refused to

---

Jackson's Inaugural Reception

1829

Andrew Jackson's inauguration impressed a Washington society woman, Mrs. Samuel H. Smith, as a solemn and sublime event. Afterwards Mrs. Smith went with a party of friends to the inaugural reception at the White House. "But what a scene did we witness!" she wrote a few days later, in a letter to an out-of-town relative.

"The *Majesty of the People* had disappeared, & a rabble, a mob, of boys, negros, women, children, scrambling, fighting, romping. What a pity, what a pity! No arrangements had been made, no police officers placed on duty & the whole house had been inundated by the rabble mob. We came too late. The President, after having been *literally* nearly pressed to death & almost suffocated & torn to pieces by the people in their eagerness to shake hands with Old Hickory, had retreated through the back way or south front & had escaped to his lodgings at Gadsby's. Cut glass & china to the amount of several thousand dollars had been broken in the struggle to get the refreshments, punch & other articles had been carried out in tubs & buckets, but had it been in hogsheads it would have been insufficient, ice-cream, & cake & lemonade, for 20,000 people, for it is said that number were there, tho' I think the estimate exaggerated. Ladies fainted, men were seen with bloody noses & such a scene of confusion took place as is impossible to describe,—those who got in could not get out by the door again, but had to scramble out of windows."

In the eyes of his followers, he—and they—were vindicated in their claim that he had been wrongfully deprived of the Presidency in 1825.

The campaign left an aftermath of ill feeling which made an extreme contrast with the so-called "good feelings" that had followed Monroe's first election. Not long after Jackson's victory at the polls, his wife died, and he blamed her death upon his political opponents, who, he felt, had broken her heart with their scandalous stories about her. Her death took the edge off his elec-

attend the inauguration of Jefferson, and the son now stayed away from the inaugural ceremonies for Jackson, spending the day on a horseback ride through the outskirts of Washington.

On that March 4, 1829, unprecedented thousands of Americans attended the ceremonies at the Capitol, and then the noisy crowd followed their hero to the White House, where at a public reception they trampled one another and even the elegantly upholstered sofas and chairs in their eagerness to shake his hand. "It was a proud day for the people," one of the Jacksonians, Amos Kendall, reported to his newspaper in Kentucky. "General Jackson is *their own* president." But most old Federalists and all lovers of political decorum were horrified. John Marshall's friend and colleague Justice Joseph Story disgustedly remarked: "The reign of King 'Mob' seemed triumphant."

New Patterns of National Politics

The rise of Jackson coincided with a revolution in national politics. Though the new President was no democratic philosopher like Jefferson, he nevertheless held certain democratic convictions, notably the conviction that government should offer "equal protection and equal benefits" to all the people. His enemies denied that he ever really championed the people's cause, but they could not well deny that he became a living symbol of democracy or that, far more than any of his predecessors, he gave a sense of participation in government to the common man.

As President, Jackson promptly set about to "reform" the personnel procedures of the federal government. For a generation, ever since the downfall of the Federalists in 1800, there had been no complete party turnover in Washington. Officeholders accordingly stayed on year after year and election after election, many of them growing gray and some of them growing corrupt in office. "Office is considered as a species of property," Jackson told Congress, "and government rather as a means of promoting individual interests than as an instrument created solely for the service of the people." He believed that official duties could be made "so plain and simple that men of intelligence may readily qualify themselves for their performance." According to him, offices belonged to the people, not to the entrenched officeholders. Or, as one of his henchmen, William L. Marcy of

New York, more cynically put it, "To the victors belong the spoils."

A corollary to the spoils system was the doctrine of rotation in office. Since ordinary men ("of intelligence") presumably were fit or could easily be fitted for government service, and since loyal members of the victorious party deserved government jobs, a particular position should not be held too long by any one person but should be passed around, or rotated, among several deserving applicants.

The partisan motives behind the spoils system and rotation in office are obvious enough. But, at least in Jackson's day, a real democratic principle also was involved. The long continuance of the same men in office bred a bureaucracy with interests of its own—interests which might be at variance with those of the public. Frequent changes within the party and occasional changes between parties, however, meant that officeholders at any given time came fresh from the citizenry and would soon return to it. Thus the government and the people would be, to a large extent, identical. Moreover, a party gaining support by the promise of government jobs would be less dependent on private wealth for financing its activities than would a party relying on the contributions of rich men and corporations. Of course, the system eventually led to abuses, and a day arrived when, with the increasing complexity of government, the basic assumption was less true than ever— the assumption that most men by nature were qualified for most governmental duties.

In actual practice, Jackson did not make such drastic removals as his partisan critics then and afterward asserted. During the entire eight years of his Presidency he removed a total of no more than one fifth of the federal officeholders, and many of these he removed for cause, such as misuse of government funds. Proportionally, Jack-

Andrew Jackson. *Albert Gallatin once described Jackson as "a tall, lank, uncouth-looking personage, with long locks of hair hanging over his face, and a cue down his back tied in an eel-skin; his dress singular, his manners and deportment that of a rough backwoodsman." Yet Daniel Webster considered him very "presidential" in appearance, and many others testified that he could be gentlemanly, distinguished, and even elegant in bearing, though he sometimes pretended to be a half-savage boor in order to get rid of unwelcome visitors. The portrait by Ralph Earl captures Jackson's finer qualities.* (COURTESY OF THE MABEL BRADY GARVAN COLLECTION, YALE UNIVERSITY ART GALLERY)

son dismissed no more of the jobholders than Jefferson had done. Nor did he appoint illiterate coon-hunters or the like to positions requiring special training or skill. When two men of equal ability, the one a party friend and the other a party foe, applied for a particular place, that place went to the party friend, and the Jacksonians no doubt could always find one of their own number who was at least as well qualified as any member of the opposition. The fact remains, nevertheless, that the Jackson administration, adapting the spoils system from some of the states, fixed it firmly upon national politics.

Eventually the Jacksonians adopted another instrumentality of democratic politics —the national nominating convention— which was originated by the earliest of the third parties in American history, the Antimasonic party. This party was a response to widespread resentment against the secret and exclusive, hence supposedly undemocratic, Society of Freemasons. Feeling rose to new heights when, in 1826, a man named William Morgan mysteriously disappeared from his home in Batavia, New York. Since Morgan had been about to publish a book purporting to expose the secrets of Freemasonry, his friends believed that vengeful Masons had done away with him. The excitement spread, and politicians in New York, Pennsylvania, and several other states seized upon it to organize a party with popular appeal. The party was anti-Jackson as well as Antimason, Jackson being a high-ranking member of the lodge. In 1831 the Antimasons held a national convention in Harrisburg, Pennsylvania, to nominate a candidate for the next year's presidential campaign. (He ran a poor third.)

Like the spoils system, the national party convention eventually became less democratic in practice than it was in theory. In theory the convention delegates, appointed by party meetings in the various states, represented the party rank and file. In practice the proceedings came to be controlled by professional politicians. Nevertheless, the adoption of the convention system was, at least in part, an effort to give the people a voice in presidential nominations.

BIBLIOGRAPHY

S. F. Bemis, *John Quincy Adams and the Union* (1956), continues and completes the distinguished biography begun with *John Quincy Adams and the Foundations of American Foreign Policy*. B. C. Clark, *John Quincy Adams: "Old Man Eloquent"* (1932), is a fairly good brief life. To get the flavor of the Adams personality, the student should go to *The Memoirs of John Quincy Adams*, edited by C. F. Adams (12 vols., 1874–1877). A one-volume selection from these memoirs is available under the title *The Diary of John Quincy Adams*, edited by Allan Nevins.

A stimulating interpretation of Jacksonian democracy may be found in A. M. Schlesinger, Jr., *The Age of Jackson* (1945). Schlesinger emphasizes the Eastern working-class aspect of the Jackson movement and views Jackson himself as a true democratic leader. T. P. Abernethy, *From Frontier to Plantation in Tennessee* (1932), provides Jackson with an aristocratic background and questions the genuineness of his democratic feelings. The background of Tennessee politics is most fairly and completely shown in C. G. Sellers, Jr., *James K. Polk: Jacksonian, 1795–1843*

(1957). A fairly straightforward and properly colorful account of Jackson's presidential career is Marquis James, *Andrew Jackson: Portrait of a President* (1937). Jackson as a popular hero and a symbol of democracy is the theme of two perceptive books: J. W. Ward, *Andrew Jackson: Symbol for an Age* (1955), and H. C. Syrett, *Andrew Jackson: His Contribution to the American Tradition* (1953).

The most profound treatment of the popularization of politics is still M. Ostrogorski, *Democracy and the Organization of Political Parties* (2 vols., 1902). Two studies of the spoils system are C. R. Fish, *The Civil Service and the Patronage* (1905), and D. G. Fowler, *The Cabinet Politician: The Postmasters General, 1829–1909* (1943). L. D. White, *The Jacksonians: A Study in Administrative History, 1829–1861* (1954), the third in a series of similar studies, is excellent on the growth of presi-

dential powers. More studies of the development of the vote are needed, but meanwhile K. H. Porter, *A History of the Suffrage in the United States* (1918), is a useful survey. J. T. Horton, *James Kent: A Study in Conservatism, 1763–1847* (1939), illustrates the thinking of those who opposed democratic trends. Louis Hartz, *The Liberal Tradition in America* (1955), is a thoughtful essay. Democratic developments in two states are traced in D. R. Fox, *The Decline of Aristocracy in the Politics in New York* (1919), which has become something of a classic; and in A. B. Darling, *Political Changes in Massachusetts, 1824–1848* (1925). Charles McCarthy's *The Antimasonic Party* (1903) is the authority on its subject. A worshipful biography of a political rocket that fizzled is J. E. D. Shipp, *Giant Days; or, The Life and Times of William H. Crawford* (1909).

CHAPTER 18

Jackson and the Nullifiers

PRESIDENT JACKSON took office with no clearly announced program to carry out. His followers—who soon began to call themselves simply Democrats—had interests so diverse that a statement of definite aims would have alienated many of the party at the outset. This is not to say that Jackson himself was wishy-washy or lacking in convictions. Far from it. Besides believing in government by and for the common man, he stood for strong presidential leadership and, while respecting what he considered the legitimate rights of the states, he was devoted to the national Union. He did not hesitate to assert his principles when South Carolina tried to put into effect the nullification (or interposition) theory of John C. Calhoun.

Calhoun: His Theory

At the age of forty-six (in 1828) Calhoun had a promising future as well as a distinguished past. A congressional leader during the War of 1812, afterwards head of the War Department for eight years (making a record that entitles him to rank as one of the few truly great Secretaries of War), then Vice President in John Quincy Adams's administration, he now was running as the vice-presidential candidate on the Jackson ticket, and he could look forward to the Presidency itself after a term or two for Jackson—if all went well.

But the tariff question placed Calhoun in a dilemma. Once he had been a forthright protectionist, coming out strongly for the tariff of 1816, but since that time many South Carolinians had changed their minds on the subject, and so had he. Carolina cotton planters were disturbed because their plantations did not pay, or at least were less profitable than it seemed they should have been. The whole state appeared to be stagnating, its population remaining almost stationary, its countryside showing signs of ruin and decay. One reason was the exhaustion of the South Carolina soil, which could not well compete with the newly opened, fertile lands of the Southwest. But the Carolinians blamed their trouble on quite an-

States it also reduced the foreign market fo American cotton. Some exasperated Caro linians were ready to seek escape from th hated law through revolution—that is

"Fort Hill": Calhoun's Home. *Throughout his long political career John C. Calhoun spent most of his time in Washington. After 1826 his permanent home—the retreat he eagerly sought in summer—was "Fort Hill" in the South Carolina back country. The house stood on a knoll overlooking the Seneca River (and still stands there, on what is now the campus of Clemson College). From the verandas could be seen alternating patches of forest and field, the red earth white with cotton in the late summer. Far to the north and northwest could be seen the outlines of the Alleghany and Blue Ridge mountains. About 50 feet behind the house, to the left in the picture, was a small building which served as Calhoun's study.*

other cause—the tariff, in particular the "tariff of abominations," the law of 1828. They reasoned that protective duties raised the prices of the things they had to buy, whether they bought them at home or from abroad, and lowered the price of the cotton they sold, most of which was exported. They had a point: in order to export, a nation has to import, and to the extent that the tariff kept foreign goods out of the United

through secession. Here was a challenge Calhoun had to meet in order to maintain his leadership in the state and make a future for himself in national politics.

Quietly he worked out a theory to justify state action in resisting the tariff law. He intended for this action, if and when it became necessary, to be strictly legal and constitutional, not revolutionary. So he had to find a basis for his plan in the Constitution itself. In his earlier career, as a nationalist, he had said the Constitution was not a thing for logicians to exercise their ingenuity upon, but should be construed with plain good sense. Now he himself resorted to subtle and ingenious logic, discovering implications in the Constitution that were not obvious to everybody—not even to the "father of the Constitution," James Madison, who denounced the Calhoun theory when he heard of it. Calhoun believed, however, that he was following the lines laid down by Madison and Jefferson in their Virginia and Kentucky Resolutions of 1798–1799. Indeed, his reasoning was quite similar to theirs, but he carried it farther than they had done, and he provided a definite procedure for state action, which they had not.

Calhoun started his reasoning with the assumption that sovereignty, the ultimate source of power, lay in the states considered as separate political communities. He went on to assume that these separate peoples had created the federal government, through their conventions that ratified the Constitution after it had been drawn up. Putting this in legal terminology, he described the states (meaning their peoples, not their governments) as the "principals," the federal government as their "agent," and the Constitution as a "compact" containing instructions within which the agent was to operate.

From these assumptions the rest of his theory followed logically enough. The Supreme Court was not competent to judge whether acts of Congress were constitutional, since the Court, like the Congress, was only a branch of an agency created by the states. No, Calhoun reasoned, the principals must decide, each for itself, whether their instructions were violated. If Congress enacted a law of doubtful constitutionality—say, a protective tariff—a state could "interpose" to frustrate the law. The people of the state could hold a convention, and if

(through their elected delegates) they decided that Congress had gone too far, they could declare the federal law null and void within their state. In that state the law would remain inoperative until three fourths of the whole number of states should ratify an amendment to the Constitution specifically assigning Congress the power in question. And if the other states should ever get around to doing this, the nullifying state would then submit—or it could secede.

Calhoun thought of nullification as a way of avoiding secession, not as a step toward it. He felt he had elaborated a "conservative principle," one tending to conserve and not to destroy the Union. It required agreement on federal policy not merely from the people of the nation as a whole, the "numerical" or "absolute" majority, but also from the peoples of the separate states, the "concurrent" majority, as he called it. Since

Calhoun's Study at "Fort Hill." *When Calhoun was home, on his South Carolina plantation, he rose about four, then rode or walked about the plantation for an hour, and read or wrote in the study until eight. After breakfast he returned to the study for the rest of the morning. In this small, simply furnished room he kept his library, prepared much of his correspondence and many of his reports and speeches, and conversed with politicians from near and far. The building was always locked when he was not in it.*

each state could veto a federal law, all the states would have to agree before any national policy could be made and carried out. Calhoun was confident that this very requirement of unanimity would cause the people of every state, North and South, to have a care for sectional interests other than their own. Thus the sections would be encouraged to cooperate, and the Union would be strengthened rather than weakened.

The legislature of South Carolina published Calhoun's first statement of his theory, anonymously, in a document entitled *The South Carolina Exposition and Protest* (1828). This condemned the recent tariff as unconstitutional, unfair, and unendurable—a law fit to be nullified. Calhoun had good reason for not wishing to be identified publicly as the author of the document. It was bound to arouse a certain amount of opposition in parts of the country, and of course he hoped to be re-elected Vice President and later to be elected President.

After the Jackson-Calhoun ticket had won its victory at the polls, Calhoun was no more eager than before to see nullification put into effect. He waited, hoping that Jackson as President would persuade Congress to make drastic reductions in tariff rates and thus mollify the outraged Carolina planters. It remained to be seen what chance Calhoun would have for the Presidency as Jackson's friend and successor. As soon as the major appointments had been made, he gained an inkling of his importance, or unimportance, in the new administration. He then realized he had a powerful rival for Jackson's favor in the person of Martin Van Buren.

Van Buren to the Fore

Van Buren, about the same age as Calhoun and equally ambitious, was quite different in background and personality. Born of Dutch ancestry in the village of Kinderhook near Albany, New York, he advanced himself through skillful maneuvering to the position of United States Senator (1820–1828). He also made himself the party boss of his state by organizing and leading the Albany Regency, the Democratic machine of New York. Though he supported Crawford for President in 1824, he afterwards became one of the most ardent of Jacksonians, doing much to carry his state for Jackson in 1828 while getting himself elected as governor. By this time he had a reputation as something of a political wizard. Short and slight, with reddish gold sideburns and a quiet manner, he gained a variety of revealing nicknames, such as "the Sage of Kinderhook," "the Little Magician," and "the Red Fox." Never giving or taking offense, he was in temperament just the opposite of the choleric Jackson, yet the two were about to become the closest of friends. Van Buren promptly resigned the governorship and went to Washington when Jackson called him to head the new cabinet as Secretary of State.

Except for Van Buren, this cabinet contained no one of more than ordinary talent. It was intended (as cabinets usually are) to represent and harmonize the sectional and factional interests within the party. No Virginian was included: for the first time since 1789 Virginia provided neither the President nor any of the Secretaries. Friends of both Van Buren and Calhoun were given places. This cabinet was not intended to form a council of advisers: Jackson did not even call cabinet meetings.

Instead, he relied on an unofficial circle of political cronies who came to be known as the "Kitchen Cabinet." Noteworthy in this group were several newspaper editors, among them Isaac Hill, a hunchbacked master of invective from New Hampshire, and Amos Kendall and Francis P. Blair from Kentucky. Blair edited (after 1830) the administration's official organ, the Washington *Globe*. The close-mouthed, asthmatic, "invisible" Kendall was said to be the genius who, behind the scenes, really ran the administration. While doubtless influential, he

was no more so than several others, especially Jackson's old Tennessee friend and
political manager William B. Lewis, who
roomed at the White House and had ready
access to the President. Soon to be the most
important of all was Van Buren, a member
of both the official and the unofficial cabinet.

Vice President Calhoun, to his dismay,
saw signs of Van Buren's growing influence
when he viewed the division of the spoils.
Not only did Van Buren get cabinet places
for himself and his friends: he also secured
the appointment of his followers to most of
the lesser offices. Already, beneath the surface, there was the beginning of a rift between the Vice President and the President.
Then Calhoun and Jackson were further
estranged, and at the same time Jackson and
Van Buren were brought closer together, in
consequence of a curious quarrel over a
woman and etiquette.

Peggy O'Neil, the bright-eyed, vivacious
daughter of a Washington tavern-keeper,
was the kind of woman whom men ad-
mire and women dislike. Andrew Jackson thought highly of Peggy when, as
Senator from Tennessee, he lived at her
father's inn, the Franklin House. Jackson's
Tennessee colleague and fellow boarder,
Senator John H. Eaton, grew extremely
fond of her. While still a girl she married
a man named Timberlake, who was away
most of the time attending to his duties as
a purser in the navy. During her husband's
absences Senator Eaton squired her about,
and after Timberlake's death at sea he took
the young widow as his wife, with Jackson's
blessing. Washington gossips told and retold scandalous stories about her relationship with Eaton while her former husband
had been still alive. All the talk would have
amounted to little if Jackson had not appointed Eaton as his Secretary of War and
thus made Mrs. Eaton a cabinet wife.

In those days the administration wives
considered themselves the elite of Washing-

ton society. For this select circle the War
Secretary's wife was morally unfit, or so
most of the others maintained. Led by Mrs.
Calhoun, they snubbed Mrs. Eaton at offi-

Martin Van Buren. *As a younger man, Van
Buren had the same shrewd, kindly expression
as in this picture, taken when he was an aging, retired politician, living as a country gentleman at "Lindenwald," his estate near Albany,
New York. The photographer was Matthew B.
Brady. As a boy in 1839, when daguerreotypes
were first introduced into the United States
from France, Brady became interested in the
new art, and later he rose to be the foremost
American photographer of the nineteenth century. A daguerreotype was made by exposing
a silver plate to light and then treating it
chemically. In 1855 Brady began using the wet-
plate process—glass plates were coated with
silver salts and had to be exposed and developed while wet. Though an improvement on
daguerreotypy, the wet-plate process required
long exposures and cumbersome equipment.
Van Buren's picture was taken by this process.*

cial balls, refused to call on her, declined to
invite her to their homes. Jackson was furi-
ous. While his nephew's wife, the mistress
of the White House, sided with the offended

wives, the President chivalrously took up Mrs. Eaton's cause. His own wife, the dead Rachel, had been slandered by his political enemies, and he was confident that Peggy

courtesy he could. Thus he more and more ingratiated himself with the President.

The Eaton affair dragged on, and finally (1831) Jackson decided to get rid of his

Mrs. Eaton and Jackson's Cabinet. *This cartoon of the 1830's pictures Peggy Eaton as a dancing girl being presented by her tavern-keeping father to the President and the secretaries. Jackson says: "Charming creature—I've not lost all my penchant for pretty women. I take 'the responsibility' of introducing her to the Cabinet." Van Buren, at the extreme right, remarks: "I like her rapid movements, her quick changes, her graceful transitions. She is of my school." Note Peggy's upswept hair-do and her stylish dress, with low-cut neck, leg-of-mutton sleeves, narrow waist, and full skirt.* (LIBRARY OF CONGRESS)

too was virtuous, an innocent victim of dirty politics. He not only defended her virtue: he demanded that his secretaries and associates concede it and treat her with respect. Even if they had been willing, they had their wives to contend with, and these ladies would not yield. Calhoun, for one, had no choice but to take sides against Mrs. Eaton, which meant taking sides against her champion, Jackson.

With Van Buren the case was different. A widower, without daughters, he had no womenfolk to worry about. From the outset he cultivated the Eatons, staged receptions for them, and showed them every

uncooperative secretaries and reorganize his cabinet. Van Buren resigned and so did two of his friends; the others took the hint and submitted their resignations too. Jackson appointed a new cabinet which on the whole was considerably stronger than the first one. Thereafter he relied more on his official advisers, less on the Kitchen Cabinet. As for Van Buren, he was sent to England as American minister, the appointment being made while the Senate was not in session. When the Senate met, there was a tie vote on the question of confirming the appointment, and Calhoun as the presiding officer broke the tie by casting his own ballot against Van Buren. This brought Van Buren home but gave no advantage to Calhoun.

Already Jackson had picked Van Buren for the presidential succession and had marked Calhoun as no friend but the worst of foes. The final break came when Jackson learned the inside story of a Monroe cabinet meeting years earlier. At the time of Jackson's Florida raid (1817) and for a long time afterward he supposed that Calhoun, as Monroe's Secretary of War, had stood up for him when others in the administration proposed to punish him for his action. The truth, as Calhoun's enemies at last convinced Jackson, was quite otherwise.

If there had been only personal differences between the two men, their parting would have been less significant than it actually was. But there were also differences of principle. At the height of the Eaton affair the opposing views of Jackson and Calhoun were dramatically revealed in consequence of a great debate on the nature of the Constitution.

The Webster-Hayne Debate

The Webster-Hayne debate, in January 1830, grew out of a Senate discussion of public lands, a discussion provoked when a Senator from Connecticut suggested that all land sales and surveys be discontinued for the time being. This suggestion immediately aroused Senator Thomas Hart Benton of Missouri, once Jackson's antagonist in a wild frontier brawl, now the Jacksonian leader in the Senate and a sturdy defender of the West. Always suspicious of New England, he charged that the proposal to stop land sales was intended to keep New England workers from going West and thus to choke off the growth and prosperity of the frontier.

A young, debonair Senator from South Carolina, Robert Y. Hayne, took up the argument after Benton. Hayne and other Southerners hoped to get Western support

for their drive to lower the tariff, and at the moment they were willing to grant abundant and cheap lands to the Westerners in exchange for such support. He hinted that the South and the West might well combine in self-defense against the Northeast.

Daniel Webster, now a Senator from Massachusetts, once had been a state-rights and antitariff man but, like Calhoun, only in reverse, he had changed his position with the changing interests of his section. The day after Hayne's speech he took the floor in an effort to head off the threatened rapprochement of the West and the South and thus to protect the interests of New England, including the tariff interest. Ignoring Benton, he directed his remarks to Hayne and, through him, to Calhoun in the Vice President's chair. He reviewed much of the history of the republic, with occasional disregard for historical facts, to prove that New England always had been the friend of the West. Referring to the tariff of 1816 he said that New England was not responsible for beginning the protectionist policy but had accepted it after other sections had fixed it upon the nation. Then, changing the subject, he spoke gravely of disunionists and disunionism in South Carolina.

Thus he challenged Hayne to meet him, not on the original grounds of the public lands and the tariff, but on the issue of state rights versus national power, an issue that could be made to seem one of treason versus patriotism. And in due time Hayne, coached by Calhoun, came back with a flashing defense of the nullification theory while Calhoun in his chair looked down upon him with occasional nods and smiles of approval, and Webster in his seat took notes, leaned back in thought, or grunted in audible dissent.

It took Webster two afternoons to deliver what schoolboys were afterward to know as the second reply to Hayne. The crowd in the gallery and on the floor, including many gaily bonneted ladies, expected a fine performance in the country's greatest show, the Senate forum, and they were not disap-

erty *and* Union, now and for ever, one and inseparable!"

He was speaking not only to the Senate and the gallery but also to the nation at

Webster Replying to Hayne. *Hayne is sitting in the front center, with his hands together. Calhoun, presiding as Vice President, leans intently on his desk, in the shadow at the extreme left. Note the bonneted ladies in the gallery and the page-boy in the left foreground. From G. P. A. Healy's painting, which hangs in Faneuil Hall, Boston.* (FRICK ART REFERENCE LIBRARY)

pointed: Webster was at his eloquent best. With infinite variety, now calm and factual, now electric with emotion, he held his audience hour after hour, sometimes sending shivers through the crowd, as when he shook his finger at the Vice President and spoke directly to him in a cavernous, rumbling voice.

"I go for the Constitution as it is, and for the Union as it is," he declaimed, as he turned to an exposition of the "true principles" of the Constitution. "It is, Sir, the people's Constitution, the people's government, made for the people, made by the people, and answerable to the people." And he meant one people, the whole nation. He concluded with the ringing appeal: "Lib-

large. Long since, with the cooperation of Chief Justice John Marshall, he had made the doctrine of national power prevail before the Supreme Court, and now he was going to educate the public. Within a few months thousands of copies of his address, in at least twenty different editions, were circulated over the country. Never before had a speech in Congress been so widely read—or so enthusiastically acclaimed.

A group of New York businessmen thanked Webster with a public dinner, and in his remarks to them he made clear that they had a more than sentimental attachment to the Union ("as it is") and the Constitution ("as it is"). "Without national character, without public credit, without systematic finance, without uniformity of commercial laws, all other advantages possessed by this city would have decayed and perished, like unripe fruit," he reminded the New Yorkers. "To speak of arresting the laws of the Union, of interposing state power in matters of commerce and revenue, of weakening the full and just authority of the general government, would be, in regard to this city, but another mode of speaking of commercial ruin, of abandoned wharfs, of vacated houses, of diminished and dispersing population, of bankrupt merchants, of mechanics without employment, and laborers without bread."

But Calhoun's followers in South Carolina had a very different conception of their own interests, and they took a very different view of the merits of the Webster-Hayne debate. They were sure that Hayne had the better of the argument. The important question at the moment, however, was what President Jackson thought, what side if any he would take.

An answer soon was given at a Democratic banquet which was supposed to honor Thomas Jefferson as the founder of the party. At the banquet the friends of Calhoun hoped to build up the alliance of South and West and strengthen his presidential prospects by identifying his principles with those of Jefferson. As was customary at such affairs, the guests settled down after dinner to an evening of drinking toasts. The President, forewarned by Van Buren, was ready with a toast of his own, which he had written down, underscoring certain words. When his turn came, he stood up and proclaimed: "Our *Federal* Union—*It must be preserved*." While he spoke he looked sternly at Calhoun. Van Buren, who stood on his chair the better to see from the far end of the table, thought he saw Calhoun's hand shake and a trickle of wine run down the outside of his glass. Calhoun responded to Jackson's toast with his own: "The Un-

ion—next to our liberty most dear. May we always remember that it can only be preserved by distributing evenly the benefits and the burthens of the Union."

Political wiseacres inferred that the President had endorsed the constitutional views of the opposition Senator, Webster, and not the views of his fellow Democrat, Calhoun.

The Veto, the Indians, and Georgia

Jackson's pro-Union and antinullification feelings, as expressed in his Jefferson's Birthday toast, did not mean that he agreed with Webster on such questions as the tariff and internal improvements, nor did it mean that he was opposed to state rights as such. On the contrary, as he had declared in his inaugural address, he believed in none but "constitutional" undertakings by the federal government. During his administration he readily vetoed laws that he thought exceeded the powers originally granted to Congress by the states; in fact, he used the veto more freely than any President before him. And he stood up for state rights when Georgia defied the Supreme Court in dealing with the Indians within its borders.

The Maysville Road Bill (1830) brought on the most significant of Jackson's vetoes. This bill, by authorizing the government to buy stock in a private company, would have given a federal subsidy for the construction of a turnpike from Maysville to Lexington, within the state of Kentucky. The Maysville pike was a segment of a projected highway which was to form a great Southwestern branch of the National Road. Nevertheless, since the pike itself was an intrastate and not an interstate project, Jackson doubted whether Congress constitutionally could give aid to it. Earlier (in 1822) President Monroe, vetoing the Cumberland Road Bill, had declared that the federal government should support only those improvements which were of general rather than local importance, and Jackson then had agreed with Monroe. Now, with Van Buren's assistance, Jackson prepared a veto message based on similar grounds. He also urged economy, denounced the selfish "scramble for appropriations," and stressed the desirability of paying off the national debt. Though Jackson also refused to sign other appropriation bills, he did not object to every proposal for federal spending to build roads or improve rivers and harbors. During his two terms such expenditures continued to mount, far exceeding those of even the John Quincy Adams administration.

The Maysville veto was not popular in the West, where better transportation was a never-ending demand, but Jackson's Indian policy was wholeheartedly approved in both the West and the South. As an old Indian fighter, Jackson was no lover of the red man, and he desired to continue and expedite the program, which Jefferson had begun, of removing all the tribes to the west of the Mississippi. The land between the Missouri and the Rockies, according to such explorers as Lewis and Clark and Stephen H. Long, was supposed to be a vast desert, unfit for white habitation. Why not leave that land for the Indians? By the Indian Removal Act of 1830 Congress proposed to exchange tribal lands within the states for new homes in the West, and by the Indian Intercourse Act of 1834 Congress marked off an Indian country and provided for a string of forts to keep the Indians inside it and the whites outside. Meanwhile the President saw that treaties, nearly a hundred in all, were negotiated with the various tribes and that reluctant tribesmen along with their women and children were moved west, with the prodding of the army.

In the process of Indian removal there was much tragedy and a certain amount of violence. When (1832) Chief Black Hawk with a thousand of his hungry Sac and Fox followers—men, women, and children—recrossed the Mississippi into Illinois to grow corn, the frontiersmen feared an invasion. Militiamen and regular troops soon drove the unfortunate Indians into Wisconsin and then slaughtered most of them as they tried to escape down the Wisconsin River. Such was the Black Hawk War, in which Abraham Lincoln was a captain of militia (he saw no action) and Jefferson Davis a lieutenant in the regular army. More serious was the Seminole War. It began when Chief Osceola led an uprising of his tribesmen (including runaway Negroes), who refused to move west in accordance with a treaty of 1833, and the fighting lasted off and on for several years. Jackson sent troops to Florida, but the Seminoles with their Negro associates were masters of guerrilla warfare in the jungly Everglades. Even after Osceola had been treacherously captured under a flag of truce and had died in prison, the red and black rebels continued to resist.

Unlike the Sacs and Foxes or the Seminoles, the Cherokees in Georgia were a civilized people, with a written language of their own (invented by the half-breed Sequoyah in 1821) and with a settled way of life as farmers. Yet the state of Georgia, after getting rid of the Creeks, was eager to remove the Cherokees also and open their millions of acres to white occupation. In 1827 these Indians adopted a constitution and declared their independence as the Cherokee Nation. Promptly the Georgia legislature extended its laws over them and directed the seizure of their territory. Hiring a prominent lawyer, the Cherokees appealed to the Supreme Court. In the case of *Cherokee Nation* v. *Georgia* (1831) Chief Justice Marshall gave the majority opinion that the Indians were "domestic dependent nations" and had a right to the land they occupied until they voluntarily ceded it to the United States. In another case, *Worcester* v. *Georgia* (1832), Marshall and the Court held that the Cherokee Nation was a definite political community with territory over which the laws of Georgia had no force and into which Georgians could not enter without permission.

President Jackson did not sympathize with the Cherokees as President Adams had done with the Creeks. Vigorously supporting Georgia's position, Jackson did nothing to aid the Indians or to see that the rulings of the Supreme Court were carried out. The Chief Justice had implied that it was the President's duty to uphold the rights of the Indians. Jackson's attitude is well expressed in the comment attributed to him: "John Marshall has made his decision; now let him enforce it." The decision was never enforced. After a few years the Cherokees signed a treaty and most of them migrated, some at the point of a bayonet, to what afterwards became Oklahoma. About a thousand fled across the state line to North Carolina, where eventually the federal government provided a reservation for them.

In a sense Georgia nullified federal authority when, proclaiming state rights, she flouted the rulings of the highest court of the United States. In doing so, nevertheless, the state had the backing of the President. But when, in the midst of the Georgia controversy, another state attempted out-and-out nullification of an act of Congress, Jackson reacted quite differently.

South Carolina Interposes

After waiting four years for Congress to undo the "tariff of abominations," the South Carolina followers of Calhoun had little patience left, and they lost that little when Congress denied them any real relief in the tariff of 1832. Few of the New England supporters of the tariff were willing to concede a thing. John Quincy Adams, now a congressman, tried to persuade Webster to accept a reduction of duties in general and a repeal of the duty on raw wool in particular. Webster refused. "He said, no, he could not do that," Adams recorded; "it had

prodigiously increased the breed of sheep, and the repeal of it would be very unpopular in New England." The wool-growers of New England must not be hurt, no matter how loudly the cotton-growers of South Carolina might complain. Though making certain changes in individual rates, the new law did not significantly lower the tariff as a whole.

Some of the South Carolinians now were ready for revolt, and had it not been for Calhoun's program and leadership, they might have taken even more drastic action than they did. Having ceased to be Jackson's friend and prospective successor, Calhoun had come out openly for nullification, elaborated the doctrine further, and induced the extremists to adopt it as their remedy. To nullify or not to nullify—that was the question in the state election of 1832. The nullifiers proved to be the majority, but their opponents (who called themselves Unionists) made up a large minority, the vote being approximately 23,000 to 17,000. Without delay the newly elected legislature called for the election of delegates to a state convention. The disheartened Unionists scarcely bothered to campaign. With large and enthusiastic majorities the convention adopted an ordinance of nullification, which declared null and void the tariffs of 1828 and 1832 and forbade the collection of duties within the state. The legislature then passed laws to enforce the ordinance and make preparations for military defense. Needing a strong man to take command at home, and another to present the South Carolina case ably in Washington, the nullifiers arranged for Hayne to become governor and for Calhoun to replace Hayne as Senator. So Calhoun resigned as Vice President.

While the nullifiers prepared for war they hoped for peace. According to the Calhoun theory the federal government had no rightful recourse, and the rest of the states could

do nothing except to amend the Constitution. When the theory was put to the test,
however, not a single state came to South
Carolina's support. A few of the Southern

hang Calhoun. Officially he proclaimed
that nullification was treason and its adherents traitors. In his proclamation, written
with the help of Edward Livingston, the

Nullification Ordinance
1832

Having failed to obtain relief from what most planters considered an
oppressive and unfair tariff, South Carolina put Calhoun's theory into practice with the following resolutions:

"Whereas the Congress of the United States, by various acts, purporting
to be acts laying duties and imposts on foreign imports, but in reality
intended for the protection of domestic manufactures, and the giving of
bounties to classes and individuals engaged in particular employments, at
the expense and to the injury and oppression of other classes and individuals, . . . hath exceeded its just powers under the Constitution,
which confers on it no authority to afford such protection, and hath violated the true meaning and intent of the Constitution, which provides for
equality in imposing the burthens of taxation upon the several States and
portions of the Confederacy. . . .

"*We, therefore, the people of the State of South Carolina, in Convention
assembled, do declare and ordain* . . . That the several acts and parts of
acts of the Congress of the United States, purporting to be laws for the
imposing of duties and imposts on the importation of foreign commodities . . . [especially the tariff acts of 1828 and 1832] . . . are unauthorized by the Constitution of the United States, and violate the true meaning
and intent thereof, and are null, void, and no law, nor binding upon this
State. . . ."

---

states were sympathetic, Virginia in particular, but none of them endorsed nullification—not even Georgia, which was noted
for its own espousal of state rights. Georgians and other Southerners of course admired Jackson for his stand on the question
of Indian removal. But whereas Jackson
had acted as if Georgia's Indian policies
were none of the federal government's business, he took a very different stand when
confronted with South Carolina's nullification attempt.

Unofficially the President threatened to

new Secretary of State, Jackson said: "I
consider, then, the power to annul a law of
the United States, assumed by one State, incompatible with the existence of the Union,
contradicted expressly by the letter of the
Constitution, unauthorized by its spirit, inconsistent with every principle on which it
is founded, and destructive of the great object for which it was formed." He assured
the people of South Carolina that there was
no way constitutionally and peaceably to
resist the nation's laws. "They who told you
that you might peaceably prevent their [the

laws'] execution deceived you—they could not have been deceived themselves." Jackson did not confine himself to mere words. Cooperating closely with the Unionists of South Carolina, he also took steps to strengthen the federal forts in the state, ordering General Winfield Scott and a warship and several revenue cutters to Charleston.

When Congress met, the President asked for specific authority with which to handle the crisis. His followers introduced a "force bill" authorizing him to use the army and navy to see that acts of Congress were obeyed. At the same time he was willing to

onized the South Carolina extremists. Violence seemed a real possibility early in 1833, as Calhoun took his place in the Senate to defend his theory and its practice. He introduced a set of resolutions on the "constitutional compact," then made a speech against the force bill.

Webster's reply to Calhoun (February 16, 1833), if less colorful than his reply to Hayne three years earlier, dwelt more fully and more cogently upon the constitutional issues at stake. The Constitution, Webster argued, was no mere compact among sovereign states that might secede at will. It was an "executed contract," an agreement to

Jackson's Proclamation

1832

"Our present Constitution was formed . . . in vain if this fatal doctrine [nullification] prevails. It was formed for important objects that are announced in the preamble, made in the name and by the authority of the people of the United States, whose delegates framed and whose conventions approved it. The most important among these objects—that which is placed first in rank, on which all the others rest—is *'to form a more perfect union.'* Now, is it possible that even if there were no express provision giving supremacy to the Constitution and laws of the United States over those of the States, can it be conceived that an instrument made for the purpose of *'forming a more perfect union'* than that of the Confederation could be so constructed by the assembled wisdom of our country as to substitute for that Confederation a form of government dependent for its existence on the local interest, the party spirit, of a State? Every man of plain, unsophisticated understanding who hears the question will give such an answer as will preserve the Union. Metaphysical subtlety, in pursuit of an impracticable theory, could alone have devised one that is calculated to destroy it. . . .

"The laws of the United States must be executed. I have no discretionary power on the subject; my duty is emphatically pronounced in the Constitution."

make concessions on the tariff question, and his followers also proposed a bill reducing the general level of duties. The force bill, like Jackson's proclamation, further antag-

set up a permanent government, supreme within its allotted sphere and acting directly upon the people as a whole. Webster dismissed secession as a revolutionary but not a constitutional right, then denounced nullification as no right at all. The nullifiers, he said, rejected "the first great principle of all republican liberty; that is, that the majority must govern." They pretended to be concerned about minority rights, but did they practice what they preached? "Look to South Carolina, at the present moment. How far are the rights of minorities there respected?" Obviously the nullificationist majority was proceeding with a "relentless disregard" for the rights of the Unionist minority—"a minority embracing, as the gentleman himself will admit, a large portion of the worth and respectability of the state."

After Calhoun came back with a vigorous restatement of his "compact" theory, he and his friends were sure that they had won the argument, just as they had been with respect to Hayne three years before. Both times Webster and his admirers were equally confident that *he* had won. In their appeals to the past, Hayne and Calhoun and Webster all stood on rather dubious grounds. As we have seen, the nullifiers found in the Constitution occult meanings that Madison, one of its chief authors, could not discover. And Webster drew from its preamble—"we the people"—inferences that historically were not justified. But Webster was on the side of the winning future: in the years ahead his ideas and not Calhoun's were to prevail.

At the moment Calhoun was in something of a predicament. South Carolina, standing alone, itself divided, could not hope to prevail if a showdown with the federal government should come. If the nullifiers meekly yielded, however, they would lose face and their leader would be politically ruined. Calhoun was saved by the timely intervention of the Great Pacificator,

Henry Clay. Newly elected to the Senate, Clay in consultation with Calhoun devised a compromise scheme by which the tariff would be lowered year after year, reaching in 1842 approximately the same level as in 1816. Calhoun was glad to endorse this plan as against the administration's tariff bill, which if passed would have redounded to the credit of Van Buren and not to the credit of either Clay or Calhoun. Finally Clay's compromise was carried, but so was the force bill, on the same day (March 1, 1833). Webster consistently opposed any concessions to the nullifiers, but Jackson was satisfied: he signed the new tariff measure as well as the force bill.

In South Carolina the Convention reassembled and repealed its ordinance of nullification as applied to the tariffs of 1828 and 1832. Then, as if to have the last word, the convention adopted a new ordinance nullifying the force act! This proceeding meant little, since the force act would not go into effect anyhow, the original ordinance (against which it was directed) having been withdrawn. The second nullification was intended to reinforce the impression that Calhoun's program was a success and was still to be reckoned with. Though Calhoun and his followers, having brought about tariff reduction, claimed a victory for nullification, the system had not worked out in the way its sponsors had intended. Calhoun had learned a lesson: no state could assert and maintain its rights by independent action. Thereafter, while continuing to talk of state rights and nullification, he devoted himself to building up a sense of Southern solidarity so that, when another trial should come, the whole section might be prepared to act as a unit in resisting federal authority.

➤➤➤➤➤➤➤➤➤➤⟵⟵⟵⟵⟵⟵⟵⟵⟵

BIBLIOGRAPHY

Sections, sectional issues, and sectional leaders are discussed by a master in F. J. Turner's *The United States, 1830–1850: the Nation and Its Sections* (1935). See also C. S. Sydnor, *The Development of Southern Sectionalism, 1819–1848* (1948).

Claude Bowers, *The Party Battles of the Jackson Period* (1922), deals interestingly in personalities, including Peggy O'Neil Timberlake Eaton. She tells her own story in *The Autobiography of Peggy Eaton* (1932) and is also the subject of a biography by Queena Pollock, *Peggy Eaton: Democracy's Mistress* (1931). Far more weighty in subject matter and in treatment is W. B. Hatcher, *Edward Livingston: Jeffersonian Republican and Jacksonian Democrat* (1940), a biography of Jackson's braintruster and Secretary of State. J. A. Garraty, *Silas Wright* (1949), reveals the career of a Jackson henchman and revises the history of the tariff of 1828.

On nullification, C. M. Wiltse's *John C. Calhoun: Nullifier, 1829–1839* (1949) is excellent in dealing with events, though a little less satisfactory in explaining theory.

Richard Hofstadter makes up for this lack in his *The American Political Tradition* (1948), which contains a chapter analyzing the Calhoun philosophy with deep perception. C. S. Boucher, *The Nullification Controversy in South Carolina* (1916), is a sympathetic account. Frederic Bancroft, *Calhoun and the South Carolina Nullification Movement* (1928), is less friendly.

H. T. Malone, *Cherokees of the Old South* (1956), presents the history of the tribesmen down to the time of their expulsion from their ancestral home. A. H. Abel, *The History of Events Resulting in Indian Consolidation West of the Mississippi* (1908), is fairly exhaustive. Grant Foreman, *Indian Removal: The Emigration of the Five Civilized Tribes* (1932), is reliable and readable. U. B. Phillips, *Georgia and State Rights* (1902), makes clear the white point of view on the Indian question. A tragic leader speaks in *Black Hawk: An Autobiography* (1955), edited by Donald Jackson. This probably contains Black Hawk's own words, though its authenticity has been questioned.

CHAPTER 19

Bank War and Panic

CRISIS FOLLOWED CRISIS during Jackson's Presidency. During his first term the big issue was that of the tariff and nullification, culminating in South Carolina's challenge to the Union. During his second term the big issue was that of banking and public finance, involving in particular the Bank of the United States. This issue brought about a realignment of factions and leaders, drawing together Webster, Clay, and Calhoun in opposition to Jackson, as the Whig party grew out of the National Republican organization to contest with the Democrats. Nevertheless, though declining a third term for himself, Jackson managed to gain a third term for his party and its principles by hand-picking his successor, Van Buren. Soon after Van Buren's inauguration the Panic of 1837 struck; and Whigs blamed it on Jackson's financial policies. It gave them added reason to doubt whether Jackson had been a wise and truly great President. On this question, histo-

rians still differ, but none of them doubts that he was an unusually powerful President, one who both as a person and as a symbol dominated the politics of his time.

Bank and the Election of 1832

The Bank of the United States was a private corporation with a charter from the federal government, which owned one fifth of the stock. It was a monopoly, having an exclusive right to hold the government's deposits. With its headquarters in Philadelphia and its branches in twenty-nine other cities, it also did a tremendous business in general banking, totaling about $70 million a year. Its services were important to the national economy because of the credit it provided for profit-making enterprises, because of its banknotes which circulated throughout the country as a dependable medium of exchange, and because of the restraining effect which its policies had upon the less well managed banks chartered by the various states.

Nicholas Biddle, president of the Bank from 1823 on, had done much to put the years after he took charge he made these decisions according, as a rule, to financial considerations. A banker, not a politician, he had no desire to mix in politics. But

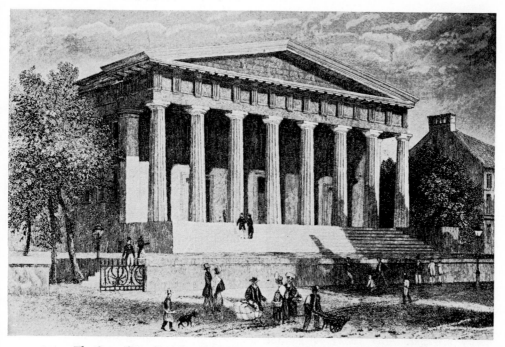

The Second Bank of the United States. *Architecturally, the home office building of the Bank, in Philadelphia, was an excellent example of the Greek Revival style. In 1818 architects were invited to submit competitive plans for "a chaste imitation of Grecian architecture." William Strickland won the competition with a design modeled on that of the Parthenon of ancient Athens. Benjamin H. Latrobe, who had submitted a similar plan, charged that Strickland had stolen the Latrobe design. After the expiration of the Bank's charter, the building became the Philadelphia Custom House.*

company on a sound and prosperous basis. A member of an aristocratic Philadelphia family, Biddle was educated at the University of Pennsylvania and thereafter devoted himself to a number of intellectual interests, including poetry. He personally owned a large proportion of the bank's stock, so much of it that together with two other large stockholders he controlled the bank. He could and did choose the officials of the branches, decide what loans were to be made, and set the interest rates. For several

he finally concluded it was necessary to do so in self-defense when, with the encouragement of Jackson, popular opposition to the Bank rose to a threatening pitch.

Opposition came from two very different groups, the "soft-money" and the "hard-money" men. The former, consisting largely of the state bankers and their friends, objected to the Bank of the United States because it restrained the state banks from issuing notes as freely as some of them would have liked, through its policy of collecting such notes and presenting them for payment in cash. These critics of the Bank desired more paper money (that is, banknotes circulating as money), not less. The other

Nicholas Biddle. *Before becoming president of the Bank of the United States, Biddle edited a literary magazine. After failing to get the Bank's federal charter renewed, he secured a state charter from Pennsylvania, but his new bank collapsed during the depression following the Panic of 1837. Biddle died penniless and disgraced in 1844. Without doubt he was a man of unusual ability as a banker, but in his "war" with Jackson he seems to have been misguided, though he has strong defenders among experts in American economic history. This portrait is from a rotogravure after a painting by Thomas Sully, a Philadelphia artist who is best known for his historical canvas, "Washington Crossing the Delaware."*

set of critics, the hard-money people, had the opposite complaint. Believing in coin as the only safe currency, these people condemned all banks of issue—all banks issuing banknotes—whether chartered by the states as all but one of them were, or by the federal government as the Bank alone was.

Jackson himself was a hard-money man. At one time in his life he had dealt in a grandiose land and mercantile speculations based on paper credit. Then a financial panic (1797) ruined his business and put him deeply into debt. Thereafter he was suspicious of all banks. During the banking controversy in Tennessee which followed the Panic of 1819, he stood consistently against all proposals to set up a state bank as a means of debtor relief. If such an institution were established, he once wrote, "the imprudent speculator may be enabled to extricate himself from his pecuniary embarrassments but the burthen must ultimately fall upon the honest farmer and industrious tradesman." As early as 1820 he said he considered the state banks and the national bank alike to be unconstitutional. After he became President he raised the question, in his inaugural address and in other statements, whether the charter of the Bank of the United States should be renewed. Unless renewed, it would expire in 1836.

To preserve the institution, Biddle began to grant banking favors to influential men in the hope of winning them to his side. At first he sought to cultivate Jackson's friends, with some success in a few instances. Then he turned more and more to Jackson's opponents. He extended loans on easy terms to several prominent newspaper editors, to a number of important state politicians, and to more than fifty Congressmen and Senators. In particular, he relied upon Senators Clay and Webster, the latter of whom was connected with the bank in various ways—as legal counsel, director of the Boston branch, frequent and heavy borrower, and Biddle's personal friend. The banker did not exploit his political adherents any more than they exploited him. Some of them virtually blackmailed and bled him, as did Webster, who wrote him at a critical moment: "I have had an application to be concerned, professionally, against the Bank, which I have declined, of course, although I believe my retainer has not been renewed or *refreshed* as usual. If it be wished that my relation to the Bank should be continued, it may be well to send me the usual retainers."

Jackson, already suspecting that Biddle had used the Bank's influence against him in the election of 1828, heard rumors enough of Biddle's subsequent activities. Still, the administration refrained from firing the first shot in the "bank war" which was about to begin. Biddle started the war. Clay, Webster, and other advisers persuaded him to apply to Congress for a recharter bill in 1832, four years ahead of the expiration date. Expecting to be the National Republican candidate, Clay desired an issue for the presidential campaign, and despite the mounting criticism of the Bank he imagined that the recharter issue would be a popular one. He assured Biddle that Congress would

pass the bank bill and that Jackson would then find himself in a dilemma from which the Bank was bound to gain its objective: a renewal of its charter. If Jackson signed the bill, well and good. If Jackson vetoed it he would lose the election, and the new administration would see to the recharter. Thus contended Clay.

After investigating the Bank and its business, Congress passed the recharter bill. At once Jackson vetoed it, sending it back to Congress with a stirring message in which he denounced the Bank as unconstitutional, undemocratic, and un-American. Though Marshall long since had asserted its constitutionality in the case of *McCulloch* v. *Maryland*, Jackson insisted that the President had as much right and duty to interpret the Constitution as did the Supreme Court. The Bank, he said, was a dangerous

---

Jackson's Bank Veto

1832

President Jackson expressed the view that the bank question was also a class question, in the following passage from his message justifying his veto of the bill for rechartering the Bank of the United States:

"There are no necessary evils in government. Its evils exist only in its abuses. If it would confine itself to equal protection, and, as Heaven does its rains, shower its favors alike on the high and the low, the rich and the poor, it would be an unqualified blessing. In the act before me [for rechartering the U.S. Bank] there seems to be a wide and unnecessary departure from these just principles. . . .

"Many of our rich men have not been content with equal protection and equal benefits, but have besought us to make them richer by act of Congress. By attempting to gratify their desires we have in the results of our legislation arrayed section against section, interest against interest, and man against man, in a fearful commotion which threatens to shake the foundations of our Union. It is time to pause in our career to review our principles, and if possible revive that devoted patriotism and spirit of compromise which distinguished the sages of the Revolution and the fathers of our Union."

monopoly which made the rich richer and the poor poorer and which threatened to overpower the people's government itself. Through the charter the government had conferred special favors on a few, but the government should afford "equal protection and equal benefits" to all the people. Besides, he warned, many of the stockholders were foreigners who through the Bank could exercise a pernicious influence upon American affairs. The veto stood, for the Bank's friends in Congress failed to obtain the two-thirds majority necessary for overriding it. And so the bank question emerged as the paramount issue of the coming election, just as Clay fondly had hoped it would.

In 1832 Clay ran as the unanimous choice of the National Republicans, who had held a nominating convention in Baltimore late the previous year. Jackson, with Van Buren as his running mate, sought re-election as the candidate of the Democratic Republicans, or Democrats. Still another candidate was in the field, representing a third party for the first time in American history. He was William Wirt, a prominent Baltimore lawyer and man of letters, the nominee of the Antimasonic party. Though he preferred Clay to Jackson, Wirt drew more votes away from the former than from the latter, though he did not draw a great many from any source, carrying only the state of Vermont. The legislature of South Carolina gave that state's electoral vote in protest to a man who was not even a candidate, John Floyd, one of Calhoun's Virginia followers. Of the remaining electoral votes, Jackson received more than five times as many as Clay.

The "Monster" Destroyed

Jackson took his decisive re-election as a sign that the people endorsed his views on the Bank of the United States. As soon as the nullification crisis had been disposed of, he determined to strike a blow at this bank-ing "monster," this dangerous money power, as he saw it. He could not put an end to the Bank before the expiration of its charter, but at least he could lessen its power by seeing to the removal of the government's deposits. By the law establishing the Bank, the Secretary of the Treasury had to give the actual order for removing them. When the incumbent Secretary refused to give the order, Jackson appointed a new one, and when this man procrastinated Jackson named a third, Roger B. Taney, previously the Attorney General and a member of the Kitchen Cabinet. Taney was more than willing to cooperate.

With Taney at the head of the Treasury Department, the process of removing the government's deposits was immediately begun, though only gradually carried out. The government stopped putting new funds in the Bank but continued paying its bills by drawing on its existing deposits, which steadily dwindled. Meanwhile the government opened accounts with a number of state banks, depositing its incoming receipts with them. These banks, including one in Baltimore with which Taney himself was associated, were chosen presumably on the basis of their financial soundness but not always without consideration of their political leanings. Jackson's enemies called them his "pet banks." By 1836 there were 89 of them.

The proud and poetic Biddle, "Czar Nicholas" to Jacksonians, was not the man to give in without a fight. "This worthy President," he wrote sarcastically, "thinks that because he has scalped Indians and imprisoned Judges, he is to have his way with the Bank. He is mistaken." Biddle had a scheme by which he intended to compel the administration to return the Bank's deposits and renew its charter as well. Single-handed, he was going to bring on an economic depression, which he could do by calling in loans and making credit scarce. The more people he could throw out of work, the better, so far as he was concerned. "Nothing but the evidence of suffering," he told the head of the Boston branch, would "produce any effect in Congress." He would excuse his action on the ground that the loss of the government deposits made it necessary. It was true that this loss, amounting to several millions, did require the Bank to reduce its lending to some extent, since the government deposits served as the basis for much of the Bank's credit. But Biddle carried his contraction of credit far beyond the needs of sound banking policy.

Throughout the winter of 1833–1834 the "Biddle panic" was on. Interest rates rose from 6 to 15 per cent, many businesses failed, and thousands of workers lost their jobs. While businessmen found it difficult or impossible to borrow from the Bank, politicians friendly to the institution continued to get easy loans. These men stood to gain political as well as pecuniary benefits from the manufactured depression, since they could derive propaganda with which to discredit Jackson. All over the country they organized meetings to adopt petitions begging for relief from Congress, petitions which delegates then brought in person to Washington, and which pro-Bank Senators or Representatives introduced with appropriately lugubrious speeches. But Jackson and the Jacksonians denied responsibility. When distressed citizens appealed to the President he answered, "Go to Biddle."

The banker finally carried his retaliation too far to suit his own friends among the anti-Jackson businessmen of the Northeast, and some of them did go to Biddle, a group of New York and Boston merchants protesting (as one of them reported) that the business community "ought not and would not sustain him in further pressure, which he very well knew was not necessary for the safety of the bank, and in which his whole object was to coerce a charter." To appease

the business community he at last reversed himself and began to grant credit in abundance and on reasonable terms. The Biddle panic was over.

King Andrew the First. *This Whig cartoon of the 1830's presents President Jackson as a tyrant with a scepter in one hand and a veto in the other; he is trampling upon the Constitution, the judiciary, internal improvements, and the Bank of the United States. His opponents called themselves "Whigs" because they pretended to be resisting a virtual king, and the Whigs in England were, traditionally, the party advocating limitations on the monarchy.* (LIBRARY OF CONGRESS)

It had failed to help the Bank. In the Senate Webster sponsored a recharter bill with modifications intended to disarm the Bank's critics. The new charter was to run for only six years, to grant no exclusive privileges, and to prohibit the issue of banknotes in denominations of less than $20. This compromise proposal, with its concessions to the foes of monopoly and of paper money, came presumably from Biddle himself. In pressing it, however, Webster had to contend against the competing plans of Clay, who insisted on a charter to last the full twenty years, and Calhoun, who talked of "unbanking the banks" somehow and a charter to run for twelve years. If the Bank men had got together, they could have put a recharter bill through the Senate, though not the House.

One thing they did accomplish, but it was only a gesture of partisan vindictiveness. This was Clay's Senate resolution solemnly censuring the President for his removal of the deposits. The resolution, adopted by a fairly close vote, asserted that the President had "assumed power not conferred by the constitution and the laws." Jackson responded with a dignified protest against his being charged with an impeachable offense while not being actually impeached and being thus given an opportunity formally to clear himself. After the Democrats got control of the Senate they undertook to strike the censure from the Senate record. With Benton taking the lead and Webster, Calhoun, and Clay filibustering in vain, the President's friends at last had the immense satisfaction of seeing the secretary of the Senate open the original manuscript journal, draw a square of broad black lines around the sentence condemning Jackson, and write across it in a bold hand the words: "Expunged by order of the Senate, this 16th day of January, 1837."

Meanwhile, the federal charter of the Bank having expired, Biddle reincorporated the institution as a state bank under the laws of Pennsylvania. No longer did it have the means of restraining note issues by other banks. Some of these banks were fairly well regulated by state laws or by the bankers themselves, particularly in New York and Massachusetts. Under the Suffolk System in Massachusetts they guaranteed one another's banknotes. But in most parts of the country and especially in the West, the discontinuance of the national bank opened the way for an unprecedented orgy of "wildcat" banking. Among the worst offenders were the government's pet banks, which generally treated the government's deposits as a windfall to be used for speculation and not as a public trust to be carefully safeguarded.

Whigs and Democrats

During the bank war the opponents of Jackson not only formally censured him in the Senate but also denounced him throughout the country for his allegedly high-handed and arbitrary actions. His opponents often referred to him as a tyrant, "King Andrew I," and they began to call themselves "Whigs," after the party which in England stood traditionally for limiting the power of the king.

The Whig party, organized in time for the congressional elections of 1834 and the presidential election of 1836, was a congeries of dissimilar groups. It included the National Republicans who had opposed Jackson in 1828 (some of these were old Federalists, others former Jeffersonian Republicans), and it included also many people who had supported Jackson in 1828 but had turned against him afterward because of his stand on internal improvements, nullification, or the Bank. Some of the Whigs, as in Virginia, were really state-rights Democrats who had broken with the President when he threatened to use force against a sister state, South Carolina. On the whole the new party was strongest among the merchants and manufacturers of the Northeast, the wealthier planters of the South, and the farmers most eager for internal improvements in the West. But the party program—internal improvements at federal expense, tariff protection, a national bank—did not appeal very strongly to the mass of voters. Throughout its existence of twenty years or so the party was able to win only two presidential elections (1840 and 1848), both of them with military heroes as its candidates.

In Jackson the Democrats had a military hero and popular leader whom no Whig could match. True, each of the two foremost Whigs, Clay and Webster, had a devoted following. The glamorous Clay, "Harry of the West," possessed a personal magnetism that won him friends throughout the country—but not enough friends ever to elect him President, though he was a candidate three times. The eloquent Webster gained fame and respect for his speeches expounding the Constitution and upholding the Union, and some of his businessmen admirers thought him a greater man than any President. But his close connection with the unpopular Bank of the United States and his dependence on rich men for his financial support disqualified him in the minds of many voters. He and Clay were bitter rivals, and their rivalry weakened the party, though at times they cooperated in politics. Sometimes associated with them and sometimes opposing them was Calhoun, the third member of what came to be known as the Great Triumvirate. Calhoun did not consider himself a Whig: after his break with Jackson he thought of himself as a no-party man. Nevertheless he joined with Webster and Clay on the Bank issue. One thing the three men and all Whigs had in common: they opposed Jackson and most of what he stood for.

Jackson and his party, in the course of his two presidential terms, developed a fairly definite and coherent political philosophy. The Jacksonians believed in laissez faire. That is, they believed that the government should let economic activities pretty much alone. They proposed the elimination of governmental favors to private enterprise, the destruction of government-granted monopolies and other corporate privileges. Then in theory the people through free and fair competition would be able to take care of themselves, each prospering in accordance with his own labor and skill. The worst of poverty and of social inequality would thus be done away with when the government ceased to help the rich and hinder the poor. While the Democrats did not advocate social revolution, they maintained that revolutionary violence might unfortunately appear unless economic inequalities were removed.

Calhoun agreed with the Democrats that the dangers of class struggle were very real, and he explored the nature and prospects of the struggle more thoroughly than anyone else of his time. Long before Karl Marx and Friedrich Engels published their *Communist Manifesto* (1848) he elaborated a similar view, though he hoped to prevent revolution whereas they intended to hasten it. In his *South Carolina Exposition and Protest* (1828) and in later writings he predicted that capitalist society would tend to divide into only two classes, "capitalists" and "operatives," that the former would expropriate and impoverish the latter, and that a revolutionary crisis would eventuate. "There is and always has been in an advanced stage of wealth and civilization," he insisted (1837), "a conflict between labor and capital." He hoped that the revolutionary danger would cause Northern businessmen to join with Southern planters in self-defense.

Webster, the leading Whig philosopher, stoutly denied the contentions of Calhoun and the Democrats. "In the old countries of Europe there is a clear and well-defined line between capital and labor," Webster conceded, but he declared there was no line so "broad, marked, and visible" in the United States. If there was any revolutionary discontent among the American people, he charged, it was due to the policies of the Jackson administration and the clamor of Democratic agitators. He maintained that the people had common interests rather than conflicting ones, at least so long as the government pursued the correct policies. He believed that a wise and active federal government, by stimulating and regulating economic activity through a national banking system, a protective tariff, and expenditures for internal improvements, could assure the economic well-being of all the people and thereby harmonize the interests of every section and class.

Thus both parties thought of themselves as representing the best interests of the whole country, though they differed in their notions of the appropriate means of achieving the general welfare. For the time being the Democrats were in power and so their policies prevailed.

Party feeling affected opinions on foreign as well as domestic affairs. When Jackson became President the trade with the British West Indies was still closed to American ships, his predecessor Adams having antagonized Great Britain by demanding completely free trade as a right rather than a privilege. As Secretary of State, Van Buren instructed the American minister in England to ask for the opening of the trade as a privilege and to say that the Adams administration had not represented public opinion. Thus Jackson succeeded where Adams had failed: the trade was opened in 1830. But anti-Jacksonians criticized the President and the Secretary of State for giving a foreign government the impression that American policy changed with a change of parties. On these grounds the Senate foes of Van Buren justified their refusal to consent to his appointment as minister to England. Of course, they themselves were mixing politics and foreign affairs as much as the administration was.

The Whigs again opposed Jackson on an issue of foreign policy when he became involved in a dispute with France. A number of American citizens held claims against the French government on account of ships seized or destroyed under Napoleon's decrees before the War of 1812. In 1831 the French government agreed to pay 25 million francs in partial satisfaction of these so-called spoliation claims. The French Chamber of Deputies, however, failed to appropriate money for making the payment. Demanding that France make good its acknowledged debt, Jackson recommended to Congress the confiscation of French property in this country. The French took this as an insult to their national honor and insisted upon an apology. Though he refused to apologize, Jackson explained that he had meant no insult. As if expecting war he asked Congress (1835) for appropriations to build up the navy and the fortifications along the coast. The Whigs, denouncing him as a warmonger, voted against such appropriations. Despite political opposition at home he won his second diplomatic victory when the Chamber of Deputies at last provided funds and the debt was paid.

At stake in the party contests of the time were not only issues of foreign and domestic policy but also questions of federal jobholding and other perquisites of political power. The Democrats had the power and the jobs; the Whigs wanted them. As the presidential election of 1836 approached, the Democrats had the advantages of patronage, Jackson's prestige, and a superior party organization. Jackson, not desiring a third term for himself, was able to choose the President to succeed him. The Democratic convention readily nominated his favorite, Van Buren.

The Whigs in 1836 could boast no such unity and discipline. Indeed, they could not even agree upon a single candidate. Their strategy, master-minded by Biddle, was to run several candidates, each of them supposedly strong in part of the country. Webster was the man for New England, and Hugh Lawson White of Tennessee was to seek the votes of the South. The third and strongest of all the Whig contenders, the one-time Indian fighter and hero of the War of 1812 from Indiana, William Henry Harrison, was counted upon in the middle states and the West. As Biddle advised: "This disease is to be treated as a local disorder—apply local remedies—if General Harrison will run better than anybody else in Pennsylvania, by all means unite upon him." None of the three candidates could expect to get a majority in the electoral college, but separately they might draw enough votes from Van Buren to prevent his getting a majority. The election would then devolve, as in 1824–1825, upon the House of Representatives, where conceivably the Whigs might be able to elect one of their men.

The three Whigs proved to be no match for the one Democrat. When the returns were in, Van Buren had 170 electoral votes to 124 for all his opponents. Again the South Carolina legislature gave that state's 11 electoral votes to a man who was not a regular candidate—Willie P. Mangum, of North Carolina. One of the Whig leaders of New York, William H. Seward, explained the victory of Van Buren thus: "The people are for him. Not so much for him as for the principle they suppose he represents. That principle is Democracy."

The Panic of 1837

At the time of the election of 1836 a nationwide boom was reaching its height. Canal enterprisers and railroad builders were busy digging ditches and laying tracks here, there, and everywhere. Prices were high and going higher, as people indulged in an orgy of spending and speculating. Money was plentiful. Much of it came from abroad, English investors buying large amounts of American corporation securities and state bonds. Most of it was manufactured by the banks, which multiplied their loans and notes with little regard to their reserves of cash, until

by 1837 bank loans outstanding amounted to five times as much as in 1830. Never had the nation seemed so prosperous.

Land as usual was a favorite speculation,

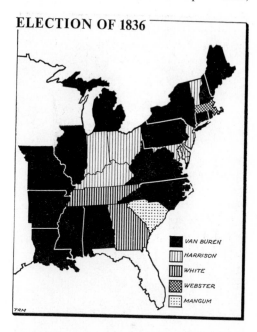

ELECTION OF 1836

VAN BUREN
HARRISON
WHITE
WEBSTER
MANGUM

especially the land sold by the federal government. After the act of 1821 had abolished installment buying and set the minimum price at $1.25 an acre, sales of public lands reached an average of 300,000 to 400,000 acres a year in the late 1820's and early 1830's. Then the business suddenly boomed. Between 1835 and 1837 nearly 40 million acres were disposed of, and the expression "doing a land-office business" came into use to describe fast selling of any kind. Nearly three fourths of the land being sold went to speculators—men acquiring large tracts in the hope of reselling at a profit—and only about a fourth of it to actual settlers. Speculators generally borrowed from the banks to make payment at the land offices.

For the time being the government profited. Receipts from land sales, which had averaged less than $2.4 million annually for the ten years preceding 1835, rose to more than $24 million in 1836. This was the government's largest source of revenue, but customs duties under the compromise tariff of 1833 added considerably to total income.

Thomas Hart Benton. *Expelled from the University of North Carolina for stealing from a roommate, Benton began life anew in Tennessee, where he was at first a close friend and then a hated foe of Andrew Jackson (the two became fast friends again during Jackson's Presidency). After moving on to St. Louis, Benton served as United States Senator from Missouri for thirty years (1821–1851), then as a Representative from that state for one term (1853–1855). In public life he was pompous, pedantic, and quarrelsome, yet extremely able, honest, and devoted to the interests of the West. In his last years he bravely fought the aggressive pro-slavery element of Missouri and the South. His two-volume autobiographical work,* Thirty Years' View *(1854–1856), gives a revealing though highly partisan account of national politics during his senatorial career. From a photograph by Matthew B. Brady.*

The government received more money than it paid out. Steadily the national debt was reduced, as Jackson insisted it should be, and finally from 1835 to 1837 the government for the first and only time in its history was out of debt. Not only that: there was also a large and growing surplus in the federal treasury.

The question for Congress and the administration was how to get rid of the treasury surplus. Tampering with the tariff was not to be considered, since the recent compromise had put to rest that touchy subject and few wanted to reopen it.

Changing the land law was a possibility, but on this subject too there were serious differences of opinion. Senator Benton, the Jacksonian from Missouri, advocated what he called "graduation." This meant gradually lowering the minimum price for unsold lands, from $1.25 to $1.00 to 75 cents to 50 cents, and finally giving away the lands that still found no buyers. Benton also favored ceding the public domain to the states within which it lay. His proposals pleased Westerners, eager for cheap land, but did not suit Easterners who desired to share in land revenues and to discourage the exodus of labor to a rapidly growing frontier. Some Easterners—such as the Connecticut Senator who in 1830 suggested a discontinuance of surveys and sales—would go so far as to halt the frontier advance. Southerners at the time were willing to appease the West but later were inclined to oppose easy land laws and rapid Western settlement. Clay devised a scheme with which he hoped to satisfy East, West, and South alike. He urged that land proceeds be divided among all the states in proportion to their population.

But why distribute only the proceeds from the sale of public lands? Why not give away to the states the entire federal surplus? This would be an effective way of getting rid of it, and the idea appealed to Congress, though the congressmen preferred to think of the distribution as a loan rather than a gift. In 1836 Congress passed and Jackson signed a distribution act providing that the surplus accumulated by the end of the year (estimated at $40 million) be paid to the states in four quarterly installments as a loan without security or interest, each state getting a share proportional to its representation in Congress. No one seriously expected the "loan" to be repaid. As the states began to receive their shares they promptly spent the money, mainly to encourage the construction of highways, railroads, and canals. The distribution of the surplus thus gave further stimulus to the speculative boom. At the same time the withdrawal of federal funds strained the "pet banks," for they had to call in a large part of their own loans in order to be able to make the transfer of funds to the state governments.

Congress did nothing to check the speculative fever, with which many congressmen themselves were badly infected, Webster for one buying up thousands of acres in the West. But the President was much concerned. Though money continued to pour into the treasury from the land offices, most of it was money of dubious value. The government was selling good land and was receiving in return a miscellaneous collection of state banknotes, none of them worth any more than the credit of the issuing bank. Jackson finally decided to act. He issued his Specie Circular (1836) announcing that in the future only hard money or the notes of specie-paying banks would be accepted in payment for public lands. This was but one sign of trouble ahead for prosperity-crazed Americans. There were also other signs, for those who cared to see them.

As Jackson reached the end of his second term the nation was still seemingly prosperous. On his last full day in office, March 3, 1837, he recognized the independence of Texas (this subject will be treated in a later chapter) and on the following day he saw his hand-picked successor, Van Buren, inaugurated as President. Soon Jackson, justifiably proud of the success of his two administrations, left for the peace and quiet of his beloved home, the Hermitage, near Nashville, Tennessee. Van Buren had been in office less than three months when the panic broke. The banks of New York, followed by those of the rest of the country, suddenly suspended specie payments (that is, they stopped paying cash on demand for their banknotes and other obligations). During the next few years hundreds of banks failed, and so did hundreds of other business firms. As unemployment grew, bread riots occurred in some of the larger cities. Prices fell, especially the price of land, which now became a burden to the recently optimistic speculators, Webster being only one of a great many who all at once found themselves "land-poor." Many railroad and canal schemes were abandoned; several of the debt-burdened state governments ceased to pay interest on their bonds and a few repudiated their debts, at least temporarily. The depression, the worst the American people ever had experienced, lasted for about five years.

The Whigs blamed Jackson for the depression. It had come, they said, because of his destruction of the national bank and his mismanagement of public finance. But they were as much to blame as he was. The distribution of the treasury surplus was a Whig measure, though Jackson signed it (with the onset of the panic, the distribution was halted before the entire surplus had been transferred to the states). This step, by weakening the pet banks, helped to bring on the crash. So did Jackson's Specie Circular, which started a general run on the banks as land buyers rushed to get cash in return for banknotes to make land-office payments. Distribution and the Specie Circular only precipitated the depression, however; they did not cause it.

The causes included those common to all depressions, the business cycle being to some extent "self-generating." Wages rose, but not so fast as prices, and thus consumption failed to keep pace with production. Costs of doing business, among them the cost of borrowed money or the interest rate, offset rising prices for the businessman and re-

States, if continued, might have lessened this overexpansion of credit, a period of financial stringency doubtless would have come anyhow, sooner or later. For the depression

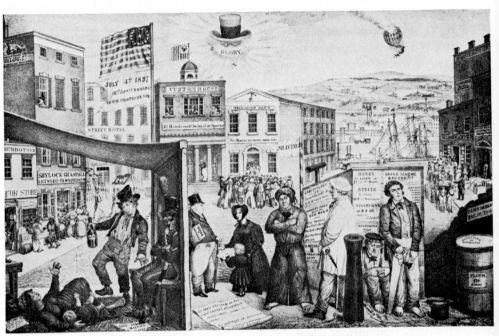

The Panic of 1837. *The banner beneath the flag reads: "July 4th 1837. 61st Anniversary of Our Independence." Militiamen parade to observe the occasion, but the people, instead of watching, are preoccupied with their troubles. Mechanics stand idle with their tools. The only busy places are the shop of "Shylock Graspall, Licensed Pawnbroker," where the unemployed seek loans with which to buy liquor; the "Mechanics' Bank," where depositors try to get cash for their worthless banknotes; and the "Sheriff's Office," where property is being sold for unpaid taxes. From a contemporary lithograph.* (COURTESY OF THE NEW-YORK HISTORICAL SOCIETY, NEW YORK CITY)

duced his margin of profit. Some causes of the Panic of 1837 were peculiar to the situation at that time. Canals and railroads were being overbuilt: heavy investments were being poured into them, but it would take years before most of these undertakings would ever bring in revenues enough to pay the cost and yield a profit, and some of the projects would never do so. Bank credit was overextended, for canal and railroad building, for land speculation, and for ordinary business. While the Bank of the United

was international, affecting England and Western Europe as well as the United States. As English investors faced a financial crisis at home, they began to withdraw funds from America, thus accounting for part of the strain on American banks. A succession of crop failures on American farms not only reduced the purchasing power of farmers but also necessitated imports of foodstuffs; to pay for these imports, additional money was drawn out of the country.

Besides its economic consequences, the

Panic of 1837 had other significant results. Hard times increased social, sectional, and political tensions. Want in the cities heightened the feeling that there existed even in America a real and dangerous class conflict —a struggle between the poor and the rich. Heavy losses suffered by Southern planters confirmed them in their conviction that national policies worked to their disadvantage, while the decline of business profits in the North intensified the belief of manufacturers that the compromise of 1833 must be undone and the tariff raised. Defaults on interest payments and outright repudiation of state bonds, many of them held by Englishmen, added to difficulties in the relations between the United States and Great Britain. Distress among the people was turned into dissatisfaction with the administration, so that the predominance of the Democrats was brought temporarily to an end after Van Buren had served but a single term. Above all, the depression gave added stimulus to a many-sided movement for social reform which already was under way.

>>->>->>->>|<<-|<<-|<<-|<<

BIBLIOGRAPHY

MARTIN VAN BUREN still awaits an adequate biography. Holmes Alexander, *The American Talleyrand* (1935), is as good as any and makes interesting reading, though it is rather superficial. Van Buren does not tell all in *The Autobiography of Martin Van Buren*, edited by J. C. Fitzpatrick (1920), but he does reveal much of the cautious and canny politician that he was. C. B. Swisher, *Roger B. Taney* (1935), is informative on Jacksonian strategy in the Bank War. W. N. Chambers, *Old Bullion Benton: Senator from the New West* (1956), provides a scholarly, critical, and readable life of Jackson's strong man in the Senate, as also does Elbert B. Smith, *Magnificent Missourian: The Life of Thomas Hart Benton* (1958).

The political opposition is the subject of two able monographs: A. C. Cole, *The Whig Party in the South* (1913), and E. M. Carroll, *Origins of the Whig Party* (1925). C. M. Fuess, *Daniel Webster* (2 vols., 1930), is the standard biography. R. N. Current, *Daniel Webster and the Rise of National Conservatism* (1955), is much briefer but gives far more attention to Webster's political philosophy. G. R. Poage, *Henry Clay and the Whig Party* (1936), traces carefully the political maneuverings of the 1830's.

G. G. Van Deusen, *The Life of Henry Clay* (1937), is excellent. G. W. Johnson, *America's Silver Age: The Statecraft of Clay, Webster, and Calhoun* (1939), is superficial but interesting. J. A. Shackford, *David Crockett: the Man and the Legend* (1956), tells the truth about the famous backwoods, buckskin Whig.

On the bank question, the most extensive work is Bray Hammond, *Banks and Politics in America from the Revolution to the Civil War* (1957). See also W. B. Smith, *Economic Aspects of the Second Bank of the United States* (1953), and R. C. H. Catterall, *The Second Bank of the United States* (1903). There are some fascinating and revealing letters in *The Correspondence of Nicholas Biddle Dealing with National Affairs, 1807–1844* (1919). S. R. Gammon, *The Presidential Campaign of 1832* (1922), is adequate.

On the boom and the depression, see R. C. McGrane, *The Panic of 1837* (1924), and W. B. Smith and A. H. Cole, *Fluctuations in American Business, 1790–1860* (1935). See also R. G. Wellington, *The Political and National Influence of the Public Lands, 1826–1842* (1914).

A Search for Heaven on Earth

AMERICA, the scene of Thomas More's sixteenth-century book *Utopia*, still seemed in the nineteenth century a land of utopian possibilities, at least to a great many Americans. They believed that their country led the rest of the world in moral as well as material progress (except for the embarrassing persistence of slavery in the South). They leapt to the defense whenever foreigners criticized American ways, as foreigners often did. Yet these progress-minded Americans themselves readily found fault with conditions in their own country when these conditions seemed to hinder the perfection of society and man. There resulted a tumultuous and variegated movement for intellectual awakening and social reform, which gained headway soon after the War of 1812, picked up momentum in the 1830's, then concentrated most of its

force on a single reform—the elimination of slavery. The reform spirit, this "freedom's ferment," never had stirred the South so much as it had the North, and with the development of an antislavery crusade Southerners resisted more strongly than ever the "isms" of the day as they rallied to a defense of their "peculiar institution." Thus the nation began increasingly to divide on moral as well as economic and political grounds.

Democracy and Civilization

"In the four quarters of the globe, who reads an American book? or goes to an American play? or looks at an American picture or statue?" So asked the English wit Sydney Smith in the *Edinburgh Review* (1820), and he assumed that the answer was obvious—nobody. Like him, many cultivated Europeans believed that the American democracy was a cultural vacuum.

On the whole, British travelers in the United States confirmed this impression.

Even when the British were complimentary, however, they were inclined to be condescending, and much of the time they were highly critical. To them the typical Yankee

Dancing the Quadrille. *This ballroom scene of the 1840's, in the Tremont Hotel, Boston, indicates that American society did not consist entirely of tobacco-spitting backwoodsmen, though it was perhaps a little behind the times. The quadrille was a square dance that had originated in France and had become fashionable in England as early as about 1815. From an illustration for the cover of a piece of sheet music.*

Occasionally these book-writing tourists had a kind word about the American and his habits. One of the most sympathetic, Harriet Martineau, author of *Society in America* (1837), admitted that the American people already had realized many ideals for which the rest of the world still strove. Though Americans had their faults, she added, they could not be discouraged by them, for they "are in possession of the glorious certainty that time and exertion will infallibly secure all wisely desired objects."

seemed filthy, rude, ignorant, quarrelsome, boastful, and greedy, as well as sickly and sallow. The Southerner seemed even worse, tyrannical and brutal, a beater of slaves. North, South, and West, the American male according to the British visitors was an inveterate tobacco chewer and spitter, with an aim that was none too good.

What these writers saw in America reflected their own prejudices as well as the objective facts. English authors, including Charles Dickens, were personally aggrieved because American publishers "pirated" their works, that is, reprinted them without paying royalties. Along with other Englishmen, men of letters also lost money by investing in state bonds which proved worthless or nearly so with the defaults and repudiations following the Panic of 1837. Quite often the interpreters of the United States to the English public were Tories who feared democracy at home and therefore wished to discredit it abroad. They were fighting against the campaign to widen the suffrage in England, a campaign which culminated in the Reform Bill of 1832 and in the Chartist movement of 1848. Reviewers of the travel books in British quarterlies gave much attention to the criticisms of American democracy and pointed out the seemingly obvious conclusion: true morality and real culture could have no place in a country where the will of the majority prevailed.

Quite different was the attitude of the young French visitor, Alexis de Tocqueville, whose two volumes on *Democracy in America* (1835–1840) still stand as the most perceptive analysis of American ways ever penned by a foreigner. Believing that political equality was the way of the future, Tocqueville toured this country to learn democracy's good and bad, its essential and nonessential elements, so that France might be better prepared for the inevitable transition to democracy. Even though he disapproved of much that he saw, he sought to understand American behavior, not to denounce it. Like the British observers, he concluded that Americans were backward in respect to science, literature, and the arts, but he did not blame their backwardness upon democracy. He wrote: "Their strictly Puritanical origin—their exclusively commercial habits—even the country they inhabit, which seems to divert their minds from the pursuit of science, literature and the arts—the proximity of Europe, which allows them to neglect these pursuits without relapsing into barbarism—a thousand special causes, of which I have only been able to point out the most important—have singularly concurred to fix the mind of the American upon purely practical objects."

Colonial attitudes persisted in America so far as things of the mind were concerned. Seldom was an American author appreciated at home until he had been praised by critics abroad, and sometimes not even then. In 1830, it has been estimated, 70 per cent of the books sold in America were published in England. By 1840 this percentage had been drastically reduced, to only about 30. In the space of one decade the American book industry had grown tremendously, though most of the books had to be subsidized or else produced for advance orders secured by subscriptions. Despite the rise of book publishing in several American cities, especially in New York, the great majority of books published and sold were written, as before, by English authors. The romantic novels of Charles Dickens and Sir Walter Scott were as much the rage in the United States as in the British Isles. Scott was a special favorite among Southerners, who often applied Scott's word "Southron" to themselves, and who viewed their own section as the contemporary land of chivalry and romance. Since the United States still was a party to no international copyright arrangement, and publishers could steal the works of favorite British writers, American authors writing for pay continued to be at a competitive disadvantage.

American writers had other outlets for their wares besides publication in books, however. Hundreds of magazines appeared and disappeared, their average life being about two years, but at any given time a large number were being published, approximately 600 in 1850. Some were successful and long-lasting, such as the *Southern Literary Messenger* (founded 1834), *Godey's Lady's Book* (1837), *Harper's New*

Monthly Magazine (1850), and the *Atlantic Monthly* (1857), besides the venerable *North American Review* (1815). In these magazines some of the greatest of native authors found a market for their works. In many other magazines, however, neither the writers nor their stories were great by any standard except popular appeal. The taste of most readers, especially women, was little different from that of their descendants who a century later were to listen to soap operas on radio or television. Sentimental and sirupy tales of struggling womanhood were favorites a hundred years ago as now.

Newspapers provided an occasional vehicle for fiction as well as journalism; for example, Harriet Beecher Stowe's *Uncle Tom's Cabin* first appeared (1851) as a serial in an antislavery weekly. Nevertheless, the main attraction of newspapers continued to lie in their news and editorial opinion. They grew rapidly in number, size, and circulation, as the United States became increasingly a nation of newspaper readers. Something new was the penny daily, the first being the New York *Sun* (1833), which soon was followed by James Gordon Bennett's New York *Herald* and Horace Greeley's New York *Tribune*. The *Sun* and the *Herald* specialized in scandal and crime, the *Tribune* in self-improvement and social uplift. With a separate weekly edition, the *Tribune* came to be a national or at least a sectional newspaper, having mail subscribers scattered throughout the North and West. The early nineteenth century was an age of personal journalism, with editors like Bennett and Greeley and lesser men over the country impressing their personalities upon their papers. "The only authors whom I acknowledge as American are the journalists," Tocqueville declared. "They, indeed, are not great writers, but they speak the language of their countrymen, and make themselves heard by them." In 1846 occurred two events that vastly facilitated the

collection and distribution of news: the introduction of the Hoe cylinder rotary printing machine and the organization of the Associated Press. The latter was a response to the spread of the telegraph, following the first practical demonstration of Samuel F. B. Morse's invention (1844).

As in the Revolutionary era, so also in the period following the War of 1812 the question of literary independence drew much discussion from American writers. Some responded to British criticisms by declaring war again—the so-called "war of the quarterlies"—in which magazine replied to magazine, the Americans defending life in the United States and denouncing the customs of England. Instead of joining in such recriminations, a few thoughtful Americans called upon their countrymen for increased originality and creative effort. "The more we receive from other countries, the greater the need of an original literature," said William Ellery Channing (1830). He went on to contend that "A people into whose minds the thoughts of foreigners are poured perpetually, needs an energy within itself to resist, to modify this mighty influence, and without it will inevitably sink under the worst bondage, will become intellectually tame and enslaved." And Ralph Waldo Emerson, in his notable Phi Beta Kappa address at Harvard (1837), urged scholars, philosophers, and men of letters to do all they could toward developing a self-reliant nationhood. But there were also arguments on the other side. Confessing that American literature was largely derivative, James Russell Lowell said (1849), "There is no degradation in such indebtedness"; and he suggested, "It may not be our destiny to produce a great literature."

Literature: A Golden Age

Foreign critics were too severe and native commentators too modest in their appraisals of American letters. In retrospect the pe-

riod from the 1820's to the 1850's has
seemed, indeed, a kind of golden age of literature in the United States. It was the time
of Washington Irving, James Fenimore

gained the esteem at least of their own
countrymen and their own generation.

Irving, author of the earliest American
literary "classics," was the first to achieve

The Spy on the Stage. *In the 1820's James Fenimore Cooper's popular
novel of the Revolutionary War,* The Spy, *was adapted as a play. This
painting was done by William Dunlap, a versatile dramatist and producer who has been called the father of the American theater.* (COUR-
TESY OF THE NEW YORK STATE HISTORICAL ASSOCIATION, COOPERSTOWN, NEW
YORK)

Cooper, Herman Melville, and Walt Whitman (all New Yorkers); Edgar Allan Poe
(a Southerner by affirmation though not by
birth); and Ralph Waldo Emerson, Henry
David Thoreau, and Nathaniel Hawthorne
(New Englanders). All these writers contributed to world literature: sooner or later
they won lasting renown abroad as well as
at home. Besides them, a number of others

foreign recognition. His *History of New
York* (1809) aimed, in his words, "to embody the traditions of the city in an amusing form," and did so in the stories of an
imaginary historian of Dutch descent, Died-
rich Knickerbocker. Irving's most famous
work, *The Sketch Book* (1819–1820), containing "Rip Van Winkle" and "The Legend
of Sleepy Hollow," made further use of the

Dutch folklore of New York. Afterwards Irving lived for a number of years in Spain and found story materials there, and still later he wrote historical works about the American West. A conservative in politics, he avoided contemporary political and social problems as literary themes. He did not disturb his readers with philosophical challenges but charmed them with his easy style and graceful art.

Cooper, a less polished but more prolific writer, turned out more then thirty novels in thirty years (1820–1850). Growing up on the New York frontier, then serving for several years in the navy, Cooper knew the forest and the sea, the settings of his adventure stories. Among the most successful were *The Spy* (1821), a novel of the Revolutionary War, and several "Leatherstocking" tales, including *The Last of the Mohicans* (1826) and *The Deerslayer* (1841). Over and over Cooper used the same formula of heroic action, breathless pursuit, and narrow escape. A born storyteller, he held his readers' attention despite the stilted dialogue of his stylized characters—the noble red man, the resourceful pioneer, the virtuous maid, and the enemy villain. He created an enduring character in the frontiersman Natty Bumppo ("Leatherstocking"). In his novels Cooper refrained from social criticism, but he also wrote essays in which, as a Democrat with aristocratic ideals, he condemned the pushing, go-getting spirit of his fellow Americans.

Melville, once a sailor and a resident of the South Seas, had a background even more adventurous than Cooper's, and he too wrote novels of adventure. But Melville was vastly more subtle and sophisticated in his writing, and he filled his stories with discursive philosophizing and with puzzling symbolism. In the best-known of his novels, *Moby Dick* (1851), Captain Ahab vengefully pursues the great white whale which has bitten his leg off; the captain catches the whale and is killed by him. Presumably the whale stands for evil, and the point of the story is that for a human being to attempt to destroy the evil in the universe is hopeless but heroic. For all the vividness of his scenes, the depth and complexity of his characters, and the richness of his style, Melville's plots moved too slowly and his meaning was too obscure for the reading public of his time. A century later he was recognized as one of the greatest novelists ever to write in the English language.

Whitman, the self-proclaimed poet of American democracy, likewise was more widely appreciated by posterity than by his contemporaries, though some of them hailed him as the most original and authentic voice of the United States. The son of a Long Island carpenter, Whitman roamed the country and supported himself by odd jobs while composing his first poems. When he hired a printer to put out a thin volume of his work, *Leaves of Grass* (1855), he could find few buyers or readers, and he scandalized most of them. His verse, unconfined by rhyme, sang exuberantly of the flesh as well as the spirit. Whitman identified himself with the American people. He wrote:

I celebrate myself, and sing myself,
And what I assume you shall assume,
For every atom belonging to me
*   as good belongs to you.*

Five more editions of *Leaves of Grass*, with added poems, appeared before Whitman's death (1892), and so did other volumes of poetry and essays. His work eventually was translated into many languages.

Poe, in a short and unhappy life which ended in 1849, made himself an even more controversial figure than Whitman. After briefly attending the University of Virginia and the United States Military Academy, Poe made a living as best he could by editing literary magazines and selling an occasional bit of writing. He devised a theory of esthetics—supposedly based on music and mathematics—which he put into practice in his haunting onomatopoetic verse, his macabre tales (he invented the detective story), and his sharp literary criticisms. His first book, *Tamerlane and Other Poems* (1827), published anonymously, brought him little money and no fame, but he gained a national reputation with "The Raven" when it appeared in a newspaper, in 1845. Some critics were contemptuous of his musical effects, and Emerson referred to him sneeringly as the "jingle man." In England, however, Alfred Lord Tennyson hailed Poe as a true, original poet, and in France Charles Baudelaire took him as an inspiration and a model. Indeed, Poe's writings influenced European literature far more than did those of any other nineteenth-century American.

New York, where Poe spent his last years, had become the literary capital of the nation after 1820. Then during the 1840's and 1850's New York, as a center of authorship, was largely eclipsed by New England, if not by the one village of Concord, Massachusetts. Why there should have been such a literary "flowering" in New England is hard to explain. Of course, there was a long tradition of literacy and scholarship in the region. Ships returning from exotic ports throughout the world, including the Far East, brought in stimulating ideas along with profitable cargoes. Travelers, among them students attending German universities, returned with the stimulus of European romanticism. And the rise of industry altered society and the countryside, unsettling old habits and beliefs and, perhaps, provoking the imagination.

Emerson, leader of the Concord literary circle, began his career as a Unitarian minister, then resigned (1833) and devoted himself to the exposition of a "transcendental" philosophy. He derived his ideas from wide reading in the works of Plato, Plotinus, seventeenth-century Neoplatonists, and writers of China, Persia, and India. He was inspired also by European travel and by conversation with English romantic authors such as Samuel Taylor Coleridge and Thomas Carlyle. From various sources Emerson put together a distinctively American philosophy of optimism, which saw reality as essentially good, and individualism, which stressed the capability of self-reliant man. Though he also wrote poetry and other works, Emerson was most noted for his platform lectures, some of which were condensed and revised for publication under the title *Essays* (1841–1844). Through both the printed and the spoken word, he reached and influenced a wide audience, though he did not convince all who read or heard him, not even all his friends. One admirer, Melville, thought him full of "oracular gibberish" at times.

Thoreau, a friend and disciple of Emerson's, built a shack in the woods on Emerson's property and lived there, beside Walden Pond, for two years. Afterwards he explained: "I went to the woods because I wished to live deliberately, to front only the essential facts of life, and see if I could not learn what it had to teach, and not, when I came to die, discover that I had not lived." He was delayed five years in finding a publisher for his account of the experience, which finally appeared as *Walden* (1854). A man of ruggedly honest principles as well as ruggedly honest prose, Thoreau meanwhile spent a night in jail for refusing to pay taxes for the support of what he considered an unjust government (the United States then being at war with Mexico). He justified his stand in *Resistance to Civil Government* (1849), an essay on "passive resistance" that afterwards influenced a number of revolutionaries abroad, among them Mahatma Gandhi in India.

Hawthorne, at different times a friend and neighbor of Emerson's and of Melville's, had an outlook more like Melville's than Emerson's. A latter-day Puritan, Hawthorne dwelt upon somber themes from the Puritan past, with a conviction that evil was a grim reality. In a series of magazine stories, collected in *Twice-Told Tales* (1837), he probed the psychology of sin, much as Jonathan Edwards might have done if Edwards had written fiction instead of theological treatises. Hawthorne's first great success was *The Scarlet Letter* (1850), which is still regarded as one of the most nearly perfect of American novels. Treating the familiar "triangle" in an unfamiliar way, this psychological novel tells of the beautiful Hester Prynne, her husband, and her lover, and their very different responses to the evil in their lives.

Besides Emerson, Thoreau, and Hawthorne there were other New England authors who, in their own time, enjoyed reputations as high as or higher than any of those three. William Cullen Bryant, as a young man in the Berkshire Hills, wrote "Thanatopsis" and other poems which brought him a reputation as America's foremost poet by 1832, after he had moved to New York to edit a newspaper, the *Evening Post*. Henry Wadsworth Longfellow, a sedate Harvard professor, appealed to popular tastes with his short poems on familiar subjects, like the village blacksmith, and his long poems elaborating historic traditions, such as *Evangeline* (1847), *The Song of Hiawatha* (1855), and *The Courtship of Miles Standish* (1858). His books sold well—a total of 300,000 copies by 1857. Oliver Wendell Holmes, another Harvard professor, a physician who taught in the Medical School, had time to write light verse and witty essays. James Russell Lowell, the first editor of the *Atlantic Monthly*, was a leading critic, essayist, and versifier. John Greenleaf Whittier, the "Quaker Poet," composed gentle, homespun verse about rural life in New England—and not so gentle verse attacking slavery in the South.

Though each section had its historians, New England had the ablest. George Bancroft celebrated the successes of what he considered God's chosen people in his ten-volume *History of the United States* (1834–1882). Like many of the intellectuals of the time, Bancroft was a Jacksonian, and his political feelings were apparent when the first volume came out, though it dealt with the colonial beginnings and not with contemporary events. The book, critics said, voted for Jackson. Works of more enduring value, because of their literary quality and their critical use of evidence, were written by William H. Prescott, Francis Parkman, and John Lothrop Motley. These writers looked outside the United States for their subject matter—to Mexico and Peru, New France, and the Dutch Republic.

Art and Sciences

In the arts of the drama, painting, sculpture, and music, and in the sciences, Americans produced much less of originality and lasting value than in literature. Yet, even in these fields, Americans were not always wholly imitative during the four decades from 1820 to 1860.

The theater became increasingly popular, though not entirely respectable, despite its efforts to appear on the side of morality through the presentation of temperance dramas like *The Drunkard* and *Ten Nights in a Bar-room*. Regular stock companies, English and American, toured the cities and larger towns. The companies depended on their stars to attract audiences. Fanny Kemble and William Charles Macready, both English, were outstanding attractions. So were the Americans Joseph Jefferson, who played the role of Rip Van Winkle before countless applauding audiences after 1859, and Edwin Forrest, famous for Shakespearean parts. Intense rivalries developed between celebrities and between their respec-

Fanny Kemble. *The most famous leading lady of her time, Frances Anne Kemble came to the United States in 1832 with her father, a prominent English actor. She married an American, Pierce Butler, and after fourteen years divorced him. She gave Shakespearean readings and performed in plays in this country and abroad. In 1833, during her first season in America, Chief Justice John Marshall and Associate Justice Joseph Story attended a couple of her performances in Washington, D.C. "We have seen Miss Kemble as Julia in 'The Hunchback,' and as Mrs. Haller in 'The Stranger,'" Story wrote. "I have never seen any female acting at all comparable to hers. She is so graceful that you forget that she is not very handsome. In [as] Mrs. Haller she threw the whole audience into tears. The chief justice shed them in common with younger eyes." Painting by Henry Inman.* (IN THE BROOKLYN MUSEUM COLLECTION)

tive fans. In 1849 a mob of Forrest's admirers marched upon a New York theater where Macready was playing, and in the ensuing riot 22 persons were killed and many more injured. The legitimate stage

often resorted to cheap showmanship so as to compete with such spectacles as circuses, minstrel shows, and "museums," containing freaks and oddities like the midget Tom Thumb. In the 1840's P. T. Barnum rose to become the leading promoter of these kinds of mass amusement.

Painters generally conformed to the sentimental taste of their customers, who demanded soft landscapes, flattering portraits, and storytelling pictures. Among the better artists, Asher B. Durand and others of the "Hudson River School" concentrated upon natural scenery, William Sidney Mount portrayed his fellow Long Islanders at work and play, and George Caleb Bingham recorded everyday scenes of life in Missouri. The most successful sculptor was Hiram Powers, whose statue of a naked woman, entitled "The Greek Slave," attracted attention and provoked controversy on moral rather than esthetic grounds.

By the 1840's New York, Philadelphia, and Boston possessed orchestras of their own, and Americans flocked to the performances of foreign celebrities such as the Norwegian violinist Ole Bull and the "Swedish Nightingale" Jenny Lind. But American composers were rare, the most successful (judged by their enduring popularity) being John Howard Payne, Lowell Mason, and Stephen C. Foster. Payne, an actor and playwright, wrote "Home, Sweet Home" for an opera (1823). Mason, a Boston music teacher, composed the tunes for "Nearer, My God, to Thee," "From Greenland's Icy Mountains," and other stately hymns. Foster wrote "Oh! Susanna," "Old Black Joe," and more than 200 other melodies, most of them to accompany his own verse. Many of these songs, written for black-face minstrel bands, convey a sense of genuine nostalgia for the plantation, though Foster was born in Pittsburgh and spent his brief and tragic life in the Northeast.

Americans were more noted for applied

science than for scientific theory. Nevertheless, from observation and experiment, some of them made significant contributions to scientific knowledge. John J. Audubon, pioneer ornithologist, published his exquisite sketches in *Birds of America* (1827–1838). Joseph Henry, the most original American scientist since Benjamin Franklin, made important discoveries in electromagnetism (thus preparing the way for Morse's invention of the telegraph). A Georgia physician, Crawford W. Long, demonstrated the practicability of ether as an anesthetic (1842).

The federal government sponsored some kinds of scientific work, though not as generously as it might have done, had Congressmen not opposed expenditures on grounds of thrift and state rights. Geographical knowledge was increased by the United States Coast Survey, begun in 1832, and by the United States Exploring Expedition, which between 1838 and 1842 surveyed extensive areas of the Pacific Ocean, under the leadership of Lieutenant Charles Wilkes. The great oceanographer, Matthew Fontaine Maury, was appointed director of the United States Naval Observatory and Hydrographic Office in 1841, and his work was thus supported by the government. In 1846 the Smithsonian Institution was founded in Washington, after an Englishman had willed his fortune of $500,000 to the United States "for the increase and diffusion of knowledge." Appropriately the noted physicist Joseph Henry became the first head of the institution.

The leading colleges, Yale and Harvard, also served as important patrons of science. At Yale Benjamin Silliman taught chemistry and mineralogy for a half century after his appointment in 1802, and for many years he edited the *American Journal of Science and Art*, after founding it in 1818. Though not a notable researcher, Silliman was an outstanding teacher who kept American students and scholars informed of scientific developments throughout the world. At Harvard the zoologist and geologist Louis Agassiz and the botanist Asa Gray not only taught but also carried on important researches in their respective fields. Through his studies of plant distribution Gray assisted the English scholar Charles Darwin in formulating the theory of evolution. When Darwin's epoch-making book *On the Origin of Species* appeared (1859), Gray endorsed and Agassiz rejected the idea that plants and animals, instead of remaining unchanged since God created them, had developed through a process of natural selection.

Spirit of Social Reform

"In no country in the world has the principle of association been more successfully used, or more unsparingly applied to a multitude of different objects, than in America," Tocqueville observed. "Societies are formed to resist enemies which are exclusively of a moral nature, and to diminish the vice of intemperance: in the United States associations are established to promote public order, commerce, industry, morality, and religion; for there is no end which the human will, seconded by the collective exertions of individuals, despairs of attaining."

Indeed, Americans organized reform societies of all kinds, not only for temperance but also for education, world peace, the care of the poor and the handicapped, the improvement of prisons, women's rights, the abolition of slavery, and dozens of other idealistic purposes. It did not take much to start a reform movement: all that was needed was a leader with an idea. Then came followers and an organization, with local societies and an occasional national or even international convention, one or more publications, fund drives and continual agitation for popular support. In the various causes there was much duplication of leadership and membership, the same person often belonging to several societies and supporting all their reforms. Often, however, the reformers worked at cross purposes. Sometimes a group disagreed and divided; often the advocates of one reform opposed advocates of a different one. This much all the reformers had in common: a sense that there were wrongs to right and a confidence that they could be righted, that man and his relationships to his fellow man could be made perfect or at least could be greatly improved.

This reform spirit derived from a variety of sources, religious and rational, domestic and foreign. The Christian doctrine of human worth, the Revolutionary philosophy of the equality of man—these were part of the general background. More immediately, the rise of industrialism in the British Isles and Western Europe as well as the United States produced social dislocations and suffering but at the same time gave promise of a more abundant life for all. No doubt, with some people, a determination to improve human welfare was stimulated by the contrast between what actually was and what apparently might be. Certainly the humanitarian stirrings of the time were to be found in many lands at once, and most conspicuously in those countries that were being most rapidly industrialized. In Europe the agitation was in some ways quite different from that in this country. There, it led to violent outbreaks, to the revolutionary attempts of 1830 and 1848. In America, where (except in the Southern states) there was no repressive government to contend with, the reformers had to fear violence only at the hands of unsympathetic mobs: reform did not mean revolt, though it culminated in the Civil War. Despite the differences in the American and European movements, American reformers often consulted and cooperated with their European counterparts, particularly with Englishmen. When it came to human betterment, cultural nationalism gave way to cosmopolitanism.

In Protestant countries the reform ethic was stronger than in Roman Catholic countries, which for the most part were less highly industrialized. Protestantism and reformism were closely related. In the United States the stimulus to reform came largely from two quite different Protestant trends —from the revivalistic, hell-fire teachings of "New Light" Calvinists, on the one hand, and on the other hand from optimistic, salvation-for-all ideas of Universalists, Unitarians, and others who completely repudiated the tenets of Calvinism.

Emerson's philosophy of "transcendentalism" contributed to the reform spirit. Emerson evolved the doctrine of the Oversoul or spiritual essence from which all things derived, including the soul of man. Since all humanity shared in this essential Being, this all-in-all, there existed a very real brotherhood of mankind. And since the Oversoul was good there could be no such thing, in the last analysis, as evil. (The later teachings of Mary Baker G. Eddy, founder of Christian Science, were in some respects similar to those of Emerson.) This philosophy, for all its obscurities and inconsistencies, had practical consequences for its believers. It made them optimistic. It taught them that they were potentially divine and could increase their divinity by identifying themselves more and more fully with the Oversoul, with Being, with Truth. It led them to believe in the perfectability of man.

Still more important as a call to reform were the preachings of the revivalist, Charles G. Finney, who was at first a Presbyterian and later a Congregationalist. In upstate New York and in Ohio, beginning in the 1820's, Finney delivered many a memorable sermon on the dangers of damnation and the possibilities of salvation—through good works as well as faith. "The church," he maintained, "must take right ground on the subject of Temperance, and Moral Reform, and all the subjects of practical morality which come up for decision from time to time." Not all the churches did so, and some reformers (known as "come-outers") left the fold and even turned against organized religion, denouncing it as a bulwark to the *status quo*. Yet many churches heeded Finney's call, especially Presbyterian and Congregational churches, which numbered more reform leaders than did any of the other Protestant sects, even the Quakers.

These leaders implied by their activities that they believed in a sort of earthly millennium as well as a heavenly one. Going a step farther, one religious prophet together with his thousands of followers expected and awaited the actual second coming of Christ. From his studies of the Bible and from other signs and calculations William Miller of Low Hampton, New York, predicted that on a certain day in 1843 Christ would appear and all true believers would ascend bodily to heaven. After new predictions and repeated disappointments he made the date indefinite. His followers formed a lasting sect, the Seventh-Day Adventists.

Miller and other prophets of the time, such as Finney and also Joseph Smith, the founder of Mormonism, were New Englanders by birth and residents of upstate New York at some stage in their careers. So, too, the great majority of reform leaders were New England born, and a large number of them lived at least temporarily in New York state. Most were descended from substantial New England families, neither rich nor poor, whose heads once had been highly respected as preachers, doctors, teachers, and farmers. With the rise of commerce and industry these families lost status in comparison with the upcoming merchants and manufacturers. The families who migrated to New York settled in counties which at first were economically dominant but which by the 1830's had fallen behind the rest of the state. These family back-

grounds indicate that the typical reformer was unconsciously a product of social changes under way in the North.

The reform spirit was far more prevalent among Whigs than among Democrats. Though it affected some of the latter too, it cannot be considered as essentially an extension of Jacksonian Democracy. The Jacksonians advocated political and economic reforms, such as the widening of the suffrage and the destruction of monopoly, but were far from unanimous in supporting social reforms, such as the abolition of slavery. Nor can the reform spirit be viewed as an outgrowth of the labor movement, except in certain cases, notably the drive for free public schools. Most reform leaders disbelieved in unions, opposed strikes, and were indifferent to the plight of the unemployed. William Lloyd Garrison, the abolitionist, denounced labor agitators for trying "to inflame the minds of our working classes against the more opulent, and to persuade men that they are contemned and oppressed by a wealthy aristocracy." A few of the "more opulent," such as the merchants Arthur and Lewis Tappan of New York and Amos and Abbott Lawrence of Boston, contributed vast sums to finance various reforms, especially abolition. This is not to say, however, that big business in general was favorable to social reform. More often than not, reform was resisted by both the laborer and the capitalist. It was essentially a middle-class movement, receiving its greatest support from the reasonably well-to-do farmers, shopkeepers, and professional people of the North and the West.

Toward Universal Education

As of 1830 no state could yet boast a general system of free public education in the modern sense, with full tax support, compulsory attendance, and enforced maintenance of schools, though Massachusetts, as in earlier times, came fairly close to it. A very high proportion of American children had the benefit of the three R's, but most of them still got their learning from church schools, proprietary institutions, private tutors, or

ers was Horace Mann, the first secretary of the Massachusetts board of education, which was established in 1837. He reorganized the state's school system, lengthened

---

Horace Mann on Education
1848

"Now surely nothing but universal education can counterwork this tendency to the domination of capital and the servility of labor. If one class possesses all the wealth and the education, while the residue of society is ignorant and poor, it matters not by what name the relation between them may be called: the latter, in fact and in truth, will be the servile dependents and subjects to the former. But, if education be equally diffused, it will draw property after it by the strongest of attractions; for such a thing never did happen, and never can happen, as that an intelligent and practical body of men should be permanently poor. Property and labor in different classes are essentially antagonistic; but property and labor in the same class are essentially fraternal."

---

members of their own families. Then, during the 1830's, a widespread demand for state-supported primary education arose. This demand came from reformers who feared the consequences of allowing every man to vote, including in many cases even the newly arrived immigrant, without making public provision for his literacy at least. The demand came also from workingmen who hoped that book learning would enable their children to rise in the world. Opposition was forthcoming, however, from taxpayers (especially childless ones) who objected to paying for the education of other people's families, and from Lutherans, Roman Catholics, and other religious groups who already supported their own church schools and did not wish to be taxed for public education besides.

Against such opposition, educational reformers made considerable headway in several of the states. The greatest of these lead-

the school year (to six months), doubled teacher's salaries, enriched the curriculum, and improved teacher training and teaching methods. Henry Barnard led the way to better schools in Connecticut and Rhode Island. In Pennsylvania a school law was passed in 1835, making state funds available for the education of all children and not merely the children of paupers, as formerly; but only the exertions of Thaddeus Stevens in the legislature saved the law from an early repeal. In New York, after William H. Seward became governor in 1839, the upstate system of school districts supporting their own schools was extended to the metropolis. This step aroused much opposition, since it gave control of some new districts to the local Roman Catholic majorities. As early as 1839 North Carolina provided for a system of common schools, though few were set up until the office of state superintendent was created and Calvin H. Wiley was elected to it in 1852. Thereafter North Carolina took the lead in public education in the South.

By the 1850's the principle of tax-supported elementary schools was accepted in all the states, and all of them were making at least a start toward putting the principle into practice. Still, there were vast differences in the quantity and quality of public schools from place to place, the poorest performances and the lowest literacy rates being found in the newly settled areas of the West and in the more sparsely populated parts of the South. Taking the country as a whole, only a small proportion of children of school age were actually going to school, one white child out of every seven in the South and one out of every six elsewhere (1860).

Most teachers were poorly paid and poorly prepared, many of them being themselves scarcely able to read, write, and cipher. In rural district schools, containing husky youths along with tender tots, what the schoolmaster needed was a strong arm rather than a well-stocked mind. If he could not thrash the most obstreperous of his pupils, he could get nowhere with his lessons. Reformers like Mann and Barnard, believing that human nature was essentially good, advocated gentleness and understanding as practiced by progressive educators in Switzerland (notably Johann Pestalozzi). Most teachers—and parents too—subscribed to the old Calvinist doctrine of inborn wickedness: they did not wish to spare the rod. Under the circumstances the majority of teaching positions continued to be filled by men, even in the elementary schools. Seldom did these men look upon teaching as a career; often they were aspiring lawyers or preachers who worked their way through college by doubling as schoolmasters in vacation periods. Nevertheless, teaching was beginning to be looked upon as a profession, and an increasing number of young women

were going into it. With Mann taking the lead, Massachusetts in 1839 established the first American state-supported teacher-training or "normal" school, at Lexington. In 1845 he brought about the formation of a state association of teachers.

Since so many teachers were poorly prepared, both they and their pupils had to rely heavily upon textbooks. Noah Webster's spellers and grammars continued to be widely used. Supplementing them and rivaling them in popularity were the six graded *Eclectic Readers* (1835–1857) prepared by William Holmes McGuffey, who was an Ohio professor and college president and then for many years a professor at the University of Virginia. The McGuffey readers were filled with moral lessons, patriotic declamations, sentimental verse, and fascinating facts. A favorite recitation piece was the following:

> *Woodman, spare that tree;*
> *Touch not a single bough.*
> *In youth it sheltered me,*
> *And I'll protect it now.*

Eventually adopted in 37 states, the McGuffey books gave thousands of schoolchildren a shared background of popular culture and helped to mold the literary tastes of the reading public.

The principle of state support was applied later to secondary than to elementary schools. By 1860 there were 22 tax-supported "free academies" in New York, more than 100 public high schools in Massachusetts, and a total of about 300 such institutions in the nation as a whole. At the same time there were approximately 6,000 private academies. Most of them were open to boys only, a few were coeducational, and a growing number were "female seminaries." Tuition rates, though low by present standards, were so high that only the youth of well-to-do families could afford to attend. Standards and curricula varied a great deal from school to school, since there was neither a public authority nor an academic tradition to enforce uniformity. Most of the academies offered courses in mathematics, public speaking, and the classics, and some of them experimented with new courses in modern languages, natural science, business training, and other practical subjects.

While the private academies were multiplying, so were the private colleges, though at a slower rate, about 80 being founded between 1830 and 1850. Almost all of these were denominational colleges, with close church connections, and their chief though not their only purpose was to prepare a learned clergy. These institutions became too numerous for their own good. Their enrollments were small, in many cases fewer than 100 in the 1850's (even Harvard and Yale had only 400 or 500 students apiece, though the College of William and Mary had nearly 1,000). Generally endowments were scanty, facilities poor, salaries low, and professors unscholarly, though self-sacrificing and sincere. None of these institutions admitted women until, in 1837, Oberlin accepted four girls as regular students and thus became the first coeducational college. Some outsiders feared that coeducation was a rash experiment that approximated free love, but the Oberlin authorities were confident that "the mutual influence of the sexes upon each other is decidedly happy in the cultivation of both mind & manners." Only a few other institutions copied Oberlin's example before the Civil War. Some of the young ladies' seminaries —notably Mount Holyoke, which the most famous of all women educators, Mary Lyon, founded in Massachusetts in 1837—eventually became full-fledged women's colleges.

The idea of state support for higher education had to contend against the prevailing concept of private, denominational control. Besides the older states with public universities (Vermont, North Carolina, Georgia,

Ohio, Virginia), many of the newer states of the Northwest and Southwest committed themselves to the support of higher learning. State universities were established in Indiana, Michigan, Kentucky, Missouri, Mississippi, Iowa, Wisconsin, Minnesota, and Louisiana before the Civil War. None of these, whether old or new, was a true university in the European sense of an institution devoted to high-level, graduate training. Many of them struggled along on meager funds and were little if any larger or more distinguished than most of the denominational colleges or even the better private academies. Privately controlled higher education remained a strong vested interest, and the great majority of college graduates received their degrees from other institutions than state universities.

The standard curriculum, whether in the private college or the state university, still emphasized the old-fashioned liberal arts. A young man who desired training for a professional career (other than the ministry) had few institutions to choose from. He could study engineering at the United States Military Academy, Rensselaer Polytechnic Institute (1824), or at Yale or Harvard, which set up engineering schools in 1846 and 1847. He could study law or medicine at one of several institutions, but no American medical school compared with the best ones abroad. In most cases, as in earlier times, he apprenticed himself to a practicing physician, learned engineering on the job (the Erie Canal was a most productive "school" for engineers), or "read law" in the office of some successful lawyer.

Adult education was furthered by the founding of numerous libraries, study clubs, and self-improvement societies of various kinds. Noteworthy was the Lyceum, which was started by Josiah Holbrook in Massachusetts (1826) and spread rapidly throughout the North. "The first step to form a Lyceum," Holbrook explained, "is for a few neighbors or citizens to agree to hold meetings for their mutual improvement." Next, they could acquire books, scientific apparatus, specimens of rocks and plants,

would lead to imitation, until communities free of crime, poverty, and other evils would cover the land. A number of religious groups, notably the Shakers, practiced a

A Lyceum Lecture. *James Pollard Espy, author of* Philosophy of Storms *(1841), is known as the father of American meteorology. Espy, his paraphernalia, and his audience—in New York about 1838—are caricatured by an unknown artist. The lecture has to do with weather, and the chart on the wall is headed: "Probability of Rain after Sunshine."* (MUSEUM OF THE CITY OF NEW YORK)

and the like. Then they could conduct experiments, carry on discussions among themselves, and sponsor public lectures. The sponsorship of lectures soon became their principal activity. Through the Lyceum many thousands of Americans were able to hear scientists like Agassiz, foreign authors like Dickens, exemplars of self-culture like the "Learned Blacksmith" Elihu Burritt, popular philosophers like Emerson, and social reformers like the abolitionist Garrison or the repentant drunkard John B. Gough.

Perfecting Society and Man

While many reformers hoped to make possible a better life by creating opportunities through education or by eliminating specific social evils, some of the more advanced thinkers aspired to start afresh and remake society by founding ideal, cooperative communities. America still seemed a spacious and unencumbered country where models of a perfect society could be set up with a good chance to succeed. Presumably success

kind of communism as a means of realizing what they considered a truly Christian life. But the impetus to communism (or communitarianism) as a way of perfecting earthly society came chiefly from nonreligious, rationalistic thinkers.

Among the communitarian philosophers, three of the most influential were Robert Owen, Charles Fourier, and John Humphrey Noyes. Owen, famous for his humanitarian policies as owner of prosperous textile mills in Scotland, reached the conclusion that faulty environment was to blame for human failings, hence that poverty and crime would not appear in a rationally planned society. In 1825 he put his principles into practice at New Harmony, on the banks of the Wabash in Indiana. Within a few years New Harmony failed as an economic enterprise, though in other respects it was a success. Fourier, a mere commercial employee in France, never visited the United States, but influenced many Americans through the writings of

Albert Brisbane, whose *Social Destiny of Man* (1840) explained the principles of Fourierism with its self-sufficient associations, or "phalanxes." One or more of these phalanxes was organized in every Northern state, the most famous of them being Brook Farm, a community of intellectuals including Hawthorne, near Boston. Noyes, a native Vermonter and a one-time Yale divinity student, founded the most bizarre and most enduring of all the utopian colonies, the Oneida Community in upstate New York (1848), where his followers carried out his unorthodox sexual theories, old men mating with young women and *vice versa*, all changing partners at his direction, supposedly in the interest of scientific breeding. Needless to say, none of these experiments set a pattern for American life.

Less thoroughgoing reforms, however, did much to alleviate the ills of society as it actually was. No evil was more glaring than the treatment of social offenders and unfortunates. Criminals of all kinds, debtors unable to pay their debts, senile paupers, and the mentally ill were crowded indiscriminately into prisons and jails which in some cases were literally holes, one jail in Connecticut being an abandoned mine shaft. From the 1820's on, the states one by one abolished imprisonment for debt, and some of them greatly improved their handling of the criminal and the insane. New York, with the erection of its new prison at Auburn (1821), introduced a system of solitary confinement by night and group work with absolute silence by day; Pennsylvania tried solitary confinement for both day and night. Though both of these systems now seem harsh, they were then hailed as progressive steps, since they gave each prisoner an opportunity to meditate upon his wrongdoing and also checked the tendency for old convicts to corrupt the young. Public hangings, supposedly a deterrent to crime, used to attract spectators by the thousands, including thieves and pickpockets busily plying their trade. In the 1830's several states began to hold executions within the privacy of prison walls, and a few states did away with capital punishment entirely. While there already existed a few mental hospitals, the insane (unless cared for at home) generally were kept in jail and treated brutally. The Boston schoolmistress Dorothea Dix, shocked by her chance visit to the Cambridge jail (1841), devoted her life to securing the establishment of insane asylums in Massachusetts and other states.

In looking for causes of insanity, pauperism, and crime, many reformers concluded that these evils could be traced largely to strong drink. Americans of earlier generations had been an alcoholically convivial people, with a remarkable per capita consumption of whiskey, hard cider, and rum. The Puritans had been hard drinkers, many respectable preachers continued to resort to stimulants, and few Americans supposed that a birth, a wedding, or a funeral could be properly observed without plenty of liquor—the story is told of drunken pallbearers who lost their way to the grave. From colonial times on, however, a few men like Cotton Mather and Dr. Benjamin Rush had spoken out against intemperance. In the early 1800's an organized temperance movement began with the formation of local societies in New England, and in 1826 the American Society for the Promotion of Temperance appeared as a coordinating agency for the various groups. The movement gained in sensationalism when (1840) six reformed drunkards of Baltimore organized the Washington Temperance Society and began to draw crowds to hear their intriguing confessions. As the temperance forces grew and spread over the country, the crusaders diverged, some advocating total abstinence and others seeing no harm in wine or beer, some favoring prohibition laws and others relying on the individual conscience. Massachusetts and other states experimented with legislation for local option, allowing communities to regulate or prohibit liquor sales, and Maine (1851)

man's perfectionist possibilities. A leading health faddist, Dr. Sylvester Graham, believed that one way to social happiness was through the eating of coarse, whole-wheat

The "Cold Water" Pledge. *Members of the Washington Temperance Society—themselves reformed drunkards—urged drinkers to join them in signing a pledge of total abstinence. This lithograph of 1846, which associates poverty with drink, is dedicated to "the Washingtonians of the United States" and is "commemorative of their Declaration of Independence from the dominion of King Alcohol."* (LIBRARY OF CONGRESS)

passed a statewide prohibition law in response to an agitation led by the Quaker merchant Neal Dow. Prohibitionists in a few other states gained similar victories, but the laws were unpopular and soon were repealed except in Maine.

To some it seemed that not only alcoholic beverages but also tobacco, coffee, and improper foods hindered the full realization of

bread (the "Graham cracker" is a faint reminder of him). Other health reformers relied on hydropathy with its regimen of bathing and water-drinking; spas like the Hot Springs in Virginia became fashionable places for taking the "water cure." Orson Fowler, the foremost exponent of phrenology (a "science" based on the notion that character and personality are revealed in the contour of the cranium), expected to bring about a "renovating of mankind" through the self-understanding that was supposed to result from the examination of bumps on

The Bloomer Costume. *An enterprising Philadelphia music publisher, taking advantage of a timely topic, brought out "The New Costume Polka" and dedicated it to Mrs. Amelia Bloomer. The cover of the sheet music was adorned with this picture of a demure yet stylish young lady wearing the clothes that Mrs. Bloomer recommended.* (LIBRARY OF CONGRESS)

the head. This science gained such popularity that practically everyone turned into an amateur phrenologist.

Whatever the social handicaps that beset man as man, those that a woman had to face were considerably worse. In America she enjoyed a freer life and greater respect than in England or Europe, yet in this country too she was legally an inferior. According to the Anglo-American common law a husband had almost absolute authority over the person and property of his wife: what was his was his, and what was hers was his also. In case of divorce he was far more

likely than she to get custody of the children. Though women worked in household and mill, they could not look forward to careers in medicine, the ministry, politics, or law. By custom they were forbidden to speak in public to a mixed audience, lest they "unsex" themselves and lose their feminine charm.

Though women were active in the reform movements, especially temperance and abolition, male reformers usually compelled them to take a back seat. This discrimination against them intensified an already growing demand for women's rights. In 1848 Lucretia Mott and Elizabeth Cady Stanton called a convention of women; it met in Seneca Falls, New York, and adopted resolutions (patterned on the Declaration of Independence) to the effect that all men *and women* are created equal and endowed with certain inalienable rights. While the feminists failed to obtain the right to vote or hold office, they made noticeable gains before the Civil War. As early as 1839, Mississippi had recognized the right of married women to control their own property; during the next two decades several other states did the same. At least one woman, Dr. Elizabeth Blackwell, gained acceptance and fame as a physician; several women, prominent among them Lucy Stone (who with her husband's approval retained her maiden name), became successful lecturers; a still larger number, including Emma Willard and Catharine Beecher, made great contributions to progressive education, especially for women. Some of the feminists, apparently thinking equality with men meant similarity to them, cut their hair short and wore more or less mannish clothes. Mrs. Amelia Bloomer, for example, attempted to popularize the skirt-and-pantalettes costume which was named for her.

Recalling the Napoleonic Wars and the War of 1812, many reformers agreed with the Quakers that one of the worst ills of the world was war. By 1819 more than a dozen local peace societies had sprung up in various parts of the United States, and in 1828 the Maine merchant William Ladd undertook to coordinate the movement by founding the American Peace Society with headquarters in New York. Later (1840) Ladd devised a peace plan embracing a Congress of Nations and a Court of Nations whose decisions were to be enforced by public opinion rather than economic or military sanctions. Meanwhile the pacifists disagreed, some approving defensive but not offensive wars, others taking a pledge of complete nonresistance. To most of the peace workers in New England, the Mexican War (1846–1848) seemed an act of proslavery aggression on the part of the United States, and they took their stand against it, Henry David Thoreau refusing to pay taxes for its support, and James Russell Lowell writing in the *Biglow Papers:* "Ez fer war, I call it murder,—there you hev it plain an' flat." But the Civil War put the pacifists in a dilemma, at least momentarily, since most of them were also abolitionists. Finally the antislavery cause took precedence over the antiwar cause, as it already had taken precedence over the rest of the reform crusades.

Antislavery and Proslavery

After the Missouri excitement of 1819–1821, Americans involved in the antislavery movement calmed down somewhat, though they continued their work and gradually increased the number of antislavery societies and members. For the next decade their program continued to be mild and gradualistic, and they were most numerous in the South, particularly in the border slave states. The most active national organization was the American Colonization Society (established in 1817), which had adherents in both the North and the South. It aimed to "colonize" freed Negroes in their homeland, and under its auspices the black republic of Li-

beria was founded on the African coast. The society received private contributions and appropriations from the legislatures of Virginia and Maryland to carry on the work, but in ten years it succeeded in transporting to Africa fewer Negroes than were being born in America each month. Northern members began to suspect that their Southern associates were more interested in strengthening slavery, by getting rid of Negroes already free, than in hastening the end of the institution by encouraging slaveowners to manumit their slaves. During the 1820's the most active crusader against slavery itself was the New Jersey Quaker Benjamin Lundy, who published the leading antislavery newspaper of the time, the *Genius of Universal Emancipation*, in Baltimore.

In 1831 Lundy's helper, the young Massachusetts-born printer William Lloyd Garrison, sounded a new and strident note with the first issue of his own paper, *The Liberator*, in Boston. From the outset Garrison condemned the thought of gradual, compensated emancipation and demanded immediate abolition, without reimbursement for slaveowners. Under his leadership the New England Anti-Slavery Society was founded in 1832 and the American Anti-Slavery Society the following year. But he shocked many friends of freedom by the extremes to which he went. He opposed the government, characterizing the Constitution as "a covenant with death and an agreement with hell," and he opposed the churches on the grounds that they were bulwarks of slavery. In 1840 he split the American Anti-Slavery Society by insisting upon the right of women to participate fully in its activities, even to speak before audiences that included men as well as women.

By that time there were in existence nearly 2,000 local societies with a total of almost 200,000 members. These societies remained alive, active, and growing after the disruption of the national organization. The movement as a whole was far bigger than Garrison. His influence was confined mainly to New England, and even in that part of the country he was but one of many impor-

this did not mean precisely what it seemed to mean. The abolitionists aimed at what they called "immediate abolition gradually accomplished." That is, they hoped to bring

---

The Liberator: *First Issue*

1831

William Lloyd Garrison made clear his fiery spirit and his uncompromising aim in the very first number of his abolitionist newspaper, *The Liberator*. He told his readers:

"I am aware that many object to the severity of my language; but is there not cause for severity? I *will* be as harsh as truth, and as uncompromising as justice. On this subject, I do not wish to think, or speak, or write with moderation. No! No! Tell a man whose house is on fire, to give a moderate alarm; tell him to moderately rescue his wife from the hands of the ravisher; tell the mother to gradually extricate her babe from the fire into which it has fallen;—but urge me not to use moderation in a cause like the present. I am in earnest—I will not equivocate—I will not excuse—I will not retreat a single inch—*AND I WILL BE HEARD.*"

---

tant leaders, a few of the others being William E. Channing, Theodore Parker, and Wendell Phillips. In New York and the Middle West the most influential was Theodore Weld, who was far more sane and sensible than Garrison and equally devoted to the cause. Converted to reform by Finney's preaching, Weld worked within the churches, especially the Presbyterian and Congregational. Through the labors of men like Weld, thousands came to disapprove slavery who never joined an antislavery society. Thus it is hard to say how many antislavery people there were at any given time, especially since "antislavery" was a term so broad as to include all kinds and degrees of opposition to slavery.

Most of the active members of organized societies were "abolitionists" in the sense that they favored immediate abolition. But

about a sudden and not a gradual end to slavery, but they did not expect to achieve this for some time. At first, they counted on "moral suasion": they were going to appeal to the conscience of the slaveholder and convince him that slaveholding was a sin. Later they turned more and more to political action, seeking to induce the Northern states and the federal government to aid the cause where possible. Employing propaganda of the deed as well as the word, they helped runaway slaves find refuge in the North or in Canada, though in doing so they did not set up any such highly organized system as the term "Underground Railroad" implies. After the Supreme Court (in *Prigg* v. *Pennsylvania*, 1842) held that the states need not aid in enforcing the federal fugitive-slave law of 1793, abolitionists secured the passage of "personal liberty laws" in several of the Northern states; these laws forbade state officials to assist in the capture and return of runaways. Above all, the antislavery societies petitioned Congress to abolish slavery in places where the federal government had jurisdiction—in the territories and the District of Columbia—and to prohibit the interstate slave trade. Not even the most ardent abolitionists supposed that Congress constitutionally could interfere with a "domestic" institution like slavery within the Southern states themselves.

While the abolitionists engaged in pressure politics, they never formed a political party with an abolition platform. In 1840 the Liberty party was launched, with the Kentucky antislavery leader James G. Birney as its presidential candidate, but this party and its successors did not campaign for outright abolition: they stood for "free soil," that is, for keeping slavery out of the territories. Some free-soilers were friends of the slave; others were Negrophobes who cared nothing about slavery but desired to make the West a white man's country. Garrison said free-soilism was really "white-manism."

In the North, where there was widespread anti-Negro if not proslavery feeling, the antislavery movement provoked much hostility during the 1830's. When Prudence Crandall undertook to admit Negro children to her private school in Connecticut, she aroused the opposition of the community, and the state supreme court decided against her in a lawsuit arising from the controversy. A mob attacked Garrison on the streets of Boston, and another (1837) killed the antislavery editor Elijah Lovejoy in Alton, Illinois. Throughout the North antislavery lecturers, risking their health if not their lives, time and again were attacked with rotten eggs or stones.

In the South the reaction was far stronger, and if no abolitionists were killed, it was only because (from the 1830's on) they dared not even venture into that part of the country. Southern planters expressed horror at the teachings of Garrison; they identified the whole antislavery movement with him and gave him far more notoriety than his importance justified. But the attitude of slaveowners was a response to developments in the South as well as the North. Even if Garrison never had existed, the slaveholders would have been prompted to strengthen the defenses of slavery, for the institution was threatened by Southern slaveless farmers and by the slaves themselves. Between 1830 and 1832 a Virginia constitutional convention and then the state legislature, responding to demands from the western part of the state, considered ending slavery through compensated emancipation but were discouraged by the tremendous expense it would have required. Meanwhile, in 1831, the Negro preacher Nat Turner led a slave insurrection in Southampton County, Virginia, and several dozen whites were slain before Turner and his followers could be captured and put to death. While slave conspiracies were common in the South, Turner's was the only one that actually culminated in rebellion. Always uneasy, always mindful of the horrors of the slave uprising in Santo Domingo (in the 1790's), Southerners now were terrified. They blamed the Turner insurrection on Garrison and his *Liberator*.

While the Southern states strengthened their slave codes, controlling the movements of slaves and prohibiting their being taught to read, Southern leaders proceeded to elaborate an intellectual defense of slavery. In 1832 Professor Thomas R. Dew of the College of William and Mary published a pamphlet outlining the slavery case; in subsequent years many others added their contributions to the cause, and in 1852 the defense was summed up in an anthology, *The Pro-Slavery Argument*. As early as 1835 John C. Calhoun boasted that Southerners had ceased to apologize for slavery as a necessary evil and had been convinced that it was "a good—a positive good." According to the proslavery argument it was good for the slave because he was an infe-

no slaves and had no direct interest in the peculiar institution. Some proslavery propagandists concluded that slavery was such a good thing it should be extended to include

---

Calhoun on Slavery

1837

"I hold that in the present state of civilization, where two races of different origin, and distinguished by color, and other physical differences, as well as intellectual, are brought together, the relation now existing in the slaveholding States between the two is, instead of an evil, a good—a positive good. I feel myself called upon to speak freely upon the subject where the honor and interests of those I represent are involved. I hold then, that there never has yet existed a wealthy and civilized society in which one portion of the community did not, in point of fact, live on the labor of the other. . . . I may say with truth that in few countries so much is left to the share of the laborer, and so little exacted from him, or where there is more kind attention paid to him in sickness or infirmities of age. Compare his condition with the tenants of the poor houses in the more civilized portions of Europe—look at the sick and the old and infirm slave, on one hand, in the midst of his family and friends, under the kind superintending care of his master and mistress, and compare it with the forlorn and wretched condition of the pauper in the poor house."

---

rior creature who needed the master's guidance and who was better off—better fed, clothed, and housed, and more secure—than the Northern factory worker. It was good for Southern society because it was the only way two races so different as the black and the white could live together in peace. It was good for the nation as a whole because the entire Southern economy depended on it, and the prosperity of the nation depended on the prosperity of the South. It was good in itself because the Bible sanctioned it—did not the Hebrews of the Old Testament own bondsmen, and did not the New Testament apostle Paul advise, "Servants, obey your masters"? These and other arguments convinced most Southerners, even those (the great majority) who owned

white workers in the North as well as black laborers in the South.

While spreading proslavery propaganda, Southern leaders tried to silence the advocates of freedom. Southern critics of slavery found it healthful to go North, among them Hinton Helper of North Carolina, James Birney of Alabama, and the Grimke sisters of South Carolina. In 1835 a mob destroyed sacks containing abolition literature in the Charleston post office, and thereafter Southern postmasters generally refused to deliver antislavery mail. Southern state legislatures passed resolutions demanding that Northern states suppress the "incendiary" agitation of the abolitionists. In Congress, Southern Representatives with the cooperation of Northerners secured the adoption of the "gag rule" (1836) according to which antislavery petitions were automatically laid on the table without being read.

As a champion of freedom of speech and petition, John Quincy Adams led a struggle against the gag rule, finally (1844) securing its repeal. Throughout the North many people who were not abolitionists began to feel that civil liberties were endangered in the entire country, not just the South. These people were inclined to sympathize with the abolitionist as a martyr for freedom in the broadest sense. They came to suspect that there really existed, as the abolitionist

claimed, a kind of "Slave Power Conspiracy" to destroy the liberties of the country as a whole. They began to wonder, as Abraham Lincoln did, whether the nation could long continue to be half slave and half free —whether the nation might not become all slave. Thus the majority of Northerners, though not necessarily for love of the Negro, eventually came to sympathize in varying degrees with the antislavery cause, while an even larger and more determined majority of Southerners rallied to the defense of the peculiar institution, thereby laying the foundation for a "solid South."

⇛⇛⇛⇛⟪⟪⟪⟪

BIBLIOGRAPHY

AN INTRODUCTION to Englishmen's comment on American ways may be obtained from *American Social History as Recorded by British Travellers*, edited by Allan Nevins (1923; new ed., 1931), and from Max Berger's *The British Traveller in America, 1836–1860* (1943). Alexis de Tocqueville, *Democracy in America* (4 vols., 1835–1840), is available in a number of editions.

Important interpretations of the literary productivity of the time may be found in Van Wyck Brooks, *The Flowering of New England, 1815–1865* (1936); F. O. Matthiessen, *American Renaissance* (1941); and Lewis Mumford, *The Golden Day* (1926). A biography of a foremost literary figure is R. L. Rusk, *The Life of Ralph Waldo Emerson* (1949).

The best survey of the reform movements as a whole is A. F. Tyler, *Freedom's Ferment: Phases of American Social History to 1860* (1944). R. E. Riegel, *Young America, 1830–1840* (1949), contains a good deal on reform agitation during that decade. R. S. Fletcher, *A History of Oberlin College from Its Foundation through the*

Civil War (2 vols., 1943), amounts to vastly more than a mere college chronicle, since it treats Oberlin as the important reform center which it was. A. M. Schlesinger, *The American as Reformer* (1950), provides a brief, thoughtful introduction to the reform spirit. The relations between religion and reformism form the themes of C. C. Cole, Jr., *The Social Ideals of the Northern Evangelists, 1826–1860* (1954), and T. L. Smith, *Revivalism and Social Reform in Mid-Nineteenth-Century America* (1957), which emphasizes the ideas of the common man rather than those of the "crackpot fringe." C. A. Johnson, *The Frontier Camp Meeting* (1955), covers the subject of revivalism in the Mississippi Valley during the first four decades of the nineteenth century.

On individual reformers and reforms, the literature is so abundant that it can be no more than sampled. A really distinguished work is Arthur Bestor's *Backwoods Utopias: The Sectarian and Owenite Phases of Communitarian Socialism in America: 1663–1829* (1950). Among the many other notable books, the following may be mentioned:

H. E. Marshall, *Dorothea Dix, Forgotten Samaritan* (1937); H. S. Commager, *Theodore Parker* (1936); J. D. Davies, *Phrenology: Fad and Science* (1955); N. K. Teeters and J. D. Shearer, *The Prison at Philadelphia* (1957), a study of the rise and decline of Pennsylvania's system of solitary confinement; Carl Bode, *The American Lyceum* (1956); and Paul Monroe, *The Founding of the American Public School System* (1940).

Betty Fladeland, *James Gillespie Birney: Slaveholder to Abolitionist* (1955), shows that not all abolitionists were "Northern fanatics." R. B. Nye, *William Lloyd Garrison and the Humanitarian Reformers* (1955), succinctly recounts the career of the most famous abolitionist and places him in the context of the reform movement as a whole. See also Nye's *Fettered Freedom: Civil Liberties and the Slavery Controversy, 1830–1860* (1949), an important work. G. H. Barnes, *The Anti-Slavery Impulse, 1833–1844* (1933), makes a case for Theodore Weld as the most important of the abolitionists. On the proslavery argument see W. S. Jenkins's *Pro-Slavery Thought in the Old South* (1935) and Harvey Wish's *George Fitzhugh: Propagandist of the Old South* (1943).

CHAPTER 21

Democratic Defeat and Whig Division

As the 1830's drew to a close and the 1840's began, the two major political parties in the country were national institutions in their organization and their principles. The Democrats and the Whigs numbered their followers in every section, and both advocated measures that stirred the support of economic groups in every area. In the Northeast, the South, and the West, the party masses studied the issues of the day, followed the careers of their favorite chieftains, and turned out at rallies to hear endless speeches. On election day the faithful were brought to the polls—persuaded, cajoled, and sometimes purchased—by intricately and efficiently organized machines that operated from the national and state level down to the cities and even precincts. The parties sought to arouse the loyalty of local factions to a national associ-

ation and to bind these cliques together to labor for the victory of that association. Thus they were a unifying influence in a Union that shortly would be troubled by sectional divergence. Even the differences between the parties tended to strengthen nationalism. Broadly speaking, the Democrats and the Whigs represented different economic aggregations in American society as a whole rather than one class or a combination of classes centered in one section.

Composition of the Parties

The Democratic party that called Van Buren its leader was very much the same party that had followed Jackson. Predominantly it was a party made up of small property holders—farmers of the West, South, and East, wage earners of the Eastern cities, small Southern planters, and some small businessmen. Under Van Buren it was even more the party of the common man than it had been in Jackson's time, for many business-minded Democrats had seceded to the Whigs after the Bank fight. Although it continued to house some conservative representatives of large property (some Southern planters, some Eastern capitalists), it was an organization with a remarkable degree of cohesion. In general, Democrats believed in equality of opportunity; being men on the make, so to speak, they favored free competition unrestricted by monopolistic charters or state franchises. They advocated territorial expansion, a broadened suffrage, and a greater degree of political democracy in state governments. The party was nationalistic in the sense that it was opposed to movements or tendencies that might disrupt or weaken the Union.

On the burning issue of the times, the banking question, most Democrats were opposed to a restoration of the Bank of the United States or to any similar financial system that would create a connection between the national government and the banking world. They favored either state-owned banks that would extend credit to farmers or state-regulated banks that would be unable to defraud poor people. The Democrats in a few states wanted to abolish all banks.

A common Democratic attitude toward banks was that of the "Locofoco" faction of the party in New York, a combination of workingmen and reformers who, with Van Buren's aid, secured control of the party machinery. (The Locofocos got their name because before a party meeting at which they feared their conservative opponents would turn off the gas lights, they provided themselves with the new "locofoco" friction matches.) The Locos believed that paper money was an invention of the bankers to cheat the people and that the practices of many banks had caused the recent panic. In

the legislature they won passage of a law providing for state regulation of banks and requiring banks to carry a certain amount of specie reserve. Although the Locofocos were stigmatized as radicals, they were in reality, at least in money matters, conservatives. Theirs was the conservatism of small capitalists who wanted to restrain big ones by the power of local government.

In contrast to the Democrats, the Whigs were, or seemed to be, a combination of many disparate elements. Their party has been called "an organized incompatibility." It is true that few political organizations have contained so many different economic groups. In the Whig ranks were the business and banking classes of the Northeast, the urban commercial and banking interests of the South as well as most of the big planters of that section, and the business-banking class and some farmers of the West. And yet the results of Whig diversity have been exaggerated. In the early 1840's the Whigs too were a party with a large measure of cohesion.

Most Whigs wanted another national bank and, failing that, they desired a liberal chartering of commercial banks (to advance credit to business) by the states. Most Whigs wanted the tariff raised in greater or lesser degree. Most Whigs, being of the well-to-do classes, feared that the numerical majority, "the mob," would support legislation threatening the interests of property; they were, however, sufficiently realistic to accept the necessity of manhood suffrage. But Whiggery appealed to others than the well-to-do. Many ordinary people in the West and in interior areas in other sections were drawn to the party because of its liberal policy on internal improvements; also, many Westerners voted Whig because they thought the party would do what the West wanted about the public lands. The dominant note of the party might be summed up as a belief that government should help the economy to expand, particularly by extending favors to the upper classes.

The differences between the Northern and Southern wings of the party have been overemphasized by historians. The usual

The Van Buren Program

The policies which the Van Buren administration tried to carry through Congress were partly an expression of the beliefs of

---

The Conservative Whigs

Although the Whigs secured the support of many plain people in elections, theirs was pre-eminently the party of the conservative propertied classes. In the words of one Whig leader: "The Whig party is governed by its leading and reflecting men. The tone of the party is derived from men of property and character, and they are in a measure held to respect property guaranteed by the Constitution and the laws of the land." Whigs liked to say that they knew each other by the instincts of gentlemen. When asked if a gentleman could not be a Democrat, one Whig answered: "Well, he is apt not to be; but if he is, he is in damned bad company."

---

picture is that the Northern wing stood for business and nationalism and the Southern branch for the planters' interests and state rights; therefore, Whigs could never agree on anything except hating people like Jackson and Van Buren. As a matter of fact, the majority of Southern Whigs in the period 1837–1844 were almost as nationalistic as their Northern colleagues. The merchant-banker class was extremely influential in some states and actually controlled the planters. The business interests and their planter allies advocated measures like a national bank and a higher tariff. So also did groups like the Louisiana sugar barons and the Kentucky hemp growers. Only a minority of Southern Whigs, a planter segment, were strong state righters. The gravest danger to Whig unity—the factor most likely to prevent the Whigs, if in power, from enacting a program—was not a North-South disagreement but the possibility that the state-rights minority might be in a position to block the will of the majority.

the equalitarian wing of the party and partly a product of the depression that began in 1837 and lasted throughout the duration of Van Buren's tenure of power. The administration commanded a solid majority in the Senate and could usually put its measures through that body with no trouble, but in the House a coalition of Whigs and conservative Democrats sometimes blocked the administration program.

There was not much the government could do to lessen the impact of the depression—hundreds of bank failures, bankruptcies in business and agriculture, falling prices, and the unemployment of 200,000 workers. The modern concept that government can successfully fight the onset of depression, and has an obligation to do so, simply did not exist at that time. Nor were there any agencies in the government as it was then organized that could have acted to combat depression conditions. The only tradition of government intervention in economic matters was the Federalist–National

Republican–Whig program of aid to business, to which Democrats were fiercely opposed. Consequently Van Buren recommended but few direct antidepression measures. He contented himself with advising Congress to authorize the borrowing of $10 million to meet expenses during the emergency, which advice the legislators agreed to, and he urged that the government should accept only specie for taxes and other due payments, which was hardly a measure calculated to raise either prices or confidence. Basically, the attitude of the administration was that the country would have to work its way through the depression until the depression worked itself out.

In formulating a program of permanent legislation, as contrasted to emergency measures resulting from the depression, the administration clearly reflected the wishes of the dominant farmer-labor segment of the party. The President urged Congress to reduce the price of public lands, and he recommended passage of a general pre-emption bill giving settlers the right to buy 160 acres at a set minimum price before land in any particular area was opened for public sale. A bill graduating land prices downward passed the Senate three times but was blocked in the House. A similar fate befell a pre-emption bill. His program of agrarian reform foiled by legislative opposition, Van Buren had to resort to executive action to please his urban followers. By presidential order he established a ten-hour work day on all federal works. For the first time in the nation's history the government had taken direct action to aid the rising labor class.

The most important measure in the President's program, and the most controversial, was his proposal for a new fiscal system. With the Bank of the United States destroyed and with Jackson's expedient of "pet banks" discredited, some kind of new system was urgently needed. Van Buren's fiscal ideas attest both his mental ingenuity and

his sincere devotion to Democratic principles. The plan he suggested, known as the "Independent Treasury" or "Subtreasury" system, was simplicity itself. Government funds would be placed in an independent treasury at Washington and in subtreasuries in specified cities throughout the country. Whenever the government had to pay out money, its own agents would handle the funds. No bank or banks would have the government's money or name to use as a basis for speculation. The connection between the government and the banking community would be broken permanently.

Van Buren placed the Independent Treasury proposal before Congress in a special session called in 1837. It encountered the immediate and bitter opposition of most Whigs and of many conservative Democrats. Twice a bill to establish an independent treasury passed the Senate only to fail in the House. Not until 1840, the last year of Van Buren's Presidency, did the administration succeed in driving the measure through both houses of Congress.

Although the Independent Treasury system was abolished by the Whigs in 1841, it was re-established by the Democrats in 1846 and remained the nation's fiscal system until the Civil War. The creation of the Independent Treasury was a momentous event in the history of the republic in its middle period of development. It signified that, in financial matters at least, the small capitalists were going to have something to say about the future economic course of the country. They had decided that the government should control its own finances and that private groups should not utilize the nation's finances for any purpose. Under the Bank of the United States, a private group associated with the government had controlled in part national finances and credit. That day was now gone. Henceforth the banking power would have to operate on its own instead of as a part of the government.

But by destroying the central bank the Democrats had eliminated the only coordinating agency in the business-banking complex. At the very time that the economic system was becoming more centralized, the banking system was decentralized.

Some Results of the Depression

The depression years that witnessed the divorce between the national government and the banking interests saw also a separation between the state governments and private enterprise. In the 1830's many of the states had entered actively into the business field. They had built and operated roads and canals, or they had supplied the credit to private concerns to construct such internal improvements. In some Southern and Western states state-owned banks had been established.

Most of the experiments in state ownership and operation failed. The "people's" banks failed, not because they were politically managed (although such was often the case), but because they could not withstand the impact of the depression. A similar fate befell most of the state-sponsored works of internal improvements. To finance these projects the states had borrowed heavily, assuming that they could repay out of anticipated profits. But in the depression there were no profits. Unable to meet their obligations, some states repudiated their debts. Many state enterprises were abandoned or operated at a loss borne by the taxpayers.

Out of the failure of the state experiments in business and out of the depression there emerged a widespread conviction that the old Federalist-Whig program of an association between government and business to expand the economy was unsound. The 1840's saw a general retreat of government from the field of business. In the banking area the trend was toward state regulation of banks, with many states adopting laws patterned after the New York Locofoco system of control. Another financial trend was toward the system of free banking. Before the depression period an individual or a company wishing to form a bank had to make special application to the legislature for permission. Now many states passed laws setting up general conditions under which any individual or company could incorporate a bank. Parallel developments occurred in other parts of the business world. As the states withdrew from the building sphere, they encouraged, necessarily, private interests to enter. New state acts—general laws of incorporation similar to the banking measures—made it easier for private groups to create large combinations. With the acceptance of principles like limited liability for stockholders, the corporation began to assume many of its modern forms. Ironically, it was the Democrats, regarded by conservatives as hostile to business, who were the principal architects of the new laws. Perhaps unconsciously, they had done much to push business along a new road of expansion.

Election of 1840

As the campaign year of 1840 approached, the Whigs scented victory. The effects of the depression still gripped the country, and the Democrats, the party in power, could be blamed for the depression. So reasoned the Whigs, who now realized that a party representing the upper income groups must, if it expected to win, pose as a party of the people. The Whigs were ready to offer themselves to the voters as the men who could save the nation from depression. As for the Democrats, they could only stand on their record, which for the last four years was a gloomy one, and behind Van Buren, who was far from being a glamorous leader.

The Whigs also realized that they would have to achieve more unity and a stronger organization than they had demonstrated in 1836; in particular, they would have to settle on one candidate who could appeal to all segments of the party and to all sections of the country. Obviously the easiest way to coordinate the party was through the new

William Henry Harrison. *At his inauguration Harrison was 68—the oldest man to become President. Although he was an extensive landowner, he had slipped into debt, and at the time of his election was supporting his family on his income as county recorder.* (LIBRARY OF CONGRESS)

mechanism of the national nominating convention, already used by the Democrats. Accordingly the Whigs held their first convention in Harrisburg, Pennsylvania, in December, 1839. Their veteran leader, Henry Clay, "Mr. Whig," expected the nomination, but the party bosses decided otherwise. Clay had too definite a record; he had been defeated too many times; he had too many enemies. Passing him over, the convention nominated William Henry Harrison of Ohio, and for Vice President, John Tyler of Virginia.

William Henry Harrison was a descendant of the Virginia aristocracy, but all of his adult life had been spent in the North-

west, where he first came as a young army officer in General Wayne's campaign against the Indians. After a short military career he resigned his commission and purchased a large tract of land near North Bend, Ohio; his father-in-law was one of the biggest land speculators in the West. Wealth and honors followed fast: secretary of the Northwest Territory, delegate to Congress, and governor of Indiana Territory and superintendent of its Indian affairs. As supervisor of the Northwest Indians he came into conflict with the great Shawnee chief, Tecumseh, over land cessions; in the war that followed Harrison won an indecisive victory over the Indians at Tippecanoe (near present-day Lafayette, Indiana). But his dubious triumph made him a national hero, and always thereafter he was known as "Old Tippecanoe." His military reputation was enhanced when he defeated the British in the Battle of the Thames in the War of 1812. After the war he served for a short period in Congress. His governmental experience might have been limited and his military abilities might be questioned, but he was undeniably a renowned Indian fighter (like Jackson) and a successful general. In short, he was a popular national figure.

The Democrats, meeting in national convention at Baltimore, nominated Van Buren, pointed proudly to their record, especially the Independent Treasury, and condemned all the works of Whigs, especially the Bank of the United States. Demonstrating that their party was, in some respects, no more united than the Whigs, the Democrats failed to nominate a vice-presidential candidate, declaring vaguely that they would leave the choice of that office to the wisdom of the voters.

The campaign of 1840 set a new pattern in American politics. It inaugurated the circus-carnival atmosphere that would mark presidential elections for years in the future and that would awe or amuse European be-holders—vast meetings, shouting parades, party badges and other insignia, and campaign songs. With the emergence of two sharply defined parties, politics was becoming professionalized. The party bosses who could organize and deliver the votes were becoming more important than the "statesmen" who delivered speeches, and victory and the spoils of office were becoming more important in the minds of many people than adherence to principle. Throughout the campaign the eager Whigs were on the offensive. They depicted themselves as the party of the people and the party that could save the nation from depression. They accused the Democrats of bringing on the depression by reckless financial legislation. They said Van Buren was an aristocrat who used cologne, drank champagne, and engaged in other undemocratic and un-American practices. A Democratic newspaper unwisely sneered that Harrison was a simple

was almost handing the election to the Whigs, and they took the cue fast. Yes, their candidate was a simple man of the people, they proclaimed, and he loved log cabins and cider (actually he was a man of substance and lived in a large and well-appointed house).

Thereafter the log cabin was an established symbol at every Whig meeting, and hard cider an established beverage. Hundreds of Whig orators bragged that they had been born in log cabins or apologized for having been brought into the world in more sumptuous edifices. Thousands of Whig auditors listened to these effusions and happily chanted the songs that turned every Whig gathering into a frenzy of enthusiasm: "Tippecanoe and Tyler too" and "Van, Van is a used-up man." Against such techniques and the lingering effects of the depression the Democrats could not fight. When the votes were counted in November, Harrison

---

The Singing Whigs

In the campaign of 1840 the Whigs introduced several political techniques that became standard instruments of democracy—mass meetings, stump speakers, popular newspapers, campaign songs. Harrison was the first presidential candidate to stump the country. A favorite song at Whig rallies ran as follows:

What has caused the great commotion, motion, motion,
   Our country through?
   It is the ball a rolling on.
For Tippecanoe and Tyler too—Tippecanoe and Tyler too,
And with them we'll beat little Van, Van, Van,
Van is a used up man,
And with them we'll beat little Van.

---

soul who would be glad to retire to a log cabin if provided with a pension and plenty of hard cider. In a country where many people lived or had lived in log cabins, this

had 234 electoral votes to 60 for Van Buren. The Whig victory was not as sweeping as it seemed; of the popular vote, which was about twice as large as in 1836, Harrison had 1,275,000 to Van Buren's 1,129,000, a majority of less than 150,000.

Harrison was never to have a chance to demonstrate what sort of President he

John Tyler. *Tall, slender, charming in manner, Tyler impressed people in personal intercourse. But in his political dealings he made a host of enemies. Henry Clay in his own time called him a "traitor" to Whiggery, and Theodore Roosevelt in a later age referred to him as "a politician of monumental littleness." His defenders have pointed out that he was a skilled administrator and diplomat.* (LIBRARY OF CONGRESS)

would have made. Although he seemed to be in good health, he was sixty-eight years old in 1841, and the strain of the campaign and the inauguration and the pressing demands of his office-seeking supporters were apparently too much for him to stand. He contracted a cold which turned into pneumonia, and he died on April 4, 1841, exactly one month after he had been inaugurated —the first President to die in office. In his brief presidential tenure he had looked for advice to the accepted leaders of the party, particularly to Clay and Webster. Webster became Secretary of State, and four of

Clay's friends went into the Cabinet. Undoubtedly Clay and Webster had expected to guide the old soldier through the political jungle. But now "Tippecanoe" was dead and "Tyler too," a practicing politician and a Southern Whig, was in the White House.

The Whigs in Power

John Tyler was the first Vice President to succeed to the office of chief executive. Although there were some who contended that he should proceed on the basis that he was merely the second officer acting as the first, he assumed that the powers as well as the title of the Presidency had descended upon him. A member of an aristocratic Virginia family, Tyler had been in politics since he was twenty-one. He had served in both houses of the Virginia legislature, in both houses of Congress, and as governor of his state. In every phase of his long political career he had cast himself in the role of representative of the conservative planter class. He went to Congress as a Democrat, but he left that party in protest at what he considered Jackson's overly equalitarian program and imperious methods. Probably one reason the Whigs put him on the ticket with Harrison was the hope that he would attract the votes of similar conservative former Democrats.

Tyler's lengthy political record would suggest that his views on specific issues must have been well-known to his party. A similar impression would follow from a superficial examination of his personality and character. In expressing opinions he seemed to speak frankly and honestly; in his manner there was a certain dogmatism that seemed to indicate deep conviction. And yet the curious fact is that in 1841 people were not sure what John Tyler believed. This was because his course had not always been straight. Although in the past he had opposed measures like a national bank, a protective tariff, and internal improvements, he was known to be a close friend of Clay, who supported these measures. In the recent campaign Tyler's statements on the bank issue had been vague but seemed to indicate, if they meant anything, that he favored a bank; Clay apparently had the impression that the new President would throw the support of the administration behind a new bank and other Whig projects. But as soon as Tyler became President he broke with Clay and fought the latter's program, which was also the program of the majority of Northern and Southern Whigs. Undoubtedly he had always been at heart an agrarian, state-rights Whig, however much he had trimmed in 1840. Undoubtedly he was also piqued at Clay because that Senator assumed that he could voice the party's principles. Whatever the case, the Tyler administration was about to reveal the great, dangerous weakness of the Whig party: the minority segment of the Southern wing—the state-rights group—could prevent the majority from enacting a positive program.

At first all seemed to be harmony among the Whigs. Tyler retained Harrison's cabinet, and continued the late President's policy of discharging Democrats from government jobs and putting Whigs in their places. In the Senate Clay offered a set of resolutions which he intended as a kind of platform for the party—a program which, if adopted, would keep the party in power. These resolutions declared for (1) repeal of the Independent Treasury Act, (2) the creation of a new Bank of the United States, (3) an increase in the tariff rates, and (4) the distribution of the proceeds of public land sales among the states.

A part of Clay's proposed platform was enacted without causing serious division in the party. With near unanimity the Whigs passed a measure, which Tyler signed, abolishing the Independent Treasury system. Clay's distribution bill, which was more of a personal matter with him than an article of party faith, aroused some opposition. Western Whigs preferred lower land prices to distribution; many Whigs, including the President, thought it was imprudent to give away federal money when the government was having trouble meeting expenses; and some Whigs, again including Tyler, feared that the consequent loss of revenue would force the passage of an extremely high, and hence politically dangerous, tariff bill. In order to get his pet measure accepted, Clay had to agree to an amendment that distribution would stop whenever it became necessary to raise tariff rates above the 20 per cent level set by the tariff of 1833. Clay hoped that later he could persuade Congress to repeal the amendment; but in this he failed, and his failure hurt him when he took up the tariff issue. Twice he carried the party in Congress with him on bills raising tariffs above the 1833 maximum rates and at the same time retaining distribution. But Tyler refused to accept any combination of distribution and higher duties; he vetoed both bills. He was demanding, in effect, that the party decide for one or the other. Faced by a choice, the Whigs took the tariff. They agreed on a bill, the tariff of 1842, which set the rates at approximately the same level as in the tariff of 1832; since the new rates were higher than those of 1833, distribution was nullified. Tyler accepted the act but with no great show of enthusiasm. With the majority of the party, however, the bill was a popular measure. Strongly protective in nature, it pleased the manufacturing and producing interests that supported the Whigs.

The Whig legislative program made a bid for the approval of another important bloc of possible supporters: the Western settlers and farmers. In the years between 1836 and 1845 the West continued its steady expansion. Emigrants in large numbers moved into the Western states and territories and into other unsettled areas. Arkansas became a state in 1836, Michigan in 1837, and Florida in 1845. The greatest rush of settlers was into the future states of Wisconsin, Iowa, and Minnesota. The West, ever growing in extent and population and hence ever increasing in political power, desired certain laws from the national government, especially a general pre-emption bill. To attract Western voters and to build up the party in the West, the Whig leadership put through Congress the Pre-emption Act of 1841, which made it possible for a man to claim 160 acres of land before they were offered publicly for sale and to pay for them later at $1.25 an acre. Sometimes called the "log cabin bill," this measure was hailed by the Whigs as a relief measure for sufferers from the depression and as a proof of their party's devotion to the welfare of the common man. The Democrats had attested the same devotion in Van Buren's administration when they had advocated an identical law.

The Fatal Whig Division

Although the Whigs enacted a more positive program than historians have usually given them credit for, the results of their success were largely nullified and the unity of their organization seriously threatened by an ugly fight in the party on the big issue of the period: the bank question. On one side in this controversy were the important party leaders and a majority of Northern and Southern Whigs. On the other were the President and a small group of agrarian, state-rights Southern Whigs, most of whom, like Tyler, were former Democrats. The tragedy of the Whigs was that the Tyler faction, a minority, controlled the Presidency and hence could veto the desires of the majority in Congress.

The Whig leadership was committed to restoring a financial system similar to the Bank of the United States. Tyler desired a kind of "state-rights national bank": one that would confine its operations to the Dis-

trict of Columbia and establish branches in the states only with their consent. Apparently sensing that Tyler did not like the idea of a national bank, the leaders framed a measure creating exactly such an institution but tried to disguise it by calling it a "Fiscal Bank." Not deceived, the President vetoed the bill. Thinking they could meet his objections by playing with words, Clay and his colleagues secured the passage of another act creating what they called a "Fiscal Corporation." Again Tyler interposed a veto. Lacking a sufficient majority to override the veto, the Whig majority knew that their plan of restoring the Bank was dead. They fumed with rage at the President, who added to their anger by vetoing a number of internal improvement bills. In an unprecedented action for a political party, a conference of congressional Whigs, attended by most of the Northern members and a majority of the Southern members, read Tyler, the titular leader of the party, out of the organization. All the cabinet members resigned except Webster, who had some diplomatic business with Great Britain that he wished to settle. To fill their places, the President appointed five men of his own stripe—former Democrats.

Below the surface of the feuds and the bitter words in Washington, a portentous new political alignment was taking shape. Tyler and the small band of conservative Southern Whigs who followed him were getting ready to join the Democrats. When the office of Secretary of State became vacant in 1843, Tyler appointed Calhoun—who had been a Democrat, had left the party in the 1830's, and had become a Democrat again. Into the common man's party of Jackson and Van Buren was about to enter a group of men who had aristocratic ideas about government, who thought that government had an obligation to protect and even expand the institution of slavery, and who believed in state rights with a single-minded, almost fanatical devotion. As the immigration of planters into the Democratic party would continue in the years ahead, the character of that party would change; it would become less equalitarian, more conservative, more Southern. Correspondingly, the Whig party would change too, becoming less agrarian and more industrial, less Southern and more Northern. The Tyler administration saw the start of an ominous trend that would end with both parties becoming less national and more sectional.

Foreign Affairs, 1837–1844

From the close of the War of 1812 to 1840 relations between the United States and Great Britain were generally friendly and sometimes intimate. After the war England realized that it would be smart to treat Canada's neighbor to the south with more respect. The diplomatic agreements demilitarizing the Great Lakes and fixing the Canadian boundary (except at the eastern and western ends) indicated that Great Britain was now prepared to regard the United States as a sovereign nation and that relations between the two countries were entering a new phase—a phase in which each would consider the other as approximately an equal.

Not that all was sweetness and light between the two English-speaking nations. On both sides of the ocean there were factors —and people—at work to produce mutual irritation; there were some sore spots in the situation which provoked dissension and were even capable of causing war. American orators and editors, especially at election times, delighted to recall the Revolution and the War of 1812 and to dilate on British perfidy and tyranny, twisting the Lion's tail, it was said, so he would roar loud enough for the Irish-American voters in New York City to hear. British travelers in this country still angered Americans by

going home and writing books or giving lectures in which they sneered at the crude American culture and the raw American ways. During the internal-improvement craze, Americans had borrowed large sums of money from English financiers; and they sometimes displayed that resentment which the debtor often has for the creditor. Correspondingly, when a number of American states defaulted on their debts in the 1830's, the English spoke bitterly of people who could not be trusted to keep a contract. The greatest potential cause of trouble between the two nations, however, was the unsettled part of the Canadian boundary: the Maine and Oregon regions. Inevitably the time was coming when the ever-expanding American people would move into those areas; inevitably when that happened a tense, explosive situation was going to result, one that might bring on war.

And yet in these years, despite all the actual and potential provocations, the two nations remained at peace. This was partly because the men in charge of both governments were generally sober and moderate individuals who realized that neither country had a fundamental grievance that justified war. It was partly, perhaps largely, because the economic relations between Britain and America were too important to risk a conflict. The United States purchased more British goods than any other country, taking 15 per cent of England's total exports. Britain, on the other hand, depended on America for many raw materials, especially cotton, to keep its industries going. Any rupture of these commercial contacts might be disastrous to the economies of both countries. A final factor working for peace, its nature hard to define and its influence almost impossible to fix, was the cultural affinity of the English-speaking nations. They would not have criticized each other so fiercely had they not felt a certain bond of similarity. Besides, the critics in both countries had the pleasure of knowing that their barbs would be understood—they were couched in the same language.

Starting in the late 1830's a series of incidents unfolded that brought the two nations into diplomatic controversy and close to actual war. In 1837 rebellion broke out in the eastern provinces of Canada. Although the insurrection was supported by only a small minority and was easily crushed, many Americans, especially on the northeastern border adjoining Canada, applauded the rebels and furnished them with material aid. Were not the Canadians doing what the Americans had done in 1776? And if they won their independence, might they not wish to join the United States? The defeated rebel leaders retired to Buffalo, New York, where they recruited Americans to their cause and organized raiding parties to cross the Niagara River. To supply their forces over the river they chartered a small American steamship, the *Caroline*. One night while the ship was moored at a wharf on the American side the Canadian authorities sent over a picked party which forcibly took possession of the *Caroline* and burned her; in the melee one American was killed.

Instantly excitement flared on both sides of the border. In Washington and London, however, the tendency was to view the matter more calmly. President Van Buren issued a proclamation asking Americans to abide by the neutrality laws, and he sent General Winfield Scott, a trusted "trouble shooter," to the border to act as a pacificator. At the same time the President was resolved to uphold American rights. He believed that the attack on the *Caroline* was an utterly indefensible act and a violation of American sovereignty. Through the State Department a protest was delivered to Britain along with a demand for an apology and reparations. The English government, although not upholding the attack, did not disavow it; nor did the British offer to pay

the compensation the American government had asked.

While the *Caroline* affair simmered to a slow boil, two new incidents stoked the flames up again. One was the question of the Maine boundary. As defined by the Treaty of 1783, this line was impossible to locate. Previous attempts to fix it by mutual agreement and by arbitration had failed. In 1838 Americans and Canadians, mostly lumberjacks, began to move into the Aroostook River region in the disputed area. A head-smashing brawl between the two parties, dignified by the title of the Aroostook War, threatened more trouble between England and America. It was averted when Van Buren sent General Scott to the "war" zone with instructions to stop the fighting. Scott persuaded the Maine and Canadian authorities to withdraw their forces until the boundary could be set by diplomatic negotiation.

The second inflammatory episode involved a Canadian named Alexander McLeod, who was suspected of being a member of the party that had boarded the *Caroline*. Being imprudent enough to enter New York, he was arrested by the state authorities and charged with murder and arson. Immediately the British government reacted with majestic rage. Admitting that the boarding party had been an official one, England contended that McLeod could not be accused of murder because he had acted under orders. The Foreign Secretary, the bellicose Lord Palmerston, demanded McLeod's release and threatened that his execution would bring "immediate and frightful" war. McLeod came to trial in the Tyler administration, when Webster was Secretary of State. Although Webster did not think McLeod was worth a war, he could do nothing to effect his freedom. The prisoner was under New York jurisdiction and had to be tried in the state courts, a peculiarity of American jurisprudence which the British did not seem to understand. Fortunately for the cause of peace—and for himself—McLeod was able to establish an alibi, and was acquitted.

Even though the McLeod case had been settled and the passions aroused by the Canadian rebellion were cooling, relations between the United States and Britain were still tense as the Tyler administration began. There were still too many festering points of disagreement that might produce war, especially with a man like Palmerston in power. England had never given satisfaction in the *Caroline* affair; the Maine dispute was obviously going to have to be ended soon; with Americans moving in large numbers into the Oregon country people in the West were demanding the occupation of that area. As if these problems were not enough, England, the leading antislavery nation and hence the leader in the attempt to stamp out the African slave trade, was asking for the right to search American merchant ships suspected of carrying black cargoes. Although the slave trade between Africa and the United States had been closed since 1809, Americans could engage in traffic between Africa and other countries. Moreover, slavers of other nations frequently sought to avoid capture by hoisting the American flag. The British had sought this right for years; always the American government, particularly sensitive on the matter of search of its vessels by England, had refused it. Complicating the situation was a practice in the domestic slave trade in the United States whereby slaves were carried by sea from port to port. Sometimes the ships in this trade were blown off their course to the British West Indies, where the authorities, acting under English law, freed the slaves. In 1841 an unusual incident occurred that aroused widespread anger in the United States, especially in the South. An American brig, the *Creole*, sailed from Virginia for New Orleans with over a hundred slaves aboard. En route the slaves mutinied, took possession of the ship, and took her to the Bahamas. Here British officials declared the bondsmen free. Although Webster protested strongly that the *Creole* had entered the port under compulsion and that hence she was under American law, England refused to return the slaves.

At this critical juncture a new government came to power in Great Britain, one that was more disposed to conciliate the United States and to settle the outstanding differences between the two countries. One of the first acts of the new ministry was to send an emissary, Lord Ashburton, to America to negotiate an agreement on the Maine boundary and other matters. Ashburton was an urbane and tactful nonprofessional diplomat and a man with a long record of friendship for the United States. In Webster, Ashburton would confront an individual very much like himself: Webster, likewise not a professional diplomat, was nevertheless a talented negotiator. Ashburton liked Americans, and Webster admired the English. Both men sincerely wished to avoid war, and to gain this objective both were willing to compromise on others. Soon after they met, they agreed to discard most of the documents and data over which previous diplomats had disagreed and to reach a decision through the medium of informal discussions. The result of their deliberations was the Webster-Ashburton Treaty of August 9, 1842.

The most important issue settled by the treaty was the Maine boundary, which was fixed at its present location. By the terms of this arrangement, the United States received about seven twelfths of the disputed area, which was about as much as it could expect. Minor rectifications in the boundary were made in the Lake Champlain area and from Lake Superior to the Lake of the Woods. These changes were based upon more recent and accurate geographical information, and were fair to the United States. As a result of Webster and Ashburton's work, the boundary was now established as far west as the Rocky Mountains; only the Oregon

both nations would maintain naval squadrons off the African coast, the American ships being charged with the duty of chasing slavers using the American flag.

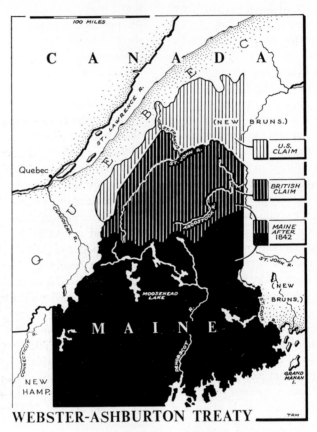

WEBSTER-ASHBURTON TREATY

country was still in dispute. The negotiators showed no disposition to deal with the knotty Oregon question.

Other issues of dissension disposed of by the treaty were the extradition of criminals and the slave trade. One section listed seven crimes for which the United States and Canada would extradite accused citizens of the other country. On the question of the slave trade, Ashburton asked for the right of British warships to "visit" suspected slave ships that were flying the American flag. Webster refused, saying that the right of visit was the same as the right of search. Finally, they compromised the difference by agreeing that

Through exchanges of notes that were not technically part of the treaty, Webster and Ashburton also eased the memories of the *Caroline* and *Creole* affairs. Ashburton expressed "regret" for the raid on the *Caroline;* he also pledged that in the future there would be no "officious interference" with American ships forced by "violence or accident" to enter British ports—presumably meaning there would be no repetition of the *Creole* episode.

The Webster-Ashburton agreements were the product of reasonable compromise. Although neither country was completely satisfied, the governments of both felt they had won enough to ratify the treaty. The treaty removed any chance of immediate war and eased the way for further agreements in the future.

In the Tyler administration the United States established diplomatic relations with a new nation—China. Ever since 1784 American ships had engaged in trade with China; by the 1840's this trade and commercial contacts with other areas in the Orient was becoming important enough to attract general attention in America. The possibilities of the China trade had also long attracted the interest of England, whose government resented the restrictions which the weak Chinese government imposed on the economic activities of foreigners. In 1842 Britain forced China to open certain ports to foreign trade. Eager to share the new privileges, American mercantile interests persuaded Tyler and Congress to send a commissioner to China to negotiate a trade treaty. The choice of the first commissioner to China was a fortunate one: Caleb Cushing turned out to be a brilliant diplomat. In the Treaty of Wanghia, concluded in 1844, he secured all the economic concessions which American interests desired. He also persuaded the Chinese to grant Americans the right of extraterritoriality—the right, if accused of crimes, to be tried by American officials rather than by Chinese judges. In the next ten years American trade with China steadily increased in volume.

The Supreme Court, 1837–1844

Although the Democrats had lost control of the executive branch of the government and were generally a minority in Congress, they had an iron grasp on the Supreme Court. Jackson had been able to appoint seven new justices; thus, of the nine members, seven were agrarian Democrats. And the Chief Justice after 1835, Roger B. Taney, was a Jacksonian of the Jacksonians. Denounced as a cheap politician and a dangerous radical

when he was chosen to head the Court, he suffered under similar criticisms during his twenty-eight years as presiding justice. After his death his reputation suffered at the hands of historians, many of whom condemned him for being too much a state-rights man and for truckling too much to the South. Only in recent years has he been recognized as a great jurist and a great Chief Justice.

Jacksonian Jurist. *"The Constitution is gone," wailed Daniel Webster when Roger B. Taney became Chief Justice of the Supreme Court in 1835. Conservatives professed to fear that Taney would plunge the judiciary into radical excesses. Actually, during his twenty-eight years on the Court, the tall, slender Marylander would demonstrate both liberal and conservative qualities. The descendant of an indentured servant who had become a planter, Taney was devoted to the ideals of an agrarian society and a limited national government. But he also believed that the states should act to control the segments of economic power represented by business.* (NATIONAL ARCHIVES)

Between the Marshall-dominated Court and the Taney-dominated Court there was no sharp break in constitutional interpretation. But there was a marked change in emphasis. Taney and the majority of his colleagues were moderate agrarian liberals. In general they tended to recognize the right of popular majorities, acting through state

cided against the state. But now Taney, speaking for the Democratic majority, supported Massachusetts. Although he advanced legal precedents to justify the deci-

---

Chief Justice Taney on the Object of Government

The accession of Taney to the Supreme Court marked a modification in the nationalistic course followed by the tribunal under Marshall. Under Taney the Court was also more inclined to take note of changing economic and social conditions. In his first constitutional opinion, the Charles River Bridge case, Taney defined the purpose of Government: "But the object and end of all government is to promote the happiness and prosperity of the community by which it is established; and it can never be assumed, that the government intended to diminish its power of accomplishing the end for which it was created. The continued existence of a government would be of no great value, if, by implications and presumptions, it was disarmed of the powers necessary to accomplish the ends of its creation, and the functions it was designed to perform, transferred to the hands of privileged corporations. While the rights of private property are sacredly guarded, we must not forget, that the community also have rights, and that the happiness and well-being of every citizen depends on their faithful preservation."

---

legislatures, to regulate private property rights and the activities of corporations. In general, without adhering at all to the doctrines of Calhoun, they were inclined to modify the nationalism of the Marshall Court.

The attitude of the Court was revealed in the case of *Charles River Bridge* v. *Warren Bridge* (1837). In briefest essence, the background of this case was as follows: one company had a charter from Massachusetts to operate a toll-bridge for a specified period of years; the legislature authorized another corporation to erect a bridge that would be toll-free; the first company contended that the state's action was invalid because it was a breach of contract. It was the old question—Could a state alter an agreement with a corporation?—which in the Dartmouth College case Marshall had de-

sion, Taney based his position broadly on Jacksonian social doctrine. The object of government, he said, was to promote happiness, and this purpose was superior to property rights; a state had power to regulate corporations if such action was necessary to achieve the well-being of the community. Although the decision opened the way to increased state control and was wildly denounced by conservatives, it really aided the development of business. Industry was not going to grow if older corporations could maintain monopolies and choke off the competition of newer companies.

Another Taney decision which enlarged state powers was *Bank of Augusta* v. *Earle* (1839). The question here was whether a corporation chartered in one state could do business in another which wished to exclude it. The Court held that under interstate comity a corporation had a general right to operate in other states, but that a state could, if it wished, exclude a foreign corporation or establish regulations for its entrance. This decision led many states to enact regulatory laws for corporations from other states. In the absence of any federal regulation of interstate commerce, these measures were the only restrictions on companies engaged in business on a regional or national scale. In other cases, notably the so-called Licence Cases (1847), the Court modified the earlier *Gibbons* v. *Ogden* decision, and held that under certain conditions the federal commerce power was not exclusive and that the states possessed a limited concurrent power to act.

The question of interstate commerce and who was to control it involved issues that bothered Southerners: the domestic slave trade and the rendition of fugitive slaves. A federal law of 1793 placed the responsibility for the return of runaway slaves upon national and state courts and required state officials to help enforce the national law. But as the antislavery movement waxed in strength, some Northern states passed "personal liberty laws" which made it difficult if not impossible to catch fugitives and banned state officers from assisting in their capture. In 1842 the constitutionality of these measures was challenged before the Court in the case of *Prigg* v. *Pennsylvania*. The Court held that the Pennsylvania law was void; no state law could impede the right of an owner to get his property back. But because the enforcement of the fugitive slave clause in the Constitution was exclusively a federal power, state authorities were not required to aid in the rendition of fugitives.

In the case involving economic issues, the court had spoken with a fair degree of unanimity. But in the Prigg case it divided. There was a majority and a minority opinion. The highest tribunal in the land was split as deeply on the slavery controversy as the whole nation would shortly be.

-)))-)))-)))-)) (((-(((-(((-(((

BIBLIOGRAPHY

MANY OF THE monographs and biographies cited in Chapters 18 and 19 continue to be useful for the period from 1837–1844. Special political studies throwing light on the Van Buren and Harrison-Tyler administrations are O. D. Lambert, *Presidential Politics in the United States, 1841–1844* (1936); H. R. Fraser, *Democracy in the Making* (1938); and R. G. Gunderson, *The Log-Cabin Campaign* (1957). The troubled course of the Whig party is traced in Carroll, *Origins of the Whig Party*, and Cole, *The Whig Party in the South*. The most penetrating analysis of the South in these years is Sydnor, *The Development of Southern Sectionalism, 1819–1848*. Three solid works on economic developments are B. H. Hibbard, *A History of the Public Land Policies* (1924); R. G. Wellington, *The Political and National Influence of the Public Lands, 1826–1842* (1914); and D. R. Dewey, *State Banking before the Civil War* (1910).

Studies of the leading political figures are numerous and, for the most part, at least adequate. Van Buren can be studied in Fitzpatrick, ed., *The Autobiography of Martin Van Buren*, and in Alexander, *The American Talleyrand*. Satisfactory biographies of Harrison are Freeman Cleaves, *Old Tippecanoe* (1939), and J. A. Green, *William Henry Harrison* (1941). Of higher quality is O. P. Chitwood, *John Tyler* (1939). Calhoun is brilliantly depicted in Wiltse, *John C. Calhoun, Sectionalist*. A penetrating analysis of Clay is Poage, *Henry Clay and the Whig Party*. Other highly useful biographies are Swisher, *Roger B. Taney;* Fuess, *Daniel Webster,* vol. 2; Chambers, *Old Bullion Benton;* and Eaton, *Henry Clay and the Art of American Politics.*

Foreign relations are treated in several ex-cellent works. Official American policy is traced in S. F. Bemis, *American Secretaries of State* (1927–1929), vol. 5. An older but still useful study is J. S. Reeves, *American Diplomacy under Tyler and Polk* (1907). Valuable monographs are A. B. Corey, *The Crisis of 1830–1842 in Canadian-American Relations* (1941); J. B. Brebner, *North Atlantic Triangle* (1945); Tyler Dennett, *Americans in Eastern Asia* (1922); and Dulles, *The Old China Trade.*

CHAPTER 22

Expansion and Conflict

I N 1845 JOHN TYLER, frustrated and embittered, retired from Washington to
his native Virginia. In 1849 another
President, James K. Polk, went home to
Tennessee serene and satisfied in the knowledge that he had carried his policies to complete victory. Not only had he induced
Congress to adopt his legislative program,
but, more important, he had contributed to
his country's greatness by adding to its domain a magnificent new physical empire.
Those four years, 1845–1849, were a period
of tremendous territorial expansion. The
tide of emigration continued to roll into the
upper Mississippi Valley, increasing the population of the states in that area and
bringing two new states, Iowa (1846) and
Wisconsin (1848), into the Union. The settled frontier had now moved to a line half-
way across the continent.

The expansive energies of the American
people were not, however, confined to the
territorial limits of the United States, even

though huge regions in the trans-Mississippi
West were still unsettled. Americans looked
longingly toward lands not clearly owned
by their government—the Oregon country
—and to lands owned by another government—Mexico—as places where they would
like to live and which they would like to
possess. That they should overlook that
part of their own country west of Missouri
was not strange. According to explorers,
this area was so arid as to be unfit for white
habitation. On maps it was called the "Great
American Desert," and under Jackson it
had been marked off as a place for Indians
to live in. And so Americans moved to frontiers outside the United States—to Oregon
in the "Far West" and to the Mexican borderlands southwest of the international
boundary. And inevitably their government
followed them, annexing or joining these
areas to the growing republic. During the
Polk administration, over one million square
miles of new territory came under Ameri-

can control, and the western boundaries of the United States advanced from the Louisiana Purchase line to the Pacific Ocean. Well might the ordinary-looking little man from Tennessee feel proud of his work. No other President except Jefferson had acquired so much for his country.

When the westward thrust of the 1840's was finished, the United States was a larger, richer, and more powerful nation. The new western empire and its immense resources opened possibilities of national development almost beyond calculation. The ultimate effect, then, of expansion would be to strengthen nationalism. But the immediate result was to weaken it; outward expansion provoked internal conflict. To the older sections, or to certain economic-political groups in them, the West appeared as a prize to be struggled for and exploited. It

of influence. In short, the West created, or was capable of creating, a dangerous disequilibrium between the sections.

Reasons for American Expansion

A contemporary editor who approvingly observed the expansionist spirit of the 1840's called it "Manifest Destiny," and his apt phrase has been adopted by historians to characterize both the mood and the process of expansion. The editor meant that it was the destiny or fate of the American people to advance into and to take possession of certain regions. Although Manifest Destiny had the virtue of elasticity and could, if necessary, be stretched to cover any coveted area, its advocates commonly gave it defined limits: the United States was preordained to control all of North America. There is significance in the mechanistic im-

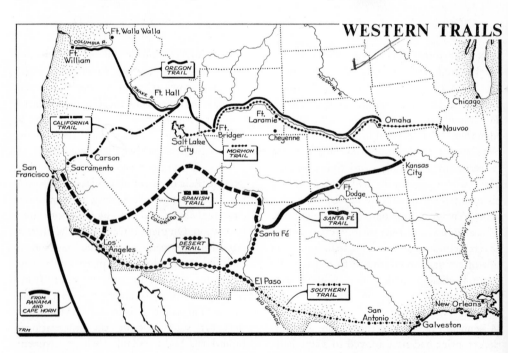

WESTERN TRAILS

could be a prize—to the section that won control; but to whichever section lost the struggle, the West could be a menace, because the loser would suffer a diminution

plications of Manifest Destiny. Expansion was not just something that humans willed; it was created by certain forces, historical, geographical, cultural, beyond their control. Although expansion could be defended logically—and it was loudly defended—it did not, being partly superhuman, particularly need justification. In this sense,

ways were better than those of other countries; therefore, they had a right and even an obligation, if they were powerful enough, to impose their ways on less able or

---

An Imperialist View of Oregon

Although most Americans justified the acquisition of Oregon and California with the simple formula of Manifest Destiny, the leading advocates of expansion foresaw more immediate commercial goals: possession of the Pacific ports would enable the United States to dominate the Pacific and Oriental trade. A principal exponent of this view was Senator Thomas Hart. Benton of Missouri. In a speech in 1848 he painted a glowing picture of Oregon and its value as a trade base: "Agricultural capabilities to sustain a great population, and to furnish the elements of commerce and manufactures —a vast and rich commerce and navigation at its hands—a peaceable sea to navigate—gentle and profitable people to trade with them—a climate of supreme and almost miraculous salubrity—a natural frontier of mountain ramparts—a triple barrier of mountains—to give her a military impregnability. . . . I now come to another advantage, common to all North America, and long since the cherished vision of my young imagination. A Russian Empress said of the Crimea: Here lies the road to Byzantium. I say to my fellow-citizens: Through the valley of the Columbia, lies the North American road to India."

American expansionism was strikingly similar to the rationale of imperialism of European nations in the nineteenth century. The most important difference between American and European imperialism was that whereas Europeans were moving to regions at a far distance from their homelands, Americans were advancing into frontiers contiguous to their own country and within the continental limits of North America.

Like other countries of Western civilization in the nineteenth century, the United States was strongly affected by nationalism, that feeling or belief of belonging to an in-group that was superior to other groups. Like the people in other nations, Americans thought that their institutions and their

fortunate peoples, who would benefit from the experience. With Americans this concept of national primacy was reinforced by a conviction, widely and deeply held, that the United States was charged with a vast mission: to demonstrate to all the Western world the virtues and the glory of democracy. This mission was peculiar to America, the world's greatest democracy. The lesson might be taught, the goal achieved, by the power of example, with other nations voluntarily adopting American ideals. But those ideals could be spread more easily and immediately by forcing them, if necessary, on peoples in regions adjacent to the United States.

In the complex of expansionism the youth of the American nation was a factor of vital importance. The United States was, so to speak, an immature giant, conscious of its strength but not quite sure of it, conscious of its destiny but fearful that a powerful

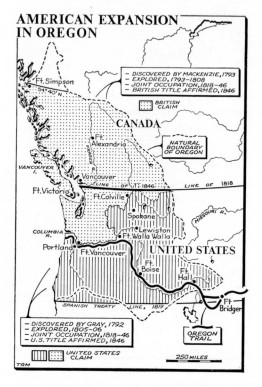

AMERICAN EXPANSION IN OREGON

- DISCOVERED BY MACKENZIE, 1793
- EXPLORED, 1793–1808
- JOINT OCCUPATION, 1818–46
- BRITISH TITLE AFFIRMED, 1846

BRITISH CLAIM

- DISCOVERED BY GRAY, 1792
- EXPLORED, 1805–06
- JOINT OCCUPATION, 1818–46
- U.S. TITLE AFFIRMED, 1846

UNITED STATES CLAIM

250 MILES

rival might block its further growth. The great fear was of England, old in the wiles of diplomacy, experienced in the ways of war. Did not Britain have a foothold in Oregon? Was she not trying to dominate the new republic of Texas, which had just overthrown Mexican rule? This uncertainty about the future, this distrust of England, caused Americans to be bumptious and boastful when talking about expansion, and caused their leaders to utter the wild, warlike statements that puzzle or disgust modern readers. Also difficult for moderns to comprehend is the seeming obsession of Americans of the 1840's to extend the nation to the Pacific. This is because we do not see the same map that they saw. On

their maps everything west of the Louisiana Purchase line was owned or claimed by a foreign power. Such a situation seemed as wrong or incomplete to them as it undoubtedly would to us today.

Expansion in Oregon

The ownership of Oregon might be in dispute, but its boundaries were clearly defined—on the north the latitude line of 54°40′, on the east the crest of the Rocky Mountains, on the south the forty-second parallel, and on the west the Pacific Ocean. Included in its half million square miles were the present states of Oregon, Washington, and Idaho, parts of Montana and Wyoming, and half of British Columbia.

At various times in the past the Oregon country had been claimed by Spain, Russia, France, England, and the United States. By the 1820's only the last two nations remained in contention for Oregon. The others had withdrawn and surrendered their rights to Britain or to the United States or to both. The American and British claims to Oregon were equally valid—or invalid. Both countries could assert title on the basis of the activities of their explorers, maritime traders, and fur traders. The English had one solid advantage: they were in actual possession of a part of the area. In 1821 the powerful British fur trading organization, the Hudson's Bay Company, under the leadership of its factor, John McLoughlin, established a post at Fort Vancouver, north of the Columbia River.

Whatever the merits of Britain's claims, she showed a disposition to compromise the controversy by effecting an agreement with the United States to divide Oregon. Several times the English government proposed the Columbia as a suitable line of division. The United States, also showing a desire to compromise, countered by suggesting that the forty-ninth parallel would be a more satisfactory boundary. This difference in official views prevented a settlement of the Oregon question in the treaty of 1818. Unable to agree on a demarcation line, the diplomats of the two powers negotiated a compact whereby the citizens of each were to have equal access to Oregon for ten years. This arrangement, called joint occupation, was renewed in 1827 for an indefinite period, with either nation empowered to end it on a year's notice.

In the 1820's and 1830's most Americans did not seem to care whether Oregon was occupied at all; only a few sought access to the territory. American fur trading companies tried, not very successfully, to compete with the Hudson's Bay Company. Various propagandists and promoters urged American title to all of Oregon. One was Hall J. Kelley, a Boston schoolmaster, who devoted most of his life to advertising the economic potential of the Oregon country; another was Nathaniel J. Wyeth, a Boston merchant, who organized two overland expeditions to Oregon. Kelley, Wyeth, and others worked hard to stir up public concern, but their efforts had little effect. The first real American interest in Oregon came as a result of the activities of missionaries. The principal religious denominations were becoming increasingly conscious of the importance of foreign missions, and hearing that the Indians of the Oregon area, who were obviously "foreigners," were eager to receive Christian teachings, they decided to send missionaries to them. Ministers like Jason Lee, Marcus Whitman, and Father

---

Emigrants on the Oregon Trail

In 1846 Francis Parkman, cultured young Easterner and future historian, traveled through the West. He described what he saw in *The Oregon Trail* (1849), a classic account of the West: "We were late in breaking up our camp on the following morning, and scarcely had we ridden a mile when we saw, far in advance of us, drawn against the horizon, a line of objects stretching at regular intervals along the level edge of the prairie. An intervening swell soon hid them from sight, until, ascending it a quarter of an hour after, we saw close before us the emigrant caravan, with its heavy white wagons creeping on in slow procession, and a large drove of cattle following behind. Half a dozen yellow-visaged Missourians, mounted on horseback, were cursing and shouting among them, their lank angular proportions enveloped in brown homespun, evidently cut and adjusted by the hands of a domestic female tailor. As we approached, they called out to us: 'How are ye, boys? Are ye for Oregon or California?' As we pushed rapidly by the wagons, children's faces were thrust out from the white coverings to look at us; while the care-worn, thin-featured matron, or the buxom girl, seated in front, suspended the knitting on which most of them were engaged to stare at us with wondering curiosity. By the side of each wagon stalked the proprietor, urging on his patient oxen, who shouldered heavily along, inch by inch, on their interminable journey."

Pierre Jean de Smet made the long journey to Oregon to establish missions. All of the missionaries located their posts south of the Columbia River; the Protestants tended to concentrate in the fertile Willamette Valley, where, being married men with families to support, they engaged in agriculture.

The missionaries described their work in

West. Amazed observers called it the "Oregon fever." Rather than being a fever, the great migration was a normal expression of the dynamic energy of a young and grow-

Migrants Crossing the Plains. *Migrants on the Western trails traveled in canvas-covered wagons. Some of the heaviest wagons weighed from 3,000 to 7,000 pounds, and required the pulling service of ten or twelve horses or oxen. Smaller wagons of the type shown in the print weighed about 2,500 pounds. A wagon train of migrants operated under the direction of a captain who assigned each wagon a position. An average day's trip for a train was from fifteen to twenty miles.* (LIBRARY OF CONGRESS)

reports and letters that were published in the influential religious journals and widely reprinted in secular newspapers. They dwelt quite as much on the rich soil and lovely climate of Oregon as on the spiritual condition of the Indians. The public reaction was almost incredible. Suddenly, and without apparent reason, vast numbers of Americans seemed to be aware of Oregon. Just as suddenly, beginning in 1841, thousands of pioneers took the trail to the Far

ing nation. In part it was a repetition of earlier frontier movements; it was also a manifestation of the new mood of expansion that was beginning to grip the country and that would have to run its course.

The emigrants to Oregon traveled the long, difficult, and often deadly route known as the Oregon Trail. It started at Independence, Missouri, at the bend of the Missouri River, and led in a northwesterly direction to the Platte River at Fort Kearney, Nebraska. At this point the trail ran west along the Platte, and its north fork into southern Wyoming, crossed the Rockies at South Pass, entered the Oregon country at the Snake River Valley, and eventually led to the Columbia. The Oregon Trail was 2,000 miles in length, it penetrated into Indian country, and it crossed mountains and semidesert regions. To the emigrants, traveling in caravans of covered wagons and accompanied by huge herds of cattle, it presented enormous problems in transportation. The average period required for the journey was from May to November. Some never lived to complete it. But the great majority got through. By 1845, 5,000 Americans were living south of the Columbia—and demanding that their government take possession of Oregon. The whole United States seemed to support their demands. Obviously the government would have to act.

Expansion in Texas

Southwest of the international boundary of the United States stretched the northern provinces of Mexico—Texas, New Mexico, and Upper California—once parts of Spain's colonial empire in North America but since 1822 states in the independent "Republic of Mexico." Under Spanish rule the provinces had been subject to only the lightest supervision from the government of the viceroyalty in Mexico, and only a few thousand white men had settled in them. The same conditions prevailed under the Republic, which lacked the power and the population to govern and settle such distant areas. At one time, after the Louisiana Purchase, the United States had advanced a claim to Texas, but had renounced it in 1819. Twice thereafter, however, in the Presidencies of J. Q. Adams and Jackson, the United States had offered to buy Texas, only to meet with indignant Mexican refusals. The mere fact that purchase was proposed indicated that American interest was focused on Texas and that eventually Manifest Destiny would point to this region. In fact, no large crystal ball was necessary to foretell that soon all the frontier provinces would fall to the United States, the one nation that had the resources to settle them.

The Mexican government invited the inevitable in Texas. In the early 1820's it encouraged American immigration by offering land grants to men like Stephen Austin who would promise to colonize a given number of families on their concessions. Probably the motive of the government was to build up the economy of Texas, and hence its tax revenues, by increasing the population with foreigners, but the experiment was to result in the loss of Texas to the United States. Thousands of Americans, attracted by reports of the rich soil in Texas, took advantage of Mexico's welcome. Most of them settled in the coastal plain area; the great majority, by the very fact of geography, came from the Southern states, sometimes bringing with them slaves, although slavery was forbidden in Mexico after 1829. By 1835 approximately 35,000 Americans were living in Texas.

Almost from the beginning there was friction between the settlers and both the Mexicans they came in contact with and the Mexican government. Whether the trouble was over land titles, taxes, or other issues, it resulted from one fundamental cause. The Americans and the Mexicans represented two different cultures which clashed when brought into close relationship. Putting it perhaps too simply, the virile, pushing Anglo-Saxon culture of the United States came into natural conflict with the older, more leisurely Latin civilization of Mexico. Inevitably the points of difference increased in number and bitterness as time went on. Finally the Mexican government, realizing that its power to control Texas was in effect being challenged by the settlers, moved to exert control. A series of restrictive measures was followed by an act abolishing the powers of the various states of the Republic, a measure that the Texans took to be aimed specifically at them. In the best American tradition they resolved to uphold their rights by rebelling. In 1836 Texas proclaimed its independence.

The aroused Mexican government announced that it was not going to let Texas go. The Mexican dictator, Santa Anna, advanced into Texas with a large army that should have been able to defeat the Texans, who even with the aid of volunteers, money, and supplies from private groups in the United States were having difficulty in organizing a resistance. Indeed, for a time it seemed that Santa Anna would crush the rebellion. A Texas garrison at the Alamo mission in San Antonio was exterminated; another at Goliad suffered substantially the same fate when the Mexicans murdered most of the force after it surrendered. But General Sam Houston, emerging as the national hero of Texas, kept a small army together, and at the battle of San Jacinto (April 21, 1836, near present-day Houston) he defeated the Mexican army and took Santa Anna prisoner. Although the Mexican government refused to recognize the captured dictator's vague promises to withdraw Mexican authority from Texas, it made no further attempts to subdue the province. Texas had won its independence.

The new Republic did not wish, however, to remain independent. It desired to become a possession of the United States, and through its president, Sam Houston, Texas asked for recognition, to be followed by annexation. Sound reasons dictated the decision of the Texas leaders. Texas, with a population of at the most 50,000, needed the protection of the United States against Mexico, which might try to reconquer the state. Texas lacked the human and material resources to support the expenses of a national government. But fundamentally Texas wanted annexation because the great majority of its people were Americans who naturally wanted to be a part of their own country.

Texas asked for annexation in Jackson's second administration. Although the President favored annexation, he proceeded cautiously. Sentiment for adding Texas to the United States was strong in all sections but particularly so in the South, where it was believed that the huge area would open new borders for cotton cultivation and, when it entered the Union as one or several states, enlarge the political influence of the South. The latter consideration was particularly important to Southern leaders like Calhoun who were becoming increasingly aware that most of the remaining territory within the present national limits would be settled and admitted as free states, thus tipping the sectional balance against the South.

But there were signs of opposition to Texas, too. Texas applied for annexation at a time when abolitionism was beginning to make its influence felt in politics, when angry talk was heard in Congress about the right of petition and the slave trade. Many Northerners felt a moral repugnance to human servitude, and openly expressed a conviction that it would be immoral to extend the dominion of slavery; others, not quite so idealistic or frank about their motives, were opposed to incorporating a region that would add to Southern votes in Congress and in the electoral college. To Jackson it seemed that annexation would cause an ugly sectional controversy and disrupt the Democratic party in an election year (1836). Furthermore, it was almost certain to bring on a war with Mexico. He did not, therefore, propose annexation to Congress, and did not even extend recognition to Texas until just before he left office in 1837.

His successor, Van Buren, also forebore, for similar reasons, to press the issue.

Refused by the United States, Texas sought recognition, support, and money in Europe. Her leaders talked about creating a vast southwestern nation, stretching to the Pacific, which would be a rival to the United States; some of them probably believed what they were saying, although it is more probable that they were trying to put additional pressure on the government in Washington. Whatever their motives, it was the kind of talk that Europe, particularly England, was charmed to hear. An independent Texas would be a counterbalance to the United States and a barrier to further American expansion; it would supply cotton for European industry and provide a market for European exports. England and France jumped to recognize Texas and to conclude trade treaties with her. The English government played with the idea of guaranteeing the independence and boundaries of the new nation.

News of Britain's interest in Texas reached the United States in 1843–1844, when Manifest Destiny was beginning to seize the imagination of large segments of the American people. The result was another attempt at annexation. President Tyler, eager to increase Southern power, persuaded Texas, not so eager to receive another possible snubbing, to apply again, and Secretary of State Calhoun submitted an annexation treaty to the Senate in April, 1844. Unfortunately for Texas, Calhoun presented annexation as if its only purpose was to extend slavery. Put forward on a sectional basis and backed by an unpopular President, the treaty had no chance, and was soundly defeated. But it was clear to all except some of the politicians, who should have known better, that the public favored annexation in some form and that, as with Oregon, the government would soon have to act in some way.

Expansion in New Mexico and California

New Mexico, the second of Mexico's frontier provinces, supported a scanty population on a semiprimitive economy. Its small metropolis and trade center, Santa Fe, was three hundred miles from the most northern settlements in Mexico. Under Spanish rule the New Mexicans had to export their few products over a thousand miles to Mexico City and Vera Cruz and from these economic centers import their meager finished goods. When Mexico became independent, she let it be known that traders from the United States would be welcome in New Mexico. An American, William Becknell, wagoned a load of merchandise to Sante Fe in 1821 and sold it at a high profit. Out of his success, widely reported in the East, arose the famous and colorful "Sante Fe trade."

The mechanics of the trade were simple. Every year the traders, who were small merchants and sometimes even enterprising farmers, gathered a stock of simple manufactured goods to be moved to Santa Fe in wagons. They collected at some central point, usually Independence, Missouri, and after reaching Council Grove traveled in an organized caravan over what soon became known as the Santa Fe Trail. Over 800 miles in length, the trail crossed the Kansas plains to the bend of the Arkansas, and followed that river upstream a short distance before dipping into New Mexico. Usually the lumbering covered wagons of the traders required six weeks to complete the trip. On the return journey, the merchants carried gold, silver, furs, and mules.

Although the profits for the individuals who engaged in the trade were often high, the total volume of this "commerce of the prairies" was not large, and the number of Americans who were concerned with it was small. Nor did the trade result in any considerable American settlement in New Mexico, although a few traders and Rocky Mountain trappers decided to make their homes there. The real significance of the

The first Americans to enter California were maritime traders and captains of the Pacific whaling ships, who put in to California harbors to barter goods or acquire

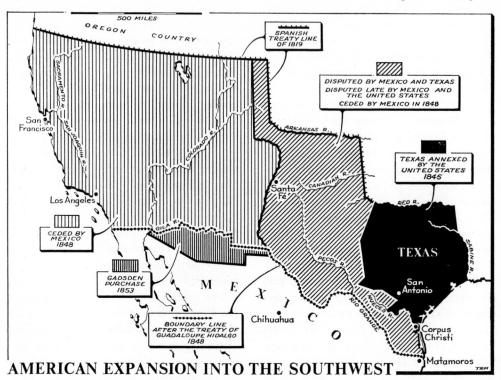

AMERICAN EXPANSION INTO THE SOUTHWEST

Santa Fe trade was not in amounts of dollars or people, but in its influence upon American concepts of expansion. It focused attention on a new area, opened up still another route to the West, and pointed another direction for Manifest Destiny.

More distant from the homeland than New Mexico and even freer from Mexican supervision, if that was possible, was the third of the northern provinces, California. In this vast, rich region lived perhaps 7,000 Mexicans, descendants of Spanish colonists, who engaged in agricultural pursuits, chiefly ranching, lived lives of primitive plenty, and carried on a skimpy trade with the outside world. Here was another area clearly marked off for the workings of American expansion.

supplies. Following them came merchants, who established stores, imported merchandise, and conducted a profitable trade with the Mexicans and Indians. A good example of the merchant adventurer is Thomas O. Larkin, who set up business in Monterey in 1832 and soon attained the status of a leading citizen. Although Larkin maintained close and friendly relations with the Mexican authorities, he secretly longed for the day when California would become an American possession. In 1844–1845 he accepted an appointment as United States consul, with instructions to arouse sentiment among the Californians for annexation.

Nearly all of the first settlers had come to California by sea, but as reports spread of its rich soil and mild climate, immigrants began to enter from the east by land. These were pioneering farmers, men of the type who were penetrating Texas and Oregon in search of greener pastures. Indeed, some of the first agricultural migrants were people who had started for Oregon and changed their destination to California. The overland route to California followed the Oregon Trail to a point near the present Wyoming-Idaho boundary where, turning southwestward, it became the California Trail, and crossing present Utah and Nevada, led through the Sierra Nevada Mountains to California. By 1845 there were 700 Americans in California, most of them concentrated in the valley of the Sacramento River. The overlord of this region, and in a sense the leader of the Americans, was John A. Sutter, once of Germany and Switzerland, who had moved to California in 1839 and had become a Mexican citizen. His headquarters at Sutter's Fort was the center of a magnificent domain where the owner ranched thousands of cattle and horses and maintained a network of small manufacturing shops to supply his armed retainers.

The United States government had shown an interest in California even before many Americans had moved there. Jackson had toyed with the idea of buying a part of the area, and so had Tyler. As with Oregon and Texas, the United States feared that Great Britain wanted to acquire or dominate California, a suspicion that was given credence by the activities of British diplomatic agents in the province. A curious incident in 1842 illustrated the direction of official American thinking. The commander of the American naval squadron in the Pacific heard (falsely, of course) that war had broken out between his country and Mexico; he also understood that a British fleet was heading for California. Executing what he thought were the wishes of the govern-

ment, he took possession of Monterey and proclaimed annexation. A highly embarrassing situation followed, with the impetuous officer and his government having to present some quick apologies. But the incident revealed to all, including Britain and Mexico, that the United States was looking yearningly at California. Equally significant was the growing desire of the American settlers there to become part of the United States.

Election of 1844

The campaign of 1844 illustrates the truth that professional politicians sometimes mistake the popular will. In that year a majority of the people obviously and unmistakably favored a program of expansion, but many of the professionals, particularly those of the conservative Whig party, who were more removed from the masses than the Democrats, did not seem to sense the expansionist mood of the country. Clay expected to be the Whig candidate, and Van Buren the Democratic nominee. Both wanted to avoid taking a stand on the annexation of Texas, because a stand, no matter on which side, was certain to lose some votes. Consequently, they issued separate statements, so similar in tone as to indicate previous consultation between the authors, opposing annexation without the consent of Mexico.

Clay's action did not harm his candidacy. The Whig convention nominated him unanimously, although the platform discreetly omitted any reference to Texas. But Van Buren had destroyed his chances with the Democrats, particularly with those from the South, who were enraged by his opposition to annexation. The Democratic convention threw him aside, and nominated James K. Polk of Tennessee, a champion of expansion. Furthermore, the Democrats, more representative of the people than the Whigs and hence more aware of popular opinion, recognized the political attractiveness of Manifest Destiny, and they clutched it to their party. The platform caught fairly the prevailing mood of expansionism in its

ELECTION OF 1844

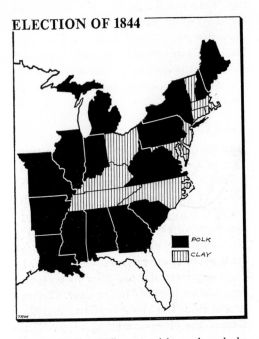

POLK
CLAY

key resolution: "That our title to the whole of the Territory of Oregon is clear and unquestionable; that no portion of the same ought to be ceded to England or any other power, and that the re-occupation of Oregon and the re-annexation of Texas at the earliest practicable period are great American measures, which this Convention recommends to the cordial support of the Democracy of the Union."

The "re's" in the resolution were clever attempts to make the proposed acquisitions seem entirely legal: Oregon had always belonged to the United States and Texas was originally a part of the Louisiana Purchase. Cleverness marked every aspect of the Democratic platform and every phase of Democratic planning for the campaign. By combining Oregon and Texas, the Democrats separated Texas from the slavery question. One territory would eventually add to the

strength of the free states, the other to the slave states. Nobody could accuse the Democrats of sectionalism; rather, they stood forward as the champions of *national* expansion. Furthermore, the platform was designed to appeal to two sections, the South and West, which acting together could control the government. In fact, the Democrats were deliberately attempting to cement an alliance of the agricultural sections on the basis of mutual interest. To the South they offered Texas and a low tariff; to the West they offered Oregon and the restoration of the Independent Treasury.

A third party appeared in the campaign, one that had been organized four years earlier. This was the Liberty party, made up mostly of Western abolitionists who demanded the abolition of slavery in the territories and in the District of Columbia. In 1840 their candidate, James G. Birney, had polled some 7,000 votes. Now Birney was running again and hoping to do better. The Liberty party was a cloud on the horizon, one that showed some Americans were sufficiently excited about the slavery issue to inject it into politics.

Throughout the campaign the Democrats, like the Whigs four years earlier, took the offensive. Sensing that in expansion they had a popular program, they emphasized expansion in their appeals to the voters. As in 1840, shouted slogans often were substituted for sober speeches, with the eager Democrats crying from platform and press for "The re-annexation of Texas and the re-occupation of Oregon" and "All of Oregon or none"; after the election the latter demand would be translated into the more dramatic cry of "Fifty-four forty or fight." Too late Clay realized that he had muffed the expansion issue, and announced that under certain circumstances he might be for the acquisition of Texas. His tardy straddling probably cost him more votes than it gained. The Democratic techniques were effective. Polk carried the election by 170 electoral votes to 105, although his popular lead was less than 40,000. Significantly, the Democrats secured a majority in both houses of Congress. If the votes meant anything, they were a mandate for expansion. Of another kind of significance was the popular vote of the Liberty party, which increased to 62,000.

President Tyler, who would remain in office until March, 1845, viewed the election as a mandate to secure the southern part, Texas, of the Democratic prize-package. He proposed to Congress, which also understood perfectly well the meaning of the election, that Texas be annexed by joint resolution of both houses, a device which would get around the necessity of obtaining two-thirds majority in the Senate for annexation by treaty. In February, 1845, Congress voted (120 to 98 in the House and 27 to 25 in the Senate) to admit Texas to the Union. Conditions were affixed: Texas could be subdivided into not more than four additional states; it had to pay its own public debts but was to retain its public lands; and it had to submit any boundary disputes in which it became involved to the United States. Texas accepted the conditions, and became a state in December, 1845.

The Acquisition of Oregon

James K. Polk has been called the first "dark horse" presidential candidate, meaning one who suddenly emerges from relative obscurity to win the race. He was not quite so obscure in 1844 as some people, particularly the Whigs, affected to believe. Born in frontier North Carolina, Polk emigrated, then in his mid-twenties, to Tennessee, thus following the pattern of the man who became his political mentor, Andrew Jackson. In Tennessee he practiced law and politics, soon becoming recognized as one of the state's Democratic leaders. Elected to the national House of Representatives,

he held his seat for fourteen consecutive years, serving for four of them as speaker. In 1839 he left national politics to become governor of Tennessee; and although defeated for re-election, he was undeniably a national figure, being prominently mentioned for the Vice Presidency in 1840 and 1844. Nobody ever accused Polk of possessing personal glamour. In appearance he was thin, worn, even grim, and his public manners comported with his looks. But he had a good mind, he worked hard at his job,

James K. Polk. *Slight of stature and unimpressive in appearance, Polk was a man of iron determination. In his daily schedule he arose at six o'clock in the morning and worked far into the night. Always frail in health, he drove himself too hard in the Presidency and left the office physically broken. Three months after his retirement he was dead.* (LIBRARY OF CONGRESS)

and above all he had an iron, implacable will. Probably no other President entered office with so clearly defined a program and accomplished so much of it as Polk. He was the ablest President between Jackson and Lincoln and perhaps the strongest chief executive before the Civil War. Like Jackson and Tyler, but to a greater degree, he assumed that he had the function of influencing Congress and the right of vetoing its actions. He completed the process begun by Jackson and Tyler of subordinating cabinet officers from "constitutional advisors" to administrative agents. And he was the first President to direct a war in all its phases—the first actual commander in chief.

When Polk assumed office, half of the Democratic platform concerning expansion, the annexation of Texas, had been carried out by Tyler. Polk turned immediately to the other half, Oregon. Although in his inaugural address he seemed to assert American title to all of Oregon, he was in reality willing to compromise—to effect a division on the line of the forty-ninth parallel. His motives are not easy to determine, and his subsequent course is sometimes hard to follow. Perhaps he felt that he had to try for a compromise because previous administrations had offered to settle on the forty-ninth parallel, thus committing him to do the same. Perhaps he reasoned that "fifty-four forty or fight" meant exactly what it said, and thus would involve a war with a major power for a minor result. Or perhaps he restrained himself on Oregon because trouble with Britain would impede other plans of expansion he had in mind for territory in Mexico. At any rate, the American government notified the British minister in Washington that it stood ready to divide Oregon on the forty-ninth parallel. The minister, amply demonstrating that he lacked the ability to be a minister, rejected the offer without referring it to London.

Abruptly Polk took a more militant attitude. Saying America should look John Bull "straight in the eye" and hinting at war, he asserted claim to all of Oregon. In his annual message to Congress, in Decem-

ber, 1845, he asked that body to give notice to England that joint occupation would end in a year. The United States, he said, would not permit a European colony to be established in North America by force or by diplomatic action. This last was a somewhat surprising restatement of the Monroe Doctrine, largely forgotten since 1823; in its reference to diplomatic intervention, Polk's pronouncement explicated the somewhat general language of the original document. Congress, with some Whigs dissenting, complied with the President's request.

Although there was some loose talk of war on both sides of the Atlantic, neither nation really wished to resort to force. The men in the British government particularly were convinced that a war for a territory most of which was already settled by Americans, would be the worst kind of folly. Accordingly, Britain advanced a proposal to divide Oregon at latitude forty-nine—that is, to accept Polk's original proposal. The President affected to believe the offer should be rejected, but he was easily persuaded by his cabinet to submit it to the Senate for advice. Probably he was relieved to shift the responsibility for making a decision onto the Senate. That body accepted the proposed agreement, and on June 15, 1846, a treaty was signed fixing the boundary at the forty-ninth parallel. (This agreement is usually called simply the Oregon Treaty, but sometimes the Buchanan-Pakenham Treaty.) The United States had secured the greater and better part of the Oregon country and certainly all that it could have legitimately expected to get.

Most of the votes against the treaty came from Senators of Polk's own party, Democrats from the Northwest. Outraged that the United States had gotten only part of Oregon, they were bitterly convinced that the President had betrayed the party's platform and sacrificed the interests of the West to those of his own South. There had been no compromise on Texas, they said. A dangerous crack had appeared in the South-West alliance.

Polk's Plans for Expansion

President Polk's dreams of expansion went beyond the Democratic platform. He entered office determined to acquire for his country New Mexico and California and possibly other parts of northern Mexico as well. He hoped to acquire them by pacific methods: through the use of diplomacy and money. But there can be no doubt that if he could not get them peaceably he was ready to resort to war. There also can be no doubt that Mexico, smarting from the loss of Texas and suffering under a government often controlled by military adventurers, was in a belligerent frame of mind and was equally ready to dissolve, not solve, its boundary problems by war. Under the circumstances, it is not surprising that the two nations shortly came to war; war between them was, if not inevitable, highly probable.

Mexico had protested the annexation of Texas, and when Texas became a state the Mexican government broke off diplomatic relations with the United States. To further embitter the situation, a dispute over Texas's boundary with Mexico now developed. Texas claimed that the Rio Grande River, from source to mouth, constituted her western and southern border, an assertion which would place much of what is now New Mexico in Texas. Mexico, not formally conceding the loss of Texas, replied that the southern border of Texas had always been the Nueces River. Polk recognized the Texas claim, and in the summer of 1845 sent a small army force under General Zachary Taylor to the Nueces line—to protect Texas, he said, against the Mexicans. The President was undoubtedly sincere in thinking he had to support the Texans, now Americans, but to Mexico his course smacked of aggression. The United States

had Texas, and now it seemed to be reaching out for New Mexico. At the same time Polk brought up the question of certain financial obligations, amounting to several million dollars, which were due American citizens in Mexico for damaged property, unsatisfied debts, and other losses. In 1841 Mexico had agreed to reimburse the claimants, but after making several payments she had announced that she simply could not continue them. Now Polk was pressing for the money. He was, the Mexicans thought suspiciously, in an unseemly hurry to settle things.

They would have been more suspicious if they had known what the President was doing in California. At the same time that Taylor was sent to the Nueces, secret instructions went to the commander of the Pacific naval squadron to seize the California ports if he heard that Mexico had declared war. A little later Consul Larkin was informed that while the government had no aggressive designs on California, if the people wanted to revolt and join the United States they would be received as brethren. The hint was not lost on Larkin, who immediately began to stir up sentiment for annexation. Still later an exploring expedition led by Captain John C. Frémont, of the army's corps of topographical engineers, entered California. The Mexican authorities, alarmed by the size of the party and its military aspects, ordered Frémont to leave. He complied, but moved only over the Oregon border.

After preparing measures that looked like war and that could lead to war, Polk resolved on a last effort to achieve his objectives by diplomacy. He dispatched to Mexico a special minister, John Slidell, a Louisiana politician, with instructions to settle all the questions in dispute between the two nations—to settle them with American money. If Mexico would acknowledge the Rio Grande boundary for Texas, the United

States would assume the damage claims against Mexico. If she would cede New Mexico, the United States would pay $5,-000,000. And for California, the United States would pay up to $25,000,000. Slidell arrived in Mexico at a time when the government was about to be changed by the customary method of revolution. The government that was going down did not dare to negotiate with him, and the one that took over, having risen to power partly by denouncing the American offer and blustering about war, did not dare even to receive him. Accordingly, Slidell notified his government that his mission had failed. Immediately after receiving Slidell's information, on January 13, 1846, Polk ordered Taylor's army to move to the Rio Grande.

It has been charged that the President sent troops into the disputed area in the hope of provoking Mexico to start a war. Of course, in his opinion the area was not in dispute but was American territory, and he had a right to occupy it. If Polk was hoping for trouble, he was disappointed for months. Taylor's army encamped on the north bank of the river near its mouth, while across the stream Mexican forces contented themselves with observing the Americans. Finally in May after Slidell had returned to Washington, Polk decided to ask Congress to declare war on the grounds that Mexico had refused to honor its financial obligations and had insulted the United States by rejecting the Slidell mission. While Polk was working on a war message, the electrifying news arrived from Taylor that Mexican troops had crossed the Rio Grande and attacked a unit of American soldiers. Immediately Polk revised his message. Instead of asking for war to redress past grievances he demanded force to defend the nation against present invasion. Ignoring some salient facts in the situation, he declared that "Mexico has passed the boundary of the United States . . . and shed

American blood upon the American soil" and that "war exists by the act of Mexico herself." Congress accepted Polk's interpretation of events, and on May 13, 1846, declared war by votes of 40 to 2 in the Senate and 174 to 14 in the House. Manifest Destiny had come to its great climax.

Although the country accepted war with apparent enthusiasm and near-unanimity, there was more opposition than appeared on the surface. The war was most popular in the Mississippi Valley states, which furnished most of the volunteer troops to fight it. In the Northeast, it was received with coolness if not disapproval, particularly by Whigs and antislavery groups. Even in the older Southern states there was a feeling that expansion was going too far, that the acquisition of too much territory would provoke sectional controversy. Opposition increased and intensified as the war continued and costs and casualties came home to the people. The Whigs in Congress supported the war appropriation bills, but they became ever bolder and more bitter in denouncing "Mr. Polk's war" and its aggressive origin and objectives.

The Mexican War

A comparison of the combatants of the Mexican War, that is, an analysis of their ability to wage war, discloses that most of the advantages were on the side of the United States. The population of the United States was about 17 million; that of Mexico, 7 million. Although the Mexican regular army outnumbered the American army 32,000 to 8,000 in 1846, the United States, with a larger manpower reservoir, was capable of putting superior forces in the field. Furthermore, the Mexican army was not as impressive as its numbers indicated. Too elaborately organized, it contained far too many generals, many of whom were corrupt and inefficient and more interested in politics than in generalship. The American economy was superior to that of Mexico, particularly in industrial production, and hence the United States was better able to supply its armed forces and to finance the costs of war. What implements of war the United States could not produce, it could import from Europe, for the American navy, small as it was, dwarfed the almost nonexistent Mexican navy. Because the United States possessed the sea power, it could transport armies to invade Mexico, striking at the long eastern coast, and supply them after they reached there.

During the war the United States raised a total armed force of a little over 100,000 troops. Of these about 60,000 were volunteers, most of whom had enlisted for a twelve-months term and consequently saw little or nothing of the war. Despite the seemingly large size of the American forces, the largest single army in the field did not number more than 14,000 men. The generals who led these forces were either senior officers who had spent their adult lives in the service or politicians who had just entered the military organization from civilian life. Some representatives of both groups proved to be capable subordinate commanders, but the best that can be said of the division and regimental officers is that they were adequate. Of the army commanders, only one, Winfield Scott, possessed outstanding ability. If the level of the general officers was ordinary, that of the lower-ranking commissioned officers was unusually high. By 1846 West Point had graduated 1,000 students, many of whom served in the war. For the first time American armies contained large numbers of professionally trained officers. The young West Pointers were the future generals of the Civil War. In the Mexican war they had their only important military experience before 1861. It was their "rehearsal for conflict."

In the opening phases of the war President Polk assumed the function of planning grand strategy, a practice which he continued almost to the end of the war. Although he sometimes conferred with the cabinet or with Scott, the army's ranking general, or with field commanders, Polk himself determined the nature of American strategy. His basic idea was to seize key areas on the Mexican frontier and then force the Mexicans to make peace on American terms. Accordingly, he ordered Taylor to cross the Rio Grande and occupy northeastern Mexico, taking as his first objective the city of Monterrey. Polk seems to have had a vague idea that from Monterrey Taylor could advance southward, if necessary, and menace Mexico City, the enemy capital. Taylor, "Old Rough and Ready," beloved by his soldiers for his courage and easy informality but ignorant of many technical aspects of war, attacked Monterrey in September, 1846; after a hard fight he captured it, but at the price of agreeing to let the garrison evacuate without pursuit. Although the country hailed Taylor as a hero, Polk was disgusted with the general, and concluded that he did not possess the ability to lead an offensive against Mexico City. Also, Polk began to realize that an advance south through the mountains would involve impossible problems of supply. As a result, Taylor, with an army of about 12,000, settled down to occupy a triangular area extending from Saltillo on the west to Tampico on the coast. The Mexicans gave no indication that their reverses were causing them to think of peace.

In the meantime two other offensives planned by Polk were in the process of execution, one aimed at New Mexico and the other at California. In the summer of 1846 a small army under Colonel Stephen W. Kearny was assembled at Fort Leavenworth (near the Missouri border in present Kansas), charged with the mission of reducing New Mexico. Kearny made the long march to Sante Fe and occupied the town with no opposition. Indeed, in the entire province there was no resistance worthy of the name. Kearny took possession in the name of the United States, sent part

tions from Polk, Kearny proceeded with a few hundred troopers to California to take charge of operations there. In California a combined revolt and war was be-

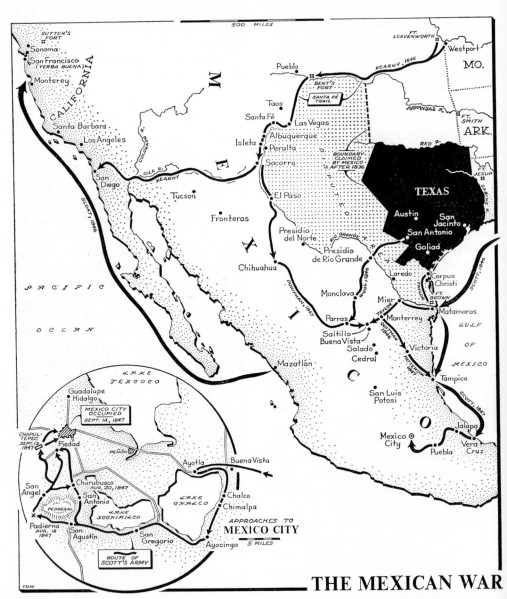

THE MEXICAN WAR

of his army (Missouri volunteers under Colonel A. W. Doniphan) south to join Taylor, and disposed other parts to garrison the province. Then, acting under instruc-

ing staged by the settlers, Frémont's exploring party, and the American navy. The settlers had proclaimed California an independent state (in the "Bear Flag Revolution"); Frémont had returned from Oregon to lead the rebels; and the navy had landed forces and annexed California to the United States. When Kearny arrived, the Americans were fighting under the direction of Commodore R. F. Stockton of the navy. Not without some difficulty, Kearny brought the disparate American elements under his command, and by the autumn of 1846 completed the conquest of California.

In addition to northeastern Mexico, the United States now had possession of the two provinces for which it had gone to war. In a sense, the objectives of the war had been achieved. The only trouble was that Mexico refused to recognize realities; she would not agree to a peace and cede the desired territory. At this point Polk turned to General Scott, the commanding general of the army and its finest soldier, for help. The President had not previously employed Scott's talents for several reasons: the two men did not get on well together; at the beginning of the war Scott had put forward a plan which Polk considered, with some justification, to be impractical; and the general was a known Whig and an open aspirant for the Presidency. But he seemed to be the only man who could bring the war to an end. Besides, to Polk's intense irritation, Taylor, the ranking hero of the war so far, had turned out to be a Whig too, and members of that party were talking him up for the White House.

Together Polk and Scott devised a plan to force the Mexicans to accept peace by capturing their capital. Scott would assemble at Tampico an army to be made up partly of troops from Taylor's army and partly of forces from other areas. The navy would transport this army down the coast to Vera Cruz, which would be seized and made into a base. From Vera Cruz, Scott would move west along the National Highway to Mexico City. Late in 1846 Scott

went to Mexico to organize his forces. Taylor, who lost about half of his army to Scott and thus was left with less than 5,000 men, was instructed to stand on the defensive.

While Scott was assembling his army off the coast, General Santa Anna, the Mexican dictator, decided to take advantage of the division of American forces by marching northward and crushing Taylor and then returning to deal with Scott. With an army

General Winfield Scott. *Few men have had as great or as long an influence on the United States army as Scott. His military career stretched from the War of 1812 to the opening of the Civil War. For twenty years, from 1841 to 1861, he was commanding general of the army. This print shows him at the beginning of his victorious campaign in Mexico. Because he was formal and on occasion even pompous, the soldiers called him "Old Fuss and Feathers."* (NATIONAL ARCHIVES)

much larger than Taylor's, Santa Anna attacked the Americans at Buena Vista (February, 1847), where "Old Rough and Ready," angered at being subordinated to

Scott, had placed his army in a dangerously exposed position. Although Santa Anna handled Taylor roughly, he could not break the American line, and had to retire from ther resistance until he was within a few miles of Mexico City. Before the capital, Santa Anna made a desperate stand, but Scott defeated him badly at Padierna and

Entrance of Scott's Army into Mexico City. *This print of the American army taking possession of the Mexican capital appeared in a history of the war written by George W. Kendall of the New Orleans* Picayune, *who was one of the first war correspondents to accompany an army.* (LIBRARY OF CONGRESS)

the field and return to defend Mexico City without his expected victory.

In the meantime Scott had taken Vera Cruz by siege and was moving inland. His campaign is one of the most brilliant in American military annals. With an army that never numbered more than 14,000 and that at times sank to 9,000, he advanced 260 miles into enemy territory, conserved the lives of his soldiers by using flanking movements instead of frontal assaults, and finally achieved his objective without losing a battle. After leaving Vera Cruz, Scott first encountered Santa Anna at Cerro Gordo, in the mountains, and inflicted a smashing reverse on the Mexicans. Scott met no fur-

Churubusco (August, 1847), and drove on the city. After capturing the fortress of Chapultepec in a hard fight, the Americans occupied, on September 14, the enemy capital. A new Mexican government came into power, one that recognized the fact of defeat and that was willing to make a peace treaty.

By a strange circumstance, a peace commissioner was present with Scott's army. Polk, in his growing anxiety to get the war finished, had sent with the invading army a presidential agent who was authorized to negotiate an agreement, on terms similar to those Polk had proposed in the Slidell mission, whenever the Mexicans seemed disposed to treat for peace. The man selected for this post was Nicholas P. Trist, chief clerk of the State Department. After the fall of Mexico City, Polk became disgusted with Trist's failure to accomplish anything, and recalled his envoy. At that moment, Trist was about to enter into negotiations with the Mexican authorities, so he disregarded the President's orders and stayed on. On February 2, 1848, he concluded the treaty of Guadalupe Hidalgo, which embodied the essence of Polk's original instructions. Mexico agreed to cede California and New Mexico and to acknowledge the Rio Grande boundary of Texas. In return, the United States contracted to assume the claims of its citizens against Mexico and to pay $15 million to Mexico.

Polk, despite his irritation with Trist, decided to submit the treaty to the Senate. After all, it secured what the United States had gone to war to get, and it was probably the only agreement Mexico would consent to. Besides, new factors were intruding in the situation and threatening ominous complications that the President wanted to avoid. Some of the expansionists in both sections were demanding that the United States hold out for the annexation of all Mexico, and this permitted the antislavery leaders to charge that Southern slaveholders were running the government for their own ends. (Actually, some antislavery men, convinced that slavery could never thrive in Mexico, favored annexation.) Acceptance of the treaty, Polk thought, would silence the extremists on both sides. Accordingly, he submitted it to the Senate with a recommendation for ratification. By a vote of 38 to 14, with a majority of both Democrats and Whigs supporting the treaty, it was approved.

Expansion in Utah

When the war ended, a portion of the territory acquired from Mexico was already settled by Americans who, oddly enough, had left their country because they were unhappy there. These people were adherents of a religious sect formally known as the "Church of Jesus Christ of Latter Day Saints," the members of which were known as Mormons. The Mormon faith had originated in western New York; it was one of the numerous new religions that flowered in America in the 1820's and 1830's. Like some others of the new sects, the Mormons believed in a tightly knit and disciplined community life directed by the church elders, and they practiced a communal form of economic life. Seeking a more congenial environment, the Mormons, under the leadership of their prophet, Joseph Smith, moved to Ohio, then to Missouri, and finally to Nauvoo, Illinois. Everywhere they met with resentment, largely caused by their economic and community organization. At Nauvoo they particularly outraged the opinions of their neighbors by introducing polygamy. Their troubles came to a climax when a mob lynched Smith.

Brigham Young, who succeeded Smith, and the elders now decided that if the Mormons were to escape further persecution they would have to move outside the United States. In 1846 almost the entire Mormon community, 12,000 emigrants, left Nauvoo for the Council Bluffs (in the vicinity of present Omaha), where they stayed until their leaders could determine upon a final destination. The place picked out by Young was the Great Salt Lake basin in Utah, distant and isolated from the authority of any government and so arid that no other people would have the courage to live there. In 1847–1848 several thousand Mormons made the long, hard trip to their new home, and by 1850 over 11,000 people were settled in and around the Mormon metropolis of Salt Lake City. It was one of the epic mass migrations of American history. Under the driving leadership of

Young, the Mormons prospered. With the aid of irrigation they successfully engaged in agriculture, they established thriving home industries, and they built up a profitable trade with emigrants on the way to California.

Although the Mormons were disillusioned to find themselves once again in the United States, they soon realized that federal control over them could be only nominal. In fact, the national government made little actual effort to govern the area. Utah was organized as a territory in 1850, but Brigham Young was appointed territorial governor. The Mormon community was almost autonomous until after the Civil War.

re-established the Independent Treasury system, thus pleasing all sections of the Democratic party and redeeming one of its platform promises. Again at Polk's demand, Congress fulfilled another platform pledge by lowering the tariff. The Walker Tariff, framed by the able Secretary of the Treasury, Robert J. Walker, reduced the average tariff rates to a level of 26.5 per cent. It delighted the South, which had at last succeeded in its long fight to get the tariff down, but it could not have been passed without the votes of Western Democrats. Naturally, the Westerners expected something in return, and specifically they expected Southern support for internal improvements. Although the Democratic plat-

The Mormons and Their Economy

The Mormons avoided the temptation to go after quick wealth which afflicted other groups in the mountain-desert region. Although their disciplined community exhibited many features of a collectivist society, they practiced, as this excerpt from an address by Brigham Young reveals, the capitalistic virtues cherished by all Americans (by "usury" Young meant "interest"): "A man has no right with property, which, according to the laws of the land, legally belongs to him, if he does not want to use it; he ought to possess no more than he can put to usury, and cause to do good to himself and his fellow-man. When will a man accumulate money enough to justify him in salting it down, or, in other words, laying it away in the chest, to lock it up, there to lie, doing no manner of good either to himself or his neighbor? It is impossible for a man ever to do it. No man should keep money or property by him that he cannot put to usury for the advancement of that property in value or amount, and for the good of the community in which he lives; if he does, it becomes a dead weight upon him, it will rust, canker, and gnaw his soul, and finally work his destruction, for his heart is set upon it."

Politics Under Polk

In domestic politics President Polk was as aggressive—and successful—as he was in foreign policy. At his insistence Congress

form had declared against a "general" program of internal improvements, Western Democrats did not think this restriction applied to their section. Two internal improvements bills passed Congress, but Polk, who sincerely believed that the national government had no legal power to finance such projects, vetoed both of them. The Westerners were disappointed and angered;

a high-tariff state, moved an amendment that slavery should be prohibited in any territory secured from Mexico. The so-called Wilmot Proviso passed the House,

---

Northwestern Resentment at Polk

When Polk vetoed an internal-improvements bill, leaders in the Old Northwest charged that Southern influence was blocking the development of their section. Cried a Chicago newspaper: "The North can and will be no longer hoodwinked. If no measures for protection and improvement of anything Northern or Western are to be suffered by our Southern masters, . . . a signal revolution will inevitably ensue. . . . The North and West will look to and take care of their own interests henceforth. . . . They will see that the power to oppress shall not again be entrusted to men who have shown themselves to be slaveholders, but not Americans. The fiat has gone forth—Southern rule is at an end."

---

as in the case of Oregon, they thought that Polk was sacrificing their interests to those of the South. Another factor that could divide the South-West alliance had appeared.

Before Polk left office, a much more dangerous issue emerged. In August, 1846, while the war was in progress, Polk had asked Congress to provide him with $2 million that he could use to purchase territory from Mexico. When the appropriation was introduced in the House, David Wilmot of Pennsylvania, an antislavery Democrat from

but failed in the Senate. It would be called up again and be debated and voted on for years. The Wilmot Proviso tended to cut across party lines and to align people in sectional blocs. Northern legislatures adopted resolutions approving it; Southern legislatures fiercely denounced it. In Congress a majority of the Democrats opposed the Proviso, but the Whigs split badly, with most Northern Whigs voting for it and most Southern Whigs against. Here was an issue that might divide the country.

≫≫-≫≫-≫≫-≫≫-≪≪-≪≪-≪≪-≪≪

BIBLIOGRAPHY

THE EXPANSION of the Western frontier is treated satisfactorily in several general works, notably in Billington, *The Far Western Frontier, 1830–1860* and *Westward Expansion* (1949); and L. R. Hafen and C. C.

Rister, *Western America* (1950). Another useful general work is Cardinal Goodwin, *The Trans-Mississippi West, 1803–1853* (1922). Other studies dealing with broad aspects of Western developments are H. N.

Smith, *Virgin Land* (1950); Everett Dick, *Vanguards of the Frontier* (1941); G. P. Garrison, *Westward Extension* (1906); and Bernard De Voto, *The Year of Decision, 1846* (1943). The relationship between territorial expansion and politics is discussed in W. E. Dodd, *Expansion and Conflict* (1915), and more recently and challengingly in N. A. Graebner, *Empire on the Pacific* (1955). A. K. Weinberg analyzes the philosophy of expansionism in *Manifest Destiny* (1935). The classic work on the fur trade is H. M. Chittenden, *The American Fur Trade of the Far West* (3 vols., 1902).

The process of expansion into specific areas has been exhaustively described by historians. For the Oregon country, see the excellent general treatment by O. O. Winther, *The Great Northwest* (1947); C. L. Skinner, *Adventurers of Oregon* (1921); M. C. Jacobs, *Winning Oregon* (1938); K. W. Porter, *John Jacob Astor* (2 vols., 1931); C. M. Drury, *Marcus Whitman* (1937); and Francis Parkman's superb source account, *The Oregon Trail* (1849 and later editions). For California, consult two outstanding general histories: John Caughey, *California* (1953); R. G. Cleland, *From Wilderness to Empire* (1944); and A. B. Hulbert's fascinating collection of documents, *The Forty-Niners* (1931). For Texas, see E. C. Barker, *Mexico and Texas, 1821–1835* (1928) and *Stephen F. Austin* (1925); R. N. Richardson, *Texas, the Lone Star State* (1943), a general history; W. R. Hogan, *The Texas Republic* (1946), excellent social history; W. C. Binkley, *The Texas Revolution* (1952); and Marquis

James, *The Raven* (1929), a biography of Sam Houston. For Utah, see W. A. Linn, *Story of the Mormons* (1902); Nels Anderson, *Desert Saints* (1942); M. R. Werner, *Brigham Young* (1925); and F. M. Brodie, *No Man Knows My Story* (1945), a biography of Joseph Smith. For New Mexico, go to R. L. Duffus, *The Santa Fe Trail* (1930) and the vivid source work, Josiah Gregg, *Commerce of the Prairies* (1954 edition, ed. by M. L. Moorhead).

Ample treatment of the background of the Mexican War is found in J. S. Reeves, *American Diplomacy under Tyler and Polk* (1907) and G. L. Rives, *The United States and Mexico, 1821–1848* (2 vols., 1913). The standard work on the war is Justin H. Smith, *The War with Mexico* (2 vols., 1919), but the best one-volume study is R. S. Henry, *Story of the Mexican War* (1950). Shorter but good accounts are N. W. Stephenson, *Texas and the Mexican War* (1921), and A. H. Bill, *Rehearsal for Conflict* (1947). E. I. McCormac, *James K. Polk* (1922), is an adequate biography, but the best source for the President is Allan Nevins, ed., *Polk, the Diary of a President* (1952). Nevins has also written a biography of a man who had an important role in the exploration of the West and in the Mexican War, *Fremont, Pathmarker of the West* (1955). Two outstanding military biographies are C. W. Elliott, *Winfield Scott* (1937), and Holman Hamilton, *Zachary Taylor, Soldier of the Republic* (1946). Brainerd Dyer, *Zachary Taylor* (1946), deals with Taylor's part in the war and also his later political career.

CHAPTER 23

The Bases of Sectionalism: The Northeast and the West

B EGINNING IN THE 1840's and increasing in intensity during the next decade, sectionalism—in a much more extreme shape than in earlier years—appeared as a potent force in American life. Sectional dissimilarities seemed to characterize American society, and sectional controversies threatened to dominate American politics. At times sectionalism seemed to endanger the very existence of the Federal Union. Significantly, these divisive factors came into play at a time when other forces —economic, cultural, geographic—were combining their influence to strengthen the bonds of national unity and to exalt the mood and the concept of nationalism. In part the angry brawls of these troubled years were only the growing pains of a young nation which was approaching, with some reluctance, an inexorable homogene-

ity. A few observers sensed dimly the mechanistic impulses that were at work in the national framework. Indeed, the aggressive attitude assumed by one section, the South, was partly the result of a determination not to be pressed into a national norm that some Southerners felt was inevitable—unless the South could in some way check the political agent of centralism: the federal government.

Because many of the ultimate results of the sectional controversy seem *now* to have been preordained, some later students of the period have concluded that the quarrels were artificial or superficial and could and should have been avoided by the men of that period. This is a hindsight viewpoint that judges past events in the light of present knowledge; it assumes that people of the past should have foreseen the course of history. The differences of peoples in past periods do not become unimportant because we think they were not worth getting excited about. The issues of the sectional controversy were real and vital to the Americans who argued them and who finally fought a terrible civil war to settle them. Nor is it certain that the outcome was fated to be what it was. There is a bare possibility that the legions of the Southern Confederacy, sallying forth to support their opinions with guns, might have altered, at least temporarily, the seeming inevitability of American history.

The Character of Sectionalism

At the risk of some oversimplification, it is possible to say that in the 1840's and 1850's the United States, in a political-geographic sense, consisted of three sections: the Northeast, the West, and the South. The Northeast was made up of the New England states and New York, Pennsylvania, and New Jersey. The West, sometimes called the Northwest, included Ohio, Indiana, Illinois, Michigan, Wisconsin, Iowa, and Minnesota; today we call this area the Middle West. The vast region known as the South, embracing every state where slavery existed, stretched from Maryland to Texas, from Missouri to Mississippi. In a previous period some of the states in this section (Arkansas or Mississippi, for example) had exhibited characteristics that justified classifying them as Western states, but during the time of the sectional controversy any state that practiced slavery has to be considered as being, at least in a political meaning, in the Southern system.

It should be noted that the boundaries of sectional division were not quite as neat or definite as the preceding paragraph might indicate. Within each section were subregions, like the Upper and Lower South, that might exhibit marked cultural differences. And there were geographic subregions, like

the Ohio River Valley, that cut over sectional lines and had their own peculiar form of entity. Particularly at the edges of the sectional divisions the lines of demarcation sometimes tended to become blurred. Parts of Ohio, such as the Western Reserve district in the northeastern area of the state, developed an economy similar to that of the neighboring Northeast and a culture similar to that of New England, from which most of its inhabitants had originally come. Missouri, a Southern state, contained many people who had emigrated from the Northern states or from Europe; its economy was partly Southern in nature and partly Western. As a result Missouri acted sometimes like a Southern state and on other occasions like a Western one.

But despite the careful qualifications that must be made in analyzing sectionalism, the fact remains that three sections existed in the United States. Indeed, as the sectional controversy developed and the Northeast and West acted together on many issues, people spoke of the country as being comprised of two sections, the North (the East and West) and the South. It is a matter of immense significance that the line of sectional division, as it came to be drawn in men's minds, ran in an east-west direction and divided the nation into a North and a South. Had it not been for the appearance of the slavery issue, it is possible that the dividing line might have run from north to south and divided the nation into an East and a West. On one side would have been the older states from Maine to Florida and on the other the newer states of the West from Wisconsin to Louisiana. If proof of the awful potency of the slavery issue is required, the evidence is apparent in slavery's power to split the natural entity of the Mississippi Valley and array the states of that area in opposite political camps.

Any analysis of the sectional controversy must emphasize the differing economic systems of the three sections, not only because many of the political issues were economic in origin, but also because the economy of each section had much to do with determining the general form of its culture. The economic systems of the sections contained within themselves a number of variations, and yet the system of each manifested a peculiar unity. Thus, in the Northeast, which had a predominantly industrial economy, there were manufacturers, bankers, merchants (in foreign and domestic trade), laborers, and farmers. In the agricultural West were farmers and, in smaller numbers and of less importance than in the East, manufacturers, bankers, and laborers. In the South, which was even more agricultural than the West, were planters, farmers, some merchants and bankers, and a few manufacturers and laborers.

The all-important fact to be grasped concerning sectional economics is that in each section a particular economic activity dominated the life of the region, and hence a particular class, the one that managed the dominant activity, tended to control the wealth of the region and to lead the other classes in politics. In the Northeast the most lucrative activity was industry, and here the leadership was generally held by the manufacturer-banker group. In the South, the great staple-producing area, the planters, sometimes working in alliance with the merchants, exercised a controlling influence. The regnant factions in both the East and South, it should be noted, were minorities. In the West, on the other hand, not only were the farmers the most numerous element in the population, but they controlled most of the wealth of the region as well; no powerful minority group comparable to the planters of the South appeared in the West to offer leadership to the farmers. The above generalizations require several qualifications. For one thing, they do not mean that members of the

same class always felt enough group identity to work together; farmers in one part of a Western state, for example, might oppose the desires of their fellows in another part. Nor do they mean that the planters of the South or the magnates of the East led other people around by their noses or had everything their own way or even wielded consistent power. In these sections there were often bitter internal divisions and struggles, and sometimes the lower economic groups were able to win control of state governments or to force the upper groups to agree to a division of power. In both sections the dominant classes, aware of the limitations placed on them by the democratic myth and themselves influenced by its precepts, strove to cajole and please the masses. This was particularly true in the South, where the planters often managed the farmers, who were the most numerous segment of the population, by giving them what they wanted or telling them what they wanted to hear. Leaders in the Northeast and South, and also in the West, were frequently able to unite their masses by convincing them that a particular program in national politics would benefit all groups in the region.

But even after taking necessary qualifications into account, it is broadly accurate to say that the salient feature of American economy before 1860 was the concentration of different economic interests in different geographic sections instead of a diffusion of these interests throughout the nation. And this was a fact of momentous and ominous significance for the peace and durability of the Federal Union. It meant that the normal class differences always present in a democracy were intensified and exacerbated because they became also sectional differences. A clash between business and agriculture, for example, was more than a contention between two classes. It was capable of developing into a controversy between the Northeast and the South. It excited two sets of opinions and emotions, and was, therefore, harder to compromise, more difficult to settle. Even without the

number of hired laborers increased from 791,000 in 1840 to 1,311,000 in 1860. In certain areas of production, particularly marked advances were scored. In the cotton

---

Urban Growth
1840–1860

In 1840 the largest cities in the country were in the Northeast and the South. But in the next two decades, as the East became increasingly industrialized, cities there shot ahead of their Southern rivals. The following figures show the comparative rates of growth:

	1840	1850	1860
New York	312,000	515,000	805,000 (1,200,000 counting Brooklyn)
Philadelphia	220,000	340,000	565,000
Boston	93,000	136,000	177,000
Baltimore	102,000	169,000	212,000
New Orleans	100,000	116,000	165,000

The most spectacular population gains were scored by the new Western cities. From 40,000 in the 1830's, Cincinnati climbed to 161,000 in 1860. In the same period St. Louis went from 10,000 to 160,000, and Chicago, astonishing everybody but itself, from 3,000 to 109,000.

---

appearance of the moral question of slavery, the political-economic issues at stake in the sectional controversy would have strained the ablest statesmanship the nation had to offer.

The Northeast: Business

Between 1840 and 1860 American industry experienced a steady and in some fields a spectacular growth. In 1840 the total value of manufactured goods produced in the United States was $483,278,000; ten years later the figure had climbed to $1,055,500,-000; and in 1860 it stood at $1,885,861,000. For the first time the value of manufactured goods was approximately equal to that of agricultural products ($994,000,000 in 1850 and $1,910,000,000 in 1860). The

textile industry the number of spindles in operation jumped from 2¼ million in 1840 to over 5 million by 1860. In the 1840's there were 1,500 woolen mills in the country, which annually produced goods valued at $20,696,999; by 1860 there were 1,900 mills whose products were valued at $68,-865,000.

The impact of the Industrial Revolution was most apparent in the states of the Northeast. Here could be seen the change from domestic or household manufactures to the factory system, the shift of economic power from merchant capitalism to industrial capitalism, the beginnings of the corporation organization in business, and many other innovations that heralded the coming of modern America. A few figures will illustrate the industrial predominance of the Northeast. Of the approximately 140,000 manufacturing establishments in the country in 1860, 74,000 were located in this section; they represented a capital investment of $682,000,000, or well over half the total national investment of a billion dollars; the annual value of their products was $1,270,-937,679, or two thirds of the national figure of $1,885,861,000; of the 1,311,000 workers in the United States about 938,000 were employed in the mills and factories of the New England and middle states.

The principal industries in the Northeast were: cotton textiles, centered in Massachusetts and Philadelphia; woolens manufacture, in Massachusetts, New York, and Connecticut; silk manufacture, in Connecti-

gines, machine tools, firearms, ships, clocks, shoes, rubber goods, and furniture. In these and other areas of industrial activity the Northeast led all other sections. But even its most highly developed industries still showed qualities of immaturity, were still far away from the production goals they would attain after 1865. The cotton manufacturers, for example, concentrated on producing goods of coarse grade, making little attempt to turn out fine items, which continued to be imported from England. Much the same situation existed in the woolens industry, which because of a short American supply of raw wool could not even meet the domestic demand for coarse goods. Technological advances and improved methods of manufacturing were expanding

Calico Printing in a New England Textile Mill. *A great technological advance in the textile industry came when cylinder printing of cotton goods was introduced. This technique supplanted block printing, done with wood blocks, and produced quickly and cheaply a more uniform design.* (BROWN BROTHERS)

cut and New Jersey; and iron and coal production, in Pennsylvania. Other important products of the area were textile machinery (sewing machines, for example), steam en-

the productivity of American factories, but as yet American industry, which exported very little, was unable to satisfy fully the wants of American consumers.

Charles Goodyear Discovers Rubber. *The India rubber industry came into being in the United States in 1830. But within a few years the companies manufacturing rubber products collapsed with losses of over $2,000,000. The trouble was that rubber by itself became sticky and soft in warm weather and brittle in cold weather. Desperately needed was a method of curing rubber that would make it impervious to heat or cold. Among those who became interested in finding such a process was Charles Goodyear, of New Haven, Connecticut. He was a common New England type of the period, not highly educated, but intensely curious and inventive. For years he conducted various tests, many of them in the kitchen of his home, without success. In 1839 he accidentally dropped a mass of rubber mixed with sulphur on top of his hot stove. It charred but did not melt. The combination of rubber, plus sulphur, plus heat was what he had been searching for. The process became known as vulcanization.* (GOODYEAR TIRE AND RUBBER COMPANY)

Technology and industrial ingenuity were, however, preparing the way for future American industrial supremacy. The machine tools used in the factories of the Northeast, such as the turret lathe, the grinding machine, and the universal milling machine, were better than those in European factories. The principle of interchangeable parts, applied earlier in gun factories by Eli Whitney and Simeon North, was being introduced into other lines of manufacturing. Coal was replacing wood as an industrial fuel, particularly in the smelting of iron. Coal was also being used in increasing amounts to generate power in the steam engines beginning in some areas of industry to replace the water power that earlier had driven most of the factory machinery in the Northeast. The production of coal, most of it mined in western Pennsylvania in the Pittsburgh area, leaped from 50,000 tons in 1820 to 14,000,000 tons in 1860.

The great technical advances in American industry owed much to American inventors; indeed, these advances could not have occurred without the contributions of the ingenious men who discovered new inventions or devised improvements on existing models. The patent records reveal the searching curiosity of American inventors and technicians in the decades before the Civil War. In 1830 the number of inventions patented was 544; in 1850 the figure rose to 993; and in 1860 it stood at 4,778. The 1840's and early 1850's witnessed a number of notable inventions and innovations. In 1844 Samuel F. B. Morse, an artist with an interest in science, completed several years of experimentation with an electric telegraph by transmitting from Baltimore to Washington the news of Polk's nomination for the presidency. Within a few years the telegraph system would connect most American cities, and a revolution in communications would be accomplished. Another individual without much scientific knowledge, Charles Goodyear, a New England hardware merchant, discovered in 1839 a method of vulcanizing rubber; his proces had been put to 500 uses by 1860, and the rubber industry was firmly established. In 1846 Richard Hoe invented the first steam cylinder press for newspapers, thereby making it possible to print more papers at a faster rate and at a cheaper cost; because of the Hoe press, Americans in North and South would be more fully informed on the issues of the sectional controversy and perhaps quicker to anger than otherwise would have been the case. Also in 1846 Elias Howe of Massachusetts constructed a sewing machine, upon which improvements were shortly made by Isaac Singer. The Howe-Singer machine was soon employed in manufacturing ready-to-wear clothing and shoes; a little later, in the Civil War, it would contribute mightily to supplying the Northern armies and would be one reason for Northern victory. Goodyear and Hoe, Howe and Singer, and many another inventor and technologist were laying the foundations for the system of mass production that after 1865 would make the United States the marvel of the industrial world.

In an earlier period the dominant economic figure in the Northeast had been the merchant capitalist—the man who engaged in foreign or domestic trade, who invested his surplus capital in banks, and who sometimes financed small-scale domestic manufactures. By 1840 merchant capitalism was in a state of decline. Not that the merchant disappeared. In cities like New York, Philadelphia, and Boston, there were important and influential mercantile groups that operated shipping lines to Southern ports, carrying away cotton, rice, sugar, and carrying back finished goods, or dispatched fleets of trading vessels to the ports of Europe and the Orient. Many of the ships in the overseas trade were the famous clippers, the most beautiful and the fastest sailing ships afloat. In their heyday in the late forties and early fifties, the clippers were capable of averaging 300 miles a day, which com-

pared favorably with the best time then being made by steamships. Although the value of American exports, almost entirely agricultural in nature, increased from $123,-609,000 in 1840 to $333,576,000 in 1860, American merchants saw in the 1850's much of their carrying trade fall into the hands of British competitors, who enjoyed the advantages of steam-driven iron ships and government subsidies.

It was not foreign rivalry, however, that caused the decline of the merchant capitalist, but rather the rise of the factory system in the United States. In manufactures the merchants saw greater opportunities for profit than in trade. They shifted their capital from mercantile investments to industry, becoming owners and operators of factories or placing their money in companies operated by others. Indeed, one reason why the Industrial Revolution developed sooner in the East than in other sections was that the merchant class had the money and the will to finance it. Many business concerns were owned by one man, by a family, or by partners. But in some areas of development, and particularly in the textile industry, the corporation form of organization appeared at an early date. In their overseas ventures the merchants had been accustomed to diversifying their risks by buying shares in a number of vessels and voyages. They employed the same device when they moved their capital from trade to manufacturing, purchasing shares in several textile companies. The corporation was capable of attracting larger capital investments than other forms of organization, and it pointed a way to expansion that business would increasingly follow.

Regardless of the forms of business organization, the industrial capitalists became the ruling class, the aristocrats of the Northeast. As they had sought and secured economic dominance, they reached for and grasped political influence. In politics, local or national, they liked to be represented by highly literate lawyers who could articulate their prejudices and philosophy. Their beau ideal of a representative was Daniel Webster of Massachusetts, whom the businessmen of the section, at considerable financial cost to themselves, supported for years in the United States Senate. Webster mirrored perfectly the conservative beliefs of the mill magnates. Although some Eastern political theorists distrusted democracy and were not above sneering at the "glittering generalities" of the Declaration of Independence, Webster had little fear of the tyranny of majority rule. He thought that the representative system and the checks of the Constitution afforded adequate protection for the propertied few against the many. Primarily he was interested in economics rather than political theory. In Webster's view the most important function of government was to stimulate the expansion of the economy by means of a national banking system, a protective tariff, and internal improvements. True, such a program would directly benefit business, but ultimately, by enlarging the national income, it would aid all classes and result in a more widespread ownership of property. With government thus acting as an agent to harmonize all special interests by creating a stable economic system, the interests of the upper income groups would be immune from attacks by the dissatisfied—for there would be few who were dissatisfied. Very definitely, the philosophy of the captains of industry did not embrace laissez faire.

The Northeast: Agriculture and Labor

The story of agriculture in the Northeast after 1840 is largely one of economic deterioration. The reason for the worsening situation is simple: the farmers of this section could not produce goods in competition with the new and richer soil of the West. As they saw their products being undersold in

the Eastern markets by Western goods, Eastern farmers turned to a system of production that aimed at a rude self-sufficiency or to the cultivation of products that would not suffer from Western competition. Many pulled up stakes and emigrated to the West or moved to the mill towns and became laborers. As a result, the rural population in many parts of the section declined.

Areas of agricultural activity in which the centers of production shifted from East to West were wheat, corn, vineyards, and the raising of cattle, sheep, and hogs. In 1840, when the total national wheat crop was 84,823,000 bushels, the leading wheat growing states were New York, Pennsylvania, Ohio, and Virginia; in 1860, with the national output standing at 183,105,000 bushels, the bulk of the crop was produced in Illinois, Indiana, Wisconsin, Ohio, and Michigan. The same pattern was true of corn, with Illinois, Ohio, and Missouri supplanting New York, Pennsylvania, and Virginia as the centers of production. In the growing of the minor grains, oats, rye, and barley, the East maintained a slight edge, although the West was forging up to a position of equality. In 1840 the most important cattle-raising areas in the country were in New York, Pennsylvania, and New England, but by the 1850's the leading cattle states were Illinois, Indiana, Ohio, and Iowa, in the West, and Texas, in the South. In similar fashion, the centers of sheep and hog production moved from East to West. Ohio replaced New York as the chief wool-producing state, and Chicago and Cincinnati became the great markets for the sale of hogs as well as cattle.

In some fields of farm production the Northeast held its own or even surpassed the West. As the urban centers of the section increased in population, many farmers turned profitably to the task of supplying foods to the city masses, engaging in truck gardening (vegetables) or fruit raising.

New York led all other states in apple production. Other lucrative fruit crops of the section were melons, berries, and peaches. New Jersey was a center of peach production, as were also Delaware and Maryland on the Southern border. Also stimulated by the rise of cities was dairy farming: the profits to be derived from supplying milk, butter, and cheese to local markets attracted many farmers in central New York, southeastern Pennsylvania, and various parts of New England. Approximately half of the dairy products of the country were produced in the East; the other half came from the West, with Ohio being the dairy center of that section. Partly because of the expansion of the dairy industry, the Northeast led other sections in the production of hay. New York was the leading hay state in the nation, and large crops were grown in Pennsylvania and New England. The Northeast also exceeded other areas in producing potatoes, but in the 1840's the crop was hit by a blight from which it never fully recovered.

Most of the workers in Northeastern factories during the decade of the forties came from the native population of the section—from the farming classes that were being pinched off the land by Western competition. Probably almost a half of the total number of laborers consisted of women and children, and in some industries, notably textiles, the percentage was much higher. The rural people who flocked to the mill towns in the hope of finding a better life soon discovered that their situation was little better, if indeed as good, as it had been back on the farms. With the exception of a few factories operated by humanitarian owners, working and living conditions were bad—as bad as they had been in the 1830's. Most mill towns were cheerless, ugly places in which to live, and most factories were unsanitary, unhealthful buildings in which to work. The average work day was 12 to 15 hours. The wages of skilled workers ranged from $4 to $10 a week; unskilled workers and women and children received $1 to $6 per week. Nor was labor strong enough in the forties to do much toward bettering working conditions. The unions attempted, with little success, to persuade state legislatures to pass laws setting a maximum work day. New Hampshire, in 1847, enacted a statute providing that no person be required to work more than ten hours in one day unless he agreed to an "express contract" calling for greater time; in the following year Pennsylvania adopted a similar law for the textile and paper industries. These measures were largely inoperative because many employers forced prospective employees to sign agreements for longer hours. Three states—Massachusetts, New Hampshire, and Pennsylvania—passed laws regulating child labor, but the statutes merely forbade the employment of minors for more than ten hours in a day without the consent of their parents. Probably the greatest legal victory achieved by labor was in a judicial case in Massachusetts. The supreme court of that state, in *Commonwealth* v. *Hunt* (1842), declared that unions were lawful organizations and that the strike was a lawful weapon. Other state courts gradually accepted the principles of the Massachusetts decision.

During the 1840's the factory labor supply of the Northeast was significantly augmented by immigrants from Europe; in fact, that decade witnessed the first great wave of European immigration to the United States. Between 1830 and 1840 only some 500,000 immigrants entered the country, with the highest yearly figure, 84,000, being reached in 1840. Then the floodgates opened. From 1840 to 1850 over 1,500,000 Europeans moved to America; in the last years of the decade the average number arriving yearly was almost 300,000. Of the 23,000,000 people in the United States in

1850, 2,210,000 were foreign-born; of these almost a million were Irish and over half a million were Germans. Special reasons explained the prevalence of immigrants from

unions had been formed by such groups as machinists, hat workers, printers, molders, stone cutters, and a few others. But these were organizations of skilled workers, rep-

Sources of Immigration, 1821–1870

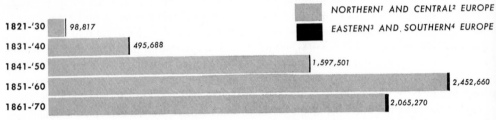

| | NORTHERN[1] AND CENTRAL[2] EUROPE |
| | EASTERN[3] AND SOUTHERN[4] EUROPE |

1821-'30	98,817
1831-'40	495,688
1841-'50	1,597,501
1851-'60	2,452,660
1861-'70	2,065,270

[1] Great Britain, Ireland, Scandinavia, Netherlands, Belgium, France, Switzerland
[2] Germany, Poland, Austria-Hungary

[3] Russia and Baltic States, Rumania, Bulgaria, Turkey
[4] Italy, Spain, Portugal, Greece

Ireland and Germany: widespread poverty caused by the economic dislocations of the Industrial Revolution; famines resulting from the failure of the potato and other crops; dislike of English rule by the Irish; and the collapse of the liberal revolutions of 1848 in Germany. The great majority of the Irish settled in the Eastern cities where they swelled the ranks of unskilled labor. Not until after 1850, however, when the tide of immigration reached even greater heights, would foreigners outnumber native-born in the labor population. Most of the Germans, having a little more money than the Irish, who had practically none, moved on to the Northwest, where they became farmers or went into business in the Western towns.

The immigrant flood helped to delay the development of the labor organizations that had experienced a vigorous growth in the thirties but that had been hard hit by the depression after 1837. Not only did immigration increase the labor supply, and thus help to cause lower wages, but many of the newcomers were willing to work for less than the wages demanded by native workers. Labor never recovered, before 1860, the ground it had lost in the lean depression years. By the 1850's several national craft

resenting only a tiny minority of labor and manifesting almost no class awareness. The overwhelming mass of laborers remained in an unorganized state.

The West

To describe and analyze the sectional anatomy of the West, or Northwest, is a simpler task than to perform the same process for the Northeast and the South. The West's economy was free of some of the complexities and conflicts that were present in the other sections. It was less diverse than that of the East, and hence had fewer class divisions. In many ways it was similar to that of the South, but it was not troubled by some of the stresses that characterized the agricultural region below the Mason and Dixon line.

There was some industry in the West, more than in the South, and in the two decades before the Civil War the section experienced a steady industrial growth. By 1860 the West had 36,785 manufacturing establishments with a capital investment of over $194,000,000; the annual value of their products was $384,606,530, and they employed 209,909 workers. Along the southern shore of Lake Erie was a flourishing industrial-commercial complex of which Cleveland was the center. Another manufacturing area was in the Ohio River valley, with the meat-packing city of Cincinnati as its nucleus. Farther west, the rising city of Chicago, destined to be the great metropolis of the section, was emerging as the national center of the agricultural machinery and meat-packing industries. The most important industrial products of the West were farm machines, flour, meats, distilled whiskey, and leather and wooden goods.

But predominantly the West was a land of family farms and small farmers. The that the average size of Western farms was 200 acres. Certainly there were very few farms of 1,000 acres or more; the large landed estate of the South, the plantation, had almost no counterpart in the West. While tenantry existed in parts of the section, the majority of the farmers owned their own land.

The leading agricultural products of the Northwest were, as previously indicated, corn, wheat, cattle, sheep, and hogs. In concentrating on these products the Western farmer was motivated by sound economic reasons; he was responding to a new eco-

St. Louis in the 1850's. *As the West grew in population and expanded its economy, its cities became larger. They began to assume the form and to exercise the functions of metropolitan centers in the East. This print shows one of the principal Western cities, St. Louis, as it appeared in the 1850's. Of the three major cities of the West, St. Louis and Cincinnati were older than Chicago and for years were more populous. But by 1860 the Lake Michigan city, experiencing a spectacular growth, was hard on their heels, and after the Civil War it would emerge as the metropolis of the section.* (COURTESY CHICAGO HISTORICAL SOCIETY)

great majority of its people were farmers, and its most important economic activity was agriculture. While the census figures do not give the complete story, it would seem nomic situation largely created by the Industrial Revolution. As the Northeast became more industrial and urban, it enlarged the domestic market for farm goods; at the same time England and certain European nations, undergoing the same process, started to import larger amounts of food from the outside. In short, there was a steadily increasing worldwide demand for farm products, which meant steadily rising farm prices. For the farmers, the forties and early fifties were years of prosperity. The expansion of agricultural markets had profound effects on sectional alignments in the United States. Of the West's total output, by far the greater part was disposed of in the Northeast; only the surplus remaining after domestic needs were satisfied was exported abroad. The new well-being of Western farmers, then, was in part sustained by Eastern purchasing power. Eastern industry, in turn, found an augmenting market for its products in a prospering West. Between the two sections there was being forged a fundamental economic relationship that was profitable to both.

The Western farmers who produced goods for outside markets were important figures in an agricultural revolution. They were participants in a transition from subsistence farming, in which the farm family tried to produce or make for itself all the necessities of life, to commercial or specialized agriculture, in which the farmer concentrated on one or several cash crops and used the proceeds of his sales to purchase his finished goods. Although many farmers clung to self-sufficiency, the trend after 1840 was toward specialization. The new methods made for an easier way of life for the farmer, and they gave him a higher standard of living. They also interlocked him more tightly into the national economy, making him more dependent upon other economic groups. Now a depression in the East might bring disaster to the West.

The swelling domestic trade between East and West could not have developed without an adequate transportation system. In the 1830's most of the goods exchanged between the two sections were carried on the Erie Canal. After 1840 railroads gradually supplanted canals and all other modes of transport. In 1840 the total railroad trackage of the country was only 2,818 miles. By that time, however, the railroads had passed their experimental stage; their advantages over water and road conveyances had been proved. As a result, there was a great expansion of construction in the forties, and by the end of the decade the trackage figure had risen to 9,021 miles. Most of the new lines were in the East and West, and several of them crossed New York state, giving the East a better connection with the West than the one furnished by the Erie Canal. The railroads enabled the Western farmers to ship their products cheaply and quickly to Eastern markets; they were one reason why Western competition forced many Eastern farmers out of business. They also lessened Western dependence on the Mississippi River as an artery of commerce, and thereby weakened the economic bonds between the Northwest and the South. The full effects of the railroads on sectional alliances, however, would not be felt until the 1850's, when an even greater outburst of construction would occur.

To answer the increasing demands for its products, the Northwest had to enlarge its productive capacities. It was able to meet the challenge, partly because its fresh, fertile soil was capable of supporting an augmented output. A more important reason was the presence, in the forties, of large blocks of still unoccupied land, which made it possible to enlarge the area under cultivation. By 1850 the growing Western population had settled the prairie regions east of the Mississippi, and was pushing beyond the river. Stimulated to greater production by rising prices and conscious of the richness of his soil, the average Western farmer engaged in wasteful, exploitative methods of farming that often resulted in rapid soil exhaustion. Hardly ever was crop rotation practiced, and the use of commercial fertilizers was almost unknown. In the farmers' defense, it should be noted that the body of knowledge concerning scientific agriculture was comparatively scanty. The federal and state governments did little to disseminate information on agrarian improvements. The most active agricultural societies were in the East, and there also the best and the most widely read farm periodicals were published.

Some improvements in farming methods did, however, find their way into use. New varieties of seed, notably Mediterranean wheat, which was hardier than the native type, were introduced in some areas; better breeds of animals, such as hogs and sheep from England and Spain, were imported to take the place of native stock. In nearly every case these and similar innovations were first tried out on Eastern farms, and later won whole or partial acceptance in the West. Of greater importance were the improvements which Americans continued to introduce in farm machines and tools. During the forties more efficient grain drills, harrows, mowers, and hayrakes were placed in wide use. The cast-iron plow, devised earlier, continued to be popular because its several parts could be replaced when broken. An even better implement appeared in 1847 when John Deere established at Moline, Illinois, a factory to manufacture plows with steel moldboards, which were more durable than those made of iron and were also self-scouring.

Two new machines appeared to herald a coming revolution in grain production. The most important was the automatic reaper, invented by Cyrus H. McCormick of Virginia. The reaper, taking the place of sickle, cradle, and hand labor, enabled a crew of six or seven men to harvest in a day as much wheat (or any other small grain) as could fifteen using the older methods. McCor-

mick, who had patented his device in 1834, established in 1847 a factory at Chicago in the heart of the grain belt. By 1850 he was turning out 3,000 reapers a year; by 1860, 20,000; and in the latter year over 100,000 reapers were in use on Western farms. Almost as helpful an aid to the grain grower was the thresher, which appeared in large numbers after 1840. Before that time, grain was flailed out by hand (7 bushels a day was a good average) or trodden out by farm animals (20 bushels a day on the average). The threshing machines could thresh 25 bushels or more in an hour. Most of the threshers were manufactured at the Jerome I. Case factory at Racine, Wisconsin. The various new machines being introduced onto American farms were, like the similar devices being adopted in industry, the instruments that would make mass production possible. But as was the case in industry, the full productive potential of the machines would not be realized until the Civil War.

The West is often called the most democratic of the three sections. The statement is accurate in the sense that the farmers, the majority, were the dominant economic class, and generally had their way in politics. What few aristocratic groups existed were small in number and scanty in influence; usually they identified themselves politically with the masses. Western democracy, however, was highly conservative in nature. It was a capitalistic, property-conscious, middle-class kind of democracy. There were contradictions in Western beliefs that were not grasped by the people who held them. An Ohio agrarian leader (Clement L. Vallandigham) could shout from the hustings: "The great dividing line was always between capital and labor—between the few who had money and wanted to use the government to protect and increase it, and the many who had little but wanted to keep it." This was the small capitalist speaking,

First Demonstration of the McCormick Reaper. *In 1831 Cyrus H. Mc-Cormick demonstrated the first successful reaper near the town of Steele's Tavern, Virginia. The amazed onlookers saw the machine cut grain much faster than men with cradle scythes could do. Two men were required to operate this reaper, one to ride the horse and one to rake the platform. Other workers followed to bind the grain. In the picture McCormick is anxiously walking behind his invention. He and his father, a substantial landowner, were profoundly interested in machines that would lighten farm labor. After improving his reaper, Mc-Cormick, with great foresight, built a manufacturing plant in Chicago, the obvious market center for farm machinery, and came to dominate the industry. He introduced many modern techniques, including a guarantee for his product, installment buying, and advertising. A favorite slogan was "Westward the course of empire takes its way—with McCormick reapers in the van."* (STATE HISTORICAL SOCIETY OF WISCONSIN AND INTERNATIONAL HARVESTER COMPANY)

the man who denounced concentrated wealth, particularly if it was in another section, because he feared its power. But the average Westerner also admired acquisitiveness, business shrewdness, thrift—the virtues that endowed men with property. He was proud of men in his own region, like Cyrus McCormick, who had achieved wealth; he thought that some day, with a little luck, he might be like McCormick.

While no one man spoke for the Western agrarians as completely as did Webster for businessmen of the East, Abraham Lincoln, an Illinois Whig, voiced many of the economic opinions of the people of his section. Lincoln favored a system in which all men would have an equal opportunity to acquire property; equal opportunity would mean a system in which most men would own property. Some would get more than others, which was all right. "I take it that it is best for all to leave each man free to acquire property as fast as he can," said Lincoln. "Some will get wealthy. I don't believe in a law to prevent a man from getting rich; it would do more harm than good. . . . When one starts poor, as most do in the race of life, free society is such that he knows he can better his condition; he knows that there is no fixed condition of labor for his whole life."

The democratic conservatism of the West was apparent in the program it advocated in national politics: internal improvements, cheap or preferably free lands, and territorial expansion. The West opposed any return to a financial system similar to the Bank of the United States, which it viewed as a hostile foreign corporation. On the tariff issue it wavered from one side to the other, generally being willing to trade votes with either in return for support of one of its pet projects; however, as industry developed in the section and the trade with the East expanded, Western sentiment for a high tariff increased. Most Westerners thought that the national government should not interfere with slavery in the South, and in overwhelming numbers they believed in white supremacy. They did not want Negroes, slave or free, in their states, and they did not want to have to compete with them in territories where they might immigrate.

➤➤➤➤➤➤➤➤➤◄◄◄◄◄◄◄◄

BIBLIOGRAPHY

C. R. Fish has sketched the outlines of American society during the era of sectionalism in *The Rise of the Common Man, 1830–1850* (1927). The emergence of the factory system is presented in a number of general and special studies. The standard work is V. S. Clark, *History of Manufactures in the United States* (3 vols., 1929). Also basic is Tryon, *Household Manufactures in the United States, 1640–1860*. Valuable general accounts are L. M. Hacker, *The Triumph of American Capitalism* (1940); and T. C. Cochran and William Miller, *The Age of Enterprise* (1942). For specific industries and special phases of business development, see Ware, *The Early New England Cotton Manufacture*; Mirsky and Nevins, *The World of Eli Whitney*;

Allan Nevins, *Abram S. Hewitt, With Some Account of Peter Cooper* (1935), good on the iron industry; Smith and Cole, *Fluctuations in American Business, 1790–1860*; and E. W. Martin, *The Standard of Living in the United States in 1860* (1942).

The story of American inventive and technological ingenuity is fully developed in Roger Burlingame, *March of the Iron Men* (1938); J. A. Kouwenhoven, *Made in America* (1948); and J. W. Oliver, *History of American Technology* (1956). Also useful are Waldemar Kaempffert (ed.), *A Popular History of American Invention* (2 vols., 1924), and Mitchell Wilson, *American Science and Invention* (1954), a pictorial record. Holland Thompson, *The Age of Invention* (1921), is a brief introduction.

Developments in transportation are best described in Taylor, *The Transportation Revolution, 1815–1860* (1951), which is also a revealing economic history of its period. Valuable for both its narrative and illustrations is Seymour Dunbar, *History of Travel in America* (4 vols., 1915, one-vol. edition, 1937). The basic work on American trade is E. R. Johnson and others, *History of Domestic and Foreign Commerce of the United States* (2 vols., 1915). A shorter treatment is A. B. Hulbert, *The Paths of Inland Commerce* (1920). For the clipper ships, see A. H. Clark, *The Clipper Ship Era, 1843–1869* (1910), and C. C. Cutler, *The Story of the American Clipper* (1930). The revolution in communications is described in R. L. Thompson, *Wiring a Continent* (1947).

The rise of the railroads to transportation dominance can be followed in Taylor's work and in Slason Thompson, *A Short History of American Railways* (1925), and J. A. Miller, *Fares Please* (1941). Two excellent studies of railroad financing are F. A. Cleveland and F. W. Powell, *Railroad Promotion and Capitalization in the United States* (1909), and A. D. Chandler, Jr., *Henry Varnum Poor* (1956). An enlightening analysis of the psychology of the railroad magnates is T. C. Cochran, *Railroad Leaders, 1845–1890* (1953). By far the best histories of specific roads in this period are P. W. Gates, *The Illinois Central Railroad and Its Colonization Work* (1934), and R. C. Overton, *Burlington West* (1941).

The standard work on labor is J. R. Commons and others, *History of Labour in the United States* (4 vols., 1918–1935). Excellent shorter accounts are Norman Ware, *The Industrial Worker, 1840–1860* (1924), and F. R. Dulles, *Labor in America* (1949). There are several good histories of immigration: G. W. Stephenson, *History of American Immigration* (1926); M. L. Hansen, *The Immigrant in American History* (1940); Carl Wittke, *We Who Built America* (1939); and Oscar Handlin, *The Uprooted* (1951).

The sectional structure of the West is ably presented in H. C. Hubbart, *The Older Middle West, 1840–1860* (1936). Basic for agricultural developments is P. W. Bidwell and J. I. Falconer, *History of Agriculture in the Northern United States, 1620–1800* (1925). Worth attention is A. H. Sanford, *The Story of Agriculture in the United States* (1916). On the introduction of technology to the farms, see W. T. Hutchinson, *Cyrus Hall McCormick* (2 vols., 1930–35).

CHAPTER 2 4

The Bases of Sectionalism: The South

O F THE THREE great sections of the country, the South was the one that possessed the highest degree of cultural unity, the one that presented the strongest appearance of sectional solidarity to the outside world. The South was an entity, even though within its vast expanse it exhibited immense differences in climate, soil, and people—more perhaps than were to be found in any other region. In addition to coherence, the South had uniqueness. While the social systems of all three sections contained many common cultural features, they also manifested certain striking variations. But no section deviated as much from the central pattern or displayed as many differences from other areas as did the South. In the story of the sectional controversy, the culture complex of the South is of pivotal importance. If the section had

not been as distinctive as it was, perhaps the Civil War would not have occurred.

The factors or qualities that gave the South its peculiar flavor are not easy to define; students of the section have not always agreed on what these ingredients were or on the influence to be assigned to each. Certain features of Southern life and of the region's social-economic complex stand out with obvious significance. The South was, and is, the hottest part of the country. Throughout most of the section the climate is warm and mild; in one part, the lower Gulf coast, it is subtropical. The growing seasons are longer than in the North, varying from six months in the Upper South to nine months in the Gulf states. The South's economy was predominantly agrarian, and was characterized by the presence of the large plantation as well as the small farm.

Southern farming was largely commercial in nature, concentrating on producing certain staple crops—cotton, tobacco, sugar, and rice—for sale to outside areas. Unlike the West, the South disposed of the bulk of its products in England and Europe instead of in the domestic market; it felt closer economic ties with England than with the Northeast. The South was a rural land, with fewer cities, towns, and villages than there were in the Northern states, and its population was more diffused than that of the North (about 13 persons per square mile in 1860 as compared with 20 in the North). The great majority of the Southern white people were Anglo-Saxon in origin and in their cultural ideals, and in preponderant numbers they were Protestant in religion.

The Determinants of Southernism

The factors just listed would have made the South somewhat different from the other sections but not uniquely different. In themselves they are insufficient to explain the qualities called "Southern" or the culture pattern of Southernism or the unity of the South. The basic determinants of Southern society must be sought elsewhere. When scholars of the region's history have looked for these determinants, they have come up with differing formulas.

Some observers have seen the South primarily as the expression of a state of mind or a way of life. According to this concept, the essence of Southernism is to be found in the section's rural character, in its people's love of the land, and in their devotion to English cultural standards. Geography and historical heritage combined to create a society similar to that once presided over by the country gentry of the British provinces. The rural South was stable and conservative, satisfied with things as they were and little given to change. In contrast to the North, Southern civilization was ordered and orderly. Class organization was sharply but not rigidly defined; some groups occupied higher positions than others, but each held a status with which it was largely satisfied. As a result, class competition was at a minimum. Above all, the physical environment was of such a nature that it sustained society without great expenditures of human energy. All classes (or almost all) enjoyed a comfortable life (some more than others) without having to work too hard. Free from the necessity of conquering his environment, the Southerner was absorbed with ways to exploit its pleasures, with the art of living. "Soil, scenery, all the color and animation of the external world, tempted a convivial race to an endless festival of the seasons," wrote the twentieth-century Virginia novelist, Ellen Glasgow. "In the midst of a changing world all immaterial aspects were condensed for the Southern planter into an incomparable heartiness and relish for life. What distinguished the Southerner . . . from his severer neighbors to the north was his ineradicable belief that pleasure is worth more than toil, that it is even worth more than profit."[1]

Other students, following the lead of the eminent historian of the plantation system, U. B. Phillips, have found the "central theme" of Southern history in the presence in the section of the Negro slaves. The South was the only area in the United States (indeed in all Western civilization with the exceptions of Brazil and Cuba), where the institution of human slavery existed. It was the only section of the nation that contained within its social organization vast numbers of a race of another color than white. Southerners might differ among themselves on political and economic questions, but on the issue of race they closed ranks with iron resolution. They were determined to keep the South a white man's

[1] Ellen Glasgow, *A Certain Measure* (New York: Harcourt, Brace, 1943), p. 135.

country, and they viewed slavery as the best means to their end. Slavery, according to this formula, was more than a labor supply system. It was also a white supremacy device, and as such it enlisted the support of the Southern white masses, including the great majority who did not own slaves. Race consciousness, then, and the compulsion felt by white Southerners to establish a system of race relations that would enable them to control the blacks were the factors that account for the oneness of the South. Slavery was an important subforce because it seemed to be the ideal instrument, ready at hand and deeply rooted in the Southern past, to sustain white civilization.

Both formulas have validity, and both are useful in arriving at an understanding of Southern unity. There can be little doubt that rural conservatism and race consciousness were essential elements in Southern culture and compelling determinants of Southernism. It should be noted, however, that the two concepts are in reality interconnected and hard to separate. For instance, would the ideal of a conservative agrarian society have developed without the presence of a plantation aristocracy? And could there have been such an aristocracy without slavery? These are questions to be pondered, even though they cannot be answered with finality.

A third analysis of Southernism remains to be considered, although it must be advanced with caution because it is concerned with speculation in the realm of human psychology. As previously indicated, the South was about the only place in Western civilization where slavery was practiced and condoned. From the 1820's on, slavery was subjected to an ever mounting and almost constant condemnation, emanating not only from the Northern states, but also from the Latin American countries, where it had been declared illegal, and from Great Britain, whose government had abolished it throughout the British Empire. The South, then, was an area of Western civilization, not a nation but a section of a nation (and in point of population a minority section), that cherished an institution at violent variance with the culture of the civilization of which it was a part. Where slavery was concerned, the South seemed to defy the opinions of its world, and that world let the South know it disapproved.

The effects of this mass reprobation on Southern psychology are hard to estimate, but they must have been tremendous. It has been surmised that the South secretly and uneasily recognized the rightness of world opinion, which is like saying that the section labored under the weight of a huge guilt complex. A more prosaic and probable diagnosis is that the South was uncomfortably aware of its separate identity and resigned to it. Probably the great majority of Southerners would have preferred to live lives similar to those of other peoples in Western civilization and to be approved instead of criticized. Undoubtedly they were sometimes nagged by misgivings about their position when they faced the moral scorn of all Western culture. But they could conceive of no escape. The only way out was to abolish slavery, an impossible course of action because they could think of nothing to put in its place to maintain white supremacy. It has been said that the South was like a man who had a wolf by the ears and did not know how to let it go. Thoughtful Southerners realized that slavery isolated their region from Western society. Said William Harper of South Carolina: "The judgment is made up. We can have no hearing before the tribunal of the civilized world. Yet, on this very account, it is more important that we, the inhabitants of the slaveholding States, insulated as we are by this institution, and cut off, in some degree, from the communion and sympathies of the world by which we are surrounded, . . .

and exposed continually to their animadversions and attacks, should thoroughly understand this subject, and our strength and weakness in relation to it."

In summary, then, the South was in some ways similar to the North and in others startlingly different. It subscribed to the democratic myth, but more than any other section it glorified aristocratic leadership. Its agricultural system was commercial and specialized, and thus in harmony with modern trends, but many of its social institutions were more feudal than modern. It was the only area in Western civilization that contained large numbers of the colored race and that was troubled by racial tensions. Perhaps the best way to describe the South is to say that in significant part it was outside the mainstream of the nineteenth century.

Social Organization

Any description and analysis of Southern social groups must be preceded by a discussion of the distribution of slave ownership among the whites, because the number of slaves held by any group largely determined its social status. Only a minority of the whites owned slaves. In 1850, when the total white population was over 6,000,000, the number of slaveholders was 347,525. In 1860, when the white population was just above 8,000,000 (the slave population was 3,950,513), the number of slaveholders had risen to only 383,637. These figures, taken in themselves, give a somewhat misleading impression. Each slaveholder was normally the head of a family averaging five members. To arrive at the number of whites having a proprietary interest in slavery, it is necessary to multiply by five the number of slaveholders. This formula shows 1,737,-625 whites connected with slave ownership in 1850, and 1,937,625 in 1860. A broadly accurate statement is that one family out of every four owned slaves.

A second fact of vital importance concerning slave proprietorship is that of the minority of whites holding slaves only a small part, another minority, owned substantial numbers of blacks. The census figures of 1850 afford a convenient point of departure from which to analyze the distribution of slave ownership.

Holders of

1 SLAVE EACH	68,820
2–4 SLAVES EACH	105,683
5–9 " "	80,765
10–19 " "	54,595
20–49 " "	29,733
50–99 " "	6,196
100–199 " "	1,479
200–299 " "	187
300–499 " "	56
500 or more	11
TOTAL NUMBER SLAVEHOLDERS	347,525

Revealing and significant conclusions leap out from these figures. Half of the total number of slaveholders owned four slaves or less; five sevenths owned nine or less. The holders of 50 or more numbered less than 8,000, and the holders of 100 or more less than 1,800. Only a negligible few owned more than 500.

The foregoing data provide a helpful, if a partial, basis from which to study the social organization of the slaveholding states. Risking the charge of setting up arbitrary standards of demarcation, one can say that eight important social groups comprised the free population of the South. These groups were the major planters, the medium and small planters, the farmers, the manufacturers and merchants, the professional classes, the highlanders of the mountain areas, the poor whites, and the free Negroes.

At the apex of the Southern system stood the major planters—the lords of the manor, the aristocrats of the South, the cotton magnates, and the sugar, rice, and tobacco nabobs. The exact ingredients that constituted a man a major planter or an area of land a large plantation have been variously defined by students of Southern history. In the South of the 1850's the most efficient eco-

siderable part of it under cultivation, to specialize in producing one of the staple crops, and, what was most important, to maintain a credit rating with the domestic or

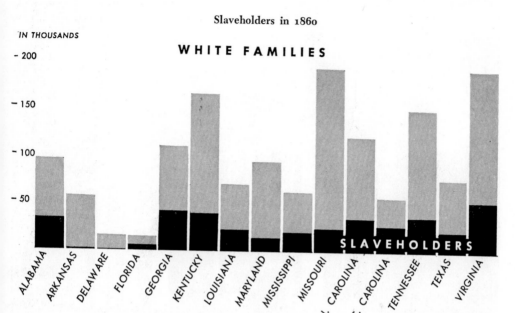

Slaveholders in 1860

nomic unit was thought to be a plantation of 1,000 acres worked by sixty to a hundred slaves. How many holdings of this size or larger existed is hard to determine, but they were many. There were 641 in Virginia, 700 in Alabama, and 900 in Georgia. (By way of contrast, in all the Northern states in 1860 there were only 787 farms of more than 1,000 acres, 262 of which were in California.) Of course, some owners of thousand-acre estates did not own sixty slaves or anywhere near that number. A very few individuals owned plantations of 5,000 and 6,000 acres, and a similar few held four or five separate plantations of 1,000 acres each.

A convenient and reasonably accurate standard of measurement for a major planter would seem to be that he had to own at least forty or fifty slaves and 800 or more acres. He would require a labor force of that size to clear his land and place a con-

foreign merchant who marketed his produce and handled the purchases of his finished goods. By the terms of this formula, there were in 1850 something over 8,000 major planters. (It may be noted that some scholars say that ownership of twenty or more slaves is sufficient to make a major planter, which would place the figure at 37,662.) Using similar principles of measurement, holders of from ten slaves to a figure in the forties can be classified as small and medium planters; over 80,000 owners fall into this category. The approximately 255,-000 individuals who held from one to nine slaves are ranked as farmers, although they possessed greater economic substance and higher social prestige than the many thousands of other farmers who owned no slaves.

The total number of planters—large, medium, and small—then, was 92,257 in 1850.

The major planters represented the social ideal of the South. Enriched by vast annual incomes, dwelling in palatial homes, surrounded by broad acres and many slaves, masters of the Northeast, their social position was higher, their political power stronger, and their leadership more unhesitatingly accepted. The factors that made

A Plantation Home of the Old South. *This Louisiana plantation house, "Richland," illustrates the lavish way of life of the planter class of the Old South and one of the architectural styles prevailing in the antebellum period. Clearly in the tradition of the Greek Revival, with its Doric columns supporting a Grecian pediment, Richland was built in 1826.* (LOUISIANA DEPARTMENT OF COMMERCE AND INDUSTRY)

they were the class to which all Southerners paid a certain deference and to which every ambitious Southerner aspired. Enabled by their wealth to practice the leisured arts, they cultivated gracious living, good manners, learning, and politics. Their social pattern determined to a considerable degree the tone of all Southern society. The medium and small planters aped the behavior modes of the major magnates; they lived in much the same manner, but less lavishly.

The planter class constituted the closest approach to an aristocracy to be found in America. In comparison with the factory planter regnancy possible deserve special mention, because the impression is sometimes given that these proud sons of the plantation system ordered common folk around in imperious fashion and ruled much in the fashion of the lords of feudal times. Such a view is highly misleading. It is true that class distinctions were more sharply drawn in the South than in other sections, that Southern society approximated in some respects a caste system, and that some Southerners spoke scornfully of the democratic faith and voiced their criticisms more openly than leaders in other regions would have dared. But it is also true that in most of the section, and particularly in the newer states, class arrangements were fairly fluid and an ambitious person could move from one class to another. Farmers nursed the hope of becoming small slaveholders, and small planters aimed to become large ones. Many achieved their goal. In fact, the great majority of the cotton lords of the Mississippi Valley states had come, in an economic meaning, from the ranks of the obscure and the ordinary. Furthermore, in most areas of the South, and again the statement applies especially in the newer states, most of the essentials of the democratic myth were accepted, or at least were widely preached, and therefore must have had some influence. Planters who wished to exercise political influence or hold political office had to take account of this reality. Whether or not they believed in majority rule, they had to affect democratic manners and to mouth principles that would please the multitudes.

Fundamentally, it would seem that the planters exercised a dominating leadership because the great majority of whites desired them to execute such a function. As the planters were the models of social aspiration in the section, so they also appeared to the masses as the natural leaders of Southern life. This was also the way, it must be quickly added, in which the planters saw themselves, and this was the role they wanted to fill. Because their wealth gave them leisure, they were able to cultivate the arts of leadership and, what was very important, spend time being leaders, time which lesser people often could not afford. The antebellum South, then, presents a spectacle not often seen in social organization— that of a ruling class, impelled by the normal power drives of a propertied minority group, wielding enormous influence with the general acquiescence and approval of other classes. Strengthening the bonds of class solidarity and also the position of the

planters was the institution of slavery and the presence of the Negroes. Slavery made all whites feel that they were members of the ruling class; at the same time they feared that any division among the dominant race involving slavery would endanger white supremacy. Finally, neither the planters nor the slaveholding system *directly* exploited the farmers. Although the great planters took a preponderant share of the section's income, they did not seem to prosper at the farmers' expense. If the Southern farmer nourished economic grievances, he saw nothing in the workings of the slavery system that caused him to blame his troubles on the planter.

The farmers, those who owned a few slaves and the greater number who owned none, constituted the majority of the white population. They were the middle class of the South. In general, they lived lives of rude plenty, devoting more attention to subsistence farming than the planters. Most of them owned their land. In fact, in the 1850's the number of non-slaveholding landowners increased at a much faster rate than the number of slaveholding owners. Although there was a tendency in some states for the planters to crowd the farmers out of the most fertile areas, it is probable that about 80 per cent of the farmers owned their holdings. Very definitely, the farming class felt that it had a stake in Southern society. Because they cherished hopes of rising to the planter group and because they were intensely race conscious, the farmers were militant defenders of slavery, being often more aggressive in their attitudes than the planters themselves.

Usually neglected or ignored in delineations of Southern society are the business classes—the manufacturers and merchants. And yet they were a social group of some numbers and of considerable importance. In 1860 there were in the Southern states 20,631 manufacturing establishments with a capital investment of $95,957,185, employing 110,-721 laborers, and turning out products with an annual value of $155,531,281. The overwhelming majority of these plants were planters' crops. These individuals, centered in towns like New Orleans, Charleston, Mobile, and Savannah, acted as selling agents for the planters, for which service they

---

The Universal Southern Support of Slavery

Northern observers of the Southern scene were astonished to see that the non-slaveholders were more ardent in their support of slavery than the planters. A North Carolinian explained their feelings: "They had in their minds a fixed and definite meaning attached to the word 'abolitionist.' They regarded it as meaning one who was in favor of setting free all the Negroes, to remain there among themselves, and to have all the rights and privileges of, and be on an equality with, the poor white man. Thus it was a question of caste, of social position. . . ."

---

small affairs, many of them being really of the domestic manufacturing type; probably many of the workers were members of farm families employed on a part-time basis. The New England states, with approximately the same number of establishments, had a capital investment of $257,477,783, employed 391,836 laborers, and produced goods annually valued at $468,599,287. Flour milling and textile and iron manufacturing were the principal Southern industries, with the principal mill areas being located in Virginia, the Carolinas, and Georgia. The Tredegar Iron Works in Richmond compared favorably with the best iron mills in the East; the value of Southern textile goods increased from $1,500,000 in 1840 to $4,500,-000 in 1860. But despite some promising beginnings, Southern industry before 1860 remained largely in a formative stage. Most Southerners showed a kind of distaste for industrialism, and most Southerners with surplus capital to invest preferred to put it in slaves and land.

More important than the budding manufacturers were the merchants, particularly the brokers or factors who marketed the charged a commission, and sometimes also as purchasing agents, for which they exacted an additional fee. Frequently the broker became a banker to the planter, furnishing money or goods on credit; in such cases the planter might be in hock to his factor for a long period during which time he would have to consign his entire crop to the broker. It is evident that the merchant, dominating as he did the credit facilities of the rural South, was in a position to exert great economic pressure on the planter. The role of the merchant in Southern life has never been fully evaluated. Evidence exists that in some states the members of the mercantile class exercised a controlling influence in politics before 1850; apparently they wielded less power and the planters more after that date. It should be noted, too, that the brokers, like other Southerners, were entranced with the plantation ideal. Many bought and operated plantations or built plantation-like homes just outside of towns.

Closely linked economically with the planters were the professional classes—lawyers, editors, doctors, and others. Because their well-being largely depended on planter prosperity, the professional groups usually agreed with and voiced the ideals of the dominant class. Indeed, many professional men were from the gentry, younger sons of plantation families who foresaw brighter careers in law or medicine than as hangers-on at home. The planters readily grasped the importance of having as allies such articulate groups as lawyers and editors. Like the mill magnates of the East, the planting lords often liked to be represented in politics by clever lawyers, of whom the South possessed an abundance. Surveying the number of lawyers in political life, some contemporary observers concluded that the real ruling class was the legal fraternity.

In the Southern mountains—the Appalachian ranges east of the Mississippi and the Ozarks west of the river—lived the Southern highlanders, the white group set most apart from the mainstream of Southern life. The culture pattern of the mountain people differed drastically from that of the inhabitants of the rest of the section and indeed from the rest of the country. It was not just that the mountaineers practiced a crude kind of subsistence agriculture or lived in what outsiders considered primitive conditions; nor was it that hardly any slaves were in the mountain areas. Rather the difference was in the physical isolation of the highlanders and in their own proud sense of seclusion from the outside world. Although the degree of their insulation has been exaggerated by some writers and was less in some areas than in others, they were, nevertheless, separated from Southern society and were largely satisfied to remain so. They held to old ways and old ideals, which included a somewhat emotional devotion to the concept of nationalism, and they refused to worship the new political gods of state rights that the South adopted after 1850. The mountain region was the only part of the South that defied the trend to-

ward sectional conformity. In the Civil War, areas like western Virginia and eastern Tennessee would be centers of resistance to Southern independence.

Occupying the lowest position in Southern white society was that tragic and degraded class known as the poor whites, who in 1850 comprised perhaps half a million of the section's population. Not to be confused with poor white people, the poor whites were distinct from the lowliest farmers and the highlanders, and ranked just a little above the slaves. Their distinguishing traits were laziness, ignorance, and lack of ambition. Found in almost every state and known variously by such uncomplimentary names as "crackers," "sand hillers," "white trash," and others, they occupied the infertile lands of the pine barrens, the red hills, and the swamps. Here they lived in miserable cabins surrounded by almost unbelievable squalor, subsisting on a poorly balanced diet which the men provided by hunting and fishing and which was sometimes supplemented by a few home-raised vegetables. The origins of this submerged class are shrouded in obscurity. One theory is that they were the weaker and less competent members of the frontier population who permitted themselves to be pushed back into the poorer lands by more enterprising individuals. A more likely explanation is that their degradation was the result of dietary deficiencies and disease. Afflicted by pellagra, hookworm, and malaria, the poor whites resorted to such degenerative activities as eating clay, a practice which in itself indicated a serious shortcoming in their diets. After 1900 modern medicine would correct their food and health habits. The diseases then practically disappeared, and so did the class known as poor whites.

Perhaps the strangest social group in Southern society was the free Negroes. In many respects, they were a displaced group. Not slaves, they were not, because of their color, completely free. They did not have the assured status which other groups, even the poor whites, possessed. Free Negroes appeared early in the history of slavery. They were former slaves who, for personal or humanitarian reasons, had been freed by their masters. Manumission was usually accomplished by will or deed, although a few bondsmen seem to have purchased their freedom. In 1860 there were some 250,000 free Negroes in the slaveholding states, of whom over half lived in Virginia and Maryland; other sizeable groups were present in Louisiana, Kentucky, Tennessee, Missouri, and North Carolina. Although a few free Negroes attained wealth and prominence (and also the ownership of slaves), most of them lived in conditions of poverty. Many avenues of economic advancement were closed to them by law or custom; for obvious reasons, the white South did not want free colored men to rise in the economic scale. In general, the whites viewed the free Negroes with distrust; their very presence seemed to endanger the institution of slavery. State laws denied citizenship to them, forbade them to assemble without white supervision or to migrate from one area to another, and placed numerous other restraints upon them. (There were about 238,-000 free Negroes in the North. They possessed the rights of state citizenship in some Northern states but not in all.) Of course, all the laws were not enforced, and the lot of the freemen was not as somber as the statutes might indicate. Many free Negroes absorbed the tenets of Southernism, and offered their support to the Southern cause when the Civil War started.

Southern Agriculture

The Southern agricultural system was organized around the production of the great staples: tobacco, rice, sugar, and cotton. These were the section's money crops, but they did not constitute by any means its only forms of agricultural effort. What might be termed general, or diversified, farming was carried on in many areas, notably in the Shenandoah Valley of Virginia and the Bluegrass region in central Kentucky. Most planters aimed to produce on the plantation the foodstuffs needed by the family and the slaves. On some large units, more acres were planted in corn than in cotton, and in 1850 half the corn crop of the country was raised in the South. The section produced 87 per cent of the nation's hemp supply (in Kentucky and Missouri) and 80 per cent of its peas and beans. Other important products of Southern husbandry were apples, peaches, peanuts, sweet potatoes, hogs, and mules. Despite the planters' efforts to achieve self-sufficiency, they could not supply all the needs of their slaves, and large amounts of corn and pork had to be imported annually from the Northwest.

But the staples dominated the economic life of the section and absorbed the attention of the majority of the people. Climatic and geographical conditions dictated the areas where each was produced. Tobacco, which needed but a fairly short growing season (six months), was grown in tidewater Maryland west of the Chesapeake, in piedmont Virginia and adjacent North Carolina, in northern and western Kentucky, in northwestern Tennessee, and in the Missouri River Valley of Missouri. Rice demanded a growing season of nine months and irrigation, and hence was restricted to the coastal region of South Carolina and Georgia. Sugar, with a similar period necessary for maturation, was concentrated in south Louisiana and a small area in east Texas (around Galveston). Cotton, which required a growing season of seven to nine months and could be produced in a variety of soil formations, embraced the largest zone of production. The Cotton Kingdom stretched from North Carolina to Texas. In this huge expanse the principal production areas were as follows: all of South Carolina except the coast; central Georgia; most of Alabama, heaviest in the center and northwest; most of Mississippi, heaviest along the Mississippi River; southwestern Tennessee; southern Arkansas; the northern three fourths of Louisiana; and eastern Texas. Smaller quantities were produced in North Carolina on both sides of the fall line, and northern Florida.

All of the Southern staples required a great deal of care, skilled or unskilled, from planting time through cultivation to harvesting. Consequently, each one could profitably employ slave labor; some could be produced only on large units of land. Tobacco culture called for almost constant care of a skilled nature. Unless slaves were cheap, tobacco could be grown most economically on small units, farms or small plantations. (Slaves were hardly ever cheap because of the demand for their services in the cotton belt.) Rice and sugar could be produced profitably only on large units. Both required the use of many slaves but no particular skilled care, and both included a manufacturing process to prepare the crop for marketing (threshing and milling with rice, refining for sugar) which demanded substantial investments in machinery and therefore were beyond the reach of the small producer. Cotton, requiring constant, unskilled attention, could be raised profitably on either small or large units. The only economic advantage that the planter possessed over the farmer was that, with more acres, he gained a greater total revenue.

From the sale of the great staples the South derived its chief sources of revenue. Into the markets of the world in the 1850's the section poured annually over 400,000 pounds of tobacco, over 360,000 hogsheads of sugar, and over 240,000 pounds of rice. But the big money crop was cotton. From 1,000,000 bales in 1830, Southern production

of cotton steadily increased until it reached 4,000,000 bales in 1860. In that year Southern cotton brought $191,000,000 in the European markets, almost two thirds of the total export trade of the United States. (By way of contrast, the annual value of the rice crop was $2,000,000.) No wonder that Southerners said smugly, "Cotton is King." The influence of cotton on the Southern economy, on slavery, and on Southern psychology was enormous and almost impossible to estimate. One writer (Anne O'Hare McCormick) has said imaginatively but without too much exaggeration: "For cotton is something more than a crop or an industry; it is a dynastic system. . . . It is mapmaker, troublemaker, history-maker. It was cotton that made the South into a section. On cotton the South built up a social and political economy essentially different from that prevailing in the rest of the country."[2]

As cotton culture expanded, the centers of production moved westward into the fresher lands of Alabama, Mississippi, Arkansas, Louisiana and Texas—the region that was often called by Southerners the Southwest. The extension of the Cotton Kingdom into this area bore certain resemblances to the rush of gold seekers into a new frontier. The prospect of tremendous profits drew settlers quickly by the thousands. Some who came were wealthy planters from the older states who transferred their assets and slaves to a cotton plantation. Most were small slaveholders or slaveless farmers who intended to become planters. Many were from the Northern states; in 1860, an estimated 350,000 people of Northern birth resided in the Southwest. The inevitable result of this migration was to deplete the population of the older states. Between 1820 and 1860 the population of Virginia, Maryland, and the Carolinas increased but little; in the same period the

[2] *New York Times Magazine*, June 1, 1930.

population of Alabama increased eightfold and of Mississippi tenfold; in 1820 the combined Alabama-Mississippi population was 200,000, but by 1860 it was 1,660,000. In the 1850's there were 388,000 Virginians and 127,000 Marylanders living in other states.

A similar shift occurred in slave population. The number of slaves in Alabama leaped from 41,000 in 1820 to 435,000 in 1860, and in Mississippi from 32,000 to 436,000. In the same period in Virginia, the increase was only from 425,000 to 490,000. It has been estimated that between 1840 and 1860, 410,000 slaves were moved from the Upper South to the cotton states. The transfer of slaves from one part of the South to another was accomplished through the medium of professional slave traders who operated as individuals or as members of firms. In long distance traffic the slaves were moved on trains or on river or ocean steamers. Sometimes they were moved afoot; in coffles of several hundreds they would be marched along Southern highways to their destination. Eventually all the slaves in the domestic trade arrived at some central market like Natchez, New Orleans, Mobile, or Galveston, where purchasers collected to bid for their ownership. From 1840 to 1860 the price for a good field hand varied from $500 to $1,700, the wide range resulting largely from falling or rising cotton prices; the average figure was probably $800. Inevitably the slave trade generated a degree of brutality in the men connected with it and in the system itself. Southern leaders condoned the trade but eased their consciences by assigning a low social position to the traders, except those who invested their profits in plantations.

Like the Western farmers, the agriculturists of the South tended to employ farming methods that exhausted the soil. Little attention was devoted to such matters as crop rotation, the use of fertilizers, or deep plowing. The same crop was planted on the same soil year after year. In defense of the Southern producer, it should be noted that some soil exhaustion was due to erosion by rain and wind, that often he planted a particular crop because all his neighbors did the same thing, and that, like all Americans, he considered it easier to migrate to new lands than to restore old ones. Furthermore, some promising advances in scientific and improved farming methods were achieved. There were agricultural societies and journals in the South, as in the other sections, and there were dedicated individuals who labored to rebuild the resources of their section. Such a man was the famous Edmund Ruffin of Virginia, advocate of fertilization, rotation, and deep plowing. The author of a work on calcareous manures and the founder of the excellent *Farmers' Register*, Ruffin was one of the best informed men in the country on agricultural questions. Through his efforts and those of others, some progress in checking soil depletion was made in the older states, but it may be doubted that their teachings had much influence in the lush, fresh Cotton Kingdom.

Slavery

Slavery was an institution established by law and regulated in detail by law. The slave codes of the Southern states forbade a slave to hold property, to leave his master's premises without permission, to be out after dark, to congregate with other slaves except at church, to carry firearms, to strike a white man even in self-defense. The codes prohibited teaching a slave to read or write, and denied the right of a slave to testify in court against a white person. They contained no provisions to legalize slave marriages or divorces. Any person showing a strain of Negro ancestry was presumed to be a slave unless he could prove otherwise. If an owner killed a slave while punishing him, the act was not considered a crime. These and dozens of other restrictions and

Slave Scenes. *The picture of the cotton pickers is of a post-Civil War date, but the harvesting techniques were the same as those used in slavery times. The other picture shows slave huts on a plantation near Savannah, Georgia. These brick dwellings were superior to the usual wooden slave dwellings.* (BROWN BROTHERS)

impositions would seem to indicate that the slaves lived under a harsh and dismal regime, which would have been the case had the laws been drastically enforced. Actually they were applied so unevenly that it is difficult to say what their effect was. Slaves did acquire property, they were taught to read and write, and they did assemble together, the laws to the contrary notwithstanding. Most slave offenses were tried by the master, who might inflict punishments ranging from some mild disciplinary action to flogging or branding. Major offenses, including crimes, were generally referred to the courts.

Just as the institution of slavery was regulated by law, so the routine of plantation life was governed by a system of rules created by custom and the planters. At the head of the administrative organization of a plantation was the owner. If he was a small planter, he directly supervised the work on his place. If he was a medium or major planter, he hired an overseer and perhaps an assistant overseer to represent him. Some planters had to employ overseers because they were too busy with politics to devote full attention to their lands, but even had this not been true the owners of the larger estates could not have administered them without the help of assistants. Almost as important in the managerial force was the "head driver," a trusted and responsible slave, who acted under the overseer as a kind of foreman. Under him might be several subdrivers. Two methods or systems of assigning slave labor were employed in plantation routine. One was the task system, most widely used in rice culture. Here a slave was allotted a particular task in the morning, say to hoe one acre; when he completed his job he was free for the rest of the day. The other was the gang system, employed on the cotton, sugar, and tobacco plantations. Under this method, the slaves were simply divided into groups, each of which was directed by a driver, and were worked for as many hours as the overseer considered a reasonable workday.

As far as physical conditions of life were concerned, the slaves were about as well off as most members of the world's laboring population. They were furnished with an adequate if rough diet, consisting mainly of corn meal, salt pork, and molasses; they were encouraged to raise gardens for their own use, and were issued fresh meats on special occasions. They received issues of cheap clothes and shoes. They lived in cabins, the slave quarters, generally constructed of wood. Medical care was provided by the plantation mistress or a doctor retained by the owner. Although the slave worked hard, beginning with light tasks as a child, his workday was no longer than that of the Northern farmer or laborer. He was given time off to hunt and fish, and he attended the church and some of the social festivities of his white family. Beginning with the abolitionists and continuing down to contemporary historians, a great deal of ink has been spilled trying to determine the evidence of brutality in slave discipline. Because of the relative scarcity of records, the answer even now cannot be final. Slaves were subjected to the severest penalties for two offenses: resisting or killing a white man, and exciting and participating in revolt. Hard punishment was also meted out to slaves who attempted to run away to the free states or to Canada. The exact number of fugitives who tried to escape or who succeeded is not known. It was undoubtedly small; but the problem of runaways caused real concern in the South, and some of the penalties inflicted on those caught approached the barbarous. As for the extent of brutality occurring in the routine of the plantation, that is, practiced by masters as part of their system of slave control, the records seem to show that there was enough to give color to some of the charges of the abolitionists. But considering the whole picture, the truth seems to be that

ance of slavery from the standpoint of the employer were never so strong as in the years just preceding the Civil War."[3]

At the same time there can be no doubt

A Southern Industrialist on Slavery

Perhaps the leading industrialist in the South was William Gregg (1800–1867) of South Carolina. A textile manufacturer, he preached that the South must industrialize or fall behind the North in economic development. Decrying the Southern preoccupation with agriculture, he wrote: "Any man who is an observer of things could hardly pass through our country without being struck with the fact that all the capital, enterprise, and intelligence is employed in directing slave labor; and the consequence is that a large portion of our poor white people are wholly neglected and are suffered to while away an existence in a state but one step in advance of the Indian of the forest."

---

most masters treated their charges with mildness and even leniency, as indeed they had every economic motive for doing.

Another question that has agitated students of the plantation system is this: Was slavery profitable? Some scholars, figuring the planter's return on his investment, have said no; they contend that whereas planters thought they were making profits of 8 to 13 per cent, they were in reality getting 3 per cent or less, barely enough to cover their maintenance and carrying charges. These writers, however, have used a computation method not employed by the planters. They take the capital invested in a plantation, estimate what the interest on it would have been if invested in another economic activity, and subtract this sum from the yearly income. The planters themselves believed they were making very satisfactory profits, which is the important thing. There is much truth in the statement of one scholar: "Far from being a decrepit institution, the economic motives for the continu-

that the slave system, or rather the economic system of which slavery was a part, retarded Southern development and posed some grave economic problems for the section. Southern capital was absorbed in slaves and plantations, "in the mere enlargement of plantation crops"; Southern assets were frozen in one form of investment, leaving little fluid capital for other economic undertakings. In 1850, when the crops of the South sold for $119 million, only $20 million was on deposit in Southern banks, and in 1860, when the crops brought in $200 million, the deposits were but $30 million. Because of the concentration on agriculture, the South had to purchase its finished goods from the outside, often from the North, and the exchange generally operated to the advantage of the North. Thoughtful Southerners realized the economic subordination of their region. "From the rattle with which

[3] L. C. Gray, *History of Agriculture in the Southern United States to 1860* (Washington: Carnegie Institution, 1933), I, p. 476.

the nurse tickles the ear of the child born in the South to the shroud that covers the cold form of the dead, everything comes to us from the North," exclaimed Albert Pike. Said a writer in *De Bow's Review:* "I think it would be safe to estimate the amount which is lost to us annually by our vassalage to the North at $100,000,000. Great God!" Not without reason is it said that the antebellum South had a colonial economy.

The Mind of the South

It might also be said that Southern culture, in the literary and aesthetic sense, was colonial. Southerners tended to take their literary cues from English or New York sources and to buy only books recommended by authorities in those places. Although the planter class bought books in large numbers, they usually purchased the works of English and Northern writers, almost ignoring the authors of their own section. They showed the same lack of appreciation for Southern magazines. Of the one hundred magazines founded in the South, only nine survived for any length of time. And of the nine, but three attained much vogue: the excellent literary journals, *The Southern Literary Messenger* (Richmond, 1834–1864) and *The Southern Quarterly Review* (New Orleans and Charleston, 1842–1857), and the magazine of Southern commercial and agricultural expansion, *De Bow's Review* (New Orleans, 1846–1880). Even these periodicals had to take second place to Northern productions. In that hotbed of Southern sentiment, Charleston, *De Bow's Review* sold an average of 173 copies, while *Harper's Magazine* was regularly purchased by 1,500 Carolinians. Said a disgusted observer (G. W. Bagby): "If the angel Gabriel had gone into the very heart of the South, if he had taken his place on the top of the office of the Charleston *Mercury* and there proclaimed the immediate approach of the Day of Judgment, that would not have hindered the hottest secessionist from buying the New York *Herald* and subscribing for *Harper's Magazine*."

In the fields of belles-lettres and science also, the South was primarily a section of consumers rather than producers. Although Southern contributions to the nation's cultural life were greater than is sometimes supposed, the fact remains that the section did not produce a literature or a body of scientific findings to compare with the Northeast or even with the Virginia of the eighteenth century. Among the reasons that account for the relative backwardness of the South is the rural character of the region. There were few cities, and not one like New York or Boston that could act as a focal point of culture, and there were few publishing facilities. The high illiteracy rate among white adults decreased the potential reading audience. In the simple nature of Southern society there were few complexities to intrigue the writer and impel him to find an explanation. The planters, the class that might have patronized a Southern literature, viewed writers with good-natured scorn; they considered oratory and statesmanship to be much more significant activities than literature. At a time when writing was becoming a recognized and respected profession in the North, Southern authors, as so many of them bitterly testified, were regarded as amusing fellows who had little to offer their society. Furthermore, after 1830 much of the creative energy of the South was channeled into the defense of slavery. Under attacks from the outside, the section felt a compulsion to glorify its image of itself and to enforce conformity to that image. Freedom of thought, which was largely accepted in the North and which Jefferson and other former Southern leaders had said was necessary in a good society, was seriously stifled in the South.

Considering the bleak reception accorded intellectuals, it is surprising that the section contained as many fine writers as it did. In the 1830's most of the outstanding authors had been from the Virginia-Maryland area: Nathaniel Beverly Tucker (*The Partisan Leader*), William Alexander Caruthers (*The Cavaliers of Virginia*), and John Pendleton Kennedy (*Swallow Barn* and *Horseshoe Robinson*). They were novelists who wrote historical romances or romantic eulogies of the plantation system in the Upper South. After 1840 the Southern literary capital shifted to Charleston. Here lived and wrote the antebellum South's most distinguished man of letters, William Gilmore Simms. Primarily a novelist, although he composed some tolerable poetry, Simms wrote over thirty works of fiction, some of them novels glorifying Charleston and South Carolina, others historical romances of the Revolution. Although *The Yemassee* is his most widely known book, his best volumes are the ones dealing with the Revolution (*The Partisan, The Forayers, Woodcraft*). Simms had a rare talent for earthy description of common folk, and his better work compares favorably with Cooper. Also at Charleston were Hugh Swinton Legaré, perhaps the best linguist in America and an authority on the history of law, and the young poets Henry Timrod and Paul Hamilton Hayne, who would achieve their chief renown after the Civil War.

Just as significant as the genteel-plantation authors and producing works that were more distinctively American were the writers of the Southern frontier. These men depicted the society of the backwoods rural areas; they described ordinary people and poor whites instead of aristocratic cavaliers; they were deliberately and sometimes painfully realistic; and they seasoned their sketches with a robust, vulgar humor that was something new in American literature. The leading light among the frontier writers was Augustus B. Longstreet of Georgia (*Georgia Scenes*). Others who wrote in the

same vein were Joseph G. Baldwin (*Flush Times of Alabama and Mississippi*) and Johnson J. Hooper (*Some Adventures of Captain Simon Suggs*). Although the Southern realists were few in number and composed but few books, they have an important place in Southern and American literature. In departing from the standards of delicate romance that characterized their times, they were originals. And in their humor they established a tradition that was uniquely American and that ultimately found a supreme exponent in Mark Twain.

In the field of natural science also the South made respectable if limited contributions. Interest in the sciences was fairly widespread, as elsewhere in the country, but because of the rural character of the section there were fewer museums, societies, and lectures than in the East. The South was no more hostile to science than any agrarian, conservative region. A Southerner, Joel R. Poinsett of South Carolina, opponent of Calhoun and introducer of the poinsettia into the United States, played a large role in establishing the Smithsonian Institution in Washington as a national center for scientific research. Some Southern scientists attained national reputations, even if they were not recognized in their own section. Among them were Joseph Le Conte of Georgia, in geology; John Bachman of South Carolina, who helped John James Audubon in his researches on the quadrupeds of North America (although Audubon lived in the North, he conducted most of his work, particularly his great study of birds, in the South); and in chemistry, J. Lawrence Smith of South Carolina, a specialist in soil chemistry, and Irish-born John W. Mallet of Alabama, a member of the Royal Society of England. Probably the ablest Southern scientist was the Virginia naval officer Matthew Fontaine Maury, who became director of the National Observatory and Hydrographical Department. In 1855 he published his brilliant study of the relationship between winds, waves, and storms, *The Physical Geography of the Sea*, and became known as the founder of the science of oceanography. Although

South were inferior to those of the East, about as good as those of the West. There were 3,000 private academies, with 200,000 students. The public school system, which

Progress of the South Toward a Minority Status

	Percentage of total population of United States	Percentage of white population of United States	Percentage of House of Representatives	Percentage of electoral college
1790	49.9	40.1	44	45
1820	46.7	35.8	42	42
1840	42.8	32.5	39	39
1860	39.1	29.9	35	35

Note: Seven of the original thirteen states were Northern. In the 1790's the number of Northern and Southern states became equal and remained so until 1850. Then the North took the lead. In 1860 there were eighteen Northern and fifteen Southern states, giving the North thirty-six votes in the Senate to the South's thirty.

Maury did his work in Washington, he was definitely a Southerner, and when the Civil War started he came home to offer his services to his native section.

It has been said (by H. C. Nixon) that in the South there were more people who could read Latin and fewer who could read English than in any part of the country. The educational system of the section reflected the aristocratic ideals of the plantation regime. In 1860 there were 260 Southern colleges and universities, public and private, with 25,000 students enrolled in them, or more than half the total number of students in the United States. The South had twice as many students per one thousand of white population in college as any other section. The Lower South had 11,000 students in its institutions of higher learning, while New England, with approximately the same population, could boast of only 3,748. Below the college level, the schools of the

developed mainly after 1840, numbered 18,000 schools and 600,000 students. One child in every seven attended a public school; the average for the rest of the country was one in five. Institutions like libraries where an enterprising individual might educate himself were fewer in the South than in the North. In Louisiana there were only 100 books to each 1,218 white people, while in Massachusetts there were 100 to each 118 persons. The South had over 500,000 white illiterates, or more than half of the country's total.

If Webster expressed the political-social creed of the Eastern businessmen and Lincoln formulated the aspirations of the Western small capitalists, who spoke for the South? Probably its truest voice was the great and grim South Carolinian, John C. Calhoun. "Whatever road one travels," writes V. L. Parrington, "one comes at last upon the austere figure of Calhoun, commanding every highway of the southern mind." There is some exaggeration here. During his lifetime many Southern leaders considered him an extremist, and it is doubtful if the complexities of his philosophy were understood by the Southern masses. Undoubtedly his influence increased after his death in 1850. In his later years Calhoun concerned himself with devising constitutional barriers to protect the minority South from the majority North. Much of his thinking was based on a concept of class struggle. He saw society as being divided into a number of clashing economic interests that might eventually destroy its unity. But no internal division, said Calhoun, would rend the South. Society there would always be stable because the laborers were slaves and a master class—the planters—were free to govern the many. Slave labor, therefore, was superior to free labor, and should be protected and extended. If the North did not understand the superiority of the Southern system, it should at least be prevented from interfering with it. To safeguard his beloved

section, Calhoun proposed a number of schemes based on what he called the "concurrent majority," by which the majority of one section could veto the will of a national majority; one method he suggested to accomplish his purpose was to have two Presidents, one from the free states and one from the slave states.

Calhoun was an original thinker, and his admirers have contended that his philosophy has permanent significance for the protection of minorities. This may be true, but in his own century his greatest importance was that, more than any man, he convinced the South it should make no compromise with the modern world, no reform of slavery, and no internal adjustment of its social system. His rigid insistence that the perfect South should never change ensured that it would remain a minority. Beguiled by Calhoun's logic, the plantation South turned introspectively to admiring itself. He helped to erect a metaphysical curtain between the South and the civilization of the Western world.

➤➤➤-➤➤-➤➤-➤➤≪-≪-≪-≪

BIBLIOGRAPHY

ALL ASPECTS of the social structure of the antebellum South are discussed with different emphases in three textbooks: W. B. Hesseltine, *The South in American History* (1943); Clement Eaton, *A History of the Old South* (1949); and F. B. Simkins, *A History of the South* (1953). More specialized studies are W. E. Dodd, *The Cotton Kingdom* (1919), brief but stimulating; R. S. Cotterill, *The Old South* (1939), unusually good; and U. B. Phillips, *Life and Labor in the Old South* (1929), a mellow description of the plantation system. A penetrating analysis of Southern political thought is J. T. Carpenter, *The South as a*

Conscious Minority, 1789–1861 (1930). In *The Mind of the South* (1941), W. J. Cash maintains that certain thought patterns have existed throughout Southern history. The student is again referred to Sydnor's fine study, *Development of Southern Sectionalism, 1819–1848*. The classic description of the South by a Northern traveler is F. L. Olmsted, *The Cotton Kingdom* (1953 edition, edited by A. M. Schlesinger).

There are two histories of slavery, each with a different viewpoint: U. B. Phillips, *American Negro Slavery* (1918), and K. M. Stampp, *The Peculiar Institution* (1956). Phillips saw many positive features in slavery, Stampp is more critical of the institution. The Southern defense of slavery is presented in W. S. Jenkins, *Pro-Slavery Thought in the Old South* (1935). Frederic Bancroft, *Slave-Trading in the Old South* (1931), is a valuable study of one aspect of the slave system. For the role of the Negro in slavery and after, see J. H. Franklin, *From Slavery to Freedom* (1947).

Southern economic life is exhaustively treated in E. Q. Hawk, *Economic History of the South* (1934). The basic work on agriculture is L. C. Gray, *History of Agriculture in the Southern United States to 1860* (2 vols., 1933). A. O. Craven, *Edmund Ruffin, Southerner* (1932), describes the career of a pioneer in scientific farming. Equally good is Broadus Mitchell, *William Gregg* (1928), a study of a pioneer Southern industrialist. Monographs that explore significant aspects of the Southern economy are Dick, *The Dixie Frontier*, and L. E. Atherton, *The Southern Country Store, 1800–1860* (1949). A book that ignores the plantation hierarchy is F. L. Owsley, *Plain Folk of the Old South* (1949). The relationship between economics and politics is ably sketched in R. R. Russel, *Economic Aspects of Southern Sectionalism, 1840–1861* (1924).

On Southern intellectual life, a basic work is Clement Eaton, *Freedom of Thought in the Old South* (1940). In *The Southern Plantation* (1924), F. P. Gaines has critically examined the plantation tradition and its influence on Southern thought. J. H. Franklin describes what he maintains is a thread of violence in Southern history in *The Militant South* (1956). Dominant intellectual influences on Southern thinking are treated in R. G. Osterweis, *Romanticism and Nationalism in the Old South* (1949). The best work on literature is J. B. Hubbell, *The South in American Literature, 1607–1900* (1954). An excellent biography of one of the South's most important intellectual figures is Frank Freidel, *Francis Lieber* (1947).

CHAPTER 25

The Politics of Sectionalism

To control American politics, a combination of two sections was required. No one section had enough votes in Congress to secure by its own strength the legislation it desired. In effecting a combination of two sections, the representatives of both had to consider first the factor of mutuality of interest, and second, the potentiality of cooperation. Regardless of what common interests two sections might have, it was unlikely they would be in complete agreement on a common program. Each, in order to get part of what it wanted, would have to concede something to the other, even though this involved modifying its sectional platform. In fine, a great deal of plain political horse-trading would have to be done. At various times the politicians had tried to create various sectional alliances. In the 1820's Henry Clay had proposed a union of East and West on the basis of the American System, and for a time this partnership functioned with a fair degree of effectiveness. Then in the 1830's a new coalition came into being, the two agricultural sections, the West and South, working together through the medium of the Democratic party. This connection, which in the beginning was loosely formed and did not include all groups in either section, operated throughout the forties. It was destroyed in the decade of the fifties.

The West-South alliance fell apart because the partners could not agree on certain issues, and neither one would make modifications to accommodate the other. One question that split them was that of internal improvements. The West, as it always had, demanded federal financial aid for railroads and other transportation projects. The South, partly because it disliked anything that enlarged the powers of the national government and partly because the proposed railroads would run in an east-west direction, was cool to internal improvements or opposed to them. A second issue of divergence concerned the national territories and the public lands. The South demanded as one of its constitutional rights that slavery be permitted to expand into the territories. This the West opposed, partly because of a moral objection to slavery but mainly because Westerners did not want to face the competition of slave labor in the territories. Infuriated by the refusal of its ally to support its rights in the territories, the South set itself to thwarting the desire of the West to secure a Homestead Act by which the government would dispose of its lands to settlers without cost. Finally, over the West-South union, as over American politics generally, hovered the slavery question, which tended to separate all the free states from the slave states and which, being largely moral in nature, was extremely difficult to compromise. By 1860 the East and the West were again acting together on most issues, and the South was left standing alone. Alone and fearful, the South seceded, and civil war followed. The breakup of the West-South alliance becomes, then, one of the most momentous events in American history.

Slavery and the New Territories

The Polk administration bowed out of office amidst a swirling controversy concerning the status of slavery in the territories acquired as a result of the war with Mexico. That controversy, precipitated by the Wilmot Proviso, would dominate the election of 1848 and continue into the administration chosen in that contest. As the dispute developed, it broadened in scope and deepened in bitterness, but always the central question remained: Should slavery be permitted to expand into the new territories? Out of the congressional debates in the closing months of Polk's incumbency, there emerged four proposed formulas to settle the issue. In considering these various plans, all of which involve complex matters of constitutional interpretation, it is perhaps helpful to note at the outset that all parties

conceded a territory could, when becoming a state, do whatever it wanted concerning slavery—exclude it or establish it. The point in contention was the status of slavery in a territory before statehood.

One formula was embodied in the Wilmot Proviso, namely that Congress had the right, and the duty, to exclude slavery from any territory under its jurisdiction. The legal argument of its supporters was that Congress, possessing the power to make regulations for the governance of national territories, obviously could determine the status of slavery in such lands. Furthermore, there were sound legal precedents for exclusion. Congress had previously banned slavery in several Northern territories and, most notably, by the Missouri Compromise, north of the 36° 30′ line in the Louisiana Purchase area. In general, the strongest advocacy of the Proviso solution came from two groups: (1) antislavery Northern Whigs, sometimes called Conscience Whigs to distinguish them from more moderate colleagues who were disposed to conciliate the South and were known therefore as Cotton Whigs; and (2) the left-wing Locofoco Democrats, centered in New York, who were now called the Barnburners because it was said that in their zeal to win control of the party they were like the farmer who burned the barn to get the rats. Essentially, the Wilmot Proviso was the program of the Northern extremists, who believed that their measure would prevent the growth of slavery and thus cause its ultimate extinction.

Diametrically opposed to the exclusionist scheme was the formula of the Southern extremists. They contended that the states jointly owned the territories and therefore that the citizens of each and every state possessed equal rights in the territories, including the right to move to them with their property, meaning particularly slave property. According to this view, Congress which was only the agent for the joint owners, had no power to prohibit the movement of slavery into the public domain or to regulate it in any way except by extending protection; neither could a territorial legislature, which was a creature of Congress, take any action to ban slavery. As might be expected, the principal proponent of this argument was Calhoun. In an effort to focus attention on his program and, if possible, to unite the South behind it, he offered in the Senate in February, 1847, a set of resolutions embodying the extreme Southern position. Although the resolutions never came to a vote, the essence of them was adopted by the Virginia legislature and several Southern state Democratic conventions. For this reason, they became known, rather extravagantly, as the Platform of the South. Actually, at this stage Calhoun's opinions had little support in his section. Some Democrats, but not all, went along with him; others, as well as most of the Southern Whigs, hoped to find a middle road between the extremes.

For the consideration of moderate men in both sections, two compromise plans were presented. One, which numbered President Polk among its advocates, proposed to run the Missouri Compromise line of 36° 30′ through the new territories to the Pacific coast, banning slavery north of the line and permitting it south. The other, first prominently espoused by Lewis Cass, Democratic Senator from Michigan, was originally called "squatter sovereignty"; later, when taken up by Stephen A. Douglas, an Illinois Senator of the same party, it was given the more dignified title of "popular sovereignty." According to this formula, the question of slavery in each territory should be left to the people there, acting through the medium of their territorial legislature. When a territory had sufficient people to entitle it to a legislature, that body could establish or exclude slavery.

The scheme of extending the Missouri Compromise line, although it possessed the sanction of historical precedent, never secured much support. But popular sovereignty, partly because it seemed to be based on sound democratic principles, carried a strong appeal in all sections. Simple and easy to understand, it seemed to be an eminently sensible solution; besides, it promised to shift the responsibility of fixing the status of slavery in the territories out of national politics and onto the people of the Western lands. The apparent simplicity of popular sovereignty was highly deceptive. Actually, it was a doctrine of considerable subtlety, and because of its importance in the record of the sectional controversy, merits careful analysis.

It was no accident that the principal champions of popular sovereignty were Western Democrats. The Democratic leaders of the West faced a peculiar political dilemma. As practicing politicians, they were moved by normal desires to win elections and by an institutional urge to preserve the national organization of their party, which meant keeping the Southern and Western wings satisfied and united. Their problem was that their constituents objected to meeting the competition of slave labor in the territories. If they indorsed exclusion (Wilmot Proviso), they would please their local supporters and split the party nationally. If they approved Calhoun's platform, they would destroy the party in the West. Either extreme position was impossible. They had to produce a formula that would seem to make a concession to the South, or, at least, that would not insult it, but one that would also reassure Western voters that slavery would be kept out of the territories.

Popular sovereignty seemed to fulfill both needs. It could be offered to the South as a concession because it would not ban slavery by national action. A federal policy of passivity held out the possibility that the

South, if enough slaveholders migrated west, could capture some of the territories. In fact, in 1848 many Southern Democrats accepted popular sovereignty's nonintervention as being essentially the same as Calhoun's brand. At the same time Western Democrats could sell the doctrine to their own people as an exclusion scheme, as in reality it was. In any contest for the territories which was based on the number of voters, the free states were bound to win: they possessed a greater and more migratory population, and established slaveholders from the Southern states were not going to move to regions where slave labor might not be profitable. As many observers remarked, nature had passed a Wilmot Proviso for the Mexican cession territory. Popular sovereignty was an ingenious design, but it had two weaknesses. By its very nature it could not be frankly and completely explained; at any moment a group which had accepted it might see the trickery involved. More serious, it ignored the profound moral sentiment against slavery that was ever growing in strength in the North.

Congress and the country debated the various formulas, but at the end of Polk's administration a decision had still not been reached. No territorial government had been provided for California and New Mexico (New Mexico included most of present New Mexico and Arizona, all of Utah and Nevada, and parts of Colorado and Wyoming). Even the organization of Oregon, so far north that obviously slavery would never enter it, was held up by the controversy. Southern members of Congress, hoping to gain some advantage in the regions farther south, blocked a terriorial bill for Oregon until August, 1848, when a free-soil government was finally authorized.

Election of 1848

The debate was partially stilled by the election of 1848. Neither of the major parties wished to make either expansion or exclusion of slavery a major issue. To do so was a sure way of losing votes in one section or another; in addition, many leaders in both parties sincerely believed that a continuation of the bitter argument would intensify sectional divisions and possibly lead to disunion. In their official pronouncements, therefore, the Democrats and the Whigs tried to avoid definite and provocative references to the slavery question.

The Democrats nominated as their candidate, Lewis Cass of Michigan, an elderly, honest, dull wheel horse of the party. In December, 1847, in a public document known as the "Nicholson Letter," Cass had advanced the idea of letting the territorial legislatures decide the status of slavery ("squatter sovereignty"), and his position made him acceptable as a compromise candidate to most Northern and Southern Democrats. Although the platform was purposely vague in its references to slavery, it was capable of being interpreted as an endorsement of squatter sovereignty. Deeply angered by both the nominee and the platform were the New York Barnburners, who had hoped to make Van Buren the standard-bearer and to secure a moderate statement against slavery expansion. (The faction in the New York Democratic party opposed to the Barnburners—that is, the regular or administration Democrats—were known as "Hunkers," presumably because they always "hunkered," or hankered, for offices.)

Equally circumspect were the Whigs, who adopted no platform and presented as their candidate a military hero with no political record—General Zachary Taylor of Louisiana. Taylor, known as "Old Rough and Ready" and "Old Zack," was "the hero of Buena Vista" and, in popular opinion, the hero of the whole Mexican War. He had the additional merit of owning a hundred slaves, a fact which was expected to make him attractive to Southern voters. A presidential boom for Taylor had started as early as 1846. Although the general was highly receptive, he announced that he would run only if allowed to maintain a position of independence to all parties. In fact, he intimated that he might accept nominations from both Whigs and Democrats. Later, when he saw he would have to identify himself with one party to be nominated, he admitted that he was a moderate Whig.

The actions of the major parties left the antislavery groups with no place to go. Ardent abolitionists and even moderates who merely opposed the expansion of slavery found it difficult to swallow either Cass or Taylor. The situation was ripe for the appearance of a third party—if the various dissatisfied elements could be brought together. The potential sources for a new party were the existing Liberty party and the antislavery members of the old organizations. Late in the campaign (August, 1848), the third-party promoters called for a national convention. To this meeting came representatives of the Liberty party and the Barnburners and some Conscience Whigs. The convention adopted a platform endorsing the principle of the Wilmot Proviso and declaring for free homesteads and a higher tariff. In order to ensure the support of the Barnburners, Van Buren was nominated for the Presidency. Because the platform emphasized "Free Soil, Free Labor, Free Speech, and Free Men," the new party became known as the Free-Soil party. Although it fell apart after 1852, its formation was an event of great significance. This was no collection of one-idea men united only by opposition to slavery. In calling for homesteads and a tariff, measures which the South opposed, the Free-Soilers were trying to attract to the antislavery cause Northern economic groups which believed the South denied them legislation they should have. There might be something incongruous in Van Buren's running on a high-tariff plat-

form, but the Free-Soil party pointed the way to a new political departure: the possibility of combining the moral idealism of antislavery with the economic aspirations of Northern industry and agriculture.

Zachary Taylor. *Of medium height and rather heavy build, Taylor was informal in his dress to the point of carelessness. In the Mexican War some of his soldiers commented that he looked more like a farmer than a general. Easy and cordial in manner, he was pre-eminently the general of the enlisted men, who admiringly called him "Old Rough and Ready."* (LIBRARY OF CONGRESS)

In comparison with the two preceding elections, the campaign was quiet and even apathetic. When the votes were counted, it was found that Taylor had won a narrow victory. He received 1,360,000 popular votes to 1,220,000 for Cass—a plurality of only 140,000—and 163 electoral votes to Cass's 127—a majority of 36. Although Van Buren did not carry a single state, he polled an impressive 291,000 votes, and the Free-Soilers elected ten members to Congress. It is also probable that Van Buren pulled enough Democratic votes away from Cass, particularly in New York, to throw the election to Taylor.

Zachary Taylor was the first man to be elected President with no previous political training or experience. He was also the first professional soldier to sit in the White House. Taylor was born in Virginia, but while he was an infant his family moved to Kentucky, where the boy grew up. In 1808, at the age of twenty-three, he secured a commission as lieutenant in the regular army, and remained in the service for forty years. After serving in the War of 1812 and various Indian wars, he capped his military career with his victories in Mexico. He lived in Louisiana and owned a cotton plantation in Mississippi. As President, Taylor demonstrated the virtues and defects inherent in his background. He had but a limited knowledge of the basic issues in American politics, and it is doubtful if he understood, at least in the beginning, all the powers and functions of his office. At first he was inclined to defer too much to the advice of others, and later to rely too heavily on his own inexperienced judgment. Not a subtle man, he did not always recognize the terrible complexities involved in certain situations, and tended to adopt what seemed to be simple solutions. Unschooled in politics, he did not, to the disgust of some Whig leaders, always play the political game by the rules; at times he seemed to consider himself as a nonpartisan President above parties and politics.

Although he came from the South and was a slaveholder, Taylor was a Southerner only in a technical sense. From his long years in the army he had acquired a national outlook and an attachment to the concept of nationalism. Unlike other Southerners, he had no great devotion to slavery or the Southern way of life and no particular loyalty to the South as a section. Not impressed with the seriousness of the slavery issue one way or another, he was not likely to be impressed by a crisis created by it. In one respect, he entered office with a great advantage. Cass and Van Buren had run on definite platforms (Cass's Nicholson letter was a personal platform)—squatter sovereignty and the Wilmot Proviso. Had either been elected and tried to apply his program, an ugly crisis would have followed. Of the three candidates, only Taylor was uncommitted to a specific plan. He was free, if he had the skill, to devise a formula that would restore sectional unity.

Crisis at Mid-Century

Because of the failure of Congress to provide civil government for the area annexed from Mexico, those regions were being administered by military officials who were responsible to the President. The situation was unsatisfactory to everybody concerned with it: to the national government, which was unable to establish efficient agencies of administration, and to the people of the new lands, who desired the benefits of civil government. It could, nevertheless, have been tolerated for a period, because the population of the territories was relatively small and was therefore capable of being governed by military authority. In the normal course of frontier expansion, several years would elapse before these regions received a substantial number of settlers. But suddenly an unforeseen economic event occurred, changing the picture dramatically almost overnight and forcing the nation to face the issue of slavery in the West.

In January, 1848, gold was accidentally discovered in the Sacramento Valley in California. As word of the strike spread, inhabitants of California and the whole Far West, fired by hopes of becoming immediate millionaires, stampeded to the area to stake out claims. By the end of summer the news had reached the eastern states and Europe. Then the gold rush really started. From the United States and, so it seemed, all the world, thousands of people, the "Forty-Niners," poured into California. Those who left from the older states could choose between three routes of travel: over-

the huge inrush of settlers. Crime was rampant, mining titles were insecure, and men enforced their own law with guns or knives. Organized bands of criminals roamed

Washing for Gold. *These miners in a Western gold camp are engaging in placer mining. The gold found in the first strikes was located in the form of particles along stream beds. Prospectors separated the gold from sand or gravel by washing the deposit in a swirl of water. Washing was done in pans or boxes.* (FROM SAMUEL BOWLES, *Our New West*)

land by covered wagon, inexpensive but involving a long journey over the Great Plains and across the Rockies: by ship around Cape Horn, quicker but more expensive; or the dangerous, difficult shortcut across the Isthmus of Panama. By all three routes, disdaining starvation, thirst, disease, and even death, the seekers after gold came —more than 80,000 of them in 1849. By the end of that year, California had a population of approximately 100,000, more than enough to entitle her to statehood.

Either statehood or some form of territorial civil government was an obvious and urgent necessity for California. The few military officials were completely unable to cope with the conditions resulting from

through the territory, and were countered by vigilance committees which themselves sometimes engaged in illegal acts. California needed desperately the order that only civil authority could give; it required laws emanating from government, and courts to interpret them.

To President Taylor, assuming office in March, 1849, statehood seemed to be the solution to California's problem. More important, statehood appealed to the old soldier as the perfect solution for the controversy over slavery in the territories. All sides conceded that a territory, as it became a state, could do whatever it wanted about slavery. With his penchant for seeking simple answers, Taylor reasoned thus: California and also New Mexico should be encouraged to frame state constitutions and apply for admission to the Union. Nobody could deny their right to dispose of slavery as they wished; they would become states, and two areas of potential sectional conflict would be removed. That both territories contained but a few Southerners and hence were certain to exclude slavery did not bother the President at all; his only thought, and it became almost an obsession, was to settle the slavery issue by getting the new acquisitions into the Union. Nor did he think that he should call Congress into session to inform that body, which would have to pass upon the applications of California and New Mexico, of his contemplated actions. He urged California and New Mexico to frame constitutions, and directed military officials in the territories to expedite statehood movements.

California needed no prodding; by October she had prepared and ratified a constitution in which slavery was prohibited. In their haste, the Californians, without waiting for congressional approval of their work, as required by law, elected a state government and representatives to Congress. New Mexico, with a smaller population and less pressing governmental problems, moved more slowly, but nevertheless by May, 1850, she too had adopted a constitution banning slavery. When Congress assembled in December, 1849, Taylor rather proudly described his efforts, and recommended that California be admitted as a free state and that New Mexico, when she was ready, be permitted to come in with complete freedom to decide the status of slavery as she wished.

Immediately it was apparent that Congress was not going to accept the President's program. For one reason, the legislative branch felt a natural jealousy of the power of the executive, a feeling that had been steadily increasing since Jackson's time;

many legislators believed that Taylor should have consulted Congress before acting. Again, this Congress, the Thirty-First, contained a number of able and even distinguished members. Among them were the three great elder statesmen whose careers stretched back to the War of 1812—Webster, Clay, and Calhoun. Present also were a group of younger men who shortly would make their own marks—Stephen A. Douglas, William H. Seward, and Salmon P. Chase from the North, and Jefferson Davis, Alexander H. Stephens, and Robert Toombs from the South. Many of these men viewed Taylor as a dangerous political amateur rushing about like a bull in a china shop; they considered themselves much better qualified to pass on delicate political issues.

Another factor in the situation was the emergence of side issues generated by the conflict over slavery in the territories. One of these concerned slavery in the District of Columbia. The antislavery people, charging that human servitude in the capital was a national disgrace, were demanding that it be abolished there; to this charge Southerners angrily replied that the institution could not be touched without the consent of Maryland, which had originally donated the land, and that to abolish it would place a stigma on the entire South. Another ancillary question involved the rendition of fugitive slaves. Since the *Prigg* v. *Pennsylvania* case, a number of Northern states had passed laws, sometimes called "personal liberty laws," forbidding their courts and police officers to assist in the return of runaways. Southern extremists, taking the position that these statutes were designed to prevent slaveholders from recovering their property, were calling for the passage of a stringent *national* fugitive slave law. A third issue related to the boundary between Texas and New Mexico. Texas claimed the portion of New Mexico east of the Rio

Grande (the Santa Fé area), although the national government during the Mexican War had assigned this region to New Mexico. To Texans it seemed that Washington was trying to steal part of their territory; they also resented the government's refusal to assume the Texas war debt. Southern extremists supported the pretensions of Texas, while their fellows in the North, eager to cut down the size of a slave state, upheld New Mexico. Observing the bitterness engendered by the various collateral questions, thoughtful men in both sections wondered if Taylor's simple solution of statehood would really settle the points of conflict between North and South.

But the biggest road block in the way of the President's program was the South—angered and frightened by the possibility that two new free states would be added to the Northern majority. With its social system under constant attack from the North and from most centers of opinion in Western culture, the South had developed a strong sense of insecurity. In 1789 the South contained 40 per cent of the nation's total white population; by 1850 it had but 31 per cent. The drop in proportion of population was accompanied by a dimunition of power in the national government. From 46 per cent of the seats in the House of Representatives in 1789, the South sank to 38 per cent in 1850; the loss in votes in the Electoral College was from 45 per cent to 38. Only in the Senate did the South still maintain equality. The number of free and slave states was equal in 1850; there were fifteen of each. But now the admission of California would upset the balance and deprive the South of its last constitutional protection—and New Mexico, Oregon, and Utah were yet to come! Many Southerners agreed with Henry W. Hilliard of Alabama when he said the South was about to enter into the condition of "a fixed, dreary, hopeless minority." Explained Jefferson Davis of Mississippi: "Now for

the first time, we are about permanently to destroy the balance of power between the sections of the Union. . . . When that barrier for the protection of the minority is about to be obliterated, I feel we have reached the point at which the decline of our Government has commenced."

Even the most extreme Southerners had always admitted the right of a state to exclude slavery. On the face of it, they could offer no valid legal arguments against California's admission. But in the heat and hate of the moment, the extremists and even some of the moderates took the position that California, and also New Mexico, had not really desired statehood but had been pressured into seeking admission by Taylor. Therefore, because their applications had been artificially stimulated, it was proper to keep them out. Responsible leaders stated that if California was admitted and if slavery was prohibited in the territories, the time had come for the South to secede from the Union. At the suggestion of Mississippi, a call went out for a Southern-rights convention to meet in June, 1850, at Nashville, Tennessee, to consider whether the South should resort to the ultimate act of secession. In the North excitement ran equally high. Every Northern state legislature but one adopted resolutions demanding that slavery be barred from the territories; public meetings all through the free states called for the Wilmot Proviso and the abolition of slavery in the District of Columbia. Such was the situation that confronted Congress and the country as the tense year of 1850 opened.

The Compromise of 1850

Faced by the threat of a national crisis, moderate men and lovers of the Union naturally turned their thoughts to the framing of a great congressional compromise that would satisfy both sections and restore sectional tranquility. Just as naturally, the pro-

moters of compromise turned for a leader
to the venerable statesman from Kentucky,
Henry Clay. Representing a border state in
the Upper South, the region that geograph-

established in the rest of the Mexican
cession region with no restrictions
upon slavery and no mention of its
status.

An Extreme Southern View on Compromise in 1850

In his last speech Calhoun insisted that the North should either agree to
everything that the South demanded as its rights or permit the minority section to depart the Union: "It is time, Senators, that there should be an open
and manly avowal on all sides, as to what is intended to be done. If the question is not now settled, it is uncertain whether it ever can hereafter be;
and we, as the representatives of the States of this Union, regarded as governments, should come to a distinct understanding as to our respective views,
in order to ascertain whether the great questions at issue can be settled or
not. If you, who represent the stronger portion, cannot agree to settle them
on the broad principle of justice and duty, say so; and let the States we both
represent agree to separate and part in peace, tell us so; and we shall know
what to do, when you reduce the question to submission or resistance. If you
remain silent, you will compel us to infer by your acts what you intend."

ically and ideologically was situated between the two extremes, Clay had every
reason to abhor sectional discord, and during his long career he had acquired a deserved reputation for his skill in reconciling
conflicting interests. Quite ready to head
the forces of conciliation, Clay believed
that Taylor's little statehood formula was
inadequate to deal with the crisis. To Clay's
way of thinking, no compromise would
have any significant or lasting effects unless
it settled all the issues in dispute between
the sections. Accordingly, he took a number of separate measures which had been
proposed by various members of both parties from North and South, and combined
them into one set of resolutions which on
January 29, 1850, he presented to the Senate.
His proposals were as follows:

a. California was to be admitted as a free
state.
b. Territorial governments were to be

c. Texas was to relinquish her claim to
New Mexico in return for the national
government's assuming her public
debt.
d. Slavery in the District of Columbia
was never to be abolished unless its
residents and those of Maryland consented and compensation was paid.
e. The slave trade in the District was to
be abolished.
f. Congress was to enact a more drastic
and effective fugitive slave law.
g. Congress was to declare that it had no
power to regulate the interstate slave
trade.

These resolutions inaugurated a debate
in the Senate, and in the House and throughout the country, that lasted until September. Clay, who had but two years to live,
started the oratorical tournament with a defense of his measures and a plea to North
and South to be mutually conciliatory and

forebearing. To the North he pointed out that the Wilmot Proviso was a needless slap in the face to the South, for slavery was not likely to enter any of the national territories. To the South he emphasized the perils inherent in secession, which was certain to be followed by civil war. To both sections he issued an urgent warning that a continuation of the present recriminations and unyielding demands could lead only to disunion. Reasonable men should avert that catastrophe by agreeing on an honorable compromise.

Early in March, Calhoun, who would die within the month, presented the views of the Southern extremists. Too ill and weak to speak, he sat grimly in his seat while a colleague read his speech. Almost ignoring Clay's proposals, he devoted his argument to what to him was the larger and the only subject—the minority South—and he asked more for his section than could be given. Because of Northern aggressions, the cords

observe the laws concerning fugitive slaves, must cease attacking slavery, and must accept an amendment to the Constitution guaranteeing a balance of power between the sections. The amendment he had in mind may have been one providing for the election of dual Presidents, one from the North and one from the South, each possessing a veto power. In short, nothing would satisfy Calhoun except abject surrender by the North.

After Calhoun came the third of the elder statesmen, Webster, who, like Clay, had but two years of life left. The address he delivered, "the Seventh of March speech," was probably the greatest forensic effort of his long oratorical career. Although he still nourished White House ambitions, Webster now sought to calm angry passions and to rally Northern moderates to support of compromise, even at the risk of alienating the strong antislavery sentiment of his na-

Whittier's Denunciation of Webster

The New England abolitionists were outraged by Webster's speech supporting the Compromise of 1850 and the Fugitive Slave Act, and they denounced him in bitter terms. Emerson said: "All the drops of his blood have eyes that look downward." Whittier expressed his feelings about Webster's speech in a poem, "Ichabod":

> All else is gone; from those great eyes
>   The soul has fled:
> When faith is lost, when honor dies,
>   The man is dead!
>
> Then, pay the reverence of old days
>   To his dead fame;
> Walk backward, with averted gaze,
>   And hide the shame!

that bound the Union were snapping, he said. What would save the Union? The North must admit that the South possessed equal rights in the territories, must agree to

tive New England. While he devoted some attention to repelling Calhoun's arguments and the notion of peaceable secession, Webster deliberately aimed most of his remarks at the North. Following Clay's lead, he appealed to the majority section not to irritate the South by insisting on a Wilmot Proviso where an ordinance of nature had al-

William H. Seward. *In the 1850's the Senator from New York was regarded as a leader of the extreme antislavery wing of the Republican party. Actually, he was much less radical than he sounded in his speeches. Like other politicians of the period, he overestimated his ability to accommodate personal differences, forgetting that popular passions aroused by Senate speeches could not be stilled by Senate cloakroom conferences.* (NATIONAL ARCHIVES)

ready excluded slavery. He reproved the abolitionists for their violent language and the Northern people for not observing their obligations under the Constitution to return fugitive slaves. In a moving peroration, he evoked a vision of a united, happy, and tranquil Union.

Other speakers, important and insignificant, moderate and extremist, entered the debate. Some recommended popular sovereignty; others advocated extending the Missouri Compromise line. Of particular import were the views of the Northern extremists, voiced by the New York Whig Seward, who maintained extremely cordial personal relations with President Taylor, and Ohio's Chase, who had been sent to the Senate by a combination of Democratic and Free-Soil votes. Almost as adamant as Calhoun, Seward demanded the immediate admission of California and the prohibition of slavery in all the territories. He attacked the existing fugitive slave law as offensive to Northern opinion, and predicted, accurately, that a more stringent measure would increase sectional discord. Boldly he declared that slavery must be restricted to its present limits as a prelude to accomplishing its ultimate extinction. His bland assumption that slavery was a dying institution angered Southerners, but they were even more enraged by his assertion that antislavery people were not bound to obey constitutional injunctions respecting slavery. There was a higher law than the Constitution, he proclaimed, the law of God, and slavery contravened divine law. Although Southerners were undoubtedly shocked by Seward's statement, the notion that human law, to be operative, must conform to superhuman law was fairly common in American thought in the nineteenth century. Seward was only giving political expression to doctrines advanced on the philosophical level by Emerson, Thoreau, and other transcendentalist thinkers.

After most of the speeches had been made, Clay's resolutions were referred to a special committee, headed by Clay, which was to frame them into acceptable laws and report back to the Senate. Early in May the committee presented three proposed bills. The first, which became known as the "Omnibus Bill," attempted to dispose of the territorial problem. It proposed that California be admitted as a free state, that the remainder of the territory acquired from Mexico be divided into two territories, New Mexico and Utah, with no restriction on or guarantee of slavery, and that Texas surrender her claim to the area contested with New Mexico for a payment of $10,000,000. The second bill provided for the effective fugitive slave law that the South wanted, and the third would have abolished the slave trade in the District of Columbia.

When the bills were introduced, it was evident that popular sentiment in all sections was slowly swinging in favor of some kind of compromise. The country was entering upon a period of prosperity—the result of an expanding foreign trade, the flow of gold from California, and a boom in railroad construction—reminiscent of the flush days of the 1830's. Conservative eco-

seemed to be abating. The Nashville convention met in June, and after adopting some tame resolutions adjourned to await final action by Congress.

For a time, however, it seemed that Congress was not going to act. All attempts to pass the Omnibus Bill failed. One reason for the impasse was Clay's faulty strategy. Although he probably could have secured majorities for the separate items in the measure, he insisted on presenting it as a package arrangement, and on this basis he met defeat. Another reason was the opposition of Taylor. The President persisted in his stand that the admission of California, and possibly New Mexico, must come first and alone; after that, it might be possible to discuss other measures. In the meantime, if the South wanted to try anything like secession, "Old Zack" was ready to use force against his native section and to lead the armed forces in person. Still a third factor holding

An Extreme Northern View on Compromise in 1850

William H. Seward, Senator from New York, expressed the feelings of those Northerners who refused to make any further concessions to the South in 1850: "I AM OPPOSED TO ANY SUCH COMPROMISE, IN ANY AND ALL THE FORMS IN WHICH IT HAS BEEN PROPOSED. Because, while admitting the purity and the patriotism of all from whom it is my misfortune to differ, I think all legislative compromises radically wrong and essentially vicious. They involve the surrender of the exercise of judgment and conscience on distinct and separate questions, at distinct and separate times, with the indispensable advantages it affords for ascertaining truth. They involve a relinquishment of the right to reconsider in future the decisions of the present, on questions prematurely anticipated. And they are a usurpation as to future questions of the province of future legislators."

nomic interests everywhere wanted to terminate the sectional dispute and concentrate the attention of the nation upon internal expansion. Even in the South excitement

back compromise was the attitude of the Northern Whigs. Partly because they were influenced by Taylor's leadership and partly because they disliked on principle Clay's territorial proposals, they opposed the Omnibus measure in overwhelming numbers; only one Northern Whig Senator followed Webster in supporting it. Despite the prom-

Millard Fillmore. *Few Presidents have exemplified the American success story as completely as Fillmore. Born in a log cabin and raised in poverty, by sheer industry he made himself into a successful lawyer and wealthy man. His support of the Compromise of 1850 alienated many Whig leaders and cost him the party's nomination in 1852. He was the last Whig President.* (LIBRARY OF CONGRESS)

inence in the debates of the great Whig chieftains, Clay and Webster, most of the votes for compromise had come from the Democrats.

During the summer two of the personal impediments to a settlement departed from the scene. On July 9, President Taylor died, the victim of a violent stomach disorder following an attack of heat prostration. He

was succeeded by the Vice President, Millard Fillmore of New York. The new chief executive was a handsome, dignified man of no great abilities; but he was also a practical professional politician who understood the importance of compromise in statecraft. At once he ranged himself on the side of the advocates of adjustment, using his powers of persuasion and patronage to swing Northern Whigs into line. At about the same time, Clay, exhausted by his labors, temporarily left Congress, and Douglas took over the leadership of the compromise forces. Discarding the Kentuckian's all-or-nothing strategy, Douglas broke up the various measures reported by Clay's committee, and presented them one by one. Offered in this manner, each item was able to command a majority. Even with Douglas's masterly direction and with a friendly President in the White House, the bills encountered rough sledding. Despite Fillmore's best efforts, many Northern Whigs continued in opposition. Most of the votes that passed them were provided by Democrats, with important assistance from some Whigs. By mid-September the series of measures that became known as the Compromise of 1850 had been enacted by both houses of Congress and signed by the President.

In its completed form the Compromise of 1850 consisted of five laws, which may be summarized as follows:

a. California was admitted as a free state.

b. New Mexico was organized as a territory, and Texas was to relinquish her claim to New Mexican territory in return for a payment of $10,000,000 from the national government.

c. Utah was organized as a territory.

d. The slave trade was abolished in the District of Columbia.

e. A new and more severe Fugitive Slave Act placed the enforcement agencies of the national government at the disposal of slaveholders.

The ambiguous phrases in the acts concerning slavery in New Mexico and Utah did not, by congressional fiat, specifically ban or authorize slavery in either territory. They were intended to invest the territorial legislatures with power to prohibit or exclude slavery in the territorial stage, and thus to extend a limited recognition to popular sovereignty.

Acceptance of the Compromise

It was one thing to pass the Compromise through Congress and another to persuade the country to accept it as a satisfactory and permanent settlement of the controversy. In both North and South the compromise leaders felt constrained to launch lavish propaganda campaigns—conducted through the media of mass meetings, newspapers, and pamphlets—to educate the public. Widely circulated and applauded was a pledge signed in January, 1851, by 44 members of Congress from both parties (of whom 34 were from the South) to oppose any candidate for public office who did not recognize the Compromise as a final adjustment. Such a declaration seemed to banish the slavery issue forever, which was what most people wanted to do with it.

In the North the task of winning popular acceptance was easier than in the South. Both the business and agricultural interests longed for a return to sectional harmony. The only provision in the Compromise that really gagged Northern opinion was the Fugitive Slave Act. By this measure, a Negro accused of being a runaway was denied trial by jury and the right to testify in his own behalf. His status was to be decided by a federal judge or by a special commissioner appointed by the federal circuit courts. He could be remanded to slavery on the bare evidence of an affidavit presented by the man who claimed to be his owner. Federal marshals were to enforce the act, and heavy penalties were to be levied on anyone assist-

ing a slave to escape. Although Southerners considered the law as only a legal recognition of their just property rights, it was deeply offensive to the moral sentiment of the North, and in the years ahead it would be a prolific producer of sectional quarrels. But at the moment the North was willing to swallow the slave-catching features of the Compromise in order to secure the whole measure. In general, the Democrats were the strongest supporters of the Compromise. Most Whigs accorded it a cool approval or kept silent.

The advocates of the Compromise in the South had to fight hard to carry the day.

Western Democrat. *In 1850 Stephen A. Douglas was emerging as a leader of the Senate and the Democrats of the Northwest. He did as much as any man to secure the adoption of the Compromise of 1850. Just over five feet in height, with massive head and shoulders, he was known as "the Little Giant."* (NATIONAL ARCHIVES)

Many Southerners honestly believed that the admission of California was but the first step in a planned conspiracy to give the North a sufficient majority in the federal system to interfere with slavery in the South. The extremists still talked of the necessity of secession. The adjourned session of the Nashville convention met in No-

the Compromise movement; in others, Democrats took the lead. In the end the Unionists won out except in South Carolina, and that state dared not act alone. The South

---

The Georgia Platform

1850

Georgia accepted the Compromise of 1850 but listed possible acts by the North that would lead her to reconsider her decision. These conditions may be taken as minimum Southern demands for sectional peace:

"Fourth. That the State of Georgia, in the judgment of this Convention, will and ought to resist, even (as a last resort) to a disruption of every tie which binds her to the Union, any future Act of Congress abolishing Slavery in the District of Columbia, without the consent and petition of the slaveholders thereof, or any Act abolishing Slavery in places within the slave-holding States, purchased by the United States for the erection of forts, magazines, arsenals, dock-yards, navy-yards, and other like purposes; or in any Act suppressing the slave-trade between slave-holding States; or in any refusal to admit as a State any Territory applying because of the existence of Slavery therein; or in any Act prohibiting the introduction of slaves into the Territories of Utah and New Mexico; or in any Act repealing or materially modifying the laws now in force for the recovery of fugitive slaves.

"Fifth. That it is the deliberate opinion of this Convention, that upon the faithful execution of the Fugitive Slave Bill by the proper authorities, depends the preservation of our much loved Union."

---

vember, 1850 (with, however, only about a third of the original delegates present), and condemned the Compromise; the members called for an all-Southern convention to decide whether the section should seek to maintain its rights in the Union or whether it should secede. Sentiment against the Compromise was particularly strong in South Carolina, Georgia, Mississippi, and Alabama. In these states special conventions were elected to determine if the situation justified secession. The supporters of drastic action styled themselves Secessionists or Southern Rightists, and the champions of conciliation assumed the names of Unionists or Conservatives. In some cases Whigs led

brought itself to accept the Compromise, but only after much agonizing, and then only conditionally. Epitomizing the feelings of its people were the resolutions of the "Georgia Platform." They declared that Georgia would acquiesce in the Compromise but—if the North disregarded the Fugitive Slave Law, or attempted to abolish slavery in the District of Columbia, or denied admission to a state because it wished to have slavery—then Georgia would consider the compact broken and would protect its rights even to the length of seceding. In the general relief all over the country at Southern acceptance of the Compromise, most Northerners seemed to miss the significant fact that a number of Southern states had strikingly reaffirmed the doctrine of state sovereignty.

The Compromise of 1850 really settled little. If the points won by both sections are computed as on a balance sheet, the North clearly had the better of the deal. The North had secured the abolition of the slave trade in the national capital. In return the South had received its desired Fugitive Slave Act, but in the future nothing would so exasperate Northern opinion against the South and turn even moderates into critics of slavery as this ineptly conceived measure which the South would have done better to forget. The North gained the admission of California as a free state, which was bound to come sooner or later regardless of Southern opposition, and in compensation the

permit both sides to vote for them, but they clearly meant that the territorial legislatures were to have full power to legislate on slavery: to exclude it or to establish it or to regulate it. That is, the status of slavery in New Mexico and Utah would be determined by the process of popular sovereignty. If one or both of the territories prohibited slavery and if a case arose involving title to slaves, the case could be appealed to the Supreme Court, which would then have to decide if Congress could bar slavery from a territory or authorize a territorial legislature to do so. Both New Mexico and Utah, when they entered the Union, could, like other states, make any disposition of slavery they wished. The territorial provisions hardly added up to a victory for either section. Rather, like the Compromise itself,

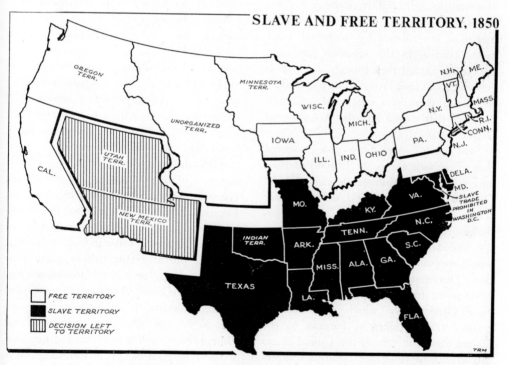

SLAVE AND FREE TERRITORY, 1850

FREE TERRITORY

SLAVE TERRITORY

DECISION LEFT TO TERRITORY

South obtained the organization of New Mexico and Utah without the Wilmot Proviso. The provisions concerning these territories were vaguely worded, in order to

they postponed a decision on fundamental issues, which was perhaps what the promoters of the measure were trying to accomplish—to buy time in the hope that in time the troublesome issues would disappear. The Compromise was a truce, and it proved to be of short and uneasy duration.

Foreign Affairs Under Taylor and Fillmore

As a result of the acquisition of California and Oregon, the United States had become a Pacific power. The rapid settlement of California following the discovery of gold and the sustained movement of migrants to Oregon indicated that a new center of American population was about to come into being in the Far West. And yet communication with this area, by horse and wagon over the plains and mountains or by water around Cape Horn, was distressingly slow and dangerously dubious. There was an imperative need to bind the Pacific coast communities more tightly to the rest of the country, and obviously this need could be met most immediately by improved water transportation. In this situation interested Americans turned their thoughts to a project which had long intrigued men's minds—the construction of a canal across Central America that would link the Atlantic and Pacific oceans.

Two possible routes for a canal presented themselves: one across the Isthmus of Panama, which lay within the domain of New Granada (later Colombia), and the other across Nicaragua, which was regarded as the more feasible. If the United States should decide to build a canal in Panama, it would encounter no international complications. During the Polk administration the government had concluded a treaty with New Granada by which that country granted transit rights in Panama to the United States; in return, the United States had agreed to recognize Granada's sovereignty in Panama and to defend the neutrality of the region. If the United States chose the Nicaragua route, which seemed likely, it would have to deal with Great Britain, which had important commercial interests in this part of the Caribbean as well as colonies: Belize, or British Honduras, and a claimed protectorate over the Mosquito Indians on the east coast of Nicaragua. Quite willing to check the ambitious Americans in rich Central America, England attempted to render her shadowy Mosquito protectorate substantial by asserting British authority over an Indian village (San Juan or Greytown), the probable eastern terminus of the proposed canal. Instantly American public opinion was aroused, and war talk flared on both sides of the Atlantic. It seemed to be the Oregon-Maine quarrel over again.

But, as in the earlier crisis, neither nation wanted to go to the length of war to defend its interests. Both preferred to negotiate the difficulty. England sent to America an able minister, Henry Lytton Bulwer, to treat with Taylor's Secretary of State, John M. Clayton. The result of their deliberations was the Clayton-Bulwer Treaty (April 19, 1850), a characteristic Anglo-American compromise. As neither nation would consent to let the other have sole control of a canal, they agreed to join in promoting a waterway, with the understanding that neither should ever fortify or exercise exclusive control over the project. An ambiguous clause in the treaty attempted to deal with England's territorial interests and ambitions in Central America. Written in purposely obscure language in order to facilitate agreement, it provided that neither party was ever to occupy or assume dominion over any part of Central America. While Great Britain understood that this meant she was not to occupy any more territory, the United States took it to mean that England would relinquish her present holdings. In a few years this provision of the treaty was to cause further discord between the two nations.

Although the treaty received ready Senate approval, it was angrily denounced by expansionists, who condemned it as a self-denying pledge, a self-granted obstacle to expansion, which need not have been given. Later generations would stigmatize it as an abject surrender to British diplomacy, and it has been called the most unpopular treaty ever concluded by the United States. Actually, when all the factors in the situation are considered, the pact was a substantial American victory. Without yielding any practical advantage or important right, the United States blocked future British expansion in Central America and British ambitions to control the proposed canal. Furthermore, the United States had persuaded the most powerful nation in the world, and the greatest colonizing power, to recognize the principles of the Monroe Doctrine.

When Fillmore became President, he appointed Webster Secretary of State. At that moment the great democratic and nationalist revolutions of 1848 in Europe were running their course, some succeeding, others petering out in failure. A vision of a republican Europe, with governments based, of course, on the model of the United States, stirred the American imagination. In the Democratic party a "Young America" movement started, dedicated to, among other objectives, aiding oppressed peoples over the seas. Politicians in both parties, particularly those who had minority groups like the Irish and Germans in their districts, contributed to the excitement by denouncing the decayed monarchies of the Old World. Webster and other moderates sensed in the situation an opportunity to make the people forget the recent sectional fight by directing their attention to events abroad. When the government of Austria officially protested against the apparent readiness of the United States to recognize the Hungarians, who were in revolt against Austria, Webster resolved to write a reply that would touch the national pride of Ameri-

cans in all sections and that would awaken Europe to the greatness of America. His answer was a triumph of spread-eagle diplomacy, an insult to Austria, and a taunt to all Europe. In one screaming passage he declared that in comparison with the extent of the United States, the possessions of Austria were "but as a patch on the earth's surface." After the Hungarian uprising collapsed, the magnetic national hero of Hungary, Louis Kossuth, came to America to seek aid for his people. He was wined and dined and lionized, and Webster spoke at a banquet in his honor; but Kossuth could secure no pledge from the government to intervene in Europe on Hungary's behalf. He departed after learning that American interest in persecuted nationality groups was confined mainly to talk.

In another area of foreign relations, Webster proceeded with less bombast and more prudence. Lying at the mouth of the Gulf of Mexico and controlling the Caribbean communications of the United States was the rich Spanish colony of Cuba. American statesmen had long been aware of the island's importance to their country, and previous administrations probably would have acted to take it if a strong foreign power had sought to oust decrepit Spain. President Polk had tried, without success, to induce Spain to sell. After the Mexican War, American interest in Cuba mounted, partly as a result of the continued influence of Manifest Destiny but mainly because of the slavery question. Observant Southerners recognized that the territories acquired from Mexico were unfit for slave labor and that the South could hope for no new slave states within the present national limits. Only to the south—to the Caribbean and Central America—could the South look for lands where slavery would be profitable, and in this region the richest prize was Cuba. Southern expansionists talked of organizing filibustering expeditions to seize the island for the United States, and New Orleans became a center where plans for Cuban conquest were hatched.

Coincidentally a filibustering leader appeared, one General Narciso López, a Venezuelan adventurer, who proposed to invade Cuba with a force of volunteer Americans, eject the Spanish, and present the island to the United States. In 1849 he prepared an expedition, but Federal officials in New Orleans and New York broke up his plans. In the following year he succeeded in reaching Cuba but had to flee to the United States when the Spanish dispersed his small force. Encouraged by Southern supporters, López made plans in 1851 for a third try. He landed in Cuba with over 400 men, mostly Americans, and almost immediately suffered a decisive defeat, he and part of his army being captured. The Spanish authorities, irritated by López's periodic visits, executed him and more than fifty of his followers. When news of López's fate reached the United States, popular indignation was widespread and intense, especially in the South. In New Orleans a mob wrecked the Spanish consulate and a Spanish newspaper office. Now it was

Spain's turn to be indignant; her government demanded reparation and an apology. Webster, fresh from insulting Austria, with whom for geographical reasons alone it was impossible to fight, did not want a war with a nation that might fight. In a conciliatory note, he admitted the wrong committed by the mob and extended satisfactory amends.

Webster might have backed down in the López affair, but it was immediately evident that his action did not mean his government was abandoning interest in Cuba. England and France, alarmed by the filibustering movements, proposed to Washington a tripartite agreement guaranteeing Spain's sovereignty in Cuba. The United States rejected the idea. Edward Everett, who succeeded Webster, explained to England and France the strategic importance of Cuba, commanding the sea approaches to the United States and dominating the Caribbean and Isthmian water routes. The American government, said Everett, could make no pledge that it would never acquire Cuba. Indeed, "Under certain contingencies it might be almost essential to our safety."

-»-»-»-»«-«-«-«

BIBLIOGRAPHY

THE PREVIOUSLY CITED monographs by Cole, Carpenter, and Dodd and the biographies of Calhoun, Webster, Clay, and Benton can be used profitably in connection with this chapter. At this point Allan Nevins' monumental history of the sectional controversy becomes a basic item; the pertinent volumes for this period are *Ordeal of the Union* (2 vols., 1947). Three books by A. O. Craven contain valuable material and challenging interpretations: *The Repressible Conflict, 1830–1861* (1939); *The Growth of Southern Nationalism, 1848–1861* (1953);

and *The Coming of the Civil War* (rev. ed., 1957). The social background of the sectional quarrel is described in A. C. Cole, *The Irrepressible Conflict, 1850–1865* (1934). On the role of the abolitionist groups in the controversy, see Theodore C. Smith, *The Liberty and Free Soil Parties in the Northwest* (1897) and D. L. Dumond, *Anti-Slavery Origins of the Civil War* (1939). An excellent state study is R. H. Shryock, *Georgia and the Union in 1850* (1926).

Much of the political history of the period is in biographies. Among the best are Holman Hamilton, *Zachary Taylor, Soldier in the White House* (1951), and Dyer, *Zachary Taylor*. Stephen A. Douglas is brilliantly presented in G. F. Milton, *The Eve of Conflict* (1934). A good account of another Democratic leader is F. B. Woodford, *Lewis Cass* (1950). Satisfactory lives of two important Southern spokesmen are U. B. Phillips, *Robert Toombs* (1913), and Rudolph von Abele, *Alexander H. Stephens*

(1946). Northern Whig leadership is delineated in biographies of two New Yorkers: Frederic Bancroft, *William H. Seward* (2 vols., 1900), and G. G. Van Deusen, *Thurlow Weed* (1947).

On foreign policy, see Bemis, *American Secretaries of State*, vols. 5 and 6, and two outstanding monographs: M. W. Williams, *Anglo-American Isthmian Diplomacy, 1815–1915* (1916), and Basil Rauch, *American Interest in Cuba, 1848–1855* (1948).

CHAPTER 26

The Drift Toward Disunion

OR APPROXIMATELY two years after the great Compromise, sectional tranquility prevailed in the country. The 1850's opened in a cycle of economic expansion. In the glow of flush times that pervaded every section, people turned with relief from the slavery controversy to the more rewarding tasks of developing the nation's material resources. Both parties in the election of 1852 pledged to observe the provisions of the Compromise, and the quarrels of the past seemed to have receded into the past. But hardly had the administration chosen in that election settled well into office when the truce of 1850 was undone. Discord again rent the Union. This time it would not cease until submitted to the final arbitration of civil war.

The Compromise was not maintained for a number of reasons, two of which were of primary influence. First, the various sections or the dominant class in each, or the politicians who represented the dominant groups, were not sufficiently devoted to the principles of the Compromise to make it work. They—the politicos or their backers —paid lip tribute to the ideals of conciliation, and in most cases sincerely so, but at the same time they tried to secure advantages for their section which made sectional reconciliation impossible. And second, the Compromise did not stop what no legislative enactment from any source could have halted—the growing conviction in men's minds that slavery was a moral wrong and an affront to the spirit of the nineteenth century. No legal wand waved by Congress could command people in the North to refrain from denouncing slavery, or Southerners to desist from glorifying it.

Sectionalism was cutting into some of the most vital areas of national life, even into organized religion. In the 1840's slavery had caused the Methodists and Baptists to split into Northern and Southern branches. In the 1850's controversy over slavery rent the

Presbyterians into bitter factions, impelling some Southern synods to secede, and stirred dangerous dissensions among the Episcopalians. Only the Roman Catholics escaped the dividing influence of the issue. As sec-

flict between opposing and enduring forces, and it means that the United States must and will, sooner or later, become either entirely a slave-holding nation, or entirely a free labor nation."

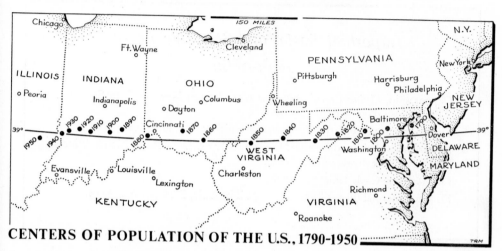

CENTERS OF POPULATION OF THE U.S., 1790-1950

tionalism manifested its increasing influence, the beleaguered South closed in even more tightly on itself. Many Southern Whigs became Democrats in the belief that the Democratic party, representing strict construction and constitutional restraints, offered a stouter protection to the minority South than their own organization; when the shift was completed the South had almost a one-party system and the Whig party had almost no Southern wing. The West-South alliance, strained in the Polk-Taylor period, finally broke and fell apart. As the controversy deepened, it became more bitter. South and North nourished dark, almost pathological suspicions of the other's motives. Charged Jefferson Davis of Mississippi: "I see nothing short of conquest on the one side, or submission on the other. . . . It is no longer the clamor of a noisy fanaticism, but the steady advance of a self-sustaining power to the goal of unlimited supremacy." Cried William H. Seward of New York: "Shall I tell you what this collision means? . . . It is an irrepressible con-

America in the Fifties

As in the forties, in the following decade the social forces promoting sectional division operated simultaneously with other and more enduring factors that were drawing the various sections closer together and stimulating the spirit of nationalism. The nation continued its phenomenal human and material expansion. Between 1850 and 1860 the population leaped from approximately 23 million to over 31 million, with a significant proportion of the increase occurring in the recently settled states just west of the Mississippi and in the Far West; some of the states and territories boasting the greatest growth had not even appeared in the census of 1840. Two new states entered the Union to swell the Northern majority, Minnesota (1858) in the booming Northwest, and on the Pacific coast Oregon (1859), whose population increased from 13,000 in 1850 to 52,000 by 1860. Oregon came in with her northern boundary fixed at the Columbia, while above the river

Washington Territory, organized in 1853, was already receiving settlers. South of Oregon the lush empire of California still drew hordes of emigrants, many of whom now

City became "cities" overnight; and the territory of Nevada was in the making.

Helping to swell the growing population were the hosts of immigrants who con-

---

Important Social and Scientific Events
1848–1860

Clipper ship, *Flying Cloud*, sets new record from New York to San Francisco of 89 days, 8 hours, 1851.

First passenger train from the East (Detroit) arrives in Chicago, 1852.

First railroad bridge over the Mississippi River, from Rock Island, Illinois, to Davenport, Iowa, opened, 1856.

First Atlantic Cable laid, 1857–1858.

First commercial oil well brought in at Titusville, Pennsylvania, 1859.

---

came to engage in agriculture; in the decade the population quadrupled, reaching a figure of 400,000. New Mexico and Utah experienced smaller but respectable population increases; to the irritation of the Mormons thousands of nonbelievers began to throng into the colony set aside for the Saints. Farther to the east the agricultural frontier was reaching out across the Great Plains to the area that later would become the states of Kansas and Nebraska. Nor was the mining frontier confined to California. In 1858 gold was discovered in the Pike's Peak region, in the area which would become Colorado, and the gold rush of the following year duplicated in spirit if not in numbers the scenes of 1849. Soon nearly 40,000 people were seeking riches in and around Denver City, the metropolis of the new El Dorado. In the same years large deposits of silver were found on the eastern slopes of the Sierra Nevada Mountains. Thousands of prospectors came to work the fabulous Comstock Lode and other ore-producing centers; Virginia City and Carson

tinued to arrive from Europe. The number who came in the fifties exceeded even that of the previous decade, reaching an estimated aggregate of over two and a half million. As before, the overwhelming majority of the newcomers hailed from Ireland and Germany. By 1860 more than a million and a half Irish had migrated to the United States, and approximately a million Germans. Other nationalities or ethnic stocks represented in the immigrant tide were Englishmen, Frenchmen, Italians, Jews, Scandinavians, Poles, and Hollanders. Most of the foreigners collected in the urban centers of the Northern states, although some of the Germans and some members of the smaller migrant groups turned to farming. Almost half of the population of New York City consisted of aliens, and in St. Louis, Chicago, and Milwaukee the foreign-born outnumbered those of native birth. Few immigrants settled in the South. Only 500,000 lived in the slave states in 1860, and a third of these were concentrated in Missouri; of the Southern cities only New Orleans contained a large number of foreign-born residents. Immigrants avoided the South partly because of the climate, partly because most of them were opposed to slavery or feared the competition of slave labor, but mostly because the bulk of them landed at Northern ports and from these points gravitated easily to areas in the North that attracted them.

In some cities and states the foreign vote assumed pivotal importance. Existing laws in many states permitted aliens to vote if they had been in the country for a year and had declared intention to seek citizenship. Particularly in the large cities, the politicians courted the immigrant voters with material favors, including outright money payments, and in some places it became common to buy votes in blocks. In general, the immigrants tended to affiliate with the Democrats, whose party they regarded as the representative of the common man.

The presence of huge numbers of aliens occasioned the appearance of the first important organized nativist movement in American history. While some natives recognized the contribution which the newcomers were making to the cultural and material development of their adopted land, many others disliked their ways and feared their influence. These critics stressed that many of the immigrants were mentally and physically defective, that they created centers of pauper population, and that their votes were corrupting politics. Laborers complained that the aliens, willing to work for low wages, were stealing their jobs. Protestants, impressed by the aptitude which the Catholic Irish demonstrated for politics, believed, or affected to believe, that the church of Rome was attaining an undue power in American government. Many Americans of older stock were honestly concerned that the foreign hordes would not assimilate into national life or would inject new and radical philosophies into the national thought pattern.

Out of these tensions and prejudices there emerged a number of secret societies to combat the alien menace. Originating in the East and later spreading to the West and South, these groups combined in 1850 to form the Supreme Order of the Star-Spangled Banner. Included in the official beliefs of the order were opposition to Catholics or aliens holding public office and support of stricter naturalization laws and literacy tests for voting. When members were asked to define their platform, they replied, because of the secrecy rule, "I know nothing," and hence were popularly called "Know-Nothings." Soon the leaders decided to seek their objectives by political methods, and formed the American party. In the East the new organization scored an immediate and astonishing success, casting in the elections of 1854 a large vote in Pennsylvania and New York and winning control of the state government in Massachusetts. Elsewhere its progress was more modest and tempered by local conditions. Western Know-Nothings, because of the presence of many German voters in the area, found it expedient to proclaim that they were not opposed to naturalized Protestants. In the South, where Catholics were few, the leaders disavowed any religious bias, and Catholics participated in the movement. The reasons for the spectacular growth of the party are easy to explain. For one thing, it seemed to point to a way to evade the slavery issue; for another, it offered a refuge to Whigs, who saw their party breaking up and who did not want to join the Democrats. But the Know-Nothings, like other similar organizations of the period, could not avoid the slavery question, and finally, by 1856, they too would split on the inevitable issue.

The most dynamic centralizing force operating in American society was the continuing revolution in communications. "The fifties," writes one historian (A. C. Cole), "saw the emerging outlines of a genuinely national system of transportation and communication."[1] In order to provide speedier mail facilities to the Pacific coast, the government contracted with John Butterfield of the Overland Mail Company; Butterfield agreed to furnish a stagecoach service between St. Louis and San Francisco, and to cover the distance in twenty-five days. Although he was able to meet the terms of

[1] A. C. Cole, *The Irrepressible Conflict, 1850–1865* (New York: Macmillan, 1934), p. 3.

the pact, an even faster arrangement was established by the freighting organization of Russell, Majors, and Waddell. This was the famous Pony Express, which operated between St. Joseph, Missouri, and Sacramento. Making its first run in 1860 from both terminals, the relays of pony riders succeeded in delivering their messages in what was then considered the incredible time of ten days. Ironically, while people were still marveling at the pony express, another medium was about to make it obsolete. The telegraph, introduced in the previous decade, seemed, because of the relatively low cost of constructing wire systems, the ideal answer to the problems of long-distance communication. By 1860 over 50,000 miles of wire connected all parts of the country, and a year later the Pacific telegraph, with 3,595 miles of wire, was open between New York and San Francisco. Nearly all of the independent lines had been absorbed into one organization, the Western Union Telegraph Company. American enthusiasm for wire communication was not limited to the confines of the nation.

Two Views of Immigration. *These two pictures from* Harper's Weekly *show the sometimes antithetical attitudes that Americans had about immigrants. The one on the left is a rather idealized representation of some immigrants departing from home for the United States. Note the handsome, almost noble features of each person. The picture above shows political workers operating at the naturalization office before an election. They are ready to testify that an immigrant has been in the United States for five years—provided the immigrant will promise his vote. The obvious Irish type in the foreground and the other foreigners are here depicted as beings of a low social order. (*FROM* Harper's Weekly, *1857 AND 1858*)

Cyrus W. Field, a New York businessman, conceived the project of laying an Atlantic cable between Newfoundland and Ireland. With financial aid from associates and en-

communications was supplied by the railroads, now recognized to be the cheapest and best form of long-distance transportation. An outburst of construction without

The Overland Mail. *Congress authorized the establishment of an overland mail line to California in 1857, providing for the payment of an annual subsidy to the carrier. John Butterfield secured the contract and organized the famous Overland Mail. On the Butterfield line, coaches of the Concord type operated between San Francisco and St. Louis or to a rail terminal west of St. Louis. They followed an indirect southern route over 2700 miles in length. The average time for a trip was twenty-five days. In addition to letters, the coaches carried passengers, who paid $100 for a rough, jolting journey. The coach in the picture is about to take off from San Francisco on the first leg of the run eastward.* (FROM *Harper's Weekly*, 1858)

couragement from the British and American governments, he completed a cable in 1858. Messages between Great Britain and the United States were exchanged, and man seemed to have accomplished another conquest of distance. But within a few weeks the cable went dead, nor could Field, who continued to believe in his idea, get it to working again. (After the Civil War, Field returned to his labors, and in 1866 succeeded in laying a permanent cable.)

The greatest transforming influence in

previous parallel occurred in the fifties. The amount of trackage tripled, going from 9,021 miles in 1850 to 30,626 in 1860. By sections the railroad mileage was as follows: in the Northeast, 9,500 miles; in the West, 11,078; in the South, 10,048. Despite its smaller figure, the East, the smallest of the sections, had the most efficient system, with twice as much trackage per square mile of land as the West and four times as much as the South. By far the largest amount of construction took place in the West, which

The Pony Express Meets the Telegraph. *On the eve of the Civil War the speed of the Pony Express in transmitting letters astonished most people. But already the pony rider was being made obsolete by an even faster medium, the telegraph. The print depicts dramatically the confrontation of the two forms of communication.* (LIBRARY OF CONGRESS)

The Pony Express

The men who rode the Pony Express were unforgettably described by Mark Twain in *Roughing It* (1871): "There was no idling time for a pony rider on duty. He rode fifty miles without stopping, by daylight, moonlight, starlight, or through the blackness of darkness—just as it happened. He rode a splendid horse that was born for a racer and fed and lodged like a gentleman; kept him at his utmost speed for ten miles, and then, as he came crashing up to the station where stood two men holding fast a fresh, impatient steed, the transfer of rider and mailbag was made in the twinkling of an eye, and away flew the eager pair and were out of sight before the spectator could get hardly the ghost of a look. Both rider and horse went 'flying light.' The rider's dress was thin and fitted close; he wore a roundabout and a skullcap and tucked his pantaloons into his boot tops like a race rider. He carried no arms—he carried nothing that was not absolutely necessary, for even the postage on his literary freight was worth *five dollars a letter*."

n 1850 had stood a poor third in aggregate miles. Now, with more than a third of the country's trackage, the West enjoyed rapid communication with the East and between its inland cities and the Great Lakes and the Mississippi-Ohio river route. The railroads

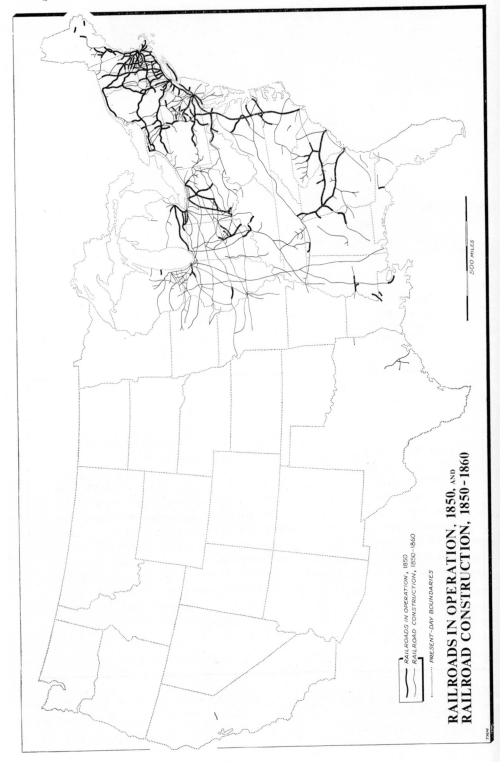

RAILROADS IN OPERATION, 1850, AND
RAILROAD CONSTRUCTION, 1850 - 1860

RAILROADS IN OPERATION, 1850
RAILROAD CONSTRUCTION, 1850-1860
.... PRESENT-DAY BOUNDARIES

500 MILES

were reaching even west of the Mississippi, which at several points was spanned by iron bridges. One line ran from Hannibal to St. Joseph on the Missouri River, and another

Wheeling. From the terminals of these lines other roads into the interior touched the Mississippi River at eight points. Other important trunk routes were the Michigan

---

Some Railroad Firsts

First common carrier railroad chartered in the United States, 1827.
First steam locomotive to run in America makes trial trip, 1829.
First train of cars hauled by a locomotive, 1830.
First Pullman sleepers introduced, 1859.
First dining cars introduced, 1863.
First transcontinental railroad completed, 1869.
First trains to be fully equipped with electric lights, 1887.
First heavy duty electric locomotive put in regular use, 1895.

---

was being built from St. Louis to Kansas City. The South's total trackage figure is somewhat deceptive. Many of its lines were short ones, and there were few through lines. Nevertheless, such towns as Charleston, Atlanta, Savannah, and Norfolk had direct connections with Memphis, and thus with the Northwest; and Richmond was connected, via the Virginia Central, with the Memphis and Charleston railroad. In addition, several independent lines furnished a continuous connection between the Ohio River and New Orleans.

A new feature in railroad development —and one that would profoundly affect the nature of sectional alignments—was the trend toward the consolidation of short lines into trunk lines. By 1853 four roads had surmounted the Appalachian barrier to connect the Northeast with the West. Two, the New York Central and the New York and Erie, gave New York City access to the Lake Erie ports. The Pennsylvania road linked Philadelphia and Pittsburgh, and the Baltimore and Ohio connected the Maryland metropolis with the Ohio River at

Central and the Michigan Southern, which entered Chicago from the east, and the Rock Island and Chicago, which connected the Great Lakes and the Mississippi. Chicago became the rail center of the West, served by fifteen lines and over a hundred daily trains. The appearance of the great trunk lines tended to divert traffic from the water routes, the Erie Canal and the Mississippi River. By lessening the dependence of the West upon the Mississippi, the railroads helped to weaken the West-South alliance; by binding more closely the East and West, they prepared the way for a coalition of those sections.

The formation of trunk lines also resulted in important technological improvements, notably in the direction of establishing a uniform gauge, or width of track. In the first decades of construction the gauge depended largely on the notions of the builders. Some adopted the English standard of 4 feet 8½ inches. Others chose gauges ranging from 3 to 6 feet. As long as there was no demand for through service, the variations were no particular problem. But when traffic began to move over long distances and over several lines, the diverse gauges, forcing a costly process of unloading and reloading, became intolerable. The trunk

Despite such vexatious problems as gauges, the railroads were able to revolutionize transportation costs and time. At the opening of the century the average

Railroads in the 1850's. *As railroads extended their lines and enlarged their business, they also sought to develop greater locomotive power and to improve their cars and service. By the 1850's locomotives had become standardized to what was known as the "American type." A locomotive of this type is shown above. Note that it has a four-wheel leading truck and two pair of driving wheels, coupled. The blunderbuss shape of the smokestack was for the purpose of catching sparks thrown by the wood-burning stoves used on all trains. The average speed of such a locomotive in passenger traffic was thirty miles an hour. To accommodate passengers on long journeys, the railroads introduced sleeping cars. They were three-decker affairs, and separate cars were provided for men and women. Pullman sleepers convertible to day use were introduced in 1857 but did not become popular until after the Civil War.* (ASSOCIATION OF AMERICAN RAILROADS)

lines necessarily had to lead the way to a standard gauge. On most of the roads between New York and Chicago the gauge was almost the same, varying only 2 inches. For through service the trunk companies employed cars with broad-tread wheels that could navigate the different widths. Although progress toward a standard gauge was made, there were in 1860 twelve different gauges on the country's railroads.

freight rate by wagon was 33¢ per ton mile; the average passenger rate was 6¢ per mile. In the stagecoach era of the 1830's a trip from Boston to New York consumed forty-one hours; from New York to St. Louis, a distance of 1,600 miles, over three weeks were required. The average coach fare for 300 miles was $15. The principal result of the advent of water transportation was to reduce freight charges. According to one estimate, the cost of traffic on the various means of transportation in 1840 were as follows: roads, 10–20¢ per mile; canals, 1½¢; lake steamers, 2–4¢; river steamers, 1½¢; railroads, 2½¢. Water transportation continued to be cheaper than railroad transportation, but the railroads could move goods in about half the time required on water. The following table will indicate the advantages in speed of the railroads between particular cities:

From	Mile Distance	Time by Water	Time by Railroads
New York to Cleveland	700	9 days	3 days
New York to Detroit	825	10 days	4 days
New York to Chicago	1,500	14½ days	6½ days
New York to St. Louis	1,600	———	12½ days

Railroad costs continued to decrease, reaching by the decade of the 1860's an average of slightly less than 2¢ per ton mile.

Capital to finance the railroad boom came from various sources. Some of it was provided by American investors, and large sums were borrowed abroad. Substantial aid was provided by local governmental units—states, cities, towns, counties—eager to have a road to serve their needs. This support took the form of loans, stock subscriptions, subsidies, and donations of land for rights of way. The railroads also obtained assistance from the federal government in the shape of public land grants. In 1850 Senator Stephen A. Douglas and other railroad-minded politicians persuaded Congress to grant lands to the state of Illinois to aid the Illinois Central, then building toward the Gulf of Mexico; Illinois was to transfer the land to the Central as it carried its construction forward. Other states and their railroad promoters demanded the same privileges, and by 1860 Congress had allotted over 30 million acres to eleven states.

There was a revolution in news as well as in communications. During the fifties Americans experienced the impact of a new kind of journalism. In increasing numbers the upper and middle classes were reading monthly magazines which featured fiction and articles by some of the country's outstanding writers. Easily the leader in this field was *Harper's New Monthly Magazine*, with 170,000 subscribers, but competition was furnished by *Putnam's Magazine* and the *Atlantic Monthly*, both founded in the fifties. Another organ that appealed to the more literate groups was the New York religious-political weekly, the *Independent*, with a circulation of nearly 100,000. For the edification of the masses there appeared the pictorial weeklies, lavishly illustrated with drawings by America's best popular artists. The pioneer among the picture journals was the *National Police Gazette*, established in 1845 by George Wilkes. It was also the most sensational, being dedicated to record "horrid murders, outrageous robberies, bold forgeries, astounding burglaries, hideous rapes, vulgar seductions." Other, although not necessarily similar, magazines reaching huge audiences were the *New York Ledger* (1851), *Leslie's Illustrated Newspaper* (1855), and *Harper's Weekly* (1857).

More important than any of the magazines in influencing American opinion were the newspapers, of which there were more than 3,000 in 1860. Originally Washington had been the national news center, and the papers published there had been government or party organs which filled their columns with dull documents and speeches. With the advent of the telegraph and the railroad and with the government's assumption of the function of public printing, the center of news transmission shifted to

New York. A new type of newspaper also appeared, one that was more attuned to the spirit and the needs of the new America. Although newspapers continued to concentrate on politics, they came to report more human interest stories and, what was very important, to record the most recent news, the happenings of yesterday, which they could not have done before the telegraph. The New York papers and to a lesser degree those of other Northern cities maintained corps of special correspondents to go into any part of the country to cover any event that seemed newsworthy. Most of the metropolitan journals were owned in whole or in part by their editors, who were also in many cases their founders; unlike modern newspapers they bore the imprint of a single personality and are often referred to as "personal" organs.

The leading Northern papers, with the names of their editor-owners in parentheses, were the New York *Tribune* (Horace Greeley), the New York *Herald* (James Gordon Bennett), the New York *Times* (Henry J. Raymond), the New York *Evening Post* (William Cullen Bryant), the Springfield (Massachusetts) *Republican* (Samuel Bowles), the Cincinnati *Commercial* (Murat Halstead), and the Chicago *Tribune* (Joseph Medill). Southern newspapers, with smaller budgets, tended to follow the older pattern of reporting slightly stale political news. The principal Southern papers were the Richmond *Whig* (J. H. Pleasants), the Charleston *Mercury* (Robert Barnwell Rhett), the Louisville *Journal* (George D. Prentice), and the New Orleans *Picayune* (George W. Kendall). The combined circulation of the New York *Tribune* and *Herald* exceeded that of all the dailies published in the South.

In one sense, the new journalism helped to feed the fires of sectional discord. The rapid reporting of detailed information regarding differences between the sections probably prompted men to anger more quickly and more often than otherwise would have been the case. But viewed in a longer perspective the revolution in news was a unifying factor in American life. As one historian of journalism (L. M. Starr) has pointed out, the ultimate result of the news revolution was to endow the American people with that mystic sense of common destiny which is conveyed only by news of great events being reported everywhere simultaneously and soon after their occurrence.[2]

Election of 1852 and After

Political organizations in the year 1852 showed the effects of sectionalism. Thousands of Southern Whigs, disgusted by the antislavery sentiments of their Northern colleagues or convinced that the Democratic party was a safer guardian of the rights of the minority section, had shifted or were in the process of shifting their political loyalties; some were finding a temporary haven in the American party. The Whig party was still national, but it was fast shedding its Southern wing. The South still had a two-party system, but one of the parties was at the point of demise. The Democrats, on the surface, were more united than the Whigs, and were strengthened by the return of the bolting Barnburners. And yet the Democrats too were troubled by internal stresses. Broadly speaking, the party was composed of three economic-political groupings: the West or Northwest (farmers, aspiring capitalists), the South (planters, farmers), and an Eastern faction made up predominantly of merchants with Southern trade interests. The Westerners wanted to subordinate the slavery issue, with popular sovereignty; while the more extreme Southerners, if sufficiently aroused by outside pressures, would want to

[2] L. M. Starr, *Bohemian Brigade* (New York: Knopf, 1954), p. 55.

emphasize it by proclaiming Calhoun's doctrine of congressional support of slavery in the territories. In this situation lurked the possibility of a division that could split the party.

At their national convention in 1852 the Democrats adopted a platform pledging their unswerving devotion to the Compromise of 1850 and their united opposition to all attempts in any "shape or color" to renew the agitation of the slavery question. Not so unanimous when it came to choosing a candidate, they wrangled through forty-nine ballots, with no one of the leading contenders—Cass, Douglas, or James Buchanan of Pennsylvania—being able to secure a two-thirds majority. Finally, the prize went to one of the more obscure aspirants, another "dark horse," Franklin Pierce of New Hampshire. The Whigs likewise endorsed the Compromise but in much milder terms and over the opposition of many Conscience Whigs. Instead of nominating a man connected with and committed to the Compromise, they named, after fifty-three ballots, General Winfield Scott, whose views were unknown and whose support by Northern delegates made him suspect to Southerners. He would be the last Whig candidate. The only party to repudiate the Compromise was the Free-Soilers—seriously weakened by the defection of the Barnburners—who offered, as their candidate, John P. Hale of New Hampshire.

Probably because they had taken a stronger stand for the Compromise, the Democrats won the election. Pierce carried twenty-seven states and Scott four, and the Democrat had 254 electoral votes to the Whig's 42, the largest majority that any candidate had attained since Monroe's victory in 1820. In the popular vote, however, Pierce's triumph was much narrower, 1,601,-000 to 1,386,000, or a majority of only about 215,000. The Free-Soilers lost almost

half the number of votes they had polled in 1848. If their votes are reckoned as part of the opposition to the Democrats, Pierce's majority was a mere 60,000.

Franklin Pierce. *Handsome and slender, Pierce looked almost boyish at the time of his inauguration. Although he had an appealing personality, he lacked firmness of character and was easily dominated by stronger men in his cabinet and in Congress.* (LIBRARY OF CONGRESS)

When Franklin Pierce was inaugurated in 1853, he was, at the age of forty-nine, the youngest man up to that time to become President. He was also generally considered to be the handsomest chief executive the country had ever had. Amiable in nature and charming in manner, he had been selected as the Democratic nominee largely for reasons of party harmony. In his short political career he had upheld few opinions and had made few enemies. A member of a well-known New Hampshire family, he had served briefly in the state legislature and in both houses of Congress. In the Mexican War he had enlisted as a private, but was soon given a commission as brigadier general. At the time of his nomination he was quietly practicing law in his native state. He lacked the qualities to be a strong or positive President. His greatest weakness was a paralyzing indecision; it was said that he would come to one conclusion in the morning and change it in the afternoon. Generally he was dominated by the strong men of his cabinet, namely Secretary of State William L. Marcy of New York, Secretary of War Jefferson Davis of Mississippi, and Attorney General Caleb Cushing of Massachusetts. Partly because of conviction and partly because he enjoyed the society of certain Southerners and let them influence him, he was inclined to espouse the views of the Southern wing of the party.

In his inaugural address, Pierce paid tribute to the principles of the Compromise and deprecated a renewal of sectional agitation and discord. He foresaw a future of peace and tranquility and prosperity. But by the following year strife between the sections, sharper and uglier than before, raged unchecked, and the great adjustment of 1850 became a forgotten thing. For the revival of the controversy President Pierce must bear some responsibility, for some of the policies of his administration helped to precipitate the quarrel. Yet it would be unfair to charge it solely to the President and his advisers. There were forces at work in American society which would have brought about a return of conflict no matter what administration or party was in power. As before remarked, there were some issues that no congressional enactment could settle.

The Compromise did not dissolve the abolitionist organizations or stop their crusade to convince the Northern masses that slavery was a sin. Since 1830 the abolitionists had been flooding the country with propaganda—mainly disseminated by popular lecturers and by widely circulated pamphlets. In the 1850's they intensified their

efforts, and partly because recent events had focused attention on slavery, they found a larger audience. They also found new allies and new and more effective media of expression. The Free-Soil upsurge had placed several members of that group in Congress, and these men—such as Charles Sumner of Massachusetts in the Senate, and Joshua R. Giddings of Ohio in the House—could denounce slavery from the vantage point of the national forum. Furthermore, they could use their congressional mailing privileges to send their speeches free to people all over the Northern states. Horace Greeley, building his New York *Tribune* into a potent public influence, regularly opened his columns to abolitionist propaganda; the weekly edition, circulating far beyond the Eastern seaboard, reached into the rural areas of every part of the North, where it was received as a form of political gospel.

But the most powerful, the most telling document in the abolitionist propaganda attack was a novel, *Uncle Tom's Cabin*, by Harriet Beecher Stowe, published in 1852. Mrs. Stowe, "Crusader in Crinoline," was a member of a famous New England ministerial family (her father and her seven brothers were preachers), and she married a minister. It has been said that she was raised and smothered in orthodox New England Calvinism. For several years she had lived in Cincinnati, and from there had made several forays into Kentucky to view slavery and plantation life. These excursions were her only direct contact with the South. Her novel, written after she and her husband had left Cincinnati for Maine, was an indictment of slavery although not of the slaveholders; her purpose was to show that the slave system was inherently brutal and had a brutalizing effect on all who were connected with it.

From the historical viewpoint, it does not particularly matter whether her book was a good or bad novel; by modern standards, it has many defects, the characters being obvious stereotypes instead of real people and the conversations and many of the situations seeming contrived and artificial. It does not even matter whether her picture of slavery was true or false. Actually, it was both, being partly compounded of fact and partly of fancy; it departed from accuracy in that it emphasized the unusual or the extreme in slavery instead of the normal. What is important is that this moving tale of poor, persecuted Uncle Tom had a terrific impact on the Northern mind. Other abolitionists had attacked slavery in the abstract or as an evil institution, but Mrs. Stowe assailed it in terms of human personalities. In such a form, her message appealed to emotions and sympathies that no previous attack had touched, and inspired other similar novels to follow. The book sold over 300,000 copies in its year of publication. Dramatized into a play which was presented by countless professional and amateur companies all over the North, it reached other thousands who may not have read its pages. It was propaganda, but propaganda on a grand, almost a noble, level. Not without reason has *Uncle Tom's Cabin* been called the most influential

---

A Militant Defense of Slavery

One of the most extreme defenders of slavery was George Fitzhugh of Virginia. Belligerently he argued that slavery was a positive good and that it should be established in the North as well as the South. His writings were read by Abraham Lincoln, who concluded from them that the South hoped to extend slavery over the entire nation: "We should indignantly hurl back upon our assailants the charge that there is something wrong and rotten in our system. From their own mouths we can show free society to be a monstrous abortion, and slavery society to be the healthy, beautiful and natural being which they are trying, unconsciously, to adopt. We deem this peculiar question of negro slavery of very little importance. The issue is made throughout the world on the general subject of slavery in the abstract. The argument has commenced. One set of ideas will govern and control after awhile the civilized world. Slavery will every where be abolished, or every where be re-instituted."

---

novel ever published in the United States.

As the abolitionist assault mounted in intensity, it enlarged in scope. From condemning slavery the abolitionists advanced to denouncing everything and everybody connected with the institution. They framed a blanket indictment of Southern religion, family life, education—in short, of Southern culture. The effect of their propaganda was to sustain and increase the sense of insecurity felt by most Southerners. Did people in the North, asked Southerners, really believe these things? And if they did, were Southern rights safe in a Union controlled by people who were so hostile to the Southern way of life? Some Southern leaders understood, of course, that the abolitionists represented only a minority in the North; but because they wanted to arouse their people to an extreme position or were hoping for disunion, they saw to it that the most extreme abolitionist statements were featured in Southern newspapers. Nor was the South without its own aggressive propagandists who indicted all of Northern culture. carry their system into the free states. The propagandists on each side had perhaps a greater influence on the other section than on their own.

An Abolitionist View of the Fugitive Slave Act. *In this abolitionist broadside a party of "slave catchers" has run down some escaping slaves and is about to murder them. The Fugitive Slave Act was bitterly resented in the North, and abolitionist depictions of its enforcements were readily believed.* (LIBRARY OF CONGRESS)

ture. George Fitzhugh of Virginia published two books, *Sociology for the South: or, the Failure of Free Society* (1854) and *Cannibals All! or, Slaves Without Masters* (1857), in which he asserted that slavery was a natural condition, and depicted slave society as immeasurably superior to free society. He thought that Northern capitalists would eventually enslave their workers, and confidently predicted that slavery would some day dominate the nation. Widely reprinted in the Northern press, Fitzhugh's doctrines, which received relatively scant attention in the South, convinced many Northerners that the slavocracy meant to

Another explosive force in national society was the Fugitive Slave Act of the Compromise. Seward had predicted in 1850 that its enforcement would offend Northern opinion and contribute to sectional bitterness. His prophecy proved grimly accurate. Many people in the North, including some who were not abolitionists, were hostile to the law from the moment it was passed, believing that it violated various procedural guarantees of the Constitution and the basic concepts of English-American law. This hostility was intensified and increased when Southerners appeared in the Northern states to pursue fugitives or to claim as former slaves Negroes who had been living for years in Northern communities. Although most Northerners were willing to give a grudging acceptance to the law, there were centers of antislavery opinion where opposition was rampant. In these areas, mobs or organized groups attempted to impede enforcement of the act. In 1851 a crowd in Boston took a runaway named Shadrach away from a federal marshal and sent him on his way to Canada. Later in the same year at Syracuse, New York, there was a similar rescue of a slave named Jerry McHenry. In 1854 in Boston a mob led by respectable and prominent men tried unsuccessfully to take one Anthony Burns from the custody of federal officers.

These displays of violence alarmed the South, but making an even stronger impact were the new personal-liberty laws passed by several Northern legislatures. The frank purpose of the statutes was to render the Fugitive Slave Act a nullity. Although differing in details, the laws agreed in attempting to interpose state power between the accused fugitive and the federal authority. Wisconsin and Massachusetts instructed state courts to issue writs of habeas corpus against any person detaining a fugitive, and granted the fugitive a judicial hearing in which the burden of proof was placed on the pursuer. The supreme court of one state, Wisconsin, in the case of *Ableman* v. *Booth* declared the national law void; and when the Supreme Court of the nation in reviewing the case decided against the state, the Wisconsin court ignored the decision of the highest tribunal. Viewing the legal and judicial barriers being thrown in the way of the one provision of the Compromise which the South considered a positive victory, Southerners were deeply angered. The North, they felt, was showing that it did not intend to observe the compact of 1850. Talk of secession began to revive.

Democratic Imperialism

In the same inaugural address in which he voiced hopes for sectional amity, President Pierce raised an issue that was certain to provoke discord. His administration, he said, would not be deterred from territorial expansion by "any timid forebodings of evil." It was possible, he continued, that for its own security the United States might have to acquire certain possessions not then under its control. Approval of expansion by a Democratic administration in which Southern influence was paramount was an infallible method of reviving the sectional dispute. Naturally, many people in the North jumped to the conclusion that Pierce meant to seize foreign territory suitable for slavery and that specifically he had his eye on Cuba. And Pierce's desire to serve the Southern interest in his party was one reason for the imperialism that characterized his foreign policy. But this is not the whole story. Pierce was also swayed by the philosophy of Manifest Destiny, which was a continuing force in American life, and by the past record of the Democratic party as an instrument of territorial expansion. Sometimes called by his admirers "Young Hickory," in imitation of Jackson, he was in spirit the heir of James K. Polk.

The aggressive program of the administration manifested itself almost immediately and in several different areas. In Central America the United States continued to press England to withdraw her claims to authority in the Nicaragua-Honduras region. Britain was quite ready to back out, but she would not be pushed out. Relations between the two governments were complicated and embittered by the activities of the most famous of all American filibusters, William Walker. This tiny (he weighed just 100 pounds), dynamic, and dangerous man appeared in Nicaragua in 1855 with a band of American adventurers, and succeeded in establishing himself as dictator. He seems to have had a vision of becoming the head of a federation of Central American states. The British government, however, suspected that he was acting as an agent for Pierce and preparing the way for American annexation; this suspicion, although without foundation, was strengthened when the President extended recognition to Walker's government.

Walker might eventually have caused real trouble between England and the United States, but his too-ambitious plans miscarried. Forced to leave Nicaragua by military pressure exerted by neighboring republics, he attempted to return in 1860. He landed in Honduras but was arrested by British naval officials. They turned him over to the Honduran authorities, who promptly had him executed by a firing squad. By that time England had renounced her claims to the Honduran islands and the Mosquito coast. Walker lasted long enough to cause trouble between the North and the South. His seizure of Nicaragua was wildly applauded in the South and approved by many leading Democrats. Not unnaturally many Northerners concluded that Pierce had sent Walker to Central America to acquire another slave state.

While the Walker business was taking place in Central America, the two English-speaking nations traded resentments on a front far removed: Britain's colony of Canada. But in this dispute a fair and friendly settlement was speedily effected. It began when American fishermen complained to Washington that Canadian authorities were restricting their rights, as guaranteed by the Convention of 1818, to ply their trade off the Newfoundland and Labrador coasts. Pierce responded by dispatching a naval force to the area to protect American interests. The situation was further complicated by Canada's grave economic difficulties. As a result of England's free trade program

and the United States' tariff policy, the colony had lost a substantial portion of its export trade. Some Canadians contended that Canada's position would be improved by union with the United States, but the majority thought that the colony should merely seek closer trade relations with her southern neighbor. The Canadian legislature asked the home government to negotiate a treaty based on reciprocal principles.

Great Britain, beset by troubles in Europe, decided to conciliate the United States on the fisheries question and at the same time to appease Canadian economic grievances. She sent to Washington to conclude a treaty a special mission headed by Lord Elgin. The result of his discussions with Secretary of State Marcy was the Canadian Reciprocity Treaty of 1854, the first agreement of its kind ever made by the American government. By its terms American fishermen were granted enlarged privileges in Canadian waters. Of more importance were the reciprocal provisions, which listed a number of commodities, most of them agricultural, which were to be admitted to both countries without tariff duties. Although the treaty operated mainly to Canada's advantage, the United States also derived some substantial benefits in the form of increased trade. Of greater significance, in terms of later developments, was the fact that Canada was being drawn into the American economic orbit.

The Pierce administration also applied its vigorous foreign policy in the middle Pacific and in Asia, and in this huge region it scored one resounding diplomatic triumph. Since the conclusion of the Treaty of Wanghia (1844), American trade with China had steadily increased; Yankee traders had also secured a foothold in other Asiatic areas, notably in Siam. Americans engaged in the Pacific trade were accustomed to stopping over for supplies and rest at the midway point of Hawaii, which was also used as a base by the American whaling fleets in the Pacific. Because of its location, Hawaii seemed a tempting prize for a European nation with important Pacific interests. The United States felt that its interests were as great as any, and several times the government had taken the position that while it had no aggressive designs on the islands, it could not permit them to be annexed by another power. These disclaimers became less frequent after the acquisition of California and Oregon gave the nation a Pacific boundary and as American investors and speculators settled in Hawaii. Instead, a great deal of talk began, in the press and out, of annexing Hawaii or seizing it by a filibuster. Secretary Marcy tried to take advantage of the new expansion boom by negotiating a treaty of annexation with the Hawaiian government, but the pact proved unacceptable to the Senate. Nevertheless, it was clear that the United States intended to maintain its influence in the middle Pacific, and observers could have predicted that some day the islands would go the way of Texas and New Mexico.

The administration's most notable Asiatic success was in opening trade relations with another nation, the island kingdom of Japan. For over two centuries Japan had followed a policy of seclusion from the outside world; only the Dutch among Occidental peoples were allowed trade privileges, and these at only one port. As America's Oriental trade grew in volume, there were demands from shippers and businessmen that the government take steps to open Japan to American commerce. In 1852 President Fillmore sent out a naval expedition commanded by Commodore Matthew C. Perry, who was instructed to sound out the Japanese on a trade agreement. Perry reached Japan the following year, and, conducting himself with great firmness and tact, delivered his message. Realizing that the island people would require time to reach a decision involving a break with their past, he did not attempt to conclude a treaty, but left after stating that he would return the next year with a stronger force.

In 1854, acting now under the sponsorship of the Pierce administration, Perry returned to Japan. He found the Japanese ready to negotiate a pact, partly because they had been impressed by Perry's display of American naval might but mainly because the more progressive Japanese leaders had decided that relations with the outside world were desirable. Perry secured a treaty which opened two ports to American trade and provided for the residence in one of them of an American consul general. As the ports were relatively inaccessible, the United States did not gain any immediate economic benefits. More important was Japan's permission to appoint a consul general. To this post Pierce named a brilliant diplomat, Townsend Harris, and gave him instructions to conclude a more comprehensive treaty. After years of patient work, Harris persuaded the Japanese to accept an agreement (in 1858) that gave the United States a more favored position than any other nation.

Although the administration's foreign policy in the episodes just recounted had been marked by a kind of eager aggressiveness, it had been a national policy; it had sought objectives which could be said to benefit the national interest. In dealing with Cuba, however, Pierce and his advisers adopted a program which, whatever their motives, seemed specifically designed to profit the South. The result was to precipitate a minor controversy in domestic politics and to place the South in the position of seeming to conspire to violate the Compromise of 1850.

Pierce's reference in his inaugural to the possibility that the United States might have to acquire certain new possessions was commonly taken to mean Cuba. This impression was strengthened when he appointed Pierre Soulé of Louisiana as minister to Spain. Soulé was known as an enthusiastic expansionist who had a special and consuming enthusiasm to secure control of Cuba. He seemed to think that the purpose of his mission was to provoke war with Spain, and in any listing of tactless American diplomats he would occupy a high place. Soon after he arrived in Madrid, Spanish officials in Cuba seized an American merchant ship, the *Black Warrior*, on the grounds that it had violated some shipping regulation. Although the United States demanded proper satisfaction, Soulé went far beyond his instructions, and delivered what amounted to an ultimatum. Spain ignored the peppery minister, and dealt directly with Washington and the ship's owners, eventually arriving at a satisfactory settlement with both.

Although the *Black Warrior* incident showed that the Pierce administration was not prepared to go to war for Cuba, the President and his advisers were determined to secure the island, if they could, by other means. In 1854 Marcy instructed Soulé to offer Spain up to $130 million for Cuba. If Spain refused to sell, Soulé was to try to "detach" Cuba from Spanish rule; by detach, Marcy meant to start a movement for Cuban independence. After independence, it was hoped, the island would join the United States. Before Soulé could act, Marcy sent additional instructions. Soulé was to meet with James Buchanan, minister to England, and John Y. Mason, minister to France, and determine ways and means of acquiring Cuba. The three men conferred at Ostend, Belgium, and later at a German town. They embodied their recommendations in a diplomatic dispatch to Marcy which shortly found its way into the newspapers and which has become known in history as the Ostend Manifesto. This remarkable document stated that the United States should endeavor to purchase Cuba for a reasonable

price. If Spain should reject an offer, the United States would have to consider if possession of Cuba was essential to national security; if the answer was yes, the United States would be justified in "wresting" the island from Spain. Publication of the essence of the dispatch in the American press caused a terrific uproar. In the North it was charged that the administration, acting as the tool of the South, was endeavoring to add a new slave state to the Union even at the risk of war. Marcy hastily disavowed any such purpose and any responsibility for the actions of his ministers. Nevertheless, it would seem that Soulé and his colleagues had proceeded in broad conformity with the spirit of Marcy's instructions. The administration had used them to test public opinion, but finding the issue too hot had to drop it.

The Kansas-Nebraska Act

By the 1850's the line of frontier settlement had reached the great bend of the Missouri. Beyond the western boundaries of Minnesota, Iowa, and Missouri stretched the vast expanse of prairie land earlier called the Great American Desert and designated as an Indian reserve. Now it was known that large sections of this region were suited to farming, and in the Northwest people were saying that the national government should open the area to settlement, provide it with territorial government, and remove the Indians. Already, settlers were beginning to trickle in, the obvious heralds of another mass migration. With the frontier line about to move farther west, the problem of communication between the older states and the trans-Mississippi West became more urgent. It was evident that the day was not far distant when a continuous string of settled areas would stretch from the Mississippi Valley to California. The new West that was in the making and the Pacific coast would have to be linked with the rest of the country by rapid transportation. When people thought of transportation in the fifties, they first thought of railroads. The magic iron rails would bind the sprawling nation together; they would also speed the settlement of the prairie region and give it economic stability.

The idea of a transcontinental railroad was not new. Such a project had been discussed in Congress and out for years, first as a means of aiding American commerce with the Orient and later, after the United States acquired a Pacific frontage, as a necessary linkage with California. On the general features of the road, there was considerable agreement. It should start at some point in the Mississippi Valley that had good connections with the East; it should follow the most practicable route to the coast; and it should be built by private interests with the aid of financial assistance from the federal government, probably in the form of land grants. Disagreement entered the picture—and disagreement of an ominous character—when people talked about the eastern terminus of the road and its specific route. Several cities pressed their claims, but the leading contenders were Chicago, St. Louis, Memphis, and New Orleans. In part this competition represented the natural and normal ambitions of these cities, and the areas of which they were the metropolises, to control the trade of the West. But it soon became something entirely different. The transcontinental railroad, like nearly everything else in the fifties, became entangled in sectionalism. It became a prize that the North and South would struggle to secure and try to deny to each other. When people talked about a road beginning at New Orleans, they referred to it as the southern route. When they discussed one starting at Chicago, they called it the northern route.

In 1853, at the request of Congress, the War Department undertook a survey of the various routes under consideration. They were four in number: (1) the northern, proceeding from Chicago; (2) the central, from St. Louis; (3) the southern, from New Orleans; and (4) a second southern route, from Memphis. The surveyors reported that from an engineering viewpoint all four routes were equally feasible. Nevertheless, they seemed to give an edge to one of the southern routes, either of which offered some undeniable advantages. Both presented few engineering problems; they led to the Pacific coast by a short route, and, as a very important consideration, they would run through areas already settled, Texas and New Mexico. The most serious objection to a southern route was that it would not follow the natural and accustomed path of emigration to the West. A northern or central road would follow this path, but would lead through unsettled, unorganized Indian country.

One argument against a southern route had been removed through the foresight of Secretary of War Davis, one of the leading promoters of a southern railroad. Surveys had indicated that a road from a southern terminus would probably have to pass through an area south of the Gila River, in Mexican territory. At Davis's suggestion, Pierce appointed James Gadsden, a Southern railroad builder, to negotiate with Mexico for the sale of this region. Gadsden persuaded the Mexican government to dispose of a strip of land that today comprises the southern portion of Arizona and part of southern New Mexico, the so-called Gadsden Purchase, which cost the United States $10 million.

One man who was interested in a transcontinental railroad was Senator Stephen A. Douglas, and his interest influenced him to introduce in Congress a fateful legislative act, one that accomplished the final destruction of the truce of 1850. As a Senator from Illinois and a resident of Chicago and, above all, as the acknowledged leader of the Northwestern Democrats, Douglas naturally wanted the transcontinental railroad for his own city and section. He realized too the potency of the principal argument urged against the northern route: that west of the Mississippi it would run largely through unsettled Indian country. In January, 1854, as chairman of the Committee on Territories, he acted to nullify this argument. He introduced a bill to organize a huge new territory, to be known as Nebraska, west of Iowa and Missouri. His railroad ambitions may not have been the only motive animating Douglas. He may have been partly moved by the expressed desires of his followers in the Northwest to get the territory organized—to provide it with government—as a means of speeding settlement.

Whatever his reasons, Douglas seemed to realize that his bill would encounter the opposition of the South, partly because of its railroad implications and partly because it would prepare the way for a new free state, the proposed territory being in the Louisiana Purchase area north of the 36° 30' line of the Missouri Compromise and hence closed to slavery. In an effort to make the measure acceptable to Southerners, Douglas inserted a provision stating that the status of slavery in the territory would be determined by the territorial legislature, that is, according to the doctrines of popular sovereignty. Theoretically at least, this would open the region to slavery; Douglas justified his position by saying that the parts of the Compromise of 1850 dealing with slavery in New Mexico and Utah had "superseded" the earlier adjustment. This concession was not enough to satisfy extreme Southern Democrats, particularly those from Missouri who were fearful that their state would be surrounded by free territory. They demanded more, and Douglas, having launched his bill, had to give more to get their support. He agreed to a clause specifi-

cally repealing the territorial section of the Missouri Compromise and to a provision creating two territories, Nebraska and Kansas, instead of one. Presumably the latter, because of its more southern location, would become a slave state. In its final form the measure was known as the Kansas-Nebraska Act.

Douglas's motives in yielding to Southern demands were condemned in 1854 and have been argued about by historians ever since. It has been charged that he was angling for Southern votes for the Democratic presidential nomination and that he hoped to profit personally from speculations in railroad stock and Chicago real estate. While he undoubtedly nourished White House ambitions, there is no evidence that he was moved at this particular time by narrow thoughts of self-advancement. The truth seems to be that he wanted something for his section, and to get it had to concede more than he wished. Of course, in his thinking popular sovereignty conceded nothing to the South. Through its operation the North, with a greater and more mobile population, would win all the territories anyway. Perhaps Douglas foresaw that the issue of slavery in the territories would rise again, and decided that popular sovereignty was the best method of dealing with the problem. He could not understand that other people did not view slavery and popular sovereignty in the same pragmatic light he did. Without a strong moral sense himself, he could not comprehend that others might become excited over a principle, might be intensely angered at what they deemed an aggressive advance by an institution they considered immoral.

If Douglas's course is hard to define, so also are the reasons that prompted Southerners to support the Kansas-Nebraska bill. They must have realized that the South did not possess the manpower resources to win even one of the new territories. Southern leaders apparently thought that migrants from Missouri would be able to secure Kansas for slavery, but in Missouri there were only something over 20,000 slaveholders, too few to provide a surplus for Kansas. It would seem that the South accepted Douglas's bill largely to gain a theoretical victory: for the satisfaction of having Congress declare open to slavery a region from which previously it had been excluded. But this paper triumph of Southern ideals carried with it elements of immediate and practical danger for the section. In the past many Southerners had contended that neither Congress nor a territorial legislature could ban slavery from a territory. Now they were conceding that a territory had the power to exclude it. Of course, many Southerners who voted for the measure did not understand it that way. They took popular sovereignty to mean the same thing as Calhoun's doctrine of noninterference by the federal government. Finally, the South, which had not initiated the bill, had let itself be placed in the position of seeking new territory for slavery expansion, of securing the repeal of an old and revered compromise—in short, of aggressively reopening the sectional controversy.

Douglas induced President Pierce to endorse his bill, and so the Kansas-Nebraska Act became an official Democratic measure. But even with the backing of the administration, it encountered stiff opposition and did not become a law until May, 1854. Nearly all the Southern members of Congress, whether Whigs or Democrats, supported the bill, and nearly all the Northern Whigs opposed it. It was a matter of great moment that the Northern Democrats split, with half of their votes in the House going for the act and half against it. Sectionalism had almost destroyed the Whig party, and now it was beginning to break down the Democrats. It was also eating away at the foundations of the South-West alliance.

Later in the session Southern votes defeated the West's Homestead bill, and Pierce vetoed a Western-sponsored internal-improvements bill. The tariff of 1857, championed by the President and reducing the rates to the lowest level since 1816, strengthened the conviction of many Westerners that the South was running the Democratic party.

Of greater importance than the opposition to the Kansas-Nebraska Act in Congress was the reaction against it in the Northern states. The whole North seemed to blaze with fury at this latest demonstration of the power of the slavocracy, and much of the fury was directed at Douglas, who, to the eyes of many Northerners, had acted as a cat's-paw for the slaveholders. No other piece of legislation in congressional history produced as many immediate, sweeping, and ominous charges as the Kansas-Nebraska Act. It destroyed the Whig party in the South except in the border states. At the same time, as many Southern Whigs became Democrats, it increased Southern influence in the Democratic party. It destroyed the popular basis of Whiggery in the North, with the result that by 1856 the national Whig party had disappeared and a conservative influence in American politics had been removed. It divided the Northern Democrats and drove many of them from the party. Most important of all, it called into being a new party that was frankly sectional in composition and creed.

Men in both the major parties who opposed Douglas's bill took to calling themselves Anti-Nebraska Democrats and Anti-Nebraska Whigs. In their anger at the South, in their fear that the slavocracy meant to push its institution into the Western territories, they were in a mood to defend their opinions by forming a new party. And in 1854 their party took shape, and it took a name—the Republican party. Exactly when and where it came into being is impossible to say. Originating in a series of spontaneous popular meetings throughout the Northwest, the Republican movement soon spread to the East. The new party showed an immediate strength that was sensational. In the elections of 1854, the Republicans, often acting in concert with the Know-Nothings, elected a majority to the House and won control of a number of Northern state governments. For the moment the Republican party was a one-idea organization: its only platform was opposition to the expansion of slavery into the territories. Composed mainly of former Whigs and Free-Soilers but including also a substantial segment of former Democrats, it represented in large part the democratic idealism of the North. But it contained, in addition, Northern power groups who felt that the South —the champion of a low tariff, the enemy of homesteads and internal improvements— was blocking their legitimate economic aspirations.

Bleeding Kansas

The pulsing popular excitement aroused in the North by the Kansas-Nebraska Act was sustained by events occurring during the next two years in Kansas. Both Nebraska and Kansas were declared open for settlement in 1854. Only a few settlers entered Nebraska, which for years remained primarily a jumping-off place for people going to the Far West. But an entirely different situation developed in Kansas. Almost immediately immigrants in substantial numbers moved into this territory. They came partly because the agricultural possibilities of Kansas had been better advertised than those of her northern neighbor. That is, and the fact needs to be emphasized, the migration to Kansas was in part a normal expansion of the farming frontier. But it was also something else. It was a contest between North and South to determine who could put the most settlers into Kansas and control the territory. The struggle for Kansas seemed to dramatize for the entire nation the struggle between freedom and slavery.

It was not, of course, quite as simple as that. Many people who came to Kansas had come to make homes and not to be contenders in an ideological contest. Many had come to enrich themselves in land speculation, and in order to further their purposes they were perfectly willing to pose as champions of lofty principles—of the Northern or Southern variety. And some had come, as their like came to every frontier, to practice the work of the lawless and the violent in a new and fluid society; they too were willing, if it served their ends, to appear as advocates of fine ideals. But there were some who came for the specific purpose of engaging in a struggle of ideologies. They were dedicated men who were determined to make Kansas free—or slave. Those who came from the North were encouraged to go by press and pulpit and the powerful organs of abolitionist propaganda; often they received financial help from organizations like the New England Emigrant Aid Company, which had been created to render such assistance. Those who came from the South were stimulated by similar influences of a Southern nature; often they received financial contributions from the communities they had left.

In any territorial contest to be decided by numbers, all the advantages were on the side of the North with its larger and more mobile population. From the beginning, by far the greater number of actual settlers in Kansas were from the free states. Most of them were farmers, and they settled in the fertile eastern section of the territory; their chief towns were Lawrence and Topeka. The migrants from the slave states, most of them from Missouri, stayed close to the Missouri River; their towns were Atchison and Leavenworth. Leaders of the Democratic party in Missouri, notably Senator David R. Atchison, openly exhorted their followers to answer the emigrant aid societies by being prepared to cross into Kansas when elections were held and vote the territory for slavery. To represent the national authority in this potentially explosive situation, President Pierce appointed three successive governors: Andrew H. Reeder, Wilson Shannon, and John W. Geary. Although all were Democrats, Reeder and Geary, after arriving in Kansas, had to concede that in an honest count the antislavery settlers would outnumber their opponents.

An honest count in Kansas seemed impossible. In the spring of 1855 elections were held for a territorial legislature. Thousands of Missourians, some traveling in armed bands, moved into Kansas and voted. Although there were probably only some 1,500 legal votes in the territory, over 6,000 votes were counted. With such conditions prevailing, the proslavery forces elected a majority to the legislature, which proceeded immediately to enact a series of laws legalizing slavery. The outraged free-staters, convinced that they could not get a fair deal from the Pierce administration, resolved on extralegal action. Without asking permission from Congress or the territorial governor, they elected delegates to a constitutional convention which met at Topeka and adopted a constitution excluding slavery. They then chose a governor and legislature, and petitioned Congress for statehood. Pierce stigmatized their movement as unlawful and akin to treason. The full weight of the government, he announced, would be thrown behind the proslavery territorial legislature.

Up to this point violence, although often threatened, had not actually appeared. Now it came with dramatic and grim suddenness. An armed force of proslavery adherents marched on Lawrence, where armed free-staters waited to meet them (the "Wakarusa War"). A clash was averted only through the personal intervention of Governor Shannon, who persuaded the Southerners to withdraw. But a few months later a proslavery federal marshal assembled a huge posse, consisting mostly of Missourians, to arrest the free-state leaders in Lawrence. The posse not only made the arrests but sacked the town. Retribution came immediately. Among the more extreme antislavery men was a fierce, fanatical old man named John Brown who considered himself as an instrument of God's will to destroy slavery. Estimating that five antislavery men had been murdered, he decided that it was his sacred duty to exact vengeance—a life for a life. He gathered six followers, and in one bloody night murdered five proslavery settlers (the "Pottawatomie massacre"). The result was to touch off civil war in Kansas—irregular, guerrilla war conducted by armed bands, some of them more interested in land claims or loot than in ideologies. Governor Geary had to employ federal troops to restore even a semblance of order.

In all, about 200 lives were lost. This figure was not excessive for a frontier area. Nevertheless, there was a difference between the violence in Kansas and that in other newly opened regions. Here men had died, or were supposed to have died, for a high moral issue. Actually, some had gone to their deaths for reasons much less noble. Nor were the issues quite as clear as sometimes presented in the Northern press, particularly by the New York papers that had correspondents on the spot to cover every outrage. The great majority of the free-state settlers were antislavery but not pro-Negro. They did not want to face the competition of slave labor or of any kind of Negro labor. When Kansas finally became a state in 1861, her constitution excluded slavery—and free Negroes. Nevertheless, in 1856 the issues in Kansas seemed clear enough to people in the North and the South. They believed (and whether or not their beliefs were completely correct is historically unimportant) that the aggressive designs of the other section were epitomized by what was happening in Kansas.

Thus "Bleeding Kansas" became a symbol of the sectional controversy.

-»»-»»-»»-»»«-«-«-«-«

BIBLIOGRAPHY

FOR THIS CHAPTER works of continuing usefulness are the histories of economic development and immigration listed in Chapter 23 and the previously cited political studies of Carpenter, Craven, Milton, and Nevins. A handy survey of the fifties is H. H. Simms, *A Decade of Sectional Controversy* (1942). An older work still worth attention is Theodore C. Smith, *Parties and Slavery* (1906). Two books by R. F. Nichols are basic for this period: *Franklin Pierce* (1931), and *The Disruption of American Democracy* (1948), a study of the Democratic party. The complex motives behind the passage of the Kansas-Nebraska Act are treated in P. O. Ray, *Repeal of the Missouri Compromise* (1909). Ray's opinions are not accepted by all historians, and the student who wishes to explore the question more thoroughly is referred to an article by R. F. Nichols in the *Mississippi Valley Historical Review*, XLIII (1956).

Books on the settlement of Kansas are numerous and sometimes controversial. G. R. Gaedert, *The Birth of Kansas* (1940), is a convenient introduction. A colorful account that carries the story through the Civil War is Jay Monaghan, *Civil War on the Western Border* (1955). A good biography is O. G. Villard, *John Brown* (1910; new edition, 1942). But all studies of the Kansas question should be checked against two monographs by J. C. Malin, *John Brown and the Legend of Fifty-Six* (1942), and *The Nebraska Question* (1953).

Several special studies relate politics to the social and economic background. Excellent on the Know-Nothings are R. A. Billington, *The Protestant Crusade, 1800–1860* (1938), and W. D. Overdyke, *The Know-*

Nothing Party in the South (1950). For the reactions of Northern merchants to the slavery controversy, see P. S. Foner, *Business and Slavery* (1941). The abolitionist psychology is explored in R. F. Wilson, *Crusader in Crinoline* (1941), a biography of Mrs. H. B. Stowe.

The political history of the 1850's can be followed in biographies of its leading figures. The best work on Douglas is Milton's previously mentioned book, but Allen Johnson, *Stephen A. Douglas* (1908), is useful. A revealing study of a Southern propagandist is Wish, *George Fitzhugh*. There is as yet no good one-volume life of Jefferson Davis, but useable are W. E. Dodd, *Jefferson Davis* (1907), and Allen Tate, *Jefferson Davis* (1929). A colorful account of Davis up to 1860 that is somewhat too laudatory is Hudson Strode, *Jefferson Davis, American Patriot* (1955).

Good for the social and economic backdrop is Cole's *Irrepressible Conflict*. Newspaper developments are treated in two texts: A. M. Lee, *The Daily Newspaper in America* (1937), and F. L. Mott, *American Journalism* (1950). A basic item for social history is Mott's multi-volume *A History of American Magazines;* for this period see vol. 1, *1741–1850* (1930) and vol. 2, *1850–1865* (1938). There are several excellent biographies of leading journalists: E. F. Brown, *Raymond of the Times* (1951); D. C. Seitz, *The James Gordon Bennetts* (1928); W. H. Hale, *Horace Greeley* (1950); and G. G. Van Deusen, *Horace Greeley* (1953). These biographies also illuminate the political history of the day.

On foreign policy, see the works previously cited of Rauch and Williams, and

Bemis, *American Secretaries of State*, vol. 6. Other good accounts whose subjects are indicated by their titles are L. B. Shippee, *Canadian-American Relations, 1849-1874* (1939); P. J. Treat, *The Diplomatic Relations between the United States and Japan, 1853-1895* (1932); Dexter Perkins, *The Monroe Doctrine, 1826-1867* (1933); and A. A. Ettinger, *The Mission to Spain of Pierre Soulé* (1932). The filibusters are treated in W. O. Scroggs, *Filibusters and Financiers* (1916), but a later study is E. S. Wallace, *Destiny and Glory* (1957).

CHAPTER 27

The Rush Toward Disunion

D URING THE PIERCE ADMINISTRATION the nation had seemed to move toward disunion in a kind of halting drift. But after the election of 1856 it would seem to rush toward the fateful goal. A series of rapidly unfolding events pushed the sections along a road that led always closer to civil war. Bitterness and hatred mounted with each incident, and men hardened their minds by the hour against compromise.

On the plains of Kansas the minions of slavery and antislavery continued to debate popular sovereignty with rifles. Their deeds were debated throughout the country and in Congress. In May, 1856, Charles Sumner of Massachusetts arose in the Senate to discuss affairs in the strife-torn territory. He entitled his speech "The Crime against Kansas." Handsome, humorless, sincere, doctrinaire, Sumner embodied the extreme element of the political antislavery movement. Elected to the Senate in 1850 by a coalition

of Free-Soilers and Democrats, he was the kind of idealist who would demand justice even though the heavens crumbled down. Or, in the more practical language of politics, he was the kind of man who could not rise above principle. Wrapped in a sense of personal righteousness, he was not easily hurt by words, and he did not realize that others might be hurt by words of his. In his address he fiercely denounced the Pierce administration, the South, and slavery; and he singled out for particular attention as a champion of slavery Senator Andrew P. Butler of South Carolina. It was an age when orators were wont to indulge freely in personal invective, but in his allusions to Butler and others, Sumner went farther than most.

Particularly enraged by the attack was Butler's nephew, Preston Brooks, a member of the House from South Carolina. He resolved to punish Sumner by a method approved by the Southern code—by publicly and physically chastizing the Senator. Approaching Sumner at his desk when the Senate was not in session, he proceeded to beat his kinsman's traducer with a cane until Sumner fell to the floor in bloody unconsciousness. The injured Senator stayed out of the Senate four years, and during his absence his state refused to elect a successor. Brooks, censured by the House, resigned and stood for re-election. He was returned by an almost unanimous vote.

Never in our history has there been as much violence, or danger of violence, as in the decade of the fifties. The Brooks-Sumner episode was but one of many. Members of Congress came to the sessions armed, pistols were sometimes pulled in the heat of argument, several fist-swinging brawls occurred between individual Northerners and Southerners and between groups from both sections, and challenges to duels were freely passed. The violence in Congress, like that in Kansas, was a symbol. It showed that Americans were becoming so agitated by their differences that they could not settle them by the normal political processes: debate and the ballot.

Election of 1856

The presidential campaign of 1856 got under way with the country convulsed by the Brooks assault and the continuing violence in Kansas. The Democrats adopted a platform that endorsed the Kansas-Nebraska Act and defended popular sovereignty as the safest solution of the slavery issue. Logically the party should have nominated one of the outstanding advocates of popular sovereignty, Pierce or perhaps Douglas. But political parties cannot always be logical in elections. The leaders wanted a man who had not made many enemies and who was not closely associated with the explosive question of "Bleeding Kansas." As a result, the nomination went to James Buchanan of Pennsylvania, a reliable party

stalwart who had been minister to England and hence had been safely out of the country during the recent troubles.

The Republicans, engaging in their first

John C. Frémont. *John C. Frémont was the Republican party's first presidential candidate. As an officer in the topographical engineering service of the army, he explored the Far West and served in the Mexican War. Because of his explorations, he was known as the "Pathfinder." He was handsome, romantic, sincere, and often unstable and hard to get along with. He represented dramatically the early idealism of the Republicans.* (PHOTO BY U.S. ARMY SIGNAL CORPS)

presidential contest, faced the campaign with a confidence born of party youth and their spectacular success in the elections of 1854. Still primarily a one-idea party, their platform consisted mainly of denunciations of the Kansas-Nebraska Act and the expansion of slavery into the territories. They did, however, approve a program of internal improvements, an indication that their leaders were beginning to grasp the advantage of combining the idealism of antislavery with the economic aspirations of the North. Just as eager as the Democrats to present a safe candidate, the Republicans nominated John C. Frémont, who, working first for the United States army and later for private interests, had made a national reputation as an explorer of the Far West. Although he was a sincere Republican, the glamorous "Pathfinder" was selected because he was a famous figure who had no political record and hence was highly available.

The American or Know-Nothing party entered the campaign with its strength seriously sapped. It was beginning to break apart on the inevitable rock of sectionalism. At its convention, many Northern delegates had withdrawn because the platform was not sufficiently firm in opposing the expansion of slavery. The remnant that was left nominated Millard Fillmore. The candidacy of the former President was endorsed by the sad remnant of another party, the few remaining Whigs who could not bring themselves to support either Buchanan or Frémont.

The campaign was the most exciting one since the contest of 1840. Its frenzied enthusiasm was due largely to the Republicans. Fully expecting to win, they conducted a campaign that featured huge mass meetings, lavish circulation of political literature, and wholesale employment of party symbols and slogans. They shouted for "Free Soil, Free Speech, and Frémont," depicted "Bleeding Kansas" as a sacrifice to the evil ambitions of the slavocracy, and charged that the South, using Northern dupes like Buchanan as its tools, was plotting to extend slavery into every part of the country. Their techniques stirred a wide response in the North, but they also caused a conservative reaction against the Republicans. Many Northern moderates, disturbed by the sectional nature of the new party and its frank sectional appeal to Northern

sentiment, decided to vote for Buchanan. They feared that the Republicans, if victorious, would indulge in rash acts that might precipitate disunion; they reasoned that the Democrats, being a conservative and a national party, were better qualified to preserve tranquility and the Union.

The results of the election seemed to indicate that the prevailing mood of the country was conservative. Buchanan, the winning candidate, polled 174 electoral votes, Frémont 114, and Fillmore 8. The Democrats also secured majorities in both houses of Congress. Buchanan carried all the slave states except Maryland (whose eight votes went to Fillmore) and five Northern states (Illinois, Indiana, New Jersey, Pennsylvania, and California). Frémont won the other eleven Northern states, and he received a large minority vote in the five states carried by Buchanan. The popular vote was 1,838,000 for Buchanan, 1,341,000 for Frémont, and 874,000 for Fillmore. In the South, including the border states, the Republicans polled practically no popular votes. The Democrats, with strength in both sections, could rightly say that they were a national party and their rivals a sectional party. But the Democrats, without their almost solid block of Southern states, would have been defeated. In a real sense, the Democratic organization had become a captive of the South. Furthermore, the Democratic victory had been uncomfortably close. A slight shift of popular votes in Pennsylvania and Illinois would have thrown those states into the Republican column and elected Frémont. The sectional Republican party, controlling most of the state governments in the larger section, could well face the future with confidence.

James Buchanan had been in politics and in public office almost continuously since he was twenty-three years old. Born into a moderately wealthy Pennsylvania family and educated in the law, he deliberately chose to become a professional politician. He had served in the Pennsylvania legislature, in the House of Representatives (for ten years), and in the Senate (for twenty years). He had been minister to Russia and England under Jackson and Pierce and Secretary of State under Polk. Always he had worked diligently for the success of the Democratic party and his own political advance. At the time of his inauguration he was nearly sixty-six, the oldest President, with the exception of Harrison, that the country has had. Undoubtedly his age and general physical infirmity had something to do with the indecision he often displayed. He also has the distinction of being the only President who never married.

With his distinguished and varied background of political experience, it would seem that he should have been an outstanding executive. Instead, he proved to be perhaps the least successful President in the nation's history. One critic called him "the most perfect imbecile that ever held office." This is a too-harsh judgment. He was a well-meaning and public-spirited man, but he lacked breadth of vision and sturdiness of character. Cast into the Presidency during one of the most critical periods in the nation's life, he seemed to be obsessed by one idea—to meet every crisis by giving the South what it wanted. In message after message he advocated the purchase of Cuba, the extension of American hegemony over Central America, and the establishment of a protectorate over northern Mexico. When Western Democrats introduced a Homestead bill, Southern votes blocked its passage. Later the Southerners, in the interests of party harmony, relented and let the bill through. Buchanan calmly and inanely vetoed the measure.

The Panic of 1857

In the year in which Buchanan took office, a financial panic struck the country, to be fol-

lowed by several years of stringent depression. The economic dislocation was in origin partly American and partly European. During the fifties the United States passed

James Buchanan. *Buchanan came to the presidency with a rich background of education and political experience. But he proved to be a weak President, largely because, like his predecessor Pierce, he had an indecisive character. In his youth Buchanan was engaged to a lady, but the engagement was broken by a quarrel. Soon after the girl died. Buchanan never married and became the only bachelor President.* (LIBRARY OF CONGRESS)

through a period of tremendous economic expansion. The productive capacities of the nation's economic plant had been increased in all fields—in industry, in transportation, and in agriculture. To a considerable degree, these capacities had been overexpanded. That is, the economy could now produce a great deal more of everything than the country could use; the business, or the demand, to sustain the enlarged facilities simply did not exist. Many of the new enterprises had been financed on credit, some of it extended by European investors; the resulting burden of indebtedness was, in many cases, too heavy to be repaid out of current revenues. Furthermore, the produc-

usual demand for American food, particularly during the Crimean War (1854–1856). When that conflict ceased, the demand fell off, with the result that agricultural prices were seriously depressed.

The Panic of 1857. *An artist for one of the illustrated weeklies sketched the reactions of businessmen on Wall Street to the Panic of 1857. Every figure but one seems to be facing ruin; the snug-looking gentleman in the front center probably had sold out just before the crash. In the background frantic citizens are beating at the doors of a closed bank.* (FROM *Harper's Weekly*, 1857)

tion boom had brought with it an orgy of speculation, principally in land. Contributing to the speculative frenzy was the inflated condition of the currency. With no central agency like the old Bank of the United States to check the issues of local banks and with no regulation of banking practices except that provided by some states, state-chartered banks were often free to overexpand their issue of bank notes; and many of them took full advantage of their opportunities. Europe had contributed to the causes of the depression by its un-

The depression affected all classes and sections. But instead of drawing the nation closer together in a sense of common misfortune, the depression sharpened sectional differences and strengthened the forces of disunion. The South, although naturally affected by the depression, was not hit as hard as the North. In this agricultural area there had been relatively little expansion of industrial facilities and less speculation than in Northern states. Moreover, the continuing world demand for cotton, accompanied by high prices, enabled the South to recoup its losses quickly and to emerge from the depression sooner than the North. The result was to confirm the opinion of Southern leaders that their economic system was superior to that of the free states; and, smarting under previous Northern criticisms of Southern society, they loudly boasted to the North of their superiority. Those Southerners who favored disunion seized the occasion to urge that the South would be better off out of a Union subject to such economic dislocations.

In the North the impact of the depression had the effect of strengthening the sectional Republican party and weakening the Democrats. Distressed economic groups—manufacturers and farmers—came to believe that the depression had been caused by unsound policies forced upon the government by Southern-controlled Democratic administrations. They thought that prosperity could be restored by a program embracing such items as a high tariff, a homestead act, and internal improvements—all measures to which the South was opposed. In short, the frustrated economic interests of the North were, by the force of circumstances, being pushed into an alliance with the antislavery impulse as represented by the Republican party. Northern resentment at what seemed to be Southern restraint of the nation's economic future was one important reason why the Democrats lost their majority in the House in the elections of 1858.

The Supreme Court and Slavery

Since the beginning of the controversy over slavery in the territories, almost every agency of government—Congress, Presidents, state legislatures—had expressed an opinion on the issue. The lone important exception was the Supreme Court of the United States. That august body now projected itself into the situation with its decision in the case of *Dred Scott v. Sanford*, handed down two days after Buchanan was

inaugurated. The highest court in the land spoke, but its voice did not calm the angry differences between North and South. Instead, the effect of the decision was to intensify the sectional quarrel.

Dred Scott was a Missouri slave, the property of an army surgeon, who on his military pilgrimages had carried Scott with him to Illinois, a free state, and to Minnesota Territory, where slavery was forbidden by the Missouri Compromise. Eventually both the owner and the slave returned to Missouri, where the surgeon died. The legal maneuvering that then ensued is extremely complicated, but the facts may be briefly summarized. Scott was persuaded by some abolitionists to bring suit in the Missouri courts for his freedom on the ground that residence in a free territory made him a free man. The state supreme court decided against him, but in the meantime the officer's widow had married an abolitionist. Ownership of Scott was now technically transferred to a New Yorker, J. F. A. Sanford. The purpose of this arrangement was to enable Scott to get his case into the federal courts with the claim that the suit lay between citizens of different states.

Scott's suit was appealed to a federal court and eventually found its way to the Supreme Court, where it was twice elaborately argued in 1856. Throughout the long period of litigation, it was evident that both parties to the dispute, which enlisted some of the most prominent political lawyers in the country, were eager to get a test case before the highest court. Regardless of the decision, Scott would be freed, as his abolitionist owners would not keep him a slave. But the case had become bigger than Scott. What both sides wanted was to secure a federal decision on the status of slavery in the territories. In a sense, the suit had become one involving the views of extreme Northerners and extreme Southerners, and both apparently felt that they would gain something from a pronouncement by the Court.

Of the nine justices, seven were Democrats (five of them being from the South), one was a Whig, and one was a Republican. At first, Chief Justice Taney and his fellow Democrats intended to decide the case against Scott on the ground that, as the supreme court of Missouri had decided, he was a slave and not a citizen. That is, the majority hoped to avoid the question of whether Scott could bring a suit and the general issue of the constitutionality of the Missouri Compromise. It became known, however, that the two non-Democratic members, John McLean and Benjamin R. Curtis, were preparing dissenting opinions supporting the power of Congress to prohibit slavery in the territories. The Democrats then determined to consider the case in its broadest aspects, and Taney was selected to deliver the majority opinion. Thus the Court was forced by its minority members to deal with what might be termed the political phase of the suit, but the zeal with which Taney and his colleagues addressed themselves to the task suggests that they were not averse to the alteration of their plans.

Each of the nine justices presented a separate opinion. The arguments of five of the Democratic members, while differing in detail, agreed on essentials, and Taney's opinion is regarded as the official decision of the Court. The Taney or majority opinion announced two important principles. First, the Chief Justice declared that Scott was not a citizen of Missouri and hence could not bring a suit in the federal courts. He was not a citizen because a Negro who was a descendant of slaves could never become a citizen of the national community. Such a person might be a citizen of a particular state, but the state could not introduce him into any national status. The framers of the Constitution, Taney asserted, had intended their document to apply only to white men; as historical proof he cited that no state had had Negro citizens at the time the Constitution was adopted. Taney was, therefore, denying federal citizenship to Negroes whose ancestors had been slaves and, at least by inference, to all Negroes. He was saying that the Constitution had created a white man's government and that, so far as the Constitution was concerned, Negroes had no rights that white men were bound to respect.

The second principle in Taney's argument was concerned with the question of whether Scott's residence in territory north of the Missouri Compromise line had made him free. Here he was dealing with the political or collateral phase of the case, and hence this section of his decision is referred to, in legal language, as an *obiter dictum*. Taney met the issue squarely: Scott's sojourn in Minnesota had not affected his status as a slave. Slaves were property, said Taney, and the Fifth Amendment prohibited Congress from taking property without "due process of law." Consequently, Congress possessed no authority to pass a law depriving persons of their slave property in the territories. The only power that Congress could exercise in regard to slavery in the territories was the obligation to protect owners in their rights. The Missouri Compromise, therefore, had always been null and void. Taney's contentions were challenged in the dissenting opinions of Curtis and McLean, who claimed that Negroes had been citizens in some states when the Constitution was adopted and who asserted that Congress possessed ample power to exclude slavery from national territories.

Few judicial opinions have stirred as much popular excitement as the decision involving this obscure Missouri Negro. The South, naturally, was elated: the highest tribunal in the land had invested with legal sanction the extreme Southern argument.

Slavery, said jubilant Southerners, could now enter any territory; moreover, Congress was obligated to protect it wherever it went. And the whole Republican plat- tion of Congress, perform the same act? The decision seemed to threaten not only the basic principle of the Republicans, but popular sovereignty as well.

Republican Denunciation of the Supreme Court

Republican anger at the Dred Scott decision was intense. Party leaders denounced the Court's reasoning and proclaimed that when the party came to power it would take action to have the decision reversed. Presumably they meant to "pack" the Court and bring a new case. A typical Republican reaction came from the Chicago *Tribune:* "That bench full of Southern lawyers which gentlemen of a political temperament call 'august tribunal' is that last entrenchment behind which despotism is sheltered; and until a national convention amends the Constitution so as to defend it against the usurpations of that body, or until the Court itself is reconstructed by the dropping off of a few of its members and the appointment of better men in their places, we have little to hope for by congressional action in the way of restricting slavery."

---

form was illegal, for surely the Republicans would respect the opinion of the Supreme Court. This was exactly what the Republicans did not intend to do. In Republican circles the decision was denounced in terms of extreme violence. The decision had been conceived in a partisan spirit by a partisan body, cried the Republicans, and deserved as much consideration as any pronouncement by a group of political hacks. As for settling the status of slavery in the territories, that section of the opinion was an *obiter dictum* and had no legal justification. Boldly the Republicans announced that when they secured control of the national government they would reverse the decision—by altering the personnel of the Court; that is, by "packing" it with new members. Northern Democrats, although they did not join in the attack on the Court, were alarmed by the decision. For if Congress could not ban slavery from a territory, how could a territorial legislature, a crea-

Bleeding Kansas Again

President Buchanan, who had known in advance the nature of the Dred Scott decision (having been tipped off by two of the Justices), had said in his inaugural address that he hoped the forthcoming opinion would end the agitation over slavery in the territories. With equal blindness, he decided that the best solution for the Kansas troubles was to force the admission of that territory as a slave state. He named as territorial governor Robert J. Walker, an able man who in the course of his career had held several important offices, including the Treasury post in Polk's cabinet. Walker was instructed to encourage a statehood movement in Kansas, and he understood that the President would support him in whatever he did.

The events that ensued after Walker's arrival in the territory followed the usual confused and complex pattern of Kansas territorial politics. The existing proslavery legislature had called an election for delegates to a constitutional convention. The governor, who intended to maintain a fair balance between both sides, urged the free-state people to vote, but they, unable to believe that a Buchanan appointee could be honest, refused to participate. As a result, the proslavery forces won control of the convention, which met in 1857 at Lecompton and framed a constitution establishing slavery. Instead of submitting the document for popular ratification or rejection, the convention decided to permit the voters to choose only between the "constitution with slavery" or the "constitution without slavery." If the latter provision carried, slavery would still exist by force of other clauses in the constitution. A negative vote would presumably prohibit the further introduction of slaves, but the constitution would be adopted and Kansas would become a slave state. As the disgusted free-staters refused to vote on such a choice, the "constitution with slavery" was approved by a vote of over 6,000. By this time, however, the antislavery groups had acquired confidence in Walker, and when an election for a new territorial legislature was called, they turned out to vote. They won a majority, partly due to the help of the governor, who threw out a number of fraudulent votes. Promptly the legislature moved to submit the entire Lecompton constitution to the voters. This time the proslavery people refused to participate, and the document was rejected by more than 10,000 votes.

Although both sides had resorted to fraud and although both still on occasion indulged in violence, the picture in Kansas was clear enough. The majority of the people did not want to see slavery established. Unfortunately Buchanan could not see, or did not want to see, the true picture. Enraged at Walker's support of the free-staters, whom he denounced as rebels, the President forced the governor to resign. He then urged Con-

gress to admit Kansas under the Lecompton constitution, and threw the full weight of the administration into a move to force the party to back his proposal. But Douglas and other Western Democrats refused to accept this perversion of popular sovereignty. Openly breaking with the administration and angering Southern Democrats, Douglas denounced the Lecompton proposition. And although Buchanan's plan passed the Senate, Western Democrats helped to block it in the House. Partly to avert further division in the party, a compromise measure, the English bill, was now offered (1858) and passed. It provided that the Lecompton constitution should be submitted to the people of Kansas for the third time. If the document was approved, Kansas was to be admitted and given a federal land grant; if it was disapproved, statehood would be postponed until the population reached 93,600, the legal ratio for a representative in Congress. Again, and for the last time, the Kansas voters decisively rejected the Lecompton constitution. Not until the closing months of Buchanan's administration, in 1861, when a number of Southern states had withdrawn from the Union, would Kansas enter the Union—as a free state. (Although Buchanan undoubtedly maneuvered to make Kansas a slave state, it should be noted that the proposed land grant, which looked like a bribe, was probably not intended as such; similar grants were offered to other territories.)

Elections of 1858 and Their Aftermath

The autumnal congressional elections of 1858 were of greater interest and importance than is usually true of such mid-term contests. Not only did they have an immediate and powerful influence on the course of the sectional controversy, but they projected into the national spotlight the man who would be the dominating figure in the tragic years just ahead when sectional strife would deepen into civil war, the man who by giving up his life in that conflict would become the great folk hero of the American democratic tradition.

For various reasons, the contest that ex-

Lincoln had been the leading Whig in Illinois. After the passage of the Kansas-Nebraska Act he had, after some hesitation, joined the new party, and he was now the

Lincoln and Douglas in Debate. *This is a depiction by a later artist, R. M. Root, of the debate between Lincoln and Douglas at Charleston. Lincoln, who was beardless until 1861, is speaking, and Douglas sits at his right. Various dignitaries of both parties are on the platform. The man behind Lincoln and to the left taking notes is probably a reporter. In the 1850's speeches were frequently recorded by men known as "stenographic reporters." They used a system of shorthand devised by Isaac Pitman and described by him in a book published in 1837,* Stenographic Sound Hand. (ILLINOIS STATE HISTORICAL LIBRARY)

cited the widest public attention was the senatorial election in Illinois. There Stephen A. Douglas, the most prominent Northern Democrat, was a candidate for re-election, and he was fighting for his political life. Since Douglas, or his successor, would be chosen by a legislature which was yet to be elected, the control of that body became a matter of paramount importance. To complicate the situation, the Buchanan administration, in order to punish Douglas for his opposition to the Lecompton constitution, entered opposition Democratic candidates against him in many legislative districts. But Douglas's greatest worry was that in the Republican candidate, Abraham Lincoln, he faced the ablest campaigner in the opposition party.

leading Republican. Although he was a distinguished personage in Illinois and was well known throughout the adjoining Western states, he was hardly a national figure, and his reputation could not compare with that of the famous Douglas. Nevertheless, he was a redoubtable opponent, and Douglas feared him. Lincoln was an extremely adroit stump speaker and the shrewdest principled politician in our history. Partly to gain prestige and partly to place Douglas on the defensive, Lincoln challenged the Senator to a series of seven joint debates. Douglas accepted, and the two candidates argued their cases before huge crowds in every congressional district in the state. The Lincoln-Douglas debates, as the oratorical jousts came to be known, were widely reported by the nation's press, and before their termination the Republican who had dared to challenge the "Little Giant" of the Democracy was a man of national prominence.

As political argumentation, as rough-and-tumble stump repartee, the debates were of a high order. They were not, and were not intended to be, objective, scholarly discussions of the issues involved. Each candidate was out to discredit the other's case and to present his own in as favorable a light as possible. And yet from out of the slashing sallies, the loaded questions, and the broad banter, there emerged a clear exposition of vital issues and some serious truths that many Americans would ponder over. Douglas devoted his principal efforts to defending popular sovereignty and attacking the Republicans. He accused them, and Lincoln, of promoting a war of sections, of wishing to interfere with slavery in the South, and of advocating social equality of the races. Lincoln, denying that these charges were true (and they were not), flung his own accusations. He accused the Democrats, and Douglas, of being in a conspiracy to extend slavery into the territories and possibly, by means of another Supreme Court decision, into the free states as well (a charge which was not true either). Lincoln was particularly effective in repeatedly drawing from Douglas the admission that he did not regard slavery as morally wrong. With singular disregard of the moral sense of the North, Douglas said time and again that he did not care whether slavery was "voted down, or voted up." All that mattered to him was that it be voted by a majority.

Lincoln's views on slavery, as expounded in the debates and in other speeches during the fifties, deserve particular attention, not merely because they were his, but because they came to represent the thinking of the conservative central core of the Republican party; they became, in effect, the official views of the party in the election of 1860.

He was opposed to slavery—on moral, political, and economic grounds. He believed that a vigorous and expanding system of slavery gave the lie to the American ideal of democracy. He thought that slavery and the aristocratic philosophy of its advocates threatened to subvert the great principle of American society: equality of opportunity. Most of all, he feared the effects of slavery on white people. Let the idea be established that Negroes were not created with an equal right to earn their bread, he said, and the next step would be to deny the right to certain groups of whites, probably laborers. It was his solicitude for the economic well-being of the white masses that impelled Lincoln to oppose the introduction of slavery into the territories. He maintained that the national lands should be preserved as places for poor white people to go to to better their condition. But these lands would not be a refuge for such people if slavery was planted in them, because free labor could not compete with slave labor.

And yet Lincoln was opposed to the abolitionists and to plans of emancipation aimed at the South. His views were eminently practical and pragmatic. To him it was tremendously important that slavery existed and was believed in by millions of people. The physical fact of slavery must be taken into account by its opponents. "Because we think it wrong, we propose a course of policy that shall deal with it as a wrong," he said. But, he added, "We have a due regard to the actual presence of it amongst us and the difficulties of getting rid of it in any satisfactory way and all the constitutional obligations thrown about it." What course of policy did Lincoln propose for dealing with slavery? He and his party would "arrest the further spread of it," that is, prevent its expansion into the territories, and thus place it in a state of "ultimate extinction." His plan, then, was to pen up slavery in the South, where it would eventually die a natural death; he hoped for a kind of patient emancipation. It was a conservative plan, one that would be years in the fulfilling. But the point should not be missed that, prior to the formation of a state constitution? Or in other words, is popular sovereignty still a legal formula despite the Dred Scott decision? The question was a deadly

---

Lincoln in the Debates with Douglas

In 1858 Carl Schurz, a German-American Republican leader, met Lincoln at Quincy, Illinois. The cultured Schurz was a little shocked at what he saw: "On his head he wore a somewhat battered stovepipe hat. His neck emerged long and sinewy from a white collar turned down over a thin black necktie. His lank, ungainly body was clad in a rusty black dress coat with sleeves that should have been longer; but his arms appeared so long that the sleeves of a 'store' coat could hardly be expected to cover them all the way down to the wrists. His black trousers, too, permitted a very full view of his large feet. On his left arm he carried a gray woolen shawl, which evidently served him for an overcoat in chilly weather. His left hand held a cotton umbrella of the bulging kind, and also a black satchel that bore the marks of long and hard usage. His right he had kept free for handshaking, of which there was no end until everybody in the car seemed to be satisfied. I had seen, in Washington, several public men of rough appearance, but none whose looks seemed quite so uncouth, not to say grotesque, as Lincoln's."

---

in Lincoln's mind, it was a fundamental or a final solution to the problem of slavery. Given time and tolerance, human servitude in the United States would disappear.

Between Lincoln and Douglas there were several points of agreement. Both were opposed to social and political equality of the races, and both wanted to keep slavery out of the territories. Their chief difference was that Douglas did not want to see slavery expand, but he was unwilling to call it wrong. Lincoln did not want it to spread, but he insisted that it be admitted wrong. The distinction may seem unimportant to modern minds, but to the men of the fifties it was vital.

In the debate at Freeport, Lincoln asked Douglas a question which made this meeting historically the most significant of all the debates. His query was: Can the people of a territory exclude slavery from its limits

trap, because no matter how Douglas answered it, he would lose something. If he disavowed popular sovereignty, he would undoubtedly be defeated for re-election and his political career would be ended. But if he reaffirmed his formula, Southern Democrats would be offended, the party split deepened, and his chances of securing the Democratic nomination in 1860 mortally damaged. Lincoln knew how Douglas would answer, for the Senator had commented on the decision in previous speeches. Lincoln's purpose was to force Douglas to make a direct and public statement of his position, one that the South could not ignore.

Boldly Douglas met the issue. The people of a territory, he said, could, by lawful means, shut out slavery prior to the formation of a state constitution. Slavery could not exist a day without the support of "local police regulations": that is, without terri-

torial laws recognizing the right of slave
ownership. The mere failure of a legislature
to enact such laws would have the practical
effect of keeping slaveholders out. Thus,

The elections went heavily against the
Democrats, who lost ground in almost
every Northern state. In some states, as in
President Buchanan's own Pennsylvania,

The Last Hours of Congress, March, 1859. *Congress adjourned in
March, 1859, in an atmosphere of tension that reflected the rising sectional bitterness in the country. Although violence was feared at the
night sessions, the closing hours passed with nothing more than excited
speeches.* (FROM *Harper's Weekly*, 1859)

despite the Dred Scott decision, a territory
could exclude slavery. Douglas's reply became known as the Freeport Doctrine or, in
the South, as the Freeport Heresy. It satisfied his followers sufficiently to win him a
return to the Senate, but throughout the
North it aroused little enthusiasm. Although
his plan of police regulations would work
out exactly as he said, it seemed a little too
expedient, a little too slick. His answer to
the fatal question practically ruined Democratic prospects of unity.

the result was due to Northern resentment
at the economic policy (low tariff) of the
Southern-controlled Democratic party. In
others the voters were registering their disapproval of the administration's proslavery
program, especially as manifested in Kansas.
The administration retained control of the
Senate but lost its majority in the House,
where the Republicans gained a plurality.
In the holdover or short session of 1858–
1859, in which the Democrats were in the
majority, and in the regular session of 1859

(elected in 1858), every demand of the Republicans and Northern Democrats was blocked by Southern votes or by presidential vetoes; these defeated measures included a tariff increase, a homestead bill, a Pacific railroad, and federal land grants to states for the endowment of agricultural colleges. The 1859 session was also marked by an uproarious hassle over the election of a speaker of the House. The brawl had its origin, curiously enough, in a book: *The Impending Crisis of the South*, by Hinton R. Helper. This work was a new and peculiar kind of attack upon slavery, and, from the Southern viewpoint, the most dangerous kind of attack the institution had yet endured. The book had been endorsed by a number of Republican Congressmen, several

they delayed the choice of a presiding officer for almost two months. The significance of the book, however, is not in its relationship to the fight over the speakership, but in its influence on Southern psychology.

Helper was a non-slaveholding white North Carolinian who had traveled in the North and who had had to leave his native section because of his opposition to slavery. *The Impending Crisis*, published in New York in 1857, was largely a statistical analysis of the effects of slavery on the South. By comparing the material development of the South and the North, Helper sought to demonstrate that slavery had retarded the South and had operated to enrich the few, the planters, at the expense of the many, the

A Southern Abolitionist

In *The Impending Crisis of the South* (1857) Hinton R. Helper, a North Carolinian, presented statistics to show that slavery was impoverishing the South. He called on the non-slaveholders to abolish the institution. But Helper was also bitterly anti-Negro. He wanted to colonize the freed slaves out of the country: "Non-slaveholders of the South! Farmers, mechanics and workingmen, we take this occasion to assure you that the slaveholders, the arrogant demagogues whom you have elected to offices of honor and profit, have hookwinked you, trifled with you, and used you as mere tools for the consummation of their wicked designs. They have purposely kept you in ignorance, and have, by moulding your passions and prejudices to suit themselves, induced you to act in direct opposition to your dearest rights and interests. By a system of the grossest subterfuge and misrepresentation, and in order to avert, for a season, the vengeance that will most assuredly overtake them ere long, they have taught you to hate the abolitionists, who are your best and only true friends. Now, as one of your own number, we appeal to you to join us in our patriotic endeavors to rescue the generous soil of the South from the usurped and desolating control of these political vampires."

of whom were possible candidates for speaker of the House. Southern Democrats contended bitterly that anyone who had approved the volume was unfit for the office;

yeoman farmers. As long as slavery existed, he contended, the white masses were doomed to live in poverty and ignorance. He exhorted the non-slaveholders to overthrow the institution and destroy the power of the slavocracy. Here was an attack that really frightened Southern leaders. It did not come from an outsider; it was not based

appearance on the national scene. Still convinced that he was God's instrument to destroy slavery, he decided to transfer his activities from Kansas to the South itself.

Thoreau on John Brown

After the Harpers Ferry raid, many abolitionists proclaimed Brown to be a martyr for freedom. Henry D. Thoreau announced his views at a church meeting in Concord: "I am here to plead his cause with you. I plead not for his life, but for his character,—his immortal life; and so it becomes your cause wholly, and is not his in the least. Some eighteen hundred years ago Christ was crucified; this morning, perchance, Captain Brown was hung. These are the two ends of a chain which is not without its links. He is not Old Brown any longer; he is an angel of light. I see now that it was necessary that the bravest and humanest man in all the country should be hung. Perhaps he saw it himself. I *almost fear* that I may yet hear of his deliverance, doubting if a prolonged life, if *any* life, can do as much good as his death."

on moral grounds; and, what was particularly ominous, it appealed to the economic self-interest of the majority of Southern whites. In the South the book was, in effect, proscribed; it was dangerous to possess a copy. What worried the defenders of slavery was the possibility that Helper's book and similar attacks would circulate in the South if the Republicans won control of the national government. For years Southern postmasters had had an unofficial understanding with national postal authorities that they did not have to deliver antislavery propaganda documents. But what if the Republicans appointed men who would see that such items were delivered? Then the South might be flooded with abolitionist tracts and its intellectual solidarity dangerously cracked.

Even more alarming to the leaders of the South was another event occurring in 1859. John Brown, the grim fanatic of the Pottawatomie killings, now made a spectacular

With encouragement and financial aid from certain Eastern abolitionists, some of whom were aware of his purpose, he devised a wild scheme to liberate the slaves. His plan was to seize a mountain fortress in Virginia from which he could make raids to free slaves; he would organize his freedmen, whom he intended to arm, into a Negro state within the South, and eventually he would force the South to concede emancipation. In short, he was out to incite a violent slave insurrection. Because he needed guns, Brown fixed on Harpers Ferry, where a United States arsenal was located, as his base of operations. In October, at the head of eighteen followers, he descended on the town and captured the arsenal. Almost immediately he was attacked by citizens and local militia companies, who were shortly reinforced by a detachment of United States marines sent to the scene by the national government. With ten of his men killed, Brown had to surrender. He was promptly tried in a Virginia court for treason against the state, found guilty, and sentenced to death by hanging. Six of his followers met a similar fate.

Probably no single event had as much influence as the Brown raid in convincing Southerners that the welfare of their section was unsafe in the Union. Despite all the eulogies of slavery that they penned and all the pictures that they drew of the contented character of the slaves, one great fear always secretly gnawed at their hearts: the possibility of a general slave insurrection. Elaborate control measures existed in every state to prevent Negroes from assembling in large groups, and Southerners believed that they could shut off an uprising before it got started, unless—unless it was instigated and encouraged from the outside. It is no exaggeration to say that Brown's foray sent horror through the South. Southerners jumped to the conclusion that the Republicans were responsible for Brown. Either they had sent him or their irresponsible "higher-law" doctrines had impelled him to embark on his mad act; other similar incursions might be expected in the future. These suspicions were, of course, untrue; prominent Republicans like Lincoln and Seward condemned Brown as a criminal. But Southerners were more impressed by the words of such abolitionists as Wendell Phillips and Ralph Waldo Emerson, who glorified Brown as a new saint. Undoubtedly his execution made him a martyr to thousands of Northerners. Virginia would have been better advised to declare him insane and confine him in an asylum.

The Great Decision of 1860

The election of 1860 was, measured by the consequences that followed after it, the most momentous choice in our history. It is the only contest in which the issues were so important that the losing side felt that it could not abide by the result and attempted to withdraw from the society of which it was a part.

As the Democrats gathered in convention at Charleston, South Carolina, in April, it was evident that the disruptive force of sectionalism was about to destroy the last remaining national political organization in the country. Most of the Southern delegates came with the determination to compel the party to adopt a platform providing for federal protection of slavery in the territories: that is, an official endorsement of the principles of the Dred Scott decision. That this would ensure defeat in the November election they did not seem to care. If the Democratic party would not recognize Southern rights, it was worthless to the South, and the South would know how to act. The Western Democrats, arriving with bitter recollections of how Southern influence had blocked their legislative demands in the recent Congress, were angered at the rule-or-ruin attitude of the Southerners. They hoped, however, to negotiate a face-saving statement on slavery that would hold the party together. On one point they were adamant: Douglas must be the party's candidate. The weak Eastern faction was ready to cooperate with whichever side promised victory in November.

The first test of strength occurred over the wording of the section in the platform concerning slavery. Two proposed planks were submitted to the convention. One, the Southern plan, demanded federal protection of slavery in the territories and asserted that neither Congress nor a territorial legislature could exclude slavery. The other, the Western plan, vaguely endorsed popular sovereignty and proposed that all questions involving slavery in the territories be left up to the Supreme Court. Essentially the Westerners were trying to avoid a party split by an evasive statement that seemed to promise something to both factions. It was not enough. When the convention adopted the Western platform, the delegations from eight Lower South states withdrew from the hall. The remaining delegates then proceeded to the selection of a candidate. Douglas led on every ballot, but he could not muster the two-thirds majority (of the original number of delegates) required by party rules. Finally the managers adjourned the convention to meet again in Baltimore in June. At the Baltimore session, most of the Southerners reappeared, only to walk out again when the credentials of other new Southern delegates were questioned; some Southerners had refused to go to Baltimore and had assembled for a meeting of their own at Richmond. The rump convention at Baltimore then nominated Douglas. The Southern bolters at Baltimore and the men in Richmond nominated John C. Breckinridge of Kentucky. Sectionalism had at last divided the historic Democratic party. There were now two Democratic candidates in the field, and, although Douglas had supporters in the South and Breckinridge in the North, one was the nominee of the Northern Democrats and the other of the Southern Democrats. Each candidate sought to disavow the regional character of his nomination by choosing a vice-presidential running mate from the other section: Douglas ran with Herschel V. Johnson of Georgia and Breckinridge with Joseph Lane of Oregon. The obvious stratagem fooled nobody.

The Republicans, stimulated by visions of victory, held their convention in Chicago in May. Although the divisions developing in the Democratic ranks seemed to spell a Republican triumph, the party managers were taking no chances on a slip-up. They were determined that the party, both in its platform and its candidate, should appear to the voters as representing conservatism, stability, and moderation; above all, they wanted to erase any possible impression that

Republicans were radical idealists. No longer was the Republican party a one-idea organization composed of grim crusaders against slavery. It now embraced, or hoped to embrace, every major interest group in the North which believed that the South, the champion of slavery, was blocking its legitimate economic aspirations. The platform reflected the new orientation of the party. It endorsed such measures as a high tariff, internal improvements, a homestead bill, and a Pacific railroad to be built with federal financial assistance. On the slavery issue, the Republicans affirmed the right of each state to control its own institutions, which was their way of saying that they did not intend to interfere with slavery in the South. But they also denied the authority of Congress or of a territorial legislature to legalize slavery in the territories, which was equivalent to saying that they still would oppose the expansion of slavery. Taking note of Southern threats of disunion, the platform declared that the Union was indissoluble and that a minority section could not withdraw from it. Clearly the Republicans, in their devotion to the concept that the central government should stimulate expansion of the economy and in their dedication to the ideals of nationalism, were the political heirs of the Federalists and the Whigs.

In their choice of a candidate the Republicans also demonstrated their purpose of appearing as a party of positive conservatism. The leading contender for the nomination was Seward, who faced the competition of a number of favorite-son candidates. The New Yorker confidently expected to win the prize. He was the most famous man of the party and a veteran enemy of slavery. But his very prominence and his long political record damaged his chances. He had made many enemies and had alienated some important pressure groups. Seward is a prime example of what happens to an architect of a political movement dedicated to effecting a change in social structure. At the moment of victory, the party discards its leader out of a fear that his radicalism will repel voters it hopes to attract. Actually Seward was not radical on the slavery issue, but his past utterances made him seem so; and hence he seemed politically unavailable. Passing him and other aspirants over, the convention nominated on the third ballot Abraham Lincoln—who was prominent enough to be respectable but obscure enough to have few foes, and who was radical enough to please the antislavery faction in the party but conservative enough to satisfy the ex-Whigs. To complete the strategy of availability, the vice-presidential nomination went to Hannibal Hamlin of Maine, a former Democrat.

As if three parties were not enough, a fourth entered the lists—the Constitutional Union party. Although posing as a new organization, it was really the last surviving remnant of the oldest conservative tradition in the country; its leaders were elder statesmen and most of its members were former Whigs. Meeting in Baltimore in May, the party nominated John Bell of Tennessee and Edward Everett of Massachusetts. The platform declared for the Constitution, the Union, and enforcement of the laws. These vague sentiments meant nothing, of course, which was the intention back of them. The Constitutional Union men, often ridiculed as the "old man's party" or the "soothing-syrup" people, were deliberately appealing to moderates, especially in the border slave states, with an evasive platform. Probably they hoped to win enough states to throw the election into the House, where a conservative might be chosen President.

The campaign demonstrated how sectionalism was warping the normal pattern of American politics. In the North the Repub-

licans conducted a campaign reminiscent of the exciting contest of 1840, replete with parades, symbols, and mass meetings. For the most part, they stressed the economic promises in their platform, and subordinated the slavery issue. Lincoln, following the customary practice of candidates, made no speeches, leaving this work to lesser party luminaries. Unlike previous candidates, he refused to issue any written statements of his views, claiming that anything he said would be seized on by Southerners and misrepresented. The two Democratic factions seemed more interested in attacking each other than in defeating the Republicans. Douglas, breaking with precedent, embarked on a speaking tour that carried him into the South. He denounced Breckinridge's supporters as disunionists and warned the South that the Union could not be broken up. The most peculiar feature of the campaign, and the one that revealed most strikingly the deep, disruptive influence of sectionalism, was the failure of any one of the four parties to develop strength on a national scale. In effect the election became a struggle between parties within sections. In the North the contest was between Lincoln and Douglas, with the other two candidates having only negligible support. In the South the issue lay between Breckinridge and Bell, with Douglas running a weak third. Lincoln's name appeared on the ballot in a few border states, but he polled hardly any votes in this area, and in ten Southern states he received not a single popular vote.

In the November election Lincoln won a majority of the electoral votes and the Presidency. The distribution of the popular and electoral votes for all candidates is so important, as indicating the possible feelings of the American people in the sectional crisis, that it deserves particular analysis. The vote stood as follows:

	ELECTORAL VOTE	POPULAR VOTE	PER CENT OF POPULAR VOTE
Lincoln	180	1,866,452	40
Douglas	12	1,375,157	29
Breckinridge	72	847,953	18
Bell	39	590,631	13
Total	303	4,680,193	

Lincoln carried every free state except New Jersey, where he took four electoral votes and Douglas three. Breckinridge had the electoral votes of every state in the Lower South and of Delaware, Maryland, and North Carolina. Bell won Kentucky, Tennessee, and Virginia. Despite his large popular vote, Douglas carried only one state, Missouri. The combined popular vote of Lincoln's opponents was almost a million more than his total. But even if all the op-

Lincoln would still have carried the populous states and would have won with a smaller electoral majority. As it was, the Republicans had elected a President, but they had failed to secure a majority in Congress; and of course they did not have the Supreme Court.

The meaning of the election is not easy to interpret. Did the votes show that a majority in both sections favored extreme action—or a conservative policy? Students

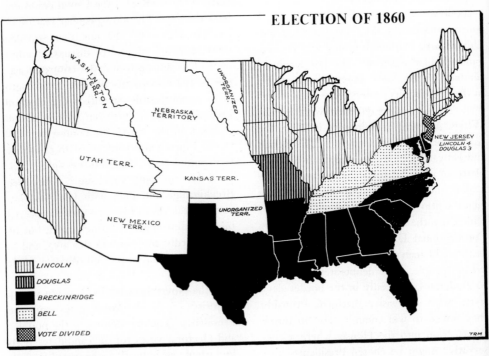

ELECTION OF 1860

NEW JERSEY
LINCOLN 4
DOUGLAS 3

LINCOLN
DOUGLAS
BRECKINRIDGE
BELL
VOTE DIVIDED

position strength had been concentrated upon one candidate, the result would have been the same. Because of the sometimes peculiar workings of the electoral system,

who believe in the latter explanation point out that in the popular vote Lincoln was a minority President and that Breckinridge's opponents polled almost 124,000 more votes in the slave states than he did. If, however, Lincoln and Breckinridge are reckoned as the candidates of the extremes, then the election was a mandate for decisive action of one kind or the other; the Northern Republican and the Southern Democrat had approximately 750,000 more votes than Douglas and Bell, the middle candidates. But undoubtedly the most significant fact about the election was that an unquestioned majority had voted to stop the expansion of slavery. Lincoln and Douglas were committed, by one formula or another, to keeping slavery out of the territories, and 69 per cent of the voters had endorsed their positions. The hard fact of this majority the South now had to face. Either the South must accede to the national will or attempt to preserve its interests by withdrawing from the nation.

The Secession of the South

During the campaign various Southern leaders had threatened that if the Republicans won the election the South would secede from the Union. Southern threats of secession had been voiced at intervals since 1850, without any action following, and Northerners had come to believe they were intended as bluffs. This time, however, the South meant them.

The concept of secession was rooted in the political philosophy which the South had developed to protect its minority status. According to this doctrine, the Union was an association of sovereign states. The individual states had once joined the Union; they could, whenever they wished, dissolve their connections with it and resume their status as separate sovereignties. For a state to leave the Union was a momentous act but a lawful one. Southerners, therefore, had devised a process—one that they considered dignified and legitimate—to accomplish secession. The governor and the legislature would take steps to call an election

for a special state convention. This body, while in session, represented the sovereign power of the state; it exercised the supreme powers of government. By a majority vote it could pass an ordinance of secession. Because the convention had been chosen by the people and invested with specific authority, it did not have to submit its decision to popular ratification.

Approximately four months elapsed between Lincoln's election on November 6 and his assumption of the Presidency on March 4, 1861. During that period seven states in the Lower South seceded. In these states there was virtually no opposition to the right of secession. The only question debated was whether the choice of a Republican President justified the exercise of the right. In the election of delegates to the conventions and in the conventions when they gathered, two factions or groups were evident. One may be termed the seceders. Better organized than their opponents, they advocated an immediate withdrawal from the Union. Their leaders—men like Robert Toombs of Georgia, William L. Yancey of Alabama, and Robert Barnwell Rhett of South Carolina—shouted that the interests of the South were no longer safe in a nation that would soon be controlled by its enemies. The South must be out of the Union, they insisted, before Lincoln took office. The other group, of whom Alexander H. Stephens of Georgia may be taken as an outstanding if not completely typical representative, counseled a wait-and-see policy. They pointed out that the Republicans did not control Congress or the Supreme Court, that even if Lincoln wished to violate Southern rights he could not move alone. Wait for evidence of a hostile intention or the power to perpetrate it, they begged. At the very least, let the South act as a unit instead of as individual states: call a Southern convention to decide on the best method to protect the section's interests. Because they endorsed collective action, members of this group were sometimes called "cooperators."

The advocates of immediate secession carried the day. It was not just that they had long been preparing for the crisis or that they were more tightly organized than their opponents. For years the Southern people had sustained a mood of impending insecurity, which, in turn, had created terrific social tensions. Now, with the election of a Republican President, the great threat so long feared seemed about to materialize. In some form or manner, the Southern way of life would be altered or even ended, perhaps not immediately but certainly in the near future. Southern notions of how this result would be accomplished might have been, with many individuals, vague and ill-defined, but the apprehension was nevertheless very real. To cope with the situation, the cooperators advised delay: a continuation of the tactics of the past. The seceders offered a simple, direct remedy that promised not only to save Southern rights but to snap at once the almost unbearable tensions that the past had generated.

South Carolina, long the hotbed of Southern separatism, led off the secession parade, its convention taking the state out of the Union on December 20, 1860, by a unanimous vote. Six other states of the Lower South soon followed. The dates of their secession and the votes in their conventions were as follows: Mississippi (January 9), 84 to 15; Florida (January 10), 62 to 7; Alabama (January 11), 61 to 39; Georgia (January 19), 208 to 89; Louisiana (January 26), 113 to 17; and Texas (February 1), 166 to 8. There was more opposition to secession than the votes indicate. In Georgia and Alabama the cooperators offered resolutions to delay action which failed by narrow majorities. In all the conventions some delegates who favored delay, seeing that their cause was hopeless, decided to vote for secession in order to demonstrate to the outside world that their state was united. Before Lincoln ever assumed the Presidency, then, seven Southern states had left the Union. Not only that, but in February, 1861, representatives of the seceded states met at Montgomery, Alabama, and formed a new, Southern nation—the Confederate States of America.

While secession was running its course in the Cotton South, the Northern populace regarded the spectacle with mingled feelings of amazement and anger. Although a few vociferous antislavery groups and individuals professed delight at getting rid of the South, most Northerners were too shocked at the moment to think in terms of a specific policy to meet the crisis. Undoubtedly the basic disposition of Northern opinion was to maintain the Union, by compromise if possible or even by force if necessary, but months of discussion would have to pass before this inclination would harden into determination.

Something of the indecision in Northern attitudes was reflected in the thinking of President Buchanan. In his message to Congress of December, 1860, delivered on the eve of the secession movement, he denied the right of a state to secede; but he added that he did not think the federal government possessed the power to coerce a state back into the Union. His policy was not as muddled as it seemed. He hoped that a program of nonaggression would avert secession except by a few states and would isolate those that withdrew. He intended to avoid a collision of arms and to maintain the symbolic authority of the national government until his successor could take office. Almost immediately South Carolina subjected the President's policy to a dangerous test. As the various states seceded, they took possession of federal property within their boundaries, but they lacked the strength to seize certain offshore forts, notably Fort Sumter in the harbor of Charleston, South Carolina, and Fort Pickens in the harbor of Pensacola, Florida. South Carolina understood Buchanan's position to mean acquiescence in its independence, and the state sent com-

the harbor, it encountered the fire of shore batteries and returned to the North. The attack on the ship was an overt act by South Carolina, virtually an act of war. But al-

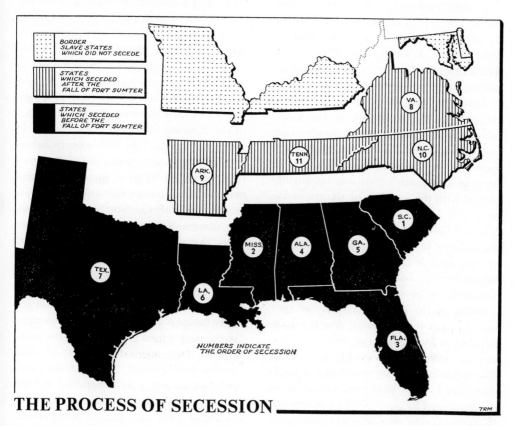

BORDER
SLAVE STATES
WHICH DID NOT SECEDE

STATES
WHICH SECEDED
AFTER THE
FALL OF FORT SUMTER

STATES
WHICH SECEDED
BEFORE THE
FALL OF FORT SUMTER

VA. 8

TENN. 11

N.C. 10

ARK. 9

S.C. 1

MISS. 2

ALA. 4

GA. 5

TEX. 7

LA. 6

FLA. 3

NUMBERS INDICATE
THE ORDER OF SECESSION

THE PROCESS OF SECESSION

TRM

missioners to Washington to ask for the surrender of Sumter, garrisoned by a small force under Major Robert Anderson. Buchanan, fearful as he was of provoking a clash, refused to yield the fort. Gradually, as he realized his conciliatory policy was not going to halt the secession movement, he assumed a stronger nationalistic stand.

In January, 1861, in another message to Congress, he denied the right of a state to secede, and in the same month he decided to succor Anderson. By his direction an unarmed merchant ship, the *Star of the West*, proceeded to Fort Sumter with troops and supplies. When the vessel attempted to enter

though the flag had been fired on, there was no great outburst of indignation in the North, which is evidence that as yet Northern opinion had not completely crystallized.

In his message of December, 1860, Buchanan recommended to Congress that it should frame compromise measures to avert secession, his idea of compromise being to give the South everything it wanted. The legislators, shocked by the threatened crisis and influenced by memories of 1850, needed no urging. The Senate and the House appointed committees to study plans of adjustment. The House committee reported back a scheme based upon a constitutional amendment that would deny forever to Congress the power to abolish slavery in the states where it existed. It was not acceptable to the South because it did not come to grips with the issue of slavery in the territories. The Senate committee concentrated its attention on a proposal submitted by Senator John J. Crittenden of Kentucky. The Crittenden Compromise, as it became known, called for a series of constitutional amendments: one would have guaranteed the permanence of slavery in the states; others were designed to satisfy Southern demands on such matters as fugitive slaves and slavery in the District of Columbia. But the heart of Crittenden's plan was his attempt to deal with the problem of slavery in the territories. He proposed to re-establish the Missouri Compromise line of 36° 30′ in all the territory of the United States then held or *thereafter acquired*. North of the line slavery was to be prohibited, south of it slavery was to be recognized. The Southern members of the committee indicated they would accept this territorial division if the Republicans, who were not averse to Crittenden's other points, would agree to it. The Republicans, after sounding out President-elect Lincoln in Illinois, voted against the proposal. Lincoln took the position that the restoration of the Missouri Compromise line would encourage the South to embark on imperialist adventures in Latin America. The committee had to report that it could not agree on a plan.

One notable attempt to effect a compromise was made outside Congress. The legislature of Virginia invited the other states to send delegates to a peace conference at Washington. Representatives from twenty-one states assembled early in February, and spent most of the month framing compromise proposals. The plan of the Peace Convention, as that body was called, followed closely the Crittenden scheme. The princi-

pal difference was that the Convention proposal tried to meet the Republican objection to the 36° 30′ line of division by providing that no new territory should be acquired without the consent of a majority of the Senators from both the free and the slave states. The sponsors of the Convention submitted their plan to the Senate, but it received almost no support. It came too late to influence the course of events.

Why did all the compromise proposals fail? Does their rejection furnish any clues to the thinking of the American people in the secession crisis? As with most questions involving historical motivation, only tentative answers can be given. But it would seem that the compromises failed for the simple reason that both the North and the South, as represented by their political agents, believed that they could not agree to any further modification of their principles. In part, this attitude was the result of long years of bitter agitation; men felt that they had yielded enough, and now they were not going to budge regardless of the consequences. Southerners sensed that none of the compromise plans touched the heart of their problem: the minority status of their section. Northerners were determined that the minority section should not be permitted to exercise a veto on national development. With the politicians, there were other considerations. Southern extremists had gone so far in stressing the necessity of secession and in describing the glories to follow Southern independence that they could not now draw back; perhaps they had become convinced by their own propaganda. If the Republicans had compromised their stand on slavery in the territories, they would have repudiated the chief plank in their platform and the issue on which they had risen to power. They would also have committed political suicide, a process in which parties rarely engage.

And so nothing had been resolved when Abraham Lincoln was inaugurated President on March 4, 1861. Lincoln came to Washington with a policy to meet the crisis. He first announced it in his inaugural address. Naturally, in this state paper which would be studied carefully in all sections and especially in the South, he did not enunciate in frank detail every point in his program. He did, however, state with reasonable candor and clarity the broad outlines of the course he intended to follow. In the address Lincoln laid down the following basic principles: the Union was older than the Constitution, no state could of its own volition leave the Union, the ordinances of secession were illegal, and acts of violence to support secession were insurrectionary or revolutionary. As to the specific situation created by secession, he declared that he meant to execute the laws in all the states and to maintain possession of federal property in the seceded states (Forts Sumter and Pickens). In summary, Lincoln was saying that if force was necessary to preserve the Union, he would employ it. He did not rule out the possibility of conciliation. He would proceed—for a period—with caution and forbearance; and if the seceded states wished to return, they were welcome. But they would have to return without any conditions of compromise being exacted from the national government. Lincoln's policy reflected accurately the opinions of the Northern people. Whatever differences separated them, they were, in overwhelming numbers, devoted to the concept of the Union. However they calculated its values, in emotional, political, or economic terms, they thought it was worth maintaining, even by war.

Lincoln soon found an opportunity to apply his policy in the case of Fort Sumter. Major Anderson was running short of supplies; unless he received fresh provisions the fort would have to be evacuated. If Lincoln permitted the loss of Sumter, the South, and perhaps the North as well, would never believe that he meant to sustain the Union. After much deliberation and against the advice of most of his civil and military advisers, he decided to dispatch to the fort a naval relief expedition. Carefully he informed the South Carolina authorities, who, of course, would have to notify the Confederate government, that ships bearing supplies were on the way. The Confederate government was in a diplomatic dilemma. If the Confederacy permitted the expedition to land, it would be placed in the position of bowing tamely to Federal authority; its people would not believe that it meant to sustain secession. But the only alternative was to reduce the fort before the ships arrived—in short, to invoke war. After hours of anguished discussion, the government decided on the latter choice. General P. G. T. Beauregard, in charge of Confederate forces at Charleston, was ordered to demand the surrender of Sumter, and, if the demand was refused, to reduce the fort. Beauregard served his summons, and Anderson rejected it. The Confederates then bombarded the fort for two days, April 12–13, 1861. On April 14, Anderson surrendered. The accusation is sometimes made that Lincoln so maneuvered the situation at Sumter as to provoke war. The charge is unjust both to Lincoln's humanity and to his political skill. He did not want war, but he foresaw that war was probable. He so maneuvered that if it came, it would be started by the other side.

After Sumter there were no doubts that war had come. Lincoln moved to increase the army and called on the states to furnish troops to restore the Union. At this juncture four more slave states seceded and joined the Confederacy: Virginia (April 17); Arkansas (May 6); Tennessee (May 7); and

North Carolina (May 20). Before Sumter these Upper South states had considered secession, but had decided that the election of Lincoln did not constitute sufficient reason to leave the Union. They were, however, committed to the doctrine of state sovereignty and to the right of secession, both of which would be things of the past if the national government had the power to coerce states back into the Union. To preserve state sovereignty, they embarked, with some reluctance, on the secession adventure. Forty-six mountain counties in northwestern Virginia refused to accept the decision of their state, established their own "loyal" government, and in 1863 secured admission to the Union as the new state of West Vir-

ginia. The four remaining slave states, Maryland, Delaware, Kentucky, and Missouri, cast their lot with the Union. In these states the people were torn between conflicting emotions: sympathy for the South and devotion to nationalism; in addition, they had close economic ties with both sections. Undoubtedly a majority in each favored the national cause. Nevertheless, the Lincoln administration kept a keen watch on their actions, and in two, Maryland and Missouri, helped to ensure their decision by employing military force. The Confederacy, then, did not represent a solid block of slave states as the embattled hosts of North and South faced each other on the eve of war.

->>>->>>->>>->> <<<-<<<-<<<-<<<

BIBLIOGRAPHY

BEARING DIRECTLY on the topics of this chapter are the previously mentioned books by Simms, Craven, Nichols, Milton, and Carpenter, and the various works on Kansas. The most comprehensive treatment is Allan Nevins, *The Emergence of Lincoln* (2 vols., 1950). A penetrating interpretive study is U. B. Phillips, *The Course of the South to Secession* (1939). In *John C. Frémont and the Republican Party* (1930), R. J. Bartlett depicts an important figure in the emerging Republican party. Economic developments are traced in G. W. Van Vleck, *The Panic of 1857* (1943). For the entrance of the Supreme Court into the slavery controversy, see Vincent Hopkins, *Dred Scott's Case* (1951), and Swisher, *Roger B. Taney.*

Again biographies serve to fill in the political record. For Lincoln before 1860, consult A. J. Beveridge, *Abraham Lincoln, 1809–1858* (2 vols., 1928), a valuable political analysis; Carl Sandburg, *Abraham Lincoln: The Prairie Years* (2 vols., 1926), a

vivid panorama of the society in which Lincoln lived; and J. G. Randall, *Lincoln the President*, vol. 1 (1945). W. E. Baringer has written two good studies of Lincoln's nomination and his course as President-elect: *Lincoln's Rise to Power* (1937) and *A House Dividing* (1945). The psychology of a Southern moderate is analyzed in J. H. Parks, *John Bell of Tennessee* (1950), and that of a Southern extremist in L. A. White, *Robert Barnwell Rhett* (1931). For the thinking of a somewhat dogmatic Republican, see J. A. Isely, *Horace Greeley and the Republican Party* (1947).

E. D. Fite, *The Presidential Campaign of 1860* (1911), is a general treatment but later and more detailed are R. H. Luthin, *The First Lincoln Campaign* (1944), and Ollinger Crenshaw, *The Slave States in the Presidential Election of 1860* (1945). The best survey of secession is D. L. Dumond, *The Secession Movement* (1931). Two superb documentary collections are Dumond, ed., *Southern Editorials on Secession* (1931), and H. C. Perkins, ed., *Northern Editorials on Secession* (2 vols., 1942). Lincoln's course during secession is analyzed from different viewpoints in D. M. Potter, *Lincoln and His Party in the Secession Crisis* (1942), and K. M. Stampp, *And the War Came* (1950). P. G. Auchampaugh describes Buchanan in the same situation in *James Buchanan and His Cabinet on the Eve of Secession* (1926).

CHAPTER 28

The Civil War: The North

THE CIVIL WAR was the first great military experience of the American people. Compared to it, the earlier struggles—the Revolution, the War of 1812, the Mexican War—were minor and episodic. In the perspective of world history, the Civil War is the first of the modern wars: it was a war of matériel as well as of men. It witnessed the employment of mass armies, railroads, the telegraph, armored ships, railroad artillery, balloons, the Gatling gun (the precursor of the machine gun), repeating rifles, trenches, and wire entanglements. Modern war is total in its impact and its effects. It compels a nation to mobilize and direct its whole resources for the end of victory. If the Civil War was not quite total, it marked a transition from the older type of warfare to the new. Unlike the leisurely, limited-objective wars of the eighteenth century, it was a rough, ruthless, war-to-the-hilt kind of fight. For both sides it was a war of ideas, and to both the outcome was

desperately important. This was a war that went all the way.

The Civil War is the most dramatic single event in our history; it has been called *the* great historical experience of the American people. That these claims have validity is evinced by the immense popular interest in the war that has existed up into contemporary times: it is the most written-about and most read-about period in American history. But the Civil War was more than a spectacular episode. It was an event of tremendous pivotal importance in the history of the nation, comparable to the Revolution of 1789 in France. More than most wars, the Civil War settled some things—and settled them permanently. It accomplished the destruction of slavery, and it made certain the triumph of industrial capitalism. Most important of all, it sustained the Union and cemented the modern American nation. In its wake it would leave some new and troublesome problems and some issues that people have been arguing about ever since. But the great result of the war—the endurance of the Union—was accepted by all important elements in American life. After 1865 no faction or class or section would even contemplate the possibility of breaking up the American nation.

The Military Potential of North and South

A comparison of the combatants on the eve of war reveals that all the great material factors were on the side of the North. And these advantages became more significant as the conflict continued and the superior economy of the North became geared for war production. The North had a larger manpower reservoir from which to draw its armed forces. In the North, or the United States, were twenty-three states with a population of approximately 22,000,000. In the South, or the Confederate States, were eleven states with a population of some 9,000,000. But it would not be accurate to say that Northern superiority in manpower was as 22 to 9. Included in the Northern total are the four "loyal" slave states (Maryland, Delaware, Kentucky, Missouri), which furnished thousands of soldiers to the Confederacy, and the Pacific Coast states, which provided no direct aid to the North. In both sections minority elements opposed the war or were reluctant to support it; in the North, the Peace Democrats (to be discussed later), and in the South, the inhabitants of the mountain areas. The exact number of each group is hard to determine; in computing the strength of the combatants, it is perhaps sufficient to say that they canceled each other out. A complicating factor in evaluating the Confederate manpower potential is the presence in the Southern population total of approximately 3,500,000 slaves, leaving a white population of something under 6,000,000. Should the comparison ratio then be 20 plus to 6? Such a figure

would be misleading. While the slaves were not directly available for military service, they were indirectly a source of important power to the Confederate war effort. They performed a substantial amount of military labor, acting as teamsters, cooks, and in other capacities in the armies, and they worked in gangs in constructing fortifications. More important, as agricultural laborers, they fulfilled a vital function in production. If they had not been present on the plantations and farms, a certain number of white men would have had to take their place.

Without attempting to fix an exact ratio, it may be said that the North enjoyed a substantial manpower superiority; obviously the North was capable of raising larger military forces than the South. The manpower advantage was not, however, the major factor that some writers have tried to make it. The Northern armies did not attain a decisive numerical majority until the last year and a half of the war. Later generations of Southerners who talked about the Confederacy being overwhelmed by sheer numbers were thinking of 1864–1865, when the odds were 5 to 1. They were nothing like that in the first half of the war. The Confederate armies increased steadily in size until 1863, reaching their greatest strength in that year, and then steadily declined. Before 1863 the Union armies, although usually larger than their opponents, were not greatly superior. In a number of important engagements the size of the contending forces was approximately equal, or the Confederate inferiority was slight. It would have been possible, in the first two years of the war, for the South to have won its independence by a purely military decision. Had things gone a little differently in some of the early battles, had fortune shifted her favors a bit, the story *might* have had another ending.

Of more decisive importance than the

manpower factor, particularly after the struggle settled into a sustained effort by both sides, was the superior potential of the Northern economic system to produce the

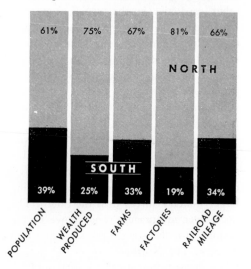

Comparison of North and South, 1860

matériel of modern war. At the beginning of the war both sections possessed adequate agricultural facilities to feed their armed forces and their civilian populations. As the conflict continued, the productive capacities of the North expanded, primarily as a result of the use on Northern farms of labor-saving machines like the reaper, drill, and thresher. Southern agricultural production, on the other hand, decreased under the strain of war. Federal occupation or devastation of large parts of the South reduced the size of the food-producing area, and the tendency of the slaves to flock into the army camps of the invaders lessened the number of agricultural laborers. But even with damaged facilities, the South, almost up to the end, was probably producing enough food to meet its minimum needs. During the last two years of the war, hunger and privation existed in the armies and among civilians in cities and towns, but most of the shortages were due to the inability of the South's

transportation system to move supplies where they were needed.

The North's greater economic potential was most fully and formidably apparent in industrial production. Almost any set of comparative figures can be chosen to illustrate the overwhelming nature of Northern superiority. In the North (in 1860) there were approximately 110,000 manufacturing establishments, representing a capital investment of $850,000,000, employing 1,130,000 workers, and turning out annually products valued at $1,500,000,000. For the South, the approximate figures were: establishments, 20,000; capital, $95,000,000; workers, 110,-000; value of products, $155,000,000. As to a comparison in a specific field of production, the woolen goods industry, which would have a vital role in supplying such military items as uniforms and blankets, may be cited. In 1860 the value of woolens made in Northern plants was $64,000,000, while the total for the South was only $4,500,000.

These and other statistics, translated into material results, meant that the Northern armies, once the economic system had been converted to war production, would have more of everything then the Southern forces. This was not true, of course, in the first year of the war, when both sides purchased large amounts of supplies, particularly arms, from Europe. After 1862 the North was able to manufacture practically all of its war materials; its dependence on Europe ceased. The South, on the other hand, had to rely on Europe all during the war, running what goods it could through the Northern naval blockade. It also tried desperately to expand its own industrial facilities. The brilliant Confederate chief of ordnance, Josiah Gorgas, accomplished wonders in building arsenals and in supplying the armies with weapons and munitions. Nevertheless, both the quantity and the quality of Confederate firearms was inferior, and the firepower of a Confederate army was rarely equal to that of its enemy. Equally important, the Southern economic system was unable to provide its soldiers, and its civilian society, with the other matériel of modern war: clothes, boots, blankets, stockings, medical supplies, and the like. Its failure in this respect was one reason why Southern morale dropped badly after 1863.

The Civil War was the first railroad war, that is, the first war in which railroads were used to mobilize men and supplies and to transport both to places where they were needed. In every respect the transportation system of the North was superior to that of the South. The North had more and better inland water transport (steamboats, barges), more surfaced roads, and more wagons and animals. But it was with the vital railroads that the North enjoyed the greatest advantage. The North had approximately 20,000 miles of railroads, while the South, containing at least as large a land area, had only 10,000 miles. The trackage figures, however, do not tell the whole story of Southern inferiority. Many of the roads had been built by small companies, and hence were short lines; there were important gaps between key points in the South, which meant that supplies had to be detoured long distances or carried between railheads by wagons. Furthermore, the gauges varied even more widely than those in the North, which prevented the interchange of equipment. The few through lines, like the connection between Richmond and Memphis and the one between Richmond and the Carolinas, ran close to the land or sea frontier, and were vulnerable to enemy raids. In the North, when locomotives, freight cars, or rails became unusable, they were replaced by new stock. But when Southern equipment was broken down by use or destroyed by the Federals, it could not be replaced. Before 1860 the South had purchased its rolling stock from Northern factories or from

Southern plants like the Tredegar Iron Works, which during the war were turning out guns. If the South lost ten locomotives, then it had to manage with that many less. As the war wore on, the Confederate railroad system steadily deteriorated, and by the last year and a half of the struggle it had almost collapsed.

The great weapon of sea power was also in the hands of the North. At the beginning of the war the United States navy was too small to exercise a significant influence on the course of the struggle: it numbered only some 90 ships of all types and 9,000 sailors. Rapid expansion soon made naval power a major military factor. By the last year of the war the navy contained approximately 670 ships and 51,000 men. No average size for the Confederate navy can be given because the frequent destruction of its ships resulted in a shifting total; its greatest personnel, however, was a mere 4,000. Northern sea power served in two important strategic functions. First, the Federal government proclaimed, when the war started, a blockade of the Southern coast. The mission of sealing off the long coastal line of the Confederacy was an impossible one for the Federal navy in the beginning. Even as the navy grew in size and after it reached its maximum, it was unable to establish a completely effective blockade. Blockade runners continued to operate in and out of such ports as Wilmington, Charleston, and Mobile. The effects of the blockade in depriving the South of supplies have been disputed; they probably have been exaggerated. Nevertheless, the blockade did hurt the South. It was a form of economic warfare, and by helping to isolate the South from the outside world it had a psychological effect on Southern morale. The second function of sea power was in aiding the Federal land forces to invade and subjugate the vast Western theater: the region between the Appalachian Mountains and the Mississippi River. In this area the larger rivers were navigable to transport boats and small ships of war. The navy carried supplies for the armies, and joined with them in attacking Confederate strong points. Some of the largest operations in the West were combined land and naval affairs. It is no great exaggeration to say that without the employment of sea power on the Western rivers the West could not have been conquered.

When the material factors are analyzed and weighed, the impression emerges that the South had absolutely no chance to win the war. The Southern struggle for independence seems a gallant but utterly rash endeavor, doomed to failure from the start by the brutal arithmetic of the situation. Actually, the material odds were not as great as at first glance they appear. As previously indicated, the South might have won a decision on the battlefield up to 1863. Southern inferiority in manpower was partially offset by other factors. The South, for the most part, fought on the defensive in its own country and commanded interior lines. The Northern invaders had to maintain long lines of communication, to supply themselves in areas where transportation was defective, and to garrison occupied regions. Furthermore, in this civil war, unlike a war with a foreign country, the North had to do more than capture the enemy capital or defeat enemy armies. It had to convince the Southern civilian population that the war was hopeless by seizing and holding most of the Confederacy; it had, in short, to conquer a people—all of which was an extremely difficult job and required a vast expenditure of men and resources.

The Confederacy had what might be called a psychological opportunity to win its independence. The South was fighting for something very concrete, very easy for its people to understand. It simply wanted to be independent, to be let alone; it had no aggressive designs on the North. The North, on the other hand, was fighting for abstract ideals: the maintenance of the Union and, later, the emancipation of the slaves. It was a more difficult task for Lincoln to hold his people in support of the war than it was for the leaders of the South. The North, at any moment it wanted, could have peace and independence by quitting the war. If the South could convince the North that it could not be conquered or that the result would not be worth the sacrifices, it might, even after 1863, win its freedom. At least once during the war it seemed that the North was convinced, was about to give up the contest.

War Economics and Finance

For the North the wartime years were a period of prosperity and expansion. Both industry and agriculture increased their productive facilities, and at the end of the war were turning out more products than at its beginning. With hardly a sign of strain, the economic system was able to supply the needs of the civilian population and to satisfy the new and huge demands of the armed forces. The Northern economy accomplished the same prodigious feat that the national economy would later perform on a larger scale in the two great wars of the twentieth century. It maintained a great war and at the same time increased the national wealth; it demonstrated a capacity to create faster than any possible destruction. The booming prosperity and the expanded facilities were direct creations of the war; they were the results of the influence of modern war on the economy. Modern war is based on matériel. It calls for the production and expenditure of vast amounts of industrial and agricultural supplies, which are acquired and dispensed by the government. Perforce the government becomes a purchaser of all kinds of goods, for which, in order to speed delivery, it offers generous prices. In the Civil War, the government of the United States, as it mobilized the national resources for war, touched in some degree almost every important segment of the nation's economy.

The most spectacular expansion of productive capacities occurred in manufacturing. Among the industries which increased their output, and their profits, in response to the stimulus of war, were the following: iron and steel, woolens, boots and shoes, arms and ammunition, railroads, petroleum, prepared foods, coal, and lumber. In many areas of industrial activity, record production totals were piled up during the war years. In 1864, 21,000,000 tons of coal were mined, as compared to 13,000,000 tons in 1860. The annual consumption of wool jumped from 85,000,000 pounds to over 200,000,000. The production of such items as iron ore, pig iron, copper, and salt exceeded by several times the highest totals of the prewar period. The volume of freight tonnage carried on the railroads and inland waterways reached unprecedented figures. Some railroads increased their traffic as much as 100 per cent. Shipments on the Erie Canal and the Great Lakes recorded even greater advances. Before the war the average annual tonnage of iron ore carried on the Lakes was only 132 tons; by 1863 the iron steamers were transporting ore to the Pittsburgh mills at the rate of 235,000 tons a year.

In large part, the increased production was accomplished by remodeling or enlarging old factories and by building new ones. In one year Philadelphia built fifty-seven new factories, and Chicago twenty-four new meat-packing houses. But much of the increase was achieved by using machines and manufacturing processes that had been introduced before the war but never fully utilized until the war forced mass production upon industry. The Howe-Singer sewing machine, for example, enabled the textile business to meet the enormous demands of the government for uniforms. In the process it created a new business: ready-made suits for men. The principle of the sewing machine as applied to the making of boots and shoes—machine stitching of soles to uppers—permanently revolutionized the shoe industry. In arms manufacturing, the principle of interchangeable parts (the invention of Eli Whitney) was employed in the arsenals of the government and in those owned by private enterprise. The results were little short of phenomenal. Before the war the combined output of the government arsenals at Springfield, Massachusetts, and Harpers Ferry, Virginia, had been only 22,000 weapons a year; by 1862 the Springfield establishment alone was turning out 200,000 rifles a year. The thirty-eight largest arms factories in the North could manufacture 5,000 rifles every day, while the maximum total for Southern plants, which was not often achieved, was only 300 a day.

The production feats of industry were almost equaled by those of agriculture. The farmers of the North were called upon to supply the government with enormous amounts of foodstuffs for the army. At the same time an urgent need for American wheat developed in Great Britain, troubled by declining production and a succession of crop failures. It was an index of the vigor of the Northern agricultural system that it was able to satisfy both the domestic and foreign demands. The wheat production of the Northern states leaped from 142,000,000 bushels in 1859 to 191,000,000 bushels by 1863, a total that exceeded the output of the entire nation before the war. The amount of wheat exported was three times greater than in the prewar years. Like increases occurred with other crops: wool production rose from 60,000,000 pounds in 1860 to 142,-000,000 pounds in 1865. Part of the enlarged agricultural volume was the result of ideal weather conditions, and part was accomplished by bringing new land under cultivation, particularly in the West. But, as was the case in industry, much of the expansion was due to the employment of machines that had been introduced before the war but not fully utilized. Now, with the government offering high prices for farm products and simultaneously inducting farm men into the army, the farmers were forced to resort to labor-saving machinery. For the first time such aids as the mower, the thresher, the drill, and the reaper were widely used. Without the reaper, the tremendous expansion of wheat production could not have occurred. By 1865 some 250,000 reapers were at work on Northern farms.

A powerful stimulant to the expanding economy was provided by the economic legislation enacted by the Republican party during the war. The Republicans represented, in an economic sense, the aspirations of Northern industry and agriculture, and, now that the war had removed Southern opposition to those aspirations, they proceeded to put into effect the kind of program their supporters expected. Most of the laws benefited business, an indication that the Eastern-industrial wing was acquiring an increasing ascendancy in the party.

The chief gains of the Western-agricultural wing were embodied in the Homestead Act (1862) and the Morrill Land Grant Act (1862), both measures which the West had long sought. The first provided that any citizen, or any alien who had declared his intention to become a citizen, could register claim to a quarter section of public land (160 acres), and, after giving proof that he had lived on it for five years, receive title on payment of a small fee. Although some Western migration occurred during the war, no great use was made of the act until the years immediately after its close. The Morrill Law was an answer to Western demands for federal aid for the promotion of agricultural education. By its terms each state was to receive 30,000 acres of public land for each of its congressional representatives, the proceeds from the donation to be used for education in agriculture, engineering, and military science. The measure provided the basis for the development of the so-called "land-grant" colleges and universities.

Industry scored its first gain a few days before President Buchanan left office. Congress passed the Morrill Tariff Act, which provided a moderate increase in duties, bringing the rates up to approximately what they had been before 1846. Later measures enacted in 1862 and 1864 were frankly protective. By the end of the war the average of duties was 47 per cent, the highest in the nation's history, and more than double the prewar rate. Other legislative victories for business were achieved in connection with railroads and immigration. With Southern opposition to a Northern transcontinental railroad now absent, the promoters of that project successfully revived their plans. Two laws (1862, 1864) created two Federal corporations: the Union Pacific Railroad Company, which was to build westward from Omaha, and the Central Pacific, which was to build eastward from California. The government would aid the companies by donating them public lands and advancing government loans. Although actual construction would have to wait until after the war, these measures represented internal improvements on a scale never dreamed of by the Federalists or the Whigs. Immigration from Europe fell off in the first years of the war, partly because of the unsettled conditions created by the war. The decrease, coupled with the military demands for manpower, threatened to cause a labor shortage, and President Lincoln and business leaders asked Congress for governmental encouragement of immigration. In 1864 Congress passed a contract labor law by which business was authorized to import laborers, paying the costs of their transportation, with the future wages and homesteads of the migrants being mortgaged to repay the costs. Over 700,000 immigrants entered the country during the war years, some coming in under the new law and others responding to the normal attractions of America.

Perhaps the most important measure affecting the business-financial community was the National Bank Act, enacted in 1863 and amended in 1864. Conceived partly as a long-range reform of the banking system and partly as a solution to the immediate financial needs of the government, the act created the National Banking System, which lasted without serious modification until 1913. Its architects, including Secretary of the Treasury Salmon P. Chase, thought of it as a law that would restore control over the currency to the national government. They argued that both for the military present and the economic future the country needed a uniform and standard banknote currency; at the outbreak of the war 1,500 banks chartered by twenty-nine states were empowered to issue notes. Furthermore, claimed Chase and his supporters, national supervision of the banking system would enable the government to market its bonds more economically, thus aiding the financing of the war.

The act spelled out a process by which a "banking association" (an existing state bank or a newly formed corporation) could secure a federal charter of incorporation and become a National Bank. Each association was required to possess a minimum amount of capital and to invest one third of its capital in government securities. Upon depositing the securities with the national treasury, it would receive, and could issue as banknotes, United States Treasury notes up to 90 per cent of the current value of the bonds. Various clauses in the law provided for federal supervision and inspection of the banks. When many of the state banks,

disliking the regulatory features, held aloof from the new system, Congress (in 1865) placed a tax on all state banknotes. This action forced state notes out of existence and induced many state banks to seek federal charters. By the end of the war the system numbered 11,582 National Banks that were circulating notes amounting to over $200,-000,000.

Although not all bankers saw it at first, the system operated to the profit of the financial class. As the banks received interest on the bonds and generally issued their notes based on the bonds in the form of loans, they enjoyed a double interest. Furthermore, the system as finally established benefited the creditor classes and regions; the East continued to have a banknote circulation out of proportion to its population. And while Secretary Chase, a former Democrat with Jacksonian notions of finance, believed his plan was an extension of the free-banking philosophy of the anti-Biddle Democrats, essentially the National Banking System was a return to the Federalist-Whig idea of a connection between the government and the financial community.

The Northern economic system being what it was, the task of financing the war should not have been a particularly difficult one. The resources to sustain the costs were more than adequate. That they were not adequately exploited was the fault of Chase, Congress, and the bankers. Their collective mistakes can be ascribed partly to mistaken estimates of the probable length of the war (at first everybody thought it would be ended in a year) and partly, perhaps largely, to inexperience in financing anything that was very expensive. It was hard for the American people, who had not paid any excise taxes since 1817, to grasp the facts of a war that came to cost $2,000,000 a day. Nor did anyone in authority clearly understand the relationship between the financial program of a nation at war and the economy. In modern war, governments try to finance a substantial portion of their expenses by taxation. The purpose is not to pay for the goods but to prevent inflation by siphoning off surplus purchasing power —to stabilize the price level, including the prices of materials to government. The Northern government proceeded on the assumption that the purpose of taxes was to pay for goods. Moreover, it resorted to the use of paper money, thus inflating prices and adding to the costs of the war. The United States fought the first modern war with none of the safeguards that modern governments apply to a wartime economy.

The North financed the war from three principal sources: taxation, loans, and paper money issues. From taxes, including the tariff, the government received approximately $667,000,000; loans, including treasury notes, accounted for $2,600,000,000; and $450,000,000 of paper currency was issued.

TAXATION

When the war started, the government was operating under a deficit. Democratic low-tariff policies and the lingering effects of the panic of 1857 had cut government revenues to a mere trickle. Chase, who disliked high taxes on principle and who feared their impact on popular morale, failed to recommend to Congress a program of new taxes to sustain the military machine. Assuming that the war would be of short duration, he urged the short-sighted policy of paying its costs mainly from loans. From any economic viewpoint his plan was unsound, but it was popular with Congress and the people. Not until 1862, when mounting war expenses forced the country to face realities, did Congress pass an adequate war tax bill. Then it enacted the Internal Revenue Act, which placed duties on practically all goods and most occupations. Embraced in its provisions were manufacturers' taxes, sales taxes, income taxes, stamp duties, and occu-

pational licenses. Although the bill was sweeping in nature, its levies were moderate: even with a boost in rates in 1864, the receipts from the measure totaled only a little more than $300,000,000.

Even though the government's halting program did not raise as much revenue by taxation as should have been the case, the war taxes marked a new departure in American finance. For the first time in the nation's history, the government levied (in 1861) an income tax: a duty of 3 per cent on incomes above $800. Later (in 1862 and 1865) the rates were increased to 5 per cent on incomes between $600 and $5,000, and to 10 per cent on incomes above the latter figure. Through the medium of the various war taxes, the hand of the government was coming to rest upon most individuals in the country. The United States was in the process of acquiring a national internal revenue system—in fact, a national tax system—one of the many nationalizing effects of the war.

LOANS

Although the government secured the bulk of its war income by borrowing, the process of selling bonds was hampered by certain conflicts between Secretary Chase and the banking community. The bankers thought that the government should sell bonds to them below par and let them resell the securities at a profit, and they favored long-term loans at a high interest rate. Chase opposed disposing of bonds at below par; he fought for a low interest rate; and he advocated short-term issues of indeterminate period: bonds redeemable after five but before twenty years (popularly known as the "five-twenties"). In order to finance the war, both sides had to yield something. Chase had to accept a high interest on some issues (7 and 6 per cent), he had to sell some bonds below par, and he had to concede some long-term loans (redeemable in from ten to forty years—the "ten-forties"). On the other hand, he did persuade the bankers to advance the huge sums the government required: the revenue from bonds was three times as much as from all other sources combined. Chase's most original contribution to bond selling was in seeking a broad popular subscription to government stocks. In America's previous wars, bonds had been sold only to banks and to a few wealthy investors. Through the agency of Jay Cooke, a Philadelphia banker, the Treasury launched a campaign to persuade the ordinary man (and woman) to buy a bond. By high-pressure propaganda techniques, Cooke disposed of $400,000,000 of the "five-twenties"—the first example of mass financing of a war in our history.

PAPER MONEY

The government first issued paper money, early in 1862, to meet what was considered a financial emergency. At that time, with war expenses soaring, tax receipts were small and bonds were selling slowly. The only solution seemed to be fiat or paper money. Accordingly, Congress passed the Legal Tender Act, authorizing the printing of $150,000,000 in paper currency, which soon came to be known as "greenbacks." Later issues brought the total to $450,000,-000, of which $431,000,000 was outstanding at the end of the war. These notes were made legal tender for all debts except import duties and interest on government bonds. As they bore no interest, were not supported by a specie reserve, and depended for redemption on the good faith of the government (and its ability to win the war), they have been labeled by fiscal experts as a forced loan from the people. Because of their volume and because their worth was affected by the military situation, the greenbacks fluctuated and declined in value. In 1864 a greenback dollar, in relation to a gold dollar, was worth only 39¢, and even at the close of the war its value had ad-

vanced to but 67¢. In short, the greenbacks caused an inflation of prices, which adversely affected laborers and people with fixed incomes. Not all groups in the North shared in the wartime prosperity.

The greenbacks were an easy answer to the government's needs for quick funds, but they added tremendously to the cost of the war. Objectively there was no good reason to employ them, but their issuance was a result of the inevitable political pressures that may build up in a democracy at war. They were to have, however, an enduring influence on the nation's economy. Together with the notes of the National Banks, they constituted a considerable part of the circulating money supply during the war. And so as another result of the Civil War, the country acquired a national currency.

Raising the Armed Forces

When the hostilities started, the regular army numbered only about 16,000 troops, and many of its units were scattered throughout the West. President Lincoln, in his first call for troops to repress what the government called the "rebellion," summoned 75,000 militia for three months, the usual period of service set for state troops by existing militia law. Lincoln realized that the war would be of longer duration. Confronted by a crisis, he met it with bold decision, even to the point of stretching his powers as commander in chief. Without constitutional sanction, he called for 42,000 volunteers for national service for three years and authorized an increase of 23,000 in the regular army. When Congress met in July, 1861, it legalized the President's acts, and, at his recommendation, provided for enlisting 500,000 volunteers to serve for three years. All in all, the government of the North, despite some minor bungling, adopted a sound military policy from the beginning. It acted to raise a large force (numbers were on the side of the North), and it avoided the mistake of short-term enlistments.

For a time the volunteering system served to bring out enough men to fill the armies.

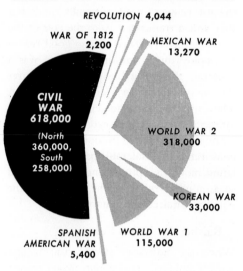

Casualties in the Civil War and Other Wars

REVOLUTION 4,044

WAR OF 1812
2,200

MEXICAN WAR
13,270

CIVIL
WAR
618,000

(North
360,000,
South
258,000)

WORLD WAR 2
318,000

KOREAN WAR
33,000

SPANISH
AMERICAN WAR
5,400

WORLD WAR 1
115,000

But after the first flush of enthusiasm had worn off, men came forward to enlist in diminishing numbers. Even the generous cash bounties held out to prospective volunteers by the federal government and by the states were insufficient lures. Finally, and with some reluctance, the government realized it would have to resort to conscription. In March, 1863, Congress enacted the first national draft law in American history (the South had employed conscription almost a year earlier). The measure provided that all able-bodied males between the ages of 20 and 45 if unmarried, between 20 and 35 if married, were liable to military service for three years. Few exemptions were permitted: only high national and state officials, preachers, and men who were the sole support of a dependant family. But it was possible to purchase exemption. A drafted man could escape service by hiring a substitute to go in his place or by paying

the government a fee of $300. These provisions were denounced as pieces of class favoritism to the upper-income groups, and eventually the cash commutation was repealed.

The law did not impose a direct draft; rather, its purpose was to spur enlistments by threatening to invoke conscription. Each state was divided into enrollment districts, and at announced intervals was assigned a quota of men to be raised. If a state, by bounties or other means, could fill the quota, it escaped the draft completely; if certain districts failed to meet their quota, a sufficient number of men were drafted to make up the difference. Some states and many districts never experienced conscription. Although the draft directly inducted only 46,-000 men, it stimulated enlistments enormously. The Federal armies increased steadily in size, reaching a maximum number in 1865. The vague statistics compiled during the war do not permit an accurate statement of the total number of men serving in the armed forces. The number of enlistments was 2,900,000, but this figure includes many who enlisted several times or served short terms. A reasonably accurate estimate is that 1,500,000 served for three years (as contrasted with 900,000 in the Confederate forces).

The casualty rate was tremendous. Indeed, if the Confederate casualties are computed in the total, in human terms the Civil War is our most costly war. The total number of deaths in the Union armies was 360,000 (in the Confederate armies 258,000). Of the Union total, approximately 110,000 were battlefield deaths: men who were killed in action or died of wounds. The remainder died of sickness or disease. The high casualty rate was due to two factors, one military and the other medical. Most military men did not understand that the weapons employed in the war—rifles and artillery with a faster rate of fire and a longer range than those used in previous wars—demanded a change in tactical thinking. With the increased firepower which armies now possessed, frontal assaults made in rigid tactical formation were becoming obsolete. Yet the generals continued to make them, with deadly results. In many battles the proportion of men killed and wounded ranged from 20 to 32 per cent. Medical knowledge and practice had improved greatly by 1861, and further progress would be registered during the war. But much remained to be discovered, particularly about the care of wounds, sanitation, and diet. Not until World War I would military medicine reach a point where fewer men died from sickness than from bullets. Doubtless the death rate in camp and hospital would have been even greater but for the work of a number of private relief organizations, the largest being the United States Sanitary Commission, which provided medical care, medical supplies, and food to the armed forces. These societies were the first instance on a large scale of organized civilian participation in a nation's war effort; they were symbols of the increasing totality of war.

To a people accustomed to a government that had hardly touched their daily lives, conscription seemed a strange and ominous thing. Opposition to the law was widespread, particularly from laborers, immigrants, and Peace Democrats. In places it erupted into violence. Demonstrators against the draft rioted in New York City for four days in 1863, killed a number of people, and held the town in their grip until subdued by troops. Some Democratic governors who supported the war (like Horatio Seymour of New York) contended that the national government had no constitutional power to conscript, and openly challenged the Lincoln administration on the issue. The government continued, however, to force men

into the army—a national army. The whole concept of state rights was being weakened by the war, in the North as well as in the South.

Wartime Politics

According to the biographer of the South's greatest general (Dr. Douglas S. Freeman), the one factor in the military situation that not even Robert E. Lee could evaluate properly was the unswerving steadfastness of purpose of Abraham Lincoln. But as the war continued, Lee came to have a picture of Lincoln as a leader endowed with immeasurable patience and persistence, and these traits in the Northern President inspired in Lee a certain fear for his cause. Lincoln possessed in ample quantity the five qualities that the historian Allan Nevins calls the conditions of statesmanship: intellectual power, moral strength, a feeling for the spirit and needs of the time, an instinctive understanding of the masses, and, in order to mold public opinion, some kind of passion—in Lincoln's case, a passion for democracy.[1]

Because he had the qualities of statesmanship, and the will to employ them, Lincoln was able to fulfill his great task—to preserve a nation. It was a more difficult task than any other American leader before or since has been called upon to meet. He had to bring the seceded states back into the Union, to conduct a bloody civil war, and to achieve a basic unity of purpose among his own divided people. Lincoln's determination that the American nation must remain unified was one of the fundamental concepts in his political philosophy. In his thinking about the Union, three ideas are apparent. One, he believed that the United States was

[1] D. S. Freeman, *R. E. Lee* (New York: Scribner's, 1935), III, p. 264; Allan Nevins, *The Statesmanship of the Civil War* (New York: Macmillan, 1953), pp. 5–9, pp. 45–6.

an organic whole, an entity that could never be artificially separated. ("Physically speaking, we cannot separate. We cannot remove our respective sections from each other, nor

idea of equality of opportunity embedded in the Declaration of Independence. ("It was that which gave promise that in due time the weights should be lifted from the shoul-

Lincoln Arriving in Washington, 1861. *On his way to Washington to be inaugurated, Lincoln was told that detectives had discovered a plot to assassinate him when he passed through Baltimore. Although skeptical of the information, he consented to abandon his published schedule and travel secretly to the capital. On arrival he was met by Congressman Elihu B. Washburn, at right, one of the few who knew of the change. Behind Lincoln are Ward H. Lamon, a self-appointed guard, and Allan Pinkerton, head of the detective agency of that name. The painting is by H. D. Stitt.* (EWING GALLOWAY)

build an impassable wall between them.") Second, he thought that America was uniquely different from other nations in that its strongest unifying bond was an idea, the

ders of all men, and that *all* should have an equal chance.") Third, he regarded the Union with reverence because it made men free in America and eventually would make them free everywhere; the United States had a mission to bring democracy by example to the world. ("We shall nobly save, or meanly lose, the last, best hope of earth.")

When Lincoln came to Washington, he was almost universally considered to be a small-time prairie politician who realized that he was unfit for his job. He strengthened this impression by his unpretentious air of humility. Actually, he was well aware of his great abilities and of his superiority over other Northern leaders. His supreme confidence in himself was demonstrated by his choice of a cabinet. The members of his official family were William H. Seward, Secretary of State; Salmon P. Chase, Secretary of the Treasury; Simon Cameron, Secretary of War, soon to be succeeded by Edwin M. Stanton; Gideon Welles, Secretary of the Navy; Edward Bates, Attorney General; Montgomery Blair, Postmaster General; and Caleb Smith, Secretary of the Interior. Representing every faction of the Republican party and every segment of Northern opinion, it was an extraordinary assemblage of advisers and a difficult set of prima donnas to manage. Three of the members, Seward, Bates, and Smith, were former Whigs; four, Chase, Cameron, Welles, and Blair, were former Democrats. Two were from slave states, Bates of Missouri and Blair of Maryland. Four, Seward, Chase, Cameron, and Bates, had been Lincoln's rivals for the nomination in 1860. The general level of ability was above average, and three of the secretaries, Seward, Chase, and Stanton, were first-rate men. Seward and Chase thought that they were abler than Lincoln and should be in his place. At the very beginning of the administration, Seward made an attempt to dominate Lincoln, failed, and became his loyal supporter. Chase never learned that the President was a bigger man than he.

Lincoln's confidence in his inner powers was revealed by his bold exercise of the war powers of his office. He had an expansive view of the role of the President in wartime. In cases where the Constitution did not stipulate who should wield certain powers, he believed that he rather than Congress should act. In order to accomplish his purposes, he was ready to violate parts of the Constitution, explaining that he would not lose the whole by being afraid to disregard a part. In this spirit he issued his proclamation of insurrection calling for troops to repress the rebellion (an act which was equivalent to a declaration of war), illegally increased the size of the regular army, and proclaimed a naval blockade of the South. It is a curious and significant fact that Lincoln and other Northern leaders, heading an established government, exhibited much more revolutionary zeal and even ruthlessness than did the new and revolutionary government they were opposing.

Among the various exercises of presidential war powers, the one that aroused the most popular criticism was the suspension of civil law in areas where resistance to the military effort seemed dangerous. Opposition to the war came from two sources: from Southern sympathizers in the Union slave states, and from the peace wing of the Democratic party. During the war there were three discernible factions among the Democrats. One was the War Democrats, who were willing to support the war and even to accept offices from the administration. After 1862, when the Republicans took to calling themselves the Union party and invited the War Democrats to join them, this group was absorbed into the dominant party and practically lost its identity. The great bulk of the Democrats preferred, however, to retain their party organization; they rendered a general support to the administration's war program but reserved the right to criticize specific acts. For purposes of classification, they may be designated as the Regular Democrats. Operating within the framework of the main party was the third faction, the Peace Democrats or, as their enemies called them, the "Copperheads."

As the strongest organized opposition to

advocated the formation of a Western confederacy, and some formed secret societies (Knights of the Golden Circle, Sons of Liberty) which allegedly engaged in treasona-

---

Lincoln's Views on Wartime Emancipation

In a public letter in 1862 to Horace Greeley of the New York *Tribune*, who had demanded an emancipation policy, Lincoln explained his subordination of the slavery issue to the larger question of the Union: "I would save the Union. I would save it the shortest way under the Constitution. . . . My paramount object in this struggle *is* to save the Union, and is *not* either to save or to destroy slavery. If I could save the Union without freeing *any* slave I would do it; and if I could save it by freeing *all* the slaves I would do it; and if I could save it by freeing some and leaving others alone I would also do that. What I do about slavery, and the colored race, I do because I believe it helps to save the Union; and what I forbear, I forbear because I do *not* believe it would help to save the Union. I shall do *less* whenever I shall believe what I am doing hurts the cause, and I shall do *more* whenever I shall believe doing more will help the cause. . . . I have here stated my purpose according to my view of *official* duty; and I intend no modification of my oft-expressed *personal* wish that all men every where could be free."

---

the war, the Peace Democrats deserve analysis. Their motivation was rooted in economic sectionalism. Centered in the Western states, they represented the old Jefferson-Jackson agrarian tradition. They feared that agriculture and the West were being subordinated to industry and the East and that state rights were going down before nationalism. Simply stated, their war policy was as follows: to call a truce in the fighting, invite the South to attend a national convention, and amend the Constitution to preserve state rights. Thus the Union would be restored and the former agrarian alliance re-established in power. Although the seceded states would never have gone along with this program, it needs to be emphasized that the Peace Democrats, in that they did not favor a division of the country, were Unionists. But there were divisions within the ranks of the Copperheads. Some of them

ble activities and constituted, to use a modern phrase, a fifth column. The precise aims of the societies never have been determined. The evidence seems to indicate that a small number of Copperheads conceived of treason but lacked the courage and ability to execute their plans.

To deal with opponents of the war, Lincoln used the weapon of military arrests. He suspended the right of habeas corpus, so that an alleged offender could be arrested and held without trial or, if tried, had to appear before a military court. At first Lincoln denied the civil process only in specified areas, but in 1862 he proclaimed that all persons who discouraged enlistments or engaged in disloyal practices would come under martial law. In all, over 13,000 persons were arrested and imprisoned for varying periods. Among those placed in custody was a Maryland secessionist leader whom Lincoln refused to release, even under a writ from Chief Justice Taney (*Ex parte Merryman*). The most prominent Copperhead in the country, Clement L. Vallandigham of Ohio, was seized by military authorities, although not at Lincoln's instigation, and later exiled to the Confederacy. (After the war, in 1866, the Supreme Court held, in *Ex parte Milligan*, that military trials in areas where the civil courts were capable of functioning were illegal.) Although the arbitrary arrests shocked many believers in civil liberty, they were essentially a part of the trend toward enforced unity that total war demands.

questions, including economic matters, they were in fundamental agreement, but they differed, and violently, on the disposition to be made of slavery. Representative leaders of the Radicals were Thaddeus Stevens of Pennsylvania, master of the party machine in the House, and Senators Charles Sumner of Massachusetts and Benjamin F. Wade of Ohio. Heading the Conservatives was President Lincoln. The Radicals wanted to seize the opportunity of the war to strike slavery down—abolish it suddenly and violently. The Conservatives, who were also antislavery, wanted to accomplish the same

THE COPPERHEAD PARTY.—IN FAVOR OF A VIGOROUS PROSECUTION OF PEACE!

An Anti-Copperhead Cartoon. *In this Civil War version of a modern political cartoon a somewhat alarmed but determined Miss Columbia faces the onslaught of the Peace Democrats or Copperheads, here depicted in their most malignant form.* (FROM *Harper's Weekly*, 1863)

There were factions too in the dominant Republican party—the Radicals and the Conservatives. The great issue that divided the Republican groups was slavery. On most

result in a different way—easily and gradually. They were temperamentally opposed to abrupt change, and they were conscious of the effects that might follow a wrenching change in race relations. They urged, therefore, a policy of gradual emancipation to be accomplished over a period of years. Lincoln made several notable although unsuccessful attempts to persuade the loyal slave states to agree to a program of compensated gradual emancipation. In short, the Radicals were determined to make the abolition of slavery an objective of the war; they would restore the Union without slavery. The Conservatives hoped to avoid turning the war into an experiment in social change; they preferred to restore the Union with slavery, but with a plan worked out for its ultimate extinction. Furthermore, in the first phase of the war Lincoln feared that the introduction of abolition as a war aim would divide Northern opinion and alienate the border slave states.

In the bitter struggle between the two factions, the Radicals won out. Time and the logic of the situation were on their side. If, as most people believed, slavery was the primary cause of the war, why should the Northern people fight and sacrifice to preserve an institution that was responsible for the war? The longer the war continued, the more certain it became that Northern opinion would demand the death of slavery. But at the beginning of the struggle, public opinion approved the Conservative position. In July, 1861, Congress adopted the Crittenden Resolution stating that the war was not being waged to interfere with the domestic institution of any state—that is, with slavery.

Nevertheless, within a year it began to be apparent that the war was affecting men's thinking about slavery, and the Radicals, gaining an ever increasing ascendancy in the party, started to whittle away at the appendages of the institution. Congress abolished slavery in the District of Columbia, with compensation to owners (April, 1862), and in the national territories (June, 1862). In the summer of 1862 the Radicals decided that Northern opinion had reached a point

where they could move against slavery in the states. In July they pushed through Congress the Confiscation Act, a measure that was in essence a bold attempt to accomplish emancipation by legislative action. The principal provisions were as follows: It declared the property of persons supporting the "rebellion" subject to forfeiture to the United States government; it declared free the slaves of persons aiding and supporting the insurrection; and it authorized the President to employ Negroes, including freed slaves, as soldiers. Although the measure was a "paper" edict so far as immediate concrete results were concerned, it marked a turning point in the war. It meant that the Republican party was coming under Radical control and that the country had come to accept emancipation as an aim of the war.

The signs were not lost on the astute master of politics in the White House. Lincoln saw that in order to achieve his larger purpose of saving the Union he would have to yield his lesser goal of preventing the sudden destruction of slavery. To preserve the nation he had to have the support of his own party and particularly of the Radicals, who were the last-ditch Unionists, the men who would never give up the war. And if a majority of the Northern people wanted slavery destroyed, as seemed the case, he could not afford to divide popular opinion by opposing their will. In July, 1862, he decided to take the leadership of the antislavery impulse away from the Radicals by putting himself at the head of it. Specifically, he prepared to issue an executive proclamation, based on his war powers as commander in chief, freeing slaves in the Confederacy. He withheld public announcement of his purpose, however, until a favorable turn in the war, when it would have a greater impact on public opinion. Although in coming to his decision Lincoln was influenced by the knowledge that emancipation would strengthen the diplomatic position of the

North with European nations, he was responding primarily to the requirements of domestic politics.

On September 22, 1862, after the battle of was under Union control, and western Virginia and southern Louisiana, which were occupied by Federal troops. Presumably these areas were omitted because they were

Lincoln and His Cabinet Reading the Emancipation Proclamation. *From left to right, sitting: Stanton, Secretary of War; Lincoln; Welles, Secretary of the Navy; Seward, Secretary of State; Bates, Attorney General. Standing: Chase, Secretary of the Treasury; Smith, Secretary of the Interior; Blair, Postmaster General.* (LIBRARY OF CONGRESS)

Antietam, the President issued his preliminary Emancipation Proclamation. In it he stated that he would issue a final document on January 1, 1863, freeing the slaves in all states that were then still in rebellion. Thus one hundred days of grace were allowed to any state or states to return to the Union. As no area in the Confederacy took advantage of his offer, Lincoln published on the first day of 1863 the final Emancipation Proclamation. This document, which is probably the most misunderstood measure in American history, declared forever free the slaves in designated areas of the Confederacy. Excepted from the edict was the whole state of Tennessee, most of which

not enemy territory and hence were not subject to the President's war powers. For a similar reason the Proclamation did not apply to the border slave states. The Proclamation freed slaves in most of the South, but it did not, in the opinion of most legal authorities and of Lincoln himself, abolish slavery as an institution. The institutional destruction of slavery would have to be accomplished, presumably, by state action or by an amendment to the Constitution.

The Emancipation Proclamation freed immediately but few slaves. Like the Confiscation Act, it would be a paper edict until it could be enforced. But its issuance announced that the war had assumed a new meaning; henceforth it was to be a war for emancipation as well as for the Union. Eventually, as Federal armies occupied large areas of the South, the Proclamation became Tennessee, Arkansas, and Louisiana. The final and inevitable action was taken early in 1865 when Congress approved the Thirteenth Amendment (ratified by the required

A Northern View of Emancipation. *This drawing originally appeared in* Harper's Weekly *and later was circulated widely as a broadside. It was, of course, a frankly Northern depiction of the significance of emancipation.* (LIBRARY OF CONGRESS)

a practical reality, and hundreds of thousands of slaves were freed by its operation. Equally important in the process of emancipation was the induction of many former slaves into the armed forces: some 186,000 served as soldiers, sailors, and laborers, thereby making a substantial contribution to the freeing of their race. Furthermore, the impulse to abolition which the Proclamation symbolized increased in intensity throughout the country, affecting even the border states. Before the end of the war slavery had been abolished in two Union slave states, Maryland and Missouri, and in three "reconstructed" or occupied Confederate states,

number of states several months after the war closed), which freed all slaves everywhere and abolished slavery as an institution.

Early in the war, and particularly after the election of 1862, in which the Republicans suffered heavy losses, the party leaders proceeded to form a broad coalition of all groups who supported the war, trying particularly to attract the War Democrats. The new organization, which was composed of a Republican core with a fringe of War Democrats, was known as the Union party. It encountered its major political test in the presidential election of 1864, which was the first national contest held in the midst of a great war. It was also one of the few occasions in the experience of democratic government, if not the only one, in which a people were offered the choice of voting to continue a war or to abandon it—and chose to keep up the fight.

Lincoln was a candidate for the Republican, or Union, nomination for a second term. He faced the opposition, however, of many of the Radicals, who remembered his tardy conversion to emancipation and who feared he would favor a mild and forgiving policy for the South at the conclusion of the war. But no rival aspirant with sufficient strength to challenge Lincoln appeared. The President was enormously popular with the masses (already the Father Abraham legend was taking form), and he had the support of most of the state machines. Secretary Chase offered himself, but his candidacy aroused little response; he withdrew from the race and eventually from the cabinet. When the Union convention met in June, it nominated Lincoln, with the chilly assent of the Radicals, and, for Vice President, Andrew Johnson of Tennessee, a War Democrat who had refused to follow his state into secession.

As the summer months wore on, all the signs indicated defeat for Lincoln. War weariness had at last settled on the Northern people: it was widely felt that the war was hopeless, that the South could not be conquered. Curiously enough, this mood of depression came at a time when the South no longer had the resources to win a military decision, when the North had only to continue fighting to finally triumph. Lincoln himself believed that he would be beaten. At this juncture some of the Radical leaders decided the moment was propitious to get rid of Lincoln as a candidate. Their plan was to persuade him to withdraw with the argument he would drag the party down to defeat; if he would not withdraw, they were ready to force him off the ticket. Then the Union national committee or another con-

vention could nominate an uncompromising Radical.

Before the Radicals could launch their scheme, rapidly changing events changed the political picture and forced a recasting of strategy. In August the Democratic convention met and nominated George B. McClellan, former Union general and an object of hatred to all good Radicals. The Peace faction got a plank into the platform denouncing the war as a failure and calling for a truce to be followed by an invitation to the South to enter a national convention. As the truce would be instituted without requiring Southern attendance as a condition, this was tantamount to recognizing the independence of the Confederacy. Although McClellan repudiated the plank, the Democrats stood before the country as the peace party. The Democratic convention gave the Radicals pause. Lincoln was bad enough, but McClellan and a peace platform were worse. They prepared to close ranks behind Lincoln as the lesser of two evils. At the same time several Northern military victories, particularly the capture of Atlanta, Georgia, early in September, rejuvenated Northern morale and gave promise of Republican success in November.

The outcome of the election was a smashing electoral triumph for Lincoln, who had 212 votes to McClellan's 21 and who carried every state except Kentucky, New Jersey, and Delaware. Lincoln's popular majority, however, was uncomfortably small, 2,213,-000 to 1,805,000 or an advantage of only 400,000. A slight shift of popular votes in some of the more populous states would have changed the result. But even if McClellan had won and had decided to comply with the peace plank (an unlikely possibility), the war would still have turned out as it did. He would not have taken office until March, 1865, and by that time the Union armies had pounded the Confederacy to defeat.

->>>->>>->>>->>-<<<-<<<-<<<-<<<

BIBLIOGRAPHY

THE LITERATURE on the Civil War is so enormous that only basic works or works dealing with particularly significant aspects of the war can be cited. The best present general treatment of the entire subject is J. G. Randall, *The Civil War and Reconstruction* (1937). C. R. Fish, *The American Civil War* (1937), is more analytical than factual. Useful introductions are G. F. Milton, *Conflict: The American Civil War* (1941), and N. W. Stephenson, *Abraham Lincoln and the Union* (1918). A valuable survey of the wartime North is E. D. Fite, *Social and Economic Conditions in the North During the Civil War* (1910). For a colorful review of Northern leaders, see Gamaliel Bradford, *Union Portraits* (1916). An impressionistic sketch of Washington during the war is Margaret Leech, *Reveille in Washington* (1941).

The best one-volume life of Lincoln is B. P. Thomas, *Abraham Lincoln* (1952). There are two outstanding multi-volume biographies: Carl Sandburg, *Abraham Lincoln: The War Years* (4 vols., 1939), and J. G. Randall, *Lincoln the President* (4 vols., 1945–1955), the last volume with R. N. Current. Sandburg distilled the essence of his work into one volume, *Abraham Lincoln* (1954), and Current did the same for Randall in *Mr. Lincoln* (1957). Two special Lincoln studies worthy of note are R. S. Harper, *Lincoln and the Press* (1951), and R. V. Bruce, *Lincoln and the Tools of War* (1956), describing Lincoln's influence on weapons adoptions.

Northern politics in all its aspects are treated in the Lincoln biographies and in T. H. Williams, *Lincoln and the Radicals* (1941); B. J. Hendrick, *Lincoln's War Cabinet* (1946); W. B. Hesseltine, *Lincoln and the War Governors* (1948); H. J. Carman and R. J. Luthin, *Lincoln and the Patronage*

(1943); Wood Gray, *The Hidden Civil War* (1942), a study of the Peace Democrats; and E. C. Kirkland, *Peacemakers of 1864* (1927), and W. F. Zornow, *Lincoln and the Party Divided* (1954), the last two dealing with the election of 1864.

A host of monographs explore special aspects of the war. The best treatment of the common soldier is B. I. Wiley, *The Life of Billy Yank* (1952), although on this subject F. A. Shannon, *Organization and Administration of the Union Army* (2 vols., 1928) is still useful. Other good studies are G. W. Adams, *Doctors in Blue* (1952); E. W. Lonn, *Desertion during the Civil War* (1928); W. B. Hesseltine, *Civil War Prisons* (1930); and W. Q. Maxwell, *Lincoln's Fifth Wheel* (1956), the Sanitary Commission. Economic developments are treated in A. M. Davis, *The Origin of the National Banking System* (1910); E. P. Oberholtzer, *Jay Cooke: Financier of the Civil War* (2 vols., 1907); W. C. Mitchell, *A History of the Greenbacks* (1903); and D. C. Barrett, *The Greenbacks and the Resumption of Specie Payments, 1862–1879* (1931).

Adequate studies of the role of the railroads are G. E. Turner, *Victory Rode the Rails* (1953), and Thomas Weber, *The Northern Railroads in the Civil War* (1952). The emerging influence of the press receives attention in B. A. Weisberger, *Reporters for the Union* (1953); Louis Starr, *Bohemian Brigade* (1954); J. C. Andrews, *The North Reports the Civil War* (1955); and Emmet Crozier, *Yankee Reporters* (1956). Benjamin Quarles relates the story of the wartime Negro in *The Negro in the Civil War* (1953), and D. T. Cornish the use of Negro troops in *The Sable Arm* (1956).

Despite the mass of books on the war, there are few good biographies of Northern civil leaders. Chase receives brilliant treatment in T. G. and M. R. Belden, *So Fell the Angels* (1956), but the student is urged to look into the Chase diaries in David Donald, ed., *Inside Lincoln's Cabinet* (1954). R. S. West, Jr., *Gideon Welles* (1943), is satisfactory, but again the student should examine a source, *The Diary of Gideon Welles* (3 vols., 1911). Two other notable diaries are Allan Nevins, ed., *The Diary of George Templeton Strong* (4 vols., 1952), by a New York businessman and Republican, and W. H. Russell, *My Diary North and South* (1863), by the famous English war correspondent (shortened version edited by Fletcher Pratt, 1954). An outstanding biography of a Radical Republican is R. N. Current, *Old Thad Stevens* (1942).

CHAPTER 29

The Civil War: The South

WHEN THE WAR STARTED, people in both South and North were gaily confident that the struggle would be of short duration. One big battle would end it all, men said, and it would be over by the time the cotton crop—or the corn—was in. In large part these cocksure attitudes were the product of a conviction that the other side was of inferior stock and could not fight. Although a sense of superiority marked both sections, it was perhaps more prevalent in the swashbuckling society of the South, where the martial tradition was stronger than in the North. Trumpeted one Southern newspaper: "They may raise plenty of men, men who prefer enlisting to starvation, scurvy fellows from the back slums of cities. . . . But these recruits are not soldiers, least of all the soldiers to meet the hot-blooded, thoroughbred, impetuous men of the South."

Thoughtful Southerners did not indulge in this kind of gasconade. They were aware of their section's inferiority in human and economic resources, and they realized the importance of the North's superior production potential. Northern material superiority might be overcome, they believed, by the skill of Southern military leadership or by the bravery of Southern arms. But even if the Southern human resources could not make up for Northern material advantages, there was still an almost certain guarantee of Confederate victory: Europe would intervene in the war on the side of the South. England and France had to have Southern cotton, and they would force the North to recognize the Confederacy. Even the most realistic Southerners were convinced of the inevitability of foreign intervention. Diplomacy was a main hope of the South, and diplomacy became, therefore, a major element in Southern military planning.

The Diplomacy of South and North

The diplomatic policies of both sides might be summarized by saying that the objectives of the South were positive and those of the

North negative. The South hoped to secure foreign recognition and to persuade England and France to break the blockade and force the United States to mediate. The North, believing that it could handle the South if unhampered by outside interference, labored to prevent recognition and intervention. In determining the factors that influenced the final outcome of the diplomatic struggle, some attention has to be given to the diplomatic personnel of the contestants. The United States, as an established nation, had the advantage of a going foreign service, while the Confederacy had to create one from the top down. Broadly speaking, the Northern diplomatic corps displayed more skill and efficiency at all levels than did its rival.

Judah P. Benjamin, who occupied the Confederate foreign office for the greater part of the war, was a clever and intelligent man, but he lacked strong convictions and confined most of his energy to administrative routine. Seward, on the other hand, after some initial blunders, learned his job well and went on to become one of the outstanding American Secretaries of State. In the key diplomatic post at London, the North was represented by a distinguished minister, Charles Francis Adams, who seemed to have inherited the diplomatic abilities of his father (John Quincy Adams) and grandfather (John Adams). He easily outshone the bucolic Confederate, James M. Mason. Perhaps the ablest Southern diplomat abroad was John Slidell, the wily czar of Louisiana politics, who as minister to France was familiarly at home in the corrupt court of the Emperor Napoleon III. In general, the Confederate diplomats in Europe were afflicted with a parochial viewpoint resulting from the South's cultural isolation. They seemed to have little appreciation of the magnitude of the antislavery sentiment in European society.

In the story of the relationship of Europe to the Civil War, the key nations are Great Britain and France. They were the great powers of Europe, and they were the powers who felt that their interests might be affected by the outcome of the war. In the other nations people followed the course of the war and sympathized with one side or the other, but their governments had nothing at stake in the struggle. England and France, who had acted together against Russia in the Crimean War, were united by an *entente*, one of the understandings of which was that questions concerning the United States fell within the sphere of British influence. Napoleon III, therefore, would not act in American affairs without the concurrence of Britain. The third power of Europe, Russia, was, like the United States, an up-and-coming nation which thought that its aspirations were being blocked by England. Feeling a community of interest with democratic America, autocratic Russia openly expressed sympathy for the Northern cause. In 1863, when war threatened to break out between Russia and England over Poland, Russia, in order to get her navy into position to attack British commerce, dispatched two fleets to American waters. One turned up at New York and the other at San Francisco, thereby creating a legend that they had come to support the United States if England and France should attempt to break the blockade.

At the beginning of the war the sympathies of the ruling classes of England and France were with the Confederacy. The landed aristocracy of Britain and most members of the manufacturing and commercial classes hoped for a Southern victory. Although their sentiments were partly motivated by a feeling of kinship for the planter aristocrats of the South, they thought as they did primarily because they disliked the ideal which the United States represented. European liberals, pressing for an extended franchise, had always pointed to the United

States as the world's most successful example of democracy—and conservatives had found this argument hard to answer. But now the great experiment was falling apart, and its failure promised to discredit democracy everywhere. Moreover, the dominant classes, and their governments, uneasily aware of the growing strength of the United States, saw in an independent Confederacy the promise of future triumphs in power politics. A divided America would mean that no single powerful nation existed in the Western hemisphere, no nation strong enough to prevent European governments from fishing in hemispheric political waters. One or the other of the American republics, and maybe both, would have to seek the diplomatic support of England or France, and would thus become a part of the European political system. Even English liberals, who were antislavery, looked kindly on the South. Puzzled by the position of the Northern government, which avowedly was waging war to restore the Union but not to destroy slavery, they concluded that the South was fighting for a cause dear to nineteenth-century liberalism: the right of self-determination.

But English and French opinion was not unanimously in favor of the South. In both countries some members of the upper classes supported the North. English liberals of a certain type, men like John Bright and Richard Cobden—usually manufacturers who were closely associated with the laboring masses—sensed that the war would have to become one to destroy slavery. They saw it as a struggle between free and slave labor, and they presented it in these terms to their followers. It was an argument that appealed to the politically conscious but unenfranchised workers, particularly those in Britain. They expressed their sympathy for the Northern cause frequently and unmistakably—in mass meetings, in resolutions, and, through the medium of Bright and other leaders, in Parliament itself. After the issuance of the Emancipation Proclamation, they intensified their activities, feeling that Lincoln had justified their faith in his purposes.

The influence on the English government of the workers' attitudes is hard to determine. Lacking direct political power, labor could not exert direct pressure on the government; it is doubtful that labor opinion was a major factor in deterring Britain from intervening in the American struggle. Rather, the wage earners rendered their most valuable service to Northern diplomacy by refusing to join in another kind of pressure: the demand that England break the blockade to obtain Southern cotton. In the minds of Southern leaders, cotton was their ace diplomatic weapon. Their analysis was as follows: the textile industry was basic to the economies of England and France, who depended on the South for the bulk of their cotton supply; deprived of Southern cotton, these countries would face economic collapse. Therefore they would have to intervene on the side of the Confederacy.

But this diplomacy based on King Cotton never worked as its champions envisioned. In 1861 English manufacturers had a surplus supply of cotton on hand (in the previous year 2,580,700 bales had been imported from the United States). The immediate effect of the blockade was to enable the textile operators to dispose of their remaining finished goods at high prices. Thereafter the supply became increasingly short (only 72,000 bales were imported from America in 1862), and many mills were forced to close. Both England and France, however, managed to avoid a complete shutdown of their textile industries by importing supplies from new sources, notably Egypt and India. Most important of all, the workers, who were among the people most directly affected by the shortage, did not clamor to have the blockade broken. Even the 500,000 English textile workers thrown out of jobs continued to support the North.

No European nation extended diplomatic recognition to the Confederacy. Nor did England and France, although several times they considered offering mediation to the American contestants, ever move to intervene in the war. A number of factors in addition to the strength of worker opinion and the weakness of cotton diplomacy restrained them. The wartime dependence of Britain on Northern wheat has previously been cited. The Emancipation Proclamation had the effect of causing opinion all over Europe to shift in favor of the North. Great Britain, as the world's leading naval power, had long relied on the weapon of blockade in war; she hesitated to interfere with the Northern blockade for fear the precedent might be used against her in the future. Moreover, England was making money out of the war. Because of sales to the belligerents, profits boomed in the textile, linen, munitions, and other industries. Confederate commerce destroyers were driving the American merchant marine from the seas, and England inherited the carrying trade of her chief maritime rival. Perhaps the principal factor preventing intervention was the military situation in America. Neither England nor France could afford to intervene unless the Confederacy seemed on the point of winning the war; otherwise they would have to reckon with the possibility of war with the North. But the South was never able to develop a prospect of certain victory. The most auspicious period for Southern hopes was in the last half of 1862, when military triumph seemed assured. But Union successes at the battles of Antietam and Stone's River checked any possibility of intervention. After the summer of 1863, there was small chance that England and France would risk anything for the side that was obviously losing—the South.

Immediately after the outbreak of hostilities, Great Britain issued a proclamation of neutrality attributing to the Confederacy the status of a belligerent. France and other nations followed suit. Although the Northern government, which officially insisted that the war was not a war but a domestic insurrection, furiously resented England's action, the British government had proceeded in conformity with accepted rules of neutrality and in accordance with the realities of the situation. The United States was fighting a *war*, a fact which Lincoln himself had recognized in his proclamation establishing a blockade. Nevertheless, the North was convinced that Britain did not intend to be truly neutral and that recognition of belligerency would be followed by recognition of Confederate independence. Thereafter during the course of the war, three areas of friction between England and the United States developed, creating three crises or near-crises, any one of which could have resulted in war between the two countries.

The first crisis, and the most dangerous one—the so-called Trent affair—occurred late in 1861. The Confederate commissioners to England and France, Mason and Slidell, had slipped through the then ineffective blockade to Havana, Cuba, where they boarded an English steamer, the *Trent*, for England. Hovering in Cuban waters was an American frigate, the *San Jacinto*, commanded by Captain Charles Wilkes, an impetuous officer who knew that the Southern diplomats were on the *Trent*. Acting without authorization from his government, Wilkes stopped the British vessel, arrested the commissioners, and bore them off in triumph to Boston. The Northern public, hungry for some success to cheer about, acclaimed him a national hero, but his rash act had placed the United States in a delicate diplomatic situation. Great Britain, reacting with ponderous offended national pride, denounced the seizure as a violation of in-

LOUIS NAPOLEON. "Ah! Ah! mon cher JONATAN, you got vipped at de Bull Run, eh?"

JOHN BULL. "Yes, 'pon my soul, you're used up now. Better give up."

JONATHAN. "Why, you Foreign Jackasses, I haven't BEGUN TO FIGHT yet!"

Jonathan Tells Off England and France. *This* Harper's Weekly *cartoon reflects the profound Northern resentment at England's and France's supposed sympathy for the South. The two are taunting the United States, personified by Brother Jonathan, with the Union defeat at Bull Run in 1861. But he lets them know what the situation is. Jonathan became a personification of the American nation in the Revolution, and Uncle Sam appeared in the War of 1812. Both were always portrayed as tall, muscular men, symbolizing the common American type. Eventually Uncle Sam supplanted Jonathan.* (FROM Harper's Weekly, 1861)

ternational law and of the rights of a neutral. The British government drafted a demand for the release of the prisoners, reparation, and an apology. As originally phrased, the demand was almost an ultimatum, to which the United States could hardly have acceded. Before it was dispatched, however, more pacifistic counsels prevailed, and the wording was altered to allow the Northern government several loopholes of escape. Lincoln and Seward, well aware that war with England would be suicidal, spun out the negotiations until American opinion had cooled off, then returned the commissioners with an indirect apology. Mason and Slidell were far more valuable to their country in a Northern prison than they ever were later in Europe. As captives they almost involved the North in war. As diplomats they accomplished little. Mason failed to win recognition for the Confederacy, was not even received officially by the government, and in 1863 departed disgustedly for France. In the latter country Slidell hobnobbed with the Emperor and other notables, but he too failed to gain recognition for the Confederacy.

The second episode—the case of the Confederate commerce destroyers—generated much friction but did not assume the proportions of a crisis. In a move to weaken the blockade, the Confederate government decided to build or buy fast ships of war to prey on Northern ocean commerce. The hope was that the North would detach ships from the blockade to hunt the destroyers. (Instead, the North took the loss of its merchant marine and maintained the blockade.) Lacking the resources to construct the vessels, the Confederacy contracted to have them built and equipped in English shipyards. Six destroyers, of which the most famous were the *Alabama*, the *Florida*, and the *Shenandoah*, were built or purchased in England, and sailed from English ports to harry Northern commerce. The British government knew what was going on, being regularly and indignantly informed by Minister Adams, but winked at the practice. Before 1863 the United States, not daring to press England too hard, had to limit its protests to charges that construction of the raiders was in violation of the laws of neutrality. These protests formed the basis, after the war, for damage claims which the United States served on Great Britain.

The third incident—the affair of the Laird rams—could have developed into a crisis, but did not because the English government suddenly decided to mend its ways. In 1863 the Confederacy placed an order with the Laird shipyards for two powerful ironclads, not commerce raiders, but formidable fighting warships with which the Confederacy meant to destroy the blockade. The loss of its ocean trade the North could absorb, but the blockade was another matter. In addition, with the course of the war definitely turning against the South, the United States could now speak with a more imperious voice. Adams was instructed to inform the English government that if the rams, or any other ships destined for the Confederacy, left port—then there would be danger of war. Adams delivered his message, but even before it was received the government had acted to detain the rams and to prevent the Confederacy from obtaining any other ships. Belatedly England realized that for a naval power she had been following a stupid policy. The infringements of neutrality which she had tolerated might create precedents that would rise to plague her in future wars in which she was a participant. Hastily she attempted to set things right by conceding she had been wrong.

If Napoleon III had had his way, France and England would have intervened in the American war at an early date. Unable to persuade Britain to act, he had to content himself with expressing sympathy for the Southern cause and permitting the Confederates to order commerce destroyers from French shipyards. The Emperor's primary motive for desiring an independent South was his ambition to establish French colonial power in the Western hemisphere: a divided America could not block his plans. He seized the opportunity of the war to set up a French-dominated empire in Mexico.

Mexico, before the war, had incurred a debt of $80 million to English, French, and Spanish bankers, an obligation that the government seemed unable or unwilling to honor. The creditors appealed to their governments to bring pressure on Mexico for payment. With the enthusiastic connivance of Napoleon, the three powers agreed to dispatch a combined land and naval force to Mexico. Late in 1861 the allies occupied several coastal towns, whereupon the Mexican government accepted terms that were satisfactory to England and Spain, and these countries withdrew their troops in April, 1862. Napoleon, however, had come to Mexico to stay. He marched his army on Mexico City and, with the support of one native political faction, proclaimed a new government (1863). At the head of his puppet state he installed a puppet emperor, an Austrian archduke, Maximilian.

Napoleon's Mexican venture was a clear violation of the Monroe Doctrine, perhaps the greatest one that has ever occurred. The United States viewed it in such a light, but for fear of provoking France into recognizing the Confederacy could do no more than register a protest. Only after the Civil War was ended did the United States feel strong enough to pressure France out of Mexico. The Confederacy, on the other hand, for obvious reasons welcomed the new Mexican regime. But, significantly, Southern opinion tended to condemn France for transgressing the Monroe Doctrine. All of which raises an interesting question: if the South had won its independence, which side would have owned the famous doctrine—or enforced it?

The Mexican imbroglio was an ominous harbinger of what would have happened in the future if the greatest power in North America had been "Balkanized."

The Confederate Government

Although the first seven Southern states to secede had left the Union as individual sovereignties, they had no intention of maintaining separate political existences. It was understood from the first that they would come together in a common confederation to which, they hoped, the states of the Upper South would eventually adhere. Accordingly, representatives of the seceded states assembled at Montgomery, Alabama, early in February, 1861, to create a Southern nation. (Actually, six states were represented at Montgomery. The delegates from Texas, the last of the seven to secede, did not arrive in time to participate in the proceedings; they did, however, affix their names to the work of the convention.)

The state-makers at Montgomery performed three important functions. They formulated a provisional constitution, which a month later they proclaimed as the permanent constitution of the Confederate States of America. They chose a provisional President and Vice President, who were approved as permanent officers in November, 1861. And they served as a provisional legislature until the permanent government came into being in February, 1862. Montgomery, "the cradle of the Confederacy," was the capital of the new nation until after Virginia seceded. Then the government moved to Richmond, partly out of deference to Virginia, partly because Richmond was one of the few Southern cities large enough to house the government.

There was significance in the name of the Southern government: it was a confederation of sovereign states, not a federation of united ones. State sovereignty was expressly recognized in the constitution. Interestingly enough, proposals to insert the right of a state to secede failed of adoption; the right was implied but never mentioned. The framers of the document could not quite bring themselves to recognize a device that might destroy their handiwork. Various clauses in the constitution reflected the state-rights orientation of the framers and the experience of the South in the old Union. The powers delegated to the central government were fewer than in the Constitution of the United States, and the reserved powers of the states were greater. Internal improvements were almost prohibited, and a protective tariff could not be levied. The principle of the concurrent voice (the power of a minority to check the majority) was sprinkled throughout the constitution. A two-thirds vote of both houses of the national legislature was necessary to admit a new state, and a similar ratio was required to enact an important appropriation bill. Any three states could demand a convention of all the states to amend the constitution, and the convention had to consider amendments proposed by three states. In structure, the Confederate government was an almost exact duplicate of the model which Southerners had just discarded. There was an executive branch, headed by a President and Vice President; a legislative branch, consisting of a two-house Congress; and a national court system.

As President the Montgomery convention elected Jefferson Davis of Mississippi, and as Vice President, Alexander H. Stephens of Georgia. Davis had been a firm but not extreme advocate of Southern rights in the former Union; he was a moderate but not an extreme secessionist. Stephens had been the leading Southern cooperator, the chief among those who had contended that secession was unnecessary; his selection was a gesture designed to induce the cooperators to support the secession adventure. In choosing their chieftains, the men at Montgomery

passed over such veteran and violent secession advocates as William L. Yancey of Alabama and Robert Barnwell Rhett of South Carolina. They were almost pathetically eager to demonstrate to their own people and to the world that the Confederacy represented conservatism.

Jefferson Davis embodied the spirit of the nation he had been called to lead. His family, which was of Southern yeoman stock, had moved from Kentucky, where he was born, to the new lush cotton lands of Mississippi, where they became rich planters almost overnight. Davis was a first-generation aristocrat. So also were most of the members of his government. The Confederacy was run by the cotton nabobs of the newer "Western" South, not by the old aristocracy of the seaboard states. Whereas Lincoln's task was to preserve a nation, Davis's was to make one. Lincoln succeeded; Davis failed. He failed partly because he lacked some of the qualities of statesmanship. He possessed integrity and a fine intelligence. Indeed, his mind was his greatest pride; he was sensitively proud of the correctness of his opinions and would support even a wrong decision to the last. He loved to dispute theoretical points to win a logical victory, and to write long, lecturing letters to people who had dared to differ with him. Patience and tact he had—until he was opposed—and then he tended to lose control of his feelings. Criticism and contradiction he regarded as almost a kind of crime. Naturally, he made many enemies, needless ones. His state papers and speeches were scholarly, logical, coldly intellectual. Nobody ever quoted them. Because he had no passion, not even for the South, he could not touch the hearts of his people.

But Davis failed primarily because he did not realize in two important respects what his task was. First, because of his military background—he was a graduate of West Point, had served in the regular army and as a volunteer officer in the Mexican War, and had been Secretary of War—he fancied himself as a military expert. He would rather have been a general than the head of state.

manded that the South act with ruthless efficiency, Davis assumed that it should observe every constitutional punctilio. Lincoln, without clear constitutional sanction, sus-

---

An English View of Jefferson Davis

William Howard Russell, war correspondent for the *Times* of London, visited the Confederate President at Montgomery, Alabama, in 1861. Although the Britisher had some reservations about Davis, he was favorably impressed with his freedom from the almost universal American habit of chewing tobacco: "I had an opportunity of observing the President very closely: he did not impress me as favorably as I had expected, though he is certainly a very different looking man from Mr. Lincoln. He is like a gentleman—has a slight, light figure, little exceeding middle height, and holds himself erect and straight. He was dressed in a rustic suit of slate-colored stuff, with a black silk handkerchief round his neck; his manner is plain, and rather reserved and drastic; his head is well formed, with a fine full forehead, square and high, covered with innumerable fine lines and wrinkles, features regular, though the cheekbones are too high, and the jaws too hollow to be handsome; the lips are thin, flexible, and curved, the chin square, well defined; the nose very regular, with wide nostrils; and the eyes deep-set, large and full—one seems nearly blind, and is partly covered with a film, owing to excruciating attacks of neuralgia and tic. Wonderful to relate, he does not chew, and is neat and clean-looking, with hair trimmed, and boots brushed."

His image of himself being what it was, he concerned himself overly much with military affairs. The point emphasized here is not that he interfered with his generals (his influence on strategy will be discussed in the next chapter), but that he spent too much time on routine items, on what one observer called "little trash." He was a good administrator who loved to administer; he was his own Secretary of War but he rarely rose above the secretarial level. Second, Davis failed to grasp the all-important fact that the Confederacy was not an established, recognized nation but a revolution. He proceeded on the basis that the Confederacy was a legal and permanent organization that could fight a war in the normal fashion of older countries. Whereas the situation de-

pended habeas corpus; Davis asked his Congress to let him suspend and received only partial permission. Watching the workings of the government, one shrewd official (R. G. H. Kean) wrote: "All the revolutionary vigor is with the enemy. . . . With us timidity—hair splitting. . . ."

The Confederate cabinet was a body of shifting personnel displaying, at best, only average ability. Davis selected the first incumbents almost entirely on a geographical basis: he wanted to include a representative from each state except his own Mississippi. This practice resulted, in some cases, in a man's being named to one post when he was better fitted for another that had to be allotted to an individual whose state had to have a member. The first Secretary of State was Robert Toombs of Georgia (the only revolutionary in the group), who did not have a diplomatic temperament but was a financial expert. He should have been Secretary of the Treasury, but, to take care of South Carolina, Davis bestowed this office on Christopher G. Memminger, a Charleston banker. Heading the War Department was Leroy P. Walker of Alabama, a lawyer who did not think there would be war and who supposedly had promised his constituents to wipe up with his handkerchief every drop of blood spilled. The Naval Department went to Florida's Stephen R. Mallory, who in the United States Senate had specialized in naval affairs and who would

which was not big enough for his talents. The Postmaster General was John H. Reagan of Texas, who ran his department with quiet efficiency. Of the original Cabinet, only Walker represented the old planter aristocracy; the rest, like Davis, were *nouveaux riches*. Three of them, Benjamin, Memminger, and Mallory, were foreign-born first-generation Americans.

The personnel of the cabinet changed rapidly and frequently. There were three Secretaries of State, two Secretaries of the Treasury, four Attorney Generals, and five Secretaries of War. Benjamin showed up in three different positions. Mallory and Reagan held their posts throughout the war,

Jefferson Davis and His Cabinet. *From left to right, sitting: Mallory, Secretary of the Navy; Benjamin, Attorney General; Davis; Reagan, Postmaster General; Memminger, Secretary of the Treasury. Standing: Walker, Secretary of War; General Lee; Vice-President Stephens; Toombs, Secretary of State.* (LIBRARY OF CONGRESS)

prove to be an able administrator. Judah P. Benjamin of Louisiana, one of the best lawyers in the country, received the relatively unimportant post of Attorney General,

and Memminger his until near the end. Toombs soon resigned, and was succeeded by R. M. T. Hunter of Virginia and then by Benjamin, who had the longest tenure in the office. Walker shortly left the War Department; his four successors, one of whom was Benjamin, were, in effect, Davis's clerks. Not a man in the cabinet ever dared to oppose the will of the President.

War Economics and Finance

In contrast to the burgeoning prosperity in the wartime North, the South in the war years underwent shortages, suffering, and sacrifice. The South, despite a frantic expansion of industrial facilities, was unable to supply the needs of its armies and civilian population. The economic experience of the Confederacy affords a prime example of the almost insuperable obstacles confronting a dominantly agricultural society in modern war. The South lacked factories, machines, industrialists who knew how to organize production, and skilled laborers. It lacked

also the resources to create new wealth. Indeed, the resources it possessed at the beginning of the conflict were largely consumed by the demands of the military machine. Such familiar examples of Southern sacrifice as church bells being cast into cannon, carpets being made into clothes, and newspapers being printed on the back of wallpaper show a nation living on its accumulated resources. Moreover, the Confederacy could not realize any revenue on its agricultural resources. The conditions of war and the blockade cut off almost at one stroke the sale of Southern exports abroad. Economically the South had to retire inward upon itself, as culturally it had retired long before the war.

The men seeking to devise measures for financing the Confederacy's war effort, Memminger and the Congressional leaders,

had to reckon with a number of hard facts. A national revenue system had to be created to collect money from a people unaccustomed to bearing large tax burdens. Southern banking houses, except in New Orleans, were fewer and smaller than those of the North. Because excess capital in the South was usually invested in slaves and land, the sum of liquid assets on deposit in banks or in individual hands was relatively small. The only specie possessed by the government was that seized in United States mints located in the South (amounting to about $1,000,000). In an attempt to secure more specie, the government dispatched an army column into New Mexico, but this force, after some initial success, was expelled. Obliged to operate against such economic handicaps, the Treasury Department quite naturally experienced perplexing difficulties as it sought to provide for the sinews of war. The Confederacy drew its war revenues from the same three sources as the North: taxation, loans, and paper money.

TAXATION

The Confederate Congress, like its counterpart in the North, showed some reluctance to enact rigorous wartime taxes. In 1861 the legislators provided for a direct tax on property to be levied through the medium of the states. If a state preferred, it could meet its quota by paying as a state. Most of the states, instead of taxing their people, assumed the tax, which they paid by issuing bonds or their own notes. In short, the first tax measure failed to really tax, and it produced a disappointing return of only $18 million. Moving more boldly in 1863, Congress passed an internal revenue tax bill which included license levies and an income tax. A unique feature of the act was a provision bearing on agriculture alone: "the tax in kind." Every farmer and planter had to

The Impact of War on the South. *Because most of the fighting in the Civil War occurred in the South, that section suffered widespread destruction of its physical resources. At the left is the demolished railroad depot in Atlanta, and at the right are the ruins of Richmond as seen across the James.* (LIBRARY OF CONGRESS)

contribute one tenth of his produce to the government. Although Congress later raised the rates in the internal revenue measure and enacted other taxes, the revenue realized from taxation was relatively small. The exact amount cannot be calculated because of problems in fixing the value of the farm products received by the government. But it has been estimated the Confederacy raised only about 1 per cent of its total income in taxes.

LOANS

The bond record of the Confederacy was little better than its tax program. Eventually the government issued bonds in such large amounts that the people suspected its ability to redeem them. Early in 1861 Congress authorized the Treasury to borrow $15 million in 8-per-cent bonds. The loan was readily subscribed, most of it by banks which paid in specie. Nearly two fifths of the amount was taken up in New Orleans, the South's only large banking center, which fell into Federal hands in 1862. Later in 1861 Congress authorized a $100 million loan to be paid in specie, paper money, or produce. The expectation was that the bulk of the proceeds would be in the form of products —"the loan in kind." The loan was subscribed, partly in paper currency and mostly in produce or pledges of produce. But many of the pledges were not redeemed or the promised products were destroyed by the enemy. It is doubtful if the government realized more than $23 million from the produce loan. Nevertheless, the principle was followed in later bond issues, with subscribers being permitted to deposit commodities with the government in exchange for bonds. The Confederacy also attempted to borrow money in Europe by pledging cotton stored in the South for future delivery. Its most notable venture in foreign finance was the famous Erlanger loan, which was supposed to net the Confederacy $15 million. Actually, Erlanger, a French financier, was interested in conducting a huge cotton speculation. The Confederate government received only $2.5 million from the loan.

PAPER MONEY

Partly because ready revenue was needed and partly because it seemed the easiest way to finance the war, the government resorted in 1861 to the issuance of paper money and treasury notes. Once it started, it could not stop. In the words of a sympathetic Southern historian (E. M. Coulter), the Confederacy with its printing-press currency was like "the drunkard who could not stay away from his drink."[1] By 1864 the staggering total of one billion dollars had been issued. In addition, states and cities issued their own notes. The inevitable result of this process was to depreciate the value of the money. Federal greenbacks, brought into the South by the invading armies, circulated at a higher premium than Confederate notes: one greenback was worth four Confederate dollars. Prices skyrocketed to astronomical heights. Some sample figures for 1863–1864 are as follows: flour, $300 a barrel; broadcloth, $125 a yard; chickens, $35 a pair; beef, $5 a pound; men's shoes, $125 a pair. Many people, particularly those who lived in towns or who had fixed incomes, could not pay these prices. They did without, and lost some of their will to victory. Undoubtedly, the inflated prices contributed to the alarming drop in popular morale which occurred in the last year and a half of the war. An official of the War Department in Richmond (J. B. Jones) wrote in his diary in 1864: "I cannot afford to have more than an ounce of meat daily for each member of my

[1] E. M. Coulter, *The Confederate States of America* (Baton Rouge: Louisiana State University Press, 1950), p. 153.

family of six. . . . The old cat goes staggering about from debility. . . . We see neither rats nor mice about the premises now. This is famine."

armies was not being increased. Most ominous of all, the twelve-months men, the veterans, showed little inclination to re-enlist. As the year 1862 opened, the Confed-

---

Hard Times in Richmond

J. B. Jones, a clerk in the Confederate War Department, kept a diary that is one of the primary Confederate sources: *A Rebel War Clerk's Diary* (1866). In this entry for 1863 he details the privations of people on fixed incomes who could not afford the inflated wartime prices:

"February 11th.—Some idea may be formed of the scarcity of food in this city from the fact that, while my youngest daughter was in the kitchen today, a young rat came out of its hole and seemed to beg for something to eat; she held out some bread, which it ate from her hand, and seemed grateful. Several others soon appeared and were as tame as kittens. Perhaps we shall have to eat them!

"18th.—One or two of the regiments of General Lee's army were in the city last night. The men were pale and haggard. They have but a quarter of a pound of meat per day. But meat has been ordered from Atlanta. I hope it is abundant there. All the necessaries of life in the city are still going up higher in price. Butter, three dollars per pound; beef, one dollar; bacon, a dollar and a quarter; sausage meat, one dollar; and even liver is selling at fifty cents per pound."

Raising the Armed Forces

Like the United States, the Confederate States first raised its armies by calling for volunteers. In 1861 Congress enacted several measures authorizing the acceptance of over 500,000 troops. Although the number coming forward did not reach this figure, the initial response was enthusiastic, and the government was convinced that volunteering would answer the manpower needs of the armed forces. However, most of the men had joined up under a provision fixing the enlistment period at twelve months; their terms would be finished in the spring of 1862. By the latter part of 1861 volunteering had dropped off badly. In the face of an expected Federal offensive, the size of the

eracy was threatened by a manpower crisis.

The government met the situation boldly. At Davis's recommendation, Congress in April enacted the First Conscription Act, which declared that all able-bodied white males between the ages of 18 and 35 were liable to military service for three years. To keep the veterans in service, the measure stated that men already in the army were to continue for three years from the date of their enlistment; that is, they got credit for one year but had to serve two more. A man who was drafted could escape his summons if he furnished a substitute to go in his place. The prices for substitutes eventually went up to as high as $10,000 in Confederate currency. The purpose of this provision was to exempt men in charge of agricultural and industrial production, but to people who could not afford substitutes it seemed like special privilege to the rich. It was repealed late in 1863 after arousing bitter class discontent.

The first draft act and later measures provided for other exemptions, mostly on an occupational basis. The government realized that conscription had to be selective, that some men had to be left on the home front to perform the functions of production. It erred in excusing men who were not doing any vital services and in permitting too many group exemptions. Several times Davis begged Congress to give a particular group a deferred status but to permit the executive branch to draft individuals from within it (which is the modern practice). The legislators, jealous of presidential power, refused. Among the groups exempted were Confederate and state officials and clerks, employees in certain industries, hospital workers, printers, teachers with twenty or more pupils, one druggist in each drugstore, doctors, editors, and factory owners. Governors at their discretion could defer officers of their militia. The various exemptions aroused wide protest, not because they were so numerous, but because people not included felt they had been discriminated against. The provision most bitterly criticized was that exempting one white man on each plantation with twenty or more slaves. Angrily denounced as the "twenty-nigger law," it caused ordinary men to say, "It's a rich man's war but a poor man's fight."

In September, 1862, Congress adopted a second conscription measure, which raised the upper age limit to 45. At the end of the year, an estimated 500,000 soldiers were in the Confederate armies. Thereafter conscription provided fewer and fewer men, and the armed forces steadily decreased in size. Federal armies seized large areas in the South, depriving the Confederacy of the manpower in the occupied regions. Military reverses in the summer of 1863 convinced many Southerners that the war was lost, causing a kind of passive resistance to the draft as men sought to avoid it by hiding in the hills and woods; desertions began to increase. The governors of certain states, notably Georgia, South Carolina, and North Carolina, who had previously contended that conscription was illegal, intensified their opposition, throwing every possible impediment in the way of execution of the draft. (Governor Zebulon M. Vance of North Carolina certified 16,000 state troops as exempt from conscription.) At the close of 1863, 465,000 men were carried on the army rolls, but probably not more than 230,000 were actually present for duty.

As 1864 opened, the situation was critical. In a desperate move, Congress lowered the age limits for drafted men to 17 and raised them to 50, reaching out, it was said, toward the cradle and the grave. Few men were obtained. War weariness and the certainty of defeat were making their influence felt. In 1864–1865 there were 100,000 desertions. An observant Confederate diarist (Mrs. Mary B. Chesnut) wrote in her journal in March, 1865: "I am sure our army is silently dispersing. Men are moving the wrong way, all the time. They slip by with no songs and no shouts now. They have given the thing up." On the army rolls, 200,000 names were carried, but at the end probably only 100,000 were actually in service. In a frantic final attempt to raise men, Congress in 1865 authorized the drafting of 300,000 slaves. The war ended before this incongruous experiment could be tried out.

With all of their defects, the Confederate conscription laws drew into the armed forces a substantial portion of the available manpower. As with the Union armies, the exact number of men in service has to be estimated from vague data. The best calculation is that 900,000 served for three years, which is a high figure for a total white population of 6,000,000. The total Southern casualties were 258,000, of which 95,000 were battlefield deaths.

differences that emerged did not take the form of party issues: the Confederacy did not last long enough for distinct parties to develop. The divisions were, however,

---

The Hatreds of War

Inevitably the war aroused resentment and even hatred. These emotions were particularly strong in the South, which experienced more directly than the North the impact of war, and were particularly expressed by Southern women, who had to fight the war at home. A Georgia girl wrote in her journal: "If all the words of hatred in every language under heaven were lumped together into one huge epithet of detestation, they could not tell how I hate Yankees. . . . Now that they have invaded our country and killed so many of our men and desecrated so many homes, I can't believe that when Christ said, 'Love your enemies,' He meant Yankees. Of course I don't want their souls to be lost, for that would be wicked, but as they are not being punished in this world, I don't see how else they are going to get their deserts."

Confederate Politics

In overwhelming numbers the Southern people were ready to support the war for Southern independence. The only important organized opposition to the war came from the inhabitants of the mountain areas, whose population was less than 10 per cent of the Southern total. One center of resistance was the extreme western part of Virginia, which was occupied by Federal troops in 1861 and became two years later the state of West Virginia. The strongest Union-sympathizing region in the limits of the Confederacy was the mountainous eastern third of Tennessee, the section known as East Tennessee. Here supporters of the national cause carried on a kind of guerrilla warfare against the occupying Confederate forces until liberated by the Federals late in 1863.

Southerners were united in their desire to sustain the war, but they were bitterly divided on how it should be conducted. The

largely political in origin and nature, but, unlike those in established countries, they were not subjected to the restraint and discipline that organized parties impose on political life. Some of the quarrels almost tore the government apart. The Confederacy would have been better off if it had had political parties.

In part, the disagreements were an inevitable reflection of the conditions of Southern culture. Most upper-class Southerners, the men who held the important civil and military posts, were proud, touchy, imperious individuals—much like Davis. As masters of a subject race, they were accustomed to giving orders, but not to being opposed or crossed. They took offense, deep personal offense, easily, and they did not submit readily to discipline, even to that exerted by their own government. Undoubtedly, much of the animosity against Davis is to be explained by his personality and the personalities of the men with whom he had to deal.

Davis made enemies of powerful men who nursed their hatred of him for years after the war was over. Something of Davis's inability to conciliate and manage people is

Creole Critic of Davis. *P. G. T. Beauregard, victor of Fort Sumter and Manassas, was the Confederacy's first hero. The dramatic Creole from south Louisiana was also one of the first Confederate leaders to become embroiled in a feud with Davis. (The roster of Davis's enemies eventually came to include many of the most important men in the South.) Beauregard and Davis quarreled constantly about military matters during the war, and continued their dispute long after its end. When Davis died in 1889, Beauregard refused to be a pallbearer at the funeral.* (L. C. HANDY STUDIOS)

seen in his relations with Congress. He vetoed thirty-eight bills, and Congress repassed thirty-seven of them. (By contrast, Lincoln vetoed only three measures.)

In part, the divisions were an inevitable product of the differences of opinion that operate in a popular government. Some people believed that Davis and his advisers were

making bad mistakes in conducting the war; others thought that certain laws of Congress were unsound or bore adversely on their interests. Naturally, Davis was blamed for military reverses. There was a great deal of criticism of both the President and Congress for holding back news of defeats from the public. Farmers resented the tax in kind and the "twenty-nigger law." Another measure that stirred tremendous criticism was the Impressment Act, which authorized the government to buy goods at prices which it set. Enacted to protect the government from the effects of its own currency, it was bitterly denounced and widely evaded.

But the great dividing force, the creator of explosive dissent, was, ironically enough, the principle of state rights—the foundation stone of Southern political philosophy —for whose conservation and consecration the South had left the old Union. State rights had become a cult with Southerners, to the point that they reacted against any sort of central control, even to controls necessary to win the war. If there was an organized faction of opposition to the government, it was that group of quixotic men who counted Vice President Stephens as their leader and who are usually known as the state-rights party. They had one simple, basic idea. They believed first in state sovereignty and then in the Confederacy. They wanted the Confederacy to win its independence, but they would not agree to sacrificing one iota of state sovereignty to achieve that goal. If victory had to be gained at the expense of state rights, they preferred defeat. Their psychology is best revealed in the words of Stephens. Addressing the Georgia legislature in a speech that blasted the administration for attempting to institute a centralized tyranny, he warned his hearers against the siren appeal of "independence first and liberty afterward." The two must stand together, he said, "and if such be our fate, let them and us all go down together in a common ruin. Without liberty, I would not turn upon my heel for independence." Continuing, he warned against the argument that a strong Southern government was preferable to a strong Northern one: "I would not turn upon my heel to choose between masters. I was not born to acknowledge a master from either the North or South."

The state-righters, standing for independence for its own sake, fought every attempt of the government to impose centralized controls, the same kind of controls to which the Northern people, with some exceptions, were submitting in order to win the war. They concentrated their fire against two powers that the central government sought to exercise: the suspension of habeas corpus, and conscription. In addition, they charged that the Davis administration was neglecting or refusing opportunities to conclude a negotiated peace with the North.

Davis realized that opposition to the war in such disaffected areas as East Tennessee could be repressed only by martial law. Always properly legal, he always went to Congress when he judged habeas corpus should be suspended, and asked for authority to dispense with the writ. The most he could wring from the legislators was permission to suspend it for a limited time or in a limited area. A bill giving him general authorization to invoke martial law was defeated. Even the bobtailed suspension which Davis secured aroused the ire of the state-righters. They denounced it as a violation of the constitution, and Stephens charged that the purpose back of the martial arrests, and behind conscription, was to establish a dictatorship.

The state-rights opposition to conscription was even more violent than to military law, and, because state authorities could interpose their authority against it, more dangerous. Recalcitrant governors like Joseph Brown of Georgia and Zebulon M. Vance of North Carolina, contending that the central government had no right to draft troops, tried in every way to obstruct the enforcement of conscription. Their chief weapon was certifying state militia troops as exempt. In the spring of 1862 an estimated 100,000 men throughout the South were held in state service. In Georgia in 1864 more men between 18 and 45 were at home than had gone into the army since 1861. When Atlanta fell to the Federals in the autumn of 1864, Brown furloughed his state troops home and refused a request from the War Department for their services. With the Confederacy tottering to destruction, he informed Richmond that the militia was "ready to defend the state against unsurpations of power as well as invasion of the enemy," and that he would not relinquish men who were the state's "only remaining protection against the encroachments of centralized power."

The idea of a negotiated peace fascinated the state-righters, especially Vice President Stephens. They never made it clear whether they were thinking of a settlement based on the return of the South to the Union or on independence. As early as 1863 they were urging the central government to seek a peace based on recognition of state sovereignty and the right of each state to control its domestic institutions—which implied a restored Union. At other times they proposed negotiations based on the independence of the Confederacy. Stephens and his friends on several occasions tried to induce the Georgia legislature to take the lead in getting other states to bring pressure on Richmond to make a peace offer. As late as February, 1865, Governor Brown favored action by Georgia and two other states to demand a national convention to amend the constitution by appointing a commander in chief in place of the President. Such a move would have meant, in effect, the deposition of Davis, and presumably would have been

608

The Beginning of the Civil War. *The war began on April 12, 1861, when Confederate forces in Charleston under General Beauregard opened fire on Fort Sumter. During the attack hundreds of excited Charlestonians crowded the rooftops to observe the spectacle. This contemporary print depicts the scene with essential accuracy. The fort, with its barracks afire, is in the center of the harbor. Off the entrance are the ships of the relief expedition, which made no attempt to enter.* (FROM *Harper's Weekly,* 1861)

followed by a peace approach to Lincoln. After studying the activities of the state-righters, one historian (H. J. Pearce, Jr.) concluded: "Despite fine words and elastic phrases couched in glittering generalities, it is plain enough that the advocates of peace were preparing the Southern mind for a peace without victory and for a very probable reunion with the North, with just so much guarantee of state sovereignty and control over 'domestic institutions' as could be wrung from the Lincoln government."

[2] H. J. Pearce, Jr., *Benjamin H. Hill* (Chicago University of Chicago Press, 1928), pp. 93–4

Historians have assigned several causes to the South's defeat in the war. They have pointed to its economic inferiority, to the collapse of its transportation system, to the breakdown of its financial arrangements. Many favor the view that the Confederacy failed because it was founded on a principle, state rights, that made failure inevitable. A confederation of sovereignties, they contend, cannot fight a modern war, cannot mobilize or direct the forces of modern war.

But wars are lost and won for many reasons. Scholars are, perhaps, too prone to explain outcomes in terms of economics and politics: the historical imperatives that seem to make the result predestined. They forget that wars are fought by humans and are often determined by human actions on the battlefields. The factories and farms of the North, writes one commentator (Bruce Catton), "were not going to appear on the firing line, and it was on the firing line that this affair must finally be settled. Up there, under the muzzles of the guns, there would be living men, as self-centered and as short-sighted and as careless of historical imperatives as any men that ever lived, and in the end it was all going to be up to them."[3] It is to the battles that we now turn to discover the ultimate cause of Southern defeat.

[3] Bruce Catton, *Glory Road* (New York: Doubleday, 1952), pp. 261–2.

➤➤➤·➤➤➤·➤➤➤·➤➤⟨⟨⟨·⟨⟨⟨·⟨⟨⟨·⟨⟨⟨

BIBLIOGRAPHY

THERE ARE good chapters on the South in the cited works of Randall and Fish. There are also a number of excellent general histories of the Confederacy. An older account that emphasizes financial and economic matters is J. C. Schwab, *The Confederate States of America* (1901). N. W. Stephenson, *The Day of the Confederacy* (1919), is a brief introduction. Among the later books are R. S. Henry, *The Story of the Confederacy* (1957), emphasizing the military side; E. M. Coulter, *The Confederate States of America* (1950), which almost ignores the military for other aspects; Clement Eaton, *A History of the Southern Confederacy* (1954), balanced although relatively brief; and two vivid volumes by Clifford Dowdey: *Experiment in Rebellion* (1946) and *The Land They Fought For* (1955). Realistic sketches of some representative Southern leaders appear in Gamaliel Bradford, *Confederate Portraits* (1914). In *The Road to Appomattox* (1956), B. I. Wiley analyzes shrewdly the factors that led to Confederate defeat.

Excellent accounts of the top leadership of the Confederacy are B. J. Hendrick, *Statesmen of the Lost Cause* (1939), and R. W. Patrick, *Jefferson Davis and His Cabinet* (1944). Frank Vandiver dissects the Confederate command system in *Rebel Brass* (1956). In addition to the biographies of Davis previously cited, see R. M. McElroy, *Jefferson Davis* (2 vols., 1937). Two Cabinet members have received satisfactory biographical treatment: R. D. Meade, *Judah P. Benjamin* (1943), and J. T. Durkin, *Stephen R. Mallory* (1954). Dissensions in the Confederacy are treated in F. L. Owsley, *State Rights in the Confederacy* (1925), and L. B. Hill, *Joseph E. Brown* (1939).

The attempt of the South to adjust its economy to war is perceptively described in C. W. Ramsdell, *Behind the Lines in the Southern Confederacy* (1944). The best account of monetary matters is R. C. Todd, *Confederate Finance* (1954), and equally authoritative is R. C. Black, *The Railroads of the Confederacy* (1952). C. H. Wesley contends that the breakdown of the railroads was a major cause of Confederate failure in *Collapse of the Confederacy* (1922). In *Ploughshares Into Swords* (1952), Frank Vandiver describes the Confederate effort to establish arms factories. An interesting account of the widespread use of substitutes is M. E. Massey, *Ersatz in the Confederacy* (1952).

Basic for the raising of the armies is A. B. Moore, *Conscription and Conflict in the Confederacy* (1924). The role of the common soldier receives ample attention in B. I. Wiley, *The Life of Johnny Reb* (1943). See also by Wiley: *Southern Negroes, 1861–1865* (1938) and *The Plain People of the Confederacy* (1943). Special aspects of the Southern war effort are treated in G. L. Tatum, *Disloyalty in the Confederacy* (1934); F. B. Simkins and J. W. Patton, *Women of the Confederacy* (1936); and H. H. Cunningham, *Doctors in Gray* (1958).

For the relation of Europe to the Civil War, see E. D. Adams, *Great Britain and the American Civil War* (2 vols., 1925; reprint, 1957), and Donaldson Jordan and E. J. Pratt, *Europe and the American Civil War* (1931). Northern diplomacy is treated in Bancroft's life of Seward previously cited, in C. F. Adams, Jr., *Charles Francis Adams* (1900), and in Jay Monaghan, *Diplomat in Carpet Slippers* (1945), which perhaps exaggerates Lincoln's influence. A specialized study is B. P. Thomas, *Russo-American Relations, 1815–1867* (1930). The standard work on Confederate diplomacy and basic for an understanding of the whole diplomatic story is F. L. Owsley, *King Cotton Diplomacy* (1931). L. M. Sears, *John Slidell* (1925), is a biography of a Southern diplomat.

To get the full flavor of the wartime South the student should examine the following diaries: J. B. Jones, *A Rebel War Clerk's Diary* (2 vols., 1935), edited by Howard Swiggett; Mary B. Chesnut, *A Diary From Dixie* (1949), edited by B. A. Williams; and R. G. H. Kean, *Inside the Confederate Government* (1957), edited by Edward Younger.

CHAPTER 30

The Civil War: The Battles

THE STUDY OF WAR has its own nomenclature. Three terms that are of basic importance are policy, strategy, and tactics. *Policy* is concerned with the purpose for which a war is fought. In a democracy, it is determined by the civil branch of the government, which decides when, against whom, and for what objective the nation will undertake war. The civil government also generally determines the number of men and the amount of matériel available to the military branch. *Strategy*, most narrowly defined, is the art of command. The commander of the nation's army, or armies, takes the men and supplies available to him, and he plans and directs operations so as to achieve his government's policy. In the nineteenth century, commanders were usually occupied with theater strategy (for a specified geographic area) or with battlefield strategy (for a particular engagement). Only rarely in the Civil War was a commander charged with the task of devising plans for the war as a whole, with what today is called "global strategy." Because strategy is designed to implement policy, the civil government in a democracy participates in forming it, at least in its broad outlines. *Tactics* is the arrangement and direction of troops in the presence of the enemy as battle is joined.

The policy of the Northern government was to restore the Union by force. Therefore the strategy had to be offensive. To achieve the purpose of the war, Northern armies would have to invade the South, defeat Confederate armies, occupy key points and large areas, and convince the Southern people that the Confederate cause was hopeless. The policy of the Southern government was to establish the independence of the Confederacy by force. To achieve its purpose, the government decided on a defensive strategy—holding as much territory as possible against Northern attacks. A strategy of defense seemed to be the most logical implementation of the South's policy, and in part it was forced on the Confederacy by the nature of Northern strategy. But the fact that the South wished to be let alone and had no aggressive designs on the North was not sufficient reason to adopt a purely defensive strategy. With equal logic and with more effect, the South might have demonstrated its capacity to win independence by employing a partially offensive strategy—by winning victories on Northern soil.

Northern and Southern Strategy

At the outset of the war, neither side had ready a previously formed plan of grand strategy. Strategic designs were worked out as the conflict developed, in the light of what the men in the high commands learned about the military situation. From the beginning, geography exercised a determining influence on the strategic planning of both contestants, affecting particularly the military thinking of the North, which had to invade and occupy the South. The geography of the South dictated that the war would have to be fought in three theaters. The Appalachian Mountain barrier, stretching from Maryland to Georgia, prevented either government from conducting unified operations east of the Mississippi River. The area east of the mountains became the Eastern theater, and the region between the mountains and the Mississippi constituted the Western theater. Beyond the river, in the states of Arkansas, Louisiana, and Texas, was the Trans-Mississippi theater. If the waters off the Southern coast from which the North maintained its naval blockade are also counted among the fighting fronts, the war was fought in four theaters.

In the Eastern theater most of the fighting took place in Virginia. The principal objective of Federal strategy on this front was to capture Richmond, the Confederate capital, and defeat the Confederate army defending it. Operations in Virginia were largely con-

ditioned by the nature of the terrain and the proximity of the rival capitals to each other. Between Washington and Richmond the marching distance was only about 130 miles. The obvious route for an invading Northern army to take extended from Washington straight down through northern Virginia. The Federals would have a short line of communications to guard, but they would have to cross several large rivers, notably the Rappahannock, which offered admirable defensive positions to the Confederates. Farther to the west, beyond the Blue Ridge Mountains, lay the Shenandoah Valley (usually called in Civil War literature simply the Valley), which ran in a general north-south direction. The Valley was an important source of food supplies to the Confederate army, but, more important, it was an alternative or secondary route between the capitals. Either side could use it as an invasion road or as a means of deceiving the other into thinking that a main thrust was about to fall from this quarter instead of farther east. The Confederates were notably successful in utilizing the Valley route to give the impression they intended to threaten Washington. Elsewhere in the Eastern theater, the Federals seized islands off the coast of the Carolinas from which to maintain the blockade or launch commando-type raids against Southern coastal communications, stabbed at the fringes of Florida, and launched a sustained although unsuccessful sea attack against Charleston.

In the vast Western theater the first objective of Northern strategy was to seize control of the line of the Mississippi River from Kentucky to the Gulf of Mexico, thus isolating the Confederate states west of the river. To achieve their goal, the Federals moved land and sea forces on the Mississippi, and conducted operations parallel to it, particularly on the Cumberland and Tennessee rivers, thereby flanking the Confederates out of their positions on the Mississippi. By the summer of 1863 the Federals had secured the Mississippi, and they then set out to attain their second strategic objective, which was to grasp the line of the Tennessee River. This stream in its 792-mile course rises in East Tennessee, flows southwest to Chattanooga, swings in a broad curve through northern Alabama, re-enters Tennessee, and runs north to join the Ohio. It presented an inviting avenue of invasion straight into the heart of the Confederacy. The key point on the Tennessee was Chattanooga, which because of its location was a gateway to the Lower South. If the Federals could occupy it, they would have a base from which to strike into Alabama or Georgia, thus cutting the Confederacy in two again. This aim was accomplished in 1864 when General Sherman moved from Chattanooga across Georgia and into the Carolinas in the great march that gutted the last resources of the Confederacy.

The Trans-Mississippi theater was a backwater of the conflict waged on the other fronts. Neither side committed heavy resources in this area. Advancing from Missouri, the Federals occupied approximately the northern half of Arkansas. In 1862 they seized New Orleans and held it and the extreme southern part of Louisiana for the rest of the war. Several ambitious plans were considered to move from New Orleans up the line of the Red River to Shreveport and from there into Texas. But the Federal high command was never able to supply enough men to execute these projects, and the one substantial offensive that was launched on the Red was turned back by the Confederates. After the Federals seized the Mississippi line in 1863, however, it was not particularly important to them to occupy the Trans-Mississippi region. By holding the Mississippi and by keeping forces in Arkansas and Louisiana, they effectively neutralized the entire theater and sealed it off from the main part of the Confederacy.

Confederate strategy, partly by choice and partly from necessity, was largely concerned with defensive measures to repel Northern offensives. The Confederate high command, which was mostly President Davis, decided not only to stand on the defensive but to defend all of the Confederacy, to meet every threatened attack. It adopted what has been called a dispersed defensive. As previously indicated, the South might have demonstrated to the North that it could not be conquered by undertaking early in the war a smashing offensive. Or, if it chose to await attack, it could have shortened its lines to hold the most defensible areas or those containing important resources. Of course, Davis, in scattering his forces over a wide circumference, was moved by practical political considerations. To abandon any part of the South might seem like a confession of weakness, might depress popular morale. But the President seemed to think primarily in defensive terms; he had almost a fixation for holding places, most of which turned out to be traps for the garrisons captured in them. On several occasions Confederate armies did go over to the offensive, did invade Northern soil. These thrusts failed, partly because they were not made in sufficient strength; in each case the attacking Southern army had to face a larger Federal force. The troops that might have tipped the balance were guarding places at home.

But it would be unfair to criticize Davis and other Confederate leaders for acting on a strategy of defense. They were the products of their culture and could not have acted otherwise. The greatest student of the art of war (the German, Clausewitz) has said that a nation will fight a war that resembles its social system. The Confederacy was based on state rights—the principle of localism—and it fought a state-rights war. Just as it was difficult for Southern political leaders to think in terms of centralism, it was hard for Confederate military directors to think in terms of a central plan of strategy or a centralized command system. It is significant that the one Confederate general who advocated massive military concentration and the abandonment of places was P. G. T. Beauregard of Louisiana, who was a Creole and the product of a French culture.

The Command Systems of North and South

The Union, as it embarked on its first great military experience and the first of the modern wars, did not have a modern command system. Indeed, in the modern sense of the phrase, the nation did not have any kind of command system. The administration of the small peacetime army was performed by the general in chief (the ranking officer of general grade) and the heads of the various bureaus and departments in the War Department: the adjutant general, the quartermaster general, and others. Although this organization was loosely referred to as "the staff of the army", or even "the general staff," it bore small if any resemblance to a modern general staff. It did not hold joint meetings or discuss common problems. No section of the staff was charged with the functions of studying strategy or formulating war plans. Its work was completely technical and routine, and each bureau head went pretty much his own way.

At the head of the organization was the general in chief, Winfield Scott, veteran of the War of 1812 and the Mexican War. Scott was 75 years old in 1861, and in such infirm health that he could barely walk. He was one of two officers in the whole service who had ever commanded troops in numbers large enough to be called an army. The other was John E. Wool, who was two years older than Scott. Besides Scott and Wool, not an officer in the North, or the South, had directed the evolutions of as large a unit as a brigade. The largest single army

that most of the younger officers had ever seen was Scott's force (or Taylor's) of 14,-000 in the Mexican War. It is a commentary on the American military system that when the Federal government assembled 30,000 troops at Washington in the summer of 1861, this was the largest army yet to appear in America.

The supreme director of the military organization was the President, the commander in chief of all the armed forces of the nation. The Northern President had been a civilian all his life; he had had no military education and no military experience except for a brief militia interlude. Yet Abraham Lincoln became a great war President, a great commander in chief. As a war director he was superior to Davis, who was a trained soldier. Lincoln illustrates the truth of Clausewitz's dictum that an acquaintance with military affairs is not the principal qualification for a director of war but that a superior mind and strength of character are better qualifications. By the power of his mind, Lincoln became a fine strategist, often showing keener strategic insight than his generals. He recognized that numbers and matériel were on his side, and immediately he moved to mobilize the maximum strength of Northern resources. He urged his generals to keep up a constant pressure on the whole strategic line of the Confederacy until a weak spot was found—and a breakthrough could be made. At an early date he realized that the proper objective of his armies was the destruction of the Confederate armies and not the occupation of Southern territory. During the first three years of the war, Lincoln performed many of the functions that in a modern command system would be done by the chief of the general staff or the joint chiefs of staff. He formulated policy, devised strategic plans, and even directed tactical movements. Some of his decisions were wise, some were wrong. But the general effect of his so-called "interfering" with the military machine was fortunate for the North. Both he and Davis have been criticized for interfering with army movements, as they had every constitutional right to do. The vital point, however, is the purpose for which they intervened. If a war director is an intelligent man and interferes to implement a sound strategy, the results will be generally good. Most of Lincoln's interferences were designed to make his generals execute a sound offensive strategy. Davis should not be criticized for interfering but for interfering to make a faulty defensive strategy more defensive.

Much of Lincoln's active direction of strategy occurred in the first years of the war before an efficient command system was devised. At the beginning, he was inclined to take the advice of General Scott. The old general, however, was unable to adjust his thinking to the requirements of mass war. Asked to present a plan of overall strategy, he came up with a scheme to blockade the South from the sea and from the line of the Mississippi River, isolating her from the outside world and gradually squeezing her into submission by economic and psychological pressure: the so-called "anaconda plan." Lincoln rejected the proposal because it would take too long to execute and because it was based on the one-idea or one-weapon principle of strategy. Scott retired from service on November 1, 1861, and to his place as general in chief Lincoln moved young George B. McClellan, who was also the commander of the Federal field army in the East, the Army of the Potomac. McClellan, who would demonstrate fatal shortcomings as a field general, did not possess the abilities to formulate strategy for all theaters of the war. The one grand strategic design he submitted was defective because it envisioned operations in only one theater, his own, and because it made places instead of enemy armies his objective. When McClellan took the field in March, 1862,

Lincoln removed him as general in chief, and did not appoint another officer to the post until July. During the interim, Lincoln, advised by Secretary of War Stanton and the Army Board (made up of the heads of the War Department bureaus), acted as his own general in chief. In July Lincoln designated General Henry W. Halleck to direct the armies. Halleck was the foremost American student of the art of war, and he had won in the West an undeserved reputation as a successful general. Lincoln intended that Halleck should be a real general in chief, that he should actually control operations. But Halleck, after a promising start, refused to take responsibility. He cast himself in the role of an adviser instead of a maker of decisions. Again Lincoln was forced to take up the function of forming and directing strategy, a task which he performed until March, 1864, when finally the nation achieved a modern command system.

In the system arrived at in 1864, Ulysses S. Grant, who had emerged as the North's greatest general, was named general in chief. Charged with directing the movements of all Union armies, Grant, because he disliked the political atmosphere of Washington, established his headquarters with the Army of the Potomac but did not technically become commander of that army. As director of the armies, Grant proved to be the man for whom Lincoln had been searching. He possessed in superb degree the ability to think of the war in overall terms and to devise strategy for the war as a whole. Because Lincoln trusted Grant, he gave the general a relatively free hand. Grant, however, always submitted the broad outlines of his plans to the President for approval before putting them in motion. Under the new arrangement, Halleck became "chief of staff," a post in which he acted as a channel of communication between Lincoln and Grant and between Grant and the departmental commanders. For Halleck, the ideal

office soldier, this was the ideal assignment. He read and briefed reports and orders for the President and for Grant, and lifted an immense administrative burden from both. The 1864 system, with a commander in chief to form the general strategy, a general in chief to give it specific shape, and a chief of staff to coordinate information, gave the United States a modern command arrangement. With the possible exception of the Prussian General Staff, it was the most efficient system then in existence.

Lincoln's active command role underlines one of the most important changes occurring in modern warfare: the emergence of the civilian in strategic planning. As war became more technological and total, strategy became a problem of directing the whole resources of a nation. It was too vast a problem for any one set of leaders, especially for the military, and civilian participation in the direction of war began and, once begun, inevitably became greater. As one example, the Northern government, in order to organize its military railroad system, had to call on the services of civilian experts. The most dramatic example of civilian intervention in military affairs in the Civil War was the Committee on the Conduct of the War, a joint investigative committee of both houses of Congress and the most powerful agency which the legislative branch has ever created to secure for itself a voice in formulating war policies. Established in December, 1861, under the chairmanship of Senator Benjamin F. Wade of Ohio and dominated by the Radical Republicans, it became the spearhead of the Radical attack on Lincoln's war program.

Although its ostensible purpose was to inquire into the causes of past defeats, the Committee devoted its major energies to efforts to control the military machine, trying particularly to force Lincoln to give the important commands to generals having Radical political ideas. The Radicals sensed that many of the Northern generals were not animated by a driving, ruthless desire for victory. They were right but for the wrong reasons. The generals in the first years of the war were influenced by the eighteenth-century concept of war as a kind of game—as chessboard maneuvers conducted in leisurely fashion and without heavy casualties. The Radicals ascribed their hesitancy to a secret sympathy for slavery, which the professionals were supposed to have imbibed at West Point. The generals favored by the Committee—most of them incompetent amateurs—would have been no improvement, but the spirit represented by the Committee helped to infuse a hard, relentless impulse into the conduct of the war. Henceforth in war, no general could assume, as McClellan did, that he could prosecute his operations as a purely military exercise with no relation to political realities.

It would be possible to summarize Southern command arrangements by saying that they consisted mainly of President Davis and that the Confederacy failed to achieve a modern command system. Early in 1862 Davis assigned General Robert E. Lee to duty at Richmond, where, "under the direction of the President," he was "charged" with the conduct of the Confederate armies. Despite the fine words, this meant only that Lee, who had a brilliant military mind, was to act as Davis's adviser, furnishing counsel when called on by the President. After serv-

The North's Greatest General. [OPPOSITE] *One observer of Ulysses S. Grant said: "He habitually wears an expression as if he had determined to drive his head through a brick wall, and was about to do it." Of average height and small stature, slouchy in dress and manner, Grant did not look like a great general, but he was, as C. F. Adams, Jr., noted, the kind of man that all would instinctively turn to in a moment of crisis.* (LIBRARY OF CONGRESS)

ing a few months, Lee went to the field, and Davis did not appoint another adviser until February, 1864. Then he selected Braxton Bragg, whom he had been forced to remove from field command after Bragg was defeated in the West. Bragg had real strategic ability, but he understood his position and restricted his function to providing technical advice. In February, 1865, the Confederate Congress, in a move directed at Davis, created the position of general in chief, which was intended for Lee. Davis, who realized the animus behind the act, named Lee to the post but took care to announce that legally he was still commander in chief. Lee accepted the job on the basis offered by the President: as a loyal subordinate instead of as the dictator some people wanted him to be. The war ended before the new command experiment could be fully tested. It is doubtful whether Lee, burdened with the command of a field army, could have formulated and directed strategy for other armies in other theaters. Preoccupied as he was with the war in his native Virginia, he might not have been able to adjust his strategic thinking to the problems of "global" strategy.

The Opening Battles: 1861

The year 1861 witnessed several small battles that accomplished large results and one big battle that had no important outcome. The small engagements occurred in Missouri and in western Virginia, the mountainous region that shortly would become the state of West Virginia. In Missouri the contending forces were headed on the one hand by Governor Claiborne Jackson and other state officials, who wanted to take the state out of the Union, and on the other by Captain (later General) Nathaniel Lyon, commanding a small regular army force at St. Louis, and Frank Blair, Jr., Republican and Unionist leader. Jackson had at his disposal those units of the state militia with Confed-

erate sympathies, and Lyon had his regulars and a number of "home-guard" outfits, which were volunteer militia loyal to Blair. Acting with quick vigor, Lyon chased the governor and his followers out of the state capital. At this point the United States and Confederate States governments, recognizing the importance of Missouri, began to send troops into the state. The command of the Northern forces was entrusted to the incompetent hands of John C. Frémont, the Republican party's first presidential candidate. Lyon, who was made of better stuff, led his column into southern Missouri, where he was defeated, and killed, by a superior Confederate force at the battle of Wilson's Creek (August 10). He had, however, seriously blunted the striking power of the Confederates, and Frémont was able to hold most of the state. For the rest of the war, the fighting in Missouri would consist mainly of guerrilla action, which often seemed to have no relation to the main conflict. The clashes of 1861 were small in the number of men engaged, but they held Missouri in the Union. If the Confederates had secured the state, lying as it did on the flank of Illinois and the Northwest, the results for the North could have been dangerous.

Into western Virginia came a Federal force which had been assembled in Ohio under the command of George B. McClellan, Crossing the Ohio River, the invaders succeeded by the end of the year in "liberating" the mountain people. Although possession of the region placed the Federals on the flank of Virginia, they could not, because of the transportation obstacles presented by the mountains, use it as a base from which to move eastward. The occupation of western Virginia was, however, an important propaganda victory for the North: a Union-sympathizing area in the Confederacy had been wrenched from Southern control.

The one big battle of the year was big only by the early standards of the war; later in the conflict it would have been considered a relatively moderate affair. It was fought in Virginia in the area between the two capitals. On the Virginia front the Federals occupied three positions. A small force held Fort Monroe on the coast between the York and James rivers. Just south of Washington was an army of over 30,000 under the command of General Irvin McDowell. In the northern end of the Shenandoah Valley were 14,000 Federals commanded by General Robert Patterson, a venerable veteran of the War of 1812 and the Mexican War. Confronting the semicircle of Federal armies were three Confederate armies: a small force opposite Fort Monroe; an army of over 20,000 under P. G. T. Beauregard based at Manassas in northern Virginia about thirty miles southwest of Washington; and 9,000 troops in the Valley, commanded by Joseph E. Johnston.

As the summer of 1861 opened, the commanders on both sides were occupied with training their levies, which, with the exception of a few regiments of regulars in the Northern army at Washington, were composed of raw recruits. Ideally, neither army should have embarked on an important campaign for several months; more time was needed to drill and equip the troops. Nevertheless, in July the Northern high command, which at this stage was largely President Lincoln, directed McDowell to undertake an offensive against the Confederates around Manassas. Usually Lincoln is depicted as acting in response to a clamor for a forward movement which had arisen in the press and among the public: the "Onward to Richmond" outcry. It is more probable that Lincoln was thinking in purely military terms. The Federals had larger forces in Virginia than the Confederates, and if McDowell's army could knock out Beauregard's (the principal Confederate force), the war might be ended immediately. The problem was to prevent other Confederate forces from coming to Beauregard's aid. The plan, as worked out, called for Patter-

---

Civil War Weapons and Tactics

Although breech-loading and repeating rifles were introduced in the war, they were not employed in large numbers. The basic infantry weapon was the Springfield rifle, a muzzle-loading, one-shot gun. Capable of killing at half a mile and most effective at 250 yards, it had a greater range and accuracy than any gun used in previous wars. A good soldier could fire two shots a minute. The basic artillery weapon was the brass "Napoleon," also a muzzle-loading, one-shot piece. With a maximum range of a mile, it was most effective at half that distance. At shorter ranges it had the deadly effect of a huge sawed-off shotgun. These weapons meant that armies packed more firepower than ever before. A force holding a strong position could stop almost any frontal assault. The traditional tactical formation of attacking in regular lines was in the process of becoming obsolete. Faced by concentrated firepower, the attackers had to advance in irregular rushes or move around the flank of the enemy. But many generals refused to realize the impact of technology upon tactics and continued to send their troops on suicidal assaults over open ground.

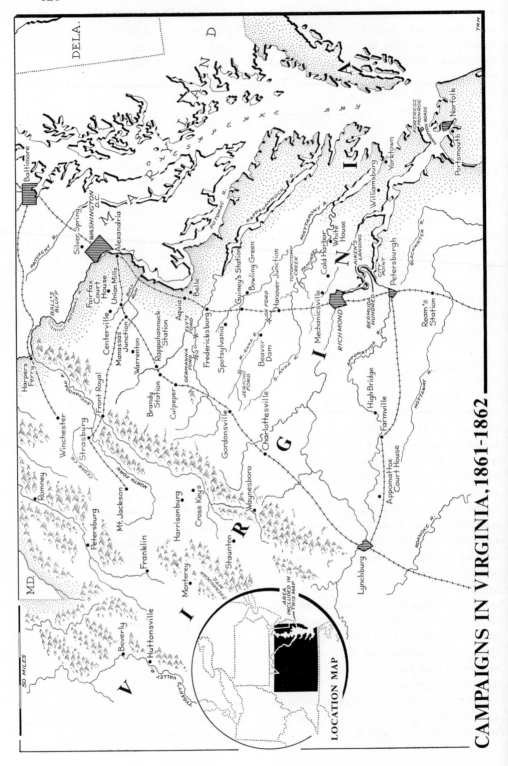

CAMPAIGNS IN VIRGINIA, 1861-1862

LOCATION MAP

AREA INCLUDED IN THIS MAP

son to contain Johnston so that McDowell could deal with Beauregard alone.

In mid-July McDowell marched his green troops toward Manassas, his movement well advertised to the Confederates by Northern newspapers and Southern spies. Beauregard retired behind Bull Run, a small stream north of Manassas, and called on the government to order Johnston to join him. The high command, however, wisely held Johnston in the Valley until McDowell's movement was more fully developed. The problem of the Confederates was to concentrate their two armies at the latest possible safe moment; if they were joined immediately, Patterson would move to McDowell, and the odds would still be in favor of the Federals. Not until McDowell approached Bull Run did the government order Johnston to Manassas. Most of Johnston's army reached Beauregard the day before the battle, making the Northern and Southern armies approximately equal in size: each numbered something over 30,000.

The Federals usually named battles for the nearest body of water in the neighborhood, the Confederates for the nearest settlement. The Northern name for the first big battle, fought on July 21, is Bull Run; the Southern title is Manassas. At Manassas or Bull Run, Johnston was the ranking Confederate officer, but he permitted Beauregard, who knew the terrain, to plan the battle. Emboldened by his reinforcements, Beauregard decided to launch an offensive, with the weight of the attack coming from his right to cut the Federals off from their base at Centreville. Oddly enough, McDowell concocted a similar plan: to attack in force on his right and turn the enemy left.

The battle might be summarized by saying that Beauregard never got his offensive into motion and that McDowell's attack almost succeeded. Because of a complex battle plan, poor staff work, and confused orders, Beauregard failed to get his troops across Bull Run in force. McDowell, on the other hand, sent a force far up the run which moved down on the weak Confederate left and threatened to drive it from the field. Hastily Beauregard had to call off his offensive and rush all available troops to the left to meet the danger rapidly developing there. The decisive phase of the battle occurred at the Henry House hill. Here the Confederates stopped a last strong Federal assault. Beauregard then ordered a counterattack. As the Confederates slashed forward, a sudden wave of panic struck through the Federal troops, wearied after hours of hot, hard fighting and demoralized by the abrupt change of events. They gave way and crossed Bull Run in a rout. Unable to get them in hand north of the stream, McDowell had to order a retreat to Washington.

No important results followed the battle. The Confederates, as disorganized by victory as the Federals were by defeat, and lacking supplies and transport, were in no condition to undertake a forward movement. Lincoln called to Washington, to replace McDowell, the victor of the fighting in western Virginia, General McClellan, and took measures to increase the army. Both sides girded themselves for the first year of real war.

The Year of Testing: 1862

In the fighting in 1862 the Federal navy played an important role, both in operations off the Southern coast and on the rivers in the Western theater. That year witnessed the introduction of several technological changes in naval construction that heralded a revolution in methods of naval warfare. Among them were an increasing reliance on steam rather than sail power, the employment of rifled ordnance and other guns firing explosive shells (a change which tended to make the prevailing wooden ships obsolete), and the introduction of ironclad vessels.

During the latter part of 1861 and the early part of 1862, the Federal navy had seized various islands off the Georgia-Carolinas coast (Port Royal, Roanoke Island, Fort Pulaski). From these bases Union ships

The Confederates constructed their ship by plating with iron a former United States frigate, the *Merrimac*, which the Yankees had scuttled in Norfolk harbor when Virginia seceded. They renamed her the *Vir-*

First Battle of Ironclads. *This print depicts, with some exaggeration, the fight between the* Monitor *and the* Merrimac. *The two contestants, in foreground, are represented with reasonable accuracy, but the damaged Union ships were not in the battle. The picture was made for public circulation by the McCormick farm machinery company, which thoughtfully included sketches of its own products in the scene.* (LIBRARY OF CONGRESS)

could blockade Southern harbors and deprive the Confederacy of the use of its own ports. Although the blockade was only in its beginning phase, the Confederate Naval Department well realized the potential effect of Northern sea power. In a bold attempt to seize the naval initiative, the Confederates introduced a new weapon—an ironclad warship. A few such vessels had been built in European navies and had operated against land fortifications, but they had not been tested in combat against other ironclads.

ginia, but in history she still is known by her original title. On March 8, 1862, the *Merrimac* came out from Norfolk to attack the blockading squadron of wooden ships in Hampton Roads. Easily the ironclad destroyed two of the Federal ships and scattered the others. Jubilation reigned in Richmond, and consternation blanketed Washington. But the Federal government, warned of the building of the *Merrimac*, had placed orders for the construction of several ironclads. One of these, the *Monitor*, arrived at Hampton Roads that night. When the *Merrimac* emerged on the following day to hunt for more victims, she was met by the *Monitor*. There then followed the first battle between ironclad ships. Neither vessel was able to damage seriously the other's armor, but the *Monitor* was able to

have caused her to founder if she had sought ocean waters; she could operate only as a harbor-defense vessel. And with the North alive to the value of ironclads and possessing superior facilities to build them, the South had lost the initiative of the new weapon.

The first decisive operations in 1862 were

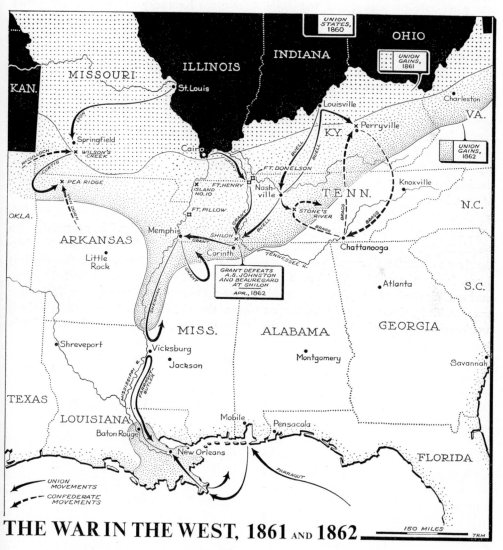

THE WAR IN THE WEST, 1861 AND 1862

prevent her foe from destroying the blockading squadron. Even if the *Merrimac* had won, the effect would have been indecisive. Technical defects in her construction would

in the Western theater. Here the Federals were trying to secure control of the Mississippi line, by moving on the river itself or parallel to it. Most of their offensives were combined land and naval affairs. To achieve their objective, the Federals advanced on the Mississippi from the north and south, moving down from Kentucky and up from the Gulf of Mexico against New Orleans. The latter operation, although not first in point of time, will be treated first, because it was a separate movement and was completed while the other was still in progress.

In April a Federal squadron of ironclads and wooden vessels commanded by David G. Farragut, destined to be the first American admiral, appeared in the Gulf. Smashing by the weak forts near the mouth of the river, Farragut ran up to New Orleans, defenseless because the Confederate high command had expected the attack to come from above, and forced the civil authorities to surrender the city (April 28–May 1). He then proceeded to Baton Rouge, which was also yielded up by its civil officials. Pursuant to orders from the Federal Naval Department, Farragut steamed up the river to meet another squadron coming down. It was thought in Washington that the ironclads alone could reduce all Confederate fortified points on the river. But after probing the defenses of Vicksburg (Mississippi), the naval officers had to report that they would need the cooperation of land forces in attacking such places. The Federals had, however, in New Orleans scored a notable success. Following Farragut came an occupying army commanded by General Benjamin F. Butler. For the rest of the war the Federals held New Orleans and the southern part of Louisiana. They had closed off the mouth of the great river to Confederate trade, they had grasped the South's largest city and greatest banking center, and they had secured a possible base for future operations.

Federal land forces in the West were under the direction of two departmental commanders. One army, with its base at Louisville, was led by General Don Carlos Buell;

all of Kentucky except the western tip was included in his department. West of the Mississippi, Henry W. Halleck, with headquarters in St. Louis, was in command. Under him in southern Missouri was a force directed by Samuel Curtis; another army subject to Halleck's control was stationed in western Kentucky under Ulysses S. Grant. The total Federal forces numbered close to 100,000, although many were not ready or equipped for service. All Confederate troops in the West were under the command of one general, Albert Sidney Johnston, who had his headquarters at Bowling Green, Kentucky. West of the Mississippi, on the Missouri-Arkansas border, was a detached left wing of 20,000 troops under Earl Van Dorn. In Kentucky the Confederate line, stretching from Columbus on the Mississippi to Bowling Green, was held by 50,000 men. A fatal weakness marked the Confederate line in Kentucky. The center, through which flowed the Tennessee and Cumberland rivers, was thrown back (southward) from the flanks, and was defended by two forts, Henry on the Tennessee and Donelson on the Cumberland. The forts had been built when Kentucky was trying to maintain a position of neutrality, and were located just over the Tennessee line. If the Federals, with the aid of naval power, could pierce the center, they would be between the two Confederate flanks and in position to destroy either.

This was exactly what the Federals did in February. Grant secured permission from Halleck to attack Fort Henry, whose defenders, awed by the ironclads accompanying the Union army, surrendered with almost no resistance (February 6). Grant then marched to Donelson while his naval auxiliary moved to the Cumberland River. At Donelson the Confederates put up a scrap, but eventually the garrison of 20,000 had to capitulate (February 16). While these sledgehammer blows were falling, Johnston seemed in a daze. Fearful that his army would be caught between Grant and Buell, who was supposed to be approaching, he ordered both flanks to retire, but before leaving he sent several thousand reinforcements into the trap at Donelson. The two wings pulled back—the right under Johnston and the left under Beauregard, who had come west to assist Johnston—and were eventually united at the railroad center of Corinth in northeast Mississippi. Grant, by the simple process of cracking the Confederate center and placing himself astride the river communications, had inflicted a near-disaster on the Confederacy. As a result of his movement, the Confederates had been forced out of Kentucky and had to yield half of Tennessee. And west of the Mississippi, Curtis crossed into Arkansas, and defeated Van Dorn at the battle of Pea Ridge (March 5–8). The South was losing control of vast chunks of territory, and the Federals were beginning to edge along the Mississippi line.

After the victories at Henry and Donelson, Halleck, who had had little to do with winning them, persuaded the government he was responsible for them, and as a reward he received the combined command of the West. He ordered Grant, with about 40,000 troops, to proceed up the Tennessee (southward), and directed Buell, who had occupied Nashville, to march to join Grant. His immediate objective was to destroy Confederate railroad communications in the Corinth area. Grant debarked his army at Pittsburg Landing, about thirty miles from Corinth. At the latter place, Johnston and Beauregard decided that their only chance to retrieve the recent reverses was to smash Grant before he was joined by Buell. Early in April they moved, 40,000 strong, toward Pittsburg Landing to deliver a surprise attack on the Federals, who were encamped between two streams flowing into the Tennessee. The battle that ensued (April 6–7) is usually known as Shiloh. The Confederates did catch Grant by surprise, and by the end of the first day's fighting drove him back to the river, but here the attack was halted. At the height of the battle Johnston was killed, and Beauregard assumed command. The next day Grant, reinforced by 25,000 of Buell's troops, went over to the offensive, and regained his original lines. Beauregard then disengaged, and withdrew to Corinth. In the tactical sense, Shiloh was an extremely narrow Union victory. The most important result was strategic in nature: the Confederates had failed to prevent a concentration of the Federal armies.

After Shiloh, Halleck, bringing reinforcements with him, came to Pittsburg Landing to direct personally the advance on Corinth. Moving with excessive caution, he took the better part of a month to reach the town and to place his army in position to take it by siege. Beauregard, rather than risk the certain entrapment of his forces, wisely evacuated his lines. The Federals now had Corinth and the railroads of which it was the hub. Furthermore, by seizing areas parallel to the Mississippi, they flanked the Confederates out of their positions on the river. By early June the Federals had occupied the river line down as far as Memphis.

At this point Halleck was called to Washington to become general in chief. Before he left, he had assigned missions to Grant and Buell, who again became departmental commanders. To Grant, the best fighting Union general yet to appear, he gave the relatively unimportant task of guarding communications in western Tennessee and northern Mississippi. To Buell, who had done practically no fighting, he assigned the vital objective of seizing Chattanooga on the Tennessee line. For the next few months Grant did little except to repel a Confederate attempt to recover Corinth. Buell took his army to Nashville to prepare his offensive. The Confederate field army in Mississippi, now commanded by Braxton Bragg (Davis had relieved Beauregard after the loss of Corinth), moved to Chattanooga,

Problem General of the North. *Short, stocky, and magnetic, George B. McClellan was known as the "Young Napoleon." He was, and still is, the most controversial Northern general of the war. Contemporaries disagreed bitterly as to his abilities, and later historians have also been divided in their judgments. Even his critics admit that he was a fine organizer, but they contend that he lacked the aggressive instinct to be a great field commander.* (NATIONAL ARCHIVES)

where it would be in position to undertake an offensive.

The Confederates held approximately the eastern half of Tennessee. Bragg's problem was to recover the rest of the state and, if possible, return the war to Kentucky. He was a brilliant strategist with a fatal weakness—he lacked the iron resolution to complete his plans. He now conceived a brilliant scheme. Instead of risking battle with Buell between Chattanooga and Nashville, he

would rapidly invade Kentucky, forcing Buell to follow and drawing him out of Tennessee. If he could reach Kentucky first, he could place himself between Buell and Louisville and force the Federals to fight on grounds of his own choosing. With Buell smashed, lustrous success would be at hand —Kentucky redeemed and the Western states open to invasion. Bragg did get to Kentucky first, he did stand between Buell and Louisville. But instead of fighting he withdrew. Buell went into the city, and, reinforced, came out looking for Bragg. The two armies met at the indecisive battle of Perryville (October 8), after which Bragg retired to Tennessee. Buell followed cautiously—he was the type of general that Lincoln said had "the slows"—and shortly the President relieved him. His successor was William S. Rosecrans. Toward the end of the year Bragg and Rosecrans, moving forward in simultaneous advances, came together in the hard-fought battle of Murfreesboro or Stone's River (December 31–January 2). Again Bragg had to retire, and this time he had to yield up some territory. Also in December Grant began a movement against Vicksburg, the key to the Mississippi defenses, but this operation belongs to the 1863 story.

In the Eastern theater in 1862 Federal operations were directed by young George B. McClellan, commander of the Army of the Potomac and the most controversial general of the war. McClellan always promised brilliant results, always seemed to be at the brink of a great success, but he never fulfilled his promises. He was a superb trainer of men but lacked the fighting instinct, necessary in a great captain, to commit his men to decisive battle. It has been said that no man could better prepare an army and lead it to the banks of the Rubicon—but somebody else would have to take it over. Furthermore, McClellan did not have a firm grasp of realities. He lived much in a military world of his own making, which he filled with superior Confederate armies about to pounce on him and destroy his army.

During the winter of 1861–1862 McClellan had remained inactive, training his army of 150,000 men near Washington. He finally settled on a plan of operations for the spring campaign. Instead of striking for Richmond

known as the Peninsula. (His movement is generally called the Peninsula campaign.) The merits of his proposal, as he presented them to the government, were as follows: he would have a relatively short land distance to cover, he could use a water line of communications on the York River, and he could utilize the support of the navy. These claims had some validity, but the plan

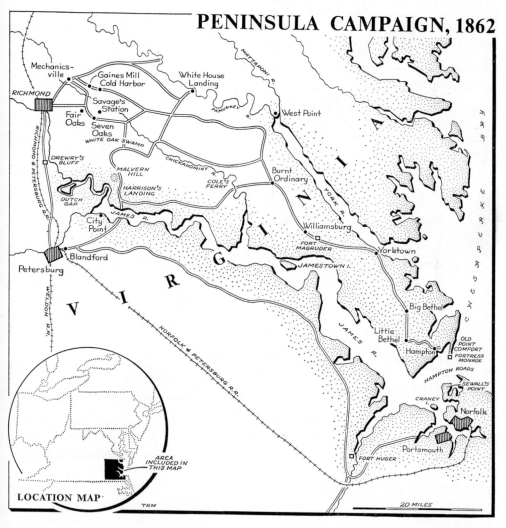

PENINSULA CAMPAIGN, 1862

by moving southward from Washington, he would have the navy transport his army to Fort Monroe on the Virginia coast in the region between the York and James rivers

aroused misgivings in Lincoln. Would not the capital be in danger, Lincoln asked, while McClellan was down in the Peninsula? The general agreed to leave enough men to make Washington safe, and a minimum figure was stipulated by the President. Late in March McClellan started putting his troops on transports bound for the Peninsula. After

decisive numerical superiority over the Confederates when he landed at Fort Monroe. But he wasted a month taking Yorktown by siege, giving the Confederate field army

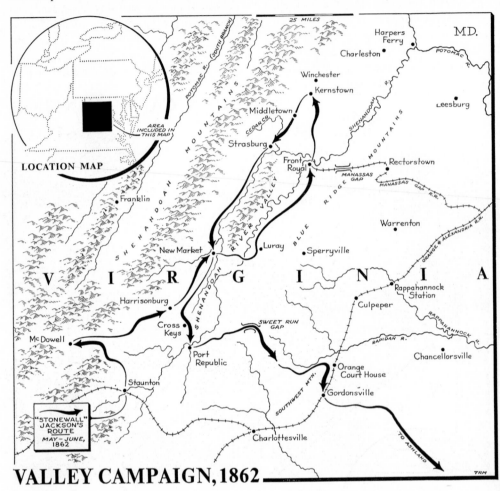

VALLEY CAMPAIGN, 1862

the general himself had departed for Virginia, Lincoln decided, on the basis of good evidence, that McClellan had not complied with the directive to leave enough men to protect Washington. Accordingly, he ordered McDowell's corps of over 30,000 men, about to embark to join McClellan, to remain south of Washington.

McClellan was thus deprived of a substantial part of his army, leaving him with something over 100,000. He had, nevertheless, a

under Joseph E. Johnston ample time to concentrate before him. He then moved forward along the line of the York. By mid-May he was within 20 miles of Richmond, and by the latter part of the month he was approaching the gates of the city. Always he pressed Lincoln to send McDowell to him, and finally the President agreed to let McDowell march to join McClellan's right wing. McClellan's army was divided by the Chickahominy River; his right was north of

A Civil War Balloon. *Signal balloons were given their first practical use in the Civil War. In this picture Professor T. C. Lowe in his hydrogen-inflated balloon is ascending behind the Union lines at Fair Oaks to view the Confederate positions. Although balloons were usually anchored to the ground, they were sometimes cut loose and allowed to drift over the enemy lines. By lightening his gas load, the pilot could ascend higher and catch a contrary wind current that would waft him back to safety.* (LIBRARY OF CONGRESS)

the stream to make contact with McDowell.

In the meantime the Confederate high command (Davis and Lee) anxiously observed the course of the campaign. They had misgivings about Johnston's strategy of drawing McClellan closer to Richmond before fighting and they were worried by the possibility that reinforcements, particularly McDowell, might join McClellan. To prevent the latter contingency, Lee devised a scheme which Davis approved. The commander of the Confederate forces in the Valley, Thomas J. ("Stonewall") Jackson, was reinforced to 17,000, and directed to move northward, giving the impression that he meant to cross the Potomac. In the brilliant Valley campaign (May 4–June 9) Jackson attacked and defeated two separate Federal armies under Frémont and Nathaniel P. Banks, and drove toward the northern end of the Valley. Partly to defend the approaches to Washington and partly to trap Jackson, Lincoln rushed forces to the Valley, including McDowell's corps. Jackson slipped back to safety before the various Federal forces could converge on him. McDowell's troops were so used up by their long march that their movement to McClellan had to be suspended. While these events were unfolding in the Valley, Johnston at last attacked McClellan at Fair Oaks or Seven Pines (May 31–June 1). The attack failed to budge McClellan, and Johnston was so seriously wounded that he had to relinquish the command. To his place Davis named the man who would lead the Army of Northern Virginia for the rest of the war, Robert E. Lee.

Lee took over at a critical moment. McClellan's army lay within a few miles of Richmond, and although McDowell's expected reinforcements were stalled in the Valley, there was always the possibility that McClellan would receive help in the near future. Lee, a brilliant field commander, realized that the Confederacy could not win its independence merely by repelling offensives. It would have to destroy a Federal army, and to achieve this purpose Lee was ready to take chances, to risk something.

Informed by his cavalry leader, J. E. B. Stuart, that one third of McClellan's army was north of the Chickahominy and two thirds south, Lee devised a daring plan. He would call Jackson from the Valley, bringing his army up to 85,000 (as compared to McClellan's 100,000), mass his forces north of the Chickahominy, and fall on the exposed Federal right and chew it to pieces. Lee's thought was that then McClellan would retreat to the York and that he could follow and smash him before he reached his base. The risk in the plan was that McClellan would discover he confronted only a small enemy force on his left and would move into Richmond.

The operation that followed, which involved several engagements, is known by the group name of the Battle of the Seven Days (June 25–July 1). It did not go off as Lee expected. He drove back the Federal right wing but was unable to destroy it. Then McClellan, instead of retiring to the York, abandoned his base there and headed southward for the James, where he had asked the navy to set up a new base. Lee followed, trying desperately to destroy the Federals, but McClellan extricated his army, even inflicting a bloody repulse on Lee at Malvern Hill. He reached Harrison's Landing on the James, where with naval support, he was safe from any attack Lee could launch.

At Harrison's Landing the Federal army was only 25 miles from Richmond, and it had a secure line of water communications. But the high command, instead of replacing McClellan with a more aggressive commander, decided to evacuate the army to northern Virginia where it would be com-

The South's Greatest General. *Robert E. Lee was a magnificent physical figure. Five feet eleven inches tall and 175 pounds in weight, he seemed larger than he was because of his massive head and wide shoulders. He was grave and reserved in manner like George Washington, his hero and model. And like Washington, he lived by a self-imposed code of high conduct. "Duty is the sublimest word in our language," he once wrote.* (LIBRARY OF CONGRESS)

bined with a smaller force under John Pope —in short, to begin a new operation on the Washington-to-Richmond "overland" route. McClellan was to command the

near Manassas: the Battle of Second Manassas or Second Bull Run (August 29–30). Lee easily halted the assault, and in a powerful counterstroke swept Pope from the field.

Confederate Dead in the Bloody Lane at Antietam. (LIBRARY OF CONGRESS)

united armies. As the Army of the Potomac left the Peninsula by water, Lee, understanding what was happening, moved his army northward with the purpose of striking Pope before he was joined by McClellan. As Lee approached, Pope retired north of the Rappahannock River. Some units of McClellan's army had reached him, and, as it developed that he might be forced into a battle, others were sent on as soon as they arrived. By a brilliant stratagem, Lee passed part of his army to Pope's rear, drawing the Federals north, and then followed with the remainder of his force. Pope, who was rash where McClellan was timid, was under the delusion he faced only Jackson's corps. Although not all of McClellan's troops had joined him, he attacked the Confederates

The beaten Federals retired to the Washington defenses, where Lincoln relieved Pope and placed all the troops around the city under McClellan's command.

Lincoln intended to employ McClellan's organizing abilities only to whip the army into shape; before it took the field he meant to replace McClellan with a fighting commander. But Lee gave the Federals no respite. Early in September he went over to the offensive, invading western Maryland. His principal purpose was to get the armies out of Virginia, whence he drew his food supplies, during the harvest season; of course, if he could win a victory in a Union state, Confederate prestige would be enormously enhanced. Obviously the Army of the Potomac was the only force available to meet this thrust, and McClellan was the only general available at the moment to lead it. With some misgivings, Lincoln let him go to meet Lee. As McClellan advanced, he had a wonderful piece of luck. He captured an order by Lee showing that the Confederate army was divided, a part of it under Jackson having gone to capture Harpers Ferry, a Federal stronghold at the head of the Valley. McClellan's move was to advance rapidly and attack before the enemy could concentrate. He moved with what was for him rapidity, but his standards of speed were peculiar. Lee had time to pull most of his army together behind Antietam Creek near the town of Sharpsburg. (The ensuing battle on September 17 is usually called Antietam.) Here McClellan, with 87,000 men, threw a series of powerful attacks at Lee's 50,000. Late in the day it seemed that the Confederate line would break, but at this moment the rest of Jackson's troops arrived from Harper's Ferry to plug the hole. Even then McClellan might have won with one more assault. But his caution asserted itself, and he called off the battle. Lee retired to Virginia, and after an interval of reorganization McClellan followed. Lincoln, disgusted by McClellan's failure to exploit his victory, removed him from command in November. It was McClellan's last military appearance in the war.

As McClellan's successor Lincoln appointed Ambrose E. Burnside, a modest mediocrity, who had been offered the position twice before and who had refused on the grounds that he was not competent for independent command. Now Burnside thought that the government desired him to fight, and fight he would. He decided to undertake a movement that was rarely risked in the war, a winter campaign. Specifically, he planned to drive at Richmond by crossing the Rappahannock at Fredericksburg, the strongest defensive point on that river. On December 13 he flung his army at Lee's defenses in a hopeless, bloody attack. At the end of a day of bitter failure and after suffering 12,000 casualties, he withdrew to the north side of the Rappahannock. Shortly he was relieved at his own request.

The war in 1862 had gone badly for the Confederacy. There had been victories in the East, but they were deceptive triumphs. The Confederates had repelled or driven the Federals, but they had not accomplished what was necessary to win the war—they had not destroyed a Federal army. The Federals withdrew to reorganize and then returned. In the West the Confederacy was losing control of the Mississippi line and of vast vital areas of territory. And all the while Southern manpower was running out.

The Year of Decision: 1863

As 1863 opened, the Federal army in the East was commanded by Burnside's successor, Joseph Hooker—"Fighting Joe," as the newspapers called him. Hooker faced a difficult military problem. His army, which numbered 120,000, lay north of the Rappahannock opposite Fredericksburg. In order to get at Lee or Richmond, Hooker had to cross the river at a point where the alert enemy could not slaughter him as it had Burnside. Avoiding the error of attempting a crossing at Fredericksburg, Hooker maneuvered opposite the town to hold Lee's attention, and crossed part of his army far up the Rappahannock. This flanking force came down on the south side, threatening to turn Lee's left. To complete his brilliant movement Hooker had only to push on to the open country around Fredericksburg—and he would have Lee in a vice. But Hooker was a good deal like Bragg: at a crucial moment he lost his nerve. So now he hesitated, and fell back to a defensive position at Chancellorsville in the desolate area of scrub trees and brush known in Virginia as the Wilderness. Here Lee came up to attack him.

The battle of Chancellorsville (May 1–5) was one of Lee's most brilliant exploits. With an army of only 60,000 (part of his force had been detached for other service),

The South's Good Soldier. *At the first battle of Manassas, Thomas J. Jackson received the name by which he is always known, "Stonewall." Another officer, rallying his troops, cried that Jackson was standing like a stone wall. Deeply religious, Jackson conceived of the South's struggle for independence as a holy war. He became Lee's most trusted subordinate, and his death after Chancellorsville was a sad blow to Confederate hopes.* (NATIONAL ARCHIVES)

he took great but justified risks. Leaving a small force at Fredericksburg to contain the Federals at that point, he moved to confront Hooker. He divided his army and sent Jackson to hit the Federal right, which was exposed, while he struck from in front. His bold purpose was to cut Hooker off from the river and destroy his army. Jackson rolled up the Federal right, but the Federals rallied and stabilized their lines. They were,

however, crowded into a small area, and they took a severe pounding from Confederate artillery. Finally Hooker, aided by a diversion from his troops at Fredericksburg, extricated his forces to the north side of the river. Again Lee had won, but not the decisive victory he had hoped for. And he had lost his ablest lieutenant. Jackson was wounded in the fighting, and died from the effects of the wound and pneumonia.

While the Federals were failing in the East, a different story was unfolding in the West, one that would influence future operations in the Eastern theater. U. S. Grant was driving at Vicksburg, the strongest Confederate fortified point on the Mississippi River and the key to the defenses that kept open a corridor of communication between the two parts of the Confederacy. Grant had started his campaign in December, 1862, and he carried it forward during the winter months of 1863. Coming down the river with naval support, he debarked his army on the Louisiana side above the city. From here he crossed to the east bank, and struck at the Confederate defenses, which were commanded by John C. Pemberton. He struck several blows, and each one failed. The terrain he was operating in north of Vicksburg was low, marshy, and laced by numerous streams and bayous, and it baffled every attempt of the army and navy to traverse it. Grant had little confidence that any of his moves would succeed; he was keeping his forces busy until the spring, when he intended to try another route to the city.

In May he unveiled his plan. The navy ran transports past the river batteries to a point below Vicksburg. The army marched down the west side, where it was met by the navy and transported to the east side. Now Grant was south of Vicksburg on relatively high and dry ground. Moving rapidly, he defeated enemy forces barring his way at Champion's Hill and the Big Black River, and closed in on Vicksburg itself. After failing to storm the strong works, he settled down to a siege, which endured for six weeks. Pemberton, realizing that his govern-

was dismayed at the prospect of losing the great river fortress. Various plans to relieve the city were discussed, the principal one being a proposal to send part of Lee's army

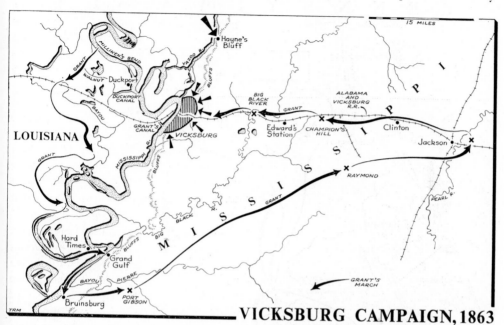

VICKSBURG CAMPAIGN, 1863

ment could not break Grant's hold and that his garrison of 30,000 was exhausted by constant fighting, surrendered on July 4. Immediately thereafter the other Confederate strong point on the river, Port Hudson (Louisiana) surrendered to a Federal force which had come up from New Orleans under N. P. Banks. At last the Federals had achieved one of their principal strategic aims: they had control of the Mississippi line. The Confederacy was split into two parts, and the Trans-Mississippi area was isolated from the main section. A great turning point in the war had been reached. At the same time the Confederacy suffered a reverse in Tennessee. Rosecrans moved forward in the so-called Tullahoma campaign, and maneuvered Bragg farther back into eastern Tennessee.

When the siege of Vicksburg began, the Confederate high command in Richmond

to Tennessee, possibly with Lee himself in command, to launch an offensive. But Lee demurred; he did not want to leave Virginia. He put forward a counter-scheme: he would invade Pennsylvania. If he could win a victory on Northern soil, he said, great results would follow. The North might abandon the war, England and France might intervene, the pressure on Vicksburg and other fronts would be broken. The government assented, and in June Lee started his movement, swinging his army west toward the Valley and then north through Maryland into Pennsylvania.

As Lee advanced, Hooker moved back to confront him, marching parallel to the line of Lee's route. But Hooker evidently had been unnerved by his experience at Chancellorsville. He seemed to be looking for a chance to escape his responsibility, and he soon found an excuse to ask to be relieved.

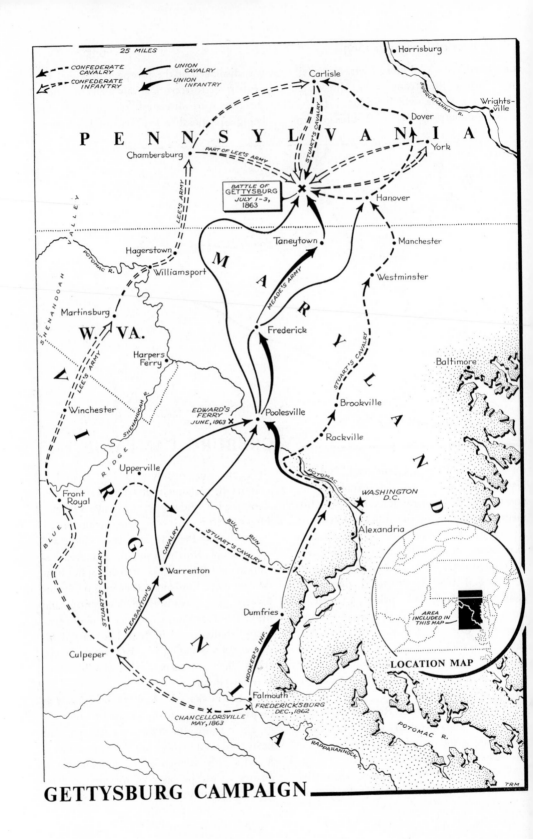

GETTYSBURG CAMPAIGN

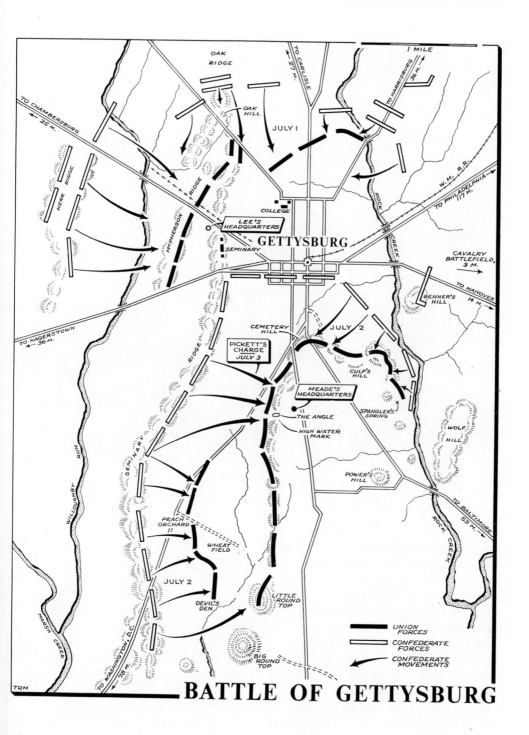

BATTLE OF GETTYSBURG

To his place Lincoln appointed a corps commander in the army, George G. Meade, a solid if unimaginative soldier. Meade followed Lee, and approached what might be line resembled an inverted fishhook, the right resting on Culp's Hill and Cemetery Hill and the front stretching along Cemetery Ridge for three miles. On the first day

Pickett's Charge at Gettysburg. *This pencil sketch by Alfred R. Waud, one of the better war artists, depicts the long line of battle that attacking forces in the war endeavored to maintain.* (LIBRARY OF CONGRESS)

called the strategic rear of the Confederate army in southern Pennsylvania. Lee, who had not expected the Federals to move so rapidly, was astounded when he learned of their nearness. With his army marching in three columns, he was in a dangerous position; hurriedly he had to concentrate his forces. Meade, realizing that Lee in enemy country had to attack or retreat, selected a strong defensive site at the little town of Gettysburg, a road hub in the region, and Lee, seeking contact with the Federals, moved toward the same spot. Here on July 1–3 was fought the most celebrated battle of the war.

The Federal army occupied a formidable position on heights south of the town. Their

(July 1) the two armies jockeyed for position around Gettysburg; the tough fighting started the following day. Lee, confident of the prowess of his troops and combative by nature, decided to attack even though he was outnumbered 90,000 to 75,000. On July 2 he threw an assault at the Federal left on Cemetery Ridge which crumpled up an advanced Federal corps but failed to reach the main line. On July 3 he mounted a greater effort: 15,000 men were to hit the center of the ridge and crack the Federal line wide open. The attacking force advanced over almost a mile of open space swept by enemy fire (the famous Pickett's charge). It was a gorgeous display of the older mode of warfare—frontal attacks by lines of infantry—which modern technology and improved weapons were making obsolete, and it was almost hopeless. Only about 5,000 men reached the ridge, and these had

enough to fight offensively. Hereafter in the East the Confederacy would have to stand on the defense.

A third turning point against the Confed-

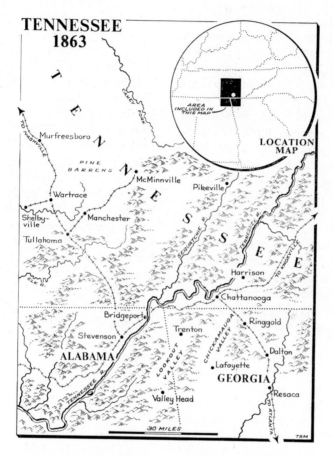

TENNESSEE 1863

LOCATION MAP

AREA INCLUDED IN THIS MAP

Murfreesboro

PINE BARRENS

McMinnville   Pikeville

Wartrace

Shelby-ville   Manchester

Tullahoma

ELK R.

Harrison

Chattanooga

Bridgeport

Stevenson   Trenton   Ringgold

ALABAMA

Lafayette

Valley Head   GEORGIA

Dalton

Resaca

TENNESSEE R.

30 MILES

TRM

to surrender or retreat. After a day of sullen waiting by both armies, Lee withdrew his shattered forces to Virginia. Meade, who had little aggressive instinct, made but a feeble pursuit. For the rest of the year the two armies maneuvered against each other in northern Virginia but never came to grips. Although Meade had undoubtedly thrown away an opportunity to end the war by not following up his victory, Gettysburg was another turning point. The total Confederate losses in the campaign were close to 25,000. Never again would Lee feel strong

eracy was reached in Tennessee. In the autumn Rosecrans moved toward Chattanooga. Bragg, in order to secure room to maneuver, evacuated the town, which was occupied by the Federals on September 9. Rosecrans, forgetting that he had not defeated Bragg, rashly plunged over the Georgia line in pursuit, where Bragg, reinforced by troops from Lee's army, was lying in wait to attack. Rosecrans barely got his scattered forces in hand before Bragg delivered his assault at Chickamauga (September 19–20). This was one of the few battles in which the Confederates enjoyed a numerical superiority (70,000 to 56,000). On the second day Bragg smashed the Federal right wide open. Rosecrans and his corps generals on that flank fled to Chattanooga even though his left continued to fight under the command of George H. Thomas, who here won the sobriquet of "the Rock of Chickamauga." Shortly Thomas too had to retire, and the beaten army fell back into the Chattanooga defenses.

Bragg did not move rapidly to exploit his victory, partly because of his heavy casualties (17,000), but eventually he advanced and occupied the heights south of Chattanooga. Mounting batteries on these points, he commanded the roads leading into the city and virtually shut off its supplies. The Federal high command, however, had ample resources to break the siege. Grant was named departmental commander of the West. Immediately he replaced Rosecrans with Thomas, and came with part of his own army to Chattanooga. The reinforced Federal army numbered 60,000, while Bragg's army was weakened by the detachment of a force for a fruitless operation against Knoxville. At the battle of Chattanooga (November 23-25) the Federals hurled Bragg from his lines on Missionary Ridge and Lookout Mountain and back into northern Georgia. They then proceeded to occupy most of East Tennessee. A second objective of Northern strategy had been achieved: possession of the Tennessee River line. From the Chattanooga base the Federals were in position to split the Confederacy again—what was left of it. Chattanooga deserves to be ranked with Vicksburg and Gettysburg. If the Confederates had recovered the Tennessee line, they would have partially redressed the other reverses; they might have prolonged the war. As it was, after 1863 the Confederacy had no chance on any front to win its independence by a military decision. Now it could hope to triumph only by exhausting the Northern will to fight.

1864–1865: The End

The campaigns of 1864–1865—the last year and a half of the war—may be studied as one piece. By 1864 all the great material advantages were on the side of the North. The Northern economic system was producing in huge amounts the supplies of war, and Northern manpower was continuing to fill up the armies. In contrast, Southern resources were dwindling fast, and Southern armies, partly because of war weariness among the people and partly because of the shrinking boundaries of the Confederacy, were steadily decreasing in numbers. The blockade was reaching the height of its power, becoming even more effective as the Federals captured most of the few ports still in Confederate possession: Mobile, Alabama (August, 1864), and Wilmington, North Carolina (January, 1865). Not the least important factor working for Northern success was the organization of the command system: all Northern land forces were now under the direction of Grant as general in chief. Henceforth the Northern armies would be moved by one brain to achieve a common purpose.

Grant's plans for 1864 called for three great offensives and several minor diversionary moves. Of the big thrusts, the Army of the Potomac, commanded by Meade but accompanied and directed by Grant, was to seek to bring Lee to decisive battle in northern Virginia. From near Chattanooga the Western army, commanded by William T. Sherman, was to advance into northern Georgia, destroy the Confederate army, now commanded by Joseph E. Johnston, and wreck the economic resources of Atlanta. From New Orleans N. P. Banks was to advance to Montgomery, Alabama, where he would be in position to join Sherman. The third offensive never came off. Banks attempted an expedition up the Red River to occupy Shreveport, Louisiana, and was so soundly trounced at Sabine Crossroads (April 8) that he could not participate in the grand design.

the beginning of the campaign, was determined to avoid a showdown unless he saw a chance to deal a decisive blow. In the Battle of the Wilderness (May 5–6) each commander struck savagely at the other; it was

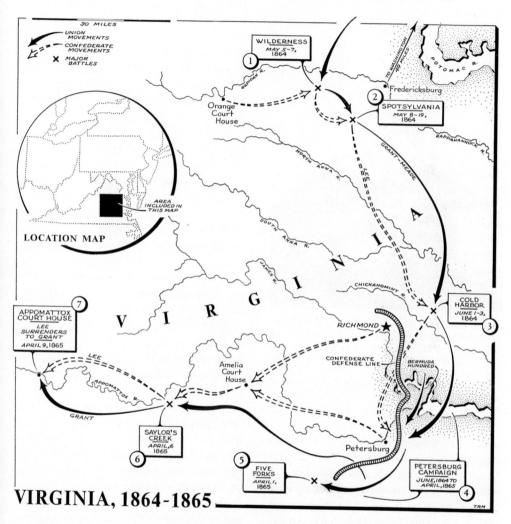

VIRGINIA, 1864-1865

The two principal offensives jumped off in May. From its position in northern Virginia the Army of the Potomac, 115,000 strong, crossed the Rappahannock and Rapidan rivers, and plunged into the Wilderness area. Grant's plan was to envelop Lee's right and force him to a showdown battle. Lee, whose army numbered about 75,000 at

a mark of the confused, grim fighting in the gloomy woods that Lee stood on the defensive in one sector while attacking in another. Both armies suffered heavy casualties, with the Federals having the greater losses. Lee, demonstrating superb defensive skill, prevented Grant from turning his right. But the Federal commander, instead of retiring to reorganize as his predecessors had done after a reverse, slid off to his left and to the southeast. He turned up at Spotsylvania Court House, where Lee moved to meet

Storm Center of the Confederacy. *Joseph E. Johnston was a small, compact man with gray hair, beard, and eyes. Like McClellan on the Northern side, he was something of a "problem general." Sensitive of his rank and rights, he became involved in continual controversy with President Davis. His soldiers called him "Uncle Joe."* (LIBRARY OF CONGRESS)

him. Here another bloody, indecisive engagement was fought (May 8–12). Again Grant sidled to his left, and again Lee slid with him. In this manner, without fighting another major clash, the two armies moved until they reached Cold Harbor, a few miles north of Richmond. At this point Grant made a last attempt to destroy Lee north of Richmond (June 1–3), and was bloodily repulsed. In a month of fighting Grant had lost in total casualties 55,000 men, and Lee, 31,000.

Now Grant had to alter his strategy. If he remained where he was, Lee would retire into the Richmond defenses to stand a siege, something Grant wanted to avoid. Masking his movements from his adversary, Grant moved southward across the James heading for Petersburg, directly south of Richmond. Petersburg was the hub of all the railroads feeding into the capital; if Grant could secure it he could force Lee to come into the open to fight for his communications. He almost succeeded. Petersburg was defended only by a small force under Beauregard, who managed, however, to hold Grant off until Lee's army could arrive. Grant now realized that he would have to resort to siege operations. He dug in, and so did Lee. The trench lines of the two armies stretched for miles above and below Petersburg. Always Grant strove to extend his left around Lee's right so as to get on the railroads that were the lifeline of the Southern army. It would be nine months until he reached his objective.

In May, Sherman, with an army of over 90,000, moved against Atlanta and Johnston's army, which numbered 60,000 at the beginning. Johnston's plan was to delay Sherman, to fight for time, and not to commit his forces unless the conditions were exceptionally favorable. Sherman's objective was to envelop Johnston and bring him to battle. The Atlanta campaign developed primarily into a game of maneuver in which Sherman tried to trap his rival, who avoided being caught. The two armies skirmished and fought almost constantly, but the only set battle was at Kennesaw Mountain (June 27). By July Sherman was approaching Atlanta, and at this point President Davis, disgusted with Johnston's strategy, replaced him in command with John B. Hood. Hood, combative by nature and well aware of the reason for his appointment, threw two successive attacks at Sherman, both of which failed. He then retired into Atlanta to stand a siege. At first Sherman resorted to siege operations, but eventually he moved part of his army south of the city to grasp its only railroad line. To avoid starvation, Hood had to evacuate. The Federal army occupied Atlanta on September 2.

Sherman had Atlanta, but he had not destroyed the enemy army. Now Hood moved northward, and struck at Sherman's railroad communications; when Sherman chased him, he withdrew. Unwilling to play hide-and-seek with Hood and eager to strike deeper into Georgia, Sherman sent 30,000 of his army to Tennessee under Thomas, and prepared to move for Savannah on the coast.

taken by sea to join Grant. At the same time Hood made a startling change in his strategy. He decided to invade Tennessee, forcing Sherman, he hoped, to follow him. He would defeat Sherman in the mountains, recover Tennessee, and then drive to the Ohio or cross the mountains to join Lee for a crushing blow at Grant—all of this with an army that numbered little more than 40,-000. It was a desperate "last-throw-of-the-dice" plan.

Hood's one scant chance for success was to get into Tennessee fast before Thomas

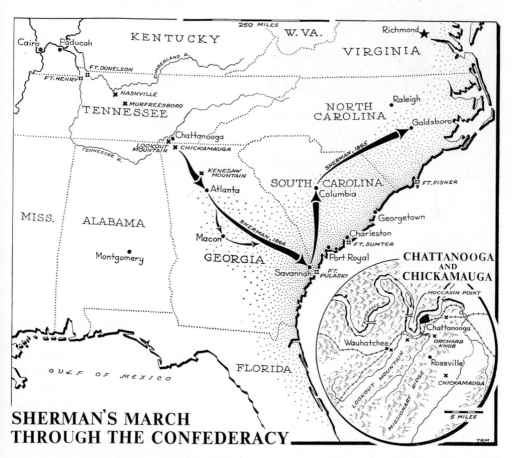

SHERMAN'S MARCH THROUGH THE CONFEDERACY

His idea was that Thomas could gather enough reinforcements to hold Hood out of Tennessee; meanwhile Sherman would march to Savannah whence he would be

could bring in reinforcements. But having devised a bold plan, he hesitated to execute it. After long delay he finally advanced into Tennessee. Confronting him and seeking to delay him was a Federal force of about 30,-000 under John M. Schofield. Hood tried strenuously to destroy this force. He caught up to it at Franklin, where on November 30

The Apostle of Modern War. *More than any American general of his time, William T. Sherman understood the nature of modern war—total warfare against the civilian population, as well as the armies, of the enemy. And no general in the Civil War did as much to inaugurate the new kind of war as did Sherman in his march through Georgia and the Carolinas. Although the spare, redheaded Sherman made himself hated in the South, he liked Southerners and after the war opposed a harsh Reconstruction policy.* (LIBRARY OF CONGRESS)

was fought an engagement which, from the Confederate viewpoint, was one of the tragic battles of the war. With no artillery support, Hood resolved to attack, across two miles of open space, the Federals, who were entrenched in a strong position. His generals, angered by Hood's remarks that their troops would not fight, seemed determined to sell their lives. A mood of doom hung over the army. In six fruitless charges Hood lost 6,000 men; eleven of his generals were killed or wounded. After that Hood might as well have gone back to Georgia. But he moved forward and took up a position south of Nashville. In the city Thomas was gathering an army that would even-

tually number over 60,000. When he was ready, he came out looking for Hood. At the Battle of Nashville (December 15–16) he smashed Hood from the field. As the Confederates retreated toward Mississippi, they were harried by the most merciless cavalry pursuit of the war. Only a few units reached Mississippi intact. The Confederate Army of Tennessee had, in effect, ceased to exist.

In the meantime Sherman was marching almost unopposed across Georgia, inaugurating a new kind of warfare. Of the Civil War generals, Sherman was the prophet of modern total war—war against the civilian population of the enemy, war intended to break the enemy people's will to resist. His army marched on a sixty-mile front, destroying property and supplies that might be used by the Confederate forces—and committing many individual depredations as well. But the greatest result of Sherman's march was psychological rather than economic. What Southerner who heard of a Union army moving at will through the heart of the South could ever believe again that the Confederacy could win the war? In Virginia soldiers in Lee's army deserted to go home to take care of their families. By December 20 Sherman was at Savannah. Here he changed his plans, winning permission from Grant to march by land to join the latter. Into South Carolina Sherman rolled, still facing slight opposition and still ripping up enemy property. He was accomplishing two objectives: destroying both Confederate resources and the railroads that brought supplies from the Lower South to Lee's army. When he advanced into North Carolina, the Confederate government got together an army of 30,000 under Johnston to oppose him, but this small force could do little more than delay his march. Nor could Lee move against him, for he was pinned down at Petersburg by Grant.

In April, 1865, Grant finally passed a part

of his army around Lee's right to the vital railroads. The Confederates evacuated Petersburg and Richmond, and Lee moved his army, now shrunk to about 25,000, westward. His one forlorn hope now was that he could reach a rail line to North Carolina and unite with Johnston. But the pursuing Federal army moved faster, and barred his escape route. Lee realized that further fighting was hopeless, and on April 9 he met Grant at Appomattox and surrendered the Army of Northern Virginia. In North Carolina Joe Johnston reached the same conclusion, and on April 26 surrendered to Sherman near Durham. Jefferson Davis, defiant to the last and unable to recognize defeat,

fled southward, and was captured in Georgia. As the news of the Confederate collapse traveled westward, other Southern generals hastened to lay down their arms. On May 4 Richard Taylor surrendered the Confederate forces in Alabama and Mississippi. On May 26 Edmund Kirby Smith, commander of the Trans-Mississippi Confederacy, surrendered at Shreveport the last important Southern army in the field. All practical resistance had ended by June 1. The Civil War, the War Between the States, the War for Southern Independence, the War for the Union, the American Iliad that had brought a new nation into being, was over.

>>>->>>->>>->>>-<<<-<<<-<<<-<<<

BIBLIOGRAPHY

Books DEALING with the military aspects of the war are so numerous as almost to defy classification. Two excellent documentary collections that catch the human interest of the story are H. S. Commager, ed., *The Blue and the Gray* (2 vols., 1950), and Otto Eisenschiml, Ralph Newman, and E. B. Long, eds., *The Civil War: The American Iliad* (2 vols., 1956). A superb pictorial presentation that includes a good narrative is David Donald, ed., *Divided We Fought* (1953). From the great account of the war by participants, *Battles and Leaders of the Civil War* (4 vols., 1887; new edition, 1956), Ned Bradford has put together a one-volume edition of the same title (1956). A good introduction but no more is William Wood, *Captains of the Civil War* (1921). J. B. Mitchell has provided a sharply etched account in *Decisive Battles of the Civil War* (1955). Top-level command problems and systems are discussed in C. R. Ballard, *The Military Genius of Abraham Lincoln* (1952); Sir Frederick Maurice, *Statesmen and Soldiers of the Civil War*

(1925); T. H. Williams, *Lincoln and His Generals* (1952); and Vandiver's *Rebel Brass*. K. P. Williams, *Lincoln Finds A General* (4 vols., 1949–1956) is a military and administrative history of the Northern military machine. For a comparative study of Northern and Southern generalship by an English student, see J. F. C. Fuller, *Grant and Lee* (1933; new edition, 1957).

Bruce Catton relates the story of the Northern Army of the Potomac in his trilogy: *Mr. Lincoln's Army* (1951), *Glory Road* (1952), and *A Stillness at Appomattox* (1954). D. S. Freeman performs the same task for the rival Army of Northern Virginia in *Lee's Lieutenants* (3 vols., 1942–1944). For the Confederate army in the West, see S. F. Horn, *The Army of Tennessee* (1941). Good studies of particular campaigns are few. Among the best are R. M. Johnston, *Bull Run* (1913); E. S. Miers, *The Web of Victory* (1955), Vicksburg; E. J. Stackpole, *They Met at Gettysburg* (1956) and *Drama on the Rappahannock* (1957), Fredericksburg; and J. G.

Barrett, *Sherman's March Through the Carolinas* (1956).

Military biographies: *North.* H. J. Eckenrode and Bryan Conrad, *George B. McClellan* (1941); W. W. Hassler, Jr., *General George B. McClellan* (1957); Lloyd Lewis, *Sherman, Fighting Prophet* (1932); W. H. Hebert, *Fighting Joe Hooker* (1944); Freeman Cleaves, *Rock of Chickamauga* (1948), Thomas; J. F. C. Fuller, *The Generalship of Ulysses S. Grant* (1929); A. L. Conger, *The Rise of U. S. Grant* (1931); and Richard O'Connor, *Sheridan the Inevitable* (1953).

Military biographies: *South.* D. S. Freeman, *R. E. Lee* (4 vols., 1934–35), a Civil War classic; Frank Vandiver, *Mighty Stonewall* (1957); J. P. Dyer, *The Gallant Hood* (1950); T. H. Williams, *Beauregard, Napoleon in Gray* (1955); R. S. Henry, *"First with the Most" Forrest* (1944); Sir Frederick Maurice, *Robert E. Lee* (1925); Burke Davis, *Gray Fox* (1956), Lee; J. W. Thomason, Jr., *Jeb Stuart* (1930); Gilbert Govan and J. W. Livingood, *A Different Valor* (1956), J. E. Johnston; J. H. Parks, *General Edmund Kirby Smith* (1954); and D. B. Sanger and T. R. Hay, *James Longstreet* (1952).

There is a substantial literature on naval operations. Among the better accounts are A. T. Mahan, *The Gulf and Inland Waters* (1883); J. T. Scharf, *History of the Confederate States Navy* (1887); W. M. Robinson, Jr., *The Confederate Privateers* (1928); J. P. Baxter, *Introduction of the Ironclad Warship* (1933); and J. D. Hill, *Sea Dogs of the Sixties* (1935). Good naval biographies are C. L. Lewis, *David Glasgow Farragut* (2 vols., 1941–1943); R. S. West, Jr., *The Second Admiral* (1937), D. D. Porter; and W. A. Roberts, *Semmes of the Alabama* (1938). Two studies that approach the most famous naval battle of the war from different viewpoints are T. C. and Ruth White, *Tin Can on a Shingle* (1957), and R. W. Daly, *How the Merrimac Won* (1957).

Many of the war figures wrote their memoirs, and some of these recollections are surprisingly good. Recommended from the huge mass of these sources are U. S. Grant, *Personal Memoirs* (2 vols., 1885; one-volume version edited by E. B. Long, 1952); W. T. Sherman, *Memoirs* (2 vols., 1875; one-volume version issued by Indiana University Press, 1957); J. W. De Forest, *A Volunteer's Adventures* (1946), edited by J. H. Croushore; E. P. Alexander, *Military Memoirs of a Confederate* (1907); Richard Taylor, *Destruction and Reconstruction* (1879; new version edited by R. B. Harwell, 1955); and H. K. Douglas, *I Rode with Stonewall* (1940).

CHAPTER 31

The Postwar Nation*

THE GUNS fell silent in 1865, and the armies of the Blue and the Gray returned to their homes, those of the South to a land desolated by defeat and those of the North to a country humming with wartime prosperity but faced with new and perplexing problems that were the outgrowth of victory. It is often thus in war. As the great epic poet of the Civil War (Stephen Vincent Benét) has written:

> The victor strikes and the beaten man
>   goes down
> But the years pass and the legend covers them both,
> The beaten cause turns into the magic
>   cause,
> The victor has his victory for his pains.[1]

*This chapter is identical with Chapter 1 of the succeeding volume, *A History of the United States: Since 1865*. See Preface.

[1] Stephen Vincent Benét, *John Brown's Body* (New York, 1928 edition), p. 189, quoted by permission of Rinehart and Company.

The Civil War had decided many things. It determined that the United States would remain one nation, and it unified that nation as it had never been unified before and placed it on the road to becoming a great world power. By destroying slavery and demonstrating that a popular government could preserve political liberties during an internal conflict, it vitalized and vindicated democracy at home and everywhere in the world. But these results were largely of a long-term or ultimate nature; their effects would not be fully felt or completely realized until long years had passed. Meanwhile, in the immediate aftermath of the war, a number of immediate problems emerged to test the statesmanship of the victors. The vast Northern armies had to be demobilized and absorbed into civilian life. The swollen wartime economy had to be converted to a peacetime basis. The powers of the national government, expanded under the pressure of war, had to be redefined for the needs of peace.

But the most urgent of the immediate problems was the South. Upon the region below the Mason-Dixon line the hand of war had left its grim imprint. Not only were its farmlands and cities ravaged by battle—the entire social organization of the section had been disrupted. By what was perhaps the most gigantic act of confiscation in history, four million slaves had been seized from their owners and made freedmen. What would their status be and who would determine that status: the white people of the Southern states or the national government? Upon what terms and by what process would the states of the defeated Confederacy be restored to the Union? The nation would have to find answers for these questions. Until the issue of the South was resolved, in one manner or another, the United States could not proceed serenely or successfully on the broad way of nationalism marked out for the future as a result of the Civil War.

The North and South at War's End

In the years after Appomattox the economic boom that had started in the North under the stimulus of war continued unabated, and the country entered upon a period of unparalleled expansion. Almost any data chosen from the census tables will serve to underline the growth that occurred. The number of manufacturing establishments, which stood at 140,000 in 1860, increased to 252,000 by 1870. The total railroad mileage of the country jumped from 30,000 miles in 1860 to over 60,000 by 1873. At the outbreak of the Civil War the size of the laboring force was 1,300,000; by 1879 it had grown to 2,732,000. In various fields of industrial activity—iron and steel, textiles, shoes, oil refining—the United States was moving toward a position of world leadership.

Four factors exercised a potent influence in sustaining the expansion of the economic system. First, Americans continued to exhibit the same technological skills that had characterized their productive activities since the 1830's, as well as the same ingenuity in devising new industrial and agricultural machines or adapting old ones to new uses that seemed to be a hallmark of the national character. Also, they continued to demonstrate their already proven abilities to organize production: to create corporations, recruit a managerial class, subdivide and specialize labor, and advertise their products to a national market. In short, Americans, more than any other people, understood the modern techniques of mass production. Second, American investors and producers had ready to hand a seemingly inexhaustible supply of raw materials: coal, iron ore, timber, oil, water power, and almost every form of metal. The American economy was young, profuse, opulent—and waiting to be exploited. Third, many of these resources were owned by a friendly and receptive national government that was willing to hand them over to private interests for exploitation and eager to aid business expansion with such measures as protective tariffs, a favorable financial policy, and subsidies of land and money. Furthermore, private enterprise operated in a sympathetic political climate. It never had to worry that the national government would inquire into its practices or attempt to regulate its activities. The years after Lee's surrender witnessed a laissez-faire Utopia. Lastly, and perhaps most important, American producers functioned in a great domestic or interior market which was guarded against outside competition by tariff walls and connected in all its parts by rail and water transportation. Moreover, it was a market which constantly expanded in size and consequently enlarged its demands. From a population of 31,000,000 in 1860, the United

States went to 39,000,000 in 1870 and to 50,000,000 by 1880. As before the war, a substantial part of the increase was the result of immigration. Between 1860 and 1880,

and uncultivated. The railroads, subjected to the strain of war and destruction by Federal armies, were in a condition of collapse, and the same was true of facilities on the in-

---

The Ruins of Columbia, South Carolina

The Southern cities suffering the greatest devastation were Columbia, Atlanta, and Charleston. Sidney Andrews, a Northern reporter, described Columbia in *The South After the War* (1866): "It is now a wilderness of ruins. Its heart is but a mass of blackened chimneys and crumbling walls. Two thirds of the buildings in the place were burned, including, without exception, everything in the business portion. Not a store, office, or shop escaped; and for a distance of three fourths of a mile on each of twelve streets there was not a building left. Every public building was destroyed, except the new and unfinished Statehouse. This is situated on the summit of tableland whereon the city is built, and commands an extensive view of the surrounding country, and must have been the first building seen by the victorious and on-marching Union army. From the summit of the ridge, on the opposite side of the river, a mile and a half away a few shells were thrown at it, apparently by way of reminder, three or four of which struck it, without doing any particular damage."

---

some 5,000,000 aliens entered the country. The bases of the economic expansion, then, were essentially sound. The postwar boom burst in 1873, largely as the result of an overexpansion of facilities; but after the depression that began in that year had worked itself out, another and an equally spectacular growth would occur.

Northern travelers in the South after 1865 were appalled when they gazed upon the desolation left in the wake of the war. Although the devastation cannot be compared with that resulting from twentieth-century warfare, it was tragic according to the measurements of the nineteenth century and, in all truth, grievous enough by the standards of any time. Cities and towns were wholly or partially gutted. Plantations and farms were wrecked or burned, and thousands of acres of agricultural land were unplanted

land waterways. In fact, with roads in a state of disrepair, with bridges destroyed, and with a shortage of wagons and horses, the entire transportation system of the region was badly disrupted. These were the physical evidences of the havoc of war. In addition, much of the personal property of Southerners had been lost with the Lost Cause. Confederate bonds and currency were now worthless, and capital that had been invested in them was gone forever. And by the emancipation of the slaves, Southerners had been deprived of property worth an estimated two billion dollars.

Matching the shattered economy of the South was the disorganization of its social system. In the months that followed the end of the war, when thousands of soldiers were drifting back to their homes—258,000 would never return and other thousands would return wounded or sick—life was seriously deranged. To many people the problem of keeping alive, of securing food and shelter, seemed the only thing that mattered. The school system practically ceased to operate, and in some areas even religious services were suspended—because the churches had been destroyed or damaged and no church funds were available. For a brief period, between the collapse of the Confederacy and the installation of federal military rule, in many parts of the section there was almost no local civil government, almost no exercise of civil political authority.

The labor system had been demolished, and several million slaves had become free laborers. Naturally confused by their abrupt change in status, they were uncertain as to their economic future and only vaguely conscious of their place and responsibilities in a free labor market. Equally uncertain were the whites, most of whom were convinced that Negroes would not work under wage arrangements. More serious from the white viewpoint was the social problem created by emancipation. Slavery, in addition to being a labor system, had been a white-supremacy device. Now, that device was gone, and although Southerners, albeit reluctantly, accepted its going, they were as determined as ever to keep the South a white man's country, to find some legal device to put in the place of slavery. In the process of racial adjustment that would ensue, in the attempt that the national government would make to fix the status of the Negro as part of its effort to control Southern politics—the phase of our history known as Reconstruction (1865–1877)—Southerners would have a unique experience. The only Americans ever defeated in war, they would become also the only Americans ever subjected to military rule and to government imposed from the outside. The episode would leave a lasting influence on the psychology of the region.

The national government had emerged from the war with new and spacious powers; but it had had no experience in handling problems of mass relief, and there was nothing in the American tradition to justify governmental rehabilitation of a stricken region. Consequently, the government took no direct action to alleviate the distress in the South or to restore the economic processes in the section. The only official agency created to deal with economic matters was the Freedmen's Bureau (set up in March, 1865), which was supposed to aid the Negroes in making the transition from slavery to freedom. Set up to function for a year after the close of the war, it was empowered to issue supplies to freedmen and loyalists, to develop educational facilities for the former slaves, and to settle Negroes on abandoned or confiscated land. Directed by General Oliver O. Howard, the bureau performed its allotted functions and more. Among other acts, its agents distributed over twenty million rations in the South; and as most of the agents were sensible if not humane men, they dispersed them to the destitute of both races, thereby rescuing many from want or starvation. In addition to this restricted form of official relief, some aid was extended by private groups, notably by agencies of the Northern churches, which sent missionaries and teachers to the South to further the religious and educational development of the colored people and also to care for the colored needy. In the area of religion occurred one of the most important social changes of Reconstruction: the secession of the Negroes from white churches and the formation of their own denominational associations.

With relative rapidity, the South recovered from the effects of war and restored its economic life. Since it was an agricultural society, its productive powers rested on the basis of land, and the land had survived the war. The chief problem was to get the plantations and farms under cultivation again. Work began at once (crops were made in 1865), and progress was steady. By 1879 the cotton crop exceeded that of 1860, part of the increase resulting from the opening of new growing areas west of the Mississippi, in Texas and Arkansas. Gradually production was expanded in the section's other principal crops: tobacco, sugar, and rice, the culture of the last shifting in the postwar period from South Carolina and Georgia to Louisiana. As the great staples, which had been the South's source of wealth before the war, again flowed into the world's markets, the region again had a cash revenue and all classes experienced a measure of well-being.

The rehabilitation of the South's agrarian economy was accomplished with relatively few changes in the nature of Southern agriculture. There was something of a shift in the distribution of land ownership, in the direction of an increase in the number of small holders. In the economic travail following the war, many planters were unable to hold on to their property and were forced to offer their land for sale at low prices. In many cases the purchasers were white yeomen. According to the census, the number of farms in Mississippi increased from 43,000 in 1860 to 68,000 by 1870, in South Carolina from 33,000 to 52,000, in Louisiana from 17,000 to 28,000. Actually, these figures are somewhat deceptive, because some of the farms listed were under 10 or 20 acres in area and were really units in a plantation, worked by tenants who were sometimes white but usually colored. The plantation system was modified, but it did not disappear. In the ownership of the system, however, an important change took place. The old planter (or the old type of planter who lived on the plantation) tended to disappear. The large land units tended to become owned and administered by merchants, banks, corporations—or by planters who

lived in towns or cities where they could devote themselves to business as well as agricultural pursuits.

During the Reconstruction period, perhaps a third or more of the farmers in the South were tenants; by 1900 the figure had increased to 70 per cent. Several factors accounted for the trend toward tenancy. The Negroes, when they became freedmen, had, of course, no property. They were forced, as a simple matter of survival, to become laborers or tenants, and most of them were unable to accumulate enough resources to rise above this status. As late as 1890, there were only 121,000 Negro landowners in the South. Probably the strongest influence promoting tenancy among both races was the lack of an adequate credit system, with a resulting scarcity of money. The National Bank System was slow to establish itself in the Southern states, and state banks were slow to recover from the effects of the war. Landlords did not have enough cash to hire laborers to work their land, and laborers could not secure loans to buy land or even raise sufficient currency to rent land on a cash basis.

Out of this situation developed an economic arrangement peculiar to the South, the share-crop and crop-lien system, in which produce and labor took the place of money. It is necessary to emphasize that there were share tenants and sharecroppers and that there was a difference between the two groups. The share tenants, most of whom were whites, worked a strip of land on a large unit, and paid as rent to the landlord one fourth to one third of their crop; they provided their own tools, seed, stock, and other supplies. The sharecroppers, most of whom were Negroes, provided nothing but their own labor. For the average cropper, the landlord would furnish all the above materials, and a horse or mule and a house as well. In addition, until the crop was harvested he would arrange credit facilities for the cropper and his family at a local country store owned by himself or a merchant. The cropper, for his part, agreed to consign from one third to one half of his crop to the landlord. Moreover, the storekeeper, the source of credit, protected his interest by taking a mortgage or lien on the tenant's share of the crop. (As time passed, the landlord and the merchant tended to become one person, and the planter-storekeeper became a major figure in the Southern credit complex.) The lien system was a necessary credit device in the postwar years; but when continued and expanded after that period, it had a hurtful influence upon Southern agriculture. The merchant or landlord, for obvious reasons, pressed the cropper to produce a single money crop, cotton, to the neglect of diversified farming and scientific farming methods. More serious were the social results of the system. The typical sharecropper was an unlettered person who did not know how to handle his own money carefully and who did not understand the mechanics of credit. Frequently, after harvesting his crop, he found himself owing money to the storekeeper and hence forced to pledge his labor to the same source for another year. Not only did the lien system prevent tenants from rising to the owning class; it also operated to bind them to particular pieces of land, to create a state of peonage. The Negro sharecropper was not a slave, but he was not completely free.

The Reconstruction period witnessed a restoration of Southern industrial facilities damaged or destroyed during the war as well as some promising beginnings in new industrial activities. Most of the rehabilitation and expansion was financed with Southern capital, with capital that often was really "local," being subscribed by the people of a town who wanted to improve their community by locating a factory in it. The only Southern enterprise that attracted

Northern and European investors was the railroads. With outside aid, the war-weakened rail system was soon put in running order again, and by 1873 over 4,000 miles of new track had been constructed. Modest but noteworthy progress was recorded in tobacco manufacturing, in the lumber industry, and in iron making; in 1880 the South produced 212,000 tons of iron. The most substantial growth occurred in textiles, which had a prewar basis to build on. Southern leaders during Reconstruction preached the economic advantage of building cotton mills where the raw material was produced, and the Southern people took this logic to heart. Practically all the mills that began to appear in Southern towns were financed by local investors. By 1880 the South could boast of 161 textile factories housing 524,000 spindles and employing 16,000 workers. But the great industrial development of the South, the development that created the "New South," would not come until after Reconstruction. And even that forward economic surge would not greatly change the nature of Southern life, would not make the South very "new." As late as 1910, only 15 per cent of all the people in the region were connected with manufacturing. For many years the South would remain, as it was in the Reconstruction era, a rural and a traditional land.

Reconstruction: Its Meaning and Motivation

"Reconstruction" was a term applied by contemporaries to the period after the war. As they employed it, Reconstruction had a strictly political connotation. It referred to the process by which the defeated states of the late Confederacy would be governed and to the conditions on which they would be restored to their former place in the Union. Historians have adopted the term and applied it to all the great transforming changes that occurred in the entire nation between 1865 and 1877, the year when Southern whites overthrew the last Republican state governments in their section and ended political Reconstruction. Actually, even if Reconstruction is considered only in its relation to the South, it had important social and economic as well as political aspects. In the social sense, it was concerned with the delicate problem of race relations and specifically with the question of who should determine the position in Southern society of the freedmen—the central government or the Southern whites acting through the media of their state governments. In the economic area, Reconstruction included both the rehabilitation of war-damaged facilities and the beginning of the transition of the region from an agricultural to an industrial economy. Whereas political Reconstruction was terminated in 1877, it may be said that social and economic Reconstruction would continue and that it has, in fact, never ceased.

In many respects the American domestic situation in 1865 resembled the conditions that prevail after any international war. There were a victorious people and a defeated people, and the victorious were faced with the problem of what kind of peace they would impose upon the defeated. When people in the North debated the terms upon which the South should be restored to the Union, they were, in a sense, arguing over the nature of a peace treaty for the defeated side. To use modern terms, they were considering the merits of a "hard" and a "soft" peace, a peace that punished the loser and forced him to conform to certain prescribed standards before he could resume his former status, or one that forgave him and permitted him to take his old place without enduring any severe penalties. The government of the United States, influenced by public opinion pulling in different directions, would experiment with several peace plans before deciding upon a final de-

sign. That final plan would be, by the standards of the times, a "hard" peace. In spirit and content, it would embody the peace program of the Radical Republicans, the dominant faction of the dominant party.

The motives that moved the Northern people to endorse one Reconstruction plan or another and finally to approve a punitive one are complex and hard to analyze. No one simple factor moved all groups in the North, and no single simple formula will explain the trends in Northern opinion. Different forces influenced different segments of the population, and the interplay of these forces in the entire matter of Reconstruction was incredibly intricate. Many persons in the North were affected by what may be termed a war psychosis and which was an inevitable aftergrowth of the war. Just as Southerners had suffered in their attempt to win independence, Northerners had sacrificed in their struggle to preserve the nation. They had endured war taxes and regulations and had seen their loved ones killed, wounded, or made prisoners. For their woes, they blamed the South or at least its leaders, and they wanted somebody punished. Some people in the North, influenced by wartime propaganda, particularly that concerning conditions in Confederate military prisons, cherished a feeling akin to hatred for all things Southern.

To some groups in the North, the status of the former slaves seemed the paramount issue. The government had freed the Negroes, they said, and now it had an obligation to follow through and see that they remained free, that they were given a fair chance to become members of American society. If in the process the government had to enforce a place for the Negro in the South, it would be but serving the requirements of justice. Closely connected with this conviction that the nation must protect the freedmen was another feeling that Reconstruction offered a Heaven-sent opportunity to recast the South in the image of the rest of the country. Here the argument was that the region below Mason and Dixon's line was backward, feudal, undemocratic—and

Architect of the Reconstruction. *Thaddeus Stevens represented the Lancaster district of Pennsylvania in the House of Representatives. Bald since a sickness in youth, he wore a wig that often fell out of place in debate. Bitter and sarcastic in speech, he ruled the Republican majority with a sure hand and drove to passage the Radical Reconstruction program.* (NATIONAL ARCHIVES)

it should be made over, made modern. Reconstruction represents the most extreme example in our history of an attempt by the majority to impose a social concept upon a minority that did not wish to be changed.

The motives that we have been discussing were those that animated ordinary folk, ordinary in that they were not powerful political personages or industrialists who might be influential enough to command the politicos. This is not to say that the politicians were not susceptible to idealism, that

they were unmoved by the situation of the freedmen, or that they were unaware of the democratic implications of the Civil War. Some of them were conscious of all these things. And some of them were affected by an anti-South psychosis that was a product of the war and the long antislavery struggle. But in the last analysis, the Reconstruction problem would have to be approached in terms of political realities; and the Reconstruction design would have to be worked out in a political body, Congress, and it would have to serve the political needs of the majority party, the Republicans, and the economic interests which they represented. Those needs dictated that the Republican party remain in power in the postwar years and that the legislative gains won during the war by the Northern economic groups composing the party—the protective tariff, the National Bank System, subsidies to railroads, and others—be maintained and expanded.

To many Republicans the issue of Reconstruction seemed starkly simple. If the government adopted a plan that permitted the South to return to the Union quickly and easily, then the Democratic strength in Congress would be increased, Southern agrarians might resurrect the old South-West alliance, the beneficent wartime legislation might be repealed, the Republican party might even be thrown from power. Some formula, some method had to be found to prevent these horrible possibilities from becoming realities. If Republican motivation does not seem to be of a very lofty nature, it should be remembered that victors hardly ever give away their victory and that American parties have never taken a cheerful view of political suicide. In many ways it was unfortunate that Reconstruction had to be designed in a political framework, but it could not have been otherwise—unless one supposes that it should have been entrusted to an all-wise dictatorship.

As the Republicans were the majority party (the Democrats were an impotent minority in the postwar period), the task of formulating a Reconstruction policy was in bers of Southern whites be disfranchised, and that the property of rich Southerners who had aided the Confederacy be confiscated and distributed among the freedmen.

Thaddeus Stevens on Reconstruction

Stevens of Pennsylvania was the Radical Republican leader in the House. Bitterly frank in speech, he announced his purposes in Reconstruction in a speech delivered in 1865: "The whole fabric of southern society *must* be changed and never can it be done if this opportunity is lost. Without this, this Government can never be, as it never has been, a true republic. Heretofore, it had more the features of aristocracy than of democracy.—The Southern States have been despotisms, not governments of the people. It is impossible that any practical equality of rights can exist where a few thousand men monopolize the whole landed property. The larger the number of small proprietors the more safe and stable the government. If the South is ever to be made a safe republic let her lands be cultivated by the toil of the owners or the free labor of intelligent citizens. This must be done though it drive her nobility into exile. If they go, all the better."

---

their hands. But even within Republican ranks there was disagreement as to the kind of peace that should be imposed upon the South. The same factions of the party (the Conservatives and the Radicals) that had clashed on wartime emancipation now confronted each other on the issue of Reconstruction. The Conservatives, led by President Lincoln at the end of the war, advocated a mild peace and the rapid restoration of the defeated states to the Union; beyond insisting that the South accept the abolition of slavery, they would not interfere with race relations or attempt to alter the social system of the South. The Radicals, directed by leaders like Thaddeus Stevens of Pennsylvania, Charles Sumner of Massachusetts, Benjamin F. Wade of Ohio, and Zachariah Chandler of Michigan, stood for a hard peace; they urged that the civil and military chieftains of the late Confederacy be subjected to severe punishment, that large num-

Above all, they wanted to keep the Southern states out of the Union until some formula could be devised to create an electorate in the South that would send Republican representatives to Congress.

Although the Radicals were a more cohesive and disciplined group during Reconstruction than they had been in the war, they did not have at the war's end a distinct and detailed peace plan worked out. It is impossible to fix the exact time when they decided that the most feasible way to establish a Republican electorate in the conquered section was to bestow the suffrage upon the Negroes. Some of the leaders, notably Sumner and Stevens, recommended this strategy from the first. Other Radicals may have agreed with them, but they hesitated to do so publicly for fear of public opinion—not all Northern states permitted Negroes to vote. But as the Reconstruction controversy developed, the Radicals moved inexorably and necessarily to advocacy of Negro suffrage, some because they thought it a matter of right, most because it promised to rivet Republican control upon the South.

Charles Sumner. *The Massachusetts Senator, sometimes called "the scholar in politics," was one of the most idealistic Republican leaders in the postwar period. He was also one of the most dogmatic and uncompromising of all politicians. Advocating a drastic Reconstruction of the South, he argued that the late Confederate states had committed political suicide by seceding and were subject to whatever form of government the national government wished to impose.* (PHOTO BY U.S. ARMY SIGNAL CORPS)

Both Republican factions, following an honored American tradition, tried to buttress their position with constitutional sanction. The Conservatives, claiming that secession was illegal, contended that the seceded states had never legally been out of the Union, were still in it, and had all the rights of states. The Radicals, the uncompromising

nationalists of the war, now insisted that the Southern states had in fact withdrawn from the nation and had therefore forfeited their rights as states. Sumner argued that by seceding the states had committed "state suicide," and Stevens bluntly referred to the defeated states as "conquered provinces." To complete the semantic confusion of Reconstruction politics, Southerners, who had fought to uphold the right of secession, demanded that they be accorded all the privileges they had previously enjoyed in the Union they had sought to dissolve.

Conservative Reconstruction

The process of Reconstruction was first put into motion during the Civil War, and the first plan of Reconstruction was presented by President Lincoln. Perhaps it is not quite accurate to say that Lincoln offered a plan. Always realistic and pragmatic, he never proceeded from the basis of dogma or theory, never bound himself to act according to a rigid blueprint. As Federal troops occupied large parts of the South, he realized that as a practical necessity civil government would have to be re-established in these areas, and he judged that as commander in chief he was the proper person to begin the restoration of civil arrangements. Moreover, he recognized that the problem of Reconstruction was without precedent in American history and would have to be dealt with without recourse to constitutional sanctions. The legal issue that agitated so many people—whether the defeated states were in or out of the Union—he dismissed as "a merely pernicious abstraction." We all agree, he said, that they are out of their proper relationship with the Union, and our sole object should be to get them back into their proper relation. Without much consideration for the effects of Reconstruction upon the future of his party, Lincoln was almost exclusively concerned with the principle that always dominated his thinking: the inviolability of the Union. His primary objective was to restore to working order the American experiment in democracy. As he had subordinated emancipation to the Union during the war, so now he would subordinate such questions as the status of the freedmen to his larger goal. Rather than a plan, Lincoln advanced a proposal or a set of suggestions for Reconstruction.

Lincoln's "plan" was embodied in a proclamation issued in December, 1863. Resting his right to reconstruct on the presidential power to pardon, he offered a general amnesty to all who would take an oath pledging future loyalty to the United States. The oath did not set up any tests for past loyalty. Lincoln said: "On principle I dislike an oath which requires a man to swear he *has* not done wrong. It rejects the Christian principle of forgiveness on terms of repentance. I think it is enough if the man does no wrong *hereafter*." Excluded from the privilege of swearing the oath (Lincoln intended the exclusion to be temporary) were high civil and military officials of the Confederacy, the leaders of the South, whom Lincoln wisely decided to keep out of the Reconstruction process for the time being. Whenever in any state 10 per cent of the number of people who had voted in 1860 took the oath, they could proceed to elect a state government that Lincoln promised to recognize; his idea here was to get Reconstruction started with a loyal minority to which other Southerners would attach themselves as they recognized the inevitability of Southern defeat. Lincoln's strong pragmatic sense permeated the entire proposal. The oath required acceptance of the wartime acts and proclamations of the President and Congress concerning slavery—which meant that Lincoln was asking the South to recognize the reality that slavery was dead—but it did not require that a state formally abolish slavery as an institution. Instead of

officially demanding abolition, Lincoln said to Southerners interested in starting Reconstruction that he hoped their states would act to ensure permanent freedom for the Negroes. In similar fashion, he wrote to Southern leaders urging them to give the ballot to intelligent Negroes or to those who had served in the Federal armies.

In three Southern states—Louisiana, Arkansas, and Tennessee—loyal governments reconstructed under the Lincoln formula were established in 1864. The required percentage of voters took the oath, slavery was abolished, and representatives were elected to Congress. Lincoln extended presidential recognition to these governments; but they would not have a firm legal status, would not be back in the Union, until they were approved by Congress, and that body was the sole judge of the qualifications of its members. The Radicals were angered and astonished at the mildness of Lincoln's program, and they were able to induce Congress to repudiate his governments. Representatives from the Lincoln states were not admitted to Congress, and the electoral votes of these states were not counted in the election of 1864. In defeating Lincoln's restoration venture, the Radicals were aided by several moderate Republicans who believed that Congress instead of the President should control Reconstruction and that Lincoln's plan did not provide adequate protection for the freedmen.

The Radicals could not stop, however, with a rejection of the President's scheme. Inevitably, people would ask what they had in mind that was better. They had to come up with a plan of their own—and at a moment when they had not thought the Reconstruction problem through and when they were uncertain that Northern opinion would accept the ideas of their more extreme leaders. Under pressure, they produced and passed (in July, 1864, while the war was still going on) the Wade-Davis Bill, which may be considered the first Radical plan of Reconstruction. This measure boldly assumed that the seceded states were out of the Union and that the function of Reconstruction belonged solely to Congress. By its provisions, the President was to appoint for each conquered state a provisional governor who would take a census of all adult white males. If a majority of those enrolled—instead of Lincoln's 10 per cent—swore an oath of allegiance, the governor was to call an election for a state constitutional convention. But the privilege of voting for delegates to this meeting was limited to those who would swear that they had never voluntarily borne arms against the United States or voluntarily aided the Confederacy; this was the so-called "iron-clad oath" that made past conduct instead of future loyalty the test of political life. The convention was required to put in the new constitution provisions abolishing slavery, disfranchising Confederate civil and military leaders, and repudiating the Confederate and state war debts. After these conditions had been met, and if Congress approved, the state was to be readmitted to the Union. While the Wade-Davis Bill was more drastic in almost every respect than the Lincoln plan, it did not, any more than the President's proposal, attempt to establish national control over race relations or Negro voting. If the Radicals sympathized with these objectives in 1864, they were not yet ready to support them openly.

The Wade-Davis Bill was passed a few days before Congress adjourned, which enabled Lincoln to dispose of it with a pocket veto. Conceding that the measure included some sound provisions, he announced that he was unwilling to be committed to any single plan of restoration. The enraged authors of the bill, Benjamin F. Wade and Henry Winter Davis, answered with a blistering denunciation of the veto, the Wade-Davis Manifesto, which warned the President not to usurp the powers of Congress. The bitterness and the strength of the Radical resistance to his plan gave Lincoln pause. Practical as always, he realized he would have to accept some of the objections of the Radicals, adopt some of their ideas. In conferences with congressional leaders and his cabinet, he began to move toward a new approach to Reconstruction, possibly one that included greater national supervision of the freedmen. What he would have eventually proposed cannot be exactly stated. On April 14, 1865, a crazed actor, John Wilkes Booth, under the delusion he was helping the South, shot the President in a Washington theater. Lincoln died early the following morning, and because of the circumstances of his death—the heroic leader, the Great Emancipator struck down in the hour of victory by an assassin—he achieved immediate martyrdom. From Washington his funeral train moved through a mourning land to Springfield, Illinois. It was a vast procession of grief, the greatest death march in history.

Coffin that passes through lanes and streets,
Through day and night with the great cloud darkening the land,
With the pomp of the inloop'd flags, with the cities draped in black.[2]

In its circuitous journey the coffin traveled 1,700 miles and was seen by over 7,000,000 people; at the numerous stops and services along the way 1,500,000 people gazed on the face of the dead martyr. In the wild excitement of the hour, it was widely assumed that Booth had been instigated to his mad act by men in the South, and the Radicals played on this theme with reckless charges implicating high Confederates. Ironically, Lincoln's death helped to kill his policy of a generous peace.

[2] Walt Whitman, *Leaves of Grass* (New York, 1940), p. 226, quoted by permission of Doubleday & Company.

Into Lincoln's place stepped Andrew Johnson, the most unfortunate of all the Presidents who accidentally inherited the office. A Southerner and former slave-holder, he became President as a bloody civil war against the South and slavery was drawing to a close. A Democrat, he became the head of a Republican administration at a time when partisan passions, held in some restraint by the exigencies of war, were about to rule the government. Born in North Carolina and a resident since his youth of Tennessee (the mountain area of the state known as East Tennessee), he represented personally and politically the poor, white farmer stock of the South. Entering politics as a Democrat, he served in the national House of Representatives, as governor of Tennessee, and as United States Senator. Throughout his political career he battled for the interests of the yeomen and against the planter aristocrats, "the bastard scrub aristocracy," as he called them in the rough, vivid language of which he was a master. When Tennessee seceded, he denounced her action and remained in his seat in the Senate, the most prominent Southerner to refuse to go with his section. He shortly became one of the most prominent War Democrats supporting the administration, and when Federal armies moved into Tennessee, Lincoln appointed him military governor of the state. In 1864 when the Republicans were looking for a War Democrat as a vice-presidential candidate—in order to make the Union party seem really national—Johnson seemed an obvious choice. He was placed on the ticket as a necessary piece of window dressing. Nobody dreamed he would ever succeed to the Presidency.

In addition to the handicaps imposed by his background, Johnson labored under other disadvantages that were the product of his political personality. Intemperate and often violent in language, stubborn and tactless in manner, he lacked Lincoln's subtle

skill in handling people. He had an above-average mind, high integrity, a capacity for hard work, and great personal—but not much political—courage. An arrant agrar-

Andrew Johnson. *Johnson, who was a tailor before going into politics, was of medium height and size. He had a dark complexion and boring black eyes. A powerful orator on the stump, he easily lost his temper when heckled and used crude and intemperate language. Sincerely devoted to his principles, he was sometimes too theoretical in upholding them.* (LIBRARY OF CONGRESS)

ian, he had little interest in the welfare of the freed Negroes, a cause dear to the idealistic element of the Republican party, or in legislation to foster industry, the principal objective of the party's powerful business wing. Moreover, while he had opposed secession, he was an old-fashioned agrarian state-righter in that he was also opposed to increasing unduly the powers of the national government. He could not accept the concept held by most Republicans—and put into partial effect by the party during the

Civil War—of a beneficent centrality in Washington subsidizing and stimulating all segments of the national economy. Finally, Johnson, unlike Lincoln, was theoretical rather than practical, dogmatic rather than pragmatic. In dealing with Reconstruction, he always stood righteously on the Constitution, even though that document obviously did not envision the unprecedented constitutional situation that existed after the war.

Johnson revealed his plan of Reconstruction soon after he took office, and proceeded to execute it during the summer of 1865 when Congress was not in session. It was applied, of course, to the states of the late Confederacy that had not come under the Lincoln plan; Johnson recognized as legal organizations the Lincoln governments in Louisiana, Arkansas, and Tennessee. In some ways his scheme resembled Lincoln's, and in others it followed the provisions of the Wade-Davis Bill. Like his predecessor, Johnson assumed that the seceded states had not left the Union and that the process of restoration should be started by the President. Also like Lincoln, he announced his design in a proclamation of amnesty which extended pardon for past conduct to all who would take a prescribed oath of allegiance. Denied the privilege of taking the oath until they received individual pardons from the President were men who had held important offices in the Confederacy (Johnson excepted more leaders than Lincoln had) and Confederates worth $20,000 or more (presumably this provision was aimed specifically at Johnson's old enemies, the planters). For each state the President appointed a provisional governor who was to invite the qualified voters, those who had sworn the oath, to elect delegates to a constitutional convention. Johnson did not specify that a minimum per cent of the former voters had to take the oath, as did the Lincoln and Wade-Davis proposals, but the implication was plain that he would require a majority.

As conditions of readmittance, the state convention had to revoke the ordinance of secession, abolish slavery, and repudiate the Confederate and state war debts. The final procedure before restoration was for a state to elect a state government and representatives to Congress. By the end of 1865 the states affected by Johnson's plan had complied with its requirements; they had established or were in process of establishing new and loyal state governments. Indeed, if the Lincoln governments are included, all of the seceded states had functioning civil governments, had been reconstructed, were ready to resume their places in the Union—if Congress should choose to recognize them when it met in December, 1865.

Congressional recognition of the political creations of Lincoln and Johnson was exactly what the Radical Republicans were determined to prevent. And many people in the North agreed with them that Presidential Reconstruction had been rushed too fast, was being accomplished too easily. Northerners were disturbed by the seeming reluctance of some members of the Southern conventions to abolish slavery and by the refusal of all the conventions to grant the suffrage to even a few Negroes. They were astounded that states claiming to be "loyal" should elect as state officials and representatives to Congress prominent leaders of the recent Confederacy; particularly hard to understand was Georgia's choice of Alexander H. Stephens, late Vice President of the Confederacy, as a United States Senator. As the year 1866 wore on, several spectacular race riots occurred in Southern cities, notably in New Orleans and Memphis, in which many more Negroes than whites were killed. Surveying these developments, many Northern people were moved to ask if the South had accepted defeat, if Southerners could be trusted to deal fairly with the freedmen. But above all, Northern opinion was aroused by the so-called Black

Codes passed by the Lincoln-Johnson legislatures in the South. Probably no single action of the South so inclined popular support to the Radicals as the enactment of these laws.

the codes were designed to govern relations between the races, to define the position of the former slaves in Southern society, and to invest the Negroes with a recognized and legal although subordinate status. The pro-

---

The Black Code of Louisiana

The sections in the Black Codes regulating Negro labor angered Northern opinion and turned many people in favor of Radical Reconstruction. The Louisiana Code had this to say:

"Sec. 1. Be it enacted by the Senate and House of Representatives of the State of Louisiana in general assembly convened, That all persons employed as laborers in agricultural pursuits shall be required, during the first ten days of the month of January of each year, to make contracts for labor for the then ensuing year, or for the year next ensuing the termination of their present contracts. All contracts for labor for agricultural purposes shall be made in writing, signed by the employer, and shall be made in the presence of a Justice of the Peace and two disinterested witnesses, in whose presence the contract shall be read to the laborer, and when assented to and signed by the latter, shall be considered as binding for the time prescribed. . . .

"Sec. 2. Every laborer shall have full and perfect liberty to choose his employer, but, when once chosen, he shall not be allowed to leave his place of employment until the fulfillment of his contract . . . and if they do so leave, without cause or permission, they shall forfeit all wages earned to the time of abandonment. . . ."

The Black Codes were the South's solution for the problem of the Negro laborer and its substitute for slavery as a white-supremacy device. Economically, the codes were intended to regulate the labor activities of a race which in white opinion would not work for wage arrangements except under compulsion. For a brief period after the war, many Negroes, confused and dazzled by the prospects of freedom, collected in towns or around army camps and did not work; they were led to believe by the speeches of some Republicans that the government was going to give land to every freedman. Some states passed their laws for the specific purpose of forcing the Negroes back to the plantations and farms. Socially,

visions of the codes varied in different states. All the acts conferred certain rights upon the colored people: to own property, to make contracts, to sue and be sued, to enter into legalized marriage. On the other hand, people of color were subject to special restrictions that did not apply to any other group. They could not, as a general rule, testify against a white person, serve on juries, or bear arms. They could enjoy the benefits of the public school system but only in separate schools, and in some states segregation in public places and conveyances was required. Various clauses in the codes reflected the conviction of the whites that the freedmen would not work unless compelled to. Negroes without steady occupation could be apprehended by local officials, fined for vagrancy, and hired out to private employers to satisfy the fine. In two states, Mississippi and South Carolina, the Negro's freedom of economic choice was seriously abridged. In Mississippi he could not own or rent land except in towns and cities, and in South Carolina he could not engage in any vocation except husbandry (agricultural labor) and domestic service. To the South, the Black Codes were a realistic approach to a great social problem. To the North, they seemed to herald a return to slavery.

Northern concern for the freedmen—plus Radical antagonism to Johnson's Reconstruction policy—was responsible for the passage by Congress in 1866 of a bill extending the life and enlarging the functions of the Freedmen's Bureau. In addition to its usual relief work, the bureau was authorized to supervise labor relations between employers and freedmen and to enforce contracts agreed to by both parties. A dispute over a contract would be decided by an agency of the bureau, by what today would be called an administrative court. All Southerners, and for that matter many Northerners, disliked this phase of the bureau's activities. Such issues as the rights of labor, it was widely held, should be settled in the civil courts. The Freedmen's Bureau was the first example in our history of government mediation in bargaining between capital and labor, a practice that was to become commonplace in the twentieth century. Johnson vetoed the measure and his action was sustained, but within a few months a second bill was passed over his veto. In ringing tones the President pointed out that the functions proposed for the Bureau violated state rights and were not sanctioned by the Constitution. He was quite right. But then the Constitution contained nothing bearing on the question of what to do with 4,000,000 freed slaves.

Radical Reconstruction

When Congress convened in December, 1865, one of the first acts of the Radical machine was to deny admission to representatives from the reconstructed states. These representatives should not be accepted, explained Radical leaders, until Congress knew more about the background of their election and the temper of Southern opinion. Accordingly, a joint committee of fifteen—the Committee on Reconstruction—was created to investigate conditions in the South and to advise Congress in framing a Reconstruction policy. It was a mark of the rapid progression of the Radicals toward a hard peace that they considered Johnson's plan inadequate, for the basic provisions of the President's scheme resembled closely the first Radical plan, the Wade-Davis Bill of the previous year.

The Radicals were prepared to defeat Johnson's program, but they felt they had to move cautiously in presenting a counterplan. They were uncertain even yet as to whether Northern opinion would support Negro suffrage imposed by national authority. As a first move, they struck at the Black Codes of Johnson's legislatures, passing in Congress the Civil Rights Bill, which forbade states to discriminate against citizens on account of race or color. Promptly Johnson vetoed the bill, and just as promptly the veto was overridden. Emboldened by their success, the Radicals struck again and harder. The Committee on Reconstruction submitted to Congress in April, 1866, a proposed amendment to the Constitution, the Fourteenth, which constituted the second Radical plan of Reconstruction.

The Fourteenth Amendment, which was adopted by Congress and sent to the states for approval in the early summer, is so important, both in its immediate bearing upon Reconstruction and in its future influence upon federal-state relationships, as to deserve particular analysis. Section 1 declared that all persons born or naturalized in the United States were citizens of the United States and of the states of their residence. This clause, which for the first time in our history set up a national definition of citizenship, was followed by the assertion that no state could abridge the rights of citizens of the United States or deprive any *person* of life, liberty, or property without due process of law or deny to any person within its jurisdiction the equal protection of the laws. In the light of later judicial developments, this provision was the most important part of the amendment; its meaning and intent would become in after years matters of dispute. Without a doubt, the framers intended to guarantee to Negroes the rights of citizenship. They may also have intended to extend the restrictions of the Bill of Rights and particularly of the Fifth Amendment, which applied only to Congress, to the states; this was the interpretation of intent which would be accepted by the federal courts in the civil-rights and segregation cases of the 1940's and 1950's. A few men on the committee probably foresaw that the word "person" could mean a "legal person"—a corporation—and that the amendment could be utilized, as it would be before the turn of the century, to protect business organizations from state regulation. Regardless of what the men on the committee had in mind, the Fourteenth Amendment was destined to have more far-reaching effects upon the structure of federal and state government than any enactment in our entire legislative history.

Section 2 provided that if a state denied the suffrage to any of its adult male inhabitants, its representation in the House of Representatives and the electoral college should suffer a proportionate reduction. To the Radicals as well as to some moderates, this clause seemed a fair and reasonable corrective to the curious effect of emancipation upon the basis of representation. By the "three-fifths compromise" of the Constitution, five slaves were counted as equal to three whites in determining a state's political population; now there were no slaves, and with representation based on total population every Southern state stood to increase its influence in Congress and the electoral college. Section 3 disqualified from any office, national or state, all persons who had previously taken an oath to support the Constitution and later had aided the Confederacy, until Congress by a two-thirds vote of each house should remove their disability. Section 4 validated the Federal debt and invalidated the Confederate debt.

In submitting the amendment for ratification Congress stipulated that it should be voted on by all the states, those that had seceded as well as those that had remained loyal. This provision put Congress in the position of permitting states that it had refused to admit to its own membership to pass on an amendment. The apparent constitutional contradiction was the result of Radical opinion that ratification would not be legal unless submitted to the total number of states. As the total number was thirty-seven, ten states could defeat the amendment; and the former Confederate states numbered eleven. Although prominent Southerners, including some who would be barred from office by the third section, advised their states to endorse the amendment and thus put an end to Reconstruction, the Southern legislatures could not bring themselves to approve a measure that would place a stigma on their late leaders. Only Tennessee ratified the amendment, winning readmittance as a reward; the other ten, joined by Kentucky and Delaware, voted it down. The Fourteenth Amendment was defeated—but only temporarily. When the times were more propitious, the Radicals would bring it up again. Meanwhile, its defeat strengthened their cause and hurt the cause of Johnson and the South. The Radicals were able to say to the North, as they did in the autumnal congressional elections of 1866: We offered the Southern people a reasonable proposal. We did not say to them that they had to let Negroes vote; only that if they did not, they would not have representation for the Negroes. They refused us. Can such a people be entrusted with self-government or admitted to a Union of loyal states?

Apparently the Northern voters were convinced by the logic of the Radical argument. They may have been equally influenced by the Radical propaganda disseminated during the campaign, which played skillfully upon the emotions and passions inherited from the war, or by Johnson's intemperate speeches made during a stumping tour to the Middle West, the President's so-called and ill-fated "swing around the circle." The elections of 1866 returned to Congress an overwhelming majority of Republicans, most of them of the Radical variety. In the Senate the line-up of the parties would be 42 Republicans to 11 Democrats; in the House, 143 Republicans to 49 Democrats. Rarely in our political history has one party so dominated the legislative branch. Now the Radicals could pass any bill over Johnson's veto; now they could enact any kind of Reconstruction plan they desired. With confidence and even arrogance, they looked forward to the struggle with the President that would ensue when Congress assembled in December, 1866.

Exploiting their victory with ruthless rapidity, the Radicals formulated their third and final plan of Reconstruction in the early months of 1867. It was embodied in an act of Congress passed on March 2 and in two supplemental acts of March 23 and July 9. All three were vetoed by Johnson and then repassed by Congress. As these bills, which for convenient classification may be termed the Reconstruction Acts of 1867, were really

parts of one piece, their provisions may be studied as a unit. The final Radical plan was based squarely on the principle that the seceded states had lost their political identity. The Lincoln-Johnson governments were declared to have no legal standing, and the ten former Confederate states (Tennessee had been readmitted) were combined into five military districts, in accordance with the conquered-province theory. In charge of each district was a military commander, supported by an army force, who was directed to prepare his provinces for readmission as states. To this end, he was to cause a registration of voters to be made, including all adult Negro males and white males who were not disfranchised for participation in "rebellion." (According to the Constitution, Congress could not legislate on suffrage in states. It could, however, fix voting privileges in conquered provinces.)

The whites who were excluded were those coming under the disability of the Fourteenth Amendment; but each voter had to swear a complicated loyalty oath, and the registrars of voters were empowered to reject men on suspicion they were not acting in good faith. A partisan registrar, if he wanted, could disqualify enough whites to guarantee a safe Republican majority. In the ten former states, 703,000 Negro and 627,000 white voters would be enrolled, and Negro voters would outnumber white in Mississippi, Louisiana, South Carolina, Alabama, and Florida. After the registration was completed in each province, the commanding general was to call on the voters of the ten subprovinces (or late states) to elect a constitutional convention to prepare a new state constitution which had to provide for Negro suffrage. If this document was ratified by the electorate of a subprovince, elections for a state government could be held. Finally, if Congress approved the constitution, if the state legislature ratified the Fourteenth Amendment, and if the amendment was adopted by the required number of states and became a part of the Constitution —then the state was to be readmitted to the Union.

In imposing Negro suffrage upon the former Confederate states, the political Radicals laid themselves open to an inevitable question from the idealistic Radicals. If it was right for Negroes to vote in the seceded states, was it not equally right that they should have the privilege everywhere in the nation, in the Southern states that had not seceded and in the states of the North? The Radicals had set in motion one of those great historical forces that once started could not be recalled. The movement for national Negro suffrage became too strong to resist. Nor did the Radicals wish to resist it, even though in some Northern states there was intense repugnance to equal rights for colored people. It suited Radical strategy to enshrine Negro suffrage, the basis of Republican strength in the South, in the Constitution, where it would be beyond the reach of repeal. Accordingly, the Radicals prepared the Fifteenth Amendment, which forbade states to deny the suffrage to any citizen because of race or color. Going into effect in 1870, it was the last touch perfecting the final Radical plan.

In the remorseless manner in which the Radicals drove through their program, in their readiness to inaugurate change regardless of social consequence, in their carelessness of constitutional niceties, we see evidences of a revolutionary spirit that would stop at nothing to attain its ends. The Radicals thought of themselves as architects of a revolution, and they did not intend to let any agency, the President or the judiciary, get in their way. They were prepared, if necessary, to establish a kind of congressional dictatorship. To curb the President, and also to facilitate Radical administration of the acts of 1867, Congress passed two palpably unconstitutional laws. One, the Ten-

ure of Office Act (1867) forbade the President to remove civil officials, including members of his cabinet, without the consent of the Senate; its principal purpose was to protect the job of Secretary of War Edwin M. Stanton, who was cooperating with the Radicals. The other, the Command of the Army Act (1867), prohibited the President from issuing military orders except through the commanding general of the army (General Grant), whose headquarters were to be in Washington and who could not be relieved or assigned elsewhere without the consent of the Senate.

When the federal judiciary seemed at the point of questioning Reconstruction legislation, the Radicals intimidated the courts. In 1866 the Supreme Court, presided over since 1864 by Chief Justice Salmon P. Chase, declared in *Ex parte Milligan* that military tribunals were illegal in regions where civil courts were functioning. Although the decision was applied to a case originating in the war, it seemed to threaten the system of military government which the Radicals were planning for the South. Radical anger at the Court was instant and intense. In Congress proposals were made to require a two-thirds majority of the justices to nullify a law of Congress, to deny the Court jurisdiction in Reconstruction cases, to reduce its membership to three, and even to abolish it. The Court took the blunt hints. When the state of Mississippi in 1867 asked for an injunction restraining Johnson from enforcing the Reconstruction Acts, the Court refused to accept jurisdiction (*Mississippi* v. *Johnson*). But in 1868 the Court agreed to hear arguments in a case involving military courts in Mississippi (*Ex parte McCardle*), which by implication involved the legality of the Reconstruction Acts. The Radicals rushed through Congress a law denying the Court appellate jurisdiction in cases concerning habeas corpus. The Court bowed by refusing to hear the case. It bowed again in

Texas v. *White* (1869), in which Chase, while accepting the Lincoln-Johnson theory that the seceded states were still in the Union, conceded that Congress possessed the

creating an imbalance in the American system of government; they were inflating the power of Congress at the expense of the other branches. Their supreme effort in this

The Impeachment of Andrew Johnson. *In this print the Senate is voting on the charges against the President. Chief Justice Chase, the presiding officer, stands at the right. At the left Senator Ross of Kansas announces he votes "Not Guilty."* (FROM *Frank Leslie's Illustrated Newspaper,* 1868)

power to determine permanent conditions of Reconstruction. Although the Supreme Court evaded the Reconstruction issue, it was not during this period an ineffective agency. In the entire history of the country before 1864 the Court had declared only two acts of Congress unconstitutional. During Chase's tenure (1864–1873), it voided ten measures of Congress.

By their aggressive moves against the executive and the judiciary, the Radicals were

direction was their attempt to remove President Johnson by the process of impeachment. Early in 1867 they began searching for evidence that Johnson had committed crimes or misdemeanors in office, the only legal grounds for impeachment, but they could find nothing upon which to base charges. Then Johnson gave them a plausible reason for action by deliberately violating the Tenure of Office Act. He suspended Secretary of War Stanton, who had worked with the Radicals against Johnson (as he had aided the same faction while holding the same office under Lincoln), and named General Grant as his successor. Johnson hoped in this manner to secure a court test case of the Tenure of Office measure, which he believed to be unconstitutional. But when the Senate refused to concur in the suspension, Grant relinquished the office to Stanton. Johnson then dismissed Stanton, but the Secretary, pointing to the action of the Senate, refused to give up the office.

In the House of Representatives the elated Radicals framed and presented to the Senate eleven charges against Johnson. The first nine accusations dealt with the President's violation of the Tenure of Office Act; the tenth and eleventh charged Johnson with making speeches calculated to bring Congress into disrespect and of not faithfully enforcing the various Reconstruction acts. In the trial before the Senate, which lasted from March 25 to May 26, 1868, Johnson's lawyers emphasized that he was justified in technically violating a law in order to force a test case and that the measure did not apply to Stanton anyway: it gave tenure to cabinet members for the term of the President by whom they had been appointed, and Stanton had been appointed by Lincoln. The House managers of the impeachment, while paying some attention to the Tenure of Office Act, harped on the theme that Johnson had opposed the will of the majority in Congress, implying that in so doing he was guilty of crimes and misdemeanors. Terrific pressure was brought upon all the Republican Senators to vote for conviction, but seven Republicans joined the twelve Democrats to vote for acquittal. On three of the charges the vote was identical, 35 to 19, one short of the required two-thirds majority. Thereupon the Radicals called off the proceedings, and the Presidency was saved from the threatened subjection to a triumphant legislative majority.

Reconstruction in the South

By 1868 six of the former Confederate states —Arkansas, North Carolina, South Carolina, Louisiana, Alabama, and Florida—had complied with the process of restoration outlined in the Reconstruction Acts and were readmitted to the Union; delaying tactics by the whites held up the return of Mississippi, Virginia, Georgia, and Texas until 1870. In all ten states, the Republicans constituted a majority and controlled the machinery of government. The Republican party in each Southern state rested on a basis of Negro voters who gratefully supported the party that had given them the suffrage and who had been organized by white leaders: Northerners who had come South for good or bad reasons and who were known as "carpetbaggers"; officials of the Union League, a propaganda arm of the national Republican organization; and some agents of the Freedmen's Bureau. Another element of white leadership in the Republican ranks, which did not remain very long, was provided by Southern whites of the upper economic classes—planters and businessmen, the so-called "scalawags"—who thought they could direct the Negro voters.

When Radical Reconstruction, with its core principle of Negro suffrage, was proposed in Congress, all Southern whites of every class were against it. But among the whites, different groups were animated by different motives. The great mass of the white people, what may be termed in an economic sense the common whites—the yeoman farmers, middle class persons, and poor whites—were opposed to Negro suffrage and to any position of equality for the Negro. They were moved by racial reasons or feelings: they simply believed that Negroes were inferior beings and should occupy an inferior place. The rich whites— the planters and businessmen—were also race conscious, but they reacted to Negro suffrage primarily in economic terms. They opposed Negro voting because it would increase the number of propertyless or laboring-class voters and would endanger the white minority. They employed two principal devices to attain their ends. One was to enter the Republican party and seek to control it. In Mississippi, for example, most of

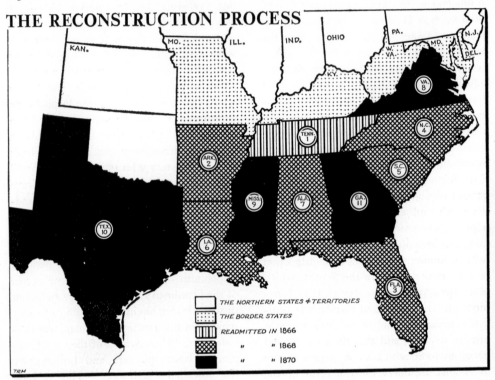

THE RECONSTRUCTION PROCESS

KAN.
MO.
ILL.
IND.
OHIO
PA.
N.J.
W. VA.
MD.
DEL.
KY.
VA. 8
TENN. 1
N.C 4
ARK 2
S.C 5
MISS. 9
AL. 7
GA. 11
TEX 10
LA. 6
FLA 3

☐ THE NORTHERN STATES & TERRITORIES
▦ THE BORDER STATES
▥ READMITTED IN 1866
▨   "   " 1868
■   "   " 1870

TRM

interests of the propertied minority. Already too many poor white men were voters, they believed; if Negro suffrage were added, the barriers against radical agrarianism could not be held.

With the passage of the Reconstruction Acts of 1867, Negro suffrage and, in many states, Negro rule became a reality. The common whites continued to oppose enlarged rights for the freedmen, and during the Reconstruction period they formed the backbone of resistance to the Republican state governments. But the upper-income whites, many of whom were former large slaveholders and were accustomed to dealing with Negroes, attempted to cooperate with the new voters and to direct their political action along lines favorable to the

the former Whigs became Republicans. "Such action is not hard to understand," writes one student (David Donald). "The Whigs were wealthy men—the large planters and the railroad and industrial promoters —who naturally turned to the party which in the state as in the nation was dominated by business interests."[3] Another stratagem was to invite the Negroes to join with interested whites in forming a new party which would be separate from the Republican or Democratic organization and which would recognize the Negro's rights. The most elaborate of these efforts, the Louisiana Unification Movement of 1873, promised

[3] David Donald, "The Scalawag in Mississippi Reconstruction," *Journal of Southern History*, X (1944), 449–50.

complete political and civil equality to the colored people.

All attempts of the rich whites to dominate the Negro vote failed, and finally the promoters joined the general white opposition to Radical Reconstruction. The attempts failed for several reasons: the reluctance of the whites, no matter how far they went in other directions, to concede social equality, and the competing leadership of the carpetbaggers who were always ready to outbid the scalawags. But fundamentally these experiments in white-colored collaboration collapsed because the contracting parties had differing economic aspirations. The Negroes, being poor people, wanted a program of social services financed by the state, which meant high taxes. The whites, representing a propertied minority, desired to reduce state services and keep taxes down to a minimum.

The financial and social record of the Reconstruction governments is a many-sided story. As many of the leaders in the conventions that framed the new state constitutions were Northerners, they put into those documents some of the most advanced provisions in the organic charters of the most progressive Northern states: provisions embodying the latest revisions in local government, judicial organization, public finance, and poor relief. These changes had the effect of modernizing Southern state government, of placing it in step with governmental trends in the rest of the country, but some of them, which looked excellent on paper, were not suited to the peculiar environment of the rural South. The financial program of the Republican governments was a compound of blatant corruption and well-designed, if sometimes impractical, social legislation. The corruption and extravagance are familiar aspects of the Reconstruction story. State budgets expanded to hitherto unknown totals, and state debts soared to previously undreamed-of

heights. In South Carolina, for example, the public debt increased from $7 million to $29 million in eight years.

In part, the corruption was the work of corrupt men. By its very nature, the Reconstruction process in the South attracted unscrupulous individuals who were eager to take what they could seize in a society in a state of revolutionary turmoil. But the economic profligacy of the Republican legislatures has to be placed in a historical setting and judged in the perspective of history. In the entire nation during the Reconstruction period, material standards seemed to transcend all others; dishonesty permeated state and city governments in the North, and the national government as well. In large measure, the corruption in the South was a phase of a national phenomenon, with the same social force—an expanding capitalism eager to secure quick results—acting as the corrupting agent. Included in the spending programs of the Reconstruction governments were subsidies for railroads and other internal improvements, some of which materialized and some of which did not—because the promoters and the politicians pocketed the subsidies. That much of the alleged corruption was a product of deep forces in contemporary society is demonstrated by the continuance of peculation in state government after Republican rule was overthrown.

The swollen state expenditures of the Reconstruction years seem huge only in comparison with the niggardly budgets of the conservative governments of the prewar era; they do not appear large when measured against the sums appropriated by later legislatures. A clearer understanding of Reconstruction emerges if one remembers that the Southern state governments represented poor people, the Negroes, and that these people had a concept, albeit a vague one, of what today would be called the welfare state. They demanded public education, public-works programs, poor relief, and other services that cost money. By the side of the thieving and the foolish spending there should be set some positive and permanent accomplishments, particularly in

The Ku Klux Klan: A Southern View. *This Klan broadside depicts the organization as most Southerners saw it. The figure with the flag and sword epitomizes white culture and has overthrown the Negro enemy. Note the incendiary torch in the hand of the Negro and the broken chains symbolizing his former slave status.* (RUTHERFORD B. HAYES LIBRARY)

education. One example is offered by South Carolina, which in 1860 had only 20,000 children in public scools; by 1873 some 50,000 white and 70,000 Negro students were enrolled in the school system.

The period of Republican control in the South varied from state to state. In some states it was overthrown by the whites almost before it began; in others it endured for years. The dates of white recovery of power in each state are as follows: Virginia, North Carolina, Georgia (1870); Texas (1873); Alabama, Arkansas (1874); Mississippi (1875); Louisiana, South Carolina, Florida (1877).

Republican power in the South rested upon three bases: the Negro vote, Republican control of the national government and particularly of the Presidency, and the presence of federal troops in the South. Should any of these be shattered or weakened, the structure of Republican rule would topple. Between 1867 and 1877 the Republicans controlled Congress for the greater part of the period, and between 1869 and 1877 a Republican President sat in the White House. Whenever in a Southern state the results of an election were disputed by Republicans and Democrats, or whenever Southern whites threatened to oust the Republicans by force, the national administration intervened to save the local Republicans. The military commander in the state concerned would be directed to install the Republican governor and legislature in office or to prevent the whites from driving them out of office. Without this support from Washington, Republican dominance in the South would have been destroyed long before it was. As the 1870's wore on, however, a rising conservative opinion in the North criticized the government for deciding elections with troops, and Republican leaders became increasingly aware that the propped-up reconstructed governments of the South were becoming a political liability.

In the states where the whites constituted a majority—the Upper South states—overthrow of Republican control was a relatively simple matter. The whites had only to organize and win the elections. Their success was facilitated by the early restoration of the suffrage to those whites who had been deprived of it by national or state action. Presidential and congressional pardons returned the privilege to numerous individuals, and in 1872 Congress, responding to public demands to forgive the penalties of the war, enacted the Amnesty Act, which restored political rights to 150,000 ex-Confederates and left only 500 excluded from political life.

who have been intrigued by their romantic hooded and robed apparel and their elaborate ritual. The national government moved quickly to stamp them out, Congress passing two Force Acts (1870–1871) and the Ku

The Ku Klux Klan: A Northern View. *This drawing in a Northern illustrated paper shows a group of Klansmen about to murder a carpetbagger whom they have abducted.* (LIBRARY OF CONGRESS)

In other states, where the Negroes were in the majority or the population difference between the races was small, the whites resorted to intimidation and violence. Frankly terroristic were the secret societies that appeared in many parts of the South, the Ku Klux Klan, the Knights of the White Camelia, and others, which attempted to frighten or physically prevent Negroes from voting. Although the societies were undoubtedly effective, their influence has probably been exaggerated by later writers

Klux Klan Act (1871) which authorized the President to use military force and martial law in areas where the orders were active. Finally, the leaders of the organizations, discovering that individual members were taking advantage of the secrecy arrangements to commit private crimes, ordered them disbanded.

More potent than the secret orders were the open semimilitary organizations that operated under such names as Rifle clubs, Red Shirts, and White Leagues. The first such society was founded in Mississippi, whence the idea spread to other states, and the procedure employed by the clubs was called the Mississippi Plan. Briefly stated,

storekeepers refused to extend them credit, employers refused to give them work. Economic pressure was a force which the Negro could not fight. If the Radicals, in bring-

---

A Carpetbag Analysis of Reconstruction

Albion W. Tourgee was an Ohio-born carpetbagger who became prominent in Reconstruction politics in North Carolina. He wrote *A Fool's Errand* (1879), probably the first novel dealing with Reconstruction. In the following passage the "Fool," the central character and a carpetbagger (undoubtedly expressing Tourgee's own ideas), explains why he thinks Reconstruction collapsed. It reveals the sense of failure and frustration felt by men like Tourgee after 1877: "We tried to superimpose the civilization, the idea of the North, upon the South at a moment's warning. We presumed, that, by the suppression of rebellion, the Southern white man had become identical with the Caucasian of the North in thought and sentiment; and that the slave, by emancipation, had become a saint and a Solomon at once. So we tried to build up communities there which should be identical in thought, sentiment, growth, and development, with those of the North. It was A Fool's Errand."

---

the plan called for the whites in each community to organize and arm, and to be prepared, if necessary, to resort to force to win elections. But the heart of the scheme was in the phrase "drawing the color line." By one method or another, legal or illegal, every white man was to be forced to join the Democratic party or leave the community. By similar methods, every Negro male was to be excluded from political action; in a few states he was permitted to vote—if he voted Democratic. Perhaps an even stronger influence than the techniques practiced by the leagues was the simple and unromantic weapon of economic pressure. The war had freed the Negro, but he was still a laborer— a hired worker or a tenant—dependent upon the whites for his livelihood. The whites readily discovered that this dependence placed the Negro in their power. Planters refused to rent land to Republican Negroes,

ing the Negro to political power, had accomplished a revolution, it was a superficial one. They failed to provide the Negro with economic power, as they might have done by giving him possession of confiscated land, and hence his rule had no lasting basis and was easily destroyed.

The Aftermath of Reconstruction

By 1876 the whites had recovered control in every Southern state except Louisiana, South Carolina, and Florida. But in each redeemed state a Republican party still existed; and as long as the Republicans controlled the national government and federal troops remained in the South, Reconstruction was still a reality. The three remaining states might stay under Republican rule; white victory in the others might be undone. In 1876 there occurred the famous presidential election in which both the Republicans and the Democrats claimed to have elected their candidate. After months of tense suspense, the issue was decided by a complicated compromise which allowed the Republicans to retain the Presidency. One result of the election was that the new chief executive, Rutherford B. Hayes, withdrew federal troops from the South in 1877. Immediately the Republican governments in Louisiana, South Carolina, and Florida fell, and white supremacy was restored in the ten states that the Radicals just a few years before had prostrated to the status of conquered provinces.

The withdrawal of the troops was a symbol that the national government was giving up its attempt to control Southern politics and to determine the place of the Negro in Southern society. The surrender, it is to be noted, was made by the Republicans. They could yield with good grace because after 1877 they had no particular need for the support of the reconstructed South. The economic legislation of the war and postwar years was safe from repeal; industry was securely entrenched in the national economy; and Republican dominance could be maintained without Southern votes. Another symbol of retreat was furnished by the Supreme Court, which in a series of decisions emasculated the Fourteenth and Fifteenth amendments of much of their significance. In the Civil Rights Cases (1883) the Court took the position that the Fourteenth Amendment prohibited states from discriminating against people on account of color but did not restrict private individuals or organizations. That is, railroads, hotels, theaters, and the like could legally practice segregation. Eventually the Court validated state legislation which discriminated against Negroes. In *Plessy* v. *Ferguson* (1896), a case involving a law that required separate seating arrangements for the races on railroads, the Court held that separate accommodations did not deprive the Negro of equal rights if the accommodations were equal. And in *Cumming* v. *County Board of Education* (1899) the Court held that laws establishing separate schools for whites and Negroes were valid if the facilities were equal for both.

The men who came to power in the South after 1877 were not in the old agrarian, planter tradition. Known as Bourbons or Redeemers, they were industrialists or would-be industrialists. They preached the industrialization of the South through the importation of Northern capital, a policy of low taxes to attract business, and a political alliance with the Northeast instead of with the South's traditional ally, the West. Controlling state governments through the medium of the Democratic party, which as a result of Reconstruction was the only party in the section, they practiced a program marked by economy in government, reduced taxes, and few social services. They did not attempt to abolish Negro suffrage but instead used the Negro vote, as men of their class had tried to use it during Reconstruction, to maintain their power. Negroes continued to vote after the return of white supremacy, but in reduced numbers. In some states they were prevented from voting by an implied threat of force; in others, their influence was nullified by tricky devices—tissue ballots and a complicated arrangement of ballot boxes—that disqualified their votes. But in many areas the colored vote was a purchased and directed vote, paid for by the Bourbons and used by them to beat down attempts of the farmers to take over control of the Democratic party.

Not until the 1890's did the Southern states attempt to disfranchise the Negroes, and the impetus for the attempt when it came was furnished by the white farmers. The farmers demanded disfranchisement because they were opposed for racial reasons to Negro voting and because they objected to the Negro vote being employed against them. The rich whites acquiesced, partly out of a desire to placate the white masses and partly because in the agrarian unrest that characterized the nineties the farmers in some states had sought to vote the Negroes on their side. The threat of competition for the Negro vote frightened all whites, and there was a general feeling that the time had come to close ranks if white supremacy was to be maintained.

In devising laws to disfranchise the Negroes, the Southern states had to take care to evade the intent of the Fifteenth Amendment. That measure did not confer suffrage upon the Negroes, but merely prohibited states from denying it because of color. The Southern problem, then, was to exclude Negroes from the franchise without seeming to base the exclusion on race. Two devices were widely employed before 1900. One was the poll tax or some form of property qualification. The other was the literacy and understanding test, which required a voter to demonstrate an ability to read and to interpret the Constitution. The reasoning behind the latter law was that local registrars could administer an impossible reading test to Negroes or rule that their interpretation of the Constitution was inadequate. Both of these devices could be used, and were used, to deny the franchise to poor white men,

who protested against tests being applied to them. So, many states passed so-called "grandfather laws," which permitted men who could not meet the literacy and property qualifications to be admitted to the suffrage if their ancestors had voted before 1867 or some date before Reconstruction began.

The Supreme Court proved as understanding in ruling on the disfranchising laws as it was in dealing with the civil rights cases. Although the Court eventually voided the grandfather laws, it validated the literacy tests (*Williams* v. *Mississippi*, 1898), and manifested a general willingness to let the Southern states define suffrage standards— provided the evasions of the Fifteenth Amendment were not too glaring. As the turn of the century approached, the South seemed to have won a complete victory over the outside influences that had sought to disturb its way of life, and Reconstruction seemed to the white South like a bad dream receding in the past. But the deep and turbulent forces generated in the years between 1865 and 1877 were only temporarily exhausted. They would appear again in American life as Americans continued to search for solutions of all the problems created by the Civil War and its troubled aftermath.

→》》→》》→》》→》》←《《←《《←《《←《《←

BIBLIOGRAPHY

MORE THAN for any other period of American history, the literature on reconstruction is marked by controversy and subjectivity. There is no good synthesis of the subject. Therefore the student may best approach reconstruction through the medium of the following articles: H. K. Beale, "On Rewriting Reconstruction History," *American Historical Review*, XLV (1940); F. B. Simkins, "New Viewpoints of Reconstruction," *Journal of Southern History*, V (1939); and T. H. Williams, "An Analysis of Some Reconstruction Attitudes," *ibid.*, XII (1946).

The first scholarly writing on reconstruction was done by W. A. Dunning and his students in the early 1900's. Dunning summarized his findings in *Reconstruction, Political and Economic* (1907). Although the Dunning school made some excellent contributions, its members tended to have a favorable orientation to Democrats and Southern whites. Dunning's ablest student, W. L. Fleming, wrote his own synthesis, *The Sequel of Appomattox* (1919), and edited a superb source collection, *A Documentary History of Reconstruction* (2 vols., 1906). Later general studies that show touches of the Dunning influence are C. G. Bowers, *The Tragic Era* (1929), colorful but superficial; G. F. Milton, *The Age of Hate* (1930); R. S. Henry, *The Story of Reconstruction* (1938); and E. M. Coulter, *The South During Reconstruction* (1947), opinionated but excellent for social and economic developments.

W. E. B. Du Bois attempted a synthesis in *Black Reconstruction* (1935). His work has value but is marred by subjectivity and an exaggerated sense of class consciousness. In *The Road to Reunion, 1865–1900* (1937), P. H. Buck traces somewhat too enthusiastically the factors that healed the wounds of war. The best account of the nation as a whole during the period is Allan Nevins, *The Emergence of Modern America, 1865–1878* (1927).

A number of special studies illuminate their own subject and the general reconstruction story. They are H. K. Beale, *The Critical Year* (1930), focusing on 1866; F. W. Klingberg, *The Southern Claims Commission* (1955); G. R. Bentley, *A History of the Freedmen's Bureau* (1955); J. B. James, *The Framing of the Fourteenth Amendment* (1956); P. A. Bruce, *The Plantation Negro as a Freedman* (1889); S. F. Horn, *The Invisible Empire* (1939), the Ku Klux Klan; and O. A. Singletary, *The Negro Militia and Reconstruction* (1957). Few good biographies for the period exist. Recommended are R. W. Winston, *Andrew Johnson* (1928), and Current, *Old Thad Stevens.* The student should examine some of the books by Northern and British visitors to the South during Reconstruction, notably Sidney Andrews, *The South Since the War* (1866); Robert Somers, *The Southern States Since the War* (1871); and J. T. Trowbridge, *A Picture of the Desolated States* (1866; new version with title *The Desolate South* edited by Gordon Carroll, 1956).

Most of the state studies of Reconstruction are dated, and new ones are needed. Best of the older works is J. W. Garner, *Reconstruction in Mississippi* (1901). In a class by itself is F. B. Simkins and R. H. Woody, *South Carolina During Reconstruction* (1932). Also recommended are J. W. Patton, *Unionism and Reconstruction in Tennessee* (1934), and T. B. Alexander, *Political Reconstruction in Tennessee* (1950).

The role of the Negro in Reconstruction and after is adequately treated in a number of books by white and Negro scholars. Franklin, *From Slavery to Freedom*, is a general history of the Negro. R. W. Logan deals with the aftermath of Reconstruction in *The Negro in American Life and Thought* (1954). A good biography is S. R. Spencer, Jr., *Booker T. Washington and the Negro's Place in American Life* (1955), but see also Washington's autobiography, *Up From Slavery* (1901). Two excellent state studies are V. L. Wharton, *The Negro in Mississippi, 1865–1890* (1947), and G. B. Tindall, *South Carolina Negroes, 1877–1900* (1952).

The emergence of the New South receives attention in P. A. Bruce, *The Rise of the New South* (1905); Holland Thompson, *The New South* (1919); and M. B. Hammond, *The Cotton Industry* (1897); but the standard work is C. V. Woodward, *Origins of the New South, 1877–1913* (1951). Tensions in Southern society are ably discussed in Roger Shugg, *Origins of Class Struggle in Louisiana* (1939); G. T. Stephenson, *Race Distinctions in American Law* (1910); Paul Lewinson, *Race, Class and Party* (1932); and Woodward, *The Strange Career of Jim Crow* (1953; paperback edition, 1957).

Appendices

THE
DECLARATION OF INDEPENDENCE

In Congress, July 4, 1776,

THE UNANIMOUS DECLARATION OF THE THIRTEEN UNITED STATES OF AMERICA

When, in the course of human events, it becomes necessary for one people to dissolve the political bands which have connected them with another, and to assume, among the powers of the earth, the separate and equal station to which the laws of nature and of nature's God entitle them, a decent respect to the opinions of mankind requires that they should declare the causes which impel them to the separation.

We hold these truths to be self-evident, that all men are created equal; that they are endowed by their Creator with certain unalienable rights; that among these, are life, liberty, and the pursuit of happiness. That, to secure these rights, governments are instituted among men, deriving their just powers from the consent of the governed; that, whenever any form of government becomes destructive of these ends, it is the right of the people to alter or to abolish it, and to institute a new government, laying its foundation on such principles, and organizing its powers in such form, as to them shall seem most likely to effect their safety and happiness. Prudence, indeed, will dictate that governments long established, should not be changed for light and transient causes; and, accordingly, all experience hath shown, that mankind are more disposed to suffer, while evils are sufferable, than to right themselves by abolishing the forms to which they are accustomed. But, when a long train of abuses and usurpations, pursuing invariably the same object, evinces a design to reduce them under absolute despotism, it is their right, it is their duty, to throw off such government and to provide new guards for their future security. Such has been the patient sufferance of these colonies, and such is now the necessity which constrains them to alter their former systems of government. The history of the present King of Great Britain is a history of repeated injuries and usurpations, all having, in direct object, the establishment of an absolute tyranny over these States. To prove this, let facts be submitted to a candid world:—

He has refused his assent to laws the most wholesome and necessary for the public good.

He has forbidden his governors to pass laws of immediate and pressing importance, unless suspended in their operation till his assent should be obtained; and, when so suspended, he has utterly neglected to attend to them.

He has refused to pass other laws for the accommodation of large districts of people, unless those people would relinquish the right of representation in the legislature; a right inestimable to them, and formidable to tyrants only.

He has called together legislative bodies at places unusual, uncomfortable, and distant from the depository of their public records, for the sole purpose of fatiguing them into compliance with his measures.

He has dissolved representative houses repeatedly for opposing, with manly firmness, his invasions on the rights of the people.

He has refused, for a long time after such dissolutions, to cause others to be elected; whereby the legislative powers, incapable of annihilation, have returned to the people at large for their exercise; the state remaining, in the meantime, exposed to all the danger of invasion from without, and convulsions within.

He has endeavored to prevent the population of these States; for that purpose, obstructing the laws for naturalization of foreigners, refusing to pass others to encourage their migration hither, and raising the conditions of new appropriations of lands.

He has obstructed the administration of justice, by refusing his assent to laws for establishing judiciary powers.

He has made judges dependent on his will alone, for the tenure of their offices, and the amount and payment of their salaries.

He has erected a multitude of new offices, and sent hither swarms of officers to harass our people, and eat out their substance.

He has kept among us, in time of peace, standing armies, without the consent of our legislatures.

He has affected to render the military independent of, and superior to, the civil power.

He has combined, with others, to subject us to a jurisdiction foreign to our Constitution, and unacknowledged by our laws; giving his assent to their acts of pretended legislation:

For quartering large bodies of armed troops among us:

For protecting them by a mock trial, from punishment, for any murders which they should commit on the inhabitants of these States:

For cutting off our trade with all parts of the world:

For imposing taxes on us without our consent:

For depriving us, in many cases, of the benefit of trial by jury:

For transporting us beyond seas to be tried for pretended offences:

For abolishing the free system of English laws in a neighboring province, establishing therein an arbitrary government, and enlarging its boundaries, so as to render it at once an example and fit instrument for introducing the same absolute rule into these colonies:

For taking away our charters, abolishing our most valuable laws, and altering, fundamentally, the powers of our governments:

For suspending our own legislatures, and declaring themselves invested with power to legislate for us in all cases whatsoever.

He has abdicated government here, by declaring us out of his protection, and waging war against us.

He has plundered our seas, ravaged our coasts, burnt our towns, and destroyed the lives of our people.

He is, at this time, transporting large armies of foreign mercenaries to complete the works of death, desolation, and tyranny, already begun, with circumstances of cruelty and perfidy scarcely paralleled in the most barbarous ages, and totally unworthy the head of a civilized nation.

He has constrained our fellow citizens, taken captive on the high seas, to bear arms against their country, to become the executioners of their friends, and brethren, or to fall themselves by their hands.

He has excited domestic insurrections amongst us, and has endeavored to bring on the inhabitants of our frontiers, the merciless Indian savages, whose known rule of warfare is an undistinguished destruction of all ages, sexes, and conditions.

In every stage of these oppressions, we have petitioned for redress, in the most humble terms; our repeated petitions have been answered only by repeated injury. A prince, whose character is thus marked by every act which may define a tyrant, is unfit to be the ruler of a free people.

Nor have we been wanting in attention to our British brethren. We have warned them, from time to time, of attempts made by their legislature to extend an unwarrantable jurisdiction over us. We have reminded them of the circumstances of our emigration and settlement here. We have appealed to their native justice and magnanimity, and we have conjured them, by the ties of our common kindred, to disavow these usurpations, which would inevitably interrupt our connections and correspondence. They, too, have been deaf to the voice of justice and consanguinity. We must, therefore, acquiesce in the necessity which denounces our separation, and hold them, as we hold the rest of mankind, enemies in war, in peace, friends.

We, therefore, the representatives of the United States of America, in general Congress assembled, appealing to the Supreme Judge of the world for the rectitude of our intentions, do, in the name, and by the authority of the good people of these colonies, solemnly publish and declare, that these united colonies are, and of right ought to be, free and independent states: that they are absolved from all allegiance to the British Crown, and that all political connection between them and the state of Great Britain is, and ought to be, totally dissolved; and that, as free and independent states, they have full power to levy war, conclude peace, contract alliances, establish commerce, and to do all other acts and things which independent states may of right do. And, for the support of this declaration, with a firm reliance on the protection of Divine Providence, we mutually pledge to each other our lives, our fortunes, and our sacred honor.

The foregoing Declaration was, by order of Congress, engrossed, and signed by the following members:

JOHN HANCOCK

NEW HAMPSHIRE

Josiah Bartlett
William Whipple
Matthew Thornton

MASSACHUSETTS BAY

Samuel Adams
John Adams
Robert Treat Paine
Elbridge Gerry

RHODE ISLAND

Stephen Hopkins
William Ellery

CONNECTICUT

Roger Sherman
Samuel Huntington
William Williams
Oliver Wolcott

NEW YORK

William Floyd
Philip Livingston
Francis Lewis
Lewis Morris

NEW JERSEY

Richard Stockton
John Witherspoon
Francis Hopkinson
John Hart
Abraham Clark

PENNSYLVANIA

Robert Morris
Benjamin Rush
Benjamin Franklin
John Morton
George Clymer
James Smith
George Taylor
James Wilson
George Ross

DELAWARE

Caesar Rodney
George Read
Thomas M'Kean

MARYLAND

Samuel Chase
William Paca
Thomas Stone
Charles Carroll,
  of Carrollton

VIRGINIA

George Wythe
Richard Henry Lee
Thomas Jefferson
Benjamin Harrison
Thomas Nelson, Jr.
Francis Lightfoot Lee
Carter Braxton

NORTH CAROLINA

William Hooper
Joseph Hewes
John Penn

SOUTH CAROLINA

Edward Rutledge
Thomas Heyward, Jr.
Thomas Lynch, Jr.
Arthur Middleton

GEORGIA

Button Gwinnett
Lyman Hall
George Walton

Resolved, That copies of the Declaration be sent to the several assemblies, conventions, and committees, or councils of safety, and to the several commanding officers of the continental troops; that it be proclaimed in each of the United States, at the head of the army.

THE CONSTITUTION OF THE
UNITED STATES OF AMERICA[1]

We the People of the United States, in Order to form a more perfect Union, establish Justice, insure domestic Tranquility, provide for the common defence, promote the general Welfare, and secure the Blessings of Liberty to ourselves and our Posterity, do ordain and establish this CONSTITUTION for the United States of America.

ARTICLE I

SECTION 1. All legislative Powers herein granted shall be vested in a Congress of the United States, which shall consist of a Senate and House of Representatives.

SECTION 2. The House of Representatives shall be composed of Members chosen every second Year by the People of the several States, and the Electors in each State shall have the Qualifications requisite for Electors of the most numerous Branch of the State Legislature.

No Person shall be a Representative who shall not have attained to the Age of twenty-five Years, and been seven Years a Citizen of the United States, and who shall not, when elected, be an Inhabitant of that State in which he shall be chosen.

[Representatives and direct Taxes[2] shall be apportioned among the several States which may be included within this Union, according to their respective Numbers, which shall be determined by adding to the whole Number of free Persons, including those bound to Service for a Term of Years, and excluding Indians not taxed, three fifths of all other Persons.][3] The actual Enumeration shall be made within three Years after the first Meeting of the Congress of the United States, and within every subsequent Term of ten Years, in such Manner as they shall by Law direct. The Number of Representatives shall not exceed one for every thirty Thousand, but each State shall have at Least one Representative; and until such enumeration shall be made, the State of New Hampshire shall be entitled to chuse three, Massachusetts eight, Rhode-Island and Providence Plantations one, Connecticut five, New York six, New Jersey four, Pennsylvania eight, Delaware one, Maryland six, Virginia ten, North Carolina five, South Carolina five, and Georgia three.

When vacancies happen in the Representation from any State, the Executive Authority thereof shall issue Writs of Election to fill such Vacancies.

The House of Representatives shall chuse their Speaker and other Officers; and shall have the sole Power of Impeachment.

SECTION 3. The Senate of the United States shall be composed of two Senators from each State, chosen by the Legislature thereof, for six Years; and each Senator shall have one Vote.

Immediately after they shall be assembled in Consequence of the first Election, they shall be divided as equally as may be into three Classes. The Seats of the Senators of the first Class shall be vacated at the Expiration of the second Year, of the second Class at the Expiration of the fourth

---

[1] This version, which follows the original Constitution in capitalization and spelling, was published by the United States Department of the Interior, Office of Education, in 1935.

[2] Altered by 16th Amendment.

[3] Negated by 14th Amendment.

Year, and of the third Class at the Expiration of the sixth Year, so that one-third may be chosen every second Year; and if Vacancies happen by Resignation, or otherwise, during the Recess of the Legislature of any State, the Executive thereof may make temporary Appointments until the next Meeting of the Legislature, which shall then fill such Vacancies.

No Person shall be a Senator who shall not have attained to the Age of thirty Years, and been nine Years a Citizen of the United States, and who shall not, when elected, be an Inhabitant of that State for which he shall be chosen.

The Vice President of the United States shall be President of the Senate, but shall have no vote, unless they be equally divided.

The Senate shall chuse their other Officers, and also a President pro tempore, in the absence of the Vice President, or when he shall exercise the Office of President of the United States.

The Senate shall have the sole Power to try all Impeachments. When sitting for that purpose, they shall be on Oath or Affirmation. When the President of the United States is tried, the Chief Justice shall preside: And no person shall be convicted without the Concurrence of two thirds of the Members present.

Judgment in Cases of Impeachment shall not extend further than to removal from Office, and disqualification to hold and enjoy any Office of honor, Trust, or Profit under the United States: but the Party convicted shall nevertheless be liable and subject to Indictment, Trial, Judgment, and Punishment, according to Law.

SECTION 4. The Times, Places and Manner of holding Elections for Senators and Representatives, shall be prescribed in each State by the Legislature thereof; but the Congress may at any time by Law make or alter such Regulations, except as to the Places of Chusing Senators.

The Congress shall assemble at least once in every Year, and such Meeting shall be on the first Monday in December, unless they shall by Law appoint a different Day.

SECTION 5. Each House shall be the Judge of the Elections, Returns and Qualifications of its own Members, and a Majority of each shall constitute a Quorum to do Business; but a smaller number may adjourn from day to day, and may be authorized to compel the Attendance of absent Members, in such Manner, and under such Penalties, as each House may provide.

Each House may determine the Rules of its Proceedings, punish its Members for disorderly Behavior, and, with the Concurrence of two thirds, expel a Member.

Each House shall keep a Journal of its Proceedings, and from time to time publish the same, excepting such Parts as may in their Judgment require Secrecy; and the Yeas and Nays of the Members of either House on any question shall, at the Desire of one fifth of those Present, be entered on the Journal.

Neither House, during the Session of Congress, shall, without the Consent of the other, adjourn for more than three days, nor to any other Place than that in which the two Houses shall be sitting.

SECTION 6. The Senators and Representatives shall receive a Compensation for their Services, to be ascertained by Law, and paid out of the Treasury of the United States. They shall in all Cases, except Treason, Felony, and Breach of the Peace, be privileged from Arrest during their Attendance at the Session of their respective Houses, and in going to and returning from the same; and for any Speech or Debate in either House, they shall not be questioned in any other Place.

No Senator or Representative shall, during the Time for which he was elected, be appointed to any civil Office under the Authority of the United States, which shall have been created, or the Emoluments whereof shall have been increased, during such time; and no Person holding any Office under the United States shall be a Member of either House during his continuance in Office.

SECTION 7. All Bills for raising Revenue

shall originate in the House of Representatives; but the Senate may propose or concur with Amendments as on other bills.

Every Bill which shall have passed the House of Representatives and the Senate, shall, before it become a Law, be presented to the President of the United States; If he approve he shall sign it, but if not he shall return it, with his Objections, to that House in which it shall have originated, who shall enter the Objections at large on their Journal, and proceed to reconsider it. If after such Reconsideration two thirds of that House shall agree to pass the bill, it shall be sent, together with the objections, to the other House, by which it shall likewise be reconsidered, and if approved by two thirds of that House, it shall become a Law. But in all such Cases the Votes of both Houses shall be determined by Yeas and Nays, and the Names of the Persons voting for and against the Bill shall be entered on the Journal of each House respectively. If any Bill shall not be returned by the President within ten Days (Sundays excepted) after it shall have been presented to him, the Same shall be a Law, in like Manner as if he had signed it, unless the Congress by their Adjournment prevent its Return, in which Case it shall not be a Law.

Every Order, Resolution, or Vote to which the Concurrence of the Senate and House of Representatives may be necessary (except on a question of Adjournment) shall be presented to the President of the United States; and before the Same shall take Effect, shall be approved by him, or being disapproved by him, shall be repassed by two thirds of the Senate and House of Representatives, according to the Rules and Limitations prescribed in the Case of a Bill.

SECTION 8. The Congress shall have Power To lay and collect Taxes, Duties, Imposts and Excises, to pay the Debts and provide for the common Defence and general Welfare of the United States; but all Duties, Imposts and Excises shall be uniform throughout the United States;

To borrow money on the credit of the United States;

To regulate Commerce with foreign Nations, and among the several States, and with the Indian Tribes;

To establish an uniform Rule of Naturalization, and uniform Laws on the subject of Bankruptcies throughout the United States;

To coin Money, regulate the Value thereof, and of foreign Coin, and fix the Standard of Weights and Measures;

To provide for the Punishment of counterfeiting the Securities and current Coin of the United States;

To establish Post Offices and post Roads;

To promote the Progress of Science and useful Arts, by securing for limited Times to Authors and Inventors the exclusive Right to their respective Writings and Discoveries;

To constitute Tribunals inferior to the Supreme Court;

To define and punish Piracies and Felonies committed on the high Seas, and Offenses against the Law of Nations;

To declare War, grant Letters of Marque and Reprisal, and make Rules concerning Captures on Land and Water;

To raise and support Armies, but no Appropriation of Money to that Use shall be for a longer Term than two Years;

To provide and maintain a Navy;

To make Rules for the Government and Regulation of the land and naval forces;

To provide for calling forth the Militia to execute the Laws of the Union, suppress Insurrections and repel Invasions;

To provide for organizing, arming, and disciplining the Militia, and for governing such Part of them as may be employed in the Service of the United States, reserving to the States respectively, the Appointment of the Officers, and the Authority of training the Militia according to the discipline prescribed by Congress;

To exercise exclusive Legislation in all Cases whatsoever, over such District (not exceeding ten Miles square) as may, by Cession of particular States, and the acceptance of Congress, become the Seat of the

Government of the United States, and to exercise like Authority over all Places purchased by the Consent of the Legislature of the State in which the Same shall be, for the Erection of Forts, Magazines, Arsenals, dock-Yards, and other needful Buildings; —And

To make all Laws which shall be necessary and proper for carrying into Execution the foregoing Powers, and all other Powers vested by this Constitution in the Government of the United States, or in any Department or Officer thereof.

SECTION 9. The Migration or Importation of such Persons as any of the States now existing shall think proper to admit, shall not be prohibited by the Congress prior to the Year one thousand eight hundred and eight, but a tax or duty may be imposed on such Importation, not exceeding ten dollars for each Person.

The privilege of the Writ of Habeas Corpus shall not be suspended, unless when in Cases of Rebellion or Invasion the public Safety may require it.

No Bill of Attainder or ex post facto Law shall be passed.

No capitation, or other direct, Tax shall be laid unless in Proportion to the Census or Enumeration herein before directed to be taken.

No Tax or Duty shall be laid on Articles exported from any State.

No Preference shall be given by any Regulation of Commerce or Revenue to the Ports of one State over those of another: nor shall Vessels bound to, or from, one State, be obliged to enter, clear, or pay Duties in another.

No Money shall be drawn from the Treasury, but in Consequence of Appropriations made by Law; and a regular Statement and Account of the Receipts and Expenditures of all public Money shall be published from time to time.

No Title of Nobility shall be granted by the United States: And no Person holding any Office of Profit or Trust under them, shall, without the Consent of the Congress, accept of any present, Emolument, Office,

or Title, of any kind whatever, from any King, Prince, or foreign State.

SECTION 10. No State shall enter into any Treaty, Alliance, or Confederation; grant Letters of Marque and Reprisal; coin Money; emit Bills of Credit; make any Thing but gold and silver Coin a Tender in Payment of Debts; pass any Bill of Attainder, ex post facto Law, or Law impairing the Obligation of Contracts, or grant any Title of Nobility.

No State shall, without the Consent of the Congress, lay any Imposts or Duties on Imports or Exports, except what may be absolutely necessary for executing its inspection Laws: and the net Produce of all Duties and Imposts, laid by any State on Imports or Exports, shall be for the Use of the Treasury of the United States; and all such Laws shall be subject to the Revision and Control of the Congress.

No State shall, without the Consent of Congress, lay any duty of Tonnage, keep Troops, or Ships of War in time of Peace, enter into any Agreement or Compact with another State, or with a foreign Power, or engage in War, unless actually invaded, or in such imminent Danger as will not admit of delay.

ARTICLE II

SECTION 1. The executive Power shall be vested in a President of the United States of America. He shall hold his Office during the Term of four years, and, together with the Vice-President, chosen for the same Term, be elected, as follows:

Each State shall appoint, in such Manner as the Legislature thereof may direct, a Number of Electors, equal to the whole Number of Senators and Representatives to which the State may be entitled in the Congress: but no Senator or Representative, or Person holding an Office of Trust or Profit under the United States, shall be appointed an Elector.

[The Electors shall meet in their respective States, and vote by Ballot for two persons, of whom one at least shall not be an Inhabitant of the same State with themselves. And they shall make a List of all the Persons voted for, and of the Number of Votes for each; which List they shall sign and certify, and transmit sealed to the Seat of the Government of the United States, directed to the President of the Senate. The President of the Senate shall, in the Presence of the Senate and House of Representatives, open all the Certificates, and the Votes shall then be counted. The Person having the greatest Number of Votes shall be the President, if such Number be a Majority of the whole Number of Electors appointed; and if there be more than one who have such Majority, and have an equal Number of Votes, then the House of Representatives shall immediately chuse by Ballot one of them for President; and if no Person have a Majority, then from the five highest on the List the said House shall in like Manner chuse the President. But in chusing the President, the Votes shall be taken by States, the Representation from each State having one Vote; a quorum for this Purpose shall consist of a Member or Members from two-thirds of the States, and a Majority of all the States shall be necessary to a Choice. In every Case, after the Choice of the President, the Person having the greatest Number of Votes of the Electors shall be the Vice President. But if there should remain two or more who have equal votes, the Senate shall chuse from them by Ballot the Vice-President.] [4]

The Congress may determine the Time of chusing the Electors, and the Day on which they shall give their Votes; which Day shall be the same throughout the United States.

No person except a natural-born Citizen, or a Citizen of the United States, at the time of the Adoption of this Constitution, shall be eligible to the Office of President; neither shall any Person be eligible to that Office who shall not have attained to the Age of thirty-five years, and been fourteen Years a Resident within the United States.

[4] Revised by 12th Amendment.

In Case of the Removal of the President from Office, or of his Death, Resignation, or Inability to discharge the Powers and Duties of the said Office, the same shall devolve on the Vice President, and the Congress may by Law provide for the Case of Removal, Death, Resignation, or Inability, both of the President and Vice President, declaring what Officer shall then act as President, and such Officer shall act accordingly, until the disability be removed, or a President shall be elected.

The President shall, at stated Times, receive for his Services a Compensation, which shall neither be increased nor diminished during the Period for which he shall have been elected, and he shall not receive within that Period any other Emolument from the United States, or any of them.

Before he enter on the execution of his Office, he shall take the following Oath or Affirmation:—"I do solemnly swear (or affirm) that I will faithfully execute the Office of President of the United States, and will, to the best of my Ability, preserve, protect, and defend the Constitution of the United States."

SECTION 2. The President shall be Commander in Chief of the Army and Navy of the United States, and of the Militia of the several States, when called into the actual Service of the United States; he may require the Opinion, in writing, of the principal Officer in each of the executive Departments, upon any subject relating to the Duties of their respective Offices, and he shall have Power to Grant Reprieves and Pardons for Offenses against the United States, except in Cases of Impeachment.

He shall have Power, by and with the Advice and Consent of the Senate, to make Treaties, provided two thirds of the Senators present concur; and he shall nominate, and by and with the Advice and Consent of the Senate, shall appoint Ambassadors, other public Ministers and Consuls, Judges of the supreme Court, and all other Officers of the United States, whose Appointments are not herein otherwise provided for, and which shall be established by Law:

but the Congress may by Law vest the Appointment of such inferior Officers, as they think proper, in the President alone, in the Courts of Law, or in the Heads of Departments.

The President shall have Power to fill up all Vacancies that may happen during the Recess of the Senate, by granting Commissions which shall expire at the End of their next Session.

SECTION 3. He shall from time to time give to the Congress Information of the State of the Union, and recommend to their Consideration such Measures as he shall judge necessary and expedient; he may, on extraordinary occasions, convene both Houses, or either of them, and in Case of Disagreement between them, with respect to the Time of Adjournment, he may adjourn them to such Time as he shall think proper; he shall receive Ambassadors and other public Ministers; he shall take Care that the Laws be faithfully executed, and shall Commission all the Officers of the United States.

SECTION 4. The President, Vice President and all civil Officers of the United States, shall be removed from Office on Impeachment for, and Conviction of, Treason, Bribery, or other high Crimes and Misdemeanors.

ARTICLE III

SECTION 1. The judicial Power of the United States, shall be vested in one supreme Court, and in such inferior Courts as the Congress may from time to time ordain and establish. The Judges, both of the supreme and inferior Courts, shall hold their Offices during good Behaviour, and shall, at stated Times, receive for their Services, a Compensation, which shall not be diminished during their Continuance in Office.

SECTION 2. The judicial Power shall extend to all Cases, in Law and Equity, arising under this Constitution, the Laws of the United States, and Treaties made, or which shall be made, under their Authority;—to all Cases affecting ambassadors, other public ministers and consuls;—to all cases of admiralty and maritime Jurisdiction;—to Controversies to which the United States shall be a Party;—to Controversies between two or more States;—between [5]—between Citizens of another State; [5]—between Citizens of different States,—between Citizens of the same State claiming Lands under Grants of different States, and between a State, or the Citizens thereof, and foreign States, Citizens or Subjects.

In all Cases affecting Ambassadors, other public Ministers and Consuls, and those in which a State shall be Party, the supreme Court shall have original Jurisdiction. In all the other Cases before mentioned, the supreme Court shall have appellate Jurisdiction, both as to Law and Fact, with such Exceptions, and under such Regulations as the Congress shall make.

The trial of all Crimes, except in Cases of Impeachment, shall be by Jury; and such Trial shall be held in the State where the said Crimes shall have been committed; but when not committed within any State, the Trial shall be at such Place or Places as the Congress may by Law have directed.

SECTION 3. Treason against the United States, shall consist only in levying War against them, or in adhering to their Enemies, giving them Aid and Comfort. No Person shall be convicted of Treason unless on the Testimony of two Witnesses to the same overt Act, or on Confession in open Court.

The Congress shall have power to declare the Punishment of Treason, but no Attainder of Treason shall work Corruption of Blood, or Forfeiture except during the Life of the Person attainted.

ARTICLE IV

SECTION 1. Full Faith and Credit shall be given in each State to the public Acts, Records, and judicial Proceedings of every other State. And the Congress may by general Laws prescribe the Manner in which

[5] Qualified by 11th Amendment.

such Acts, Records and Proceedings shall be proved, and the Effect thereof.

Section 2. The Citizens of each State shall be entitled to all Privileges and Immunities of Citizens in the several States.

A Person charged in any State with Treason, Felony, or other Crime, who shall flee from Justice, and be found in another State, shall on demand of the executive Authority of the State from which he fled, be delivered up, to be removed to the State having Jurisdiction of the crime.

No Person held to Service or Labour in one State, under the Laws thereof, escaping into another, shall, in Consequence of any Law or Regulation therein, be discharged from such Service or Labour, but shall be delivered up on Claim of the Party to whom such Service or Labour may be due.

Section 3. New States may be admitted by the Congress into this Union; but no new State shall be formed or erected within the Jurisdiction of any other State; nor any State be formed by the Junction of two or more States, or parts of States, without the Consent of the Legislatures of the States concerned as well as of the Congress.

The Congress shall have Power to dispose of and make all needful Rules and Regulations respecting the Territory or other Property belonging to the United States; and nothing in this Constitution shall be so construed as to Prejudice any Claims of the United States, or of any particular State.

Section 4. The United States shall guarantee to every State in this Union a Republican Form of Government, and shall protect each of them against Invasion; and on Application of the Legislature, or of the Executive (when the Legislature cannot be convened) against domestic Violence.

ARTICLE V

The Congress, whenever two-thirds of both Houses shall deem it necessary, shall propose Amendments to this Constitution, or, on the Application of the Legislatures of two-thirds of the several States, shall call a Convention for proposing Amendments,

which, in either Case, shall be valid to all Intents and Purposes, as part of this Constitution, when ratified by the Legislatures of three-fourths of the several States, or by Conventions in three-fourths thereof, as the one or the other Mode of Ratification may be proposed by the Congress; Provided that no Amendment which may be made prior to the Year One thousand eight hundred and eight shall in any Manner affect the first and fourth Clauses in the Ninth Section of the first Article; and that no State, without its Consent, shall be deprived of its equal Suffrage in the Senate.

ARTICLE VI

All Debts contracted and Engagements entered into, before the Adoption of this Constitution, shall be as valid against the United States under this Constitution, as under the Confederation.

This Constitution, and the Laws of the United States which shall be made in Pursuance thereof; and all Treaties made, or which shall be made, under the Authority of the United States, shall be the supreme Law of the Land; and the Judges in every State shall be bound thereby, any Thing in the Constitution or Laws of any State to the Contrary notwithstanding.

The Senators and Representatives before mentioned, and the Members of the several State Legislatures, and all executive and judicial Officers, both of the United States and of the several States, shall be bound by Oath or Affirmation to support this Constitution; but no religious Test shall ever be required as a qualification to any Office or public Trust under the United States.

ARTICLE VII

The Ratification of the Conventions of nine States shall be sufficient for the Establishment of this Constitution between the States so ratifying the same.

Done in Convention by the Unanimous Consent of the States present the Seventeenth Day of September in the Year of our Lord one thousand seven hundred and Eighty seven, and of the Independence of the United States of America the Twelfth. In Witness whereof We have hereunto subscribed our Names.[6]

GEORGE WASHINGTON
President and deputy from Virginia

NEW HAMPSHIRE
John Langdon
Nicholas Gilman

MASSACHUSETTS
Nathaniel Gorham
Rufus King

CONNECTICUT
William Samuel Johnson
Roger Sherman

NEW YORK
Alexander Hamilton

NEW JERSEY
William Livingston
David Brearley
William Paterson
Jonathan Dayton

PENNSYLVANIA
Benjamin Franklin
Thomas Mifflin
Robert Morris
George Clymer
Thomas FitzSimons
Jared Ingersoll
James Wilson
Gouverneur Morris

DELAWARE
George Read
Gunning Bedford, Jr.
John Dickinson
Richard Bassett
Jacob Broom

MARYLAND
James McHenry
Daniel of St. Thomas Jenifer
Daniel Carroll

VIRGINIA
John Blair
James Madison, Jr.

[6] These are the full names of the signers, which in some cases are not the signatures on the document.

NORTH CAROLINA
William Blount
Richard Dobbs Spaight
Hugh Williamson

SOUTH CAROLINA
John Rutledge
Charles Cotesworth Pinckney
Charles Pinckney
Pierce Butler

GEORGIA
William Few
Abraham Baldwin

ARTICLES IN ADDITION TO, AND AMENDMENT OF, THE CONSTITUTION OF THE UNITED STATES OF AMERICA, PROPOSED BY CONGRESS, AND RATIFIED BY THE LEGISLATURES OF THE SEVERAL STATES, PURSUANT TO THE FIFTH ARTICLE OF THE ORIGINAL CONSTITUTION [7]

[ARTICLE I]

Congress shall make no law respecting an establishment of religion, or prohibiting the free exercise thereof; or abridging the freedom of speech, or of the press; or the right of the people peaceably to assemble, and to petition the Government for a redress of grievances.

[ARTICLE II]

A well regulated Militia, being necessary to the security of a free State, the right of the people to keep and bear Arms shall not be infringed.

[ARTICLE III]

No Soldier shall, in time of peace, be quartered in any house, without the consent of the Owner, nor in time of war, but in a manner to be prescribed by law.

[ARTICLE IV]

The right of the people to be secure in their persons, houses, papers, and effects, against unreasonable searches and seizures, shall not be violated, and no Warrants shall issue, but upon probable cause, supported

[7] This heading appears only in the joint resolution submitting the first ten amendments.

by Oath or affirmation, and particularly describing the place to be searched, and the persons or things to be seized.

[ARTICLE V]

No person shall be held to answer for a capital or otherwise infamous crime, unless on a presentment or indictment of a Grand Jury, except in cases arising in the land or naval forces, or in the Militia, when in actual service in time of War or public danger; nor shall any person be subject for the same offence to be twice put in jeopardy of life or limb; nor shall be compelled in any criminal case to be a witness against himself, nor be deprived of life, liberty, or property, without due process of law; nor shall private property be taken for public use, without just compensation.

[ARTICLE VI]

In all criminal prosecutions, the accused shall enjoy the right to a speedy and public trial, by an impartial jury of the State and district wherein the crime shall have been committed, which district shall have been previously ascertained by law, and to be informed of the nature and cause of the accusation; to be confronted with the witnesses against him; to have compulsory process for obtaining witnesses in his favor, and to have the Assistance of Counsel for his defence.

[ARTICLE VII]

In suits at common law, where the value in controversy shall exceed twenty dollars, the right of trial by jury shall be preserved, and no fact tried by a jury, shall be otherwise reexamined in any Court of the United States, than according to the rules of the common law.

[ARTICLE VIII]

Excessive bail shall not be required, nor excessive fines imposed, nor cruel and unusual punishments inflicted.

[ARTICLE IX]

The enumeration in the Constitution, of certain rights, shall not be construed to deny or disparage others retained by the people.

[ARTICLE X]

The powers not delegated to the United States by the Constitution, nor prohibited by it to the States, are reserved to the States respectively, or to the people.

[Amendments I–X, in force 1791.]

[ARTICLE XI] [8]

The Judicial power of the United States shall not be construed to extend to any suit in law or equity, commenced or prosecuted against one of the United States by Citizens of another State, or by Citizens or Subjects of any Foreign State.

[ARTICLE XII] [9]

The Electors shall meet in their respective States and vote by ballot for President and Vice-President, one of whom, at least, shall not be an inhabitant of the same State with themselves; they shall name in their ballots the person voted for as President, and in distinct ballots the person voted for as Vice-President, and they shall make distinct lists of all persons voted for as President, and of all persons voted for as Vice-President, and of the number of votes for each, which lists they shall sign and certify, and transmit sealed to the seat of the government of the United States, directed to the President of the Senate;—The President of the Senate shall, in the presence of the Senate and House of Representatives, open all the certificates and the votes shall then be counted;—The person having the greatest number of votes for President, shall be the President, if such number be a majority of the whole number of Electors appointed; and if no person have such majority, then from the persons having the highest numbers not exceeding three on the list of those voted for as President, the House of Representatives shall choose immediately, by ballot, the President. But in choosing the President, the

---

[8] Adopted in 1798.
[9] Adopted in 1804.

votes shall be taken by states, the representation from each state having one vote; a quorum for this purpose shall consist of a member or members from two-thirds of the states, and a majority of all the states shall be necessary to a choice. And if the House of Representatives shall not choose a President whenever the right of choice shall devolve upon them, before the fourth day of March next following, then the Vice-President shall act as President, as in the case of the death or other constitutional disability of the President.—The person having the greatest number of votes as Vice-President, shall be the Vice-President, if such number be a majority of the whole number of Electors appointed, and if no person have a majority, then from the two highest numbers on the list, the Senate shall choose the Vice-President; a quorum for the purpose shall consist of two-thirds of the whole number of Senators, and a majority of the whole number shall be necessary to a choice. But no person constitutionally ineligible to the office of President shall be eligible to that of Vice-President of the United States.

ARTICLE XIII [10]

SECTION 1. Neither slavery nor involuntary servitude, except as a punishment for crime whereof the party shall have been duly convicted, shall exist within the United States, or any place subject to their jurisdiction.

SECTION 2. Congress shall have power to enforce this article by appropriate legislation.

ARTICLE XIV [11]

SECTION 1. All persons born or naturalized in the United States, and subject to the jurisdiction thereof, are citizens of the United States and of the State wherein they reside. No State shall make or enforce any law which shall abridge the privileges or immunities of citizens of the United States;

[10] Adopted in 1865.
[11] Adopted in 1868.

nor shall any State deprive any person of life, liberty, or property, without due process of law; nor deny to any person within its jurisdiction the equal protection of the laws.

SECTION 2. Representatives shall be apportioned among the several States according to their respective numbers, counting the whole number of persons in each State, excluding Indians not taxed. But when the right to vote at any election for the choice of electors for President and Vice-President of the United States, Representatives in Congress, the Executive and Judicial officers of a State, or the members of the Legislature thereof, is denied to any of the male inhabitants of such State, being twenty-one years of age, and citizens of the United States, or in any way abridged, except for participation in rebellion, or other crime, the basis of representation therein shall be reduced in the proportion which the number of such male citizens shall bear to the whole number of male citizens twenty-one years of age in such State.

SECTION 3. No person shall be a Senator or Representative in Congress, or elector of President and Vice-President, or hold any office, civil or military, under the United States, or under any State, who, having previously taken an oath, as a member of Congress, or as an officer of the United States, or as a member of any State legislature, or as an executive or judicial officer of any State, to support the Constitution of the United States, shall have engaged in insurrection or rebellion against the same, or given aid or comfort to the enemies thereof. But Congress may by a vote of two-thirds of each House, remove such disability.

SECTION 4. The validity of the public debt of the United States, authorized by law, including debts incurred for payment of pensions and bounties for services in suppressing insurrection or rebellion, shall not be questioned. But neither the United States nor any State shall assume or pay any debt or obligation incurred in aid of insurrection or rebellion against the United States, or any claim for the loss or emancipation of any slave; but all such debts, obligations, and claims shall be held illegal and void.

SECTION 5. The Congress shall have the power to enforce, by appropriate legislation, the provisions of this article.

ARTICLE XV [12]

SECTION 1. The right of citizens of the United States to vote shall not be denied or abridged by the United States or by any State on account of race, color, or previous condition of servitude—

SECTION 2. The Congress shall have power to enforce this article by appropriate legislation.

ARTICLE XVI [13]

The Congress shall have power to lay and collect taxes on incomes, from whatever source derived, without apportionment among the several States, and without regard to any census or enumeration.

ARTICLE XVII [14]

The Senate of the United States shall be composed of two Senators from each State, elected by the people thereof, for six years; and each Senator shall have one vote. The electors in each State shall have the qualifications requisite for electors of the most numerous branch of the State legislatures.

When vacancies happen in the representation of any State in the Senate, the executive authority of such State shall issue writs of election to fill such vacancies: *Provided*, That the legislature of any State may empower the executive thereof to make temporary appointments until the people fill the vacancies by election as the legislature may direct.

This amendment shall not be so con-

strued as to affect the election or term of any Senator chosen before it becomes valid as part of the Constitution.

ARTICLE XVIII [15]

SECTION 1. After one year from the ratification of this article the manufacture, sale, or transportation of intoxicating liquors within, the importation thereof into, or the exportation thereof from the United States and all territory subject to the jurisdiction thereof for beverage purposes is hereby prohibited.

SECTION 2. The Congress and the several States shall have concurrent power to enforce this article by appropriate legislation.

SECTION 3. This article shall be inoperative unless it shall have been ratified as an amendment to the Constitution by the legislatures of the several States, as provided in the Constitution, within seven years from the date of the submission hereof to the States by the Congress.

ARTICLE XIX [16]

The right of citizens of the United States to vote shall not be denied or abridged by the United States or by any State on account of sex.

Congress shall have power to enforce this article by appropriate legislation.

ARTICLE XX [17]

SECTION 1. The terms of the President and Vice-President shall end at noon on the 20th day of January, and the terms of Senators and Representatives at noon on the 3d day of January, of the years in which such terms would have ended if this article had not been ratified; and the terms of their successors shall then begin.

SECTION 2. The Congress shall assemble at least once in every year, and such meeting shall begin at noon on the 3d day of January, unless they shall by law appoint a different day.

[12] Proclaimed March 30, 1870.
[13] Passed July, 1909.
[14] Passed May, 1912, in place of Article I, Section 3, clause I, of the Constitution and that part of clause 2 of the same Section which pertains to the filling of vacancies.

[15] Passed December 3, 1917.
[16] Adopted in 1920.
[17] Adopted in 1933.

SECTION 3. If, at the time fixed for the beginning of the term of the President, the President elect shall have died, the Vice-President elect shall become President. If a President shall not have been chosen before the time fixed for the beginning of his term, or if the President elect shall have failed to qualify, then the Vice-President elect shall act as President until a President shall have qualified; and the Congress may by law provide for the case wherein neither a President elect nor a Vice-President elect shall have qualified, declaring who shall then act as President, or the manner in which one who is to act shall be selected, and such person shall act accordingly until a President or Vice-President shall have qualified.

SECTION 4. The Congress may by law provide for the case of the death of any of the persons from whom the House of Representatives may choose a President whenever the right of choice shall have devolved upon them, and for the case of the death of any of the persons from whom the Senate may choose a Vice-President whenever the right of choice shall have devolved upon them.

SECTION 5. Sections 1 and 2 shall take effect on the 15th day of October following the ratification of this article.

SECTION 6. This article shall be inoperative unless it shall have been ratified as an amendment to the Constitution by the legislatures of three-fourths of the several States within seven years from the date of its submission.

ARTICLE XXI [18]

SECTION 1. The eighteenth article of amendment to the Constitution of the United States is hereby repealed.

SECTION 2. The transportation or importation into any State, Territory, or possession of the United States for delivery or use therein of intoxicating liquors, in violation of the laws thereof, is hereby prohibited.

SECTION 3. This article shall be inoperative unless it shall have been ratified as an amendment to the Constitution by conventions in the several States, as provided in the Constitution, within seven years from the date of the submission hereof to the States by the Congress.

ARTICLE XXII [19]

No person shall be elected to the office of the President more than twice, and no person who has held the office of President, or acted as President, for more than two years of a term to which some other person was elected President shall be elected to the office of the President more than once.

But this Article shall not apply to any person holding the office of President when this Article was proposed by the Congress, and shall not prevent any person who may be holding the office of President, or acting as President, during the term within which this Article becomes operative from holding the office of President or acting as President during the remainder of such term.

[18] Adopted in 1933.
[19] Adopted in 1951.

Sovereigns of England and Great Britain, 1485–1820

The ruler was King (or Queen) of England until 1707, except for the interregnum of 1649–1660, during which Oliver Cromwell made himself Lord Protector. The ruler was King (or Queen) of Great Britain after the union of England and Scotland in 1707, and King (or Queen) of Great Britain and Ireland after 1800.

HENRY VII, *1485–1509*
HENRY VIII, *1509–1547*
EDWARD VI, *1547–1553*
MARY, *1553–1558*
ELIZABETH, *1558–1603*
JAMES I (VI OF SCOTLAND), *1603–1625*
CHARLES I, *1625–1649*
   OLIVER CROMWELL, *1650–1658*

RICHARD CROMWELL, *1658–1659*

CHARLES II, *1660–1685*

JAMES II, *1685–1688*

WILLIAM III AND MARY II, *1689–1694*

WILLIAM III, *1694–1702*

ANNE, *1702–1714*

GEORGE I, *1714–1727*

GEORGE II, *1727–1760*

GEORGE III, *1760–1820*

Admission of States to the Union

(In the case of the first thirteen, the date given is that of ratification of the Constitution.)

1.	Delaware	Dec. 7, 1787	26.	Michigan	Jan. 26, 1837
2.	Pennsylvania	Dec. 12, 1787	27.	Florida	Mar. 3, 1845
3.	New Jersey	Dec. 18, 1787	28.	Texas	Dec. 29, 1845
4.	Georgia	Jan. 2, 1788	29.	Iowa	Dec. 28, 1846
5.	Connecticut	Jan. 9, 1788	30.	Wisconsin	May 29, 1848
6.	Massachusetts	Feb. 6, 1788	31.	California	Sept. 9, 1850
7.	Maryland	Apr. 28, 1788	32.	Minnesota	May 11, 1858
8.	South Carolina	May 23, 1788	33.	Oregon	Feb. 14, 1859
9.	New Hampshire	June 21, 1788	34.	Kansas	Jan. 29, 1861
10.	Virginia	June 25, 1788	35.	West Virginia	June 19, 1863
11.	New York	July 26, 1788	36.	Nevada	Oct. 31, 1864
12.	North Carolina	Nov. 21, 1789	37.	Nebraska	Mar. 1, 1867
13.	Rhode Island	May 29, 1790	38.	Colorado	Aug. 1, 1876
14.	Vermont	Mar. 4, 1791	39.	North Dakota	Nov. 2, 1889
15.	Kentucky	June 1, 1792	40.	South Dakota	Nov. 2, 1889
16.	Tennessee	June 1, 1796	41.	Montana	Nov. 8, 1889
17.	Ohio	Mar. 1, 1803	42.	Washington	Nov. 11, 1889
18.	Louisiana	Apr. 30, 1812	43.	Idaho	July 3, 1890
19.	Indiana	Dec. 11, 1816	44.	Wyoming	July 10, 1890
20.	Mississippi	Dec. 10, 1817	45.	Utah	Jan. 4, 1896
21.	Illinois	Dec. 3, 1818	46.	Oklahoma	Nov. 16, 1907
22.	Alabama	Dec. 14, 1819	47.	New Mexico	Jan. 6, 1912
23.	Maine	Mar. 15, 1820	48.	Arizona	Feb. 14, 1912
24.	Missouri	Aug. 10, 1821	49.	Alaska	Jan. 3, 1959
25.	Arkansas	June 15, 1836			

Presidential Elections,
1789–1876

YEAR	CANDIDATES	PARTIES	POPULAR VOTE	ELEC- TORAL VOTE
1789	GEORGE WASHINGTON (*Va.*)			69
	John Adams			34
	Others			35
1792	GEORGE WASHINGTON (*Va.*)			132
	John Adams			77
	George Clinton			50
	Others			5
1796	JOHN ADAMS (*Mass.*)	Federalist		71
	Thomas Jefferson	Democratic- Republican		68
	Thomas Pinckney	Fed.		59
	Aaron Burr	Dem.-Rep.		30
	Others			48
1800	THOMAS JEFFERSON (*Va.*)	Dem.-Rep.		73
	Aaron Burr	Dem.-Rep.		73
	John Adams	Fed.		65
	C. C. Pinckney	Fed.		64
	John Jay	Fed.		1
1804	THOMAS JEFFERSON (*Va.*)	Dem.-Rep.		162
	C. C. Pinckney	Fed.		14
1808	JAMES MADISON (*Va.*)	Dem.-Rep.		122
	C. C. Pinckney	Fed.		47
	George Clinton	Dem.-Rep.		6
1812	JAMES MADISON (*Va.*)	Dem.-Rep.		128
	De Witt Clinton	Fed.		89
1816	JAMES MONROE (*Va.*)	Dem.-Rep.		183
	Rufus King	Fed.		34
1820	JAMES MONROE (*Va.*)	Dem.-Rep.		231
	John Quincy Adams	Dem.-Rep.		1
1824	JOHN Q. ADAMS (*Mass.*)	Dem.-Rep.	108,740	84
	Andrew Jackson	Dem.-Rep.	153,544	99
	William H. Crawford	Dem.-Rep.	46,618	41
	Henry Clay	Dem.-Rep.	47,136	37
1828	ANDREW JACKSON (*Tenn.*)	Democrat	647,286	178
	John Quincy Adams	National Republican	508,064	83
1832	ANDREW JACKSON (*Tenn.*)	Democrat	687,502	219
	Henry Clay	Whig	530,189	49
	John Floyd	Whig		11
	William Wirt	Anti-Mason	33,108	7

YEAR	CANDIDATES	PARTIES	POPULAR VOTE	ELEC-TORAL VOTE
1836	MARTIN VAN BUREN (*N.Y.*)	Democrat	762,678	170
	W. H. Harrison	Whig ⎫		73
	Hugh L. White	Whig ⎬	735,651	26
	Daniel Webster	Whig ⎭		14
	W. P. Mangum	Whig		11
1840	WILLIAM H. HARRISON (*Ohio*)	Whig	1,275,016	234
	Martin Van Buren	Democrat	1,129,102	60
	J. G. Birney	Liberty	7,069	
1844	JAMES K. POLK (*Tenn.*)	Democrat	1,337,243	170
	Henry Clay	Whig	1,299,062	105
	J. G. Birney	Liberty	62,300	
1848	ZACHARY TAYLOR (*La.*)	Whig	1,360,099	163
	Lewis Cass	Democrat	1,220,544	127
	Martin Van Buren	Free Soil	291,263	
1852	FRANKLIN PIERCE (*N.H.*)	Democrat	1,601,274	254
	Winfield Scott	Whig	1,386,580	42
	John P. Hale	Free Soil	155,825	
1856	JAMES BUCHANAN (*Pa.*)	Democrat	1,838,169	174
	John C. Frémont	Republican	1,341,264	114
	Millard Fillmore	American	874,534	8
1860	ABRAHAM LINCOLN (*Ill.*)	Republican	1,866,452	180
	Stephen A. Douglas	Democrat	1,375,157	12
	John C. Breckinridge	Democrat	847,953	72
	John Bell	Union	590,631	39
1864	ABRAHAM LINCOLN (*Ill.*)	Republican	2,213,655	212
	George McClellan	Democrat	1,805,237	21
1868	ULYSSES S. GRANT (*Ill.*)	Republican	3,012,833	214
	Horatio Seymour	Democrat	2,703,249	80
1872	ULYSSES S. GRANT (*Ohio*)	Republican	3,597,132	286
	Horace Greeley	Democrat; Liberal Republican.	2,834,125	66
1876	RUTHERFORD B. HAYES (*Ohio*)	Republican	4,036,298	185
	Samuel J. Tilden	Democrat	4,300,590	184

President	Vice President	Secretary of State	Secretary of Treasury
1. George Washington, Federalist . 1789	John Adams, Federalist 1789	T. Jefferson . . . . . . 1789 E. Randolph . . . . . 1794 T. Pickering 1795	Alex. Hamilton . . . 1 Oliver Wolcott 1
2. John Adams, Federalist 1797	Thomas Jefferson, Republican 1797	T. Pickering . . . . . 1797 John Marshall 1800	Oliver Wolcott . . . . 1 Samuel Dexter 1
3. Thomas Jefferson, Republican . . 1801	Aaron Burr, Republican . . . . 1801 George Clinton, Republican 1805	James Madison . . . 1801	Samuel Dexter . . . . 1 Albert Gallatin 1
4. James Madison, Republican 1809	George Clinton, Republican . . . . . . 1809 Elbridge Gerry, Republican 1813	Robert Smith . . . . 1809 James Monroe . . . 1811	Albert Gallatin . . . . 1 G. W. Campbell . . . 1 A. J. Dallas . . . . . . 1 W. H. Crawford . . 1
5. James Monroe, Republican 1817	D. D. Tompkins, Republican 1817	J. Q. Adams 1817	W. H. Crawford . . . 1
6. John Quincy Adams, Nat'l Rep. 1825	John C. Calhoun, Republican 1825	Henry Clay 1825	Richard Rush 1
7. Andrew Jackson, Democratic . . . 1829	John C. Calhoun, Democratic . . . . . 1829 Martin Van Buren, Democratic . . . 1833	M. Van Buren . . . 1829 E. Livingston . . . . 1831 Louis McLane . . . 1833 John Forsyth 1834	Sam. D. Ingham . . 1 Louis McLane . . . . 1 W. J. Duane . . . . . 1 Roger B. Taney . . . 1 Levi Woodbury . . . 1
8. Martin Van Buren, Democratic . 1837	Richard M. Johnson, Democratic . . 1837	John Forsyth 1837	Levi Woodbury . . . 1
9. William H. Harrison, Whig 1841	John Tyler, Whig 1841	Daniel Webster . . . 1841	Thos. Ewing 1
10. John Tyler, Whig and Democratic 1841		Daniel Webster . . . 1841 Hugh S. Legare . . . 1843 Abel P. Upshur . . . 1843 John C. Calhoun . . 1844	Thos. Ewing . . . . . . 1 Walter Forward . . . 1 John C. Spencer . . . 1 Geo. M. Bibb 1
11. James K. Polk, Democratic 1845	George M. Dallas, Democratic 1845	James Buchanan . . 1845	Robt. J. Walker . . . 1
12. Zachary Taylor, Whig 1849	Millard Fillmore, Whig 1849	John M. Clayton . 1849	Wm. M. Meredith . 1
13. Millard Fillmore, Whig 1850		Daniel Webster . . . 1850 Edward Everett . . 1852	Thomas Corwin . . . 1
14. Franklin Pierce, Democratic . . . 1853	William R. D. King, Democratic . . 1853	W. L. Marcy 1853	James Guthrie 1
15. James Buchanan, Democratic . . 1857	John C. Breckinridge, Democratic . . 1857	Lewis Cass . . . . . . 1857 J. S. Black 1860	Howell Cobb . . . . . 1 Philip F. Thomas . . 1 John A. Dix 1
16. Abraham Lincoln, Republican . . 1861	Hannibal Hamlin, Republican . . . . . 1861 Andrew Johnson, Unionist 1865	W. H. Seward 1861	Salmon P. Chase . . 1 W. P. Fessenden . . . 1 Hugh McCulloch . . 1
17. Andrew Johnson, Unionist 1865		W. H. Seward 1865	Hugh McCulloch . . 1
18. Ulysses S. Grant, Republican . . 1869	Schuyler Colfax, Republican . . . . . . 1869 Henry Wilson, Republican 1873	E. B. Washburne. 1869 Hamilton Fish 1869	Geo. S. Boutwell . . 1 W. A. Richardson . 1 Benj. H. Bristow . . 1 Lot M. Morrill 1
19. Rutherford B. Hayes, Republican 1877	William A. Wheeler, Republican . . . 1877	W. M. Evarts 1877	John Sherman 1

CRETARY OF WAR	ATTORNEY-GENERAL	POSTMASTER-GENERAL*	SECRETARY OF NAVY	SECRETARY OF INTERIOR
ry Knox.....1789 ickering....1795 McHenry....1796	E. Randolph.......1789 Wm. Bradford.....1794 Charles Lee.......1795	Samuel Osgood....1789 Tim. Pickering.....1791 Jos. Habersham....1795	Established April 30, 1798.	Established March 3, 1849.
McHenry....1797 Marshall....1800 'l Dexter.....1800 riswold......1801	Charles Lee.......1797 Theo. Parsons.....1801	Jos. Habersham....1797	Benj. Stoddert.......1798	
earborn.....1801	Levi Lincoln.......1801 Robert Smith......1805 J. Breckinridge....1805 C. A. Rodney......1807	Jos. Habersham....1801 Gideon Granger....1801	Benj. Stoddert.......1801 Robert Smith.......1801 J. Crowninshield.....1805	
Eustis......1809 rmstrong.....1813 es Monroe....1814 I. Crawford..1815	C. A. Rodney......1809 Wm. Pinkney......1811 Richard Rush....1814	Gideon Granger....1809 R. J. Meigs, Jr.....1814	Paul Hamilton......1809 William Jones.......1813 B. W. Crowninshield..1814	
Shelby.....1817 Graham.....1817 Calhoun....1817	Richard Rush.....1817 William Wirt......1817	R. J. Meigs, Jr.....1817 John McLean......1823	B. W. Crowninshield..1817 Smith Thompson....1818 S. L. Southard.......1823	
Barbour.....1825 B. Porter...1828	William Wirt......1825	John McLean......1825	S. L. Southard.......1825	
H. Eaton...1829 s Cass.......1831 Butler......1837	John M. Berrien...1829 Roger B. Taney....1831 B. F. Butler.......1833	Wm. T. Barry.....1829 Amos Kendall.....1835	John Branch........1829 Levi Woodbury......1831 Mahlon Dickerson...1834	
R. Poinsett...1837	B. F. Butler.......1837 Felix Grundy......1838 H. D. Gilpin.......1840	Amos Kendall.....1837 John M. Niles.....1840	Mahlon Dickerson...1837 Jas. K. Paulding.....1838	
Bell........1841	J. J. Crittenden....1841	Francis Granger....1841	George E. Badger....1841	
Bell........1841 McLean....1841 Spencer.....1841 M. Porter....1843 Wilkins.....1844	J. J. Crittenden....1841 Hugh S. Legare....1841 John Nelson.......1843	Francis Granger....1841 C. A. Wickliffe.....1841	George E. Badger....1841 Abel P. Upshur......1841 David Henshaw....1843 Thomas W. Gilmer...1844 John Y. Mason......1844	
L. Marcy...1845	John Y. Mason.....1845 Nathan Clifford....1846 Isaac Toucey......1848	Cave Johnson.....1845	George Bancroft.....1845 John Y. Mason......1846	
. Crawford..1849	Reverdy Johnson...1849	Jacob Collamer....1849	Wm. B. Preston......1849	Thomas Ewing.....1849
. Conrad....1850	J. J. Crittenden....1850	Nathan K. Hall....1850 Sam D. Hubbard...1852	Wm. A. Graham.....1850 John P. Kennedy....1852	A. H. Stuart.......1850
rson Davis...1853	Caleb Cushing.....1853	James Campbell...1853	James C. Dobbin....1853	R'bt. McClelland...1853
B. Floyd....1857 ph Holt......1861	J. S. Black........1857 Edw. M. Stanton...1860	Aaron V. Brown...1857 Joseph Holt.......1859	Isaac Toucey........1857	Jacob Thompson...1857
ameron......1861 I. Stanton....1862	Edward Bates......1861 Titian J. Coffey....1863 James Speed.......1864	Horatio King......1861 M'tgomery Blair...1861 Wm. Dennison.....1864	Gideon Welles.......1861	Caleb B. Smith.....1861 John P. Usher......1863
I. Stanton....1865 . Grant......1867 homas.......1868 . Schofield...1868	James Speed.......1865 Henry Stanbery....1866 Wm. M. Evarts....1868	Wm. Dennison.....1865 A. W. Randall.....1866	Gideon Welles.......1865	John P. Usher......1865 James Harlan......1865 O. H. Browning....1866
Rawlins.....1869 . Sherman...1869 V. Belknap..1869 onso Taft....1876 . Cameron....1876	E. R. Hoar........1869 A. T. Ackerman....1870 Geo. H. Williams..1871 Edw. Pierrepont...1875 Alphonso Taft.....1876	J. A. J. Creswell....1869 Jas. W. Marshall...1874 Marshall Jewell....1874 James N. Tyner....1876	Adolph E. Borie.....1869 Geo. M. Robeson.....1869	Jacob D. Cox......1869 C. Delano.........1870 Zach. Chandler.....1875
. McCrary...1877 . Ramsey....1879	Chas. Devens.......1877	David M. Key.....1877 Horace Maynard...1880	R. W. Thompson.....1877 Nathan Goff, Jr......1881	Carl Schurz........1877

The Postmaster-General did not become a cabinet member until 1829.

Chief Justices of the Supreme Court,
1789–1888

John Jay, N.Y.	1789–1795	Roger B. Taney, Md.	1836–1864
John Rutledge, S.C.	1795	Salmon P. Chase, Ohio	1864–1873
Oliver Ellsworth, Conn.	1795–1799	Morrison R. Waite, Ohio	1874–1888
John Marshall, Va.	1801–1835		

Speakers of the House of Representatives,
1789–1876

F. A. C. Muhlenberg, Pennsylvania	1789–1791	John W. Taylor, New York	1825–1827
Jonathan Trumbull, Connecticut	1791–1793	Andrew Stevenson, Virginia	1827–1834
F. A. C. Muhlenberg, Pennsylvania	1793–1795	John Bell, Tennessee	1834–1835
Jonathan Dayton, New Jersey	1795–1799	James K. Polk, Tennessee	1835–1839
Theodore Sedgwick, Massachusetts	1799–1801	R. M. T. Hunter, Virginia	1839–1841
Nathaniel Macon, North Carolina	1801–1807	John White, Kentucky	1841–1843
Joseph B. Varnum, Massachusetts	1807–1811	John W. Jones, Virginia	1843–1845
Henry Clay, Kentucky	1811–1814	John W. Davis, Indiania	1845–1847
Langdon Cheves, South Carolina	1814–1815	R. C. Winthrop, Massachusetts	1847–1849
Henry Clay, Kentucky	1815–1820	Howell Cobb, Georgia	1845–1851
John W. Taylor, New York	1820–1821	Linn Boyd, Kentucky	1851–1855
Philip P. Barbour, Virginia	1821–1823	N. P. Banks, Massachusetts	1856–1857
Henry Clay, Kentucky	1823–1825	James L. Orr, South Carolina	1857–1859
		William Pennington, New Jersey	1860–1861
		Galusha A. Grow, Pennsylvania	1861–1863
		Schuyler Colfax, Indiana	1863–1869
		James G. Blaine, Maine	1869–1875
		Michael C. Kerr, Indiana	1875–1876

Population of the United States, 1790–1880

Division and State	1790	1800	1810	1820	1830	1840	1850	1860	1870	1880
UNITED STATES	3,929,214	5,308,483	7,239,881	9,638,453	12,866,020	17,069,453	23,191,876	31,443,321	39,818,449	50,155,783
GEOGRAPHIC DIVISIONS										
New England	1,009,408	1,233,011	1,471,973	1,660,071	1,954,717	2,234,822	2,728,116	3,135,283	3,487,924	4,010,529
Middle Atlantic	952,632	1,402,565	2,014,702	2,699,845	3,587,664	4,526,260	5,898,735	7,458,985	8,810,806	10,496,878
South Atlantic	1,851,806	2,286,494	2,674,891	3,061,063	3,645,752	3,925,299	4,679,090	5,364,703	5,853,610	7,597,197
East South Central	109,368	335,407	708,590	1,190,489	1,815,969	2,575,445	3,363,271	4,020,991	4,404,445	5,585,151
West South Central			77,618	167,680	246,127	449,985	940,251	1,747,667	2,029,965	3,334,220
East North Central		51,006	272,324	792,719	1,470,018	2,924,728	4,523,260	6,926,884	9,124,517	11,206,668
West North Central			19,783	66,586	140,455	426,814	880,335	2,169,832	3,856,594	6,157,443
Mountain							72,927	174,923	315,385	653,119
Pacific							105,871	444,053	675,125	1,114,578
NEW ENGLAND										
Maine	96,540	151,719	228,705	298,335	399,455	501,793	583,169	628,279	626,915	648,936
New Hampshire	141,885	183,858	214,460	244,161	269,328	284,574	317,976	326,073	318,300	346,991
Vermont	85,425	154,465	217,895	235,981	280,652	291,948	314,120	315,098	330,551	332,286
Massachusetts	378,787	422,845	472,040	523,287	610,408	737,699	994,514	1,231,066	1,457,351	1,783,085
Rhode Island	68,825	69,122	76,931	83,059	97,199	108,830	147,545	174,620	217,353	276,531
Connecticut	237,946	251,002	261,942	275,248	297,675	309,978	370,792	460,147	537,454	622,700
MIDDLE ATLANTIC										
New York	340,120	589,051	959,049	1,372,812	1,918,608	2,428,921	3,097,394	3,880,735	4,382,759	5,082,871
New Jersey	184,139	211,149	245,562	277,575	320,823	373,306	489,555	672,035	906,096	1,131,116
Pennsylvania	434,373	602,365	810,091	1,049,458	1,348,233	1,724,033	2,311,786	2,906,215	3,521,951	4,282,891
SOUTH ATLANTIC										
Delaware	59,096	64,273	72,674	72,749	76,748	78,085	91,532	112,216	125,015	146,608
Maryland	319,728	341,548	380,546	407,350	447,040	470,019	583,034	687,049	780,894	934,943
Dist. of Columbia		14,093	24,023	33,039	39,834	43,712	51,687	75,080	131,700	177,624
Virginia	747,610	880,200	974,600	1,065,366	1,211,405	1,239,797	1,421,661	1,596,318	1,225,163	1,512,565
West Virginia									442,014	618,457
North Carolina	393,751	478,103	555,500	638,829	737,987	753,419	869,039	992,622	1,071,361	1,399,750
South Carolina	249,073	345,591	415,115	502,741	581,185	594,398	668,507	703,708	705,606	995,577
Georgia	82,548	162,686	252,433	340,989	516,823	691,392	906,185	1,057,286	1,184,109	1,542,180
Florida					34,730	54,477	87,445	140,424	187,748	269,493
EAST SOUTH CENTRAL										
Kentucky	73,677	220,955	406,511	564,317	687,917	779,828	982,405	1,155,684	1,321,011	1,648,690
Tennessee	35,691	105,602	261,727	422,823	681,904	829,210	1,002,717	1,109,801	1,258,520	1,542,359
Alabama				127,901	309,527	590,756	771,623	964,201	996,992	1,262,505
Mississippi		8,850	40,352	75,448	136,621	375,651	606,526	791,305	827,922	1,131,597
WEST SOUTH CENTRAL										
Arkansas			1,062	14,273	30,388	97,574	209,897	435,450	484,471	802,525
Louisiana			76,556	153,407	215,739	352,411	517,762	708,002	726,915	939,946
Texas							212,592	604,215	818,579	1,591,749
EAST NORTH CENTRAL										
Ohio		45,365	230,760	581,434	937,903	1,519,467	1,980,329	2,339,511	2,665,260	3,198,062
Indiana		5,641	24,520	147,178	343,031	685,866	988,416	1,350,428	1,680,637	1,978,301
Illinois			12,282	55,211	157,445	476,183	851,470	1,711,951	2,539,891	3,077,871
Michigan			4,762	8,896	31,639	212,267	397,654	749,113	1,184,059	1,636,937
Wisconsin						30,945	305,391	775,881	1,054,670	1,315,497
WEST NORTH CENTRAL										
Minnesota							6,077	172,023	439,706	780,773
Iowa						43,112	192,214	674,913	1,194,020	1,624,615
Missouri			19,783	66,586	140,455	383,702	682,044	1,182,012	1,721,295	2,168,380
North Dakota									2,405	36,909
South Dakota									11,776	98,268
Nebraska								28,841	122,993	452,402
Kansas								107,206	364,399	996,096
MOUNTAIN										
Montana									20,595	39,159
Idaho									14,999	32,610
Wyoming									9,118	20,789
Colorado								34,277	39,864	194,327
New Mexico							61,547	93,516	91,874	119,565
Arizona									9,658	40,440
Utah							11,380	40,273	86,786	143,963
Nevada								6,857	42,491	62,266
PACIFIC										
Washington								11,594	23,955	75,116
Oregon							13,294	52,465	90,923	174,768
California							92,597	379,994	560,247	864,694

General Bibliography

BOOK LISTS The chapter bibliographies in this volume provide references to selected books bearing upon the subjects of the particular chapters. This general bibliography includes certain of the more important books dealing with American history as a whole or with some fairly long period or broad phase of it. Most of the books listed here and on previous pages contain bibliographies of their own, and these are useful for the further pursuit of any topic the student may be interested in. The most recent and inclusive bibliographical volume is the *Harvard Guide to American History*, edited by Oscar Handlin and associates at Harvard University (1954). The student should bear in mind, however, that any list of books becomes "dated" the moment it is published; it remains useful only for finding items already in print at that time. For finding more recently published books—together with appraisals of them—the student is referred to the *American Historical Review* and the *Mississippi Valley Historical Review*, both of which appear quarterly.

MAPS AND STATISTICS The standard map collection for American history is C. O. Paullin's *Atlas of the Historical Geography of the United States* (1932). Briefer collections, designed for the student, are the *American History Atlas*, edited by A. B. Hart, D. M. Matteson, and H. E. Bolton (1942), which embodies a traditional approach to map-making; and the *Historical Atlas of the United States*, edited by C. L. Lord and E. H. Lord (rev. ed., 1953), which contains more variety and a more modern touch. Well chosen census data is given in *Historical Statistics of the United States, 1789–1945*, prepared by the Bureau of the Census with the co-operation of the Social Science Research Council (1949).

ORIGINAL SOURCES The kinds of records that history is made from are copiously illustrated in *American History Told by Contemporaries* edited by A. B. Hart (5 vols., 1897–1929). A standard compilation, especially valuable for official records and court decisions, is H. S. Commager's *Documents of American History* (rev. ed., 1949). Less extensive but more varied in their selections are *Readings in American History*, edited by Oscar Handlin (1957); *The Shaping of the American Tradition*, edited by L. Hacker and H. Zahler (1947); and *The People Shall Judge*, edited by the staff in Social Sciences I at the University of Chicago (2 vols., 1949). Great issues and dilemmas of the past are presented with both contemporary documents and subsequent historical interpretations in *Problems in American Civilization*, sponsored by the Department of American Studies at Amherst College (29 vols., 1949–1957); and in *Problems in American History*, edited by R. W. Leopold and A. S. Link (rev. ed., 1957).

THE PICTORIAL RECORD Pictures, which give a sense of reality to the past as nothing else can, are to be found abundantly in *The Pageant of America*, edited by R. H. Gabriel (15 vols., 1925–1929); the *Album of American History*, edited by J. T. Adams (4 vols., 1944–1948); and *Life in America*, edited by M. B. Davidson (2 vols., 1951).

GEOGRAPHICAL INFLUENCES E. C. Semple, *American History and Its Geographic Conditions* (rev. ed., 1933), though originally published more than half a century ago, is still useful as a general introduction. H. R. Brown, *Historical Geography of the United States* (1948) traces in fascinating detail the interplay of environment and settlement, region by region. A special kind of geographical interpretation is that of Frederick Jackson Turner, who influenced the thinking of a whole generation of historians with his essays, gathered together in *The Frontier in American History* (1920) and *The Significance of Sections in American History* (1932). What happened to the "free land," which Turner believed had determined the course of American history, is told by R. E. Robbins in *Our Landed Heritage* (1942). The most recent and thorough volume tracing the frontier movement is R. A. Billington's *Westward Expansion* (1949).

HISTORIES: COMPREHENSIVE American history is told in brief lives of men who made it in the *Dictionary of American Biography*, edited by Allen Johnson and Dumas Malone (21 vols., 1928–1944). A handy reference is the *Dictionary of American History*, edited by J. T. Adams and R. V. Coleman (5 vols., 1940). *The American Nation: A History*, edited by A. B. Hart (28 vols., 1904–1916), each volume written by a leading authority, was for many years a standard set. As is usual with such co-operative histories, the individual volumes vary in quality; some are still valuable, others obsolete. *The New American Nation Series*, edited by H. S. Commager and R. B. Morris (40-odd volumes projected, 1954–   ), undertakes to incorporate the latest scholarship and will largely replace the old series. The *Chronicles of America* (50 vols. edited by Allen Johnson, 1918–1921; 6 additional vols. edited by Allan Nevins, 1950–1951) are written in a popular vein by well informed authors. *A History of the South*, edited by W. H. Stephenson and E. M. Coulter (12 vols. projected, 1947–   ), is detailed and authoritative for the part of the country it treats.

POLITICAL AND CONSTITUTIONAL R. H. Gabriel, *The Course of American Democratic Thought* (rev. ed., 1956), interprets political philosophy. W. E. Binkley, *American Political Parties* (rev. ed., 1945), surveys the externals of politics. Richard Hofstadter, *The American Political Tradition* (1948), probes the thinking and motivation of political leaders. Two general accounts of constitutional history are A. H. Kelly and W. A. Harbison, *The American Constitution* (1948), and C. B. Swisher, *American Constitutional Development* (1943). H. C. Hockett, *The Constitutional History of the United States, 1776–1826* (2 vols., 1939), is a detailed treatment of the first half century. Charles Warren, *The Supreme Court and the Constitution* (2 vols. 1937), is the most comprehensive general work.

DIPLOMATIC Documents illustrating the history of foreign relations are contained in *The Record of American Diplomacy*, edited by R. J. Bartlett (rev. ed., 1954), and in *The Shaping of American Diplomacy*, edited by W. A. Williams (1956); the Williams book also gives selections from the writings of diplomatic historians. Textbooks are J. W. Pratt, *A History of the United States Foreign Policy* (1955); S. F. Bemis, *A Diplomatic History of the United States* (rev. ed., 1955); and T. A. Bailey, *A Diplomatic History of the American People* (rev. ed., 1958), which pursues the thesis that public opinion determines foreign policy. Area studies include Dexter Perkins, *History of the Monroe Doctrine* (rev. ed., 1955); S. F. Bemis, *The Latin American Policy of the United States* (1943); and A. W. Griswold, *The Far Eastern Policy of the United States* (1938). The ideas and arguments justifying American expansion are analyzed by A. J. Weinberg, *Manifest Destiny* (1935).

MILITARY AND NAVAL G. T. Davis gives a somewhat critical account of naval development in *A Navy Second to None* (1940). Harold and Margaret Sprout treat the same subject more enthusiastically in *The Rise of American Naval Power* (1942) and *Toward a New Order of Sea Power* (1943). In *Military Heritage of America* (1956) R. E. and T. N. Dupuy provide an able introduction to the study of the military history of the United States. In *Arms and Men* (1956) Walter Millis puts the development of American strategy into the broad setting of technological and other changes. A. A. Ekirch, Jr., tells the story of the changing problems of civil and military relationships in *The Civilian and the Military* (1956).

ECONOMIC *The Economic History of the United States* is told by experts in a series edited by Henry David and others (9 vols. projected, 1945–   ). Convenient summaries are H. U. Faulkner, *American Economic History* (rev. ed., 1954); and E. C. Kirkland, *A History of American Economic Life* (rev. ed., 1951). Aspects of the subject are treated with thoroughness by B. H. Meyer and others, *History of Transportation in the United States before 1860* (1917); E. R. Johnson and others,

History of Domestic and Foreign Commerce of the United States (2 vols., 1915); V. S. Clark, *History of Manufactures in the United States* (3 vols., 1929); L. C. Gray, *History of Agriculture in the Southern United States to 1860* (2 vols., 1925); and P. W. Bidwell and J. I. Falconer, *History of Agriculture in the Northern United States, 1620–1860* (1925). The first three hundred years of American farming are well summarized by E. E. Edwards in the Department of Agriculture's *Yearbook of Agriculture* for 1940. Financial history is surveyed in W. J. Schultz and M. B. Caine, *Financial Development of the United States* (1937). Seymour Dunbar's *History of Travel in America* (4 vols., 1915) is both readable and authoritative. Sidney Ratner's *American Taxation: Its History* (1942) is comprehensive.

TECHNOLOGICAL J. W. Oliver, *History of American Technology* (1956) is a fairly detailed and factual treatment, without illustrations. *A Popular History of American Invention*, edited by Waldemar Kaempffert (2 vols., 1924), is a useful introduction to the subject, though neither complete nor entirely accurate. Roger Burlingame relates technological invention to political and social history in *March of the Iron Men* (1938) and *Engines of Democracy* (1940). Siegfried Giedion, *Mechanization Takes Command* (1948), provocatively interprets the influence of technology upon the American home.

BUSINESS AND LABOR The role of business in American history as a whole is emphasized by T. C. Cochran and William Miller in *The Age of Enterprise* (1942). Business thinking, as well as general economic thought, is set forth in Joseph Dorfman's *The Economic Mind in American Civilization* (3 vols., 1946–1949). L. M. Hacker presents one interpretation of the stages of business development in *The Triumph of American Capitalism* (1940), and N. S. B. Gras presents another interpretation in *Business and Capitalism* (1946). The worker's place in history is revealed through original records in the *Documentary History of American Industrial Society*, edited by J. R. Commons and others (10 vols., 1910–1911). Commons and his associates also are authors of the comprehensive *History of Labor in the United States* (4 vols., 1918–1935), which is based mainly on the documents cited above. An interpretive account of labor organization is Selig Perlman's *History of Trade Unionism in the United States* (1922). A useful bibliography is Henrietta M. Larson's *Guide to Business History* (1948).

SOCIAL A pioneering co-operative work is *A History of American Life*, edited by A. M. Schlesinger and D. R. Fox (13 vols., 1927–1948). General accounts of church history are W. W. Sweet, *The Story of Religion in America* (rev. ed., 1939); and W. L. Sperry, *Religion in America* (1946). A. W. Calhoun's *A Social History of the American Family* (3 vols., 1917–1919) is the only thing of its kind, as is Dixon Wecter's *The Saga of American Society* (1936), which is a history of "high society." Aspects of the use of leisure are recounted in F. R. Dulles, *America Learns to Play* (1940), and J. A. Krout, *Annals of American Sport* (1940). Other phases of social history are treated in F. R. Packard, *History of Medicine in the United States* (2 vols., 1931); and J. H. Franklin, *From Slavery to Freedom: A History of American Negroes* (1948).

IMMIGRATION This phase of social history receives a broad, general treatment in Carl Wittke, *We Who Built America* (1940), which stresses the immigrant contribution. M. L. Hansen, *The Immigrant in American History* (1940), is a collection of essays reinterpreting the subject. The same author's *The Atlantic Migration, 1607–1860* (1940) was projected as the first volume of a comprehensive history, which Hansen's untimely death left uncompleted. Oscar Handlin, *The Uprooted* (1951), reveals the heart and soul of the immigrants, especially

those from Eastern Europe in the twentieth century. The reaction of natives to immigrant arrivals is told by R. A. Billington, *The Protestant Crusade, 1800–1860* (1938); and John Higham, *Strangers in the Land* (1938), which takes up where Billington's book leaves off.

INTELLECTUAL Charles and Mary Beard, in *The Rise of American Civilization* (2 vols., rev. ed., 1933), make a brilliant effort to integrate the history of ideas with history in general. In *The American Spirit* (1942) the same authors elaborate upon their conception of what is distinctive in American ideas. Merle Curti, *The Growth of American Thought* (rev. ed., 1951), is a thorough, inclusive account. V. L. Parrington, *Main Currents in American Thought* (3 vols., 1927–1930), organizes the story biographically and presents it from the point of view of a Jeffersonian liberal. The history of schools is summarized by E. W. Knight, *Education in the United States* (rev. ed., 1951). Higher education is treated by Merle Curti, *Social Ideals of American Educators* (1935); and by Richard Hofstadter and W. P. Metzger, *The Development of Academic Freedom in the United States* (1955). Both of these books are considerably broader than their titles indicate. Americans do not have the reputation of being a philosophical people, yet they have had their philosophers, as H. W. Schneider shows in *A History of American Philosophy* (1946).

LITERARY AND ARTISTIC H. L. Mencken, *The American Language* (3 vols., 1936–1948), deals lovingly and entertainingly with words and their history. Standard works on their respective subjects are F. L. Mott's *A History of American Magazines* (4 vols., 1930–1957) and his *American Journalism* (rev. ed., 1950). The history of literature and the fine arts may be traced in the following: R. E. Spiller and others, *Literary History of the United States* (3 vols., 1943); A. H. Quinn, *A History of the American Drama* (rev. ed., 1943); J. T.

Howard, *Our American Music* (rev. ed., 1946); O. W. Larkin, *Art and Life in America* (1949); Alexander Eliot, *Three Hundred Years of American Painting* (1957); Edgar P. Richardson, *History of American Painting* (1956); and T. E. Tallmadge, *The Story of Architecture in America* (rev. ed., 1936).

Paperback Editions

Numerous books in American history, most of which are in the reading lists, are available in soft-cover editions at moderate prices. If not obtainable at local bookstores, they may be ordered directly from the publisher. Among the books are:

Adams, Henry, *The United States in 1800* (Cornell)

American Heritage Reader (Dell)

Angle, Paul, ed., *The Lincoln Reader* (Pocket Books)

Baldwin, Joseph, *Flush Times of Alabama and Mississippi* (Sagamore)

Becker, C. L., *The Declaration of Independence* (Vintage)

Bemis, S. F., *The Diplomacy of the American Revolution* (Indiana University)

Bowen, C. D., *John Adams and the American Revolution* (Universal Library)

Brebner, J. B., *The Explorers of North America, 1492–1806* (Anchor)

Brockway, T. P., *Basic Documents in United States Foreign Policy* (Anvil)

Bryce, James, edited and abridged by L. M. Hacker, *The American Commonwealth* (Sagamore)

Burlingame, Roger, *Benjamin Franklin* (New American Library)

Butcher, M. J., *The Negro in American Culture* (New American Library)

Canby, Courtlandt, ed., *Lincoln and the Civil War: A Profile and a History* (Dell)

Cash, W. J., *The Mind of the South* (Anchor)

Charnwood, Lord, *Abraham Lincoln* (Pocket Books)

Chinard, Gilbert, *Thomas Jefferson: The Apostle of Americanism* (Ann Arbor)

Commager, H. S., *America in Perspective* (New American Library)

Crane, V. W., *The Southern Frontier, 1670–1732* (Ann Arbor)

Crèvecoeur, J. H. St. J. de, *Letters from an American Farmer* (Dutton)

Ellis, J. T., *American Catholicism* (Chicago)

Franklin, Benjamin, *Autobiography of Benjamin Franklin* (Pocket Books)

Glazer, Nathan, *American Judaism* (Chicago)

Handlin, Oscar, *Race and Nationality in American Life* (Anchor)

Heffner, R. D., *A Documentary History of the United States* (New American Library)

Hofstadter, Richard, *The American Political Tradition* (Vintage)

Hofstadter, Richard, ed., *Great Issues in American History: A Documentary Record*, Vol. I (Vintage)

Jameson, J. F., *The American Revolution*

Considered as a Social Movement (Beacon)

Johnson, Gerald, *Andrew Jackson* (Bantam)

Kemmerer, D. L., and Hunter, M. H., *Economic History of the United States* (Littlefield, Adams & Co.)

Kraus, Michael, *The North Atlantic Civilization* (Anvil)

Leech, Margaret, *Reveille in Washington* (Universal Library)

Logan, R. W., *The Negro in the United States* (Anvil)

Miller, Perry, ed., *The American Puritans: Their Prose and Poetry* (Anchor)

Miller, Perry, *The American Transcendentalists* (Anchor)

Millis, Walter, *Arms and Men* (New American Library)

Morgan, E. S., *The Birth of the Republic: 1763–89* (Chicago)

Morison, S. E., *Christopher Columbus, Mariner* (New American Library)

Morris, R. B., *The American Revolution: A Short History* (Anvil)

Morris, R. B., *Basic Documents in American History* (Anvil)

Morris, Richard, ed., *Basic Ideas of Alexander Hamilton* (Pocket Books)

Padover, S. K., *Jefferson* (New American Library)

Parkman, Francis, *The Oregon Trail* (New American Library)

Pratt, Fletcher, *Short History of the Civil War* (Pocket Books)

Rose, Arnold, *The Negro in America* (Beacon)

Rossiter, Clinton, *American Presidency* (New American Library)

Rossiter, Clinton, *The First American Revolution* (Harvest)

Rourke, Constance, *American Humor: A Study of the National Character* (Anchor)

Schlesinger, A. M., Jr., *The Age of Jackson*, abridged (New American Library)

Shannon, Fred, *American Farmers' Movements* (Anvil)

Small, Major A. R., *The Road to Richmond* (University of California)

Smith, H. N., *Virgin Land* (Vintage)

Swisher, C. B., *Historic Decisions of the Supreme Court* (Anvil)

Tate, Allen, *Stonewall Jackson* (Ann Arbor)

Tocqueville, Alexis de, *Democracy in America*, abridged (Vintage)

Wertenbaker, T. J., *The Puritan Oligarchy* (Universal Library)

Williams, T. Harry, ed., *Abraham Lincoln, Selected Speeches, Messages and Letters* (Rinehart)

Woodward, C. Vann, *Reunion and Reaction* (Anchor)

Index